# Beginning Python

## From Novice to Professional, Second Edition

Magnus Lie Hetland

Apress®

**Beginning Python: From Novice to Professional, Second Edition**

**Copyright © 2008 by Magnus Lie Hetland**

ISBN-13 (paperback): 978-1-59059-982-2

ISBN-13 (electronic): 978-1-4302-0634-7

Printed and bound in the United States of America 9 8 7 6 5

Trademarked names may appear in this book. Rather than use a trademark symbol with every occurrence of a trademarked name, we use the names only in an editorial fashion and to the benefit of the trademark owner, with no intention of infringement of the trademark.

Lead Editor: Frank Pohlmann
Technical Reviewers: Gregg Bolinger, Richard Taylor
Editorial Board: Clay Andres, Steve Anglin, Ewan Buckingham, Tony Campbell, Gary Cornell, Jonathan Gennick, Matthew Moodie, Joseph Ottinger, Jeffrey Pepper, Frank Pohlmann, Ben Renow-Clarke, Dominic Shakeshaft, Matt Wade, Tom Welsh
Project Manager: Richard Dal Porto
Copy Editor: Marilyn Smith
Associate Production Director: Kari Brooks-Copony
Production Editor: Liz Berry
Compositor: Pat Christenson
Proofreader: April Eddy
Indexer: John Collin
Cover Designer: Kurt Krames
Manufacturing Director: Tom Debolski

Distributed to the book trade worldwide by Springer-Verlag New York, Inc., 233 Spring Street, 6th Floor, New York, NY 10013. Phone 1-800-SPRINGER, fax 201-348-4505, e-mail orders-ny@springer-sbm.com, or visit http://www.springeronline.com.

For information on translations e-mail info@apress.com, or visit http://www.apress.com.

Apress and friends of ED books may be purchased in bulk for academic, corporate, or promotional use. eBook versions and licenses are also available for most titles. For more information, reference our Special Bulk Sales–eBook Licensing web page at http://www.apress.com/info/bulksales.

The source code for this book is available to readers at http://www.apress.com.

# Contents at a Glance

About the Author ........................................................... xxiii

About the Technical Reviewer ............................................... xxv

Preface .................................................................... xxvii

Introduction ............................................................... xxix

**CHAPTER 1**  Instant Hacking: The Basics ................................... 1

**CHAPTER 2**  Lists and Tuples ............................................. 31

**CHAPTER 3**  Working with Strings ......................................... 53

**CHAPTER 4**  Dictionaries: When Indices Won't Do ......................... 69

**CHAPTER 5**  Conditionals, Loops, and Some Other Statements ............. 83

**CHAPTER 6**  Abstraction ................................................. 113

**CHAPTER 7**  More Abstraction ............................................ 141

**CHAPTER 8**  Exceptions .................................................. 161

**CHAPTER 9**  Magic Methods, Properties, and Iterators ................... 175

**CHAPTER 10**  Batteries Included ......................................... 209

**CHAPTER 11**  Files and Stuff ............................................ 261

**CHAPTER 12**  Graphical User Interfaces .................................. 277

**CHAPTER 13**  Database Support ........................................... 293

**CHAPTER 14**  Network Programming ........................................ 305

**CHAPTER 15**  Python and the Web ......................................... 321

**CHAPTER 16**  Testing, 1-2-3 ............................................. 349

**CHAPTER 17**  Extending Python ........................................... 365

**CHAPTER 18**  Packaging Your Programs .................................... 383

**CHAPTER 19**  Playful Programming ........................................ 393

**CHAPTER 20**  Project 1: Instant Markup .................................. 403

**CHAPTER 21**  Project 2: Painting a Pretty Picture ....................... 425

**CHAPTER 22**  Project 3: XML for All Occasions ........................... 435

**CHAPTER 23**  Project 4: In the News ..................................... 453

**CHAPTER 24**    Project 5: A Virtual Tea Party . . . . . . . . . . . . . . . . . . . . . . . . . . . . . . 469

**CHAPTER 25**    Project 6: Remote Editing with CGI . . . . . . . . . . . . . . . . . . . . . . . . . 489

**CHAPTER 26**    Project 7: Your Own Bulletin Board . . . . . . . . . . . . . . . . . . . . . . . . . 499

**CHAPTER 27**    Project 8: File Sharing with XML-RPC . . . . . . . . . . . . . . . . . . . . . . 517

**CHAPTER 28**    Project 9: File Sharing II—Now with GUI! . . . . . . . . . . . . . . . . . . . 537

**CHAPTER 29**    Project 10: Do-It-Yourself Arcade Game . . . . . . . . . . . . . . . . . . . . 547

**APPENDIX A**    The Short Version . . . . . . . . . . . . . . . . . . . . . . . . . . . . . . . . . . . . . . 569

**APPENDIX B**    Python Reference . . . . . . . . . . . . . . . . . . . . . . . . . . . . . . . . . . . . . . 579

**APPENDIX C**    Online Resources . . . . . . . . . . . . . . . . . . . . . . . . . . . . . . . . . . . . . . 595

**APPENDIX D**    Python 3.0 . . . . . . . . . . . . . . . . . . . . . . . . . . . . . . . . . . . . . . . . . . . . 599

**INDEX** . . . . . . . . . . . . . . . . . . . . . . . . . . . . . . . . . . . . . . . . . . . . . . . . . . . . . . . . . 607

# Contents

About the Author . . . . . . . . . . . . . . . . . . . . . . . . . . . . . . . . . . . . . . . . . . . . . . . . . . . . . . . . . . . xxiii

About the Technical Reviewer . . . . . . . . . . . . . . . . . . . . . . . . . . . . . . . . . . . . . . . . . . . . . . . xxv

Preface . . . . . . . . . . . . . . . . . . . . . . . . . . . . . . . . . . . . . . . . . . . . . . . . . . . . . . . . . . . . . . . . . xxvii

Introduction . . . . . . . . . . . . . . . . . . . . . . . . . . . . . . . . . . . . . . . . . . . . . . . . . . . . . . . . . . . . . xxix

**■CHAPTER 1    Instant Hacking: The Basics** . . . . . . . . . . . . . . . . . . . . . . . . . . . . . . 1

Installing Python . . . . . . . . . . . . . . . . . . . . . . . . . . . . . . . . . . . . . . . . . . . . . . . . . . . 1
    Windows . . . . . . . . . . . . . . . . . . . . . . . . . . . . . . . . . . . . . . . . . . . . . . . . . . . 1
    Linux and UNIX . . . . . . . . . . . . . . . . . . . . . . . . . . . . . . . . . . . . . . . . . . . . . 3
    Macintosh . . . . . . . . . . . . . . . . . . . . . . . . . . . . . . . . . . . . . . . . . . . . . . . . . 5
    Other Distributions . . . . . . . . . . . . . . . . . . . . . . . . . . . . . . . . . . . . . . . . . 5
    Keeping in Touch and Up-to-Date . . . . . . . . . . . . . . . . . . . . . . . . . . . . . 7
The Interactive Interpreter . . . . . . . . . . . . . . . . . . . . . . . . . . . . . . . . . . . . . . . . 7
Algo . . . What? . . . . . . . . . . . . . . . . . . . . . . . . . . . . . . . . . . . . . . . . . . . . . . . . 9
Numbers and Expressions . . . . . . . . . . . . . . . . . . . . . . . . . . . . . . . . . . . . . . . 9
    Large Integers . . . . . . . . . . . . . . . . . . . . . . . . . . . . . . . . . . . . . . . . . . . . 11
    Hexadecimals and Octals . . . . . . . . . . . . . . . . . . . . . . . . . . . . . . . . . . . 12
Variables . . . . . . . . . . . . . . . . . . . . . . . . . . . . . . . . . . . . . . . . . . . . . . . . . . . . 13
Statements . . . . . . . . . . . . . . . . . . . . . . . . . . . . . . . . . . . . . . . . . . . . . . . . . . 13
Getting Input from the User . . . . . . . . . . . . . . . . . . . . . . . . . . . . . . . . . . . . . 14
Functions . . . . . . . . . . . . . . . . . . . . . . . . . . . . . . . . . . . . . . . . . . . . . . . . . . . 16
Modules . . . . . . . . . . . . . . . . . . . . . . . . . . . . . . . . . . . . . . . . . . . . . . . . . . . . 17
    cmath and Complex Numbers . . . . . . . . . . . . . . . . . . . . . . . . . . . . . . . 18
    Back to the __future__ . . . . . . . . . . . . . . . . . . . . . . . . . . . . . . . . . . . . 19
Saving and Executing Your Programs . . . . . . . . . . . . . . . . . . . . . . . . . . . . . 19
    Running Your Python Scripts from a Command Prompt . . . . . . . . . 20
    Making Your Scripts Behave Like Normal Programs . . . . . . . . . . . 20
    Comments . . . . . . . . . . . . . . . . . . . . . . . . . . . . . . . . . . . . . . . . . . . . . . . 22

Strings . . . . . . . . . . . . . . . . . . . . . . . . . . . . . . . . . . . . . . . . . . . . . . . . . . . . 22
    Single-Quoted Strings and Escaping Quotes . . . . . . . . . . . . . . . . . . 23
    Concatenating Strings . . . . . . . . . . . . . . . . . . . . . . . . . . . . . . . . . . . . . 24
    String Representations, str and repr . . . . . . . . . . . . . . . . . . . . . . . . . 24
    input vs. raw_input . . . . . . . . . . . . . . . . . . . . . . . . . . . . . . . . . . . . . . . 26
    Long Strings, Raw Strings, and Unicode . . . . . . . . . . . . . . . . . . . . . . 26
A Quick Summary . . . . . . . . . . . . . . . . . . . . . . . . . . . . . . . . . . . . . . . . . . 29
    New Functions in This Chapter . . . . . . . . . . . . . . . . . . . . . . . . . . . . . . 30
    What Now? . . . . . . . . . . . . . . . . . . . . . . . . . . . . . . . . . . . . . . . . . . . . . . 30

■CHAPTER 2   **Lists and Tuples** . . . . . . . . . . . . . . . . . . . . . . . . . . . . . . . . . . . . . . . 31

Sequence Overview . . . . . . . . . . . . . . . . . . . . . . . . . . . . . . . . . . . . . . . . . 31
Common Sequence Operations . . . . . . . . . . . . . . . . . . . . . . . . . . . . . . . 32
    Indexing . . . . . . . . . . . . . . . . . . . . . . . . . . . . . . . . . . . . . . . . . . . . . . . . 32
    Slicing . . . . . . . . . . . . . . . . . . . . . . . . . . . . . . . . . . . . . . . . . . . . . . . . . 34
    Adding Sequences . . . . . . . . . . . . . . . . . . . . . . . . . . . . . . . . . . . . . . . . 37
    Multiplication . . . . . . . . . . . . . . . . . . . . . . . . . . . . . . . . . . . . . . . . . . . . 37
    Membership . . . . . . . . . . . . . . . . . . . . . . . . . . . . . . . . . . . . . . . . . . . . . 38
    Length, Minimum, and Maximum . . . . . . . . . . . . . . . . . . . . . . . . . . . . 40
Lists: Python's Workhorse . . . . . . . . . . . . . . . . . . . . . . . . . . . . . . . . . . . 40
    The list Function . . . . . . . . . . . . . . . . . . . . . . . . . . . . . . . . . . . . . . . . . 40
    Basic List Operations . . . . . . . . . . . . . . . . . . . . . . . . . . . . . . . . . . . . . 41
    List Methods . . . . . . . . . . . . . . . . . . . . . . . . . . . . . . . . . . . . . . . . . . . . 43
Tuples: Immutable Sequences . . . . . . . . . . . . . . . . . . . . . . . . . . . . . . . 49
    The tuple Function . . . . . . . . . . . . . . . . . . . . . . . . . . . . . . . . . . . . . . . 50
    Basic Tuple Operations . . . . . . . . . . . . . . . . . . . . . . . . . . . . . . . . . . . 50
    So What's the Point? . . . . . . . . . . . . . . . . . . . . . . . . . . . . . . . . . . . . . . 51
A Quick Summary . . . . . . . . . . . . . . . . . . . . . . . . . . . . . . . . . . . . . . . . . . 51
    New Functions in This Chapter . . . . . . . . . . . . . . . . . . . . . . . . . . . . . . 52
    What Now? . . . . . . . . . . . . . . . . . . . . . . . . . . . . . . . . . . . . . . . . . . . . . . 52

■CHAPTER 3   **Working with Strings** . . . . . . . . . . . . . . . . . . . . . . . . . . . . . . . . . . . 53

Basic String Operations . . . . . . . . . . . . . . . . . . . . . . . . . . . . . . . . . . . . . 53
String Formatting: The Short Version . . . . . . . . . . . . . . . . . . . . . . . . . . . 53

String Formatting: The Long Version. . . . . . . . . . . . . . . . . . . . . . . . . . . . . 56
    Simple Conversion . . . . . . . . . . . . . . . . . . . . . . . . . . . . . . . . . . . . . . 57
    Width and Precision . . . . . . . . . . . . . . . . . . . . . . . . . . . . . . . . . . . . . 57
    Signs, Alignment, and Zero-Padding . . . . . . . . . . . . . . . . . . . . . . . . 58
String Methods . . . . . . . . . . . . . . . . . . . . . . . . . . . . . . . . . . . . . . . . . . . 60
    find. . . . . . . . . . . . . . . . . . . . . . . . . . . . . . . . . . . . . . . . . . . . . . . . . 60
    join. . . . . . . . . . . . . . . . . . . . . . . . . . . . . . . . . . . . . . . . . . . . . . . . 61
    lower . . . . . . . . . . . . . . . . . . . . . . . . . . . . . . . . . . . . . . . . . . . . . . . 62
    replace . . . . . . . . . . . . . . . . . . . . . . . . . . . . . . . . . . . . . . . . . . . . . 63
    split . . . . . . . . . . . . . . . . . . . . . . . . . . . . . . . . . . . . . . . . . . . . . . . 63
    strip . . . . . . . . . . . . . . . . . . . . . . . . . . . . . . . . . . . . . . . . . . . . . . . 64
    translate . . . . . . . . . . . . . . . . . . . . . . . . . . . . . . . . . . . . . . . . . . . 64
A Quick Summary. . . . . . . . . . . . . . . . . . . . . . . . . . . . . . . . . . . . . . . . . 66
    New Functions in This Chapter. . . . . . . . . . . . . . . . . . . . . . . . . . . . 66
    What Now?. . . . . . . . . . . . . . . . . . . . . . . . . . . . . . . . . . . . . . . . . . . 67

**CHAPTER 4**    **Dictionaries: When Indices Won't Do**. . . . . . . . . . . . . . . . . . 69

Dictionary Uses. . . . . . . . . . . . . . . . . . . . . . . . . . . . . . . . . . . . . . . . . . . 69
Creating and Using Dictionaries . . . . . . . . . . . . . . . . . . . . . . . . . . . . . . 70
    The dict Function. . . . . . . . . . . . . . . . . . . . . . . . . . . . . . . . . . . . . . 71
    Basic Dictionary Operations . . . . . . . . . . . . . . . . . . . . . . . . . . . . . . 71
    String Formatting with Dictionaries . . . . . . . . . . . . . . . . . . . . . . . . 73
    Dictionary Methods. . . . . . . . . . . . . . . . . . . . . . . . . . . . . . . . . . . . 74
A Quick Summary. . . . . . . . . . . . . . . . . . . . . . . . . . . . . . . . . . . . . . . . . 81
    New Functions in This Chapter. . . . . . . . . . . . . . . . . . . . . . . . . . . . 81
    What Now?. . . . . . . . . . . . . . . . . . . . . . . . . . . . . . . . . . . . . . . . . . . 81

**CHAPTER 5**    **Conditionals, Loops, and Some Other Statements**. . . . . . . 83

More About print and import. . . . . . . . . . . . . . . . . . . . . . . . . . . . . . . . . 83
    Printing with Commas . . . . . . . . . . . . . . . . . . . . . . . . . . . . . . . . . . 83
    Importing Something As Something Else . . . . . . . . . . . . . . . . . . . . 84
Assignment Magic . . . . . . . . . . . . . . . . . . . . . . . . . . . . . . . . . . . . . . . . 85
    Sequence Unpacking . . . . . . . . . . . . . . . . . . . . . . . . . . . . . . . . . . . 85
    Chained Assignments. . . . . . . . . . . . . . . . . . . . . . . . . . . . . . . . . . . 87
    Augmented Assignments. . . . . . . . . . . . . . . . . . . . . . . . . . . . . . . . 87

Blocks: The Joy of Indentation . . . . . . . . . . . . . . . . . . . . . . . . . . . . . . . . . 88
Conditions and Conditional Statements . . . . . . . . . . . . . . . . . . . . . . . . . 88
    So That's What Those Boolean Values Are For . . . . . . . . . . . . . . . . 89
    Conditional Execution and the if Statement . . . . . . . . . . . . . . . . . . . 90
    else Clauses. . . . . . . . . . . . . . . . . . . . . . . . . . . . . . . . . . . . . . . . . . . . 90
    elif Clauses. . . . . . . . . . . . . . . . . . . . . . . . . . . . . . . . . . . . . . . . . . . . . 91
    Nesting Blocks. . . . . . . . . . . . . . . . . . . . . . . . . . . . . . . . . . . . . . . . . . 91
    More Complex Conditions . . . . . . . . . . . . . . . . . . . . . . . . . . . . . . . . . 92
    Assertions. . . . . . . . . . . . . . . . . . . . . . . . . . . . . . . . . . . . . . . . . . . . . . 97
Loops . . . . . . . . . . . . . . . . . . . . . . . . . . . . . . . . . . . . . . . . . . . . . . . . . . . . 97
    while Loops . . . . . . . . . . . . . . . . . . . . . . . . . . . . . . . . . . . . . . . . . . . . 98
    for Loops. . . . . . . . . . . . . . . . . . . . . . . . . . . . . . . . . . . . . . . . . . . . . . . 99
    Iterating Over Dictionaries . . . . . . . . . . . . . . . . . . . . . . . . . . . . . . . 100
    Some Iteration Utilities . . . . . . . . . . . . . . . . . . . . . . . . . . . . . . . . . . 100
    Breaking Out of Loops . . . . . . . . . . . . . . . . . . . . . . . . . . . . . . . . . . 102
    else Clauses in Loops. . . . . . . . . . . . . . . . . . . . . . . . . . . . . . . . . . . 105
List Comprehension—Slightly Loopy . . . . . . . . . . . . . . . . . . . . . . . . . . 105
And Three for the Road . . . . . . . . . . . . . . . . . . . . . . . . . . . . . . . . . . . . 107
    Nothing Happened! . . . . . . . . . . . . . . . . . . . . . . . . . . . . . . . . . . . . . 107
    Deleting with del . . . . . . . . . . . . . . . . . . . . . . . . . . . . . . . . . . . . . . . 107
    Executing and Evaluating Strings with exec and eval. . . . . . . . . . 108
A Quick Summary. . . . . . . . . . . . . . . . . . . . . . . . . . . . . . . . . . . . . . . . . 111
    New Functions in This Chapter. . . . . . . . . . . . . . . . . . . . . . . . . . . . 112
    What Now?. . . . . . . . . . . . . . . . . . . . . . . . . . . . . . . . . . . . . . . . . . . . 112

■CHAPTER 6    **Abstraction**. . . . . . . . . . . . . . . . . . . . . . . . . . . . . . . . . . . . . . . 113

Laziness Is a Virtue. . . . . . . . . . . . . . . . . . . . . . . . . . . . . . . . . . . . . . . . 113
Abstraction and Structure . . . . . . . . . . . . . . . . . . . . . . . . . . . . . . . . . . 114
Creating Your Own Functions . . . . . . . . . . . . . . . . . . . . . . . . . . . . . . . 115
    Documenting Functions . . . . . . . . . . . . . . . . . . . . . . . . . . . . . . . . . 116
    Functions That Aren't Really Functions . . . . . . . . . . . . . . . . . . . . . 117
The Magic of Parameters . . . . . . . . . . . . . . . . . . . . . . . . . . . . . . . . . . 117
    Where Do the Values Come From? . . . . . . . . . . . . . . . . . . . . . . . . 118
    Can I Change a Parameter?. . . . . . . . . . . . . . . . . . . . . . . . . . . . . . 118
    Keyword Parameters and Defaults. . . . . . . . . . . . . . . . . . . . . . . . . 123
    Collecting Parameters . . . . . . . . . . . . . . . . . . . . . . . . . . . . . . . . . . 125
    Reversing the Process . . . . . . . . . . . . . . . . . . . . . . . . . . . . . . . . . . 128
    Parameter Practice . . . . . . . . . . . . . . . . . . . . . . . . . . . . . . . . . . . . . 129
Scoping. . . . . . . . . . . . . . . . . . . . . . . . . . . . . . . . . . . . . . . . . . . . . . . . . 131

Recursion . . . . . . . . . . . . . . . . . . . . . . . . . . . . . . . . . . . . . . . . . . . . . 133
    Two Classics: Factorial and Power . . . . . . . . . . . . . . . . . . . . . . . . . 134
    Another Classic: Binary Search . . . . . . . . . . . . . . . . . . . . . . . . . . . 136
A Quick Summary . . . . . . . . . . . . . . . . . . . . . . . . . . . . . . . . . . . . . . . . . 139
    New Functions in This Chapter . . . . . . . . . . . . . . . . . . . . . . . . . . . . 140
    What Now? . . . . . . . . . . . . . . . . . . . . . . . . . . . . . . . . . . . . . . . . . . . 140

**CHAPTER 7**   **More Abstraction** . . . . . . . . . . . . . . . . . . . . . . . . . . . . . . . . . . . 141

The Magic of Objects . . . . . . . . . . . . . . . . . . . . . . . . . . . . . . . . . . . . . . 141
    Polymorphism . . . . . . . . . . . . . . . . . . . . . . . . . . . . . . . . . . . . . . . . 142
    Encapsulation . . . . . . . . . . . . . . . . . . . . . . . . . . . . . . . . . . . . . . . . 145
    Inheritance . . . . . . . . . . . . . . . . . . . . . . . . . . . . . . . . . . . . . . . . . . 147
Classes and Types . . . . . . . . . . . . . . . . . . . . . . . . . . . . . . . . . . . . . . . 147
    What Is a Class, Exactly? . . . . . . . . . . . . . . . . . . . . . . . . . . . . . . . . 147
    Making Your Own Classes . . . . . . . . . . . . . . . . . . . . . . . . . . . . . . . 148
    Attributes, Functions, and Methods . . . . . . . . . . . . . . . . . . . . . . . . 150
    Privacy Revisited . . . . . . . . . . . . . . . . . . . . . . . . . . . . . . . . . . . . . 150
    The Class Namespace . . . . . . . . . . . . . . . . . . . . . . . . . . . . . . . . . . 152
    Specifying a Superclass . . . . . . . . . . . . . . . . . . . . . . . . . . . . . . . . 153
    Investigating Inheritance . . . . . . . . . . . . . . . . . . . . . . . . . . . . . . . . 154
    Multiple Superclasses . . . . . . . . . . . . . . . . . . . . . . . . . . . . . . . . . . 155
    Interfaces and Introspection . . . . . . . . . . . . . . . . . . . . . . . . . . . . . 156
Some Thoughts on Object-Oriented Design . . . . . . . . . . . . . . . . . . . . . 157
A Quick Summary . . . . . . . . . . . . . . . . . . . . . . . . . . . . . . . . . . . . . . . . . 158
    New Functions in This Chapter . . . . . . . . . . . . . . . . . . . . . . . . . . . . 159
    What Now? . . . . . . . . . . . . . . . . . . . . . . . . . . . . . . . . . . . . . . . . . . . 159

**CHAPTER 8**   **Exceptions** . . . . . . . . . . . . . . . . . . . . . . . . . . . . . . . . . . . . . . . . . 161

What Is an Exception? . . . . . . . . . . . . . . . . . . . . . . . . . . . . . . . . . . . . . 161
Making Things Go Wrong . . . Your Way . . . . . . . . . . . . . . . . . . . . . . . . 161
    The raise Statement . . . . . . . . . . . . . . . . . . . . . . . . . . . . . . . . . . . 162
    Custom Exception Classes . . . . . . . . . . . . . . . . . . . . . . . . . . . . . . . 163
Catching Exceptions . . . . . . . . . . . . . . . . . . . . . . . . . . . . . . . . . . . . . . 163
    Look, Ma, No Arguments! . . . . . . . . . . . . . . . . . . . . . . . . . . . . . . . . 164
    More Than One except Clause . . . . . . . . . . . . . . . . . . . . . . . . . . . . 165
    Catching Two Exceptions with One Block . . . . . . . . . . . . . . . . . . . . 166
    Catching the Object . . . . . . . . . . . . . . . . . . . . . . . . . . . . . . . . . . . . 166
    A Real Catchall . . . . . . . . . . . . . . . . . . . . . . . . . . . . . . . . . . . . . . . 167

When All Is Well. . . . . . . . . . . . . . . . . . . . . . . . . . . . . . . . . . . . . . . . . 168
And Finally . . . . . . . . . . . . . . . . . . . . . . . . . . . . . . . . . . . . . . . . . . . . . 169
Exceptions and Functions . . . . . . . . . . . . . . . . . . . . . . . . . . . . . . . . . . . . . . 170
The Zen of Exceptions . . . . . . . . . . . . . . . . . . . . . . . . . . . . . . . . . . . . . . . . 171
A Quick Summary. . . . . . . . . . . . . . . . . . . . . . . . . . . . . . . . . . . . . . . . . . . . . 173
New Functions in This Chapter. . . . . . . . . . . . . . . . . . . . . . . . . . . . . 174
What Now?. . . . . . . . . . . . . . . . . . . . . . . . . . . . . . . . . . . . . . . . . . . . . . 174

■CHAPTER 9    **Magic Methods, Properties, and Iterators** . . . . . . . . . . . . . . 175

Before We Begin . . . . . . . . . . . . . . . . . . . . . . . . . . . . . . . . . . . . . . . . . . . . 175
Constructors . . . . . . . . . . . . . . . . . . . . . . . . . . . . . . . . . . . . . . . . . . . . . . . 176
Overriding Methods in General, and the Constructor
in Particular. . . . . . . . . . . . . . . . . . . . . . . . . . . . . . . . . . . . . . . . 177
Calling the Unbound Superclass Constructor. . . . . . . . . . . . . . . . . . 179
Using the super Function. . . . . . . . . . . . . . . . . . . . . . . . . . . . . . . . . 180
Item Access. . . . . . . . . . . . . . . . . . . . . . . . . . . . . . . . . . . . . . . . . . . . . . . 182
The Basic Sequence and Mapping Protocol. . . . . . . . . . . . . . . . . . . 182
Subclassing list, dict, and str . . . . . . . . . . . . . . . . . . . . . . . . . . . . . 185
More Magic . . . . . . . . . . . . . . . . . . . . . . . . . . . . . . . . . . . . . . . . . . . . . . . 187
Properties. . . . . . . . . . . . . . . . . . . . . . . . . . . . . . . . . . . . . . . . . . . . . . . . . 187
The property Function . . . . . . . . . . . . . . . . . . . . . . . . . . . . . . . . . . . 188
Static Methods and Class Methods . . . . . . . . . . . . . . . . . . . . . . . . . 189
__getattr__, __setattr__, and Friends . . . . . . . . . . . . . . . . . . . . . . 191
Iterators . . . . . . . . . . . . . . . . . . . . . . . . . . . . . . . . . . . . . . . . . . . . . . . . . . 192
The Iterator Protocol. . . . . . . . . . . . . . . . . . . . . . . . . . . . . . . . . . . . . 192
Making Sequences from Iterators . . . . . . . . . . . . . . . . . . . . . . . . . . 194
Generators. . . . . . . . . . . . . . . . . . . . . . . . . . . . . . . . . . . . . . . . . . . . . . . . 194
Making a Generator . . . . . . . . . . . . . . . . . . . . . . . . . . . . . . . . . . . . . 195
A Recursive Generator . . . . . . . . . . . . . . . . . . . . . . . . . . . . . . . . . . . 196
Generators in General. . . . . . . . . . . . . . . . . . . . . . . . . . . . . . . . . . . . 197
Generator Methods. . . . . . . . . . . . . . . . . . . . . . . . . . . . . . . . . . . . . . 198
Simulating Generators . . . . . . . . . . . . . . . . . . . . . . . . . . . . . . . . . . . 199
The Eight Queens . . . . . . . . . . . . . . . . . . . . . . . . . . . . . . . . . . . . . . . . . . 200
Generators and Backtracking . . . . . . . . . . . . . . . . . . . . . . . . . . . . . 200
The Problem. . . . . . . . . . . . . . . . . . . . . . . . . . . . . . . . . . . . . . . . . . . 201
State Representation . . . . . . . . . . . . . . . . . . . . . . . . . . . . . . . . . . . . 202
Finding Conflicts . . . . . . . . . . . . . . . . . . . . . . . . . . . . . . . . . . . . . . . 202
The Base Case. . . . . . . . . . . . . . . . . . . . . . . . . . . . . . . . . . . . . . . . . 203
The Recursive Case . . . . . . . . . . . . . . . . . . . . . . . . . . . . . . . . . . . . . 204
Wrapping It Up. . . . . . . . . . . . . . . . . . . . . . . . . . . . . . . . . . . . . . . . . 205

A Quick Summary . . . . . . . . . . . . . . . . . . . . . . . . . . . . . . . . . . . . . . . . . . . . 206

    New Functions in This Chapter . . . . . . . . . . . . . . . . . . . . . . . . . . . . . 207

    What Now? . . . . . . . . . . . . . . . . . . . . . . . . . . . . . . . . . . . . . . . . . . . . . . 207

**CHAPTER 10**   **Batteries Included** . . . . . . . . . . . . . . . . . . . . . . . . . . . . . . . . . . . 209

Modules . . . . . . . . . . . . . . . . . . . . . . . . . . . . . . . . . . . . . . . . . . . . . . . . . . . . 209

    Modules Are Programs . . . . . . . . . . . . . . . . . . . . . . . . . . . . . . . . . . . . 209

    Modules Are Used to Define Things . . . . . . . . . . . . . . . . . . . . . . . . . 211

    Making Your Modules Available . . . . . . . . . . . . . . . . . . . . . . . . . . . . 214

    Packages . . . . . . . . . . . . . . . . . . . . . . . . . . . . . . . . . . . . . . . . . . . . . . 217

Exploring Modules . . . . . . . . . . . . . . . . . . . . . . . . . . . . . . . . . . . . . . . . . . . 218

    What's in a Module? . . . . . . . . . . . . . . . . . . . . . . . . . . . . . . . . . . . . . 218

    Getting Help with help . . . . . . . . . . . . . . . . . . . . . . . . . . . . . . . . . . . 219

    Documentation . . . . . . . . . . . . . . . . . . . . . . . . . . . . . . . . . . . . . . . . . 220

    Use the Source . . . . . . . . . . . . . . . . . . . . . . . . . . . . . . . . . . . . . . . . . 221

The Standard Library: A Few Favorites . . . . . . . . . . . . . . . . . . . . . . . . . . . 221

    sys . . . . . . . . . . . . . . . . . . . . . . . . . . . . . . . . . . . . . . . . . . . . . . . . . . . 222

    os . . . . . . . . . . . . . . . . . . . . . . . . . . . . . . . . . . . . . . . . . . . . . . . . . . . . 223

    fileinput . . . . . . . . . . . . . . . . . . . . . . . . . . . . . . . . . . . . . . . . . . . . . . . 225

    Sets, Heaps, and Deques . . . . . . . . . . . . . . . . . . . . . . . . . . . . . . . . . 227

    time . . . . . . . . . . . . . . . . . . . . . . . . . . . . . . . . . . . . . . . . . . . . . . . . . . 232

    random . . . . . . . . . . . . . . . . . . . . . . . . . . . . . . . . . . . . . . . . . . . . . . . 234

    shelve . . . . . . . . . . . . . . . . . . . . . . . . . . . . . . . . . . . . . . . . . . . . . . . . 238

    re . . . . . . . . . . . . . . . . . . . . . . . . . . . . . . . . . . . . . . . . . . . . . . . . . . . . 242

    Other Interesting Standard Modules . . . . . . . . . . . . . . . . . . . . . . . . 258

A Quick Summary . . . . . . . . . . . . . . . . . . . . . . . . . . . . . . . . . . . . . . . . . . . . 259

    New Functions in This Chapter . . . . . . . . . . . . . . . . . . . . . . . . . . . . . 260

    What Now? . . . . . . . . . . . . . . . . . . . . . . . . . . . . . . . . . . . . . . . . . . . . 260

**CHAPTER 11**   **Files and Stuff** . . . . . . . . . . . . . . . . . . . . . . . . . . . . . . . . . . . . . . . 261

Opening Files . . . . . . . . . . . . . . . . . . . . . . . . . . . . . . . . . . . . . . . . . . . . . . . 261

    File Modes . . . . . . . . . . . . . . . . . . . . . . . . . . . . . . . . . . . . . . . . . . . . . 261

    Buffering . . . . . . . . . . . . . . . . . . . . . . . . . . . . . . . . . . . . . . . . . . . . . . 263

The Basic File Methods . . . . . . . . . . . . . . . . . . . . . . . . . . . . . . . . . . . . . . . 263

    Reading and Writing . . . . . . . . . . . . . . . . . . . . . . . . . . . . . . . . . . . . . 264

    Piping Output . . . . . . . . . . . . . . . . . . . . . . . . . . . . . . . . . . . . . . . . . . 264

    Reading and Writing Lines . . . . . . . . . . . . . . . . . . . . . . . . . . . . . . . . 266

    Closing Files . . . . . . . . . . . . . . . . . . . . . . . . . . . . . . . . . . . . . . . . . . . 267

    Using the Basic File Methods . . . . . . . . . . . . . . . . . . . . . . . . . . . . . . 268

Iterating over File Contents.................................................... 270
    Doing It Byte by Byte ..................................................... 270
    One Line at a Time ....................................................... 271
    Reading Everything....................................................... 271
    Lazy Line Iteration with fileinput........................................ 272
    File Iterators ........................................................... 272
A Quick Summary............................................................... 274
    New Functions in This Chapter........................................... 275
    What Now?............................................................... 275

■CHAPTER 12    **Graphical User Interfaces**................................. 277

A Plethora of Platforms ......................................................... 277
Downloading and Installing wxPython ........................................... 278
Building a Sample GUI Application............................................... 279
    Getting Started.......................................................... 280
    Windows and Components ............................................... 281
    Labels, Titles, and Positions ............................................ 282
    More Intelligent Layout.................................................. 284
    Event Handling.......................................................... 286
    The Finished Program ................................................... 286
But I'd Rather Use .............................................................. 288
    Using Tkinter ........................................................... 289
    Using Jython and Swing.................................................. 290
    Using Something Else.................................................... 290
A Quick Summary............................................................... 291
    What Now?............................................................... 291

■CHAPTER 13    **Database Support** ......................................... 293

The Python Database API ....................................................... 294
    Global Variables......................................................... 294
    Exceptions ............................................................. 295
    Connections and Cursors................................................ 296
    Types................................................................... 297
SQLite and PySQLite ........................................................... 298
    Getting Started.......................................................... 300
    A Sample Database Application .......................................... 300
A Quick Summary............................................................... 303
    New Functions in This Chapter........................................... 304
    What Now?............................................................... 304

■**CHAPTER 14**    **Network Programming** . . . . . . . . . . . . . . . . . . . . . . . . . . . . . . . . . 305

A Handful of Networking Modules . . . . . . . . . . . . . . . . . . . . . . . . . . . . . . . 305
    The socket Module . . . . . . . . . . . . . . . . . . . . . . . . . . . . . . . . . . . . . . 306
    The urllib and urllib2 Modules . . . . . . . . . . . . . . . . . . . . . . . . . . . 308
    Other Modules . . . . . . . . . . . . . . . . . . . . . . . . . . . . . . . . . . . . . . . . . 310
SocketServer and Friends . . . . . . . . . . . . . . . . . . . . . . . . . . . . . . . . . . . . 310
Multiple Connections . . . . . . . . . . . . . . . . . . . . . . . . . . . . . . . . . . . . . . . 311
    Forking and Threading with SocketServer . . . . . . . . . . . . . . . . . . 313
    Asynchronous I/O with select and poll . . . . . . . . . . . . . . . . . . . . . 313
Twisted . . . . . . . . . . . . . . . . . . . . . . . . . . . . . . . . . . . . . . . . . . . . . . . . . . 316
    Downloading and Installing Twisted . . . . . . . . . . . . . . . . . . . . . . . . 317
    Writing a Twisted Server . . . . . . . . . . . . . . . . . . . . . . . . . . . . . . . . 317
A Quick Summary . . . . . . . . . . . . . . . . . . . . . . . . . . . . . . . . . . . . . . . . . . 319
    New Functions in This Chapter . . . . . . . . . . . . . . . . . . . . . . . . . . . 320
    What Now? . . . . . . . . . . . . . . . . . . . . . . . . . . . . . . . . . . . . . . . . . . . 320

■**CHAPTER 15**    **Python and the Web** . . . . . . . . . . . . . . . . . . . . . . . . . . . . . . . . . . . 321

Screen Scraping . . . . . . . . . . . . . . . . . . . . . . . . . . . . . . . . . . . . . . . . . . . 321
    Tidy and XHTML Parsing . . . . . . . . . . . . . . . . . . . . . . . . . . . . . . . . 322
    Beautiful Soup . . . . . . . . . . . . . . . . . . . . . . . . . . . . . . . . . . . . . . . . 327
Dynamic Web Pages with CGI . . . . . . . . . . . . . . . . . . . . . . . . . . . . . . . . 328
    Step 1. Preparing the Web Server . . . . . . . . . . . . . . . . . . . . . . . . . 328
    Step 2. Adding the Pound Bang Line . . . . . . . . . . . . . . . . . . . . . . . 329
    Step 3. Setting the File Permissions . . . . . . . . . . . . . . . . . . . . . . . 329
    CGI Security Risks . . . . . . . . . . . . . . . . . . . . . . . . . . . . . . . . . . . . . 330
    A Simple CGI Script . . . . . . . . . . . . . . . . . . . . . . . . . . . . . . . . . . . . 331
    Debugging with cgitb . . . . . . . . . . . . . . . . . . . . . . . . . . . . . . . . . . 331
    Using the cgi Module . . . . . . . . . . . . . . . . . . . . . . . . . . . . . . . . . . . 333
    A Simple Form . . . . . . . . . . . . . . . . . . . . . . . . . . . . . . . . . . . . . . . 334
One Step Up: mod_python . . . . . . . . . . . . . . . . . . . . . . . . . . . . . . . . . . . 336
    Installing mod_python . . . . . . . . . . . . . . . . . . . . . . . . . . . . . . . . . . 337
    CGI Handler . . . . . . . . . . . . . . . . . . . . . . . . . . . . . . . . . . . . . . . . . 338
    PSP . . . . . . . . . . . . . . . . . . . . . . . . . . . . . . . . . . . . . . . . . . . . . . . . 339
    The Publisher . . . . . . . . . . . . . . . . . . . . . . . . . . . . . . . . . . . . . . . . 341
Web Application Frameworks . . . . . . . . . . . . . . . . . . . . . . . . . . . . . . . . . 343
Web Services: Scraping Done Right . . . . . . . . . . . . . . . . . . . . . . . . . . . . 344
    RSS and Friends . . . . . . . . . . . . . . . . . . . . . . . . . . . . . . . . . . . . . . 345
    Remote Procedure Calls with XML-RPC . . . . . . . . . . . . . . . . . . . . 345
    SOAP . . . . . . . . . . . . . . . . . . . . . . . . . . . . . . . . . . . . . . . . . . . . . . 346

A Quick Summary. . . . . . . . . . . . . . . . . . . . . . . . . . . . . . . . . . . . . . . . . . . 346
    New Functions in This Chapter. . . . . . . . . . . . . . . . . . . . . . . . . . . . . 347
    What Now?. . . . . . . . . . . . . . . . . . . . . . . . . . . . . . . . . . . . . . . . . . . . 347

**CHAPTER 16**  **Testing, 1-2-3**. . . . . . . . . . . . . . . . . . . . . . . . . . . . . . . . . . . 349

Test First, Code Later. . . . . . . . . . . . . . . . . . . . . . . . . . . . . . . . . . . . . . 349
    Precise Requirement Specification . . . . . . . . . . . . . . . . . . . . . . . . 350
    Planning for Change . . . . . . . . . . . . . . . . . . . . . . . . . . . . . . . . . . . 351
    The 1-2-3 (and 4) of Testing. . . . . . . . . . . . . . . . . . . . . . . . . . . . . 352
Tools for Testing . . . . . . . . . . . . . . . . . . . . . . . . . . . . . . . . . . . . . . . . . 352
    doctest . . . . . . . . . . . . . . . . . . . . . . . . . . . . . . . . . . . . . . . . . . . . . 353
    unittest . . . . . . . . . . . . . . . . . . . . . . . . . . . . . . . . . . . . . . . . . . . . . 355
Beyond Unit Tests. . . . . . . . . . . . . . . . . . . . . . . . . . . . . . . . . . . . . . . . 358
    Source Code Checking with PyChecker and PyLint . . . . . . . . . . . 359
    Profiling. . . . . . . . . . . . . . . . . . . . . . . . . . . . . . . . . . . . . . . . . . . . . 362
A Quick Summary. . . . . . . . . . . . . . . . . . . . . . . . . . . . . . . . . . . . . . . . . 364
    New Functions in This Chapter. . . . . . . . . . . . . . . . . . . . . . . . . . . . 364
    What Now?. . . . . . . . . . . . . . . . . . . . . . . . . . . . . . . . . . . . . . . . . . . 364

**CHAPTER 17**  **Extending Python**. . . . . . . . . . . . . . . . . . . . . . . . . . . . . . . . 365

The Best of Both Worlds . . . . . . . . . . . . . . . . . . . . . . . . . . . . . . . . . . . 365
The Really Easy Way: Jython and IronPython . . . . . . . . . . . . . . . . . . . 367
Writing C Extensions . . . . . . . . . . . . . . . . . . . . . . . . . . . . . . . . . . . . . . 369
    A Swig of . . . SWIG. . . . . . . . . . . . . . . . . . . . . . . . . . . . . . . . . . . . 371
    Hacking It on Your Own . . . . . . . . . . . . . . . . . . . . . . . . . . . . . . . . 375
A Quick Summary. . . . . . . . . . . . . . . . . . . . . . . . . . . . . . . . . . . . . . . . . 380
    New Functions in This Chapter. . . . . . . . . . . . . . . . . . . . . . . . . . . . 381
    What Now?. . . . . . . . . . . . . . . . . . . . . . . . . . . . . . . . . . . . . . . . . . . 381

**CHAPTER 18**  **Packaging Your Programs** . . . . . . . . . . . . . . . . . . . . . . . . . . 383

Distutils Basics . . . . . . . . . . . . . . . . . . . . . . . . . . . . . . . . . . . . . . . . . . 383
Wrapping Things Up. . . . . . . . . . . . . . . . . . . . . . . . . . . . . . . . . . . . . . . 386
    Building an Archive File . . . . . . . . . . . . . . . . . . . . . . . . . . . . . . . . . 386
    Creating a Windows Installer or an RPM Package. . . . . . . . . . . . . 387
Compiling Extensions. . . . . . . . . . . . . . . . . . . . . . . . . . . . . . . . . . . . . . 388
Creating Executable Programs with py2exe . . . . . . . . . . . . . . . . . . . . 389

A Quick Summary . . . . . . . . . . . . . . . . . . . . . . . . . . . . . . . . . . . . . . . . . . . . . 390
    New Functions in This Chapter . . . . . . . . . . . . . . . . . . . . . . . . . . . . . . . 391
    What Now? . . . . . . . . . . . . . . . . . . . . . . . . . . . . . . . . . . . . . . . . . . . . . . . 391

■CHAPTER 19    **Playful Programming** . . . . . . . . . . . . . . . . . . . . . . . . . . . . . . . . . . . 393

Why Playful? . . . . . . . . . . . . . . . . . . . . . . . . . . . . . . . . . . . . . . . . . . . . . . . . 393
The Jujitsu of Programming . . . . . . . . . . . . . . . . . . . . . . . . . . . . . . . . . . . . 393
Prototyping . . . . . . . . . . . . . . . . . . . . . . . . . . . . . . . . . . . . . . . . . . . . . . . . . 394
Configuration . . . . . . . . . . . . . . . . . . . . . . . . . . . . . . . . . . . . . . . . . . . . . . . 396
    Extracting Constants . . . . . . . . . . . . . . . . . . . . . . . . . . . . . . . . . . . . . . 396
    Configuration Files . . . . . . . . . . . . . . . . . . . . . . . . . . . . . . . . . . . . . . . 396
Logging . . . . . . . . . . . . . . . . . . . . . . . . . . . . . . . . . . . . . . . . . . . . . . . . . . . 399
If You Can't Be Bothered . . . . . . . . . . . . . . . . . . . . . . . . . . . . . . . . . . . . . . 400
If You Want to Learn More . . . . . . . . . . . . . . . . . . . . . . . . . . . . . . . . . . . . . 400
A Quick Summary . . . . . . . . . . . . . . . . . . . . . . . . . . . . . . . . . . . . . . . . . . . . 401
    What Now? . . . . . . . . . . . . . . . . . . . . . . . . . . . . . . . . . . . . . . . . . . . . . . . 401

■CHAPTER 20    **Project 1: Instant Markup** . . . . . . . . . . . . . . . . . . . . . . . . . . . . . 403

What's the Problem? . . . . . . . . . . . . . . . . . . . . . . . . . . . . . . . . . . . . . . . . . 403
Useful Tools . . . . . . . . . . . . . . . . . . . . . . . . . . . . . . . . . . . . . . . . . . . . . . . . 404
Preparations . . . . . . . . . . . . . . . . . . . . . . . . . . . . . . . . . . . . . . . . . . . . . . . 405
First Implementation . . . . . . . . . . . . . . . . . . . . . . . . . . . . . . . . . . . . . . . . . 406
    Finding Blocks of Text . . . . . . . . . . . . . . . . . . . . . . . . . . . . . . . . . . . . 406
    Adding Some Markup . . . . . . . . . . . . . . . . . . . . . . . . . . . . . . . . . . . . . 407
Second Implementation . . . . . . . . . . . . . . . . . . . . . . . . . . . . . . . . . . . . . . . 408
    Handlers . . . . . . . . . . . . . . . . . . . . . . . . . . . . . . . . . . . . . . . . . . . . . . . 409
    A Handler Superclass . . . . . . . . . . . . . . . . . . . . . . . . . . . . . . . . . . . . . 410
    Rules . . . . . . . . . . . . . . . . . . . . . . . . . . . . . . . . . . . . . . . . . . . . . . . . . . 412
    A Rule Superclass . . . . . . . . . . . . . . . . . . . . . . . . . . . . . . . . . . . . . . . . 413
    Filters . . . . . . . . . . . . . . . . . . . . . . . . . . . . . . . . . . . . . . . . . . . . . . . . . 413
    The Parser . . . . . . . . . . . . . . . . . . . . . . . . . . . . . . . . . . . . . . . . . . . . . 413
    Constructing the Rules and Filters . . . . . . . . . . . . . . . . . . . . . . . . . . . 415
    Putting It All Together . . . . . . . . . . . . . . . . . . . . . . . . . . . . . . . . . . . . . 418
Further Exploration . . . . . . . . . . . . . . . . . . . . . . . . . . . . . . . . . . . . . . . . . . 423
    What Now? . . . . . . . . . . . . . . . . . . . . . . . . . . . . . . . . . . . . . . . . . . . . . . 424

■CHAPTER 21    **Project 2: Painting a Pretty Picture** . . . . . . . . . . . . . . . . . . . . . 425

What's the Problem? . . . . . . . . . . . . . . . . . . . . . . . . . . . . . . . . . . . . . . . . 425
Useful Tools . . . . . . . . . . . . . . . . . . . . . . . . . . . . . . . . . . . . . . . . . . . . . . . 426
Preparations . . . . . . . . . . . . . . . . . . . . . . . . . . . . . . . . . . . . . . . . . . . . . . 426
First Implementation . . . . . . . . . . . . . . . . . . . . . . . . . . . . . . . . . . . . . . . 427
    Drawing with ReportLab . . . . . . . . . . . . . . . . . . . . . . . . . . . . . 427
    Constructing Some PolyLines . . . . . . . . . . . . . . . . . . . . . . . . . 429
    Writing the Prototype . . . . . . . . . . . . . . . . . . . . . . . . . . . . . . . 430
Second Implementation . . . . . . . . . . . . . . . . . . . . . . . . . . . . . . . . . . . . 431
    Getting the Data . . . . . . . . . . . . . . . . . . . . . . . . . . . . . . . . . . . . 432
    Using the LinePlot Class . . . . . . . . . . . . . . . . . . . . . . . . . . . . . 432
Further Exploration . . . . . . . . . . . . . . . . . . . . . . . . . . . . . . . . . . . . . . . . 434
    What Now? . . . . . . . . . . . . . . . . . . . . . . . . . . . . . . . . . . . . . . . . . 434

■CHAPTER 22    **Project 3: XML for All Occasions** . . . . . . . . . . . . . . . . . . . 435

What's the Problem? . . . . . . . . . . . . . . . . . . . . . . . . . . . . . . . . . . . . . . . . 435
Useful Tools . . . . . . . . . . . . . . . . . . . . . . . . . . . . . . . . . . . . . . . . . . . . . . . 436
Preparations . . . . . . . . . . . . . . . . . . . . . . . . . . . . . . . . . . . . . . . . . . . . . . 437
First Implementation . . . . . . . . . . . . . . . . . . . . . . . . . . . . . . . . . . . . . . . 438
    Creating a Simple Content Handler . . . . . . . . . . . . . . . . . . . . 439
    Creating HTML Pages . . . . . . . . . . . . . . . . . . . . . . . . . . . . . . . 442
Second Implementation . . . . . . . . . . . . . . . . . . . . . . . . . . . . . . . . . . . . 444
    A Dispatcher Mix-In Class . . . . . . . . . . . . . . . . . . . . . . . . . . . 444
    Factoring Out the Header, Footer, and Default Handling . . . . . . . 446
    Support for Directories . . . . . . . . . . . . . . . . . . . . . . . . . . . . . . 447
    The Event Handlers . . . . . . . . . . . . . . . . . . . . . . . . . . . . . . . . . 448
Further Exploration . . . . . . . . . . . . . . . . . . . . . . . . . . . . . . . . . . . . . . . . 451
    What Now? . . . . . . . . . . . . . . . . . . . . . . . . . . . . . . . . . . . . . . . . . 452

■CHAPTER 23    **Project 4: In the News** . . . . . . . . . . . . . . . . . . . . . . . . . . . . . . . 453

What's the Problem? . . . . . . . . . . . . . . . . . . . . . . . . . . . . . . . . . . . . . . . . 453
Useful Tools . . . . . . . . . . . . . . . . . . . . . . . . . . . . . . . . . . . . . . . . . . . . . . . 454
Preparations . . . . . . . . . . . . . . . . . . . . . . . . . . . . . . . . . . . . . . . . . . . . . . 454
First Implementation . . . . . . . . . . . . . . . . . . . . . . . . . . . . . . . . . . . . . . . 455

Second Implementation.......................................... 458
Further Exploration............................................ 467
    What Now?.............................................. 468

■**CHAPTER 24**   **Project 5: A Virtual Tea Party** ........................... 469

What's the Problem? ......................................... 469
Useful Tools................................................. 470
Preparations ................................................ 470
First Implementation ........................................ 471
    The ChatServer Class ................................... 471
    The ChatSession Class.................................. 473
    Putting It Together..................................... 475
Second Implementation........................................ 477
    Basic Command Interpretation ........................... 477
    Rooms................................................. 478
    Login and Logout Rooms................................. 479
    The Main Chat Room .................................... 479
    The New Server........................................ 480
Further Exploration........................................... 486
    What Now?.............................................. 487

■**CHAPTER 25**   **Project 6: Remote Editing with CGI** ...................... 489

What's the Problem? ......................................... 489
Useful Tools................................................. 490
Preparations ................................................ 490
First Implementation ......................................... 490
Second Implementation........................................ 491
    Creating the File Name Form ............................ 492
    Writing the Editor Script................................ 492
    Writing the Save Script................................. 494
    Running the Editor...................................... 496
Further Exploration........................................... 497
    What Now?.............................................. 498

■CHAPTER 26    **Project 7: Your Own Bulletin Board** . . . . . . . . . . . . . . . . . . . . . 499

What's the Problem? . . . . . . . . . . . . . . . . . . . . . . . . . . . . . . . . . . . . . . . . . . 499
Useful Tools. . . . . . . . . . . . . . . . . . . . . . . . . . . . . . . . . . . . . . . . . . . . . . . . . 500
Preparations . . . . . . . . . . . . . . . . . . . . . . . . . . . . . . . . . . . . . . . . . . . . . . . . 500
First Implementation . . . . . . . . . . . . . . . . . . . . . . . . . . . . . . . . . . . . . . . . . . 502
Second Implementation. . . . . . . . . . . . . . . . . . . . . . . . . . . . . . . . . . . . . . . . 506
    Writing the Main Script. . . . . . . . . . . . . . . . . . . . . . . . . . . . . . . . . 507
    Writing the View Script. . . . . . . . . . . . . . . . . . . . . . . . . . . . . . . . . 508
    Writing the Edit Script. . . . . . . . . . . . . . . . . . . . . . . . . . . . . . . . . . 510
    Writing the Save Script. . . . . . . . . . . . . . . . . . . . . . . . . . . . . . . . . 511
    Trying It Out . . . . . . . . . . . . . . . . . . . . . . . . . . . . . . . . . . . . . . . . . . 513
Further Exploration . . . . . . . . . . . . . . . . . . . . . . . . . . . . . . . . . . . . . . . . . . . 515
    What Now?. . . . . . . . . . . . . . . . . . . . . . . . . . . . . . . . . . . . . . . . . . . 515

■CHAPTER 27    **Project 8: File Sharing with XML-RPC** . . . . . . . . . . . . . . . . . . 517

What's the Problem? . . . . . . . . . . . . . . . . . . . . . . . . . . . . . . . . . . . . . . . . . . 517
Useful Tools. . . . . . . . . . . . . . . . . . . . . . . . . . . . . . . . . . . . . . . . . . . . . . . . . 518
Preparations . . . . . . . . . . . . . . . . . . . . . . . . . . . . . . . . . . . . . . . . . . . . . . . . 519
First Implementation . . . . . . . . . . . . . . . . . . . . . . . . . . . . . . . . . . . . . . . . . . 519
    Implementing a Simple Node . . . . . . . . . . . . . . . . . . . . . . . . . . . . 520
    Trying Out the First Implementation . . . . . . . . . . . . . . . . . . . . . . . 525
Second Implementation. . . . . . . . . . . . . . . . . . . . . . . . . . . . . . . . . . . . . . . . 527
    Creating the Client Interface . . . . . . . . . . . . . . . . . . . . . . . . . . . . . 527
    Raising Exceptions . . . . . . . . . . . . . . . . . . . . . . . . . . . . . . . . . . . . 528
    Validating File Names. . . . . . . . . . . . . . . . . . . . . . . . . . . . . . . . . . . 529
    Trying Out the Second Implementation. . . . . . . . . . . . . . . . . . . . . 534
Further Exploration. . . . . . . . . . . . . . . . . . . . . . . . . . . . . . . . . . . . . . . . . . . 534
    What Now?. . . . . . . . . . . . . . . . . . . . . . . . . . . . . . . . . . . . . . . . . . . 535

■CHAPTER 28    **Project 9: File Sharing II—Now with GUI!** . . . . . . . . . . . . . . . 537

What's the Problem? . . . . . . . . . . . . . . . . . . . . . . . . . . . . . . . . . . . . . . . . . . 537
Useful Tools. . . . . . . . . . . . . . . . . . . . . . . . . . . . . . . . . . . . . . . . . . . . . . . . . 537
Preparations . . . . . . . . . . . . . . . . . . . . . . . . . . . . . . . . . . . . . . . . . . . . . . . . 538
First Implementation . . . . . . . . . . . . . . . . . . . . . . . . . . . . . . . . . . . . . . . . . . 538
Second Implementation. . . . . . . . . . . . . . . . . . . . . . . . . . . . . . . . . . . . . . . . 541
Further Exploration. . . . . . . . . . . . . . . . . . . . . . . . . . . . . . . . . . . . . . . . . . . 545
    What Now?. . . . . . . . . . . . . . . . . . . . . . . . . . . . . . . . . . . . . . . . . . . 545

■CHAPTER 29    **Project 10: Do-It-Yourself Arcade Game** ................ 547

What's the Problem? ......................................... 547
Useful Tools................................................ 548
    pygame.................................................. 548
    pygame.locals .......................................... 549
    pygame.display ......................................... 549
    pygame.font............................................. 550
    pygame.sprite .......................................... 550
    pygame.mouse ........................................... 550
    pygame.event ........................................... 550
    pygame.image........................................... 551
Preparations ............................................... 551
First Implementation ........................................ 551
Second Implementation....................................... 556
Further Exploration ......................................... 567
    What Now?............................................... 567

■APPENDIX A    **The Short Version**................................... 569

The Basics ................................................. 569
Functions .................................................. 571
Objects and Stuff ........................................... 572
Some Loose Ends............................................. 576

■APPENDIX B    **Python Reference**................................... 579

Expressions ................................................ 579
Statements.................................................. 589
    Simple Statements ...................................... 589
    Compound Statements..................................... 592

■APPENDIX C    **Online Resources** .................................. 595

Python Distributions......................................... 595
Python Documentation......................................... 596
Useful Toolkits and Modules................................... 596
Newsgroups, Mailing Lists, and Blogs ......................... 597

■**APPENDIX D   Python 3.0** ................................................. 599

Strings and I/O ................................................ 599
    Strings, Bytes, and Encodings ............................. 599
    Console I/O ................................................ 600
    New String Formatting ..................................... 600
Classes and Functions ......................................... 601
    Function Annotation ....................................... 601
    Abstract Base Classes ..................................... 601
    Class Decorators and New Metaclass Syntax ................. 601
    Keyword-Only Parameters ................................... 602
    Nonlocal Variables ........................................ 602
Iterables, Comprehensions, and Views .......................... 603
    Extended Iterable Unpacking ............................... 603
    Dictionary and Set Comprehension .......................... 603
    Dictionary Views .......................................... 603
    Iterator Return Values .................................... 603
Things That Have Gone ......................................... 604
Some Minor Issues ............................................. 604
The Standard Library .......................................... 604
Other Stuff ................................................... 605

■**INDEX** ..................................................... 607

# About the Author

 **MAGNUS LIE HETLAND** is an associate professor of algorithms at the Norwegian University of Science and Technology (NTNU). Even though he loves learning new programming languages—even quite obscure ones—Magnus has been a devoted Python fan and an active member of the Python community for many years, and is the author of the popular online tutorials "Instant Python" and "Instant Hacking." His publications include the forerunner to this book, *Practical Python* (Apress, 2002), as well as several scientific papers. When he isn't busy staring at a computer screen, he may be found reading (even while bicycling), acting (in a local theater group), or gaming (mostly role-playing games).

# About the Technical Reviewer

**RICHARD TAYLOR** is a senior analyst at QinetiQ Ltd in the UK, where he specializes in open systems architectures for command and control systems. He has been developing in Python since about 1994, and has used Python to build many large-scale commercial and research applications. When not working, Richard indulges his keen interest in genealogy and open source software, and is a regular contributor to the GRAMPS (Genealogical Research and Analysis Management Programming System) project.

# Preface

**H**ere it is—a shiny new edition of *Beginning Python*. If you count its predecessor, *Practical Python*, this is actually the third edition, and a book I've been involved with for the better part of a decade. During this time, Python has seen many interesting changes, and I've done my best to update my introduction to the language. At the moment, Python is facing perhaps its most marked transition in a very long time: the introduction of version 3. As I write this, the final release isn't out yet, but the features are clearly defined and working versions are available. One interesting challenge linked to this language revision is that it isn't backward-compatible. In other words, it doesn't simply add features that I could pick and choose from in my writing. It also changes the existing language, so that certain things that are true for Python 2.5 no longer hold.

Had it been clear that the entire Python community would instantly switch to the new version and update all its legacy code, this would hardly be a problem. Simply describe the new language! However, a lot of code written for older versions exists, and much will probably still be written, until version 3 is universally accepted as The Way To Go™.

So, how have I gotten myself out of this pickle? First of all, even though there are incompatible changes, *most* of the language remains the same. Therefore, if I wrote entirely about Python 2.5, it would be *mostly* correct for Python 3 (and even more so for its companion release, 2.6). As for the parts that will no longer be correct, I have been a bit conservative and assumed that full adoption of version 3 will take some time. I have based the book primarily on 2.5, and noted things that will change throughout the text. In addition, I've included Appendix D, which gives you an overview of the main changes. I think this will work out for most readers.

In writing this second edition, I have had a lot of help from several people. Just as with the previous two versions (the first edition, and, before it, *Practical Python*), Jason Gilmore got me started and played an important role in getting the project on the road. As it has moved along, Richard Dal Porto, Frank Pohlmann, and Dominic Shakeshaft have been instrumental in keeping it going. Richard Taylor has certainly played a crucial role in ensuring that the code is correct (and if it still isn't, I'm the one to blame), and Marilyn Smith has done a great job tuning my writing. My thanks also go out to other Apress staff, including Liz Berry, Beth Christmas, Steve Anglin, and Tina Nielsen, as well as various readers who have provided errata and helpful suggestions, including Bob Helmbold and Waclaw Kusnierczyk. I am also, of course, still thankful to all those who helped in getting the first two incarnations of this book on the shelves.

## Preface to the First Edition

A few years ago, Jason Gilmore approached me about writing a book for Apress. He had read my online Python tutorials and wanted me to write a book in a similar style. I was flattered, excited, and just a little nervous. The one thing that worried me the most was how much time it would take, and how much it would interfere with my studies (I was a Ph.D student at the time). It turned out to be quite an undertaking, and it took me a lot longer to finish than I had expected.

Luckily, it didn't interfere too much with my school work, and I managed to get my degree without any delays.

Last year, Jason contacted me again. Apress wanted an expanded and revised version of my book. Was I interested? At the time, I was busy settling into a new position as associate processor, while spending all my spare time portraying Peer Gynt, so again time became the major issue. Eventually (after things had settled down a bit, and I had a bit more time to spare), I agreed to do the book, and this (as I'm sure you've gathered) is the result. Most of the material is taken from the first version of the book, *Practical Python* (Apress, 2002). The existing material has been completely revised, based on recent changes in the Python language, and several new chapters have been added. Some of the old material has also been redistributed to accommodate the new structure. I've received a lot of positive feedback from readers about the first version. I hope I've been able to keep what people liked and to add more of the same.

Without the persistent help and encouragement from several people, this book would never have been written. My heartfelt thanks go out to all of them. In particular, I would like to thank the team that has worked directly with me in the process of writing the book: Jason Gilmore, for getting the project off the ground and steering it in the right direction; Beckie Stones, for keeping everything together; Jeremy Jones and Matt Moodie for their technical comments and insights; and Linda Marousek for being so patient with me. I'm also grateful to the rest of the team for making the process as smooth as it has been. But this book wouldn't be what it is without several people who worked with me on the previous version: I'd like to thank Jason Gilmore and Alex Martelli for their excellent technical editing (Jason on the entire book, and Alex on the first half) and for going above and beyond the call of duty in dispensing advice and suggestions; Erin Mulligan and Tory McLearn for holding my hand through the process and for nudging me along when that was needed; Nancy Rapoport for her help polishing my prose; and Grace Wong for providing answers when no one else could. Pete Shinners gave me several helpful suggestions on the game in Project 10, for which I am very grateful. My morale has also been heavily boosted by several encouraging emails from satisfied readers—thanks! Finally, I would like to thank my family and friends, and my girlfriend Ranveig, for putting up with me while I was writing this book.

# Introduction

I've started this introduction with a few quotes to set the tone for the book, which is rather informal. In the hope of making it an easy read, I've tried to approach the topic of Python programming with a healthy dose of humor, and true to the traditions of the Python community, much of this humor is related to Monty Python sketches. As a consequence, some of my examples may seem a bit silly; I hope you will bear with me. (And, yes, the name Python is derived from Monty Python, not from snakes belonging to the family *Pythonidae*.)

In this introduction, I give you a quick look at what Python is, why you should use it, who uses it, who this book's intended audience is, and how the book is organized.

So, what is Python, and why should you use it? To quote an official blurb (available from `http://python.org/doc/essays/blurb.html`), it is "an interpreted, object-oriented, high-level programming language with dynamic semantics." Many of these terms will become clear as you read this book, but the gist is that Python is a programming language that knows how to stay out of your way when you write your programs. It enables you to implement the functionality you want without any hassle, and lets you write programs that are clear and readable (much more so than programs in most other currently popular programming languages).

Even though Python might not be as fast as compiled languages such as C or C++, what you save in programming time will probably be worth using it, and in most programs, the speed difference won't be noticeable anyway. If you are a C programmer, you can easily implement the critical parts of your program in C at a later date, and have them interoperate with the Python parts. If you haven't done any programming before (and perhaps are a bit confused by my references to C and C++), Python's combination of simplicity and power makes it an ideal choice as a place to start.

So, who uses Python? Since Guido van Rossum created the language in the early 1990s, its following has grown steadily, and interest has increased markedly in the past few years. Python is used extensively for system administration tasks (it is, for example, a vital component of several Linux distributions), but it is also used to teach programming to complete beginners. The US National Aeronautics and Space Administration (NASA) uses Python both for development and as a scripting language in several of its systems. Industrial Light & Magic uses Python in its production of special effects for large-budget feature films. Yahoo! uses it (among other things) to manage its discussion groups. Google has used it to implement many components of its web crawler and search engine. Python is being used in such diverse areas as computer games and bioinformatics. Soon one might as well ask, "Who *isn't* using Python?"

This book is for those of you who want to learn how to program in Python. It is intended to suit a wide audience, from neophyte programmer to advanced computer wiz. If you have never programmed before, you should start by reading Chapter 1 and continue until you find that things get too advanced for you (if, indeed, they do). Then you should start practicing and write some programs of your own. When the time is right, you can return to the book and proceed with the more intricate stuff.

If you already know how to program, some of the introductory material might not be new to you (although there will probably be some surprising details here and there). You could skim through the early chapters to get an idea of how Python works, or perhaps read through Appendix A, which is based on my online Python tutorial "Instant Python." It will get you up to speed on the most important Python concepts. After getting the big picture, you could jump straight to Chapter 10 (which describes the Python standard libraries).

The last ten chapters present ten programming projects, which show off various capabilities of the Python language. These projects should be of interest to beginners and experts alike. Although some of the material in the later projects may be a bit difficult for an inexperienced programmer, following the projects in order (after reading the material in the first part of the book) should be possible.

The projects touch upon a wide range of topics, most of which will be very useful to you when writing programs of your own. You will learn how to do things that may seem completely out of reach to you at this point, such as creating a chat server, a peer-to-peer file sharing system, or a full-fledged graphical computer game. Although much of the material may seem hard at first glance, I think you will be surprised by how easy most of it really is. If you would like to download the source code, it's available from the Source Code/Download section of the Apress web site (`http://www.apress.com`).

Well, that's it. I always find long introductions boring myself, so I'll let you continue with your Pythoneering, either in Chapter 1 or in Appendix A. Good luck, and happy hacking.

# CHAPTER 1

∎∎∎

# Instant Hacking: The Basics

It's time to start hacking.[1] In this chapter, you learn how to take control of your computer by speaking a language it understands: Python. Nothing here is particularly difficult, so if you know the basic principles of how your computer works, you should be able to follow the examples and try them out yourself. I'll go through the basics, startiwng with the excruciatingly simple, but because Python is such a powerful language, you'll soon be able to do pretty advanced things.

First, I show you how to get the software you need. Then I tell you a bit about algorithms and their main components. Throughout these sections, there are numerous small examples (most of them using only simple arithmetic) that you can try out in the Python interactive interpreter (covered in the section "The Interactive Interpreter" in this chapter). You learn about variables, functions, and modules, and after handling these topics, I show you how to write and run larger programs. Finally, I deal with strings, an important aspect of almost any Python program.

## Installing Python

Before you can start programming, you need some new software. What follows is a short description of how to download and install Python. If you want to jump into the installation process without detailed guidance, you can simply visit `http://www.python.org/download` to get the most recent version of Python.

### Windows

To install Python on a Windows machine, follow these steps:

1. Open a web browser and go to `http://www.python.org`.

2. Click the Download link.

3. You should see several links here, with names such as Python 2.5.*x* and Python 2.5.*x* Windows installer. Click the Windows installer link to download the installer file. (If you're running on an Itanium or AMD machine, you need to choose the appropriate installer.)

---

1. *Hacking* is not the same as *cracking*, which is a term describing computer crime. The two are often confused. Hacking basically means "having fun while programming." For more information, see Eric Raymond's article "How to Become a Hacker" at `http://www.catb.org/~esr/faqs/hacker-howto.html`.

■**Note**  If you can't find the link mentioned in step 3, click the link with the highest version among those with names like Python 2.5.*x*. For Python 2.5, you could simply go to `http://www.python.org/2.5`. Follow the instructions for Windows users. This will entail downloading a file called `python-2.5.x.msi` (or something similar), where 2.5.*x* should be the version number of the newest release.

4. Store the Windows Installer file somewhere on your computer, such as `C:\download\python-2.5.x.msi`. (Just create a directory where you can find it later.)

5. Run the downloaded file by double-clicking it in Windows Explorer. This brings up the Python install wizard, which is really easy to use. Just accept the default settings, wait until the installation is finished, and you're ready to roll!

Assuming that the installation went well, you now have a new program in your Windows Start menu. Run the Python Integrated Development Environment (IDLE) by selecting Start ➤ Programs ➤ Python[2] ➤ IDLE (Python GUI).

You should now see a window that looks like the one shown in Figure 1-1. If you feel a bit lost, simply select Help ➤ IDLE Help from the menu to get a simple description of the various menu items and basic usage. For more documentation on IDLE, check out `http://www.python.org/idle`. (Here you will also find more information on running IDLE on platforms other than Windows.) If you press F1, or select Help ➤ Python Docs from the menu, you will get the full Python documentation. (The document there of most use to you will probably be the Library Reference.) All the documentation is searchable.

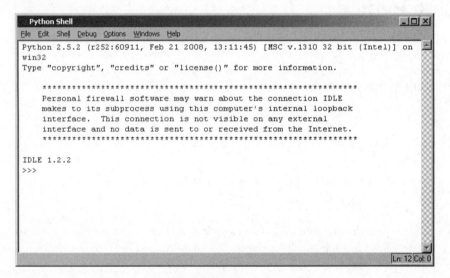

**Figure 1-1.** *The IDLE interactive Python shell*

---

2. This menu option will probably include your version number, as in Python 2.5.

Once you have the IDLE interactive Python shell running, you can continue with the section "The Interactive Interpreter," later in this chapter.

---

## WINDOWS INSTALLER

Python for Microsoft Windows is distributed as a Windows Installer file, and requires that your Windows version supports Windows Installer 2.0 (or later). If you don't have Windows Installer, it can be downloaded freely for Windows 95, 98, ME, NT 4.0, and 2000. Windows XP and later versions of Windows already have Windows Installer, and many older machines will, too. There are download instructions for the Installer on the Python download page.

Alternatively, you could go to the Microsoft download site, `http://www.microsoft.com/downloads`, and search for "Windows Installer" (or simply select it from the download menu). Choose the most recent version for your platform and follow the download and installation instructions.

If you're uncertain about whether you have Windows Installer, simply try executing step 5 of the previous installation instructions: double-click the MSI file. If you get the install wizard, everything is okay. See `http://www.python.org/2.5/msi.html` for advanced features of the Windows Installer related to Python installation.

---

# Linux and UNIX

In most Linux and UNIX installations (including Mac OS X), a Python interpreter will already be present. You can check whether this is the case for you by running the python command at the prompt, as follows:

```
$ python
```

Running this command should start the interactive Python interpreter, with output similar to the following:

```
Python 2.5.1 (r251:54869, Apr 18 2007, 22:08:04)
[GCC 4.0.1 (Apple Computer, Inc. build 5367)] on darwin
Type "help", "copyright", "credits" or "license" for more information.
>>>
```

---

**Note** To exit the interactive interpreter, use Ctrl-D (press the Ctrl key and while keeping that depressed, press D).

---

If there is no Python interpreter installed, you will probably get an error message similar to the following:

```
bash: python: command not found
```

In that case, you need to install Python yourself, as described in the following sections.

## Using a Package Manager

Several package systems and installation mechanisms exist for Linux. If you're running a Linux system with some form of package manager, chances are you can get Python through it.

---

■**Note**  You will probably need to have administrator privileges (a root account) in order to install Python using a package manager in Linux.

---

For example, if you're running Debian Linux, you should be able to install Python with the following command:

```
$ apt-get install python
```

If you're running Gentoo Linux, you should be able to use Portage, like this:

```
$ emerge python
```

In both cases, $ is, of course, the bash prompt.

---

■**Note**  Many other package managers out there have automatic download capabilities, including Yum, Synaptic (specific to Ubuntu Linux), and other Debian-style managers. You should probably be able to get recent versions of Python through these.

---

## Compiling from Sources

If you don't have a package manager, or would rather not use it, you can compile Python yourself. This may be the method of choice if you are on a UNIX box but you don't have root access (installation privileges). This method is very flexible, and enables you to install Python wherever you want, including in your own home directory. To compile and install Python, follow these steps:

1.  Go to the download page (refer to steps 1 and 2 in the instructions for installing Python on a Windows system).

2.  Follow the instructions for downloading the sources.

3.  Download the file with the extension .tgz. Store it in a temporary location. Assuming that you want to install Python in your home directory, you may want to put it in a directory such as ~/python. Enter this directory (e.g., using cd ~/python).

4.  Unpack the archive with the command tar -xzvf Python-2.5.tgz (where 2.5 is the version number of the downloaded source code). If your version of tar doesn't support the z option, you may want to uncompress the archive with gunzip first, and then use tar -xvf afterward. If there is something wrong with the archive, try downloading it again. Sometimes errors occur during download.

5. Enter the unpacked directory:

```
$ cd Python-2.5
```

Now you should be able to execute the following commands:

```
./configure --prefix=$(pwd)
make
make install
```

You should end up with an executable file called python in the current directory. (If this doesn't work, consult the README file included in the distribution.) Put the current directory in your PATH environment variable, and you're ready to rock.

To find out about the other configuration directives, execute this command:

```
./configure --help
```

## Macintosh

If you're using a Macintosh with a recent version of Mac OS X, you'll have a version of Python installed already. Just open the Terminal application and enter the command python to start it. Even if you would like to install a newer version of Python, you should leave this one alone, as it is used in several parts of the operating system. You could use either MacPorts (http://macports.org) or Fink (http://finkproject.org), or you could use the distribution from the Python web site, by following these steps:

1. Go to the standard download page (see steps 1 and 2 from the Windows instructions earlier in this chapter).

2. Follow the link for the Mac OS X installer. There should also be a link to the MacPython download page, which has more information. The MacPython page also has versions of Python for older versions of the Mac OS.

3. Once you've downloaded the installer .dmg file, it will probably mount automatically. If not, simply double-click it. In the mounted disk image, you'll find an installer package (.mpkg) file. If you double-click this, the installation wizard will open, which will take you through the necessary steps.

## Other Distributions

You now have the standard Python distribution installed. Unless you have a particular interest in alternative solutions, that should be all you need. If you are curious (and, perhaps, feeling a bit courageous), read on.

Several Python distributions are available in addition to the official one. The most well-known of these is probably ActivePython, which is available for Linux, Windows, Mac OS X, and several UNIX varieties. A slightly less well-known but quite interesting distribution is Stackless Python. These distributions are based on the standard implementation of Python, written in the C programming language. Two distributions that take a different approach are Jython and IronPython. If you're interested in development environments other than IDLE, Table 1-1 lists some options.

**Table 1-1.** *Some Integrated Development Environments (IDEs) for Python*

| Environment | Description | Web Site |
| --- | --- | --- |
| IDLE | The standard Python environment | http://www.python.org/idle |
| Pythonwin | Windows-oriented environment | http://www.python.org/download/windows |
| ActivePython | Feature-packed; contains Pythonwin IDE | http://www.activestate.com |
| Komodo | Commercial IDE | http://www.activestate.com[3] |
| Wingware | Commercial IDE | http://www.wingware.com |
| BlackAdder | Commercial IDE and (Qt) GUI builder | http://www.thekompany.com |
| Boa Constructor | Free IDE and GUI builder | http://boa-constructor.sf.net |
| Anjuta | Versatile IDE for Linux/UNIX | http://anjuta.sf.net |
| Arachno Python | Commercial IDE | http://www.python-ide.com |
| Code Crusader | Commercial IDE | http://www.newplanetsoftware.com |
| Code Forge | Commercial IDE | http://www.codeforge.com |
| Eclipse | Popular, flexible, open source IDE | http://www.eclipse.org |
| eric | Free IDE using Qt | http://eric-ide.sf.net |
| KDevelop | Cross-language IDE for KDE | http://www.kdevelop.org |
| VisualWx | Free GUI builder | http://visualwx.altervista.org |
| wxDesigner | Commercial GUI builder | http://www.roebling.de |
| wxGlade | Free GUI builder | http://wxglade.sf.net |

ActivePython is a Python distribution from ActiveState (http://www.activestate.com). At its core, it's the same as the standard Python distribution for Windows. The main difference is that it includes a lot of extra goodies (modules) that are available separately. It's definitely worth a look if you are running Windows.

---

3. Komodo has been made open source, so free versions are also available.

Stackless Python is a reimplementation of Python, based on the original code, but with some important internal changes. To a beginning user, these differences won't matter much, and one of the more standard distributions would probably be more useful. The main advantages of Stackless Python are that it allows deeper levels of recursion and more efficient multithreading. As mentioned, both of these are rather advanced features, not needed by the average user. You can get Stackless Python from `http://www.stackless.com`.

Jython (`http://www.jython.org`) and IronPython (`http://www.codeplex.com/IronPython`) are different—they're versions of Python implemented in other languages. Jython is implemented in Java, targeting the Java Virtual Machine, and IronPython is implemented in C#, targeting the .NET and MONO implementations of the common language runtime (CLR). At the time of writing, Jython is quite stable, but lagging behind Python—the current Jython version is 2.2, while Python is at 2.5. There are significant differences in these two versions of the language. IronPython is still rather young, but it is quite usable, and it is reported to be faster than standard Python on some benchmarks.

## Keeping in Touch and Up-to-Date

The Python language evolves continuously. To find out more about recent releases and relevant tools, the `python.org` web site is an invaluable asset. To find out what's new in a given release, go to the page for the given release, such as `http://python.org/2.5` for release 2.5. There you will also find a link to Andrew Kuchling's in-depth description of what's new for the release, with a URL such as `http://python.org/doc/2.5/whatsnew` for release 2.5. If there have been new releases since this book went to press, you can use these web pages to check out any new features.

---

■**Tip**  For a summary of what's changed in the more radically new release 3.0, see `http://docs.python.org/dev/3.0/whatsnew/3.0.html`.

---

If you want to keep up with newly released third-party modules or software for Python, check out the Python email list `python-announce-list`; for general discussions about Python, try `python-list`, but be warned: this list gets a *lot* of traffic. Both of these lists are available at `http://mail.python.org`. If you're a Usenet user, these two lists are also available as the newsgroups `comp.lang.python.announce` and `comp.lang.python`, respectively. If you're totally lost, you could try the `python-help` list (available from the same place as the two other lists) or simply email `help@python.org`. Before you do, you really ought to see if your question is a frequently asked one, by consulting the Python FAQ, at `http://python.org/doc/faq`, or by performing a quick Web search.

# The Interactive Interpreter

When you start up Python, you get a prompt similar to the following:

```
Python 2.5.1 (r251:54869, Apr 18 2007, 22:08:04)
[GCC 4.0.1 (Apple Computer, Inc. build 5367)] on darwin
```

```
Type "help", "copyright", "credits" or "license" for more information.
>>>
```

---

■**Note** The exact appearance of the interpreter and its error messages will depend on which version you are using.

---

This might not seem very interesting, but believe me—it is. This is your gateway to hacker-dom—your first step in taking control of your computer. In more pragmatic terms, it's an interactive Python interpreter. Just to see if it's working, try the following:

```
>>> print "Hello, world!"
```

When you press the Enter key, the following output appears:

```
Hello, world!
>>>
```

---

■**Note** If you are familiar with other computer languages, you may be used to terminating every line with a semicolon. There is no need to do so in Python. A line is a line, more or less. You may add a semicolon if you like, but it won't have any effect (unless more code follows on the same line), and it is not a common thing to do.

---

What happened here? The >>> thingy is the prompt. You can write something in this space, like print "Hello, world!". If you press Enter, the Python interpreter prints out the string "Hello, world!" and you get a new prompt below that.

---

■**Note** The term "printing" in this context refers to writing text to the screen, not producing hard copies with a printer.

---

What if you write something completely different? Try it out:

```
>>> The Spanish Inquisition
SyntaxError: invalid syntax
>>>
```

Obviously, the interpreter didn't understand that.[4] (If you are running an interpreter other than IDLE, such as the command-line version for Linux, the error message will be slightly

---

4. After all, no one expects the Spanish Inquisition . . .

dfferent.) The interpreter also indicates what's wrong: it will emphasize the word *Spanish* by giving it a red background (or, in the command-line version, by using a caret, ^).

If you feel like it, play around with the interpreter some more. For some guidance, try entering the command help at the prompt and pressing Enter. As mentioned, you can press F1 for help about IDLE. Otherwise, let's press on. After all, the interpreter isn't much fun when you don't know what to tell it, is it?

# Algo . . . What?

Before you start programming in earnest, I'll try to give you an idea of what computer programming is. Simply put, it's telling a computer what to do. Computers can do a lot of things, but they aren't very good at thinking for themselves. They really need to be spoon-fed the details. You need to feed the computer an algorithm in some language it understands. *Algorithm* is just a fancy word for a procedure or recipe—a detailed description of how to do something. Consider the following:

```
SPAM with SPAM, SPAM, Eggs, and SPAM:
First, take some SPAM.
Then add some SPAM, SPAM, and eggs.
If a particularly spicy SPAM is desired, add some SPAM.
Cook until done - Check every 10 minutes.
```

This recipe may not be very interesting, but how it's constructed is. It consists of a series of instructions to be followed in order. Some of the instructions may be done directly ("take some SPAM"), while some require some deliberation ("If a particularly spicy SPAM is desired"), and others must be repeated several times ("Check every 10 minutes.")

Recipes and algorithms consist of ingredients (objects, things), and instructions (statements). In this example, SPAM and eggs were the ingredients, while the instructions consisted of adding SPAM, cooking for a given length of time, and so on. Let's start with some reasonably simple Python ingredients and see what you can do with them.

# Numbers and Expressions

The interactive Python interpreter can be used as a powerful calculator. Try the following:

```
>>> 2 + 2
```

This should give you the answer 4. That wasn't too hard. Well, what about this:

```
>>> 53672 + 235253
288925
```

Still not impressed? Admittedly, this is pretty standard stuff. (I'll assume that you've used a calculator enough to know the difference between 1+2*3 and (1+2)*3.) All the usual arithmetic operators work as expected—almost. There is one potential trap here, and that is integer division (in Python versions prior to 3.0):

```
>>> 1/2
0
```

What happened here? One integer (a nonfractional number) was divided by another, and the result was rounded down to give an integer result. This behavior can be useful at times, but often (if not most of the time), you need ordinary division. What do you do to get that? There are two possible solutions: use real numbers (numbers with decimal points) rather than integers, or tell Python to change how division works.

Real numbers are called *floats* (or *floating-point numbers*) in Python. If either one of the numbers in a division is a float, the result will be, too:

```
>>> 1.0 / 2.0
0.5

>>> 1/2.0
0.5
>>> 1.0/2
0.5

>>> 1/2.
0.5
```

If you would rather have Python do proper division, you could add the following statement to the beginning of your program (writing full programs is described later) or simply execute it in the interactive interpreter:

```
>>> from __future__ import division
```

---

**Note**  In case it's not entirely clear, the `future` in the instruction is surrounded by two underscores on both sides: `__future__`.

---

Another alternative, if you're running Python from the command line (e.g., on a Linux machine), is to supply the command-line switch -Qnew. In either case, division will suddenly make a bit more sense:

```
>>> 1 / 2
0.5
```

Of course, the single slash can no longer be used for the kind of integer division shown earlier. A separate operator will do this for you—the double slash:

```
>>> 1 // 2
0
```

The double slash consistently performs integer division, even with floats:

```
>>> 1.0 // 2.0
0.0
```

There is a more thorough explanation of the __future__ stuff in the section "Back to the __future__," later in this chapter.

Now you've seen the basic arithmetic operators (addition, subtraction, multiplication, and division), but one more operator is quite useful at times:

```
>>> 1 % 2
1
```

This is the remainder (modulus) operator. x % y gives the remainder of x divided by y. Here are a few more examples:

```
>>> 10 / 3
3
>>> 10 % 3
1
>>> 9 / 3
3
>>> 9 % 3
0
>>> 2.75 % 0.5
0.25
```

Here 10/3 is 3 because the result is rounded down. But 3 × 3 is 9, so you get a remainder of 1. When you divide 9 by 3, the result is exactly 3, with no rounding. Therefore, the remainder is 0. This may be useful if you want to check something "every 10 minutes" as in the recipe earlier in the chapter. You can simply check whether minute % 10 is 0. (For a description on how to do this, see the sidebar "Sneak Peek: The if Statement," later in this chapter.) As you can see from the final example, the remainder operator works just fine with floats as well.

The last operator is the exponentiation (or power) operator:

```
>>> 2 ** 3
8
>>> -3 ** 2
-9
>>> (-3) ** 2
9
```

Note that the exponentiation operator binds tighter than the negation (unary minus), so -3**2 is in fact the same as -(3**2). If you want to calculate (-3)**2, you must say so explicitly.

## Large Integers

Python can handle really large integers:

```
>>> 1000000000000000000
1000000000000000000L
```

What happened here? The number suddenly got an L tacked onto the end.

---

**Note** If you're using a version of Python older than 2.2, you get the following behavior:

```
>>> 1000000000000000000
OverflowError: integer literal too large
```

The newer versions of Python are more flexible when dealing with big numbers.

---

Ordinary integers can't be larger than 2147483647 (or smaller than –2147483648). If you want really big numbers, you must use longs. A *long* (or *long integer*) is written just like an ordinary integer but with an L at the end. (You can, in theory, use a lowercase l as well, but that looks all too much like the digit 1, so I'd advise against it.)

In the previous example, Python converted the integer to a long, but you can do that yourself, too. Let's try that big number again:

```
>>> 1000000000000000000L
1000000000000000000L
```

Of course, this is only useful in old versions of Python that aren't capable of figuring this stuff out.

Well, can you do math with these monster numbers, too? Sure thing. Consider the following:

```
>>> 1987163987163981639186L * 198763981726391826L + 23
394976626432005567613000143784791693659L
```

As you can see, you can mix long integers and plain integers as you like. In all likelihood, you won't have to worry about the difference between longs and ints unless you're doing type checking, as described in Chapter 7—and that's something you should almost never do.

## Hexadecimals and Octals

To conclude this section, I should mention that hexadecimal numbers are written like this:

```
>>> 0xAF
175
```

and octal numbers like this:

```
>>> 010
8
```

The first digit in both of these is zero. (If you don't know what this is all about, just close your eyes and skip to the next section—you're not missing anything important.)

---

**Note** For a summary of Python's numeric types and operators, see Appendix B.

---

# Variables

Another concept that might be familiar to you is *variables*. If math makes you queasy, don't worry: variables in Python are easy to understand. A variable is basically a name that represents (or refers to) some value. For example, you might want the name x to represent 3. To make it so, simply execute the following:

```
>>> x = 3
```

This is called an *assignment*. We assign the value 3 to the variable x. Another way of putting this is to say that we bind the variable x to the value (or object) 3. After you've assigned a value to a variable, you can use the variable in expressions:

```
>>> x * 2
6
```

Note that you need to assign a value to a variable before you use it. After all, it doesn't make any sense to use a variable if it doesn't represent a value, does it?

---

**Note**  Variable names can consist of letters, digits, and underscore characters ( _ ). A variable can't begin with a digit, so Plan9 is a valid variable name, whereas 9Plan is not.

---

# Statements

Until now we've been working (almost) exclusively with expressions, the ingredients of the recipe. But what about statements—the instructions?

In fact, I've cheated. I've introduced two types of statements already: the print statement, and assignments. So, what's the difference between a statement and an expression? Well, an expression *is* something, while a statement *does* something (or, rather, tells the computer to do something). For example, 2*2 *is* 4, whereas print 2*2 *prints* 4. What's the difference? After all, they behave very similarly. Consider the following:

```
>>> 2*2
4
>>> print 2*2
4
```

As long as you execute this in the interactive interpreter, the results are similar, but that is only because the interpreter always prints out the values of all expressions (using the same representation as repr—see the section "String Representations, str and repr" later in this chapter). That is not true of Python in general. Later in this chapter, you'll see how to make programs that run without this interactive prompt, and simply putting an expression such as 2*2 in your program won't do anything interesting.[5] Putting print 2*2 in there, on the other hand, will print out 4.

---

5. In case you're wondering—yes, it *does* do something. It calculates the product of 2 and 2. However, the result isn't kept anywhere or shown to the user; it has no *side effects*, beyond the calculation itself.

> **Note** In Python 3.0, `print` is a function, which means you need to write `print(42)` instead of `print 42`, for example. Other than that, it works more or less like the statement, as described here.

The difference between statements and expressions may be more obvious when dealing with assignments. Because they are not expressions, they have no values that can be printed out by the interactive interpreter:

```
>>> x = 3
>>>
```

As you can see, you get a new prompt immediately. Something has changed, however; x is now bound to the value 3.

This is a defining quality of statements in general: they change things. For example, assignments change variables, and `print` statements change how your screen looks.

Assignments are, perhaps, the most important type of statement in any programming language, although it may be difficult to grasp their importance right now. Variables may just seem like temporary "storage" (like the pots and pans of a cooking recipe), but the real power of variables is that you don't need to know what values they hold in order to manipulate them.[6] For example, you know that x * y evaluates to the product of x and y, even though you may have no knowledge of what x and y are. So, you may write programs that use variables in various ways without knowing the values they will eventually hold (or refer to) when the program is run.

# Getting Input from the User

You've seen that you can write programs with variables without knowing their values. Of course, the interpreter must know the values eventually. So how can it be that we don't? The interpreter knows only what we tell it, right? Not necessarily.

You may have written a program, and someone else may use it. You cannot predict what values users will supply to the program. Let's take a look at the useful function `input`. (I'll have more to say about functions in a minute.)

```
>>> input("The meaning of life: ")
The meaning of life: 42
42
```

What happens here is that the first line (`input(...)`) is executed in the interactive interpreter. It prints out the string `"The meaning of life: "` as a new prompt. I type 42 and press

---

6. Note the quotes around storage. Values aren't stored in variables—they're stored in some murky depths of computer memory, and are referred to by variables. As will become abundantly clear as you read on, more than one variable can refer to the same value.

Enter. The resulting value of input is that very number, which is automatically printed out in the last line. That may not seem very useful, but look at the following:

```
>>> x = input("x: ")
x: 34
>>> y = input("y: ")
y: 42
>>> print x * y
1428
```

Here, the statements at the Python prompts (>>>) could be part of a finished program, and the values entered (34 and 42) would be supplied by some user. Your program would then print out the value 1428, which is the product of the two. And you didn't have to know these values when you wrote the program, right?

---

**Note**  This is much more useful when you save your programs in a separate file so other users can execute them. You learn to do that later in this chapter, in the section "Saving and Executing Your Programs."

---

### SNEAK PEEK: THE IF STATEMENT

To make things a bit more fun, I'll give you a sneak peek of something you aren't really supposed to learn about until Chapter 5: the if statement. The if statement lets you perform an action (another statement) if a given condition is true. One type of condition is an equality test, using the equality operator ==. Yes, it's a *double* equality sign. The single one is used for assignments, remember?

You simply put this condition after the word if and then separate it from the following statement with a colon:

```
>>> if 1 == 2: print 'One equals two'
...
>>> if 1 == 1: print 'One equals one'
...
One equals one
>>>
```

As you can see, nothing happens when the condition is false. When it is true, however, the following statement (in this case, a print statement) is executed. Note also that when using if statements in the interactive interpreter, you need to press Enter twice before it is executed. (The reason for this will become clear in Chapter 5—don't worry about it for now.)

So, if the variable time is bound to the current time in minutes, you could check whether you're "on the hour" with the following statement:

```
if time % 60 == 0: print 'On the hour!'
```

# Functions

In the section on numbers and expressions, I used the exponentiation operator (**) to calculate powers. The fact is that you can use a *function* instead, called pow:

```
>>> 2**3
8
>>> pow(2,3)
8
```

A function is like a little program that you can use to perform a specific action. Python has a lot of functions that can do many wonderful things. In fact, you can make your own functions, too (more about that later); therefore, we often refer to standard functions such as pow as *built-in* functions.

Using a function as I did in the preceding example is called *calling* the function. You supply it with *parameters* (in this case, 2 and 3) and it *returns* a value to you. Because it returns a value, a function call is simply another type of *expression*, like the arithmetic expressions discussed earlier in this chapter.[7] In fact, you can combine function calls and operators to create more complicated expressions:

```
>>> 10 + pow(2, 3*5)/3.0
10932.666666666666
```

---

**■Note**   The exact number of decimals may vary depending on which version of Python you are using.

---

Several built-in functions can be used in numeric expressions like this. For example, abs gives the absolute value of a number, and round rounds floating-point numbers to the nearest integer:

```
>>> abs(-10)
10
>>> 1/2
0
>>> round(1.0/2.0)
1.0
```

Notice the difference between the two last expressions. Integer division always rounds down, whereas round rounds to the nearest integer. But what if you want to round a given number down? For example, you might know that a person is 32.9 years old, but you would like to round that down to 32 because she isn't really 33 yet. Python has a function for this (called floor)—it just isn't available directly. As is the case with many useful functions, it is found in a *module*.

---

7.  Function calls can also be used as statements if you simply ignore the return value.

# Modules

You may think of modules as extensions that can be imported into Python to extend its capabilities. You import modules with a special command called (naturally enough) `import`. The function mentioned in the previous section, `floor`, is in a module called `math`:

```
>>> import math
>>> math.floor(32.9)
32.0
```

Notice how this works: we import a module with `import`, and then use the functions from that module by writing `module.function`.

If you want the age to be an integer (`32`) and not a float (`32.0`), you can use the function `int`:[8]

```
>>> int(math.floor(32.9))
32
```

---

▨**Note**  Similar functions exist to convert to other types (for example, `long` and `float`). In fact, these aren't completely normal functions—they're *type objects*. I'll have more to say about types later. The opposite of `floor` is `ceil` (short for "ceiling"), which finds the smallest integral value larger than or equal to the given number.

---

If you are sure that you won't import more than one function with a given name (from different modules), you might not want to write the module name each time you call the function. Then you can use a variant of the `import` command:

```
>>> from math import sqrt
>>> sqrt(9)
3.0
```

After using `from module import function`, you can use the function without its module prefix.

---

▨**Tip**  You may, in fact, use variables to refer to functions (and most other things in Python). For example, by performing the assignment `foo = math.sqrt`, you can start using `foo` to calculate square roots; for example, `foo(4)` yields `2.0`.

---

---

8. The `int` function/type will actually round down while converting to an integer, so when converting to an integer, using `math.floor` is superfluous; you could simply use `int(32.9)`.

# cmath and Complex Numbers

The sqrt function is used to calculate the square root of a number. Let's see what happens if we supply it with a negative number:

```
>>> from math import sqrt
>>> sqrt(-1)
Traceback (most recent call last):
  File "<pyshell#23>", line 1, in ?
    sqrt(-1)
ValueError: math domain error
```

or, on some platforms:

```
>>> sqrt(-1)
nan
```

---

■**Note**  nan is simply a special value meaning "not a number."

---

Well, that's reasonable. You can't take the square root of a negative number—or can you? Indeed you can. The square root of a negative number is an imaginary number. (This is a standard mathematical concept—if you find it a bit too mind-bending, feel free to skip ahead.) So why couldn't sqrt deal with it? Because it deals only with floats, and imaginary numbers (and complex numbers, the sum of real and imaginary numbers) are something completely different—which is why they are covered by a different module, cmath (for complex math):

```
>>> import cmath
>>> cmath.sqrt(-1)
1j
```

Notice that I didn't use from ... import ... here. If I had, I would have lost my ordinary sqrt. Name clashes like these can be sneaky, so unless you really want to use the from version, you should probably stick with a plain import.

The value 1j is an imaginary number. These numbers are written with a trailing j (or J), just like longs use L. Without delving into the theory of complex numbers, let me just show a final example of how you can use them:

```
>>> (1+3j) * (9+4j)
(-3+31j)
```

As you can see, the support for complex numbers is built into the language.

---

■**Note**  There is no separate type for imaginary numbers in Python. They are treated as complex numbers whose real component is zero.

---

## Back to the \_\_future\_\_

It has been rumored that Guido van Rossum (Python's creator) has a time machine, because quite often when people request features in the language, the features have already been implemented. Of course, we aren't all allowed into this time machine, but Guido has been kind enough to build a part of it into Python, in the form of the magic module \_\_future\_\_. From it, we can import features that will be standard in Python in the future but that aren't part of the language yet. You saw this in the section about numbers and expressions, and you'll be bumping into it from time to time throughout this book.

# Saving and Executing Your Programs

The interactive interpreter is one of Python's great strengths. It makes it possible to test solutions and to experiment with the language in real time. If you want to know how something works, just try it! However, everything you write in the interactive interpreter is lost when you quit. What you really want to do is write programs that both you and other people can run. In this section, you learn how to do just that.

First of all, you need a text editor, preferably one intended for programming. (If you use something like Microsoft Word, which I don't really recommend, be sure to save your code as plain text.) If you are already using IDLE, you're in luck. With IDLE, you can simply create a new editor window with File ➤ New Window. Another window appears, without an interactive prompt. Whew!

Start by entering the following:

```
print "Hello, world!"
```

Now select File ➤ Save to save your program (which is, in fact, a plain text file). Be sure to put it somewhere where you can find it later. You might want to create a directory where you put all your Python projects, such as C:\python in Windows. In a UNIX environment, you might use a directory like ~/python. Give your file any reasonable name, such as hello.py. The .py ending is important.

---

■**Note**  If you followed the installation instructions earlier in this chapter, you may have put your Python installation in ~/python already, but because that has a subdirectory of its own (such as ~/python/ Python-2.5/), this shouldn't cause any problems. If you would rather put your own programs somewhere else, feel free to use a directory such as ~/my_python_programs.

---

Got that? Don't close the window with your program in it. If you did, just open it again (File ➤ Open). Now you can run it with Edit ➤ Run script, or by pressing Ctrl+F5. (If you aren't using IDLE, see the next section about running your programs from the command prompt.)

What happens? Hello, world! is printed in the interpreter window, which is exactly what we wanted. The interpreter prompt may be gone (depending on the version you're using), but you can get it back by pressing Enter (in the interpreter window).

Let's extend our script to the following:

```
name = raw_input("What is your name? ")
print "Hello, " + name + "!"
```

---

**Note** Don't worry about the difference between `input` and `raw_input`—I'll get to that.

---

If you run this (remember to save it first), you should see the following prompt in the interpreter window:

```
What is your name?
```

Enter your name (for example, Gumby) and press Enter. You should get something like this:

```
Hello, Gumby!
```

Fun, isn't it?

## Running Your Python Scripts from a Command Prompt

Actually, there are several ways to run your programs. First, let's assume that you have a DOS window or a UNIX shell prompt before you, and that the directory containing the Python executable (called `python.exe` in Windows, and `python` in UNIX) or the directory *containing* the executable (in Windows) has been put in your PATH environment variable.[9] Also, let's assume that your script from the previous section (`hello.py`) is in the current directory. Then you can execute your script with the following command in Windows:

```
C:\>python hello.py
```

or UNIX:

```
$ python hello.py
```

As you can see, the command is the same. Only the system prompt changes.

---

**Note** If you don't want to mess with environment variables, you can simply specify the full path of the Python interpreter. In Windows, you might do something like this:

```
C:\>C:\Python25\python hello.py
```

---

## Making Your Scripts Behave Like Normal Programs

Sometimes you want to execute a Python program (also called a *script*) the same way you execute other programs (such as your web browser or text editor), rather than explicitly using the

---

9.  If you don't understand this sentence, you should perhaps skip the section. You don't really need it.

Python interpreter. In UNIX, there is a standard way of doing this: have the first line of your script begin with the character sequence #! (called *pound bang* or *shebang*) followed by the absolute path to the program that interprets the script (in our case Python). Even if you didn't quite understand that, just put the following in the first line of your script if you want it to run easily on UNIX:

```
#!/usr/bin/env python
```

This should run the script, regardless of where the Python binary is located.

---

**Note** In some operating systems if you install a recent version of Python (e.g., 2.5) you will still have an old one lying around (e.g.,1.5.2), which is needed by some system programs (so you can't uninstall it). In such cases, the /usr/bin/env trick is not a good idea, as you will probably end up with your programs being executed by the old Python. Instead, you should find the exact location of your new Python executable (probably called python or python2) and use the full path in the pound bang line, like this:

```
#!/usr/bin/python2
```

The exact path may vary from system to system.

---

Before you can actually run your script, you must make it executable:

```
$ chmod a+x hello.py
```

Now it can be run like this (assuming that you have the current directory in your path):

```
$ hello.py
```

If this doesn't work, try using ./hello.py instead, which will work even if the current directory (.) is not part of your execution path.

If you like, you can rename your file and remove the py suffix to make it look more like a normal program.

## What About Double-Clicking?

In Windows, the suffix (.py) is the key to making your script behave like a program. Try double-clicking the file hello.py you saved in the previous section. If Python was installed correctly, a DOS window appears with the prompt "What is your name?" Cool, huh?[10] (You'll see how to make your programs look better, with buttons, menus, and so on, later.)

There is one problem with running your program like this, however. Once you've entered your name, the program window closes before you can read the result. The window closes when the program is finished. Try changing the script by adding the following line at the end:

```
raw_input("Press <enter>")
```

---

10. This behavior depends on your operating system and the installed Python interpreter. If you've saved the file using IDLE in Mac OS X, for example, double-clicking the file will simply open it in the IDLE code editor.

Now, after running the program and entering your name, you should have a DOS window with the following contents:

```
What is your name? Gumby
Hello, Gumby!
Press <enter>
```

Once you press the Enter key, the window closes (because the program is finished). Just as a teaser, rename your file hello.pyw. (This is Windows-specific.) Double-click it as before. What happens? Nothing! How can that be? I will tell you later in the book—I promise.

## Comments

The hash sign (#) is a bit special in Python. When you put it in your code, everything to the right of it is ignored (which is why the Python interpreter didn't choke on the /usr/bin/env stuff used earlier). Here is an example:

```
# Print the circumference of the circle:
print 2 * pi * radius
```

The first line here is called a *comment*, which can be useful in making programs easier to understand—both for other people and for yourself when you come back to old code. It has been said that the first commandment of programmers is "Thou Shalt Comment" (although some less charitable programmers swear by the motto "If it was hard to write, it should be hard to read"). Make sure your comments say significant things and don't simply restate what is already obvious from the code. Useless, redundant comments may be worse than none. For example, in the following, a comment isn't really called for:

```
# Get the user's name:
user_name = raw_input("What is your name?")
```

It's always a good idea to make your code readable on its own as well, even without the comments. Luckily, Python is an excellent language for writing readable programs.

# Strings

Now what was all that raw_input and "Hello, " + name + "!" stuff about? Let's tackle the "Hello" part first and leave raw_input for later.

The first program in this chapter was simply

```
print "Hello, world!"
```

It is customary to begin with a program like this in programming tutorials. The problem is that I haven't really explained how it works yet. You know the basics of the print statement (I'll have more to say about that later), but what is "Hello, world!"? It's called a *string* (as in "a string of characters"). Strings are found in almost every useful, real-world Python program and have many uses. Their main use is to represent bits of text, such as the exclamation "Hello, world!"

# Single-Quoted Strings and Escaping Quotes

Strings are values, just as numbers are:

```
>>> "Hello, world!"
'Hello, world!'
```

There is one thing that may be a bit surprising about this example, though: when Python printed out our string, it used single quotes, whereas we used double quotes. What's the difference? Actually, there is no difference:

```
>>> 'Hello, world!'
'Hello, world!'
```

Here, we use single quotes, and the result is the same. So why allow both? Because in some cases it may be useful:

```
>>> "Let's go!"
"Let's go!"
>>> '"Hello, world!" she said'
'"Hello, world!" she said'
```

In the preceding code, the first string contains a single quote (or an apostrophe, as we should perhaps call it in this context), and therefore we can't use single quotes to enclose the string. If we did, the interpreter would complain (and rightly so):

```
>>> 'Let's go!'
SyntaxError: invalid syntax
```

Here, the string is `'Let'`, and Python doesn't quite know what to do with the following s (or the rest of the line, for that matter).

In the second string, we use double quotes as part of our sentence. Therefore, we have to use single quotes to enclose our string, for the same reasons as stated previously. Or, actually we don't *have* to. It's just convenient. An alternative is to use the backslash character (\) to escape the quotes in the string, like this:

```
>>> 'Let\'s go!'
"Let's go!"
```

Python understands that the middle single quote is a character *in* the string and not the *end* of the string. (Even so, Python chooses to use double quotes when printing out the string.) The same works with double quotes, as you might expect:

```
>>> "\"Hello, world!\" she said"
'"Hello, world!" she said'
```

Escaping quotes like this can be useful, and sometimes necessary. For example, what would you do without the backslash if your string contained both single and double quotes, as in the string `'Let\'s say "Hello, world!"'`?

---

■**Note**  Tired of backslashes? As you will see later in this chapter, you can avoid most of them by using long strings and raw strings (which can be combined).

---

## Concatenating Strings

Just to keep whipping this slightly tortured example, let me show you another way of writing the same string:

```
>>> "Let's say " '"Hello, world!"'
'Let\'s say "Hello, world!"'
```

I've simply written two strings, one after the other, and Python automatically concatenates them (makes them into one string). This mechanism isn't used very often, but it can be useful at times. However, it works only when you actually write both strings at the same time, directly following one another:

```
>>> x = "Hello, "
>>> y = "world!"
>>> x y
SyntaxError: invalid syntax
```

In other words, this is just a special way of writing strings, not a general method of concatenating them. How, then, do you concatenate strings? Just like you add numbers:

```
>>> "Hello, " + "world!"
'Hello, world!'
>>> x = "Hello, "
>>> y = "world!"
>>> x + y
'Hello, world!'
```

## String Representations, str and repr

Throughout these examples, you have probably noticed that all the strings printed out by Python are still quoted. That's because it prints out the value as it might be written in Python code, not how you would like it to look for the user. If you use print, however, the result is different:

```
>>> "Hello, world!"
'Hello, world!'
>>> 10000L
10000L
>>> print "Hello, world!"
Hello, world!
>>> print 10000L
10000
```

As you can see, the long integer 10000L is simply the number 10000 and should be written that way when presented to the user. But when you want to know what value a variable refers to, you may be interested in whether it's a normal integer or a long, for example.

What is actually going on here is that values are converted to strings through two different mechanisms. You can use both mechanisms yourself, through the functions str and repr. str simply converts a value into a string in some reasonable fashion that will probably be understood by a user, for example.[11] repr creates a string that is a representation of the value as a legal Python expression. Here are a few examples:

```
>>> print repr("Hello, world!")
'Hello, world!'
>>> print repr(10000L)
10000L
>>> print str("Hello, world!")
Hello, world!
>>> print str(10000L)
10000
```

A synonym for repr(x) is `x` (here, you use backticks, not single quotes). This can be useful when you want to print out a sentence containing a number:

```
>>> temp = 42
>>> print "The temperature is " + temp
Traceback (most recent call last):
  File "<pyshell#61>", line 1, in ?
    print "The temperature is " + temp
TypeError: cannot add type "int" to string
>>> print "The temperature is " + `temp`
The temperature is 42
```

---

■**Note**  Backticks are removed in Python 3.0, so even though you may find backticks in old code, you should probably stick with repr yourself.

---

The first print statement doesn't work because you can't add a string to a number. The second one, however, works because I have converted temp to the string "42" by using the backticks. (I could have just as well used repr, which means the same thing, but may be a bit clearer. Actually, in this case, I could also have used str. Don't worry too much about this right now.)

In short, str, repr, and backticks are three ways of converting a Python value to a string. The function str makes it look good, while repr (and the backticks) tries to make the resulting string a legal Python expression.

---

11. Actually, str is a type, just like int and long. repr, however, is simply a function.

## input vs. raw_input

Now you know what "Hello, " + name + "!" means. But what about raw_input? Isn't input good enough? Let's try it. Enter the following in a separate script file:

```
name = input("What is your name? ")
print "Hello, " + name + "!"
```

This is a perfectly valid program, but as you will soon see, it's a bit impractical. Let's try to run it:

```
What is your name? Gumby
Traceback (most recent call last):
  File "C:/python/test.py", line 2, in ?
    name = input("What is your name? ")
  File "<string>", line 0, in ?
NameError: name 'Gumby' is not defined
```

The problem is that input assumes that what you enter is a valid Python expression (it's more or less the inverse of repr). If you write your name as a string, that's no problem:

```
What is your name? "Gumby"
Hello, Gumby!
```

However, it's just a bit too much to ask that users write their name in quotes like this. Therefore, we use raw_input, which treats all input as raw data and puts it into a string:

```
>>> input("Enter a number: ")
Enter a number: 3
3
>>> raw_input("Enter a number: ")
Enter a number: 3
'3'
```

Unless you have a special need for input, you should probably use raw_input.

## Long Strings, Raw Strings, and Unicode

Before ending this chapter, I want to tell you about a few other ways of writing strings. These alternate string syntaxes can be useful when you have strings that span several lines or contain various special characters.

### Long Strings

If you want to write a really long string, one that spans several lines, you can use triple quotes instead of ordinary quotes:

```
print '''This is a very long string.
It continues here.
And it's not over yet.
"Hello, world!"
Still here.'''
```

You can also use triple double quotes, `"""like this"""`. Note that because of the distinctive enclosing quotes, both single and double quotes are allowed inside, without being backslash-escaped.

---

**Tip** Ordinary strings can also span several lines. If the last character on a line is a backslash, the line break itself is "escaped" and ignored. For example:

```
print "Hello, \
world!"
```

would print out `Hello, world!`. The same goes for expressions and statements in general:

```
>>> 1 + 2 + \
    4 + 5
12
>>> print \
    'Hello, world'
Hello, world
```

---

## Raw Strings

*Raw strings* aren't too picky about backslashes, which can be very useful sometimes.[12] In ordinary strings, the backslash has a special role: it *escapes* things, letting you put things into your string that you couldn't normally write directly. For example, a new line is written \n, and can be put into a string like this:

```
>>> print 'Hello,\nworld!'
Hello,
world!
```

This is normally just dandy, but in some cases, it's not what you want. What if you wanted the string to include a backslash followed by an n? You might want to put the DOS pathname `C:\nowhere` into a string:

```
>>> path = 'C:\nowhere'
>>> path
'C:\nowhere'
```

This looks correct, until you print it and discover the flaw:

```
>>> print path
C:
owhere
```

---

12. Raw strings can be especially useful when writing regular expressions. More about those in Chapter 10.

Not exactly what we were after, is it? So what do we do? We can escape the backslash itself:

```
>>> print 'C:\\nowhere'
C:\nowhere
```

This is just fine. But for long paths, you wind up with a lot of backslashes:

```
path = 'C:\\Program Files\\fnord\\foo\\bar\\baz\\frozz\\bozz'
```

Raw strings are useful in such cases. They don't treat the backslash as a special character at all. Every character you put into a raw string stays the way you wrote it:

```
>>> print r'C:\nowhere'
C:\nowhere
>>> print r'C:\Program Files\fnord\foo\bar\baz\frozz\bozz'
C:\Program Files\fnord\foo\bar\baz\frozz\bozz
```

As you can see, raw strings are prefixed with an r. It would seem that you can put anything inside a raw string, and that is almost true. Quotes must be escaped as usual, although that means that you get a backslash in your final string, too:

```
>>> print r'Let\'s go!'
Let\'s go!
```

The one thing you can't have in a raw string is a lone, final backslash. In other words, the last character in a raw string cannot be a backslash unless you escape it (and then the backslash you use to escape it will be part of the string, too). Given the previous example, that ought to be obvious. If the last character (before the final quote) is an unescaped backslash, Python won't know whether or not to end the string:

```
>>> print r"This is illegal\"
SyntaxError: invalid token
```

Okay, so it's reasonable, but what if you want the last character in your raw string to be a backslash? (Perhaps it's the end of a DOS path, for example.) Well, I've given you a whole bag of tricks in this section that should help you solve that problem, but basically you need to put the backslash in a separate string. A simple way of doing that is the following:

```
>>> print r'C:\Program Files\foo\bar' '\\'
C:\Program Files\foo\bar\
```

Note that you can use both single and double quotes with raw strings. Even triple-quoted strings can be raw.

### Unicode Strings

The final type of string constant is the *Unicode string* (or Unicode *object*—they don't really belong to the same type as strings). If you don't know what Unicode is, you probably don't need to know about this. (If you want to find out more about it, you can go to the Unicode web site, www.unicode.org.) Normal strings in Python are stored internally as 8-bit ASCII, while Unicode strings are stored as 16-bit Unicode. This allows for a more varied set of characters, including special characters from most languages in the world. I'll restrict my treatment of Unicode strings to the following:

```
>>> u'Hello, world!'
u'Hello, world!'
```

As you can see, Unicode strings use the prefix u, just as raw strings use the prefix r.

---

**Note** In Python 3.0, all strings will be Unicode strings.

---

# A Quick Summary

This chapter covered quite a bit of material. Let's take a look at what you've learned before moving on.

**Algorithms**: An algorithm is a recipe telling you exactly how to perform a task. When you program a computer, you are essentially describing an algorithm in a language the computer can understand, such as Python. Such a machine-friendly description is called a program, and it mainly consists of expressions and statements.

**Expressions**: An expression is a part of a computer program that represents a value. For example, 2+2 is an expression, representing the value 4. Simple expressions are built from *literal values* (such as 2 or "Hello") by using *operators* (such as + or %) and *functions* (such as pow). More complicated expressions can be created by combining simpler expressions (e.g., (2+2)*(3-1)). Expressions may also contain *variables*.

**Variables**: A variable is a name that represents a value. New values may be assigned to variables through *assignments* such as x = 2. An assignment is a kind of *statement*.

**Statements**: A statement is an instruction that tells the computer to *do* something. That may involve changing variables (through assignments), printing things to the screen (such as print "Hello, world!"), importing modules, or a host of other stuff.

**Functions**: Functions in Python work just like functions in mathematics: they may take some arguments, and they return a result. (They may actually do lots of interesting stuff before returning, as you will find out when you learn to write your own functions in Chapter 6.)

**Modules**: Modules are extensions that can be imported into Python to extend its capabilities. For example, several useful mathematical functions are available in the math module.

**Programs**: You have looked at the practicalities of writing, saving, and running Python programs.

**Strings**: Strings are really simple—they are just pieces of text. And yet there is a lot to know about them. In this chapter, you've seen many ways to write them, and in Chapter 3 you learn many ways of using them.

## New Functions in This Chapter

| Function | Description |
| --- | --- |
| abs(number) | Returns the absolute value of a number |
| cmath.sqrt(number) | Returns the square root; works with negative numbers |
| float(object) | Converts a string or number to a floating-point number |
| help() | Offers interactive help |
| input(prompt) | Gets input from the user |
| int(object) | Converts a string or number to an integer |
| long(object) | Converts a string or number to a long integer |
| math.ceil(number) | Returns the ceiling of a number as a float |
| math.floor(number) | Returns the floor of a number as a float |
| math.sqrt(number) | Returns the square root; doesn't work with negative numbers |
| pow(x, y[, z]) | Returns x to the power of y (modulo z) |
| raw_input(prompt) | Gets input from the user, as a string |
| repr(object) | Returns a string representation of a value |
| round(number[, ndigits]) | Rounds a number to a given precision |
| str(object) | Converts a value to a string |

## What Now?

Now that you know the basics of expressions, let's move on to something a bit more advanced: data structures. Instead of dealing with simple values (such as numbers), you'll see how to bunch them together in more complex structures, such as lists and dictionaries. In addition, you'll take another close look at strings. In Chapter 5, you learn more about statements, and after that you'll be ready to write some really nifty programs.

# CHAPTER 2

■■■

# Lists and Tuples

**T**his chapter introduces a new concept: *data structures*. A data structure is a collection of data elements (such as numbers or characters, or even other data structures) that is structured in some way, such as by numbering the elements. The most basic data structure in Python is the *sequence*. Each element of a sequence is assigned a number—its position, or *index*. The first index is zero, the second index is one, and so forth.

---

**■Note** When you count or number things in your daily life, you probably start counting from 1. The numbering scheme used in Python may seem odd, but it is actually quite natural. One of the reasons for this, as you see later in the chapter, is that you can *also* count from the end: the last item of a sequence is numbered –1, the next-to-last –2, and so forth. That means you can count forward *or* backward from the first element, which lies at the beginning, or 0. Trust me, you get used to it.

---

This chapter begins with an overview of sequences, and then covers some operations that are common to all sequences, including lists and tuples. These operations will also work with strings, which will be used in some of the examples, although for a full treatment of string operations, you have to wait until the next chapter.

After dealing with these basics, we start working with lists and see what's special about them. After lists, we come to tuples, which are very similar to lists, except that you can't change them.

## Sequence Overview

Python has six built-in types of sequences. This chapter concentrates on two of the most common ones: *lists* and *tuples*. The other built-in sequence types are strings (which I revisit in the next chapter), Unicode strings, buffer objects, and xrange objects.

The main difference between lists and tuples is that you can change a list, but you can't change a tuple. This means a list might be useful if you need to add elements as you go along, while a tuple can be useful if, for some reason, you can't allow the sequence to change. Reasons for the latter are usually rather technical, having to do with how things work internally in Python. That's why you may see built-in functions returning tuples. For your own programs, chances are you can use lists instead of tuples in almost all circumstances. (One notable exception, as described in Chapter 4, is using tuples as dictionary keys. There lists aren't allowed, because you aren't allowed to modify keys.)

Sequences are useful when you want to work with a collection of values. You might have a sequence representing a person in a database, with the first element being their name, and the second their age. Written as a list (the items of a list are separated by commas and enclosed in square brackets), that would look like this:

```
>>> edward = ['Edward Gumby', 42]
```

But sequences can contain other sequences, too, so you could make a list of such persons, which would be your database:

```
>>> edward = ['Edward Gumby', 42]
>>> john = ['John Smith', 50]
>>> database = [edward, john]
>>> database
[['Edward Gumby', 42], ['John Smith', 50]]
```

---

**Note** Python has a basic notion of a kind of data structure called a *container*, which is basically any object that can contain other objects. The two main kinds of containers are sequences (such as lists and tuples) and mappings (such as dictionaries). While the elements of a sequence are numbered, each element in a mapping has a name (also called a key). You learn more about mappings in Chapter 4. For an example of a container type that is neither a sequence nor a mapping, see the discussion of sets in Chapter 10.

---

# Common Sequence Operations

There are certain things you can do with all sequence types. These operations include *indexing*, *slicing*, *adding*, *multiplying*, and checking for *membership*. In addition, Python has built-in functions for finding the length of a sequence, and for finding its largest and smallest elements.

---

**Note** One important operation not covered here is *iteration*. To iterate over a sequence means to perform certain actions repeatedly, once per element in the sequence. To learn more about this, see the section "Loops" in Chapter 5.

---

## Indexing

All elements in a sequence are numbered—from zero and upwards. You can access them individually with a number, like this:

```
>>> greeting = 'Hello'
>>> greeting[0]
'H'
```

---

■**Note**  A string is just a sequence of characters. The index 0 refers to the first element, in this case the letter *H*.

---

This is called *indexing*. You use an index to fetch an element. All sequences can be indexed in this way. When you use a negative index, Python counts *from the right*; that is, from the last element. The last element is at position –1 (not –0, as that would be the same as the first element):

```
>>> greeting[-1]
'o'
```

String literals (and other sequence literals, for that matter) may be indexed directly, without using a variable to refer to them. The effect is exactly the same:

```
>>> 'Hello'[1]
'e'
```

If a function call returns a sequence, you can index it directly. For instance, if you are simply interested in the fourth digit in a year entered by the user, you could do something like this:

```
>>> fourth = raw_input('Year: ')[3]
Year: 2005
>>> fourth
'5'
```

Listing 2-1 contains a sample program that asks you for a year, a month (as a number from 1 to 12), and a day (1 to 31), and then prints out the date with the proper month name and so on.

**Listing 2-1.** *Indexing Example*

```
# Print out a date, given year, month, and day as numbers

months = [
    'January',
    'February',
    'March',
    'April',
    'May',
    'June',
    'July',
    'August',
    'September',
    'October',
    'November',
    'December'
]
```

```
# A list with one ending for each number from 1 to 31
endings = ['st', 'nd', 'rd'] + 17 * ['th'] \
        + ['st', 'nd', 'rd'] +  7 * ['th'] \
        + ['st']

year    = raw_input('Year: ')
month   = raw_input('Month (1-12): ')
day     = raw_input('Day (1-31): ')

month_number = int(month)
day_number = int(day)

# Remember to subtract 1 from month and day to get a correct index
month_name = months[month_number-1]
ordinal = day + endings[day_number-1]

print month_name + ' ' + ordinal + ', ' + year
```

An example of a session with this program might be as follows:

---

```
Year: 1974
Month (1-12): 8
Day (1-31): 16
August 16th, 1974
```

---

The last line is the output from the program.

## Slicing

Just as you use indexing to access individual elements, you can use *slicing* to access *ranges* of elements. You do this by using *two* indices, separated by a colon:

```
>>> tag = '<a href="http://www.python.org">Python web site</a>'
>>> tag[9:30]
'http://www.python.org'
>>> tag[32:-4]
'Python web site'
```

As you can see, slicing is very useful for extracting parts of a sequence. The numbering here is very important. The *first* index is the number of the first element you want to include. However, the *last* index is the number of the first element *after* your slice. Consider the following:

```
>>> numbers = [1, 2, 3, 4, 5, 6, 7, 8, 9, 10]
>>> numbers[3:6]
[4, 5, 6]
>>> numbers[0:1]
[1]
```

In short, you supply two indices as limits for your slice, where the first is *inclusive* and the second is *exclusive*.

## A Nifty Shortcut

Let's say you want to access the last three elements of numbers (from the previous example). You could do it explicitly, of course:

```
>>> numbers[7:10]
[8, 9, 10]
```

Now, the index 10 refers to element 11—which does not exist, but is one step after the last element you want. Got it?

This is fine, but what if you want to count from the end?

```
>>> numbers[-3:-1]
[8, 9]
```

It seems you cannot access the last element this way. How about using 0 as the element "one step beyond" the end?

```
>>> numbers[-3:0]
[]
```

Not exactly the desired result. In fact, any time the leftmost index in a slice comes later in the sequence than the second one (in this case, the third-to-last coming later than the first), the result is always an empty sequence. Luckily, you can use a shortcut: if the slice continues to the end of the sequence, you may simply leave out the last index:

```
>>> numbers[-3:]
[8, 9, 10]
```

The same thing works from the beginning:

```
>>> numbers[:3]
[1, 2, 3]
```

In fact, if you want to copy the entire sequence, you may leave out *both* indices:

```
>>> numbers[:]
[1, 2, 3, 4, 5, 6, 7, 8, 9, 10]
```

Listing 2-2 contains a small program that prompts you for a URL, and (assuming it is of the form http://www.somedomainname.com) extracts the domain name.

**Listing 2-2.** *Slicing Example*

```
# Split up a URL of the form http://www.something.com

url = raw_input('Please enter the URL: ')
domain = url[11:-4]

print "Domain name: " + domain
```

Here is a sample run of the program:

```
Please enter the URL: http://www.python.org
Domain name: python
```

## Longer Steps

When slicing, you specify (either explicitly or implicitly) the start and end points of the slice. Another parameter (added to the built-in types in Python 2.3), which normally is left implicit, is the step length. In a regular slice, the step length is one, which means that the slice "moves" from one element to the next, returning all the elements between the start and end:

```
>>> numbers[0:10:1]
[1, 2, 3, 4, 5, 6, 7, 8, 9, 10]
```

In this example, you can see that the slice includes another number. This is, as you may have guessed, the step size, made explicit. If the step size is set to a number greater than one, elements will be skipped. For example, a step size of two will include only every other element of the interval between the start and the end:

```
>>> numbers[0:10:2]
[1, 3, 5, 7, 9]
numbers[3:6:3]
[4]
```

You can still use the shortcuts mentioned earlier. For example, if you want every fourth element of a sequence, you need to supply only a step size of four:

```
>>> numbers[::4]
[1, 5, 9]
```

Naturally, the step size can't be zero—that wouldn't get you anywhere—but it *can* be *negative*, which means extracting the elements from right to left:

```
>>> numbers[8:3:-1]
[9, 8, 7, 6, 5]
>>> numbers[10:0:-2]
[10, 8, 6, 4, 2]
>>> numbers[0:10:-2]
[]
>>> numbers[::-2]
[10, 8, 6, 4, 2]
>>> numbers[5::-2]
[6, 4, 2]
>>> numbers[:5:-2]
[10, 8]
```

Getting things right here can involve a bit of thinking. As you can see, the first limit (the leftmost) is still *inclusive*, while the second (the rightmost) is *exclusive*. When using a negative step size, you need to have a first limit (start index) that is *higher* than the second one. What may be a bit confusing is that when you leave the start and end indices implicit, Python does the "right thing"—for a positive step size, it moves from the beginning toward the end, and for a negative step size, it moves from the end toward the beginning.

## Adding Sequences

Sequences can be concatenated with the addition (plus) operator:

```
>>> [1, 2, 3] + [4, 5, 6]
[1, 2, 3, 4, 5, 6]
>>> 'Hello, ' + 'world!'
'Hello, world!'
>>> [1, 2, 3] + 'world!'
Traceback (innermost last):
  File "<pyshell#2>", line 1, in ?
    [1, 2, 3] + 'world!'
TypeError: can only concatenate list (not "string") to list
```

As you can see from the error message, you can't concatenate a list and a string, although both are sequences. In general, you cannot concatenate sequences of different types.

## Multiplication

Multiplying a sequence by a number *x* creates a new sequence where the original sequence is repeated *x* times:

```
>>> 'python' * 5
'pythonpythonpythonpythonpython'
>>> [42] * 10
[42, 42, 42, 42, 42, 42, 42, 42, 42, 42]
```

### None, Empty Lists, and Initialization

An empty list is simply written as two brackets ([])—there's nothing in it. But what if you want to have a list with room for ten elements but with nothing useful in it? You could use [42]*10, as before, or perhaps more realistically [0]*10. You now have a list with ten zeros in it. Sometimes, however, you would like a value that somehow means "nothing," as in "we haven't put anything here yet." That's when you use None. None is a Python value and means exactly that— "nothing here." So if you want to initialize a list of length 10, you could do the following:

```
>>> sequence = [None] * 10
>>> sequence
[None, None, None, None, None, None, None, None, None, None]
```

Listing 2-3 contains a program that prints (to the screen) a "box" made up of characters, which is centered on the screen and adapted to the size of a sentence supplied by the user. The code may look complicated, but it's basically just arithmetic—figuring out how many spaces, dashes, and so on you need in order to place things correctly.

**Listing 2-3.** *Sequence (String) Multiplication Example*

```
# Prints a sentence in a centered "box" of correct width

# Note that the integer division operator (//) only works in Python
# 2.2 and newer. In earlier versions, simply use plain division (/)


sentence = raw_input("Sentence: ")

screen_width = 80
text_width   = len(sentence)
box_width    = text_width + 6
left_margin  = (screen_width - box_width) // 2

print
print ' ' * left_margin + '+'   + '-' * (box_width-2)  +   '+'
print ' ' * left_margin + '|   ' + ' ' * text_width     + '   |'
print ' ' * left_margin + '|   ' +      sentence        + '   |'
print ' ' * left_margin + '|   ' + ' ' * text_width     + '   |'
print ' ' * left_margin + '+'   + '-' * (box_width-2)  +   '+'
print
```

The following is a sample run:

Sentence: He's a very naughty boy!

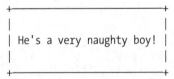

Membership

To check whether a value can be found in a sequence, you use the in operator. This operator is a bit different from the ones discussed so far (such as multiplication or addition). It checks whether something is true and returns a value accordingly: True for true and False for false. Such operators are called *Boolean operators*, and the truth values are called *Boolean values*. You learn more about Boolean expressions in the section on conditional statements in Chapter 5.

Here are some examples that use the in operator:

```
>>> permissions = 'rw'
>>> 'w' in permissions
True
>>> 'x' in permissions
```

```
False
>>> users = ['mlh', 'foo', 'bar']
>>> raw_input('Enter your user name: ') in users
Enter your user name: mlh
True
>>> subject = '$$$ Get rich now!!! $$$'
>>> '$$$' in subject
True
```

The first two examples use the membership test to check whether 'w' and 'x', respectively, are found in the string permissions. This could be a script on a UNIX machine checking for writing and execution permissions on a file. The next example checks whether a supplied user name (mlh) is found in a list of users. This could be useful if your program enforces some security policy. (In that case, you would probably want to use passwords as well.) The last example checks whether the string subject contains the string '$$$'. This might be used as part of a spam filter, for example.

---

**Note**  The example that checks whether a string contains '$$$' is a bit different from the others. In general, the in operator checks whether an object is a member (that is, an element) of a sequence (or some other collection). However, the only members or elements of a string are its characters. So, the following makes perfect sense:

```
>>> 'P' in 'Python'
True
```

In fact, in earlier versions of Python this was the only membership check that worked with strings—finding out whether a character is in a string. Trying to check for a longer substring, such as '$$$', would give you an error message (it would raise a TypeError), and you'd have to use a string method. You learn more about those in Chapter 3. In Python 2.3 and later, however, you can use the in operator to check whether any string is a substring of another.

---

Listing 2-4 shows a program that reads in a user name and checks the entered PIN code against a database (a list, actually) that contains pairs (more lists) of names and PIN codes. If the name/PIN pair is found in the database, the string 'Access granted' is printed. (The if statement was mentioned in Chapter 1 and will be fully explained in Chapter 5.)

**Listing 2-4.** *Sequence Membership Example*

```
# Check a user name and PIN code

database = [
    ['albert', '1234'],
    ['dilbert', '4242'],
    ['smith',  '7524'],
    ['jones',  '9843']
]
```

```
username = raw_input('User name: ')
pin = raw_input('PIN code: ')

if [username, pin] in database: print 'Access granted'
```

## Length, Minimum, and Maximum

The built-in functions len, min, and max can be quite useful. The function len returns the number of elements a sequence contains. min and max return the smallest and largest element of the sequence, respectively. (You learn more about comparing objects in Chapter 5, in the section "Comparison Operators.")

```
>>> numbers = [100, 34, 678]
>>> len(numbers)
3
>>> max(numbers)
678
>>> min(numbers)
34
>>> max(2, 3)
3
>>> min(9, 3, 2, 5)
2
```

How this works should be clear from the previous explanation, except possibly the last two expressions. In those, max and min are not called with a sequence argument; the numbers are supplied directly as arguments.

# Lists: Python's Workhorse

In the previous examples, I've used lists quite a bit. You've seen how useful they are, but this section deals with what makes them different from tuples and strings: lists are *mutable*—that is, you can change their contents—and they have many useful specialized *methods*.

## The list Function

Because strings can't be modified in the same way as lists, sometimes it can be useful to create a list from a string. You can do this with the list function:[1]

```
>>> list('Hello')
['H', 'e', 'l', 'l', 'o']
```

Note that list works with all kinds of sequences, not just strings.

---

1. It's actually a *type*, not a function, but the difference isn't important right now.

**Tip** To convert a list of characters such as the preceding code back to a string, you would use the following expression:

```
''.join(somelist)
```

where `somelist` is your list. For an explanation of what this really means, see the section about `join` in Chapter 3.

## Basic List Operations

You can perform all the standard sequence operations on lists, such as indexing, slicing, concatenating, and multiplying. But the interesting thing about lists is that they can be modified. In this section, you see some of the ways you can change a list: item assignments, item deletion, slice assignments, and list methods. (Note that not all list methods actually change their list.)

### Changing Lists: Item Assignments

Changing a list is easy. You just use ordinary assignment as explained in Chapter 1. However, instead of writing something like x = 2, you use the indexing notation to assign to a specific, existing position, such as x[1] = 2.

```
>>> x = [1, 1, 1]
>>> x[1] = 2
>>> x
[1, 2, 1]
```

**Note** You cannot assign to a position that doesn't exist; if your list is of length 2, you cannot assign a value to index 100. To do that, you would have to make a list of length 101 (or more). See the section "None, Empty Lists, and Initialization," earlier in this chapter.

### Deleting Elements

Deleting elements from a list is easy, too. You can simply use the `del` statement:

```
>>> names = ['Alice', 'Beth', 'Cecil', 'Dee-Dee', 'Earl']
>>> del names[2]
>>> names
['Alice', 'Beth', 'Dee-Dee', 'Earl']
```

Notice how Cecil is completely gone, and the length of the list has shrunk from five to four.

The del statement may be used to delete things other than list elements. It can be used with dictionaries (see Chapter 4) or even variables. For more information, see Chapter 5.

## Assigning to Slices

Slicing is a very powerful feature, and it is made even more powerful by the fact that you can assign to slices:

```
>>> name = list('Perl')
>>> name
['P', 'e', 'r', 'l']
>>> name[2:] = list('ar')
>>> name
['P', 'e', 'a', 'r']
```

So you can assign to several positions at once. You may wonder what the big deal is. Couldn't you just have assigned to them one at a time? Sure, but when you use slice assignments, you may also replace the slice with a sequence whose length is different from that of the original:

```
>>> name = list('Perl')
>>> name[1:] = list('ython')
>>> name
['P', 'y', 't', 'h', 'o', 'n']
```

Slice assignments can even be used to *insert* elements without replacing any of the original ones:

```
>>> numbers = [1, 5]
>>> numbers[1:1] = [2, 3, 4]
>>> numbers
[1, 2, 3, 4, 5]
```

Here, I basically "replaced" an empty slice, thereby really inserting a sequence. You can do the reverse to delete a slice:

```
>>> numbers
[1, 2, 3, 4, 5]
>>> numbers[1:4] = []
>>> numbers
[1, 5]
```

As you may have guessed, this last example is equivalent to del numbers[1:4]. (Now why don't you try a slice assignment with a step size different from 1? Perhaps even a negative one?)

# List Methods

You've encountered functions already, but now it's time to meet a close relative: *methods*.

A method is a function that is tightly coupled to some object, be it a list, a number, a string, or whatever. In general, a method is called like this:

```
object.method(arguments)
```

As you can see, a method call looks just like a function call, except that the object is put before the method name, with a dot separating them. (You get a much more detailed explanation of what methods really are in Chapter 7.)

Lists have several methods that allow you to examine or modify their contents.

## append

The append method is used to append an object to the end of a list:

```
>>> lst = [1, 2, 3]
>>> lst.append(4)
>>> lst
[1, 2, 3, 4]
```

You might wonder why I have chosen such an ugly name as lst for my list. Why not call it list? I could do that, but as you might remember, list is a built-in function.[2] If I use the name for a list instead, I won't be able to call the function anymore. You can generally find better names for a given application. A name such as lst really doesn't tell you anything. So if your list is a list of prices, for instance, you probably ought to call it something like prices, prices_of_eggs, or pricesOfEggs.

It's also important to note that append, like several similar methods, changes the list *in place*. This means that it does *not* simply return a new, modified list; instead, it modifies the old one directly. This is usually what you want, but it may sometimes cause trouble. I'll return to this discussion when I describe sort later in the chapter.

## count

The count method counts the occurrences of an element in a list:

```
>>> ['to', 'be', 'or', 'not', 'to', 'be'].count('to')
2
>>> x = [[1, 2], 1, 1, [2, 1, [1, 2]]]
>>> x.count(1)
2
>>> x.count([1, 2])
1
```

---

2. Actually, from version 2.2 of Python, list is a type, not a function. (This is the case with tuple and str as well.) For the full story on this, see the section "Subclassing list, dict, and str" in Chapter 9.

## extend

The extend method allows you to append several values at once by supplying a sequence of the values you want to append. In other words, your original list has been extended by the other one:

```
>>> a = [1, 2, 3]
>>> b = [4, 5, 6]
>>> a.extend(b)
>>> a
[1, 2, 3, 4, 5, 6]
```

This may seem similar to concatenation, but the important difference is that the extended sequence (in this case, a) is modified. This is not the case in ordinary concatenation, in which a completely new sequence is returned:

```
>>> a = [1, 2, 3]
>>> b = [4, 5, 6]
>>> a + b
[1, 2, 3, 4, 5, 6]
>>> a
[1, 2, 3]
```

As you can see, the concatenated list looks exactly the same as the extended one in the previous example, yet a hasn't changed this time. Because ordinary concatenation must make a new list that contains copies of a and b, it isn't quite as efficient as using extend if what you want is something like this:

```
>>> a = a + b
```

Also, this isn't an in-place operation—it won't modify the original.

The effect of extend can be achieved by assigning to slices, as follows:

```
>>> a = [1, 2, 3]
>>> b = [4, 5, 6]
>>> a[len(a):] = b
>>> a
[1, 2, 3, 4, 5, 6]
```

While this works, it isn't quite as readable.

## index

The index method is used for searching lists to find the index of the first occurrence of a value:

```
>>> knights = ['We', 'are', 'the', 'knights', 'who', 'say', 'ni']
>>> knights.index('who')
4
>>> knights.index('herring')
Traceback (innermost last):
  File "<pyshell#76>", line 1, in ?
    knights.index('herring')
ValueError: list.index(x): x not in list
```

When you search for the word 'who', you find that it's located at index 4:

```
>>> knights[4]
'who'
```

However, when you search for 'herring', you get an exception because the word is not found at all.

### insert

The insert method is used to insert an object into a list:

```
>>> numbers = [1, 2, 3, 5, 6, 7]
>>> numbers.insert(3, 'four')
>>> numbers
[1, 2, 3, 'four', 5, 6, 7]
```

As with extend, you can implement insert with slice assignments:

```
>>> numbers = [1, 2, 3, 5, 6, 7]
>>> numbers[3:3] = ['four']
>>> numbers
[1, 2, 3, 'four', 5, 6, 7]
```

This may be fancy, but it is hardly as readable as using insert.

### pop

The pop method removes an element (by default, the last one) from the list and returns it:

```
>>> x = [1, 2, 3]
>>> x.pop()
3
>>> x
[1, 2]
>>> x.pop(0)
1
>>> x
[2]
```

---

■**Note**  The pop method is the only list method that both modifies the list *and* returns a value (other than None).

---

Using pop, you can implement a common data structure called a *stack*. A stack like this works just like a stack of plates. You can put plates on top, and you can remove plates from the top. The last one you put into the stack is the first one to be removed. (This principle is called *last-in, first-out*, or LIFO.)

The generally accepted names for the two stack operations (putting things in and taking them out) are *push* and *pop*. Python doesn't have push, but you can use append instead. The pop and append methods reverse each other's results, so if you push (or append) the value you just popped, you end up with the same stack:

```
>>> x = [1, 2, 3]
>>> x.append(x.pop())
>>> x
[1, 2, 3]
```

---

**■Tip** If you want a first-in, first-out (FIFO) queue, you can use insert(0, ...) instead of append. Alternatively, you could keep using append but substitute pop(0) for pop(). An even better solution would be to use a deque from the collections module. See Chapter 10 for more information.

---

## remove

The remove method is used to remove the first occurrence of a value:

```
>>> x = ['to', 'be', 'or', 'not', 'to', 'be']
>>> x.remove('be')
>>> x
['to', 'or', 'not', 'to', 'be']
>>> x.remove('bee')
Traceback (innermost last):
  File "<pyshell#3>", line 1, in ?
    x.remove('bee')
ValueError: list.remove(x): x not in list
```

As you can see, only the first occurrence is removed, and you cannot remove something (in this case, the string 'bee') if it isn't in the list to begin with.

It's important to note that this is one of the "nonreturning in-place changing" methods. It modifies the list, but returns nothing (as opposed to pop).

## reverse

The reverse method reverses the elements in the list. (Not very surprising, I guess.)

```
>>> x = [1, 2, 3]
>>> x.reverse()
>>> x
[3, 2, 1]
```

Note that reverse changes the list and does not return anything (just like remove and sort, for example).

---

**Tip** If you want to iterate over a sequence in reverse, you can use the `reversed` function. This function doesn't return a list, though; it returns an iterator. (You learn more about iterators in Chapter 9.) You can convert the returned object with `list`:

```
>>> x = [1, 2, 3]
>>> list(reversed(x))
[3, 2, 1]
```

---

### sort

The `sort` method is used to sort lists in place.[3] Sorting "in place" means changing the original list so its elements are in sorted order, rather than simply returning a sorted copy of the list:

```
>>> x = [4, 6, 2, 1, 7, 9]
>>> x.sort()
>>> x
[1, 2, 4, 6, 7, 9]
```

You've encountered several methods already that modify the list without returning anything, and in most cases that behavior is quite natural (as with append, for example). But I want to emphasize this behavior in the case of `sort` because so many people seem to be confused by it. The confusion usually occurs when users want a sorted copy of a list while leaving the original alone. An intuitive (but *wrong*) way of doing this is as follows:

```
>>> x = [4, 6, 2, 1, 7, 9]
>>> y = x.sort() # Don't do this!
>>> print y
None
```

Because `sort` modifies x but returns nothing, you end up with a sorted x and a y containing None. One correct way of doing this would be to *first* bind y to a copy of x, and then sort y, as follows:

```
>>> x = [4, 6, 2, 1, 7, 9]
>>> y = x[:]
>>> y.sort()
>>> x
[4, 6, 2, 1, 7, 9]
>>> y
[1, 2, 4, 6, 7, 9]
```

Recall that x[:] is a slice containing all the elements of x, effectively a copy of the entire list. Simply assigning x to y wouldn't work because both x and y would refer to the same list:

```
>>> y = x
>>> y.sort()
```

---

3.  In case you're interested: from Python 2.3 on, the `sort` method uses a stable sorting algorithm.

```
>>> x
[1, 2, 4, 6, 7, 9]
>>> y
[1, 2, 4, 6, 7, 9]
```

Another way of getting a sorted copy of a list is using the sorted function:

```
>>> x = [4, 6, 2, 1, 7, 9]
>>> y = sorted(x)
>>> x
[4, 6, 2, 1, 7, 9]
>>> y
[1, 2, 4, 6, 7, 9]
```

This function can actually be used on any sequence, but will always return a list:[4]

```
>>> sorted('Python')
['P', 'h', 'n', 'o', 't', 'y']
```

If you want to sort the elements in reverse order, you can use sort (or sorted), followed by a call to the reverse method, or you could use the reverse argument, described in the following section.

### Advanced Sorting

If you want to have your elements sorted in a specific manner (other than sort's default behavior, which is to sort elements in ascending order, according to Python's default comparison rules, as explained in Chapter 5), you can define your own *comparison function*, of the form compare(x,y), which returns a negative number when x < y, a positive number when x > y, and zero when x == y (according to your definition). You can then supply this as a parameter to sort. The built-in function cmp provides the default behavior:

```
>>> cmp(42, 32)
1
>>> cmp(99, 100)
-1
>>> cmp(10, 10)
0
>>> numbers = [5, 2, 9, 7]
>>> numbers.sort(cmp)
>>> numbers
[2, 5, 7, 9]
```

The sort method has two other optional arguments: key and reverse. If you want to use them, you normally specify them by name (so-called *keyword arguments*; you learn more about those in Chapter 6). The key argument is similar to the cmp argument: you supply a function and it's used in the sorting process. However, instead of being used directly for determining whether

---

4.  The sorted function can, in fact, be used on any iterable object. You learn more about iterable objects in Chapter 9.

one element is smaller than another, the function is used to create a *key* for each element, and the elements are sorted according to these keys. So, for example, if you want to sort the elements according to their lengths, you use len as the key function:

```
>>> x = ['aardvark', 'abalone', 'acme', 'add', 'aerate']
>>> x.sort(key=len)
>>> x
['add', 'acme', 'aerate', 'abalone', 'aardvark']
```

The other keyword argument, reverse, is simply a truth value (True or False; you learn more about these in Chapter 5) indicating whether the list should be sorted in reverse:

```
>>> x = [4, 6, 2, 1, 7, 9]
>>> x.sort(reverse=True)
>>> x
[9, 7, 6, 4, 2, 1]
```

The cmp, key, and reverse arguments are available in the sorted function as well. In many cases, using custom functions for cmp or key will be useful. You learn how to define your own functions in Chapter 6.

---

■**Tip**  If you would like to read more about sorting, you may want to check out Andrew Dalke's "Sorting Mini-HOWTO," found at http://wiki.python.org/moin/HowTo/Sorting.

---

# Tuples: Immutable Sequences

Tuples are sequences, just like lists. The only difference is that tuples *can't be changed*.[5] (As you may have noticed, this is also true of strings.) The tuple syntax is simple—if you separate some values with commas, you automatically have a tuple:

```
>>> 1, 2, 3
(1, 2, 3)
```

As you can see, tuples may also be (and often are) enclosed in parentheses:

```
>>> (1, 2, 3)
(1, 2, 3)
```

The empty tuple is written as two parentheses containing nothing:

```
>>> ()
()
```

---

5. There are some technical differences in the way tuples and lists work behind the scenes, but you probably won't notice it in any practical way. And tuples don't have methods the way lists do. Don't ask me why.

So, you may wonder how to write a tuple containing a single value. This is a bit peculiar—you have to include a comma, even though there is only one value:

```
>>> 42
42
>>> 42,
(42,)
>>> (42,)
(42,)
```

The last two examples produce tuples of length one, while the first is not a tuple at all. The comma is crucial. Simply adding parentheses won't help: (42) is exactly the same as 42. One lonely comma, however, can change the value of an expression completely:

```
>>> 3*(40+2)
126
>>> 3*(40+2,)
(42, 42, 42)
```

## The tuple Function

The tuple function works in pretty much the same way as list: it takes one sequence argument and converts it to a tuple.[6] If the argument is already a tuple, it is returned unchanged:

```
>>> tuple([1, 2, 3])
(1, 2, 3)
>>> tuple('abc')
('a', 'b', 'c')
>>> tuple((1, 2, 3))
(1, 2, 3)
```

## Basic Tuple Operations

As you may have gathered, tuples aren't very complicated—and there isn't really much you can do with them except create them and access their elements, and you do this the same as with other sequences:

```
>>> x = 1, 2, 3
>>> x[1]
2
>>> x[0:2]
(1, 2)
```

As you can see, slices of a tuple are also tuples, just as list slices are themselves lists.

---

6. Like list, tuple isn't really a function—it's a type. And, as with list, you can safely ignore this for now.

## So What's the Point?

By now you are probably wondering why anyone would ever want such a thing as an immutable (unchangeable) sequence. Can't you just stick to lists and leave them alone when you don't want them to change? Basically, yes. However, there are two important reasons why you need to know about tuples:

- They can be used as keys in mappings (and members of sets); lists can't be used this way. You'll learn more mappings in Chapter 4.

- They are returned by some built-in functions and methods, which means that you have to deal with them. As long as you don't try to change them, "dealing" with them most often means treating them just like lists (unless you need methods such as index and count, which tuples don't have).

In general, lists will probably be adequate for all your sequencing needs.

# A Quick Summary

Let's review some of the most important concepts covered in this chapter:

**Sequences**: A sequence is a data structure in which the elements are numbered (starting with zero). Examples of sequence types are lists, strings, and tuples. Of these, lists are mutable (you can change them), whereas tuples and strings are immutable (once they're created, they're fixed). Parts of a sequence can be accessed through slicing, supplying two indices, indicating the starting and ending position of the slice. To change a list, you assign new values to its positions, or use assignment to overwrite entire slices.

**Membership**: Whether a value can be found in a sequence (or other container) is checked with the operator in. Using in with strings is a special case—it will let you look for substrings.

**Methods**: Some of the built-in types (such as lists and strings, but not tuples) have many useful methods attached to them. These are a bit like functions, except that they are tied closely to a specific value. Methods are an important aspect of object-oriented programming, which we look at in Chapter 7.

## New Functions in This Chapter

| Function | Description |
| --- | --- |
| cmp(x, y) | Compares two values |
| len(seq) | Returns the length of a sequence |
| list(seq) | Converts a sequence to a list |
| max(args) | Returns the maximum of a sequence or set of arguments |
| min(args) | Returns the minimum of a sequence or set of arguments |
| reversed(seq) | Lets you iterate over a sequence in reverse |
| sorted(seq) | Returns a sorted list of the elements of seq |
| tuple(seq) | Converts a sequence to a tuple |

## What Now?

Now that you're acquainted with sequences, let's move on to character sequences, also known as *strings*.

■ ■ ■

# CHAPTER 3

# Working with Strings

**Y**ou've seen strings before, and know how to make them. You've also looked at how to access their individual characters by indexing and slicing. In this chapter, you see how to use them to format other values (for printing, for example), and take a quick look at the useful things you can do with string methods, such as splitting, joining, searching, and more.

## Basic String Operations

All the standard sequence operations (indexing, slicing, multiplication, membership, length, minimum, and maximum) work with strings, as you saw in the previous chapter. Remember, however, that strings are immutable, so all kinds of item or slice assignments are illegal:

```
>>> website = 'http://www.python.org'
>>> website[-3:] = 'com'
Traceback (most recent call last):
  File "<pyshell#19>", line 1, in ?
    website[-3:] = 'com'
TypeError: object doesn't support slice assignment
```

## String Formatting: The Short Version

If you are new to Python programming, chances are you won't need all the options that are available in Python string formatting, so I'll give you the short version here. If you are interested in the details, take a look at the section "String Formatting: The Long Version," which follows. Otherwise, just read this and skip down to the section "String Methods."

String formatting uses the (aptly named) string formatting operator, the percent (%) sign.

---

■**Note** As you may remember, % is also used as a modulus (remainder) operator.

---

To the left of the %, you place a string (the format string); to the right of it, you place the value you want to format. You can use a single value such as a string or a number, you can use a tuple of values (if you want to format more than one), or, as I discuss in the next chapter, you can use a dictionary. The most common case is the tuple:

```
>>> format = "Hello, %s. %s enough for ya?"
>>> values = ('world', 'Hot')
>>> print format % values
Hello, world. Hot enough for ya?
```

> ■**Note** If you use a list or some other sequence instead of a tuple, the sequence will be interpreted as a single value. Only tuples and dictionaries (discussed in Chapter 4) will allow you to format more than one value.

The %s parts of the format string are called *conversion specifiers*. They mark the places where the values are to be inserted. The s means that the values should be formatted as if they were strings; if they aren't, they'll be converted with str. This works with most values. For a list of other specifier types, see Table 3-1 later in the chapter.

> ■**Note** To actually include a percent sign in the format string, you must write %% so Python doesn't mistake it for the beginning of a conversion specifier.

If you are formatting real numbers (floats), you can use the f specifier type and supply the *precision* as a . (dot), followed by the number of decimals you want to keep. The format specifier always ends with a type character, so you must put the precision before that:

```
>>> format = "Pi with three decimals: %.3f"
>>> from math import pi
>>> print format % pi
Pi with three decimals: 3.142
```

## TEMPLATE STRINGS

The string module offers another way of formatting values: template strings. They work more like variable substitution in many UNIX shells, with $foo being replaced by a keyword argument called foo (for more about keyword arguments, see Chapter 6), which is passed to the template method substitute:

```
>>> from string import Template
>>> s = Template('$x, glorious $x!')
>>> s.substitute(x='slurm')
'slurm, glorious slurm!'
```

If the replacement field is part of a word, the name must be enclosed in braces, in order to clearly indicate where it ends:

```
>>> s = Template("It's ${x}tastic!")
>>> s.substitute(x='slurm')
"It's slurmtastic!"
```

In order to insert a dollar sign, use $$:

```
>>> s = Template("Make $$ selling $x!")
>>> s.substitute(x='slurm')
'Make $ selling slurm!'
```

Instead of using keyword arguments, you can supply the value-name pairs in a dictionary (see Chapter 4):

```
>>> s = Template('A $thing must never $action.')
>>> d = {}
>>> d['thing'] = 'gentleman'
>>> d['action'] = 'show his socks'
>>> s.substitute(d)
'A gentleman must never show his socks.'
```

There is also a method called safe_substitute that will not complain about missing values or incorrect uses of the $ character.[1]

---

1. For more information, see Section 4.1.2, "Template strings," of the Python Library Reference (http://python.org/doc/lib/node40.html).

# String Formatting: The Long Version

The right operand of the formatting operator may be anything; if it is either a tuple or a mapping (like a dictionary), it is given special treatment. We haven't looked at mappings (such as dictionaries) yet, so let's focus on tuples here. We'll use mappings in formatting in Chapter 4, where they're discussed in greater detail.

If the right operand is a tuple, each of its elements is formatted separately, and you need a conversion specifier for each of the values.

---

**Note** If you write the tuple to be converted as part of the conversion expression, you must enclose it in parentheses to avoid confusing Python:

```
>>> '%s plus %s equals %s' % (1, 1, 2)
'1 plus 1 equals 2'
>>> '%s plus %s equals %s' % 1, 1, 2 # Lacks parentheses!
Traceback (most recent call last):
  File "<stdin>", line 1, in ?
TypeError: not enough arguments for format string
```

---

A basic conversion specifier (as opposed to a full conversion specifier, which may contain a mapping key as well; see Chapter 4 for more information) consists of the items that follow. Note that the order of these items is crucial.

- **The % character**: This marks the beginning of the conversion specifier.

- **Conversion flags**: These are optional and may be -, indicating left alignment; +, indicating that a sign should precede the converted value; " " (a space character), indicating that a space should precede positive numbers; or 0, indicating that the conversion should be zero-padded.

- **The minimum field width**: This is also optional and specifies that the converted string will be at least this wide. If this is an * (asterisk), the width will be read from the value tuple.

- **A . (dot) followed by the precision**: This is also optional. If a real number is converted, this many decimals should be shown. If a string is converted, this number is the *maximum field width*. If this is an * (asterisk), the precision will be read from the value tuple.

- **The conversion type**: This can be any of the types listed in Table 3-1.

**Table 3-1.** *String Formatting Conversion Types*

| Conversion Type | Meaning |
| --- | --- |
| d, i | Signed integer decimal |
| o | Unsigned octal |
| u | Unsigned decimal |

| Conversion Type | Meaning |
| --- | --- |
| x | Unsigned hexadecimal (lowercase) |
| X | Unsigned hexadecimal (uppercase) |
| e | Floating-point exponential format (lowercase) |
| E | Floating-point exponential format (uppercase) |
| f, F | Floating-point decimal format |
| g | Same as e if exponent is greater than –4 or less than precision; f otherwise |
| G | Same as E if exponent is greater than –4 or less than precision; F otherwise |
| c | Single character (accepts an integer or a single character string) |
| r | String (converts any Python object using repr) |
| s | String (converts any Python object using str) |

The following sections discuss the various elements of the conversion specifiers in more detail.

## Simple Conversion

The simple conversion, with only a conversion type, is really easy to use:

```
>>> 'Price of eggs: $%d' % 42
'Price of eggs: $42'
>>> 'Hexadecimal price of eggs: %x' % 42
'Hexadecimal price of eggs: 2a'
>>> from math import pi
>>> 'Pi: %f...' % pi
'Pi: 3.141593...'
>>> 'Very inexact estimate of pi: %i' % pi
'Very inexact estimate of pi: 3'
>>> 'Using str: %s' % 42L
'Using str: 42'
>>> 'Using repr: %r' % 42L
'Using repr: 42L'
```

## Width and Precision

A conversion specifier may include a field width and a precision. The width is the minimum number of characters reserved for a formatted value. The precision is (for a numeric conversion) the number of decimals that will be included in the result or (for a string conversion) the maximum number of characters the formatted value may have.

These two parameters are supplied as two integer numbers (width first, then precision), separated by a . (dot). Both are optional, but if you want to supply only the precision, you must also include the dot:

```
>>> '%10f' % pi      # Field width 10
'  3.141593'
```

```
>>> '%10.2f' % pi     # Field width 10, precision 2
'      3.14'
>>> '%.2f' % pi       # Precision 2
'3.14'
>>> '%.5s' % 'Guido van Rossum'
'Guido'
```

You can use an * (asterisk) as the width or precision (or both). In that case, the number will be read from the tuple argument:

```
>>> '%.*s' % (5, 'Guido van Rossum')
'Guido'
```

## Signs, Alignment, and Zero-Padding

Before the width and precision numbers, you may put a "flag," which may be either zero, plus, minus, or blank. A zero means that the number will be zero-padded:

```
>>> '%010.2f' % pi
'0000003.14'
```

It's important to note here that the leading zero in 010 in the preceding code does *not* mean that the width specifier is an octal number, as it would in a normal Python number. When you use 010 as the width specifier, it means that the width should be 10 and that the number should be zero-padded, not that the width should be 8:

```
>>> 010
8
```

A minus sign (-) left-aligns the value:

```
>>> '%-10.2f' % pi
'3.14      '
```

As you can see, any extra space is put on the right-hand side of the number.

A blank (" ") means that a blank should be put in front of positive numbers. This may be useful for aligning positive and negative numbers:

```
>>> print ('% 5d' % 10) + '\n' + ('% 5d' % -10)F
   10
  -10
```

Finally, a plus (+) means that a sign (either plus or minus) should precede both positive and negative numbers (again, useful for aligning):

```
>>> print ('%+5d' % 10) + '\n' + ('%+5d' % -10)
  +10
  -10
```

In the example shown in Listing 3-1, I use the asterisk width specifier to format a table of fruit prices, where the user enters the total width of the table. Because this information is supplied by the user, I can't hard-code the field widths in my conversion specifiers. By using the asterisk, I can have the field width read from the converted tuple.

**Listing 3-1.** *String Formatting Example*

```
# Print a formatted price list with a given width

width = input('Please enter width: ')

price_width = 10
item_width = width - price_width

header_format = '%-*s%*s'
format        = '%-*s%*.2f'

print '=' * width

print header_format % (item_width, 'Item', price_width, 'Price')

print '-' * width

print format % (item_width, 'Apples', price_width, 0.4)
print format % (item_width, 'Pears', price_width, 0.5)
print format % (item_width, 'Cantaloupes', price_width, 1.92)
print format % (item_width, 'Dried Apricots (16 oz.)', price_width, 8)
print format % (item_width, 'Prunes (4 lbs.)', price_width, 12)

print '=' * width
```

The following is a sample run of the program:

```
Please enter width: 35
===================================
Item                          Price
-----------------------------------
Apples                         0.40
Pears                          0.50
Cantaloupes                    1.92
Dried Apricots (16 oz.)        8.00
Prunes (4 lbs.)               12.00
===================================
```

# String Methods

You have already encountered methods in lists. Strings have a much richer set of methods, in part because strings have "inherited" many of their methods from the string module where they resided as functions in earlier versions of Python (and where you may still find them, if you feel the need).

Because there are so many string methods, only some of the most useful ones are described here. For a full reference, see Appendix B. In the description of the string methods, you will find references to other, related string methods in this chapter (marked "See also") or in Appendix B.

---

### BUT STRING ISN'T DEAD

Even though string methods have completely upstaged the string module, the module still includes a few constants and functions that *aren't* available as string methods. The maketrans function is one example and will be discussed together with the translate method in the material that follows. The following are some useful constants available from string.[2]

- string.digits: A string containing the digits 0–9

- string.letters: A string containing all letters (uppercase and lowercase)

- string.lowercase: A string containing all lowercase letters

- string.printable: A string containing all printable characters

- string.punctuation: A string containing all punctuation characters

- string.uppercase: A string containing all uppercase letters

Note that the string constant letters (such as string.letters) are *locale-dependent* (that is, their exact values depend on the language for which Python is configured).[3] If you want to make sure you're using ASCII, you can use the variants with ascii_ in their names, such as string.ascii_letters.

---

## find

The find method finds a substring within a larger string. It returns the leftmost index where the substring is found. If it is *not* found, –1 is returned:

```
>>> 'With a moo-moo here, and a moo-moo there'.find('moo')
7
>>> title = "Monty Python's Flying Circus"
>>> title.find('Monty')
0
```

---

2. For a more thorough description of the module, check out Section 4.1 of the Python Library Reference (http://python.org/doc/lib/module-string.html).

3. In Python 3.0, string.letters and friends will be removed. You will need to use constants like string.ascii_letters instead.

```
>>> title.find('Python')
6
>>> title.find('Flying')
15
>>> title.find('Zirquss')
-1
```

In our first encounter with membership in Chapter 2, we created part of a spam filter by using the expression '$$$' in subject. We could also have used find (which would also have worked prior to Python 2.3, when in could be used only when checking for single character membership in strings):

```
>>> subject = '$$$ Get rich now!!! $$$'
>>> subject.find('$$$')
0
```

---

■**Note**  The string method find does *not* return a Boolean value. If find returns 0, as it did here, it means that it *has* found the substring, at index zero.

---

You may also supply a starting point for your search and, optionally, an ending point:

```
>>> subject = '$$$ Get rich now!!! $$$'
>>> subject.find('$$$')
0
>>> subject.find('$$$', 1) # Only supplying the start
20
>>> subject.find('!!!')
16
>>> subject.find('!!!', 0, 16) # Supplying start and end
-1
```

Note that the range specified by the start and stop values (second and third parameters) includes the first index but not the second. This is common practice in Python.

*In Appendix B*: rfind, index, rindex, count, startswith, endswith.

## join

A very important string method, join is the inverse of split. It is used to join the elements of a sequence:

```
>>> seq = [1, 2, 3, 4, 5]
>>> sep = '+'
>>> sep.join(seq) # Trying to join a list of numbers
Traceback (most recent call last):
  File "<stdin>", line 1, in ?
TypeError: sequence item 0: expected string, int found
```

```
>>> seq = ['1', '2', '3', '4', '5']
>>> sep.join(seq) # Joining a list of strings
'1+2+3+4+5'
>>> dirs = '', 'usr', 'bin', 'env'
>>> '/'.join(dirs)
'/usr/bin/env'
>>> print 'C:' + '\\'.join(dirs)
C:\usr\bin\env
```

As you can see, the sequence elements that are to be joined must all be strings. Note how in the last two examples I use a list of directories and format them according to the conventions of UNIX and DOS/Windows simply by using a different separator (and adding a drive name in the DOS version).

*See also*: split.

## lower

The lower method returns a lowercase version of the string:

```
>>> 'Trondheim Hammer Dance'.lower()
'trondheim hammer dance'
```

This can be useful if you want to write code that is case insensitive—that is, code that ignores the difference between uppercase and lowercase letters. For instance, suppose you want to check whether a user name is found in a list. If your list contains the string 'gumby' and the user enters his name as 'Gumby', you won't find it:

```
>>> if 'Gumby' in ['gumby', 'smith', 'jones']: print 'Found it!'
...
>>>
```

Of course, the same thing will happen if you have stored 'Gumby' and the user writes 'gumby', or even 'GUMBY'. A solution to this is to convert all names to lowercase both when storing and searching. The code would look something like this:

```
>>> name = 'Gumby'
>>> names = ['gumby', 'smith', 'jones']
>>> if name.lower() in names: print 'Found it!'
...
Found it!
>>>
```

*See also*: translate.
*In Appendix B*: islower, capitalize, swapcase, title, istitle, upper, isupper.

| **TITLE CASING** |
| --- |

One relative of `lower` is the `title` method (see Appendix B), which title cases a string—that is, all words start with uppercase characters, and all other characters are lowercased. However, the word boundaries are defined in a way that may give some unnatural results:

```
>>> "that's all folks".title()
"That'S All, Folks"
```

An alternative is the `capwords` function from the `string` module:

```
>>> import string
>>> string.capwords("that's all, folks")
"That's All, Folks"
```

Of course, if you want a truly correctly capitalized title (which depends on the style you're using—possibly lowercasing articles, coordinating conjunctions, prepositions with fewer than five letters, and so forth), you're basically on your own.

## replace

The replace method returns a string where all the occurrences of one string have been replaced by another:

```
>>> 'This is a test'.replace('is', 'eez')
'Theez eez a test'
```

If you have ever used the "search and replace" feature of a word processing program, you will no doubt see the usefulness of this method.

*See also*: translate.

*In Appendix B*: expandtabs.

## split

A very important string method, split is the inverse of join, and is used to split a string into a sequence:

```
>>> '1+2+3+4+5'.split('+')
['1', '2', '3', '4', '5']
>>> '/usr/bin/env'.split('/')
['', 'usr', 'bin', 'env']
>>> 'Using    the    default'.split()
['Using', 'the', 'default']
```

Note that if no separator is supplied, the default is to split on all runs of consecutive whitespace characters (spaces, tabs, newlines, and so on).

*See also*: join.

*In Appendix B*: rsplit, splitlines.

## strip

The strip method returns a string where whitespace on the left and right (but not internally) has been stripped (removed):

```
>>> '        internal whitespace is kept        '.strip()
'internal whitespace is kept'
```

As with lower, strip can be useful when comparing input to stored values. Let's return to the user name example from the section on lower, and let's say that the user inadvertently types a space after his name:

```
>>> names = ['gumby', 'smith', 'jones']
>>> name = 'gumby '
>>> if name in names: print 'Found it!'
...
>>> if name.strip() in names: print 'Found it!'
...
Found it!
>>>
```

You can also specify which characters are to be stripped, by listing them all in a string parameter:

```
>>> '*** SPAM * for * everyone!!! ***'.strip(' *!')
'SPAM * for * everyone'
```

Stripping is performed only at the ends, so the internal asterisks are not removed.

*In Appendix B*: lstrip, rstrip.

## translate

Similar to replace, translate replaces parts of a string, but unlike replace, translate works only with single characters. Its strength lies in that it can perform several replacements simultaneously, and can do so more efficiently than replace.

There are quite a few rather technical uses for this method (such as translating newline characters or other platform-dependent special characters), but let's consider a simpler (although slightly more silly) example. Let's say you want to translate a plain English text into one with a German accent. To do this, you must replace the character *c* with *k*, and *s* with *z*.

Before you can use `translate`, however, you must make a *translation table*. This translation table is a full listing of which characters should be replaced by which. Because this table (which is actually just a string) has 256 entries, you won't write it out yourself. Instead, you'll use the function `maketrans` from the `string` module.

The `maketrans` function takes two arguments: two strings of equal length, indicating that each character in the first string should be replaced by the character in the same position in the second string. Got that? In the case of our simple example, the code would look like the following:

```
>>> from string import maketrans
>>> table = maketrans('cs', 'kz')
```

### WHAT'S IN A TRANSLATION TABLE?

A translation table is a string containing one replacement letter for each of the 256 characters in the ASCII character set:

```
>>> table = maketrans('cs', 'kz')
>>> len(table)
256
>>> table[97:123]
'abkdefghijklmnopqrztuvwxyz'
>>> maketrans('', '')[97:123]
'abcdefghijklmnopqrstuvwxyz'
```

As you can see, I've sliced out the part of the table that corresponds to the lowercase letters. Take a look at the alphabet in the table and that in the empty translation (which doesn't change anything). The empty translation has a normal alphabet, while in the preceding code, the letter *c* has been replaced by *k*, and *s* has been replaced by *z*.

Once you have this table, you can use it as an argument to the `translate` method, thereby translating your string:

```
>>> 'this is an incredible test'.translate(table)
'thiz iz an inkredible tezt'
```

An optional second argument can be supplied to `translate`, specifying letters that should be deleted. If you wanted to emulate a really fast-talking German, for instance, you could delete all the spaces:

```
>>> 'this is an incredible test'.translate(table, ' ')
'thizizaninkredibletezt'
```

*See also*: `replace`, `lower`.

## PROBLEMS WITH NON-ENGLISH STRINGS

Sometimes string methods such as `lower` won't work quite the way you want them to—for instance, if you happen to use a non-English alphabet. Let's say you want to convert the uppercase Norwegian word *BØLLEFRØ* to its lowercase equivalent:

```
>>> print 'BØLLEFRØ'.lower()
bØllefrØ
```

As you can see, this didn't really work because Python doesn't consider *Ø* a real letter. In this case, you can use `translate` to do the translation:

```
>>> table = maketrans('ÆØÅ', 'æøå')
>>> word = 'KÅPESØM'
>>> print word.lower()
kÅpesØm
>>> print word.translate(table)
KåPESøM
>>> print word.translate(table).lower()
kåpesøm
```

Then again, simply using Unicode might solve your problems:

```
>>> print u'ærnæringslære'.upper()
ÆRNÆRINGSLÆRE
```

You might also want to check out the `locale` module for some internationalization functionality.

# A Quick Summary

In this chapter, you have seen two important ways of working with strings:

**String formatting**: The modulo operator (%) can be used to splice values into a string that contains conversion flags, such as %s. You can use this to format values in many ways, including right or left justification, setting a specific field width and precision, adding a sign (plus or minus), or left-padding with zeros.

**String methods**: Strings have a plethora of methods. Some of them are extremely useful (such as split and join), while others are used less often (such as istitle or capitalize).

## New Functions in This Chapter

| Function | Description |
|---|---|
| string.capwords(s[, sep]) | Splits s with split (using sep), capitalize items, and join with a single space |
| string.maketrans(from, to) | Makes a translation table for translate |

## What Now?

Lists, strings, and dictionaries are three of the most important data types in Python. You've seen lists and strings, so guess what's next? In the next chapter, you see how dictionaries not only support indices, but other kinds of keys (such as strings or tuples) as well. Dictionaries also support a few methods, although not as many as strings.

# CHAPTER 4

■ ■ ■

# Dictionaries: When Indices Won't Do

**Y**ou've seen that lists are useful when you want to group values into a structure and refer to each value by number. In this chapter, you learn about a data structure in which you can refer to each value by name. This type of structure is called a *mapping*. The only built-in mapping type in Python is the dictionary. The values in a dictionary don't have any particular order but are stored under a key, which may be a number, a string, or even a tuple.

## Dictionary Uses

The name *dictionary* should give you a clue about the purpose of this structure. An ordinary book is made for reading from start to finish. If you like, you can quickly open it to any given page. This is a bit like a Python list. On the other hand, dictionaries—both real ones and their Python equivalent—are constructed so that you can look up a specific word (key) easily, to find its definition (value).

A dictionary is more appropriate than a list in many situations. Here are some examples of uses of Python dictionaries:

- Representing the state of a game board, with each key being a tuple of coordinates

- Storing file modification times, with file names as keys

- A digital telephone/address book

Let's say you have a list of people:

```
>>> names = ['Alice', 'Beth', 'Cecil', 'Dee-Dee', 'Earl']
```

What if you wanted to create a little database where you could store the telephone numbers of these people—how would you do that? One way would be to make another list. Let's say you're storing only their four-digit extensions. Then you would get something like this:

```
>>> numbers = ['2341', '9102', '3158', '0142', '5551']
```

Once you've created these lists, you can look up Cecil's telephone number as follows:

```
>>> numbers[names.index('Cecil')]
3158
```

---

### INTEGERS VS. STRINGS OF DIGITS

You might wonder why I have used strings to represent the telephone numbers—why not integers? Consider what would happen to Dee-Dee's number then:

```
>>> 0142
98
```

Not exactly what we wanted, is it? As mentioned briefly in Chapter 1, octal numbers are written with an initial zero. It is impossible to write decimal numbers like that.

```
>>> 0912
  File "<stdin>", line 1
    0912
       ^
SyntaxError: invalid syntax
```

The lesson is this: telephone numbers (and other numbers that may contain leading zeros) should be represented as *strings of digits*—not integers.

---

It works, but it's a bit impractical. What you *really* would want to do is something like the following:

```
>>> phonebook['Cecil']
3158
```

Guess what? If phonebook is a dictionary, you can do just that.

# Creating and Using Dictionaries

Dictionaries are written like this:

```
phonebook = {'Alice': '2341', 'Beth': '9102', 'Cecil': '3258'}
```

Dictionaries consist of pairs (called *items*) of *keys* and their corresponding *values*. In this example, the names are the keys and the telephone numbers are the values. Each key is separated from its value by a colon (:), the items are separated by commas, and the whole thing is enclosed in curly braces. An empty dictionary (without any items) is written with just two curly braces, like this: {}.

---

■**Note**  Keys are unique within a dictionary (and any other kind of mapping). Values do not need to be unique within a dictionary.

---

# The dict Function

You can use the `dict` function[1] to construct dictionaries from other mappings (for example, other dictionaries) or from sequences of (`key, value`) pairs:

```
>>> items = [('name', 'Gumby'), ('age', 42)]
>>> d = dict(items)
>>> d
{'age': 42, 'name': 'Gumby'}
>>> d['name']
'Gumby'
```

It can also be used with *keyword arguments*, as follows:

```
>>> d = dict(name='Gumby', age=42)
>>> d
{'age': 42, 'name': 'Gumby'}
```

Although this is probably the most useful application of `dict`, you can also use it with a mapping argument to create a dictionary with the same items as the mapping. (If used without any arguments, it returns a new empty dictionary, just like other similar functions such as `list`, `tuple`, and `str`.) If the other mapping is a dictionary (which is, after all, the only built-in mapping type), you can use the dictionary method `copy` instead, as described later in this chapter.

# Basic Dictionary Operations

The basic behavior of a dictionary in many ways mirrors that of a sequence:

- `len(d)` returns the number of items (key-value pairs) in d.
- `d[k]` returns the value associated with the key k.
- `d[k] = v` associates the value v with the key k.
- `del d[k]` deletes the item with key k.
- `k in d` checks whether there is an item in d that has the key k.

Although dictionaries and lists share several common characteristics, there are some important distinctions:

**Key types**: Dictionary keys don't have to be integers (though they may be). They may be any immutable type, such as floating-point (real) numbers, strings, or tuples.

**Automatic addition**: You can assign a value to a key, even if that key isn't in the dictionary to begin with; in that case, a new item will be created. You cannot assign a value to an index outside the list's range (without using append or something like that).

**Membership**: The expression k in d (where d is a dictionary) looks for a *key*, not a *value*. The expression v in l, on the other hand (where l is a list) looks for a *value*, not an *index*.

---

1. The `dict` function isn't really a function at all. It is a type, just like `list`, `tuple`, and `str`.

This may seem a bit inconsistent, but it is actually quite natural when you get used to it. After all, if the dictionary has the given key, checking the corresponding value is easy.

---

**■Tip**  Checking for key membership in a dictionary is much more efficient than checking for membership in a list. The difference is greater the larger the data structures are.

---

The first point—that the keys may be of any immutable type—is the main strength of dictionaries. The second point is important, too. Just look at the difference here:

```
>>> x = []
>>> x[42] = 'Foobar'
Traceback (most recent call last):
  File "<stdin>", line 1, in ?
IndexError: list assignment index out of range
>>> x = {}
>>> x[42] = 'Foobar'
>>> x
{42: 'Foobar'}
```

First, I try to assign the string 'Foobar' to position 42 in an empty list—clearly impossible because that position does not exist. To make this possible, I would have to initialize x with [None]*43 or something, rather than simply []. The next attempt, however, works perfectly. Here I assign 'Foobar' to the key 42 of an empty dictionary. You can see there's no problem here. A new item is simply added to the dictionary, and I'm in business.

Listing 4-1 shows the code for the telephone book example.

**Listing 4-1.** *Dictionary Example*

```
# A simple database

# A dictionary with person names as keys. Each person is represented as
# another dictionary with the keys 'phone' and 'addr' referring to their phone
# number and address, respectively.

people = {

    'Alice': {
        'phone': '2341',
        'addr': 'Foo drive 23'
    },

    'Beth': {
        'phone': '9102',
        'addr': 'Bar street 42'
    },
```

```
    'Cecil': {
        'phone': '3158',
        'addr': 'Baz avenue 90'
    }

}

# Descriptive labels for the phone number and address. These will be used
# when printing the output.
labels = {
    'phone': 'phone number',
    'addr': 'address'
}

name = raw_input('Name: ')

# Are we looking for a phone number or an address?
request = raw_input('Phone number (p) or address (a)? ')

# Use the correct key:
if request == 'p': key = 'phone'
if request == 'a': key = 'addr'

# Only try to print information if the name is a valid key in
# our dictionary:
if name in people: print "%s's %s is %s." % \
    (name, labels[key], people[name][key])
```

Here is a sample run of the program:

```
Name: Beth
Phone number (p) or address (a)? p
Beth's phone number is 9102.
```

## String Formatting with Dictionaries

In Chapter 3, you saw how you could use string formatting to format all the values in a tuple. If you use a dictionary (with only strings as keys) instead of a tuple, you can make the string formatting even snazzier. After the % character in each conversion specifier, you add a key (enclosed in parentheses), which is followed by the other specifier elements:

```
>>> phonebook
{'Beth': '9102', 'Alice': '2341', 'Cecil': '3258'}
>>> "Cecil's phone number is %(Cecil)s." % phonebook
"Cecil's phone number is 3258."
```

Except for the added string key, the conversion specifiers work as before. When using dictionaries like this, you may have any number of conversion specifiers, as long as all the given keys are found in the dictionary. This sort of string formatting can be very useful in template systems (in this case using HTML):

```
>>> template = '''<html>
    <head><title>%(title)s</title></head>
    <body>
    <h1>%(title)s</h1>
    <p>%(text)s</p>
    </body>'''
>>> data = {'title': 'My Home Page', 'text': 'Welcome to my home page!'}
>>> print template % data
<html>
<head><title>My Home Page</title></head>
<body>
<h1>My Home Page</h1>
<p>Welcome to my home page!</p>
</body>
```

---

■**Note**  The string.Template class (mentioned in Chapter 3) is also quite useful for this kind of application.

---

## Dictionary Methods

Just like the other built-in types, dictionaries have methods. While these methods can be very useful, you probably will not need them as often as the list and string methods. You might want to skim this section first to get an idea of which methods are available, and then come back later if you need to find out exactly how a given method works.

### clear

The clear method removes all items from the dictionary. This is an in-place operation (like list.sort), so it returns nothing (or, rather, None):

```
>>> d = {}
>>> d['name'] = 'Gumby'
>>> d['age'] = 42
>>> d
{'age': 42, 'name': 'Gumby'}
```

```
>>> returned_value = d.clear()
>>> d
{}
>>> print returned_value
None
```

Why is this useful? Let's consider two scenarios. Here's the first one:

```
>>> x = {}
>>> y = x
>>> x['key'] = 'value'
>>> y
{'key': 'value'}
>>> x = {}
>>> y
{'key': 'value'}
```

And here's the second scenario:

```
>>> x = {}
>>> y = x
>>> x['key'] = 'value'
>>> y
{'key': 'value'}
>>> x.clear()
>>> y
{}
```

In both scenarios, x and y originally refer to the same dictionary. In the first scenario, I "blank out" x by assigning a new, empty dictionary to it. That doesn't affect y at all, which still refers to the original dictionary. This may be the behavior you want, but if you really want to remove all the elements of the *original* dictionary, you must use clear. As you can see in the second scenario, y is then also empty afterward.

## copy

The copy method returns a new dictionary with the same key-value pairs (a *shallow copy*, since the values themselves are the *same*, not copies):

```
>>> x = {'username': 'admin', 'machines': ['foo', 'bar', 'baz']}
>>> y = x.copy()
>>> y['username'] = 'mlh'
>>> y['machines'].remove('bar')
>>> y
{'username': 'mlh', 'machines': ['foo', 'baz']}
>>> x
{'username': 'admin', 'machines': ['foo', 'baz']}
```

As you can see, when you replace a value in the copy, the original is unaffected. *However,* if you *modify* a value (in place, without replacing it), the original is changed as well because the same value is stored there (like the `'machines'` list in this example).

One way to avoid that problem is to make a *deep copy,* copying the values, any values they contain, and so forth as well. You accomplish this using the function deepcopy from the copy module:

```
>>> from copy import deepcopy
>>> d = {}
>>> d['names'] = ['Alfred', 'Bertrand']
>>> c = d.copy()
>>> dc = deepcopy(d)
>>> d['names'].append('Clive')
>>> c
{'names': ['Alfred', 'Bertrand', 'Clive']}
>>> dc
{'names': ['Alfred', 'Bertrand']}
```

### fromkeys

The fromkeys method creates a new dictionary with the given keys, each with a default corresponding value of None:

```
>>> {}.fromkeys(['name', 'age'])
{'age': None, 'name': None}
```

This example first constructs an empty dictionary and then calls the fromkeys method on that, in order to create *another* dictionary—a somewhat redundant strategy. Instead, you can call the method directly on dict, which (as mentioned before) is the *type* of all dictionaries. (The concept of types and classes is discussed more thoroughly in Chapter 7.)

```
>>> dict.fromkeys(['name', 'age'])
{'age': None, 'name': None}
```

If you don't want to use None as the default value, you can supply your own default:

```
>>> dict.fromkeys(['name', 'age'], '(unknown)')
{'age': '(unknown)', 'name': '(unknown)'}
```

### get

The get method is a forgiving way of accessing dictionary items. Ordinarily, when you try to access an item that is not present in the dictionary, things go very wrong:

```
>>> d = {}
>>> print d['name']
Traceback (most recent call last):
  File "<stdin>", line 1, in ?
KeyError: 'name'
```

Not so with get:

```
>>> print d.get('name')
None
```

As you can see, when you use get to access a nonexistent key, there is no exception. Instead, you get the value None. You may supply your own "default" value, which is then used instead of None:

```
>>> d.get('name', 'N/A')
'N/A'
```

If the key *is* there, get works like ordinary dictionary lookup:

```
>>> d['name'] = 'Eric'
>>> d.get('name')
'Eric'
```

Listing 4-2 shows a modified version of the program from Listing 4-1, which uses the get method to access the "database" entries.

**Listing 4-2.** *Dictionary Method Example*

```
# A simple database using get()

# Insert database (people) from Listing 4-1 here.

labels = {
    'phone': 'phone number',
    'addr': 'address'
}

name = raw_input('Name: ')

# Are we looking for a phone number or an address?
request = raw_input('Phone number (p) or address (a)? ')

# Use the correct key:
key = request # In case the request is neither 'p' nor 'a'
if request == 'p': key = 'phone'
if request == 'a': key = 'addr'

# Use get to provide default values:
person = people.get(name, {})
label = labels.get(key, key)
result = person.get(key, 'not available')

print "%s's %s is %s." % (name, label, result)
```

An example run of this program follows. Notice how the added flexibility of get allows the program to give a useful response, even though the user enters values we weren't prepared for:

```
Name: Gumby
Phone number (p) or address (a)? batting average
Gumby's batting average is not available.
```

## has_key

The has_key method checks whether a dictionary has a given key. The expression d.has_key(k) is equivalent to k in d. The choice of which to use is largely a matter of taste, although has_key is on its way out of the language (it will be gone in Python 3.0).

Here is an example of how you might use has_key:

```
>>> d = {}
>>> d.has_key('name')
False
>>> d['name'] = 'Eric'
>>> d.has_key('name')
True
```

## items and iteritems

The items method returns all the items of the dictionary as a list of items in which each item is of the form (key, value). The items are not returned in any particular order:

```
>>> d = {'title': 'Python Web Site', 'url': 'http://www.python.org', 'spam': 0}
>>> d.items()
[('url', 'http://www.python.org'), ('spam', 0), ('title', 'Python Web Site')]
```

The iteritems method works in much the same way, but returns an *iterator* instead of a list:

```
>>> it = d.iteritems()
>>> it
<dictionary-iterator object at 169050>
>>> list(it) # Convert the iterator to a list
[('url', 'http://www.python.org'), ('spam', 0), ('title', 'Python Web Site')]
```

Using iteritems may be more efficient in many cases (especially if you want to *iterate* over the result). For more information on iterators, see Chapter 9.

## keys and iterkeys

The keys method returns a list of the keys in the dictionary, while iterkeys returns an iterator over the keys.

## pop

The pop method can be used to get the value corresponding to a given key, and then remove the key-value pair from the dictionary:

```
>>> d = {'x': 1, 'y': 2}
>>> d.pop('x')
1
>>> d
{'y': 2}
```

## popitem

The popitem method is similar to list.pop, which pops off the last element of a list. Unlike list.pop, however, popitem pops off an arbitrary item because dictionaries don't have a "last element" or any order whatsoever. This may be very useful if you want to remove and process the items one by one in an efficient way (without retrieving a list of the keys first):

```
>>> d
{'url': 'http://www.python.org', 'spam': 0, 'title': 'Python Web Site'}
>>> d.popitem()
('url', 'http://www.python.org')
>>> d
{'spam': 0, 'title': 'Python Web Site'}
```

Although popitem is similar to the list method pop, there is no dictionary equivalent of append (which adds an element to the end of a list). Because dictionaries have no order, such a method wouldn't make any sense.

## setdefault

The setdefault method is somewhat similar to get, in that it retrieves a value associated with a given key. In addition to the get functionality, setdefault *sets* the value corresponding to the given key if it is not already in the dictionary:

```
>>> d = {}
>>> d.setdefault('name', 'N/A')
'N/A'
>>> d
{'name': 'N/A'}
>>> d['name'] = 'Gumby'
>>> d.setdefault('name', 'N/A')
'Gumby'
>>> d
{'name': 'Gumby'}
```

As you can see, when the key is missing, setdefault returns the default and updates the dictionary accordingly. If the key is present, its value is returned and the dictionary is left unchanged. The default is optional, as with get; if it is left out, None is used:

```
>>> d = {}
>>> print d.setdefault('name')
None
>>> d
{'name': None}
```

## update

The update method updates one dictionary with the items of another:

```
>>> d = {
        'title': 'Python Web Site',
        'url': 'http://www.python.org',
        'changed': 'Mar 14 22:09:15 MET 2008'
    }
>>> x = {'title': 'Python Language Website'}
>>> d.update(x)
>>> d
{'url': 'http://www.python.org', 'changed':
'Mar 14 22:09:15 MET 2008', 'title': 'Python Language Website'}
```

The items in the supplied dictionary are added to the old one, supplanting any items there with the same keys.

The update method can be called in the same way as the dict function (or type constructor), as discussed earlier in this chapter. This means that update can be called with a mapping, a sequence (or other iterable object) of (key, value) pairs, or keyword arguments.

## values and itervalues

The values method returns a list of the values in the dictionary (and itervalues returns an iterator of the values). Unlike keys, the list returned by values may contain duplicates:

```
>>> d = {}
>>> d[1] = 1
>>> d[2] = 2
>>> d[3] = 3
>>> d[4] = 1
>>> d.values()
[1, 2, 3, 1]
```

# A Quick Summary

In this chapter, you learned about the following:

**Mappings**: A mapping enables you to label its elements with any immutable object, the most usual types being strings and tuples. The only built-in mapping type in Python is the dictionary.

**String formatting with dictionaries**: You can apply the string formatting operation to dictionaries by including names (keys) in the formatting specifiers. When using tuples in string formatting, you need to have one formatting specifier for each element in the tuple. When using dictionaries, you can have fewer specifiers than you have items in the dictionary.

**Dictionary methods**: Dictionaries have quite a few methods, which are called in the same way as list and string methods.

## New Functions in This Chapter

| Function | Description |
| --- | --- |
| dict(seq) | Creates dictionary from (key, value) pairs (or a mapping or keyword arguments) |

## What Now?

You now know a lot about Python's basic data types and how to use them to form expressions. As you may remember from Chapter 1, computer programs have another important ingredient—statements. They're covered in detail in the next chapter.

# CHAPTER 5

∎∎∎

# Conditionals, Loops, and Some Other Statements

**B**y now, I'm sure you are getting a bit impatient. All right—all these data types are just dandy, but you can't really do much with them, can you?

Let's crank up the pace a bit. You've already encountered a few statement types (print statements, import statements, and assignments). Let's first take a look at some more ways of using these before diving into the world of *conditionals* and *loops*. Then you'll see how *list comprehensions* work almost like conditionals and loops, even though they are expressions, and finally you'll take a look at pass, del, and exec.

## More About print and import

As you learn more about Python, you may notice that some aspects of Python that you thought you knew have hidden features just waiting to pleasantly surprise you. Let's take a look at a couple of such nice features in print[1] and import.

---

∎**Tip**  For many applications, logging (using the logging module) will be more appropriate than using print. See Chapter 19 for more details.

---

### Printing with Commas

You've seen how print can be used to print an expression, which is either a string or automatically converted to one. But you can actually print more than one expression, as long as you separate them with commas:

```
>>> print 'Age:', 42
Age: 42
```

As you can see, a space character is inserted between each argument.

---

1. In Python 3.0, print is no longer a statement at all—it's a function (with essentially the same functionality).

---

**■Note** The arguments of `print` do *not* form a tuple, as one might expect:

```
>>> 1, 2, 3
(1, 2, 3)
>>> print 1, 2, 3
1 2 3
>>> print (1, 2, 3)
(1, 2, 3)
```

---

This behavior can be very useful if you want to combine text and variable values without using the full power of string formatting:

```
>>> name = 'Gumby'
>>> salutation = 'Mr.'
>>> greeting = 'Hello,'
>>> print greeting, salutation, name
Hello, Mr. Gumby
```

If the greeting string had no comma, how would you get the comma in the result? You couldn't just use

```
print greeting, ',', salutation, name
```

because that would introduce a space before the comma. One solution would be the following:

```
print greeting + ',', salutation, name
```

which simply adds the comma to the greeting.

If you add a comma at the end, your next `print` statement will continue printing on the same line. For example, the statements

```
print 'Hello,',
print 'world!'
```

print out `Hello, world!`.[2]

## Importing Something As Something Else

Usually, when you import something from a module, you either use

```
import somemodule
```

or

```
from somemodule import somefunction
```

or

---

2. This will work only in a script, and not in an interactive Python session. In the interactive session, each statement will be executed (and print its contents) separately.

```
from somemodule import somefunction, anotherfunction, yetanotherfunction
```

or

```
from somemodule import *
```

The fourth version should be used only when you are certain that you want to import *everything* from the given module. But what if you have two modules, each containing a function called open, for example—what do you do then? You could simply import the modules using the first form, and then use the functions as follows:

```
module1.open(...)
module2.open(...)
```

But there is another option: you can add an as clause to the end and supply the name you want to use, either for the entire module:

```
>>> import math as foobar
>>> foobar.sqrt(4)
2.0
```

or for the given function:

```
>>> from math import sqrt as foobar
>>> foobar(4)
2.0
```

For the open functions, you might use the following:

```
from module1 import open as open1
from module2 import open as open2
```

■**Note**  Some modules, such as os.path, are arranged hierarchically (inside each other). For more about module structure, see the section on packages in Chapter 10.

# Assignment Magic

The humble assignment statement also has a few tricks up its sleeve.

## Sequence Unpacking

You've seen quite a few examples of assignments, both for variables and for parts of data structures (such as positions and slices in a list, or slots in a dictionary), but there is more. You can perform several different assignments *simultaneously*:

```
>>> x, y, z = 1, 2, 3
>>> print x, y, z
1 2 3
```

Doesn't sound useful? Well, you can use it to switch the contents of two (or more) variables:

```
>>> x, y = y, x
>>> print x, y, z
2 1 3
```

Actually, what I'm doing here is called *sequence unpacking* (or *iterable unpacking*). I have a sequence (or an arbitrary iterable object) of values, and I unpack it into a sequence of variables. Let me be more explicit:

```
>>> values = 1, 2, 3
>>> values
(1, 2, 3)
>>> x, y, z = values
>>> x
1
```

This is particularly useful when a function or method returns a tuple (or other sequence or iterable object). Let's say that you want to retrieve (and remove) an arbitrary key-value pair from a dictionary. You can then use the popitem method, which does just that, returning the pair as a tuple. Then you can unpack the returned tuple directly into two variables:

```
>>> scoundrel = {'name': 'Robin', 'girlfriend': 'Marion'}
>>> key, value = scoundrel.popitem()
>>> key
'girlfriend'
>>> value
'Marion'
```

This allows functions to return more than one value, packed as a tuple, easily accessible through a single assignment. The sequence you unpack must have exactly as many items as the targets you list on the left of the = sign; otherwise Python raises an exception when the assignment is performed:

```
>>> x, y, z = 1, 2
Traceback (most recent call last):
  File "<stdin>", line 1, in <module>
ValueError: need more than 2 values to unpack
>>> x, y, z = 1, 2, 3, 4
Traceback (most recent call last):
  File "<stdin>", line 1, in <module>
ValueError: too many values to unpack
```

■ **Note** Python 3.0 has another unpacking feature: you can use the star operator (*), just as in function argument lists (see Chapter 6). For example, `a, b, rest* = [1, 2, 3, 4]` will result in `rest` gathering whatever remains after assigning values to a and b. In this case, `rest` will be `[3, 4]`. The starred variable may also be placed first, and it will always contain a list. The right-hand side of the assignment may be any iterable object.

## Chained Assignments

Chained assignments are used as a shortcut when you want to bind several variables to the same value. This may seem a bit like the simultaneous assignments in the previous section, except that here you are dealing with only one value:

```
x = y = somefunction()
```

which is the same as

```
y = somefunction()
x = y
```

Note that the preceding statements may *not* be the same as

```
x = somefunction()
y = somefunction()
```

For more information, see the section about the identity operator (is), later in this chapter.

## Augmented Assignments

Instead of writing x = x + 1, you can just put the expression operator (in this case +) before the assignment operator (=) and write x += 1. This is called an *augmented assignment*, and it works with all the standard operators, such as *, /, %, and so on:

```
>>> x = 2
>>> x += 1
>>> x *= 2
>>> x
6
```

It also works with other data types (as long as the binary operator itself works with those data types):

```
>>> fnord = 'foo'
>>> fnord += 'bar'
>>> fnord *= 2
>>> fnord
'foobarfoobar'
```

Augmented assignments can make your code more compact and concise, and in many cases, more readable.

# Blocks: The Joy of Indentation

A block isn't really a type of statement but something you're going to need when you tackle the next two sections.

A block is a *group* of statements that can be executed if a condition is true (conditional statements), or executed several times (loops), and so on. A block is created by *indenting* a part of your code; that is, putting spaces in front of it.

---

**Note**  You can use tab characters to indent your blocks as well. Python interprets a tab as moving to the next tab stop, with one tab stop every eight spaces, but the standard and preferable style is to use spaces only, not tabs, and specifically four spaces per each level of indentation.

---

Each line in a block must be indented by *the same amount*. The following is pseudocode (not real Python code) that shows how the indenting works:

```
this is a line
this is another line:
    this is another block
    continuing the same block
    the last line of this block
phew, there we escaped the inner block
```

In many languages, a special word or character (for example, begin or {) is used to start a block, and another (such as end or }) is used to end it. In Python, a colon (:) is used to indicate that a block is about to begin, and then every line in that block is indented (by the same amount). When you go back to the same amount of indentation as some enclosing block, you know that the current block has ended. (Many programming editors and IDEs are aware of how this block indenting works, and can help you get it right without much effort.)

Now I'm sure you are curious to know how to use these blocks. So, without further ado, let's have a look.

# Conditions and Conditional Statements

Until now, you've written programs in which each statement is executed, one after the other. It's time to move beyond that and let your program choose whether or not to execute a block of statements.

# So That's What Those Boolean Values Are For

Now you are finally going to need those *truth values* (also called *Boolean* values, after George Boole, who did a lot of smart stuff on truth values) that you've been bumping into repeatedly.

---

**Note** If you've been paying close attention, you noticed the sidebar in Chapter 1, "Sneak Peek: The if Statement," which describes the if statement. I haven't really introduced it formally until now, and as you'll see, there is a bit more to it than what I've told you so far.

---

The following values are considered by the interpreter to mean *false* when evaluated as a Boolean expression (for example, as the condition of an if statement):

```
False    None    0    ""    ()    []    {}
```

In other words, the standard values False and None, numeric zero of all types (including float, long, and so on), empty sequences (such as empty strings, tuples, and lists), and empty dictionaries are all considered to be false. *Everything else*[3] is interpreted as *true*, including the special value True.[4]

Got it? This means that every value in Python can be interpreted as a truth value, which can be a bit confusing at first, but it can also be extremely useful. And even though you have all these truth values to choose from, the "standard" truth values are True and False. In some languages (such as C and Python prior to version 2.3), the standard truth values are 0 (for *false*) and 1 (for *true*). In fact, True and False aren't that different—they're just glorified versions of 0 and 1 that *look* different but act the same:

```
>>> True
True
>>> False
False
>>> True == 1
True
>>> False == 0
True
>>> True + False + 42
43
```

So now, if you see a logical expression returning 1 or 0 (probably in an older version of Python), you will know that what is *really* meant is True or False.

---

3. At least when we're talking about built-in types—as you see in Chapter 9, you can influence whether objects you construct yourself are interpreted as true or false.
4. As Python veteran Laura Creighton puts it, the distinction is really closer to *something* vs. *nothing*, rather than *true* vs. *false*.

The Boolean values True and False belong to the type bool, which can be used (just like, for example, list, str, and tuple) to convert other values:

```
>>> bool('I think, therefore I am')
True
>>> bool(42)
True
>>> bool('')
False
>>> bool(0)
False
```

Because any value can be used as a Boolean value, you will most likely rarely (if ever) need such an explicit conversion (that is, Python will automatically convert the values for you, so to speak).

---

■**Note** Although [] and "" are both false (that is, bool([])==bool("")==False), they are not equal (that is, []!=""). The same goes for other false objects of different types (for example, ()!=False).

---

## Conditional Execution and the if Statement

Truth values can be combined (which you'll see in a while), but let's first see what you can use them for. Try running the following script:

```
name = raw_input('What is your name? ')
if name.endswith('Gumby'):
    print 'Hello, Mr. Gumby'
```

This is the if statement, which lets you do *conditional execution*. That means that if the *condition* (the expression after if but before the colon) evaluates to *true* (as defined previously), the following block (in this case, a single print statement) is executed. If the condition is *false*, then the block is *not* executed (but you guessed that, didn't you?).

---

■**Note** In the sidebar "Sneak Peek: The if Statement" in Chapter 1, the statement was written on a single line. That is equivalent to using a single-line block, as in the preceding example.

---

## else Clauses

In the example from the previous section, if you enter a name that ends with "Gumby," the method name.endswith returns True, making the if statement enter the block, and the greeting is printed. If you want, you can add an alternative, with the else clause (called a *clause* because it isn't really a separate statement, just a part of the if statement):

```
name = raw_input('What is your name? ')
if name.endswith('Gumby'):
    print 'Hello, Mr. Gumby'
else:
    print 'Hello, stranger'
```

Here, if the first block isn't executed (because the condition evaluated to false), you enter the second block instead. This really shows how easy it is to read Python code, doesn't it? Just read the code aloud (from if), and it sounds just like a normal (or perhaps not *quite* normal) sentence.

## elif Clauses

If you want to check for several conditions, you can use elif, which is short for "else if." It is a combination of an if clause and an else clause—an else clause with a condition:

```
num = input('Enter a number: ')
if num > 0:
    print 'The number is positive'
elif num < 0:
    print 'The number is negative'
else:
    print 'The number is zero'
```

---

■**Note**  Instead of input(...), you might want to use int(raw_input(...)). For the difference between input and raw_input, see Chapter 1.

---

## Nesting Blocks

Let's throw in a few bells and whistles. You can have if statements inside other if statement blocks, as follows:

```
name = raw_input('What is your name? ')
if name.endswith('Gumby'):
    if name.startswith('Mr.'):
        print 'Hello, Mr. Gumby'
    elif name.startswith('Mrs.'):
        print 'Hello, Mrs. Gumby'
    else:
        print 'Hello, Gumby'
else:
    print 'Hello, stranger'
```

Here, if the name ends with "Gumby," you check the start of the name as well—in a separate if statement inside the first block. Note the use of elif here. The last alternative (the else clause) has no condition—if no other alternative is chosen, you use the last one. If you want to, you can leave out either of the else clauses. If you leave out the inner else clause, names that don't start with either "Mr." or "Mrs." are ignored (assuming the name was "Gumby"). If you drop the outer else clause, strangers are ignored.

## More Complex Conditions

That's really all there is to know about if statements. Now let's return to the conditions themselves, because they are the really interesting part of conditional execution.

### Comparison Operators

Perhaps the most basic operators used in conditions are the *comparison operators*. They are used (surprise, surprise) to compare things. The comparison operators are summarized in Table 5-1.

**Table 5-1.** *The Python Comparison Operators*

| Expression | Description |
|---|---|
| x == y | x equals y. |
| x < y | x is less than y. |
| x > y | x is greater than y. |
| x >= y | x is greater than or equal to y. |
| x <= y | x is less than or equal to y. |
| x != y | x is not equal to y. |
| x is y | x and y are the same object. |
| x is not y | x and y are different objects. |
| x in y | x is a member of the container (e.g., sequence) y. |
| x not in y | x is not a member of the container (e.g., sequence) y. |

### COMPARING INCOMPATIBLE TYPES

In theory, you can compare any two objects x and y for relative size (using operators such as < and <=) and obtain a truth value. However, such a comparison makes sense only if x and y are of the same or closely related types (such as two integers or an integer and a floating-point number).

Just as it doesn't make much sense to add an integer to a string, checking whether an integer is less than a string seems rather pointless. Oddly, in Python versions prior to 3.0 you are allowed to do this. You really should stay away from such comparisons, as the result is totally arbitrary and may change between each execution of your program. In Python 3.0, comparing incompatible types in this way is no longer allowed.

> ■**Note** If you stumble across the expression x <> y somewhere, this means x != y. The <> operator is deprecated, however, and you should avoid using it.

Comparisons can be *chained* in Python, just like assignments—you can put several comparison operators in a chain, like this: 0 < age < 100.

> ■**Tip** When comparing things, you can also use the built-in function cmp, as described in Chapter 2.

Some of these operators deserve some special attention and will be described in the following sections.

### The Equality Operator

If you want to know if two things are equal, use the equality operator, written as a double equality sign, ==:

```
>>> "foo" == "foo"
True
>>> "foo" == "bar"
False
```

Double? Why can't you just use a *single* equality sign, as they do in mathematics? I'm sure you're clever enough to figure this out for yourself, but let's try it:

```
>>> "foo" = "foo"
SyntaxError: can't assign to literal
```

The single equality sign is the assignment operator, which is used to *change* things, which is *not* what you want to do when you compare things.

### is: The Identity Operator

The is operator is interesting. It seems to work just like ==, but it doesn't:

```
>>> x = y = [1, 2, 3]
>>> z = [1, 2, 3]
>>> x == y
True
>>> x == z
True
>>> x is y
True
>>> x is z
False
```

Until the last example, this looks fine, but then you get that strange result: x is not z, even though they are equal. Why? Because is tests for *identity*, rather than *equality*. The variables x and y have been bound to the *same list*, while z is simply bound to another list that happens to contain the same values in the same order. They may be equal, but they aren't the *same object*.

Does that seem unreasonable? Consider this example:

```
>>> x = [1, 2, 3]
>>> y = [2, 4]
>>> x is not y
True
>>> del x[2]
>>> y[1] = 1
>>> y.reverse()
```

In this example, I start with two different lists, x and y. As you can see, x is not y (just the inverse of x is y), which you already know. I change the lists around a bit, and though they are now equal, they are still two separate lists:

```
>>> x == y
True
>>> x is y
False
```

Here, it is obvious that the two lists are equal but not identical.

To summarize: use == to see if two objects are *equal*, and use is to see if they are *identical* (the same object).

---

■**Caution**  Avoid the use of is with basic, immutable values such as numbers and strings. The result is unpredictable because of the way Python handles these objects internally.

---

### in: The Membership Operator

I have already introduced the in operator (in Chapter 2, in the section "Membership"). It can be used in conditions, just like all the other comparison operators:

```
name = raw_input('What is your name? ')
if 's' in name:
    print 'Your name contains the letter "s".'
else:
    print 'Your name does not contain the letter "s".'
```

### String and Sequence Comparisons

Strings are compared according to their order when sorted alphabetically:

```
>>> "alpha" < "beta"
True
```

YOU MAY ALSO LIKE...

Programming in Python 3: A Complete...
    by Mark Summerfield

Python Cookbook
    by Alex Martelli

Foundations of Agile Python Development
    by Jeff Younker

Python Pocket Reference
    by Mark Lutz

Python Web Development with Django...
    by Jeff Forcier

(see the standard library documentation for the

t messy. (Actually, characters are sorted by
can be found with the ord function, whose
uppercase and lowercase letters, use the

manner, except that instead of characters, you
may have other types of elements:

```
>>> [1, 2] < [2, 1]
True
```

If the sequences contain other sequences as elements, the same rule applies to these
sequence elements:

```
>>> [2, [1, 4]] < [2, [1, 5]]
True
```

## Boolean Operators

Now, you have plenty of things that return truth values. (In fact, given the fact that all values
can be interpreted as truth values, *all* expressions return them.) But you may want to check for
more than one condition. For example, let's say you want to write a program that reads a number and checks whether it's between 1 and 10 (inclusive). You could do it like this:

```
number = input('Enter a number between 1 and 10: ')
if number <= 10:
    if number >= 1:
        print 'Great!'
    else:
        print 'Wrong!'
else:
    print 'Wrong!'
```

This would work, but it's clumsy. The fact that you have to write print 'Wrong!' in two
places should alert you to this clumsiness. Duplication of effort is not a good thing. So what do
you do? It's so simple:

```
number = input('Enter a number between 1 and 10: ')
if number <= 10 and number >= 1:
    print 'Great!'
else:
    print 'Wrong!'
```

---

■**Note** I could (and quite probably should ) have made this example even simpler by using the following chained comparison: `1 <= number <= 10`.

---

The and operator is a so-called Boolean operator. It takes two truth values, and returns true if both are true, and false otherwise. You have two more of these operators, `or` and `not`. With just these three, you can combine truth values in any way you like:

```
if ((cash > price) or customer_has_good_credit) and not out_of_stock:
    give_goods()
```

## SHORT-CIRCUIT LOGIC AND CONDITIONAL EXPRESSIONS

The Boolean operators have one interesting property: they evaluate only what they need to evaluate. For example, the expression `x and y` requires both x and y to be true; so if x is false, the expression returns false immediately, without worrying about y. Actually, if x is false, it returns x; otherwise, it returns y. (Can you see how this gives the expected meaning?) This behavior is called *short-circuit logic* (or *lazy evaluation*): the Boolean operators are often called logical operators, and as you can see, the second value is sometimes "short-circuited." This works with `or`, too. In the expression `x or y`, if x is true, it is returned; otherwise, y is returned. (Can you see how this makes sense?) Note that this means that any code you have (such as a function call) after a Boolean operator may not be executed at all.

So, how is this useful? Primarily, it avoids executing code uselessly, but it can also be used for some nifty tricks. Let's say users are supposed to enter their name, but may opt to enter nothing, and in that case, you want to use the default value `'<unknown>'`. You could use an `if` statement, but you could also state things very succinctly:

```
name = raw_input('Please enter your name: ') or '<unknown>'
```

In other words, if the return value from `raw_input` is true (not an empty string), it is assigned to name (nothing changes); otherwise, the default `'<unknown>'` is assigned to name.

This sort of short-circuit logic can be used to implement the so-called *ternary operator* (or conditional operator), commonly used in languages such as C and Java.[5] As of version 2.5, Python has a built-in conditional expression, though, which looks like this:

```
a if b else c
```

If b is true, a is returned; otherwise, c is returned. (Note that this operator cannot be used directly to get the same result as in the `raw_input` example without introducing a temporary variable.)

---

5. For a thorough explanation, see Alex Martelli's recipe on the subject in the Python Cookbook (http://aspn.activestate.com/ASPN/Cookbook/Python/Recipe/52310).

## Assertions

There is a useful relative of the if statement, which works more or less like this (pseudocode):

```
if not condition:
    crash program
```

Now, why on earth would you want something like that? Simply because it's better that your program crashes when an error condition emerges than at a much later time. Basically, you can require that certain things be true (for example, when checking required properties of parameters to your functions or as an aid during initial testing and debugging). The keyword used in the statement is assert:

```
>>> age = 10
>>> assert 0 < age < 100
>>> age = -1
>>> assert 0 < age < 100
Traceback (most recent call last):
  File "<stdin>", line 1, in ?
AssertionError
```

It can be useful to put the assert statement in your program as a checkpoint, if you know something *must* be true for your program to work correctly.

A string may be added after the condition, to explain the assertion:

```
>>> age = -1
>>> assert 0 < age < 100, 'The age must be realistic'
Traceback (most recent call last):
  File "<stdin>", line 1, in ?
AssertionError: The age must be realistic
```

# Loops

Now you know how to do something if a condition is true (or false), but how do you do something several times? For example, you might want to create a program that reminds you to pay the rent every month, but with the tools we have looked at until now, you would need to write the program like this (pseudocode):

```
send mail
wait one month
send mail
wait one month
send mail
wait one month
(...and so on)
```

But what if you wanted it to continue doing this until you stopped it? Basically, you want something like this (again, pseudocode):

```
while we aren't stopped:
    send mail
    wait one month
```

Or, let's take a simpler example. Let's say that you want to print out all the numbers from 1 to 100. Again, you could do it the stupid way:

```
print 1
print 2
print 3
...
print 99
print 100
```

But you didn't start using Python because you wanted to do stupid things, right?

## while Loops

In order to avoid the cumbersome code of the preceding example, it would be useful to be able to do something like this:

```
x = 1
while x <= 100:
    print x
    x += 1
```

Now, how do you do that in Python? You guessed it—you do it just like that. Not that complicated, is it? You could also use a loop to ensure that the user enters a name, as follows:

```
name = ''
while not name:
    name = raw_input('Please enter your name: ')
print 'Hello, %s!' % name
```

Try running this, and then just pressing the Enter key when asked to enter your name. You'll see that the question appears again, because name is still an empty string, which evaluates to *false*.

---

**Tip** What would happen if you entered just a space character as your name? Try it. It is accepted because a string with one space character is not empty, and therefore not false. This is definitely a flaw in our little program, but easily corrected: just change while not name to while not name or name.isspace(), or perhaps, while not name.strip().

---

# for Loops

The while statement is very flexible. It can be used to repeat a block of code while *any condition* is true. While this may be very nice in general, sometimes you may want something tailored to your specific needs. One such need is to perform a block of code *for each* element of a set (or, actually, sequence or other iterable object) of values.

---

■**Note** Basically, an *iterable* object is any object that you can iterate over (that is, use in a for loop). You learn more about iterables and iterators in Chapter 9, but for now, you can simply think of them as sequences.

---

You can do this with the for statement:

```
words = ['this', 'is', 'an', 'ex', 'parrot']
for word in words:
    print word
```

or

```
numbers = [0, 1, 2, 3, 4, 5, 6, 7, 8, 9]
for number in numbers:
    print number
```

Because iterating (another word for *looping*) over a range of numbers is a common thing to do, Python has a built-in function to make ranges for you:

```
>>> range(0, 10)
[0, 1, 2, 3, 4, 5, 6, 7, 8, 9]
```

Ranges work like slices. They include the first limit (in this case 0), but not the last (in this case 10). Quite often, you want the ranges to start at 0, and this is actually assumed if you supply only one limit (which will then be the last):

```
>>> range(10)
[0, 1, 2, 3, 4, 5, 6, 7, 8, 9]
```

The following program writes out the numbers from 1 to 100:

```
for number in range(1,101):
    print number
```

Notice that this is much more compact than the while loop I used earlier.

---

■**Tip** If you can use a for loop rather than a while loop, you should probably do so.

---

The xrange function works just like range in loops, but where range creates the whole sequence at once, xrange creates only one number at a time.[6] This can be useful when iterating over *huge* sequences more efficiently, but in general, you don't need to worry about it.

## Iterating Over Dictionaries

To loop over the keys of a dictionary, you can use a plain for statement, just as you can with sequences:

```
d = {'x': 1, 'y': 2, 'z': 3}
for key in d:
    print key, 'corresponds to', d[key]
```

In Python versions before 2.2, you would have used a dictionary method such as keys to retrieve the keys (since direct iteration over dictionaries wasn't allowed). If only the values were of interest, you could have used d.values instead of d.keys. You may remember that d.items returns key-value pairs as tuples. One great thing about for loops is that you can use sequence unpacking in them:

```
for key, value in d.items():
    print key, 'corresponds to', value
```

---

**Note** As always, the order of dictionary elements is undefined. In other words, when iterating over either the keys or the values of a dictionary, you can be sure that you'll process all of them, but you can't know in which order. If the order is important, you can store the keys or values in a separate list and, for example, sort it before iterating over it.

---

## Some Iteration Utilities

Python has several functions that can be useful when iterating over a sequence (or other iterable object). Some of these are available in the itertools module (mentioned in Chapter 10), but there are some built-in functions that come in quite handy as well.

### Parallel Iteration

Sometimes you want to iterate over two sequences at the same time. Let's say that you have the following two lists:

```
names = ['anne', 'beth', 'george', 'damon']
ages = [12, 45, 32, 102]
```

---

6.  In Python 3.0, range will be turned into an xrange-style function.

If you want to print out names with corresponding ages, you *could* do the following:

```
for i in range(len(names)):
    print names[i], 'is', ages[i], 'years old'
```

Here, i serves as a standard variable name for loop indices (as these things are called).

A useful tool for parallel iteration is the built-in function zip, which "zips" together the sequences, returning a list of tuples:

```
>>> zip(names, ages)
[('anne', 12), ('beth', 45), ('george', 32), ('damon', 102)]
```

Now I can unpack the tuples in my loop:

```
for name, age in zip(names, ages):
    print name, 'is', age, 'years old'
```

The zip function works with as many sequences as you want. It's important to note what zip does when the sequences are of different lengths: it stops when the shortest sequence is used up:

```
>>> zip(range(5), xrange(100000000))
[(0, 0), (1, 1), (2, 2), (3, 3), (4, 4)]
```

I wouldn't recommend using range instead of xrange in the preceding example. Although only the first five numbers are needed, range calculates all the numbers, and that may take a lot of time. With xrange, this isn't a problem because it calculates only those numbers needed.

## Numbered Iteration

In some cases, you want to iterate over a sequence of objects and at the same time have access to the index of the current object. For example, you might want to replace every string that contains the substring 'xxx' in a list of strings. There would certainly be many ways of doing this, but let's say you want to do something along the following lines:

```
for string in strings:
    if 'xxx' in string:
        index = strings.index(string) # Search for the string in the list of strings
        strings[index] = '[censored]'
```

This would work, but it seems unnecessary to search for the given string before replacing it. Also, if you didn't replace it, the search might give you the wrong index (that is, the index of some previous occurrence of the same word). A better version would be the following:

```
index = 0
for string in strings:
    if 'xxx' in string:
```

```
        strings[index] = '[censored]'
    index += 1
```

This also seems a bit awkward, although acceptable. Another solution is to use the built-in function enumerate:

```
for index, string in enumerate(strings):
    if 'xxx' in string:
        strings[index] = '[censored]'
```

This function lets you iterate over index-value pairs, where the indices are supplied automatically.

### Reversed and Sorted Iteration

Let's look at another couple of useful functions: reversed and sorted. They're similar to the list methods reverse and sort (with sorted taking arguments similar to those taken by sort), but they work on any sequence or iterable object, and instead of modifying the object in place, they return reversed and sorted versions:

```
>>> sorted([4, 3, 6, 8, 3])
[3, 3, 4, 6, 8]
>>> sorted('Hello, world!')
[' ', '!', ',', 'H', 'd', 'e', 'l', 'l', 'l', 'o', 'o', 'r', 'w']
>>> list(reversed('Hello, world!'))
['!', 'd', 'l', 'r', 'o', 'w', ' ', ',', 'o', 'l', 'l', 'e', 'H']
>>> ''.join(reversed('Hello, world!'))
'!dlrow ,olleH'
```

Note that although sorted returns a list, reversed returns a more mysterious iterable object. You don't need to worry about what this really means; you can use it in for loops or methods such as join without any problems. You just can't index or slice it, or call list methods on it directly. In order to perform those tasks, you need to convert the returned object, using the list type, as shown in the previous example.

## Breaking Out of Loops

Usually, a loop simply executes a block until its condition becomes false, or until it has used up all sequence elements. But sometimes you may want to interrupt the loop, to start a new iteration (one "round" of executing the block), or to simply end the loop.

### break

To end (break out of) a loop, you use break. Let's say you wanted to find the largest square (the result of an integer multiplied by itself) below 100. Then you start at 100 and iterate downwards to 0. When you've found a square, there's no need to continue, so you simply break out of the loop:

```
from math import sqrt
for n in range(99, 0, -1):
    root = sqrt(n)
    if root == int(root):
        print n
        break
```

If you run this program, it will print out 81 and stop. Notice that I've added a third argument to range—that's the *step*, the difference between every pair of adjacent numbers in the sequence. It can be used to iterate downwards as I did here, with a negative step value, and it can be used to skip numbers:

```
>>> range(0, 10, 2)
[0, 2, 4, 6, 8]
```

## continue

The continue statement is used less often than break. It causes the current iteration to end, and to "jump" to the beginning of the next. It basically means "skip the rest of the loop body, but don't end the loop." This can be useful if you have a large and complicated loop body and several possible reasons for skipping it. In that case, you can use continue, as follows:

```
for x in seq:
    if condition1: continue
    if condition2: continue
    if condition3: continue

    do_something()
    do_something_else()
    do_another_thing()
    etc()
```

In many cases, however, simply using an if statement is just as good:

```
for x in seq:
    if not (condition1 or condition2 or condition3):
        do_something()
        do_something_else()
        do_another_thing()
        etc()
```

Even though continue can be a useful tool, it is not essential. The break statement, however, is something you should get used to, because it is used quite often in concert with while True, as explained in the next section.

## The while True/break Idiom

The for and while loops in Python are quite flexible, but every once in a while, you may encounter a problem that makes you wish you had more functionality. For example, let's say you want to do something when a user enters words at a prompt, and you want to end the loop when no word is provided. One way of doing that would be like this:

```
word = 'dummy'
while word:
    word = raw_input('Please enter a word: ')
    # do something with the word:
    print 'The word was ' + word
```

Here is an example of a session:

```
Please enter a word: first
The word was first
Please enter a word: second
The word was second
Please enter a word:
```

This works just as desired. (Presumably, you would do something more useful with the word than print it out, though.) However, as you can see, this code is a bit ugly. To enter the loop in the first place, you need to assign a dummy (unused) value to word. Dummy values like this are usually a sign that you aren't doing things quite right. Let's try to get rid of it:

```
word = raw_input('Please enter a word: ')
while word:
    # do something with the word:
    print 'The word was ' + word
    word = raw_input('Please enter a word: ')
```

Here the dummy is gone, but I have repeated code (which is also a bad thing): I need to use the same assignment and call to raw_input in two places. How can I avoid that? I can use the while True/break idiom:

```
while True:
    word = raw_input('Please enter a word: ')
    if not word: break
    # do something with the word:
    print 'The word was ' + word
```

The while True part gives you a loop that will never terminate by itself. Instead, you put the condition in an if statement inside the loop, which calls break when the condition is fulfilled. Thus, you can terminate the loop anywhere inside the loop instead of only at the beginning (as with a normal while loop). The if/break line splits the loop naturally in two parts: the first takes care of setting things up (the part that would be duplicated with a normal while loop), and the other part makes use of the initialization from the first part, provided that the loop condition is true.

Although you should be wary of using break too often in your code (because it can make your loops harder to read, especially if you put more than one break in a single loop), this specific technique is so common that most Python programmers (including yourself) will probably be able to follow your intentions.

## else Clauses in Loops

When you use break statements in loops, it is often because you have "found" something, or because something has "happened." It's easy to do something when you break out (like print n), but sometimes you may want to do something if you *didn't* break out. But how do you find out? You could use a Boolean variable, set it to False before the loop, and set it to True when you break out. Then you can use an if statement afterward to check whether you did break out:

```
broke_out = False
for x in seq:
    do_something(x)
    if condition(x):
        broke_out = True
        break
    do_something_else(x)
if not broke_out:
    print "I didn't break out!"
```

A simpler way is to add an else clause to your loop—it is only executed if you didn't call break. Let's reuse the example from the preceding section on break:

```
from math import sqrt
for n in range(99, 81, -1):
    root = sqrt(n)
    if root == int(root):
        print n
        break
else:
    print "Didn't find it!"
```

Notice that I changed the lower (exclusive) limit to 81 to test the else clause. If you run the program, it prints out "Didn't find it!" because (as you saw in the section on break) the largest square below 100 is 81. You can use continue, break, and else clauses with both for loops and while loops.

# List Comprehension—Slightly Loopy

List comprehension is a way of making lists from other lists (similar to *set comprehension*, if you know that term from mathematics). It works in a way similar to for loops and is actually quite simple:

```
>>> [x*x for x in range(10)]
[0, 1, 4, 9, 16, 25, 36, 49, 64, 81]
```

The list is composed of x*x for each x in range(10). Pretty straightforward? What if you want to print out only those squares that are divisible by 3? Then you can use the modulo operator—y % 3 returns zero when y is divisible by 3. (Note that x*x is divisible by 3 only if x is divisible by 3.) You put this into your list comprehension by adding an if part to it:

```
>>> [x*x for x in range(10) if x % 3 == 0]
[0, 9, 36, 81]
```

You can also add more for parts:

```
>>> [(x, y) for x in range(3) for y in range(3)]
[(0, 0), (0, 1), (0, 2), (1, 0), (1, 1), (1, 2), (2, 0), (2, 1), (2, 2)]
```

As a comparison, the following two for loops build the same list:

```
result = []
for x in range(3):
    for y in range(3)
        result.append((x, y))
```

This can be combined with an if clause, just as before:

```
>>> girls = ['alice', 'bernice', 'clarice']
>>> boys = ['chris', 'arnold', 'bob']
>>> [b+'+'+g for b in boys for g in girls if b[0] == g[0]]
['chris+clarice', 'arnold+alice', 'bob+bernice']
```

This gives the pairs of boys and girls who have the same initial letter in their first name.

---

**Note**  Using normal parentheses instead of brackets will not give you a "tuple comprehension." In Python 2.3 and earlier, you'll simply get an error; in more recent versions, you'll end up with a *generator*. See the sidebar "Loopy Generators" in Chapter 9 for more information.

---

## A BETTER SOLUTION

The boy/girl pairing example isn't particularly efficient because it checks every possible pairing. There are many ways of solving this problem in Python. The following was suggested by Alex Martelli:

```
girls = ['alice', 'bernice', 'clarice']
boys = ['chris', 'arnold', 'bob']
letterGirls = {}
for girl in girls:
    letterGirls.setdefault(girl[0], []).append(girl)
print [b+'+'+g for b in boys for g in letterGirls[b[0]]]
```

This program constructs a dictionary, called letterGirls, where each entry has a single letter as its key and a list of girls' names as its value. (The setdefault dictionary method is described in the previous chapter.) After this dictionary has been constructed, the list comprehension loops over all the boys and looks up all the girls whose name begins with the same letter as the current boy. This way, the list comprehension doesn't need to try out every possible combination of boy and girl and check whether the first letters match.

# And Three for the Road

To end the chapter, let's take a quick look at three more statements: pass, del, and exec.

## Nothing Happened!

Sometimes you need to do nothing. This may not be very often, but when it happens, it's good to know that you have the pass statement:

```
>>> pass
>>>
```

Not much going on here.

Now, why on earth would you want a statement that does nothing? It can be useful as a placeholder while you are writing code. For example, you may have written an if statement and you want to try it, but you lack the code for one of your blocks. Consider the following:

```
if name == 'Ralph Auldus Melish':
    print 'Welcome!'
elif name == 'Enid':
    # Not finished yet...
elif name == 'Bill Gates':
    print 'Access Denied'
```

This code won't run because an empty block is illegal in Python. To fix this, simply add a pass statement to the middle block:

```
if name == 'Ralph Auldus Melish':
    print 'Welcome!'
elif name == 'Enid':
    # Not finished yet...
    pass
elif name == 'Bill Gates':
    print 'Access Denied'
```

---

**Note** An alternative to the combination of a comment and a pass statement is to simply insert a string. This is especially useful for unfinished functions (see Chapter 6) and classes (see Chapter 7) because they will then act as *docstrings* (explained in Chapter 6).

---

## Deleting with del

In general, Python deletes objects that you don't use anymore (because you no longer refer to them through any variables or parts of your data structures):

```
>>> scoundrel = {'age': 42, 'first name': 'Robin', 'last name': 'of Locksley'}
>>> robin = scoundrel
>>> scoundrel
```

```
{'age': 42, 'first name': 'Robin', 'last name': 'of Locksley'}
>>> robin
{'age': 42, 'first name': 'Robin', 'last name': 'of Locksley'}
>>> scoundrel = None
>>> robin
{'age': 42, 'first name': 'Robin', 'last name': 'of Locksley'}
>>> robin = None
```

At first, robin and scoundrel are both bound to the same dictionary. So when I assign None to scoundrel, the dictionary is still available through robin. But when I assign None to robin as well, the dictionary suddenly floats around in the memory of the computer with no name attached to it. There is no way I can retrieve it or use it, so the Python interpreter (in its infinite wisdom) simply deletes it. (This is called *garbage collection*.) Note that I could have used any value other than None as well. The dictionary would be just as gone.

Another way of doing this is to use the del statement (which we used to delete sequence and dictionary elements in Chapters 2 and 4, remember?). This not only removes a reference to an object, but it also removes the name itself:

```
>>> x = 1
>>> del x
>>> x
Traceback (most recent call last):
  File "<pyshell#255>", line 1, in ?
    x
NameError: name 'x' is not defined
```

This may seem easy, but it can actually be a bit tricky to understand at times. For instance, in the following example, x and y refer to the same list:

```
>>> x = ["Hello", "world"]
>>> y = x
>>> y[1] = "Python"
>>> x
['Hello', 'Python']
```

You might assume that by deleting x, you would also delete y, but that is *not* the case:

```
>>> del x
>>> y
['Hello', 'Python']
```

Why is this? x and y referred to the *same* list, but deleting x didn't affect y at all. The reason for this is that you delete only the *name*, not the list itself (the value). In fact, there is no way to delete values in Python—and you don't really need to, because the Python interpreter does it by itself whenever you don't use the value anymore.

## Executing and Evaluating Strings with exec and eval

Sometimes you may want to create Python code "on the fly" and execute it as a statement or evaluate it as an expression. This may border on dark magic at times—consider yourself warned.

---

■**Caution**  In this section, you learn to execute Python code stored in a string. This is a potential security hole of great dimensions. If you execute a string where parts of the contents have been supplied by a user, you have little or no control over what code you are executing. This is especially dangerous in network applications, such as Common Gateway Interface (CGI) scripts, which you will learn about in Chapter 15.

---

### exec

The statement for executing a string is exec:[7]

```
>>> exec "print 'Hello, world!'"
Hello, world!
```

However, using this simple form of the exec statement is rarely a good thing. In most cases, you want to supply it with a *namespace*—a place where it can put its variables. You want to do this so that the code doesn't corrupt *your* namespace (that is, change your variables). For example, let's say that the code uses the name sqrt:

```
>>> from math import sqrt
>>> exec "sqrt = 1"
>>> sqrt(4)
Traceback (most recent call last):
  File "<pyshell#18>", line 1, in ?
    sqrt(4)
TypeError: object is not callable: 1
```

Well, why would you do something like that in the first place? The exec statement is mainly useful when you build the code string on the fly. And if the string is built from parts that you get from other places, and possibly from the user, you can rarely be certain of exactly what it will contain. So to be safe, you give it a dictionary, which will work as a namespace for it.

---

■**Note**  The concept of namespaces, or *scopes*, is a very important one. You will look at it in depth in the next chapter, but for now, you can think of a namespace as a place where you keep your variables, much like an invisible dictionary. So when you execute an assignment like x = 1, you store the key x with the value 1 in the *current namespace*, which will often be the global namespace (which we have been using, for the most part, up until now), but doesn't have to be.

---

You do this by adding in `<scope>`, where `<scope>` is some dictionary that will function as the namespace for your code string:

```
>>> from math import sqrt
>>> scope = {}
```

---

7. In Python 3.0, exec is a function, not a statement.

```
>>> exec 'sqrt = 1' in scope
>>> sqrt(4)
2.0
>>> scope['sqrt']
1
```

As you can see, the potentially destructive code does not overwrite the sqrt function. The function works just as it should, and the sqrt variable resulting from the exec'ed assignment is available from the scope.

Note that if you try to print out scope, you see that it contains a *lot* of stuff because the dictionary called __builtins__ is automatically added and contains all built-in functions and values:

```
>>> len(scope)
2
>>> scope.keys()
['sqrt', '__builtins__']
```

### eval

A built-in function that is similar to exec is eval (for "evaluate"). Just as exec executes a series of Python *statements*, eval evaluates a Python *expression* (written in a string) and returns the resulting value. (exec doesn't return anything because it is a statement itself.) For example, you can use the following to make a Python calculator:

```
>>> eval(raw_input("Enter an arithmetic expression: "))
Enter an arithmetic expression: 6 + 18 * 2
42
```

---

**■Note** The expression eval(raw_input(...)) is, in fact, equivalent to input(...). In Python 3.0, raw_input is renamed to input.

---

You can supply a namespace with eval, just as with exec, although expressions rarely rebind variables in the way statements usually do. (In fact, you can supply eval with *two* namespaces, one global and one local. The global one must be a dictionary, but the local one may be any mapping.)

---

**■Caution** Even though expressions don't rebind variables *as a rule*, they certainly can (for example, by calling functions that rebind global variables). Therefore, using eval with an untrusted piece of code is no safer than using exec. There is, at present, no safe way of executing untrusted code in Python. One alternative is to use an implementation of Python such as Jython (see Chapter 17) and use the some native mechanism such as the Java sandbox.

---

**PRIMING THE SCOPE**

When supplying a namespace for exec or eval, you can also put some values in before actually using the namespace:

```
>>> scope = {}
>>> scope['x'] = 2
>>> scope['y'] = 3
>>> eval('x * y', scope)
6
```

In the same way, a scope from one exec or eval call can be used again in another one:

```
>>> scope = {}
>>> exec 'x = 2' in scope
>>> eval('x*x', scope)
4
```

Actually, exec and eval are not used all that often, but they can be nice tools to keep in your back pocket (figuratively, of course).

# A Quick Summary

In this chapter, you've seen several kinds of statements:

**Printing**: You can use the print statement to print several values by separating them with commas. If you end the statement with a comma, later print statements will continue printing on the same line.

**Importing**: Sometimes you don't like the name of a function you want to import—perhaps you've already used the name for something else. You can use the import...as... statement, to locally rename a function.

**Assignments**: You've seen that through the wonder of sequence unpacking and chained assignments, you can assign values to several variables at once, and that with augmented assignments, you can change a variable in place.

**Blocks**: Blocks are used as a means of grouping statements through indentation. They are used in conditionals and loops, and as you see later in the book, in function and class definitions, among other things.

**Conditionals**: A conditional statement either executes a block or not, depending on a condition (Boolean expression). Several conditionals can be strung together with if/elif/else. A variation on this theme is the conditional expression, a if b else c.

**Assertions**: An assertion simply asserts that something (a Boolean expression) is true, optionally with a string explaining why it must be so. If the expression happens to be false, the assertion brings your program to a halt (or actually raises an exception—more on that in Chapter 8). It's better to find an error early than to let it sneak around your program until you don't know where it originated.

**Loops**: You either can execute a block for each element in a sequence (such as a range of numbers) or continue executing it while a condition is true. To skip the rest of the block and continue with the next iteration, use the continue statement; to break out of the loop, use the break statement. Optionally, you may add an else clause at the end of the loop, which will be executed if you didn't execute any break statements inside the loop.

**List comprehension**: These aren't really statements—they are expressions that look a lot like loops, which is why I grouped them with the looping statements. Through list comprehension, you can build new lists from old ones, applying functions to the elements, filtering out those you don't want, and so on. The technique is quite powerful, but in many cases, using plain loops and conditionals (which will always get the job done) may be more readable.

**pass, del, exec, and** eval: The pass statement does nothing, which can be useful as a placeholder, for example. The del statement is used to delete variables or parts of a data structure, but cannot be used to delete values. The exec statement is used to execute a string as if it were a Python program. The built-in function eval evaluates an expression written in a string and returns the result.

## New Functions in This Chapter

| Function | Description |
| --- | --- |
| chr(n) | Returns a one-character string when passed ordinal n_ ($0 \leq n < 256$) |
| eval(source[, globals[, locals]]) | Evaluates a string as an expression and returns the value |
| enumerate(seq) | Yields (index, value) pairs suitable for iteration |
| ord(c) | Returns the integer ordinal value of a one-character string |
| range([start,] stop[, step]) | Creates a list of integers |
| reversed(seq) | Yields the values of seq in reverse order, suitable for iteration |
| sorted(seq[, cmp][, key][, reverse]) | Returns a list with the values of seq in sorted order |
| xrange([start,] stop[, step]) | Creates an xrange object, used for iteration |
| zip(seq1,_seq2,...) | Creates a new sequence suitable for parallel iteration |

## What Now?

Now you've cleared the basics. You can implement any algorithm you can dream up; you can read in parameters and print out the results. In the next couple of chapters, you learn about something that will help you write larger programs without losing the big picture. That something is called *abstraction*.

# CHAPTER 6

■ ■ ■

# Abstraction

In this chapter, you learn how to group statements into functions, which enables you to tell the computer how to do something, and to tell it only once. You won't need to give it the same detailed instructions over and over. The chapter provides a thorough introduction to parameters and scoping, and you learn what recursion is and what it can do for your programs.

## Laziness Is a Virtue

The programs we've written so far have been pretty small, but if you want to make something bigger, you'll soon run into trouble. Consider what happens if you have written some code in one place and need to use it in another place as well. For example, let's say you wrote a snippet of code that computed some *Fibonacci numbers* (a series of numbers in which each number is the sum of the two previous ones):

```
fibs = [0, 1]
for i in range(8):
    fibs.append(fibs[-2] + fibs[-1])
```

After running this, fibs contains the first ten Fibonacci numbers:

```
>>> fibs
[0, 1, 1, 2, 3, 5, 8, 13, 21, 34]
```

This is all right if what you want is to calculate the first ten Fibonacci numbers once. You could even change the for loop to work with a dynamic range, with the length of the resulting sequence supplied by the user:

```
fibs = [0, 1]
num = input('How many Fibonacci numbers do you want? ')
for i in range(num-2):
    fibs.append(fibs[-2] + fibs[-1])
print fibs
```

---

**Note** Remember that you can use raw_input if you want to read in a plain string. In this case, you would then need to convert it to an integer by using the int function.

---

But what if you also want to use the numbers for something else? You could certainly just write the same loop again when needed, but what if you had written a more complicated piece of code, such as one that downloaded a set of web pages and computed the frequencies of all the words used? Would you still want to write all the code several times, once for each time you needed it? No, real programmers don't do that. Real programmers are lazy. Not lazy in a bad way, but in the sense that they don't do unnecessary work.

So what do real programmers do? They make their programs more *abstract*. You could make the previous program more abstract as follows:

```
num = input('How many numbers do you want? ')
print fibs(num)
```

Here, only what is specific to *this program* is written concretely (reading in the number and printing out the result). Actually, computing the Fibonacci numbers is done in an abstract manner: you simply tell the computer to do it. You don't say specifically how it should be done. You create a function called fibs, and use it when you need the functionality of the little Fibonacci program. It saves you a lot of effort if you need it in several places.

## Abstraction and Structure

Abstraction can be useful as a labor saver, but it is actually more important than that. It is the key to making computer programs understandable to humans (which is essential, whether you're writing them or reading them). The computers themselves are perfectly happy with very concrete and specific instructions, but humans generally aren't. If you ask me for directions to the cinema, for example, you wouldn't want me to answer, "Walk 10 steps forward, turn 90 degrees to your left, walk another 5 steps, turn 45 degrees to your right, walk 123 steps." You would soon lose track, wouldn't you?

Now, if I instead told you to "Walk down this street until you get to a bridge, cross the bridge, and the cinema is to your left," you would certainly understand me. The point is that you already know how to walk down the street and how to cross a bridge. You don't need explicit instructions on how to do either.

You structure computer programs in a similar fashion. Your programs should be quite abstract, as in "Download page, compute frequencies, and print the frequency of each word." This is easily understandable. In fact, let's translate this high-level description to a Python program right now:

```
page = download_page()
freqs = compute_frequencies(page)
for word, freq in freqs:
    print word, freq
```

From reading this, you can understand what the program does. However, you haven't explicitly said anything about *how* it should do it. You just tell the computer to download the page and compute the frequencies. The specifics of these operations will need to be written somewhere else—in separate *function definitions*.

# Creating Your Own Functions

A function is something you can call (possibly with some parameters—the things you put in the parentheses), which performs an action and returns a value.[1] In general, you can tell whether something is callable or not with the built-in function `callable`:

```
>>> import math
>>> x = 1
>>> y = math.sqrt
>>> callable(x)
False
>>> callable(y)
True
```

> ■**Note**  The function `callable` no longer exists in Python 3.0. With that version, you will need to use the expression `hasattr(func, __call__)`. For more information about `hasattr`, see Chapter 7.

As you know from the previous section, creating functions is central to structured programming. So how do you define a function? You do this with the `def` (or "function definition") statement:

```
def hello(name):
    return 'Hello, ' + name + '!'
```

After running this, you have a new function available, called `hello`, which returns a string with a greeting for the name given as the only parameter. You can use this function just like you use the built-in ones:

```
>>> print hello('world')
Hello, world!
>>> print hello('Gumby')
Hello, Gumby!
```

Pretty neat, huh? Consider how you would write a function that returned a list of Fibonacci numbers. Easy! You just use the code from before, and instead of reading in a number from the user, you receive it as a parameter:

```
def fibs(num):
    result = [0, 1]
    for i in range(num-2):
        result.append(result[-2] + result[-1])
    return result
```

---

1. Actually, functions in Python don't always return values. More on this later in the chapter.

After running this statement, you've basically told the interpreter how to calculate Fibonacci numbers. Now you don't have to worry about the details anymore. You simply use the function fibs:

```
>>> fibs(10)
[0, 1, 1, 2, 3, 5, 8, 13, 21, 34]
>>> fibs(15)
[0, 1, 1, 2, 3, 5, 8, 13, 21, 34, 55, 89, 144, 233, 377]
```

The names num and result are quite arbitrary in this example, but return is important. The return statement is used to return something from the function (which is also how we used it in the preceding hello function).

## Documenting Functions

If you want to document your functions so that you're certain that others will understand them later on, you can add comments (beginning with the hash sign, #). Another way of writing comments is simply to write strings by themselves. Such strings can be particularly useful in some places, such as immediately after a def statement (and at the beginning of a module or a class—you learn more about classes in Chapter 7 and modules in Chapter 10). If you put a string at the beginning of a function, it is stored as part of the function and is called a *docstring*. The following code demonstrates how to add a docstring to a function:

```
def square(x):
    'Calculates the square of the number x.'
    return x*x
```

The docstring may be accessed like this:

```
>>> square.__doc__
'Calculates the square of the number x.'
```

---

■**Note**  __doc__ is a function attribute. You'll learn a lot more about attributes in Chapter 7. The double underscores in the attribute name mean that this is a special attribute. Special or "magic" attributes like this are discussed in Chapter 9.

---

A special built-in function called help can be quite useful. If you use it in the interactive interpreter, you can get information about a function, including its docstring:

```
>>> help(square)
Help on function square in module __main__:

square(x)
    Calculates the square of the number x.
```

You meet the help function again in Chapter 10.

## Functions That Aren't Really Functions

Functions, in the mathematical sense, always return something that is calculated from their parameters. In Python, some functions don't return anything. In other languages (such as Pascal), such functions may be called other things (such as *procedures*), but in Python, a function is a function, even if it technically isn't. Functions that don't return anything simply don't have a return statement. Or, if they *do* have return statements, there is no value after the word return:

```
def test():
    print 'This is printed'
    return
    print 'This is not'
```

Here, the return statement is used simply to end the function:

```
>>> x = test()
This is printed
```

As you can see, the second print statement is skipped. (This is a bit like using break in loops, except that you break out of the function.) But if test doesn't return anything, what does x refer to? Let's see:

```
>>> x
>>>
```

Nothing there. Let's look a bit closer:

```
>>> print x
None
```

That's a familiar value: None. So all functions *do* return something; it's just that they return None when you don't tell them what to return. I guess I was a bit unfair when I said that some functions aren't really functions.

---

■**Caution**  Don't let this default behavior trip you up. If you return values from inside if statements and the like, be sure you've covered every case, so you don't accidentally return None when the caller is expecting a sequence, for example.

---

# The Magic of Parameters

Using functions is pretty straightforward, and creating them isn't all that complicated either. The way parameters work may, however, seem a bit like magic at times. First, let's do the basics.

# Where Do the Values Come From?

Sometimes, when defining a function, you may wonder where parameters get their values. In general, you shouldn't worry about that. Writing a function is a matter of providing a service to whatever part of your program (and possibly even other programs) might need it. Your task is to make sure the function does its job if it is supplied with acceptable parameters, and preferably fails in an obvious manner if the parameters are wrong. (You do this with `assert` or exceptions in general. More about exceptions in Chapter 8.)

---

**Note** The variables you write after your function name in def statements are often called the **formal** parameters of the function. The values you supply when you **call** the function are called the **actual** parameters, or **arguments**. In general, I won't be too picky about the distinction. If it is important, I will call the actual parameters *values* to distinguish them from the formal parameters.

---

# Can I Change a Parameter?

So, your function gets a set of values through its parameters. Can you change them? And what happens if you do? Well, the parameters are just variables like all others, so this works as you would expect. Assigning a new value to a parameter inside a function won't change the outside world at all:

```
>>> def try_to_change(n):
        n = 'Mr. Gumby'

>>> name = 'Mrs. Entity'
>>> try_to_change(name)
>>> name
'Mrs. Entity'
```

Inside try_to_change, the parameter n gets a new value, but as you can see, that doesn't affect the variable name. After all, it's a completely different variable. It's just as if you did something like this:

```
>>> name = 'Mrs. Entity'
>>> n = name # This is almost what happens when passing a parameter
>>> n = 'Mr. Gumby' # This is done inside the function
>>> name
'Mrs. Entity'
```

Here, the result is obvious. While the variable n is changed, the variable name is not. Similarly, when you rebind (assign to) a parameter inside a function, variables outside the function will not be affected.

---

**Note** Parameters are kept in what is called a **local scope**. Scoping is discussed later in this chapter.

---

Strings (and numbers and tuples) are *immutable*, which means that you can't modify them (that is, you can only replace them with new values). Therefore, there isn't much to say about them as parameters. But consider what happens if you use a mutable data structure such as a list:

```
>>> def change(n):
        n[0] = 'Mr. Gumby'

>>> names = ['Mrs. Entity', 'Mrs. Thing']
>>> change(names)
>>> names
['Mr. Gumby', 'Mrs. Thing']
```

In this example, the parameter is changed. There is one crucial difference between this example and the previous one. In the previous one, we simply gave the local variable a new value, but in this one, we actually *modify* the list to which the variable names is bound. Does that sound strange? It's not really that strange. Let's do it again without the function call:

```
>>> names = ['Mrs. Entity', 'Mrs. Thing']
>>> n = names # Again pretending to pass names as a parameter
>>> n[0] = 'Mr. Gumby' # Change the list
>>> names
['Mr. Gumby', 'Mrs. Thing']
```

You've seen this sort of thing before. When two variables refer to the same list, they . . . refer to the same list. It's really as simple as that. If you want to avoid this, you must make a *copy* of the list. When you do slicing on a sequence, the returned slice is always a copy. Thus, if you make a slice of the *entire list*, you get a copy:

```
>>> names = ['Mrs. Entity', 'Mrs. Thing']
>>> n = names[:]
```

Now n and names contain two *separate* (nonidentical) lists that are *equal*:

```
>>> n is names
False
>>> n == names
True
```

If you change n now (as you did inside the function change), it won't affect names:

```
>>> n[0] = 'Mr. Gumby'
>>> n
['Mr. Gumby', 'Mrs. Thing']
>>> names
['Mrs. Entity', 'Mrs. Thing']
```

Let's try this trick with change:

```
>>> change(names[:])
>>> names
['Mrs. Entity', 'Mrs. Thing']
```

Now the parameter n contains a copy, and your original list is safe.

---

**Note** In case you're wondering, names that are local to a function, including parameters, do not clash with names outside the function (that is, global ones). For more information about this, see the discussion of scoping, later in this chapter.

---

### Why Would I Want to Modify My Parameters?

Using a function to change a data structure (such as a list or a dictionary) can be a good way of introducing abstraction into your program. Let's say you want to write a program that stores names and that allows you to look up people by their first, middle, or last names. You might use a data structure like this:

```
storage = {}
storage['first'] = {}
storage['middle'] = {}
storage['last'] = {}
```

The data structure storage is a dictionary with three keys: 'first', 'middle', and 'last'. Under each of these keys, you store another dictionary. In these subdictionaries, you'll use names (first, middle, or last) as keys, and insert lists of people as values. For example, to add me to this structure, you could do the following:

```
>>> me = 'Magnus Lie Hetland'
>>> storage['first']['Magnus'] = [me]
>>> storage['middle']['Lie'] = [me]
>>> storage['last']['Hetland'] = [me]
```

Under each key, you store a list of people. In this case, the lists contain only me.

Now, if you want a list of all the people registered who have the middle name Lie, you could do the following:

```
>>> storage['middle']['Lie']
['Magnus Lie Hetland']
```

As you can see, adding people to this structure is a bit tedious, especially when you get more people with the same first, middle, or last names, because then you need to extend the list that is already stored under that name. Let's add my sister, and let's assume you don't know what is already stored in the database:

```
>>> my_sister = 'Anne Lie Hetland'
>>> storage['first'].setdefault('Anne', []).append(my_sister)
>>> storage['middle'].setdefault('Lie', []).append(my_sister)
>>> storage['last'].setdefault('Hetland', []).append(my_sister)
>>> storage['first']['Anne']
['Anne Lie Hetland']
```

```
>>> storage['middle']['Lie']
['Magnus Lie Hetland', 'Anne Lie Hetland']
```

Imagine writing a large program filled with updates like this. It would quickly become quite unwieldy.

The point of abstraction is to hide all the gory details of the updates, and you can do that with functions. Let's first make a function to initialize a data structure:

```
def init(data):
    data['first'] = {}
    data['middle'] = {}
    data['last'] = {}
```

In the preceding code, I've simply moved the initialization statements inside a function. You can use it like this:

```
>>> storage = {}
>>> init(storage)
>>> storage
{'middle': {}, 'last': {}, 'first': {}}
```

As you can see, the function has taken care of the initialization, making the code much more readable.

---

■**Note**  The keys of a dictionary don't have a specific order, so when a dictionary is printed out, the order may vary. If the order is different in your interpreter, don't worry about it.

---

Before writing a function for storing names, let's write one for getting them:

```
def lookup(data, label, name):
    return data[label].get(name)
```

With lookup, you can take a label (such as 'middle') and a name (such as 'Lie') and get a list of full names returned. In other words, assuming my name was stored, you could do this:

```
>>> lookup(storage, 'middle', 'Lie')
['Magnus Lie Hetland']
```

It's important to notice that the list that is returned is the same list that is stored in the data structure. So if you change the list, the change also affects the data structure. (This is not the case if no people are found; then you simply return None.)

Now it's time to write the function that stores a name in your structure (don't worry if it doesn't make sense to you immediately):

```
def store(data, full_name):
    names = full_name.split()
    if len(names) == 2: names.insert(1, '')
    labels = 'first', 'middle', 'last'
```

```
    for label, name in zip(labels, names):
        people = lookup(data, label, name)
        if people:
            people.append(full_name)
        else:
            data[label][name] = [full_name]
```

The store function performs the following steps:

1. You enter the function with the parameters data and full_name set to some values that you receive from the outside world.

2. You make yourself a list called names by splitting full_name.

3. If the length of names is 2 (you have only a first and a last name), you insert an empty string as a middle name.

4. You store the strings 'first', 'middle', and 'last' as a tuple in labels. (You could certainly use a list here; it's just convenient to drop the brackets.)

5. You use the zip function to combine the labels and names so they line up properly, and for each pair (label, name), you do the following:

   • Fetch the list belonging to the given label and name.

   • Append full_name to that list, or insert a new list if needed.

Let's try it out:

```
>>> MyNames = {}
>>> init(MyNames)
>>> store(MyNames, 'Magnus Lie Hetland')
>>> lookup(MyNames, 'middle', 'Lie')
['Magnus Lie Hetland']
```

It seems to work. Let's try some more:

```
>>> store(MyNames, 'Robin Hood')
>>> store(MyNames, 'Robin Locksley')
>>> lookup(MyNames, 'first', 'Robin')
['Robin Hood', 'Robin Locksley']
>>> store(MyNames, 'Mr. Gumby')
>>> lookup(MyNames, 'middle', '')
['Robin Hood', 'Robin Locksley', 'Mr. Gumby']
```

As you can see, if more people share the same first, middle, or last name, you can retrieve them all together.

---

■**Note**  This sort of application is well suited to object-oriented programming, which is explained in the next chapter.

---

### What If My Parameter Is Immutable?

In some languages (such as C++, Pascal, and Ada), rebinding parameters and having these changes affect variables outside the function is an everyday thing. In Python, it's not directly possible; you can modify only the parameter objects themselves. But what if you have an immutable parameter, such as a number?

Sorry, but it can't be done. What you should do is return all the values you need from your function (as a tuple, if there is more than one). For example, a function that increments the numeric value of a variable by one could be written like this:

```
>>> def inc(x): return x + 1
...
>>> foo = 10
>>> foo = inc(foo)
>>> foo
11
```

If you *really* wanted to modify your parameter, you could use a trick such as wrapping your value in a list, like this:

```
>>> def inc(x): x[0] = x[0] + 1
...
>>> foo = [10]
>>> inc(foo)
>>> foo
[11]
```

Simply returning the new value would be a cleaner solution, though.

## Keyword Parameters and Defaults

The parameters we've been using until now are called *positional parameters* because their positions are important—more important than their names, in fact. The techniques introduced in this section let you sidestep the positions altogether, and while they may take some getting used to, you will quickly see how useful they are as your programs grow in size.

Consider the following two functions:

```
def hello_1(greeting, name):
    print '%s, %s!' % (greeting, name)

def hello_2(name, greeting):
    print '%s, %s!' % (name, greeting)
```

They both do *exactly* the same thing, only with their parameter names reversed:

```
>>> hello_1('Hello', 'world')
Hello, world!
>>> hello_2('Hello', 'world')
Hello, world!
```

Sometimes (especially if you have many parameters) the order may be hard to remember. To make things easier, you can supply the *name* of your parameter:

```
>>> hello_1(greeting='Hello', name='world')
Hello, world!
```

The order here doesn't matter at all:

```
>>> hello_1(name='world', greeting='Hello')
Hello, world!
```

The names *do*, however (as you may have gathered):

```
>>> hello_2(greeting='Hello', name='world')
world, Hello!
```

The parameters that are supplied with a name like this are called *keyword parameters*. On their own, the key strength of keyword parameters is that they can help clarify the role of each parameter. Instead of needing to use some odd and mysterious call like this:

```
>>> store('Mr. Brainsample', 10, 20, 13, 5)
```

you could use this:

```
>>> store(patient='Mr. Brainsample', hour=10, minute=20, day=13, month=5)
```

Even though it takes a bit more typing, it is absolutely clear what each parameter does. Also, if you get the order mixed up, it doesn't matter.

What really makes keyword arguments rock, however, is that you can give the parameters in the function default values:

```
def hello_3(greeting='Hello', name='world'):
    print '%s, %s!' % (greeting, name)
```

When a parameter has a default value like this, you don't need to supply it when you call the function! You can supply none, some, or all, as the situation might dictate:

```
>>> hello_3()
Hello, world!
>>> hello_3('Greetings')
Greetings, world!
>>> hello_3('Greetings', 'universe')
Greetings, universe!
```

As you can see, this works well with positional parameters, except that you must supply the greeting if you want to supply the name. What if you want to supply *only* the name, leaving the default value for the greeting? I'm sure you've guessed it by now:

```
>>> hello_3(name='Gumby')
Hello, Gumby!
```

Pretty nifty, huh? And that's not all. You can combine positional and keyword parameters. The only requirement is that all the positional parameters come first. If they don't, the interpreter won't know which ones they are (that is, which position they are supposed to have).

For example, our `hello` function might require a name, but allow us to (optionally) specify the greeting and the punctuation:

```
def hello_4(name, greeting='Hello', punctuation='!'):
    print '%s, %s%s' % (greeting, name, punctuation)
```

This function can be called in many ways. Here are some of them:

```
>>> hello_4('Mars')
Hello, Mars!
>>> hello_4('Mars', 'Howdy')
Howdy, Mars!
>>> hello_4('Mars', 'Howdy', '...')
Howdy, Mars...
>>> hello_4('Mars', punctuation='.')
Hello, Mars.
>>> hello_4('Mars', greeting='Top of the morning to ya')
Top of the morning to ya, Mars!
>>> hello_4()
Traceback (most recent call last):
  File "<pyshell#64>", line 1, in ?
    hello_4()
TypeError: hello_4() takes at least 1 argument (0 given)
```

That's pretty flexible, isn't it? And we didn't really need to do much to achieve it either. In the next section we get even *more* flexible.

## Collecting Parameters

Sometimes it can be useful to allow the user to supply any number of parameters. For example, in the name-storing program (described in the section "Why Would I Want to Modify My Parameters?" earlier in this chapter), you can store only one name at a time. It would be nice to be able to store more names, like this:

```
>>> store(data, name1, name2, name3)
```

For this to be useful, you should be allowed to supply as many names as you want. Actually, that's quite possible.

Try the following function definition:

```
def print_params(*params):
    print params
```

Here, I seemingly specify only one parameter, but it has an odd little star (or asterisk) in front of it. What does that mean? Let's call the function with a single parameter and see what happens:

```
>>> print_params('Testing')
('Testing',)
```

You can see that what is printed out is a tuple because it has a comma in it. (Those tuples of length one are a bit odd, aren't they?) So using a star in front of a parameter puts it in a tuple? The plural in params ought to give a clue about what's going on:

```
>>> print_params(1, 2, 3)
(1, 2, 3)
```

The star in front of the parameter puts all the values into the same tuple. It gathers them up, so to speak. You may wonder if we can combine this with ordinary parameters. Let's write another function:

```
def print_params_2(title, *params):
    print title
    print params
```

and try it:

```
>>> print_params_2('Params:', 1, 2, 3)
Params:
(1, 2, 3)
```

It works! So the star means "Gather up the rest of the positional parameters." I bet if I don't give any parameters to gather, params will be an empty tuple:

```
>>> print_params_2('Nothing:')
Nothing:
()
```

Indeed. How useful! Does it handle keyword arguments (the same as parameters), too?

```
>>> print_params_2('Hmm...', something=42)
Traceback (most recent call last):
  File "<pyshell#60>", line 1, in ?
    print_params_2('Hmm...', something=42)
TypeError: print_params_2() got an unexpected keyword argument 'something'
```

Doesn't look like it. So we probably need another "gathering" operator for keyword arguments. What do you think that might be? Perhaps **?

```
def print_params_3(**params):
    print params
```

At least the interpreter doesn't complain about the function. Let's try to call it:

```
>>> print_params_3(x=1, y=2, z=3)
{'z': 3, 'x': 1, 'y': 2}
```

Yep, we get a dictionary rather than a tuple. Let's put them all together:

```
def print_params_4(x, y, z=3, *pospar, **keypar):
    print x, y, z
    print pospar
    print keypar
```

This works just as expected:

```
>>> print_params_4(1, 2, 3, 5, 6, 7, foo=1, bar=2)
1 2 3
(5, 6, 7)
{'foo': 1, 'bar': 2}
>>> print_params_4(1, 2)
1 2 3
()
{}
```

By combining all these techniques, you can do quite a lot. If you wonder how some combination might work (or whether it's allowed), just try it! (In the next section, you see how * and ** can be used when a function is called as well, regardless of whether they were used in the function definition.)

Now, back to the original problem: how you can use this in the name-storing example. The solution is shown here:

```
def store(data, *full_names):
    for full_name in full_names:
        names = full_name.split()
        if len(names) == 2: names.insert(1, '')
        labels = 'first', 'middle', 'last'
        for label, name in zip(labels, names):
            people = lookup(data, label, name)
            if people:
                people.append(full_name)
            else:
                data[label][name] = [full_name]
```

Using this function is just as easy as using the previous version, which accepted only one name:

```
>>> d = {}
>>> init(d)
>>> store(d, 'Han Solo')
```

But now you can also do this:

```
>>> store(d, 'Luke Skywalker', 'Anakin Skywalker')
>>> lookup(d, 'last', 'Skywalker')
['Luke Skywalker', 'Anakin Skywalker']
```

## Reversing the Process

Now you've learned about gathering up parameters in tuples and dictionaries, but it is in fact possible to do the "opposite" as well, with the same two operators, * and **. What might the opposite of parameter gathering be? Let's say we have the following function available:

```
def add(x, y): return x + y
```

---

■**Note** You can find a more efficient version of this function in the `operator` module.

---

Also, let's say you have a tuple with two numbers that you want to add:

```
params = (1, 2)
```

This is more or less the opposite of what we did previously. Instead of gathering the parameters, we want to *distribute* them. This is simply done by using the * operator at the "other end"—that is, when calling the function rather than when defining it:

```
>>> add(*params)
3
```

This works with parts of a parameter list, too, as long as the expanded part is last. You can use the same technique with dictionaries, using the ** operator. Assuming that you have defined hello_3 as before, you can do the following:

```
>>> params = {'name': 'Sir Robin', 'greeting': 'Well met'}
>>> hello_3(**params)
Well met, Sir Robin!
```

Using * (or **) both when you define and call the function will simply pass the tuple or dictionary right through, so you might as well not have bothered:

```
>>> def with_stars(**kwds):
        print kwds['name'], 'is', kwds['age'], 'years old'

>>> def without_stars(kwds):
        print kwds['name'], 'is', kwds['age'], 'years old'
```

```
>>> args = {'name': 'Mr. Gumby', 'age': 42}
>>> with_stars(**args)
Mr. Gumby is 42 years old
>>> without_stars(args)
Mr. Gumby is 42 years old
```

As you can see, in with_stars, I use stars both when defining and calling the function. In without_stars, I don't use the stars in either place but achieve exactly the same effect. So the stars are really useful only if you use them *either* when defining a function (to allow a varying number of arguments) *or* when calling a function (to "splice in" a dictionary or a sequence).

---

**Tip**  It may be useful to use these splicing operators to "pass through" parameters, without worrying too much about how many there are, and so forth. Here is an example:

```
def foo(x, y, z, m=0, n=0):
    print x, y, z, m, n
def call_foo(*args,**kwds):
    print "Calling foo!"
    foo(*args,**kwds)
```

This can be particularly useful when calling the constructor of a superclass (see Chapter 9 for more on that).

---

## Parameter Practice

With so many ways of supplying and receiving parameters, it's easy to get confused. So let me tie it all together with an example. First, let's define some functions:

```
def story(**kwds):
    return 'Once upon a time, there was a ' \
           '%(job)s called %(name)s.' % kwds

def power(x, y, *others):
    if others:
        print 'Received redundant parameters:', others
    return pow(x, y)

 def interval(start, stop=None, step=1):
    'Imitates range() for step > 0'
    if stop is None:              # If the stop is not supplied...
        start, stop = 0, start    # shuffle the parameters
    result = []
```

```
    i = start                   # We start counting at the start index
    while i < stop:             # Until the index reaches the stop index...
        result.append(i)        # ...append the index to the result...
        i += step               # ...increment the index with the step (> 0)
    return result
```

Now let's try them out:

```
>>> print story(job='king', name='Gumby')
Once upon a time, there was a king called Gumby.
>>> print story(name='Sir Robin', job='brave knight')
Once upon a time, there was a brave knight called Sir Robin.
>>> params = {'job': 'language', 'name': 'Python'}
>>> print story(**params)
Once upon a time, there was a language called Python.
>>> del params['job']
>>> print story(job='stroke of genius', **params)
Once upon a time, there was a stroke of genius called Python.
>>> power(2,3)
8
>>> power(3,2)
9
>>> power(y=3,x=2)
8
>>> params = (5,) * 2
>>> power(*params)
3125
>>> power(3, 3, 'Hello, world')
Received redundant parameters: ('Hello, world',)
27
>>> interval(10)
[0, 1, 2, 3, 4, 5, 6, 7, 8, 9]
>>> interval(1,5)
[1, 2, 3, 4]
>>> interval(3,12,4)
[3, 7, 11]
>>> power(*interval(3,7))
Received redundant parameters: (5, 6)
81
```

Feel free to experiment with these functions and functions of your own until you are confident that you understand how this stuff works.

# Scoping

What *are* variables, really? You can think of them as names referring to values. So, after the assignment x = 1, the name x refers to the value 1. It's almost like using dictionaries, where keys refer to values, except that you're using an "invisible" dictionary. Actually, this isn't far from the truth. There is a built-in function called vars, which returns this dictionary:

```
>>> x = 1
>>> scope = vars()
>>> scope['x']
1
>>> scope['x'] += 1
>>> x
2
```

---

■**Caution** In general, you should not modify the dictionary returned by vars because, according to the official Python documentation, the result is undefined. In other words, you might not get the result you're after.

---

This sort of "invisible dictionary" is called a *namespace* or *scope*. So, how many namespaces are there? In addition to the global scope, each function call creates a new one:

```
>>> def foo(): x = 42
...
>>> x = 1
>>> foo()
>>> x
1
```

Here foo changes (rebinds) the variable x, but when you look at it in the end, it hasn't changed after all. That's because when you call foo, a *new* namespace is created, which is used for the block *inside* foo. The assignment x = 42 is performed in this inner scope (the *local* namespace), and therefore it doesn't affect the x in the outer (*global*) scope. Variables that are used inside functions like this are called *local variables* (as opposed to global variables). The parameters work just like local variables, so there is no problem in having a parameter with the same name as a global variable:

```
>>> def output(x): print x
...
>>> x = 1
>>> y = 2
>>> output(y)
2
```

So far, so good. But what if you want to access the global variables inside a function? As long as you only want to *read* the value of the variable (that is, you don't want to rebind it), there is generally no problem:

```
>>> def combine(parameter): print parameter + external
...
>>> external = 'berry'
>>> combine('Shrub')
Shrubberry
```

---

■**Caution**  Referencing global variables like this is a source of many bugs. Use global variables with care.

---

### THE PROBLEM OF SHADOWING

Reading the value of global variables is not a problem in general, but one thing may make it problematic. If a local variable or parameter exists with the same name as the global variable you want to access, you can't do it directly. The global variable is *shadowed* by the local one.

If needed, you can still gain access to the global variable by using the function globals, a close relative of vars, which returns a dictionary with the global variables. (locals returns a dictionary with the local variables.)

For example, if you had a global variable called parameter in the previous example, you couldn't access it from within combine because you have a parameter with the same name. In a pinch, however, you could have referred to it as globals()['parameter']:

```
>>> def combine(parameter):
        print parameter + globals()['parameter']
...
>>> parameter = 'berry'
>>> combine('Shrub')
Shrubberry
```

*Rebinding* global variables (making them refer to some new value) is another matter. If you assign a value to a variable inside a function, it automatically becomes local unless you tell Python otherwise. And how do you think you can tell it to make a variable global?

```
>>> x = 1
>>> def change_global():
        global x
        x = x + 1

>>> change_global()
>>> x
2
```

Piece of cake!

## NESTED SCOPES

Python functions may be nested—you can put one inside another.[2] Here is an example:

```
def foo():
    def bar():
        print "Hello, world!"
    bar()
```

Nesting is normally not all that useful, but there is one particular application that stands out: using one function to "create" another. This means that you can (among other things) write functions like the following:

```
def multiplier(factor):
    def multiplyByFactor(number):
        return number*factor
    return multiplyByFactor
```

One function is inside another, and the outer function *returns the inner one*; that is, the function itself is returned—it is not called. What's important is that the returned function still has access to the scope where it was defined; in other words, it carries its environment (and the associated local variables) with it!

Each time the outer function is called, the inner one gets redefined, and each time, the variable `factor` may have a new value. Because of Python's nested scopes, this variable from the outer local scope (of `multiplier`) is accessible in the inner function later on, as follows:

```
>>> double = multiplier(2)
>>> double(5)
10
>>> triple = multiplier(3)
>>> triple(3)
9
>>> multiplier(5)(4)
20
```

A function such as `multiplyByFactor` that stores its enclosing scopes is called a **closure**.

Normally, you cannot rebind variables in outer scopes. In Python 3.0, however, the keyword `nonlocal` is introduced. It is used in much the same way as `global`, and lets you assign to variables in outer (but non-global) scopes.

# Recursion

You've learned a lot about making functions and calling them. You also know that functions can call other functions. What *might* come as a surprise is that functions can call *themselves*.

---

2.  This topic is a bit advanced; if you're new to functions and scopes, you may want to skip it for now.

If you haven't encountered this sort of thing before, you may wonder what this word *recursion* is. It simply means referring to (or, in our case, "calling") yourself. A humorous definition goes like this:

*recursion \ri-'k&r-zh&n\ n: see recursion.*

Recursive definitions (including recursive function definitions) include references to the term they are defining. Depending on the amount of experience you have with it, recursion can be either mind-boggling or quite straightforward. For a deeper understanding of it, you should probably buy yourself a good textbook on computer science, but playing around with the Python interpreter can certainly help.

In general, you don't want recursive definitions like the humorous one of the word *recursion*, because you won't get anywhere. You look up recursion, which again tells you to look up recursion, and so on. A similar function definition would be

```
def recursion():
    return recursion()
```

It is obvious that this doesn't *do* anything—it's just as silly as the mock dictionary definition. But what happens if you run it? You're welcome to try. You'll find that the program simply crashes (raises an exception) after a while. Theoretically, it should simply run forever. However, each time a function is called, it uses up a little memory, and after enough function calls have been made (before the previous calls have returned), there is no more room, and the program ends with the error message `maximum recursion depth exceeded`.

The sort of recursion you have in this function is called *infinite recursion* (just as a loop beginning with `while True` and containing no break or `return` statements is an *infinite loop*) because it never ends (in theory). What you want is a recursive function that does something useful. A useful recursive function usually consists of the following parts:

- A base case (for the smallest possible problem) when the function returns a value directly

- A *recursive case*, which contains one or more recursive calls on *smaller parts of the problem*

The point here is that by breaking the problem up into smaller pieces, the recursion can't go on forever because you always end up with the smallest possible problem, which is covered by the base case.

So you have a function calling itself. But how is that even possible? It's really not as strange as it might seem. As I said before, each time a function is called, a new namespace is created for that specific call. That means that when a function calls "itself," you are actually talking about two different functions (or, rather, the same function with two different namespaces). You might think of it as one creature of a certain species talking to another one of the same species.

## Two Classics: Factorial and Power

In this section, we examine two classic recursive functions. First, let's say you want to compute the *factorial* of a number $n$. The factorial of $n$ is defined as $n \times (n–1) \times (n–2) \times \ldots \times 1$. It's used in many mathematical applications (for example, in calculating how many different ways there are of putting *n* people in a line). How do you calculate it? You could always use a loop:

```
def factorial(n):
    result = n
    for i in range(1,n):
        result *= i
    return result
```

This works and is a straightforward implementation. Basically, what it does is this: first, it sets the result to *n*; then, the result is multiplied by each number from 1 to *n*–1 in turn; finally, it returns the result. But you can do this differently if you like. The key is the mathematical definition of the factorial, which can be stated as follows:

- The factorial of 1 is 1.

- The factorial of a number *n* greater than 1 is the product of *n* and the factorial of *n*–1.

As you can see, this definition is exactly equivalent to the one given at the beginning of this section.

Now consider how you implement this definition as a function. It is actually pretty straightforward, once you understand the definition itself:

```
def factorial(n):
    if n == 1:
        return 1
    else:
        return n * factorial(n-1)
```

This is a direct implementation of the definition. Just remember that the function call `factorial(n)` is a different entity from the call `factorial(n-1)`.

Let's consider another example. Assume you want to calculate powers, just like the built-in function pow, or the operator **. You can define the (integer) power of a number in several different ways, but let's start with a simple one: `power(x,n)` (x to the power of n) is the number x multiplied by itself n-1 times (so that x is used as a factor n times). So `power(2,3)` is 2 multiplied with itself twice, or $2 \times 2 \times 2 = 8$.

This is easy to implement:

```
def power(x, n):
    result = 1
    for i in range(n):
        result *= x
    return result
```

This is a sweet and simple little function, but again you can change the definition to a recursive one:

- `power(x, 0)` is 1 for all numbers x.

- `power(x, n)` for n > 0 is the product of x and `power(x, n-1)`.

Again, as you can see, this gives exactly the same result as in the simpler, iterative definition.

Understanding the definition is the hardest part—implementing it is easy:

```
def power(x, n):
    if n == 0:
        return 1
    else:
        return x * power(x, n-1)
```

Again, I have simply translated my definition from a slightly formal textual description into a programming language (Python).

---

■**Tip**  If a function or an algorithm is complex and difficult to understand, clearly defining it in your own words before actually implementing it can be very helpful. Programs in this sort of "almost-programming-language" are often referred to as **pseudocode**.

---

So what is the point of recursion? Can't you just use loops instead? The truth is yes, you can, and in most cases, it will probably be (at least slightly) more efficient. But in many cases, recursion can be more readable—sometimes *much* more readable—especially if one understands the recursive definition of a function. And even though you could conceivably avoid ever writing a recursive function, as a programmer you will most likely have to understand recursive algorithms and functions created by others, at the very least.

## Another Classic: Binary Search

As a final example of recursion in practice, let's have a look at the algorithm called *binary search*.

You probably know of the game where you are supposed to guess what someone is thinking about by asking 20 yes-or-no questions. To make the most of your questions, you try to cut the number of possibilities in (more or less) half. For example, if you know the subject is a person, you might ask, "Are you thinking of a woman?" You don't start by asking, "Are you thinking of John Cleese?" unless you have a very strong hunch. A version of this game for those more numerically inclined is to guess a number. For example, your partner is thinking of a number between 1 and 100, and you have to guess which one it is. Of course, you could do it in a hundred guesses, but how many do you really need?

As it turns out, you need only seven questions. The first one is something like "Is the number greater than 50?" If it is, then you ask, "Is it greater than 75?" You keep halving the interval (splitting the difference) until you find the number. You can do this without much thought.

The same tactic can be used in many different contexts. One common problem is to find out whether a number is to be found in a (sorted) sequence, and even to find out where it is. Again, you follow the same procedure: "Is the number to the right of the middle of the sequence?" If it isn't, "Is it in the second quarter (to the right of the middle of the left half)?" and so on. You keep an upper and a lower limit to where the number *may* be, and keep splitting that interval in two with every question.

The point is that this algorithm lends itself naturally to a recursive definition and implementation. Let's review the definition first, to make sure we know what we're doing:

- If the upper and lower limits are the same, they both refer to the correct position of the number, so return it.

- Otherwise, find the middle of the interval (the average of the upper and lower bound), and find out if the number is in the right or left half. Keep searching in the proper half.

The key to the recursive case is that the numbers are sorted, so when you have found the middle element, you can just compare it to the number you're looking for. If your number is larger, then it must be to the right, and if it is smaller, it must be to the left. The recursive part is "Keep searching in the proper half," because the search will be performed in exactly the manner described in the definition. (Note that the search algorithm returns the position where the number *should* be—if it's not present in the sequence, this position will, naturally, be occupied by another number.)

You're now ready to implement a binary search:

```
def search(sequence, number, lower, upper):
    if lower == upper:
        assert number == sequence[upper]
        return upper
    else:
        middle = (lower + upper) // 2
        if number > sequence[middle]:
            return search(sequence, number, middle+1, upper)
        else:
            return search(sequence, number, lower, middle)
```

This does exactly what the definition said it should: if lower == upper, then return upper, which is the upper limit. Note that you assume (assert) that the number you are looking for (number) has actually been found (number == sequence[upper]). If you haven't reached your base case yet, you find the middle, check whether your number is to the left or right, and call search recursively with new limits. You could even make this easier to use by making the limit specifications optional. You simply add the following conditional to the beginning of the function definition:

```
def search(sequence, number, lower=0, upper=None):
    if upper is None: upper = len(sequence)-1
    ...
```

Now, if you don't supply the limits, they are set to the first and last positions of the sequence. Let's see if this works:

```
>>> seq = [34, 67, 8, 123, 4, 100, 95]
>>> seq.sort()
>>> seq
[4, 8, 34, 67, 95, 100, 123]
>>> search(seq, 34)
2
```

```
>>> search(seq, 100)
5
```

But why go to all this trouble? For one thing, you could simply use the list method index, and if you wanted to implement this yourself, you could just make a loop starting at the beginning and iterating along until you found the number.

Sure, using index is just fine. But using a simple loop may be a bit inefficient. Remember I said you needed seven questions to find one number (or position) among 100? And the loop obviously needs 100 questions in the worst-case scenario. "Big deal," you say. But if the list has 100,000,000,000,000,000,000,000,000,000,000 elements, and the same number of questions with a loop (perhaps a somewhat unrealistic size for a Python list), this sort of thing starts to matter. Binary search would then need only 117 questions. Pretty efficient, huh? [3]

---

■**Tip** You can actually find a standard implementation of binary search in the bisect module.

---

## THROWING FUNCTIONS AROUND

By now, you are probably used to using functions just like other objects (strings, number, sequences, and so on) by assigning them to variables, passing them as parameters, and returning them from other functions. Some programming languages (such as Scheme or Lisp) use functions in this way to accomplish almost everything. Even though you usually don't rely that heavily on functions in Python (you usually make your own kinds of objects—more about that in the next chapter), you *can*.

Python has a few functions that are useful for this sort of "functional programming": map, filter, and reduce.[4] (In Python 3.0, these are moved to the functools module.) The map and filter functions are not really all that useful in current versions of Python, and you should probably use list comprehensions instead. You can use map to pass all the elements of a sequence through a given function:

```
>>> map(str, range(10)) # Equivalent to [str(i) for i in range(10)]
['0', '1', '2', '3', '4', '5', '6', '7', '8', '9']
```

You use filter to filter out items based on a Boolean function:

```
>>> def func(x):
...     return x.isalnum()
...
>>> seq = ["foo", "x41", "?!", "***"]
>>> filter(func, seq)
['foo', 'x41']
```

---

3. In fact, with the estimated number of particles in the observable universe at $10^{87}$, you would need only about 290 questions to discern between them!
4. There is also apply, but that was really only needed before we had the splicing discussed previously.

For this example, using a list comprehension would mean you didn't need to define the custom function:

```
>>> [x for x in seq if x.isalnum()]
['foo', 'x41']
```

Actually, there is a feature called *lambda expressions*,[5] which lets you define simple functions in-line (primarily used with map, filter, and reduce):

```
>>> filter(lambda x: x.isalnum(), seq)
['foo', 'x41']
```

Isn't the list comprehension more readable, though?

The reduce function cannot easily be replaced by list comprehensions, but you probably won't need its functionality all that often (if ever). It combines the first two elements of a sequence with a given function, combines the result with the third element, and so on until the entire sequence has been processed and a single result remains. For example, if you wanted to sum all the numbers of a sequence, you could use reduce with lambda x, y: x+y (still using the same numbers):[6]

```
>>> numbers = [72, 101, 108, 108, 111, 44, 32, 119, 111, 114, 108, 100, 33]
>>> reduce(lambda x, y: x+y, numbers)
1161
```

Of course, here you could just as well have used the built-in function sum.

# A Quick Summary

In this chapter, you've learned several things about abstraction in general, and functions in particular:

**Abstraction**: Abstraction is the art of hiding unnecessary details. You can make your program more abstract by defining functions that handle the details.

**Function definition**: Functions are defined with the def statement. They are blocks of statements that receive values (parameters) from the "outside world" and may return one or more values as the result of their computation.

**Parameters**: Functions receive what they need to know in the form of parameters—variables that are set when the function is called. There are two types of parameters in Python: positional parameters and keyword parameters. Parameters can be made optional by giving them default values.

---

5. The name "lambda" comes from the Greek letter, which is used in mathematics to indicate an anonymous function.
6. Actually, instead of this lambda function, you could import the function add from the operator module, which has a function for each of the built-in operators. Using functions from the operator module is always more efficient than using your own functions.

**Scopes**: Variables are stored in scopes (also called *namespaces*). There are two main scopes in Python: the global scope and the local scope. Scopes may be nested.

**Recursion**: A function can call itself—and if it does, it's called *recursion*. Everything you can do with recursion can also be done by loops, but sometimes a recursive function is more readable.

**Functional programming**: Python has some facilities for programming in a functional style. Among these are lambda expressions and the map, filter, and reduce functions.

## New Functions in This Chapter

| Function | Description |
| --- | --- |
| map(func, seq [, seq, ...]) | Applies the function to all the elements in the sequences |
| filter(func, seq) | Returns a list of those elements for which the function is true |
| reduce(func, seq [, initial]) | Equivalent to func(func(func(seq[0], seq[1]), seq[2]), ...) |
| sum(seq) | Returns the sum of all the elements of seq |
| apply(func[, args[, kwargs]]) | Calls the function, optionally supplying argument |

## What Now?

The next chapter takes abstractions to another level, through *object-oriented programming*. You learn how to make your own types (or *classes*) of objects to use alongside those provided by Python (such as strings, lists, and dictionaries), and you learn how this enables you to write better programs. Once you've worked your way through the next chapter, you'll be able to write some really *big* programs without getting lost in the source code.

# CHAPTER 7

■■■

# More Abstraction

In the previous chapters, you looked at Python's main built-in object types (numbers, strings, lists, tuples, and dictionaries); you peeked at the wealth of built-in functions and standard libraries; and you even created your own functions. Now, only one thing seems to be missing—making your own objects. And that's what you do in this chapter.

You may wonder how useful this is. It might be cool to make your own kinds of objects, but what would you use them for? With all the dictionaries and sequences and numbers and strings available, can't you just use them and make the functions do the job? Certainly, but making your own objects (and especially types or *classes* of objects) is a central concept in Python—so central, in fact, that Python is called an *object-oriented* language (along with Smalltalk, C++, Java, and many others). In this chapter, you learn how to make objects. You learn about polymorphism and encapsulation, methods and attributes, superclasses, and inheritance— you learn a lot. So let's get started.

---

■**Note** If you're already familiar with the concepts of object-oriented programming, you probably know about *constructors*. Constructors will not be dealt with in this chapter; for a full discussion, see Chapter 9.

---

## The Magic of Objects

In object-oriented programming, the term *object* loosely means a collection of data (attributes) with a set of methods for accessing and manipulating those data. There are several reasons for using objects instead of sticking with global variables and functions. Some of the most important benefits of objects include the following:

- **Polymorphism**: You can use the same operations on objects of different classes, and they will work as if "by magic."

- **Encapsulation**: You hide unimportant details of how objects work from the outside world.

- **Inheritance**: You can create specialized classes of objects from general ones.

In many presentations of object-oriented programming, the order of these concepts is different. Encapsulation and inheritance are presented first, and then they are used to model real-world objects. That's all fine and dandy, but in my opinion, the most interesting feature of object-oriented programming is polymorphism. It is also the feature that confuses most people (in my experience). Therefore I'll start with polymorphism, and try to show that this concept alone should be enough to make you like object-oriented programming.

## Polymorphism

The term *polymorphism* is derived from a Greek word meaning "having multiple forms." Basically, that means that even if you don't know what kind of object a variable refers to, you may still be able to perform operations on it that will work differently depending on the type (or class) of the object. For example, assume that you are creating an online payment system for a commercial web site that sells food. Your program receives a "shopping cart" of goods from another part of the system (or other similar systems that may be designed in the future)—all you need to worry about is summing up the total and billing some credit card.

Your first thought may be to specify exactly how the goods must be represented when your program receives them. For example, you may want to receive them as tuples, like this:

```
('SPAM', 2.50)
```

If all you need is a descriptive tag and a price, this is fine. But it's not very flexible. Let's say that some clever person starts an auctioning service as part of the web site—where the price of an item is gradually reduced until someone buys it. It would be nice if the user could put the object in her shopping cart, proceed to the checkout (your part of the system), and just wait until the price was right before clicking the Pay button.

But that wouldn't work with the simple tuple scheme. For that to work, the object would need to check its current price (through some network magic) each time your code asked for the price—it couldn't be frozen like in a tuple. You can solve that by making a function:

```
# Don't do it like this...
def getPrice(object):
    if isinstance(object, tuple):
        return object[1]
    else:
        return magic_network_method(object)
```

---

■**Note**   The type/class checking and use of `isinstance` here is meant to illustrate a point—namely that type checking isn't generally a satisfactory solution. Avoid type checking if you possibly can. The function `isinstance` is described in the section "Investigating Inheritance," later in this chapter.

---

In the preceding code, I use the function `isinstance` to find out whether the object is a tuple. If it is, its second element is returned; otherwise, some "magic" network method is called.

Assuming that the network stuff already exists, you've solved the problem—for now. But this still isn't very flexible. What if some clever programmer decides that she'll represent the price as a string with a hex value, stored in a dictionary under the key `'price'`? No problem—you just update your function:

```
# Don't do it like this...
def getPrice(object):
    if isinstance(object, tuple):
        return object[1]
    elif isinstance(object, dict):
        return int(object['price'])
    else:
        return magic_network_method(object)
```

Now, surely you must have covered every possibility? But let's say someone decides to add a new type of dictionary with the price stored under a different key. What do you do now? You could certainly update getPrice again, but for how long could you continue doing that? Every time someone wanted to implement some priced object differently, you would need to reimplement your module. But what if you already sold your module and moved on to other, cooler projects—what would the client do then? Clearly, this is an inflexible and impractical way of coding the different behaviors.

So what do you do instead? You let the objects handle the operation themselves. It sounds really obvious, but think about how much easier things will get. Every new object type can retrieve or calculate its own price and return it to you—all you have to do is ask for it. And this is where polymorphism (and, to some extent, encapsulation) enters the scene.

## Polymorphism and Methods

You receive an object and have no idea of how it is implemented—it may have any one of many "shapes." All you know is that you can ask for its price, and that's enough for you. The way you do that should be familiar:

```
>>> object.getPrice()
2.5
```

Functions that are bound to object attributes like this are called *methods*. You've already encountered them in the form of string, list, and dictionary methods. There, too, you saw some polymorphism:

```
>>> 'abc'.count('a')
1
>>> [1, 2, 'a'].count('a')
1
```

If you had a variable x, you wouldn't need to know whether it was a string or a list to call the count method—it would work regardless (as long as you supplied a single character as the argument).

Let's do an experiment. The standard library random contains a function called choice that selects a random element from a sequence. Let's use that to give your variable a value:

```
>>> from random import choice
>>> x = choice(['Hello, world!', [1, 2, 'e', 'e', 4]])
```

After performing this, x can either contain the string 'Hello, world!' *or* the list [1, 2, 'e', 'e', 4]—you don't know, and you don't have to worry about it. All you care about is how many times you find 'e' in x, and you can find that out regardless of whether x is a list or a string. By calling the count method as before, you find out just that:

```
>>> x.count('e')
2
```

In this case, it seems that the list won out. But the point is that you didn't need to check. Your only requirement was that x has a method called count that takes a single character as an argument and returned an integer. If someone else had made his own class of objects that had this method, it wouldn't matter to you—you could use his objects just as well as the strings and lists.

## Polymorphism Comes in Many Forms

Polymorphism is at work every time you can "do something" to an object without having to know exactly what kind of object it is. This doesn't apply only to methods—we've already used polymorphism a lot in the form of built-in operators and functions. Consider the following:

```
>>> 1+2
3
>>> 'Fish'+'license'
'Fishlicense'
```

Here, the plus operator (+) works fine for both numbers (integers in this case) and strings (as well as other types of sequences). To illustrate the point, let's say you wanted to make a function called add that added two things together. You could simply define it like this (equivalent to, but less efficient than, the add function from the operator module):

```
def add(x, y):
    return x+y
```

This would also work with many kinds of arguments:

```
>>> add(1, 2)
3
>>> add('Fish', 'license')
'Fishlicense'
```

This might seem silly, but the point is that the arguments can be *anything that supports addition.*[1] If you want to write a function that prints a message about the length of an object, all that's required is that it *has* a length (that the len function will work on it):

```
def length_message(x):
    print "The length of", repr(x), "is", len(x)
```

As you can see, the function also uses repr, but repr is one of the grand masters of polymorphism—it works with anything. Let's see how:

```
>>> length_message('Fnord')
The length of 'Fnord' is 5
>>> length_message([1, 2, 3])
The length of [1, 2, 3] is 3
```

Many functions and operators are polymorphic—probably most of yours will be, too, even if you don't intend them to be. Just by using polymorphic functions and operators, the polymorphism "rubs off." In fact, virtually the only thing you can do to destroy this polymorphism is to do explicit type checking with functions such as type, `, and issubclass. If you can, you *really* should avoid destroying polymorphism this way. What matters should be that an object acts the way you want, not whether it is of the right type (or class).

---

■**Note**  The form of polymorphism discussed here, which is so central to the Python way of programming, is sometimes called "duck typing." The term derives from the phrase, "If it quacks like a duck …" For more information, see http://en.wikipedia.org/wiki/Duck_typing.

---

## Encapsulation

*Encapsulation* is the principle of hiding unnecessary details from the rest of the world. This may sound like polymorphism—there, too, you use an object without knowing its inner details. The two concepts are similar because they are both *principles of abstraction.* They both help you deal with the components of your program without caring about unnecessary detail, just as functions do.

But encapsulation isn't the same as polymorphism. Polymorphism enables you to call the methods of an object without knowing its class (type of object). Encapsulation enables you to use the object without worrying about how it's constructed. Does it still sound similar? Let's construct an example *with* polymorphism, but *without* encapsulation. Assume that you have a class called OpenObject (you learn how to create classes later in this chapter):

```
>>> o = OpenObject() # This is how we create objects...
>>> o.setName('Sir Lancelot')
>>> o.getName()
'Sir Lancelot'
```

---

1. Note that these objects need to support addition with each other. So calling add(1, 'license') would not work.

You create an object (by calling the class as if it were a function) and bind the variable o to it. You can then use the methods setName and getName (assuming that they are methods that are supported by the class OpenObject). Everything seems to be working perfectly. However, let's assume that o stores its name in the global variable globalName:

```
>>> globalName
'Sir Lancelot'
```

This means that you need to worry about the contents of globalName when you use instances (objects) of the class OpenObject. In fact, you must make sure that no one changes it:

```
>>> globalName = 'Sir Gumby'
>>> o.getName()
'Sir Gumby'
```

Things get even more problematic if you try to create more than one OpenObject because they will all be messing with the same variable:

```
>>> o1 = OpenObject()
>>> o2 = OpenObject()
>>> o1.setName('Robin Hood')
>>> o2.getName()
'Robin Hood'
```

As you can see, setting the name of one automatically sets the name of the other—not exactly what you want.

Basically, you want to treat objects as abstract. When you call a method, you don't want to worry about anything else, such as not disturbing global variables. So how can you "encapsulate" the name within the object? No problem. You make it an *attribute*.

Attributes are variables that are a part of the object, just like methods; actually, methods are almost like attributes bound to functions. (You'll see an important difference between methods and functions in the section "Attributes, Functions, and Methods," later in this chapter.) If you rewrite the class to use an attribute instead of a global variable, and you rename it ClosedObject, it works like this:

```
>>> c = ClosedObject()
>>> c.setName('Sir Lancelot')
>>> c.getName()
'Sir Lancelot'
```

So far, so good. But for all you know, this could still be stored in a global variable. Let's make another object:

```
>>> r = ClosedObject()
>>> r.setName('Sir Robin')
r.getName()
'Sir Robin'
```

Here, you can see that the new object has its name set properly, which is probably what you expected. But what has happened to the first object now?

```
>>> c.getName()
'Sir Lancelot'
```

The name is still there! This is because the object has its own *state*. The state of an object is described by its attributes (like its name, for example). The methods of an object may change these attributes. So it's like lumping together a bunch of functions (the methods) and giving them access to some variables (the attributes) where they can keep values stored between function calls.

You'll see even more details on Python's encapsulation mechanisms in the section "Privacy Revisited," later in the chapter.

## Inheritance

Inheritance is another way of dealing with laziness (in the positive sense). Programmers want to avoid typing the same code more than once. We avoided that earlier by making functions, but now I will address a more subtle problem. What if you have a class already, and you want to make one that is very similar? Perhaps one that adds only a few methods? When making this new class, you don't want to need to copy all the code from the old one over to the new one.

For example, you may already have a class called Shape, which knows how to draw itself on the screen. Now you want to make a class called Rectangle, which *also* knows how to draw itself on the screen, but which can, in addition, calculate its own area. You wouldn't want to do all the work of making a new draw method when Shape has one that works just fine. So what do you do? You let Rectangle *inherit* the methods from Shape. You can do this in such a way that when draw is called on a Rectangle object, the method from the Shape class is called automatically (see the section "Specifying a Superclass," later in this chapter).

# Classes and Types

By now, you're getting a feeling for what classes are—or you *may* be getting impatient for me to tell you how to make the darn things. Before jumping into the technicalities, let's have a look at what a class is, and how it is different from (or similar to) a type.

## What *Is* a Class, Exactly?

I've been throwing around the word *class* a lot, using it more or less synonymously with words such as *kind* or *type*. In many ways that's exactly what a class is—a kind of object. All objects *belong* to a class and are said to be *instances* of that class.

So, for example, if you look outside your window and see a bird, that bird is an instance of the class "birds." This is a very general (abstract) class that has several *sub*classes; your bird might belong to the subclass "larks." You can think of the class "birds" as the set of all birds, while the class "larks" is just a subset of that. When the objects belonging to one class form a subset of the objects belonging to another class, the first is called a *subclass* of the second. Thus, "larks" is a subclass of "birds." Conversely, "birds" is a *superclass* of "larks."

> ■**Note**  In everyday speech, we denote classes of objects with plural nouns such as "birds" and "larks." In
> Python, it is customary to use singular, capitalized nouns such as `Bird` and `Lark`.

When stated like this, subclasses and superclasses are easy to understand. But in object-oriented programming, the subclass relation has important implications because a class is defined by what methods it supports. All the instances of a class have these methods, so all the instances of all *subclasses* must *also* have them. Defining subclasses is then only a matter of defining *more* methods (or, perhaps, overriding some of the existing ones).

For example, `Bird` might supply the method `fly`, while `Penguin` (a subclass of `Bird`) might add the method `eatFish`. When making a `Penguin` class, you would probably also want to *override* a method of the superclass, namely the `fly` method. In a `Penguin` instance, this method should either do nothing, or possibly raise an exception (see Chapter 8), given that penguins can't fly.

> ■**Note**  In older versions of Python, there was a sharp distinction between types and classes. Built-in
> objects had types; your custom objects had classes. You could create classes, but not types. In recent ver-
> sions of Python, things are starting to change. The division between basic types and classes is blurring. You
> can now make subclasses (or subtypes) of the built-in types, and the types are behaving more like classes.
> Chances are you won't notice this change much until you become more familiar with the language. If you're
> interested, you can find more information on the topic in Chapter 9.

## Making Your Own Classes

Finally, you get to make your own classes! Here is a simple example:

```
__metaclass__ = type # Make sure we get new style classes

class Person:

    def setName(self, name):
        self.name = name

    def getName(self):
        return self.name

    def greet(self):
        print "Hello, world! I'm %s." % self.name
```

This example contains three method definitions, which are like function definitions except that they are written inside a class statement. Person is, of course, the name of the class. The class statement creates its own namespace where the functions are defined. (See the section "The Class Namespace" later in this chapter.) All this seems fine, but you may wonder what this self parameter is. It refers to the object itself. And what object is that? Let's make a couple of instances and see:

```
>>> foo = Person()
>>> bar = Person()
>>> foo.setName('Luke Skywalker')
>>> bar.setName('Anakin Skywalker')
>>> foo.greet()
Hello, world! I'm Luke Skywalker.
>>> bar.greet()
Hello, world! I'm Anakin Skywalker.
```

Okay, so this example may be a bit obvious, but perhaps it clarifies what self is. When I call setName and greet on foo, foo itself is automatically passed as the first parameter in each case—the parameter that I have so fittingly called self. You may, in fact, call it whatever you like, but because it is always the object itself, it is almost always called self, by convention.

It should be obvious why self is useful, and even necessary here. Without it, none of the methods would have access to the object itself—the object whose attributes they are supposed to manipulate. As before, the attributes are also accessible from the outside:

```
>>> foo.name
'Luke Skywalker'
>>> bar.name = 'Yoda'
>>> bar.greet()
Hello, world! I'm Yoda.
```

■**Tip**  Another way of viewing this is that foo.greet() is simply a convenient way of writing Person.greet(foo), if you know that foo is an instance of Person.

## Attributes, Functions, and Methods

The self parameter (mentioned in the previous section) is, in fact, what distinguishes methods from functions. Methods (or, more technically, *bound* methods) have their first parameter bound to the instance they belong to, so you don't have to supply it. While you can certainly bind an attribute to a plain function, it won't have that special self parameter:

```
>>> class Class:
        def method(self):
            print 'I have a self!'

>>> def function():
        print "I don't..."

>>> instance = Class()
>>> instance.method()
I have a self!
>>> instance.method = function
>>> instance.method()
I don't...
```

Note that the self parameter is not dependent on calling the method the way I've done until now, as instance.method. You're free to use another variable that refers to the same method:

```
>>> class Bird:
        song = 'Squaawk!'
        def sing(self):
            print self.song

>>> bird = Bird()
>>> bird.sing()
Squaawk!
>>> birdsong = bird.sing
>>> birdsong()
Squaawk!
```

Even though the last method call looks exactly like a function call, the variable birdsong refers to the bound method bird.sing, which means that it still has access to the self parameter (that is, it is still bound to the same instance of the class).

## Privacy Revisited

By default, you can access the attributes of an object from the "outside." Let's revisit the example from the earlier discussion on encapsulation:

```
>>> c.name
'Sir Lancelot'
>>> c.name = 'Sir Gumby'
```

```
>>> c.getName()
'Sir Gumby'
```

Some programmers are okay with this, but some (like the creators of Smalltalk, a language where attributes of an object are accessible only to the methods of the same object) feel that it breaks with the principle of encapsulation. They believe that the state of the object should be *completely hidden* (inaccessible) to the outside world. You might wonder why they take such an extreme stand. Isn't it enough that each object manages its own attributes? Why should you hide them from the world? After all, if you just used the name attribute directly on ClosedObject (the class of c in this case), you wouldn't need to make the setName and getName methods.

The point is that other programmers may not know (and perhaps shouldn't know) what's going on inside your object. For example, ClosedObject may send an email message to some administrator every time an object changes its name. This could be part of the setName method. But what happens when you set c.name directly? Nothing happens—no email message is sent. To avoid this sort of thing, you have *private* attributes. These are attributes that are not accessible outside the object; they are accessible only through *accessor* methods, such as getName and setName.

---

■**Note** In Chapter 9, you learn about *properties*, a powerful alternative to accessors.

---

Python doesn't support privacy directly, but relies on the programmer to know when it is safe to modify an attribute from the outside. After all, you should know how to use an object before using that object. It *is*, however, possible to achieve something like private attributes with a little trickery.

To make a method or attribute private (inaccessible from the outside), simply start its name with two underscores:

```
class Secretive:

    def __inaccessible(self):
        print "Bet you can't see me..."

    def accessible(self):
        print "The secret message is:"
        self.__inaccessible()
```

Now __inaccessible is inaccessible to the outside world, while it can still be used inside the class (for example, from accessible):

```
>>> s = Secretive()
>>> s.__inaccessible()
Traceback (most recent call last):
  File "<pyshell#112>", line 1, in ?
    s.__inaccessible()
AttributeError: Secretive instance has no attribute '__inaccessible'
```

```
>>> s.accessible()
The secret message is:
Bet you can't see me...
```

Although the double underscores are a bit strange, this seems like a standard private method, as found in other languages. What's not so standard is what actually happens. Inside a class definition, all names beginning with a double underscore are "translated" by adding a single underscore and the class name to the beginning:

```
>>> Secretive._Secretive__inaccessible
<unbound method Secretive.__inaccessible>
```

If you know how this works behind the scenes, it is still possible to access private methods outside the class, even though you're not supposed to:

```
>>> s._Secretive__inaccessible()
Bet you can't see me...
```

So, in short, you can't be sure that others won't access the methods and attributes of your objects, but this sort of name-mangling is a pretty strong signal that they *shouldn't*.

If you don't want the name-mangling effect, but you still want to send a signal for other objects to stay away, you can use a *single* initial underscore. This is mostly just a convention, but has some practical effects. For example, names with an initial underscore aren't imported with starred imports (from module import *).[2]

## The Class Namespace

The following two statements are (more or less) equivalent:

```
def foo(x): return x*x
foo = lambda x: x*x
```

Both create a function that returns the square of its argument, and both bind the variable foo to that function. The name foo may be defined in the global (module) scope, or it may be local to some function or method. The same thing happens when you define a class: all the code in the class statement is executed in a special namespace—the *class namespace*. This namespace is accessible later by all members of the class. Not all Python programmers know that class definitions are simply code sections that are executed, but it can be useful information. For example, you aren't restricted to def statements inside the class definition block:

```
>>> class C:
        print 'Class C being defined...'


Class C being defined...
>>>
```

---

2. Some languages support several *degrees* of privacy for its member variables (attributes). Java, for example, has four different levels. Python doesn't really have equivalent privacy support, although single and double initial underscores do to some extent give you two levels of privacy.

Okay, that was a bit silly. But consider the following:

```
class MemberCounter:
    members = 0
    def init(self):
        MemberCounter.members += 1
```

```
>>> m1 = MemberCounter()
>>> m1.init()
>>> MemberCounter.members
1
>>> m2 = MemberCounter()
>>> m2.init()
>>> MemberCounter.members
2
```

In the preceding code, a variable is defined in the class scope, which can be accessed by all the members (instances), in this case to count the number of class members. Note the use of init to initialize all the instances: I'll automate that (that is, turn it into a proper constructor) in Chapter 9.

This class scope variable is accessible from every instance as well, just as methods are:

```
>>> m1.members
2
>>> m2.members
2
```

What happens when you rebind the members attribute in an instance?

```
>>> m1.members = 'Two'
>>> m1.members
'Two'
>>> m2.members
2
```

The new members value has been written into an attribute in m1, shadowing the class-wide variable. This mirrors the behavior of local and global variables in functions, as discussed in the sidebar "The Problem of Shadowing" in Chapter 6.

## Specifying a Superclass

As I discussed earlier in the chapter, subclasses expand on the definitions in their superclasses. You indicate the superclass in a class statement by writing it in parentheses after the class name:

```
class Filter:
    def init(self):
        self.blocked = []
    def filter(self, sequence):
        return [x for x in sequence if x not in self.blocked]
```

```
class SPAMFilter(Filter): # SPAMFilter is a subclass of Filter
    def init(self): # Overrides init method from Filter superclass
        self.blocked = ['SPAM']
```

Filter is a general class for filtering sequences. Actually it doesn't filter out anything:

```
>>> f = Filter()
>>> f.init()
>>> f.filter([1, 2, 3])
[1, 2, 3]
```

The usefulness of the Filter class is that it can be used as a base class (superclass) for other classes, such as SPAMFilter, which filters out 'SPAM' from sequences:

```
>>> s = SPAMFilter()
>>> s.init()
>>> s.filter(['SPAM', 'SPAM', 'SPAM', 'SPAM', 'eggs', 'bacon', 'SPAM'])
['eggs', 'bacon']
```

Note two important points in the definition of SPAMFilter:

- I override the definition of init from Filter by simply providing a new definition.

- The definition of the filter method carries over (is inherited) from Filter, so you don't need to write the definition again.

The second point demonstrates why inheritance is useful: I can now make a number of different filter classes, all subclassing Filter, and for each one I can simply use the filter method I have already implemented. Talk about useful laziness . . .

## Investigating Inheritance

If you want to find out whether a class is a subclass of another, you can use the built-in method issubclass:

```
>>> issubclass(SPAMFilter, Filter)
True
>>> issubclass(Filter, SPAMFilter)
False
```

If you have a class and want to know its base classes, you can access its special attribute __bases__:

```
>>> SPAMFilter.__bases__
(<class __main__.Filter at 0x171e40>,)
>>> Filter.__bases__
()
```

In a similar manner, you can check whether an object is an instance of a class by using isinstance:

```
>>> s = SPAMFilter()
>>> isinstance(s, SPAMFilter)
True
>>> isinstance(s, Filter)
True
>>> isinstance(s, str)
False
```

---

■**Note**  Using isinstance is usually not good practice. Relying on polymorphism is almost always better.

---

As you can see, s is a (direct) member of the class SPAMFilter, but it is also an indirect member of Filter because SPAMFilter is a subclass of Filter. Another way of putting it is that all SPAMFilters are Filters. As you can see in the preceding example, isinstance also works with types, such as the string type (str).

If you just want to find out which class an object belongs to, you can use the __class__ attribute:

```
>>> s.__class__
<class __main__.SPAMFilter at 0x1707c0>
```

---

■**Note**  If you have a new-style class, either by setting __metaclass__ = type or subclassing object, you could also use type(s) to find the class of your instance.

---

## Multiple Superclasses

I'm sure you noticed a small detail in the previous section that may have seemed odd: the plural form in __bases__. I said you could use it to find the base classes of a class, which implies that it may have more than one. This is, in fact, the case. To show how it works, let's create a few classes:

```
class Calculator:
    def calculate(self, expression):
        self.value = eval(expression)

class Talker:
    def talk(self):
        print 'Hi, my value is', self.value

class TalkingCalculator(Calculator, Talker):
    pass
```

The subclass (TalkingCalculator) does nothing by itself; it inherits all its behavior from its superclasses. The point is that it inherits both calculate from Calculator and talk from Talker, making it a talking calculator:

```
>>> tc = TalkingCalculator()
>>> tc.calculate('1+2*3')
>>> tc.talk()
Hi, my value is 7
```

This is called *multiple inheritance*, and can be a very powerful tool. However, unless you know you need multiple inheritance, you may want to stay away from it, as it can, in some cases, lead to unforeseen complications.

If you are using multiple inheritance, there is one thing you should look out for: if a method is implemented differently by two or more of the superclasses (that is, you have two different methods with the same name), you must be careful about the order of these super-classes (in the class statement). The methods in the earlier classes *override* the methods in the later ones. So if the Calculator class in the preceding example had a method called talk, it would override (and make inaccessible) the talk method of the Talker. Reversing their order, like this:

```
class TalkingCalculator(Talker, Calculator): pass
```

would make the talk method of the Talker accessible. If the superclasses share a common superclass, the order in which the superclasses are visited while looking for a given attribute or method is called the *method resolution order* (MRO), and follows a rather complicated algorithm. Luckily, it works very well, so you probably don't need to worry about it.

## Interfaces and Introspection

The "interface" concept is related to polymorphism. When you handle a polymorphic object, you only care about its interface (or "protocol")—the methods and attributes known to the world. In Python, you don't explicitly specify which methods an object needs to have to be acceptable as a parameter. For example, you don't write interfaces explicitly (as you do in Java); you just assume that an object can do what you ask it to do. If it can't, the program will fail.

Usually, you simply require that objects conform to a certain interface (in other words, implement certain methods), but if you want to, you can be quite flexible in your demands. Instead of just calling the methods and hoping for the best, you can check whether the required methods are present, and if not, perhaps do something else:

```
>>> hasattr(tc, 'talk')
True
>>> hasattr(tc, 'fnord')
False
```

In the preceding code, you find that tc (a TalkingCalculator, as described earlier in this chapter) has the attribute talk (which refers to a method), but not the attribute fnord. If you wanted to, you could even check whether the talk attribute was callable:

```
>>> callable(getattr(tc, 'talk', None))
True
```

```
>>> callable(getattr(tc, 'fnord', None))
False
```

---

**■Note** The function `callable` is no longer available in Python 3.0. Instead of `callable(x)`, you can use `hasattr(x, '__call__')`.

---

Note that instead of using `hasattr` in an `if` statement and accessing the attribute directly, I'm using `getattr`, which allows me to supply a default value (in this case None) that will be used if the attribute is not present. I then use `callable` on the returned object.

---

**■Note** The inverse of `getattr` is `setattr`, which can be used to set the attributes of an object:

```
>>> setattr(tc, 'name', 'Mr. Gumby')
>>> tc.name
'Mr. Gumby'
```

---

If you want to see all the values stored in an object, you can examine its `__dict__` attribute. And if you *really* want to find out what an object is made of, you should take a look at the `inspect` module. It is meant for fairly advanced users who want to make object browsers (programs that enable you to browse Python objects in a graphical manner) and other similar programs that require such functionality. For more information on exploring objects and modules, see the section "Exploring Modules" in Chapter 10.

# Some Thoughts on Object-Oriented Design

Many books have been written about object-oriented program design, and although that's not the focus of this book, I'll give you some pointers:

- Gather what belongs together. If a function manipulates a global variable, the two of them might be better off in a class, as an attribute and a method.

- Don't let objects become too intimate. Methods should mainly be concerned with the attributes of their own instance. Let other instances manage their own state.

- Go easy on the inheritance, *especially* multiple inheritance. Inheritance is useful at times, but can make things unnecessarily complex in some cases. And multiple inheritance can be very difficult to get right and even harder to debug.

- Keep it simple. Keep your methods small. As a rule of thumb, it should be possible to read (and understand) most of your methods in, say, 30 seconds. For the rest, try to keep them shorter than one page or screen.

When determining which classes you need and which methods they should have, you may try something like this:

1. Write down a description of your problem (what should the program do?). Underline all the nouns, verbs, and adjectives.

2. Go through the nouns, looking for potential classes.

3. Go through the verbs, looking for potential methods.

4. Go through the adjectives, looking for potential attributes.

5. Allocate methods and attributes to your classes.

Now you have a first sketch of an *object-oriented model*. You may also want to think about what responsibilities and relationships (such as inheritance or cooperation) the classes and objects will have. To refine your model, you can do the following:

1. Write down (or dream up) a set of *use cases*—scenarios of how your program may be used. Try to cover all the functionality.

2. Think through every use case step by step, making sure that everything you need is covered by your model. If something is missing, add it. If something isn't quite right, change it. Continue until you are satisfied.

When you have a model you think will work, you can start hacking away. Chances are you'll need to revise your model or revise parts of your program. Luckily, that's easy in Python, so don't worry about it. Just dive in. (If you would like some more guidance in the ways of object-oriented programming, check out the list of suggested books in Chapter 19.)

# A Quick Summary

This chapter has given you more than just information about the Python language; it has introduced you to several concepts that may have been completely foreign to you. Here's a summary:

**Objects**: An object consists of attributes and methods. An attribute is merely a variable that is part of an object, and a method is more or less a function that is stored in an attribute. One difference between (bound) methods and other functions is that methods always receive the object they are part of as their first argument, usually called self.

**Classes**: A class represents a set (or kind) of objects, and every object (instance) has a class. The class's main task is to define the methods its instances will have.

**Polymorphism**: Polymorphism is the characteristic of being able to treat objects of different types and classes alike—you don't need to know which class an object belongs to in order to call one of its methods.

**Encapsulation**: Objects may hide (or encapsulate) their internal state. In some languages, this means that their state (their attributes) is available only through their methods. In

Python, all attributes are publicly available, but programmers should still be careful about accessing an object's state directly, since they might unwittingly make the state inconsistent in some way.

**Inheritance**: One class may be the subclass of one or more other classes. The subclass then inherits all the methods of the superclasses. You can use more than one superclass, and this feature can be used to compose orthogonal (independent and unrelated) pieces of functionality. A common way of implementing this is using a core superclass along with one or more *mix-in* superclasses.

**Interfaces and introspection**: In general, you don't want to prod an object too deeply. You rely on polymorphism, and call the methods you need. However, if you want to find out what methods or attributes an object has, there are functions that will do the job for you.

**Object-oriented design**: There are many opinions about how (or whether!) to do object-oriented design. No matter where you stand on the issue, it's important to understand your problem thoroughly, and to create a design that is easy to understand.

## New Functions in This Chapter

| Function | Description |
| --- | --- |
| `callable(object)` | Determines if the object is callable (such as a function or a method) |
| `getattr(object, name[, default])` | Gets the value of an attribute, optionally providing a default |
| `hasattr(object, name)` | Determines if the object has the given attribute |
| `isinstance(object, class)` | Determines if the object is an instance of the class |
| `issubclass(A, B)` | Determines if A is a subclass of B |
| `random.choice(sequence)` | Chooses a random element from a nonempty sequence |
| `setattr(object, name, value)` | Sets the given attribute of the object to value |
| `type(object)` | Returns the type of the object |

## What Now?

You've learned a lot about creating your own objects and how useful that can be. Before diving headlong into the magic of Python's special methods (Chapter 9), let's take a breather with a little chapter about exception handling.

# CHAPTER 8

■■■

# Exceptions

**W**hen writing computer programs, it is usually possible to discern between a normal course of events and something that's exceptional (out of the ordinary). Such exceptional events might be errors (such as trying to divide a number by zero) or simply something you might not expect to happen very often. To handle such exceptional events, you might use conditionals everywhere the events might occur (for example, have your program check whether the denominator is zero for every division). However, this would not only be inefficient and inflexible, but would also make the programs illegible. You might be tempted to ignore these exceptional events and just hope they won't occur, but Python offers a powerful alternative through its exception objects.

In this chapter, you learn how to create and raise your own exceptions, as well as how to handle exceptions in various ways.

## What Is an Exception?

To represent exceptional conditions, Python uses *exception objects*. When it encounters an error, it *raises* an exception. If such an exception object is not handled (or *caught*), the program terminates with a so-called *traceback* (an error message):

```
>>> 1/0
Traceback (most recent call last):
  File "<stdin>", line 1, in ?
ZeroDivisionError: integer division or modulo by zero
```

If such error messages were all you could use exceptions for, they wouldn't be very interesting. The fact is, however, that each exception is an instance of some class (in this case ZeroDivisionError), and these instances may be raised and caught in various ways, allowing you to trap the error and do something about it instead of just letting the entire program fail.

## Making Things Go Wrong . . . Your Way

As you've seen, exceptions are raised automatically when something is wrong. Before looking at how to deal with those exceptions, let's take a look at how you can raise exceptions yourself—and even create your own kinds of exceptions.

# The raise Statement

To raise an exception, you use the raise statement with an argument that is either a class (which should subclass Exception) or an instance. When using a class, an instance is created automatically Here is an example, using the built-in exception class Exception:

```
>>> raise Exception
Traceback (most recent call last):
  File "<stdin>", line 1, in ?
Exception
>>> raise Exception('hyperdrive overload')
Traceback (most recent call last):
  File "<stdin>", line 1, in ?
Exception: hyperdrive overload
```

The first example, raise Exception, raises a generic exception with no information about what went wrong. In the last example, I added the error message hyperdrive overload.

Many built-in classes are available. You can find a description of all of them in the Python Library Reference, in the section "Built-in Exceptions." You can also explore them yourself with the interactive interpreter. You can find all the built-in exceptions in the module exceptions (as well as in the built-in namespace). To list the contents of a module, you can use the dir function, which is described in Chapter 10:

```
>>> import exceptions
>>> dir(exceptions)
['ArithmeticError', 'AssertionError', 'AttributeError', ...]
```

In your interpreter, this list will be quite a lot longer; I've deleted most of the names in the interest of brevity. All of these exception classes can be used in your raise statements:

```
>>> raise ArithmeticError
Traceback (most recent call last):
  File "<stdin>", line 1, in ?
ArithmeticError
```

Table 8-1 describes some of the most important built-in exception classes.

**Table 8-1.** *Some Built-in Exceptions*

| Class Name | Description |
| --- | --- |
| Exception | The base class for all exceptions |
| AttributeError | Raised when attribute reference or assignment fails |
| IOError | Raised when trying to open a nonexistent file (among other things) |
| IndexError | Raised when using a nonexistent index on a sequence |
| KeyError | Raised when using a nonexistent key on a mapping |
| NameError | Raised when a name (variable) is not found |

| Class Name | Description |
| --- | --- |
| SyntaxError | Raised when the code is ill-formed |
| TypeError | Raised when a built-in operation or function is applied to an object of the wrong type |
| ValueError | Raised when a built-in operation or function is applied to an object with the correct type, but with an inappropriate value |
| ZeroDivisionError | Raised when the second argument of a division or modulo operation is zero |

## Custom Exception Classes

Although the built-in exceptions cover a lot of ground and are sufficient for many purposes, there are times when you might want to create your own. For example, in the hyperdrive overload example, wouldn't it be more natural to have a specific HyperdriveError class representing error conditions in the hyperdrive? It might seem that the error message is sufficient, but as you will see in the next section ("Catching Exceptions"), you can selectively handle certain types of exceptions based on their class. Thus, if you wanted to handle hyperdrive errors with special error-handling code, you would need a separate class for the exceptions.

So, how do you create exception classes? Just like any other class—but be sure to subclass Exception (either directly or indirectly, which means that subclassing any other built-in exception is okay). Thus, writing a custom exception basically amounts to something like this:

```
class SomeCustomException(Exception): pass
```

Really not much work, is it? (If you want, you can certainly add methods to your exception class as well.)

# Catching Exceptions

As mentioned earlier, the interesting thing about exceptions is that you can handle them (often called *trapping* or *catching* the exceptions). You do this with the try/except statement. Let's say you have created a program that lets the user enter two numbers and then divides one by the other, like this:

```
x = input('Enter the first number: ')
y = input('Enter the second number: ')
print x/y
```

This would work nicely until the user enters zero as the second number:

```
Enter the first number: 10
Enter the second number: 0
Traceback (most recent call last):
  File "exceptions.py", line 3, in ?
    print x/y
ZeroDivisionError: integer division or modulo by zero
```

To catch the exception and perform some error handling (in this case simply printing a more user-friendly error message), you could rewrite the program like this:

```
try:
    x = input('Enter the first number: ')
    y = input('Enter the second number: ')
    print x/y
except ZeroDivisionError:
    print "The second number can't be zero!"
```

It might seem that a simple if statement checking the value of y would be easier to use, and in this case, it might indeed be a better solution. But if you added more divisions to your program, you would need one if statement per division; by using try/except, you need only one error handler.

---

**Note** Exceptions propagate out of functions to where they're called, and if they're not caught there either, the exceptions will "bubble up" to the top level of the program. This means that you can use try/except to catch exceptions that are raised in other people's functions. For more details, see the section "Exceptions and Functions," later in this chapter.

---

## Look, Ma, No Arguments!

If you have caught an exception but you want to raise it again (pass it on, so to speak), you can call raise without any arguments. (You can also supply the exception explicitly if you catch it, as explained in the section "Catching the Object," later in this chapter.)

As an example of how this might be useful, consider a calculator class that has the capability to "muffle" ZeroDivisionError exceptions. If this behavior is turned on, the calculator prints out an error message instead of letting the exception propagate. This is useful if the calculator is used in an interactive session with a user, but if it is used internally in a program, raising an exception would be better. Therefore, the muffling can be turned off. Here is the code for such a class:

```
class MuffledCalculator:
    muffled = False
    def calc(self, expr):
        try:
            return eval(expr)
        except ZeroDivisionError:
            if self.muffled:
                print 'Division by zero is illegal'
            else:
                raise
```

---

**Note** If division by zero occurs and muffling is turned on, the calc method will (implicitly) return None. In other words, if you turn on muffling, you should not rely on the return value.

---

The following is an example of how this class may be used, both with and without muffling:

```
>>> calculator = MuffledCalculator()
>>> calculator.calc('10/2')
5
>>> calculator.calc('10/0') # No muffling
Traceback (most recent call last):
  File "<stdin>", line 1, in ?
  File "MuffledCalculator.py", line 6, in calc
    return eval(expr)
  File "<string>", line 0, in ?
ZeroDivisionError: integer division or modulo by zero
>>> calculator.muffled = True
>>> calculator.calc('10/0')
Division by zero is illegal
```

As you can see, when the calculator is not muffled, the ZeroDivisionError is caught but passed on.

## More Than One except Clause

If you run the program from the previous section again and enter a nonnumeric value at the prompt, another exception occurs:

```
Enter the first number: 10
Enter the second number: "Hello, world!"
Traceback (most recent call last):
  File "exceptions.py", line 4, in ?
    print x/y
TypeError: unsupported operand type(s) for /: 'int' and 'str'
```

Because the except clause looked for only ZeroDivisionError exceptions, this one slipped through and halted the program. To catch this exception as well, you can simply add another except clause to the same try/except statement:

```
try:
    x = input('Enter the first number: ')
    y = input('Enter the second number: ')
    print x/y
except ZeroDivisionError:
    print "The second number can't be zero!"
except TypeError:
    print "That wasn't a number, was it?"
```

This time using an if statement would be more difficult. How do you check whether a value can be used in division? There are a number of ways, but by far the best way is, in fact, to simply divide the values to see if it works.

Also notice how the exception handling doesn't clutter the original code. Adding a lot of `if` statements to check for possible error conditions could easily have made the code quite unreadable.

## Catching Two Exceptions with One Block

If you want to catch more than one exception type with one block, you can specify them all in a tuple, as follows:

```
try:
    x = input('Enter the first number: ')
    y = input('Enter the second number: ')

    print x/y
except (ZeroDivisionError, TypeError, NameError):
    print 'Your numbers were bogus...'
```

In the preceding code, if the user either enters a string or something other than a number, or if the second number is zero, the same error message is printed. Simply printing an error message isn't very helpful, of course. An alternative could be to keep asking for numbers until the division works. I show you how to do that in the section "When All Is Well," later in this chapter.

Note that the parentheses around the exceptions in the except clause are important. A common error is to omit these parentheses, in which case you may end up with something other than what you want. For an explanation, see the next section, "Catching the Object."

## Catching the Object

If you want access to the exception object itself in an except clause, you can use two arguments instead of one. (Note that even when you are catching multiple exceptions, you are supplying except with only one argument—a tuple.) This can be useful (for example) if you want your program to keep running, but you want to log the error somehow (perhaps just printing it out to the user). The following is a sample program that prints out the exception (if it occurs), but keeps running:

```
try:
    x = input('Enter the first number: ')
    y = input('Enter the second number: ')
    print x/y
except (ZeroDivisionError, TypeError), e:
    print e
```

---

■**Note**  In Python 3.0, the except clause will be written except (ZeroDivisionError, TypeError) as e.

---

The except clause in this little program again catches two types of exceptions, but because you also explicitly catch the object itself, you can print it out so the user can see what happened. (You see a more useful application of this later in this chapter, in the section "When All Is Well.")

## A Real Catchall

Even if the program handles several types of exceptions, some may still slip through. For example, using the same division program, simply try to press Enter at the prompt, without writing anything. You should get an error message and some information about what went wrong (a *stack trace*), somewhat like this:

```
Traceback (most recent call last):
  File 'exceptions.py', line 3, in ?
    x = input('Enter the first number: ')
  File '<string>', line 0

    ^
SyntaxError: unexpected EOF while parsing
```

This exception got through the try/except statement—and rightly so. You hadn't foreseen that this could happen and weren't prepared for it. In these cases, it is better that the program crash immediately (so you can see what's wrong) than that it simply hide the exception with a try/except statement that isn't meant to catch it.

However, if you *do* want to catch *all* exceptions in a piece of code, you can simply omit the exception class from the except clause:

```
try:
    x = input('Enter the first number: ')
    y = input('Enter the second number: ')
    print x/y
except:
    print 'Something wrong happened...'
```

Now you can do practically whatever you want:

```
Enter the first number: "This" is *completely* illegal 123
Something wrong happened...
```

---

■**Caution**  Catching all exceptions like this is risky business because it will hide errors you haven't thought of as well as those you're prepared for. It will also trap attempts by the user to terminate execution by Ctrl-C, attempts by functions you call to terminate by sys.exit, and so on. In most cases, it would be better to use except Exception, e and perhaps do some checking on the exception object, e.

---

## When All Is Well

In some cases, it can be useful to have a block of code that is executed *unless* something bad happens; as with conditionals and loops, you can add an else clause to the try/except statement:

```
try:
    print 'A simple task'
except:
    print 'What? Something went wrong?'
else:
    print 'Ah... It went as planned.'
```

If you run this, you get the following output:

```
A simple task
Ah... It went as planned.
```

With this else clause, you can implement the loop hinted at in the section "Catching Two Exceptions with One Block," earlier in this chapter:

```
while True:
    try:
        x = input('Enter the first number: ')
        y = input('Enter the second number: ')
        value = x/y
        print 'x/y is', value
    except:
        print 'Invalid input. Please try again.'
    else:
        break
```

Here, the loop is broken (by the break statement in the else clause) only when no exception is raised. In other words, as long as something wrong happens, the program keeps asking for new input. The following is an example run:

```
Enter the first number: 1
Enter the second number: 0
Invalid input. Please try again.
Enter the first number: 'foo'
Enter the second number: 'bar'
Invalid input. Please try again.
Enter the first number: baz
Invalid input. Please try again.
Enter the first number: 10
Enter the second number: 2
x/y is 5
```

As mentioned previously, an alternative to using an empty except clause is to catch all exceptions of the Exception class (which will catch all exceptions of any subclass as well). You cannot be 100 percent certain that you'll catch everything then, because the code in your try/except statement may be naughty and use the old-fashioned string exceptions, or perhaps create a custom exception that doesn't subclass Exception. However, if you go with the except Exception version, you can use the technique from the section "Catching the Object," earlier in this chapter, to print out a more instructive error message in your little division program:

```
while True:
    try:
        x = input('Enter the first number: ')
        y = input('Enter the second number: ')
        value = x/y
        print 'x/y is', value
    except Exception, e:
        print 'Invalid input:', e
        print 'Please try again'
    else:
        break
```

The following is a sample run:

```
Enter the first number: 1
Enter the second number: 0
Invalid input: integer division or modulo by zero
Please try again
Enter the first number: 'x'
Enter the second number: 'y'
Invalid input: unsupported operand type(s) for /: 'str' and 'str'
Please try again
Enter the first number: quuux
Invalid input: name 'quuux' is not defined
Please try again
Enter the first number: 10
Enter the second number: 2
x/y is 5
```

## And Finally . . .

Finally, there is the finally clause. You use it to do housekeeping after a possible exception. It is combined with a try clause:

```
x = None
try:
    x = 1/0
```

```
finally:
    print 'Cleaning up...'
    del x
```

In the preceding example, you are *guaranteed* that the `finally` clause will be executed, no matter what exceptions occur in the try clause. The reason for initializing x before the `try` clause is that otherwise it would never be assigned a value because of the `ZeroDivisionError`. This would lead to an exception when using `del` on it within the `finally` clause, which you *wouldn't* catch.

If you run this, the cleanup comes *before* the program crashes and burns:

```
Cleaning up...
Traceback (most recent call last):
  File "C:\python\div.py", line 4, in ?
    x = 1/0
ZeroDivisionError: integer division or modulo by zero
```

While using `del` to remove a variable is a rather silly kind of cleanup, the `finally` clause may be quite useful for closing files or network sockets and the like. (More on those in Chapter 14.)

You can also combine try, except, `finally`, and `else` (or just three of them) in a single statement:

```
try:
    1/0
except NameError:
    print "Unknown variable"
else:
    print "That went well!"
finally:
    print "Cleaning up."
```

---

■**Note** In Python versions prior to 2.5, the `finally` clause had to be used on its own—it couldn't be used in the same `try` statement as an `except` clause. If you wanted both, you needed to wrap two statements. From Python 2.5 onwards, you can combine these to your heart's content, though.

---

# Exceptions and Functions

Exceptions and functions work together quite naturally. If an exception is raised inside a function, and isn't handled there, it propagates (*bubbles up*) to the place where the function was called. If it isn't handled there either, it continues propagating until it reaches the main program (the global scope), and if there is no exception handler there, the program halts with a stack trace. Let's take a look at an example:

```
>>> def faulty():
...     raise Exception('Something is wrong')
...
```

```
>>> def ignore_exception():
...     faulty()
...

>>> def handle_exception():
...     try:
...         faulty()
...     except:
...         print 'Exception handled'
...
>>> ignore_exception()
Traceback (most recent call last):
  File '<stdin>', line 1, in ?
  File '<stdin>', line 2, in ignore_exception
  File '<stdin>', line 2, in faulty
Exception: Something is wrong
>>> handle_exception()
Exception handled
```

As you can see, the exception raised in `faulty` propagates through `faulty` and `ignore_exception`, and finally causes a stack trace. Similarly, it propagates through to `handle_exception`, but there it is handled with a `try`/`except` statement.

# The Zen of Exceptions

Exception handling isn't very complicated. If you know that some part of your code may cause a certain kind of exception, and you don't simply want your program to terminate with a stack trace if and when that happens, then you add the necessary `try`/`except` or `try`/`finally` statements (or some combination thereof) to deal with it, as needed.

Sometimes, you can accomplish the same thing with conditional statements as you can with exception handling, but the conditional statements will probably end up being less natural and less readable. On the other hand, some things that might seem like natural applications of `if`/`else` may in fact be implemented much better with `try`/`except`. Let's take a look at a couple of examples.

Let's say you have a dictionary and you want to print the value stored under a specific key, if it is there. If it isn't there, you don't want to do anything. The code might be something like this:

```
def describePerson(person):
    print 'Description of', person['name']
    print 'Age:', person['age']
    if 'occupation' in person:
        print 'Occupation:', person['occupation']
```

If you supply this function with a dictionary containing the name Throatwobbler Mangrove and the age 42 (but no occupation), you get the following output:

```
Description of Throatwobbler Mangrove
Age: 42
```

If you add the occupation "camper," you get the following output:

```
Description of Throatwobbler Mangrove
Age: 42
Occupation: camper
```

The code is intuitive, but a bit inefficient (although the main concern here is really code simplicity). It has to look up the key 'occupation' twice—once to see whether the key exists (in the condition) and once to get the value (to print it out). An alternative definition is as follows:

```
def describePerson(person):
    print 'Description of', person['name']
    print 'Age:', person['age']
    try:
        print 'Occupation: ' + person['occupation']
    except KeyError: pass
```

**■Note**  I use + instead of a comma for printing the occupation here; otherwise, the string 'Occupation:' would have been printed before the exception is raised.

Here, the function simply assumes that the key 'occupation' is present. If you assume that it normally is, this saves some effort. The value will be fetched and printed—no extra fetch to check whether it is indeed there. If the key doesn't exist, a KeyError exception is raised, which is trapped by the except clause.

You may also find try/except useful when checking whether an object has a specific attribute. Let's say you want to check whether an object has a write attribute, for example. Then you could use code like this:

```
try:
    obj.write
except AttributeError:
    print 'The object is not writeable'
else:
    print 'The object is writeable'
```

Here the try clause simply accesses the attribute without doing anything useful with it. If an AttributeError is raised, the object doesn't have the attribute; otherwise, it has the attribute. This is a natural alternative to the getattr solution introduced in Chapter 7 (in the section "Interfaces and Introspection"). Which one you prefer is largely a matter of taste. Indeed, getattr is internally implemented in exactly this way: it tries to access the attribute and catches the AttributeError that this attempt may raise.

Note that the gain in efficiency here isn't great. (It's more like really, really tiny.) In general (unless your program is having performance problems), you shouldn't worry about that sort of optimization too much. The point is that using try/except statements is in many cases much more natural (more "Pythonic") than if/else, and you should get into the habit of using them where you can.[1]

# A Quick Summary

The main topics covered in this chapter are as follows:

**Exception objects**: Exceptional situations (such as when an error has occurred) are represented by exception objects. These can be manipulated in several ways, but if ignored, they terminate your program.

**Warnings**: Warnings are similar to exceptions, but will (in general) just print out an error message.

**Raising exceptions**: You can raise exceptions with the raise statement. It accepts either an exception class or an exception instance as its argument. You can also supply two arguments (an exception and an error message). If you call raise with no arguments in an except clause, it "reraises" the exception caught by that clause.

**Custom exception classes**: You can create your own kinds of exceptions by subclassing Exception.

**Catching exceptions**: You catch exceptions with the except clause of a try statement. If you don't specify a class in the except clause, all exceptions are caught. You can specify more than one class by putting them in a tuple. If you give two arguments to except, the second is bound to the exception object. You can have several except clauses in the same try/except statement, to react differently to different exceptions.

else **clauses**: You can use an else clause in addition to except. The else clause is executed if no exceptions are raised in the main try block.

finally: You can use try/finally if you need to make sure that some code (for example, cleanup code) is executed, regardless of whether or not an exception is raised. This code is then put in the finally clause.

**Exceptions and functions**: When you raise an exception inside a function, it propagates to the place where the function was called. (The same goes for methods.)

---

1. The preference for try/except in Python is often explained through Rear Admiral Grace Hopper's words of wisdom, "It's easier to ask forgiveness than permission." This strategy of simply trying to do something and dealing with any errors, rather than doing a lot of checking up front, is called the *Leap Before You Look* idiom.

## New Functions in This Chapter

| Function | Description |
| --- | --- |
| `warnings.filterwarnings(action, ...)` | Used to filter out warnings |

## What Now?

While you might think that the material in this chapter was exceptional (pardon the pun), the next chapter is truly magical. Well, *almost* magical.

■■■

# CHAPTER 9

# Magic Methods, Properties, and Iterators

In Python, some names are spelled in a peculiar manner, with two leading and two trailing underscores. You have already encountered some of these (__future__, for example). This spelling signals that the name has a special significance—you should never invent such names for your own programs. One very prominent set of such names in the language consists of the *magic* (or special) method names. If your object implements one of these methods, that method will be called under specific circumstances (exactly which will depend on the name) by Python. There is rarely any need to call these methods directly.

This chapter deals with a few important magic methods (most notably the __init__ method and some methods dealing with item access, allowing you to create sequences or mappings of your own). It also tackles two related topics: properties (dealt with through magic methods in previous versions of Python, but now handled by the property function), and iterators (which use the magic method __iter__ to enable them to be used in for loops). You'll find a meaty example at the end of the chapter, which uses some of the things you have learned so far to solve a fairly difficult problem.

## Before We Begin . . .

A while ago (in version 2.2), the way Python objects work changed quite a bit. This change has several consequences, most of which won't be important to you as a beginning Python programmer.[1] One thing is worth noting, though: even if you're using a recent version of Python, some features (such as properties and the super function) won't work on "old-style" classes. To make your classes "new-style," you should either put the assignment __metaclass__ = type at the top of your modules (as mentioned in Chapter 7) or (directly or indirectly) subclass the built-in class (or, actually, type) object (or some other new-style class). Consider the following two classes:

```
class NewStyle(object):
    more_code_here
```

---

1. For a thorough description of the differences between old-style and new-style classes, see Chapter 8 in Alex Martelli's *Python in a Nutshell* (O'Reilly & Associates, 2003).

```
class OldStyle:
    more_code_here
```

Of these two, NewStyle is a new-style class; OldStyle is an old-style class. If the file began with __metaclass__ = type, though, both classes would be new-style.

---

■**Note**   You can also assign to the __metaclass__ variable in the class scope of your class. That would set the metaclass of only that class. Metaclasses are the classes of other classes (or types)—a rather advanced topic. For more information about metaclasses, take a look at the (somewhat technical) article called "Unifying types and classes in Python 2.2" by Guido van Rossum (http://python.org/2.2/descrintro.html), or do a web search for the term "python metaclasses."

---

I do not explicitly set the metaclass (or subclass object) in all the examples in this book. However, if you do not specifically need to make your programs compatible with old versions of Python, I advise you to make all your classes new-style, and consistently use features such as the super function (described in the section "Using the super Function," later in this chapter).

---

■**Note**   There are no "old-style" classes in Python 3.0, and no need to explicitly subclass object or set the metaclass to type. All classes will implicitly be subclasses of object—directly, if you don't specify a superclass, or indirectly otherwise.

---

# Constructors

The first magic method we'll take a look at is the constructor. In case you have never heard the word *constructor* before, it's basically a fancy name for the kind of initializing method I have already used in some of the examples, under the name init. What separates constructors from ordinary methods, however, is that the constructors are called automatically right after an object has been created. Thus, instead of doing what I've been doing up until now:

```
>>> f = FooBar()
>>> f.init()
```

constructors make it possible to simply do this:

```
>>> f = FooBar()
```

Creating constructors in Python is really easy; simply change the init method's name from the plain old init to the magic version, __init__:

```
class FooBar:
    def __init__(self):
        self.somevar = 42
```

```
>>> f = FooBar()
>>> f.somevar
42
```

Now, that's pretty nice. But you may wonder what happens if you give the constructor some parameters to work with. Consider the following:

```
class FooBar:
    def __init__(self, value=42):
        self.somevar = value
```

How do you think you could use this? Because the parameter is optional, you certainly could go on like nothing had happened. But what if you wanted to use it (or you hadn't made it optional)? I'm sure you've guessed it, but let me show you anyway:

```
>>> f = FooBar('This is a constructor argument')
>>> f.somevar
'This is a constructor argument'
```

Of all the magic methods in Python, __init__ is quite certainly the one you'll be using the most.

---

■**Note** Python has a magic method called __del__, also known as the *destructor*. It is called just before the object is destroyed (garbage-collected), but because you cannot really know when (or if) this happens, I advise you to stay away from __del__ if at all possible.

---

## Overriding Methods in General, and the Constructor in Particular

In Chapter 7, you learned about inheritance. Each class may have one or more superclasses, from which they inherit behavior. If a method is called (or an attribute is accessed) on an instance of class B and it is not found, its superclass A will be searched. Consider the following two classes:

```
class A:
    def hello(self):
        print "Hello, I'm A."
```

```
class B(A):
    pass
```

Class A defines a method called hello, which is inherited by class B. Here is an example of how these classes work:

```
>>> a = A()
>>> b = B()
>>> a.hello()
Hello, I'm A.
>>> b.hello()
Hello, I'm A.
```

Because B does not define a hello method of its own, the original message is printed when hello is called.

One basic way of adding functionality in the subclass is simply to add methods. However, you may want to customize the inherited behavior by overriding some of the superclass's methods. For example, it is possible for B to override the hello method. Consider this modified definition of B:

```
class B(A):
    def hello(self):
        print "Hello, I'm B."
```

Using this definition, b.hello() will give a different result:

```
>>> b = B()
>>> b.hello()
Hello, I'm B.
```

Overriding is an important aspect of the inheritance mechanism in general, and may be especially important for constructors. Constructors are there to initialize the state of the newly constructed object, and most subclasses will need to have initialization code of their own, in addition to that of the superclass. Even though the mechanism for overriding is the same for all methods, you will most likely encounter one particular problem more often when dealing with constructors than when overriding ordinary methods: if you override the constructor of a class, you need to call the constructor of the superclass (the class you inherit from) or risk having an object that isn't properly initialized.

Consider the following class, Bird:

```
class Bird:
    def __init__(self):
        self.hungry = True
    def eat(self):
        if self.hungry:
            print 'Aaaah...'
            self.hungry = False
        else:
            print 'No, thanks!'
```

This class defines one of the most basic capabilities of all birds: eating. Here is an example of how you might use it:

```
>>> b = Bird()
>>> b.eat()
Aaaah...
>>> b.eat()
No, thanks!
```

As you can see from this example, once the bird has eaten, it is no longer hungry. Now consider the subclass SongBird, which adds singing to the repertoire of behaviors:

```
class SongBird(Bird):
    def __init__(self):
        self.sound = 'Squawk!'
    def sing(self):
        print self.sound
```

The SongBird class is just as easy to use as Bird:

```
>>> sb = SongBird()
>>> sb.sing()
Squawk!
```

Because SongBird is a subclass of Bird, it inherits the eat method, but if you try to call it, you'll discover a problem:

```
>>> sb.eat()
Traceback (most recent call last):
  File "<stdin>", line 1, in ?
  File "birds.py", line 6, in eat
    if self.hungry:
AttributeError: SongBird instance has no attribute 'hungry'
```

The exception is quite clear about what's wrong: the SongBird has no attribute called hungry. Why should it? In SongBird, the constructor is overridden, and the new constructor doesn't contain any initialization code dealing with the hungry attribute. To rectify the situation, the SongBird constructor must call the constructor of its superclass, Bird, to make sure that the basic initialization takes place. There are basically two ways of doing this: by calling the unbound version of the superclass's constructor or by using the super function. In the next two sections, I explain both techniques.

## Calling the Unbound Superclass Constructor

The approach described in this section is, perhaps, mainly of historical interest. With current versions of Python, using the super function (as explained in the following section) is clearly the way to go (and with Python 3.0, it will be even more so). However, much existing code uses the approach described in this section, so you need to know about it. Also, it can be quite instructive—it's a nice example of the difference between bound and unbound methods.

Now, let's get down to business. If you find the title of this section a bit intimidating, relax. Calling the constructor of a superclass is, in fact, very easy (and useful). I'll start by giving you the solution to the problem posed at the end of the previous section:

```python
class SongBird(Bird):
    def __init__(self):
        Bird.__init__(self)
        self.sound = 'Squawk!'
    def sing(self):
        print self.sound
```

Only one line has been added to the SongBird class, containing the code Bird.__init__ (self). Before I explain what this really means, let me just show you that this really works:

```python
>>> sb = SongBird()
>>> sb.sing()
Squawk!
>>> sb.eat()
Aaaah...
>>> sb.eat()
No, thanks!
```

But why does this work? When you retrieve a method from an instance, the self argument of the method is automatically *bound* to the instance (a so-called bound method). You've seen several examples of that. However, if you retrieve the method directly from the class (such as in Bird.__init__), there is no instance to which to bind. Therefore, you are free to supply any self you want to. Such a method is called *unbound*, which explains the title of this section.

By supplying the current instance as the self argument to the unbound method, the song-bird gets the full treatment from its superclass's constructor (which means that it has its hungry attribute set).

## Using the super Function

If you're not stuck with an old version of Python, the super function is really the way to go. It works only with new-style classes, but you should be using those anyway. It is called with the current class and instance as its arguments, and any method you call on the returned object will be fetched from the superclass rather than the current class. So, instead of using Bird in the SongBird constructor, you can use super(SongBird, self). Also, the __init__ method can be called in a normal (bound) fashion.

---

**■Note** In Python 3.0, super can be called without any arguments, and will do its job as if "by magic."

---

The following is an updated version of the bird example:

```
__metaclass__ = type # super only works with new-style classes

class Bird:
    def __init__(self):
        self.hungry = True
    def eat(self):
        if self.hungry:
            print 'Aaaah...'
            self.hungry = False
        else:
            print 'No, thanks!'

class SongBird(Bird):
    def __init__(self):
        super(SongBird, self).__init__()
        self.sound = 'Squawk!'
    def sing(self):
        print self.sound
```

This new-style version works just like the old-style one:

```
>>> sb = SongBird()
>>> sb.sing()
Squawk!
>>> sb.eat()
Aaaah...
>>> sb.eat()
No, thanks!
```

## WHAT'S SO SUPER ABOUT SUPER?

In my opinion, the super function is more intuitive than calling unbound methods on the superclass directly, but that is not its only strength. The super function is actually quite smart, so even if you have multiple super-classes, you only need to use super once (provided that all the superclass constructors also use super). Also, some obscure situations that are tricky when using old-style classes (for example, when two of your super-classes share a superclass) are automatically dealt with by new-style classes and super. You don't need to understand exactly how it works internally, but you should be aware that, in most cases, it is clearly superior to calling the unbound constructors (or other methods) of your superclasses.

So, what does super return, really? Normally, you don't need to worry about it, and you can just pretend it returns the superclass you need. What it actually does is return a *super object*, which will take care of method resolution for you. When you access an attribute on it, it will look through all your superclasses (and super-superclasses, and so forth until it finds the attribute (or raises an AttributeError).

# Item Access

Although __init__ is by far the most important special method you'll encounter, many others are available to enable you to achieve quite a lot of cool things. One useful set of magic methods described in this section allows you to create objects that behave like sequences or mappings.

The basic sequence and mapping protocol is pretty simple. However, to implement all the functionality of sequences and mappings, there are many magic methods to implement. Luckily, there are some shortcuts, but I'll get to that.

---

■**Note** The word *protocol* is often used in Python to describe the rules governing some form of behavior. This is somewhat similar to the notion of *interfaces* mentioned in Chapter 7. The protocol says something about which methods you should implement and what those methods should do. Because polymorphism in Python is based on only the object's behavior (and not on its *ancestry*, for example, its class or superclass, and so forth), this is an important concept: where other languages might require an object to belong to a certain class or to implement a certain interface, Python often simply requires it to follow some given protocol. So, to *be* a sequence, all you have to do is follow the sequence protocol.

---

## The Basic Sequence and Mapping Protocol

Sequences and mappings are basically collections of *items*. To implement their basic behavior (protocol), you need two magic methods if your objects are immutable, or four if they are mutable:

__len__(self): This method should return the number of items contained in the collection. For a sequence, this would simply be the number of elements. For a mapping, it would be the number of key-value pairs. If __len__ returns zero (and you don't implement __nonzero__, which overrides this behavior), the object is treated as *false* in a Boolean context (as with empty lists, tuples, strings, and dictionaries).

__getitem__(self, key): This should return the value corresponding to the given key. For a sequence, the key should be an integer from zero to $n-1$ (or, it could be negative, as noted later), where $n$ is the length of the sequence. For a mapping, you could really have any kind of keys.

__setitem__(self, key, value): This should store value in a manner associated with key, so it can later be retrieved with __getitem__. Of course, you define this method only for mutable objects.

__delitem__(self, key): This is called when someone uses the del statement on a part of the object, and should delete the element associated with key. Again, only mutable objects (and not all of them—only those for which you want to let items be removed) should define this method.

Some extra requirements are imposed on these methods:

- For a sequence, if the key is a negative integer, it should be used to count from the end. In other words, treat x[-n] the same as x[len(x)-n].

- If the key is of an inappropriate type (such as a string key used on a sequence), a TypeError may be raised.

- If the index of a sequence is of the right type, but outside the allowed range, an IndexError should be raised.

Let's have a go at it—let's see if we can create an infinite sequence:

```
def checkIndex(key):
    """
    Is the given key an acceptable index?

    To be acceptable, the key should be a non-negative integer. If it
    is not an integer, a TypeError is raised; if it is negative, an
    IndexError is raised (since the sequence is of infinite length).
    """
    if not isinstance(key, (int, long)): raise TypeError
    if key<0: raise IndexError


class ArithmeticSequence:
    def __init__(self, start=0, step=1):
        """
        Initialize the arithmetic sequence.

        start   - the first value in the sequence
        step    - the difference between two adjacent values
        changed - a dictionary of values that have been modified by
                  the user
        """
        self.start = start                  # Store the start value
        self.step = step                    # Store the step value
        self.changed = {}                   # No items have been modified

    def __getitem__(self, key):
        """
        Get an item from the arithmetic sequence.
        """
        checkIndex(key)

        try: return self.changed[key]       # Modified?
        except KeyError:                    # otherwise...
            return self.start + key*self.step   # ...calculate the value
```

```
    def __setitem__(self, key, value):
        """
        Change an item in the arithmetic sequence.
        """
        checkIndex(key)

        self.changed[key] = value                 # Store the changed value
```

This implements an *arithmetic sequence*—a sequence of numbers in which each is greater than the previous one by a constant amount. The first value is given by the constructor parameter start (defaulting to zero), while the step between the values is given by step (defaulting to one). You allow the user to change some of the elements by keeping the exceptions to the general rule in a dictionary called changed. If the element hasn't been changed, it is calculated as self.start + key*self.step.

Here is an example of how you can use this class:

```
>>> s = ArithmeticSequence(1, 2)
>>> s[4]
9
>>> s[4] = 2
>>> s[4]
2
>>> s[5]
11
```

Note that I want it to be illegal to delete items, which is why I haven't implemented __del__:

```
>>> del s[4]
Traceback (most recent call last):
  File "<stdin>", line 1, in ?
AttributeError: ArithmeticSequence instance has no attribute '__delitem__'
```

Also, the class has no __len__ method because it is of infinite length.

If an illegal type of index is used, a TypeError is raised, and if the index is the correct type but out of range (that is, negative in this case), an IndexError is raised:

```
>>> s["four"]
Traceback (most recent call last):
  File "<stdin>", line 1, in ?
  File "arithseq.py", line 31, in __getitem__
    checkIndex(key)
  File "arithseq.py", line 10, in checkIndex
    if not isinstance(key, int): raise TypeError
```

```
TypeError
>>> s[-42]
Traceback (most recent call last):
  File "<stdin>", line 1, in ?
  File "arithseq.py", line 31, in __getitem__
    checkIndex(key)
  File "arithseq.py", line 11, in checkIndex
    if key<0: raise IndexError
IndexError
```

The index checking is taken care of by a utility function I've written for the purpose, checkIndex.

One thing that might surprise you about the checkIndex function is the use of isinstance (which you should rarely use because type or class checking goes against the grain of Python's polymorphism). I've used it because the language reference explicitly states that the index should be an integer (this includes long integers). And complying with standards is one of the (very few) valid reasons for using type checking.

---

**Note**  You can simulate slicing, too, if you like. When slicing an instance that supports __getitem__, a slice object is supplied as the key. Slice objects are described in the Python Library Reference (http://python.org/doc/lib) in Section 2.1, "Built-in Functions," under the slice function. Python 2.5 also has the more specialized method called __index__, which allows you to use noninteger limits in your slices. This is mainly useful only if you wish to go beyond the basic sequence protocol, though.

---

## Subclassing list, dict, and str

While the four methods of the basic sequence/mapping protocol will get you far, the official language reference also recommends that several other magic and ordinary methods be implemented (see the section "Emulating container types" in the Python Reference Manual, http://www.python.org/doc/ref/sequence-types.html), including the __iter__ method, which I describe in the section "Iterators," later in this chapter. Implementing all these methods (to make your objects fully polymorphically equivalent to lists or dictionaries) is a lot of work and hard to get right. If you want custom behavior in only *one* of the operations, it makes no sense that you should need to reimplement all of the others. It's just programmer laziness (also called common sense).

So what should you do? The magic word is *inheritance*. Why reimplement all of these things when you can inherit them? The standard library comes with three ready-to-use implementations of the sequence and mapping protocols (UserList, UserString, and UserDict), and in current versions of Python, you can subclass the built-in types themselves. (Note that this is mainly useful if your class's behavior is close to the default. If you need to reimplement most of the methods, it might be just as easy to write a new class.)

So, if you want to implement a sequence type that behaves similarly to the built-in lists, you can simply subclass list.

---

■**Note**  When you subclass a built-in type such as list, you are indirectly subclassing object. Therefore your class is automatically new-style, which means that features such as the super function are available.

---

Let's just do a quick example—a list with an access counter:

```
class CounterList(list):
    def __init__(self, *args):
        super(CounterList, self).__init__(*args)
        self.counter = 0
    def __getitem__(self, index):
        self.counter += 1
        return super(CounterList, self).__getitem__(index)
```

The CounterList class relies heavily on the behavior of its subclass superclass (list). Any methods not overridden by CounterList (such as append, extend, index, and so on) may be used directly. In the two methods that *are* overridden, super is used to call the superclass version of the method, adding only the necessary behavior of initializing the counter attribute (in __init__) and updating the counter attribute (in __getitem__).

---

■**Note**  Overriding __getitem__ is not a bulletproof way of trapping user access because there are other ways of accessing the list contents, such as through the pop method.

---

Here is an example of how CounterList may be used:

```
>>> cl = CounterList(range(10))
>>> cl
[0, 1, 2, 3, 4, 5, 6, 7, 8, 9]
>>> cl.reverse()
>>> cl
[9, 8, 7, 6, 5, 4, 3, 2, 1, 0]
>>> del cl[3:6]
>>> cl
[9, 8, 7, 3, 2, 1, 0]
>>> cl.counter
0
>>> cl[4] + cl[2]
9
>>> cl.counter
2
```

As you can see, CounterList works just like list in most respects. However, it has a counter attribute (initially zero), which is incremented each time you access a list element. After performing the addition cl[4] + cl[2], the counter has been incremented twice, to the value 2.

# More Magic

Special (magic) names exist for many purposes—what I've shown you so far is just a small taste of what is possible. Most of the magic methods available are meant for fairly advanced use, so I won't go into detail here. However, if you are interested, it is possible to emulate numbers, make objects that can be called as if they were functions, influence how objects are compared, and much more. For more information about which magic methods are available, see section "Special method names" in the Python Reference Manual (http://www.python.org/doc/ref/specialnames.html).

# Properties

In Chapter 7, I mentioned *accessor methods*. Accessors are simply methods with names such as getHeight and setHeight, and are used to retrieve or rebind some attribute (which may be private to the class—see the section "Privacy Revisited" in Chapter 7). Encapsulating state variables (attributes) like this can be important if certain actions must be taken when accessing the given attribute. For example, consider the following Rectangle class:

```
class Rectangle:
    def __init__(self):
        self.width = 0
        self.height = 0
    def setSize(self, size):
        self.width, self.height = size
    def getSize(self):
        return self.width, self.height
```

Here is an example of how you can use the class:

```
>>> r = Rectangle()
>>> r.width = 10
>>> r.height = 5
>>> r.getSize()
(10, 5)
>>> r.setSize((150, 100))
>>> r.width
150
```

The getSize and setSize methods are accessors for a fictitious attribute called size—which is simply the tuple consisting of width and height. (Feel free to replace this with something more exciting, such as the area of the rectangle or the length of its diagonal.) This code isn't directly wrong, but it is flawed. The programmer using this class shouldn't need to worry about how it is implemented (encapsulation). If you someday wanted to change the implementation so that size was a real attribute and width and height were calculated on the fly, you would need to wrap *them* in accessors, and any programs using the class would also have to be rewritten. The client code (the code using your code) should be able to treat all your attributes in the same manner.

So what is the solution? Should you wrap all your attributes in accessors? That is a possibility, of course. However, it would be impractical (and kind of silly) if you had a lot of simple attributes, because you would need to write many accessors that did nothing but retrieve or set these attributes, with no useful action taken. This smells of *copy-paste* programming, or *cookie-cutter code,* which is clearly a bad thing (although quite common for this specific problem in certain languages). Luckily, Python can hide your accessors for you, making all of your attributes look alike. Those attributes that are defined through their accessors are often called *properties.*

Python actually has two mechanisms for creating properties in Python. I'll focus on the most recent one, the property function, which works only on new-style classes. Then I'll give you a short description of how to implement properties with magic methods.

## The property Function

Using the property function is delightfully simple. If you have already written a class such as Rectangle from the previous section, you need to add only a single line of code (in addition to subclassing object, or using __metaclass__ = type):

```
__metaclass__ = type

class Rectangle:
    def __init__(self):
        self.width = 0
        self.height = 0
    def setSize(self, size):
        self.width, self.height = size
    def getSize(self):
        return self.width, self.height
    size = property(getSize, setSize)
```

In this new version of Rectangle, a property is created with the property function with the accessor functions as arguments (the *getter* first, then the *setter*), and the name size is then bound to this property. After this, you no longer need to worry about how things are implemented, but can treat width, height, and size the same way:

```
>>> r = Rectangle()
>>> r.width = 10
>>> r.height = 5
>>> r.size
(10, 5)
>>> r.size = 150, 100
>>> r.width
150
```

As you can see, the `size` attribute is still subject to the calculations in `getSize` and `setSize`, but it looks just like a normal attribute.

---

■**Note**  If your properties are behaving oddly, make sure you're using a new-style class (by subclassing `object` either directly or indirectly—or by setting the metaclass directly). If you aren't, the *getter* part of the property will still work, but the *setter* may not (depending on your Python version). This can be a bit confusing.

---

In fact, the `property` function may be called with zero, one, three, or four arguments as well. If called without any arguments, the resulting property is neither readable nor writable. If called with only one argument (a getter method), the property is readable only. The third (optional) argument is a method used to *delete* the attribute (it takes no arguments). The fourth (optional) argument is a docstring. The parameters are called `fget`, `fset`, `fdel`, and `doc`—you can use them as keyword arguments if you want a property that, say, is only writable and has a docstring.

Although this section has been short (a testament to the simplicity of the `property` function), it is very important. The moral is this: with new-style classes, you should use `property` rather than accessors.

### BUT HOW DOES IT WORK?

In case you're curious about how `property` does its magic, I'll give you an explanation here. If you don't care, just skip ahead.

The fact is that `property` isn't really a function—it's a class whose instances have some magic methods that do all the work. The methods in question are `__get__`, `__set__`, and `__delete__`. Together, these three methods define the so-called *descriptor protocol*. An object implementing any of these methods is a descriptor. The special thing about descriptors is how they are accessed. For example, when reading an attribute (specifically, when accessing it in an instance, but when the attribute is defined in the class), if the attribute is bound to an object that implements `__get__`, the object won't simply be returned; instead, the `__get__` method will be called and the resulting value will be returned. This is, in fact, the mechanism underlying properties, bound methods, static and class methods (see the following section for more information), and `super`. A brief description of the descriptor protocol may be found in the Python Reference Manual (`http://python.org/doc/ref/descriptors.html`). A more thorough source of information is Raymond Hettinger's How-To Guide for Descriptors (`http://users.rcn.com/python/download/Descriptor.htm`).

## Static Methods and Class Methods

Before discussing the old way of implementing properties, let's take a slight detour, and look at another couple of features that are implemented in a similar manner to the new-style properties. Static methods and class methods are created by wrapping methods in objects of the `staticmethod` and `classmethod` types, respectively. Static methods are defined without `self` arguments, and they can be called directly on the class itself. Class methods are defined with a self-like parameter normally called `cls`. You can call class methods directly on the class object too, but the `cls` parameter then automatically is bound to the class. Here is a simple example:

```
__metaclass__ = type

class MyClass:

    def smeth():
        print 'This is a static method'
    smeth = staticmethod(smeth)

    def cmeth(cls):
        print 'This is a class method of', cls
    cmeth = classmethod(cmeth)
```

The technique of wrapping and replacing the methods manually like this is a bit tedious. In Python 2.4, a new syntax was introduced for wrapping methods like this, called *decorators*. (They actually work with any callable objects as wrappers, and can be used on both methods and functions.) You specify one or more decorators (which are applied in reverse order) by listing them above the method (or function), using the @ operator:

```
__metaclass__ = type

class MyClass:

    @staticmethod
    def smeth():
        print 'This is a static method'

    @classmethod
    def cmeth(cls):
        print 'This is a class method of', cls
```

Once you've defined these methods, they can be used like this (that is, without instantiating the class):

```
>>> MyClass.smeth()
This is a static method
>>> MyClass.cmeth()
This is a class method of <class '__main__.MyClass'>
```

Static methods and class methods haven't historically been important in Python, mainly because you could always use functions or bound methods instead, in some way, but also because the support hasn't really been there in earlier versions. So even though you may not see them used much in current code, they do have their uses (such as factory functions, if you've heard of those), and you may well think of some new ones.

## __getattr__, __setattr__, and Friends

It's possible to intercept every attribute access on an object. Among other things, you could use this to implement properties with old-style classes (where property won't necessarily work as it should). To have code executed when an attribute is accessed, you must use a couple of magic methods. The following four provide all the functionality you need (in old-style classes, you only use the last three):

__getattribute__(self, name): Automatically called when the attribute name is accessed. (This works correctly on new-style classes only.)

__getattr__(self, name): Automatically called when the attribute name is accessed and the object has no such attribute.

__setattr__(self, name, value): Automatically called when an attempt is made to bind the attribute name to value.

__delattr__(self, name): Automatically called when an attempt is made to delete the attribute name.

Although a bit trickier to use (and in some ways less efficient) than property, these magic methods are quite powerful, because you can write code in one of these methods that deals with several properties. (If you have a choice, though, stick with property.)

Here is the Rectangle example again, this time with magic methods:

```
class Rectangle:
    def __init__(self):
        self.width = 0
        self.height = 0
    def __setattr__(self, name, value):
        if name == 'size':
            self.width, self.height = value
        else:
            self.__dict__[name] = value
    def __getattr__(self, name):
        if name == 'size':
            return self.width, self.height
        else:
            raise AttributeError
```

As you can see, this version of the class needs to take care of additional administrative details. When considering this code example, it's important to note the following:

- The __setattr__ method is called even if the attribute in question is not size. Therefore, the method must take both cases into consideration: if the attribute is size, the same operation is performed as before; otherwise, the magic attribute __dict__ is used. It contains a dictionary with all the instance attributes. It is used instead of ordinary attribute assignment to avoid having __setattr__ called again (which would cause the program to loop endlessly).

- The __getattr__ method is called only if a normal attribute is not found, which means that if the given name is not size, the attribute does not exist, and the method raises an AttributeError. This is important if you want the class to work correctly with built-in functions such as hasattr and getattr. If the name *is* size, the expression found in the previous implementation is used.

---

**■Note** Just as there is an "endless loop" trap associated with __setattr__, there is a trap associated with __getattribute__. Because it intercepts *all* attribute accesses (in new-style classes), it will intercept accesses to __dict__ as well! The only safe way to access attributes on self inside __getattribute__ is to use the __getattribute__ method of the superclass (using super).

---

# Iterators

I've mentioned iterators (and iterables) briefly in preceding chapters. In this section, I go into some more detail. I cover only one magic method, __iter__, which is the basis of the iterator protocol.

## The Iterator Protocol

To *iterate* means to repeat something several times—what you do with loops. Until now I have iterated over only sequences and dictionaries in for loops, but the truth is that you can iterate over other objects, too: objects that implement the __iter__ method.

The __iter__ method returns an iterator, which is any object with a method called next, which is callable without any arguments. When you call the next method, the iterator should return its "next value." If the method is called, and the iterator has no more values to return, it should raise a StopIteration exception.

---

**■Note** The iterator protocol is changed a bit in Python 3.0. In the new protocol, iterator objects should have a method called __next__ rather than next, and a new built-in function called next may be used to access this method. In other words, next(it) is the equivalent of the pre-3.0 it.next().

---

What's the point? Why not just use a list? Because it may often be overkill. If you have a function that can compute values one by one, you may need them only one by one—not all at once, in a list, for example. If the number of values is large, the list may take up too much memory. But there are other reasons: using iterators is more general, simpler, and more elegant. Let's take a look at an example you couldn't do with a list, simply because the list would need to be of infinite length!

Our "list" is the sequence of Fibonacci numbers. An iterator for these could be the following:

```
class Fibs:
    def __init__(self):
        self.a = 0
        self.b = 1
    def next(self):
        self.a, self.b = self.b, self.a+self.b
        return self.a
    def __iter__(self):
        return self
```

Note that the iterator implements the __iter__ method, which will, in fact, return the iterator itself. In many cases, you would put the __iter__ method in *another* object, which you would use in the for loop. That would then return your iterator. It is recommended that iterators implement an __iter__ method of their own in addition (returning self, just as I did here), so they themselves can be used directly in for loops.

---

■**Note**  In formal terms, an object that implements the __iter__ method is *iterable*, and the object implementing next is the *iterator*.

---

First, make a Fibs object:

```
>>> fibs = Fibs()
```

You can then use it in a for loop—for example, to find the smallest Fibonacci number that is greater than 1,000:

```
>>> for f in fibs:
        if f > 1000:
            print f
            break
...
1597
```

Here, the loop stops because I issue a break inside it; if I didn't, the for loop would never end.

---

■**Tip**  The built-in function `iter` can be used to get an iterator from an iterable object:

```
>>> it = iter([1, 2, 3])
>>> it.next()
1
>>> it.next()
2
```

It can also be used to create an iterable from a function or other callable object (see the Python Library Reference, `http://docs.python.org/lib/`, for details).

---

## Making Sequences from Iterators

In addition to *iterating* over the iterators and iterables (which is what you normally do), you can convert them to sequences. In most contexts in which you can use a sequence (except in operations such as indexing or slicing), you can use an iterator (or an iterable object) instead. One useful example of this is explicitly converting an iterator to a list using the `list` constructor:

```
>>> class TestIterator:
        value = 0
        def next(self):
            self.value += 1
            if self.value > 10: raise StopIteration
            return self.value
        def __iter__(self):
            return self
...
>>> ti = TestIterator()
>>> list(ti)
[1, 2, 3, 4, 5, 6, 7, 8, 9, 10]
```

# Generators

Generators (also called *simple generators* for historical reasons) are relatively new to Python, and are (along with iterators) perhaps one of the most powerful features to come along for years. However, the generator concept is rather advanced, and it may take a while before it "clicks" and you see how it works or how it would be useful for you. Rest assured that while generators can help you write really elegant code, you can certainly write any program you wish without a trace of generators.

A generator is a kind of iterator that is defined with normal function syntax. Exactly how generators work is best shown through example. Let's first have a look at how you make them and use them, and then take a peek under the hood.

## Making a Generator

Making a generator is simple; it's just like making a function. I'm sure you are starting to tire of the good old Fibonacci sequence by now, so let me do something else. I'll make a function that flattens nested lists. The argument is a list that may look something like this:

```
nested = [[1, 2], [3, 4], [5]]
```

In other words, it's a list of lists. My function should then give me the numbers in order. Here's a solution:

```
def flatten(nested):
    for sublist in nested:
        for element in sublist:
            yield element
```

Most of this function is pretty simple. First, it iterates over all the sublists of the supplied nested list; then it iterates over the elements of each sublist in order. If the last line had been print element, for example, the function would have been easy to understand, right?

So what's new here is the yield statement. Any function that contains a yield statement is called a *generator*. And it's not just a matter of naming; it will behave quite differently from ordinary functions. The difference is that instead of returning *one* value, as you do with return, you can yield *several* values, one at a time. Each time a value is yielded (with yield), the function *freezes*; that is, it stops its execution at exactly that point and waits to be reawakened. When it is, it resumes its execution at the point where it stopped.

I can make use of all the values by iterating over the generator:

```
>>> nested = [[1, 2], [3, 4], [5]]
>>> for num in flatten(nested):
        print num

...
1
2
3
4
5
```

or

```
>>> list(flatten(nested))
[1, 2, 3, 4, 5]
```

## LOOPY GENERATORS

In Python 2.4, a relative of list comprehension (see Chapter 5) was introduced: *generator comprehension* (or *generator expressions*). It works in the same way as list comprehension, except that a list isn't constructed (and the "body" isn't looped over immediately). Instead, a generator is returned, allowing you to perform the computation step by step:

```
>>> g = ((i+2)**2 for i in range(2,27))
>>> g.next()
16
```

As you can see, this differs from list comprehension in the use of plain parentheses. In a simple case such as this, I might as well have used a list comprehension. However, if you wish to "wrap" an iterable object (possibly yielding a huge number of values), a list comprehension would void the advantages of iteration by immediately instantiating a list.

A neat bonus is that when using generator comprehension directly inside a pair of existing parentheses, such as in a function call, you don't need to add another pair. In other words, you can write pretty code like this:

```
sum(i**2 for i in range(10))
```

## A Recursive Generator

The generator I designed in the previous section could deal only with lists nested two levels deep, and to do that it used two for loops. What if you have a set of lists nested arbitrarily deeply? Perhaps you use them to represent some tree structure, for example. (You can also do that with specific tree classes, but the strategy is the same.) You need a for loop for each level of nesting, but because you don't know how many levels there are, you must change your solution to be more flexible. It's time to turn to the magic of recursion:

```
def flatten(nested):
    try:
        for sublist in nested:
            for element in flatten(sublist):
                yield element
    except TypeError:
        yield nested
```

When flatten is called, you have two possibilities (as is always the case when dealing with recursion): the *base* case and the *recursive* case. In the base case, the function is told to flatten a single element (for example, a number), in which case the for loop raises a TypeError (because you're trying to iterate over a number), and the generator simply yields the element.

If you are told to flatten a list (or any iterable), however, you need to do some work. You go through all the sublists (some of which may not really be lists) and call flatten on them. Then you yield all the elements of the flattened sublists by using another for loop. It may seem slightly magical, but it works:

```
>>> list(flatten([[[1],2],3,4,[5,[6,7]],8]))
[1, 2, 3, 4, 5, 6, 7, 8]
```

There is one problem with this, however. If `nested` is a string-like object (string, Unicode, UserString, and so on), it is a sequence and will not raise `TypeError`, yet you do *not* want to iterate over it.

---

■**Note**   There are two main reasons why you shouldn't iterate over string-like objects in the `flatten` function. First, you want to treat string-like objects as atomic values, not as sequences that should be flattened. Second, iterating over them would actually lead to infinite recursion because the first element of a string is another string of length one, and the first element of *that* string is the string itself!

---

To deal with this, you must add a test at the beginning of the generator. Trying to concatenate the object with a string and seeing if a `TypeError` results is the simplest and fastest way to check whether an object is string-like.[2] Here is the generator with the added test:

```
def flatten(nested):
    try:
        # Don't iterate over string-like objects:
        try: nested + ''
        except TypeError: pass
        else: raise TypeError
        for sublist in nested:
            for element in flatten(sublist):
                yield element
    except TypeError:
        yield nested
```

As you can see, if the expression `nested + ''` raises a `TypeError`, it is ignored; however, if the expression does *not* raise a `TypeError`, the `else` clause of the inner `try` statement raises a `TypeError` of its own. This causes the string-like object to be yielded as is (in the outer `except` clause). Got it?

Here is an example to demonstrate that this version works with strings as well:

```
>>> list(flatten(['foo', ['bar', ['baz']]]))
['foo', 'bar', 'baz']
```

Note that there is no type checking going on here. I don't test whether `nested` *is* a string (which I could do by using `isinstance`), only whether it *behaves* like one (that is, it can be concatenated with a string).

## Generators in General

If you followed the examples so far, you know how to use generators, more or less. You've seen that a generator is a function that contains the keyword `yield`. When it is called, the code in the function body is not executed. Instead, an iterator is returned. Each time a value is requested,

---

2. Thanks to Alex Martelli for pointing out this idiom and the importance of using it here.

the code in the generator is executed until a yield or a return is encountered. A yield means that a value should be yielded. A return means that the generator should stop executing (without yielding anything more; return can be called without arguments only when used inside a generator).

In other words, generators consist of two separate components: the *generator-function* and the *generator-iterator*. The generator-function is what is defined by the def statement containing a yield. The generator-iterator is what this function returns. In less precise terms, these two entities are often treated as one and collectively called *a generator*.

```
>>> def simple_generator():
        yield 1
...
>>> simple_generator
<function simple_generator at 153b44>
>>> simple_generator()
<generator object at 1510b0>
```

The iterator returned by the generator-function can be used just like any other iterator.

## Generator Methods

A relatively new feature of generators (added in Python 2.5) is the ability to supply generators with values after they have started running. This takes the form of a communications channel between the generator and the "outside world," with the following two end points:

- The outside world has access to a method on the generator called send, which works just like next, except that it takes a single argument (the "message" to send—an arbitrary object).

- Inside the suspended generator, yield may now be used as an *expression*, rather than a *statement*. In other words, when the generator is resumed, yield returns a value—the value sent from the outside through send. If next was used, yield returns None.

Note that using send (rather than next) makes sense only after the generator has been suspended (that is, after it has hit the first yield). If you need to give some information to the generator before that, you can simply use the parameters of the generator-function.

---

■**Tip**  If you *really* want to use send on a newly started generator, you can use it with None as its parameter.

---

Here's a rather silly example that illustrates the mechanism:

```
def repeater(value):
    while True:
        new = (yield value)
        if new is not None: value = new
```

Here's an example of its use:

```
r = repeater(42)
r.next()
42
r.send("Hello, world!")
"Hello, world!"
```

Note the use of parentheses around the yield expression. While not strictly necessary in some cases, it is probably better to be safe than sorry, and simply always enclose yield expressions in parentheses if you are using the return value in some way.

Generators also have two other methods (in Python 2.5 and later):

- The throw method (called with an exception type, an optional value and traceback object) is used to raise an exception inside the generator (at the yield expression).

- The close method (called with no arguments) is used to stop the generator.

The close method (which is also called by the Python garbage collector, when needed) is also based on exceptions. It raises the GeneratorExit exception at the yield point, so if you want to have some cleanup code in your generator, you can wrap your yield in a try/finally statement. If you wish, you can also catch the GeneratorExit exception, but then you must reraise it (possibly after cleaning up a bit), raise another exception, or simply return. Trying to yield a value from a generator after close has been called on it will result in a RuntimeError.

---

**■Tip**  For more information about generator methods, and how these actually turn generators into simple *coroutines*, see PEP 342 (http://www.python.org/dev/peps/pep-0342/).

---

## Simulating Generators

If you need to use an older version of Python, generators aren't available. What follows is a simple recipe for simulating them with normal functions.

Starting with the code for the generator, begin by inserting the following line at the beginning of the function body:

```
result = []
```

If the code already uses the name result, you should come up with another. (Using a more descriptive name may be a good idea anyway.) Then replace all lines of this form:

```
yield some_expression
```

with this:

```
result.append(some_expression)
```

Finally, at the end of the function, add this line:

```
return result
```

Although this may not work with all generators, it works with most. (For example, it fails with infinite generators, which of course can't stuff their values into a list.)

Here is the flatten generator rewritten as a plain function:

```
def flatten(nested):
    result = []
    try:
        # Don't iterate over string-like objects:
        try: nested + ''
        except TypeError: pass
        else: raise TypeError
        for sublist in nested:
            for element in flatten(sublist):
                result.append(element)
    except TypeError:
        result.append(nested)
    return result
```

# The Eight Queens

Now that you've learned about all this magic, it's time to put it to work. In this section, you see how to use generators to solve a classic programming problem.

## Generators and Backtracking

Generators are ideal for complex recursive algorithms that gradually build a result. Without generators, these algorithms usually require you to pass a half-built solution around as an extra parameter so that the recursive calls can build on it. With generators, all the recursive calls need to do is yield their part. That is what I did with the preceding recursive version of flatten, and you can use the exact same strategy to traverse graphs and tree structures.

In some applications, however, you don't get the answer right away; you need to try several alternatives, and you need to do that on *every* level in your recursion. To draw a parallel from real life, imagine that you have an important meeting to attend. You're not sure where it is, but you have two doors in front of you, and the meeting room has to be behind one of them. You choose the left and step through. There, you face another two doors. You choose the left, but it turns out to be wrong. So you *backtrack*, and choose the right door, which also turns out to be wrong (excuse the pun). So, you backtrack again, to the point where you started, ready to try the right door there.

## GRAPHS AND TREES

If you have never heard of graphs and trees before, you should learn about them as soon as possible, because they are very important concepts in programming and computer science. To find out more, you should probably get a book about computer science, discrete mathematics, data structures, or algorithms. For some concise definitions, you can check out the following web pages:

- http://mathworld.wolfram.com/Graph.html

- http://mathworld.wolfram.com/Tree.html

- http://www.nist.gov/dads/HTML/tree.html

- http://www.nist.gov/dads/HTML/graph.html

A quick web search or some browsing in Wikipedia (http://wikipedia.org) will turn up a lot of material.

This strategy of backtracking is useful for solving problems that require you to try every combination until you find a solution. Such problems are solved like this:

```
# Pseudocode
for each possibility at level 1:
    for each possibility at level 2:
        ...
            for each possibility at level n:
                is it viable?
```

To implement this directly with for loops, you need to know how many levels you'll encounter. If that is not possible, you use recursion.

## The Problem

This is a much loved computer science puzzle: you have a chessboard and eight queen pieces to place on it. The only requirement is that none of the queens threatens any of the others; that is, you must place them so that no two queens can capture each other. How do you do this? Where should the queens be placed?

This is a typical backtracking problem: you try one position for the first queen (in the first row), advance to the second, and so on. If you find that you are unable to place a queen, you backtrack to the previous one and try another position. Finally, you either exhaust all possibilities or find a solution.

In the problem as stated, you are provided with information that there will be only eight queens, but let's assume that there can be any number of queens. (This is more similar to real-world backtracking problems.) How do you solve that? If you want to try to solve it yourself, you should stop reading now, because I'm about to give you the solution.

---

**Note** You can find much more efficient solutions for this problem. If you want more details, a web search should turn up a wealth of information. A brief history of various solutions may be found at `http://www.cit.gu.edu.au/~sosic/nqueens.html`.

---

## State Representation

To represent a possible solution (or part of it), you can simply use a tuple (or a list, for that matter). Each element of the tuple indicates the position (that is, column) of the queen of the corresponding row. So if `state[0] == 3`, you know that the queen in row one is positioned in column four (we are counting from zero, remember?). When working at one level of recursion (one specific row), you know only which positions the queens above have, so you may have a state tuple whose length is less than eight (or whatever the number of queens is).

---

**Note** I could well have used a list instead of a tuple to represent the state. It's mostly a matter of taste in this case. In general, if the sequence is small and static, tuples may be a good choice.

---

## Finding Conflicts

Let's start by doing some simple abstraction. To find a configuration in which there are no conflicts (where no queen may capture another), you first must define what a conflict is. And why not define it as a function while you're at it?

The `conflict` function is given the positions of the queens *so far* (in the form of a state tuple) and determines if a position for the *next* queen generates any new conflicts:

```
def conflict(state, nextX):
    nextY = len(state)
    for i in range(nextY):
        if abs(state[i]-nextX) in (0, nextY-i):
            return True
    return False
```

The `nextX` parameter is the suggested horizontal position (x coordinate, or column) of the next queen, and `nextY` is the vertical position (y coordinate, or row) of the next queen. This function does a simple check for each of the previous queens. If the next queen has the same x coordinate, or is on the same diagonal as (`nextX`, `nextY`), a conflict has occurred, and `True` is returned. If no such conflicts arise, `False` is returned. The tricky part is the following expression:

```
abs(state[i]-nextX) in (0, nextY-i)
```

It is true if the horizontal distance between the next queen and the previous one under consideration is either zero (same column) or equal to the vertical distance (on a diagonal). Otherwise, it is false.

## The Base Case

The Eight Queens problem can be a bit tricky to implement, but with generators it isn't so bad. If you aren't used to recursion, I wouldn't expect you to come up with this solution by yourself, though. Note also that this solution isn't particularly efficient, so with a very large number of queens, it might be a bit slow.

Let's begin with the base case: the last queen. What would you want her to do? Let's say you want to find all possible solutions. In that case, you would expect her to produce (generate) all the positions she could occupy (possibly none) given the positions of the others. You can sketch this out directly:

```python
def queens(num, state):
    if len(state) == num-1:
        for pos in range(num):
            if not conflict(state, pos):
                yield pos
```

In human-speak, this means, "If all queens but one have been placed, go through all possible positions for the last one, and return the positions that don't give rise to any conflicts." The num parameter is the number of queens in total, and the state parameter is the tuple of positions for the previous queens. For example, let's say you have four queens, and that the first three have been given the positions 1, 3, and 0, respectively, as shown in Figure 9-1. (Pay no attention to the white queen at this point.)

**Figure 9-1.** *Placing four queens on a 4 × 4 board*

As you can see in the figure, each queen gets a (horizontal) row, and the queens' positions are numbered across the top (beginning with zero, as is normal in Python):

```
>>> list(queens(4, (1,3,0)))
[2]
```

It works like a charm. Using list simply forces the generator to yield all of its values. In this case, only one position qualifies. The white queen has been put in this position in Figure 9-1. (Note that color has no special significance and is not part of the program.)

## The Recursive Case

Now let's turn to the recursive part of the solution. When you have your base case covered, the recursive case may correctly assume (by induction) that all results from lower levels (the queens with higher numbers) are correct. So what you need to do is add an else clause to the if statement in the previous implementation of the queens function.

What results do you expect from the recursive call? You want the positions of all the lower queens, right? Let's say they are returned as a tuple. In that case, you probably need to change your base case to return a tuple as well (of length one)—but I get to that later.

So, you're supplied with one tuple of positions from "above," and for each legal position of the current queen, you are supplied with a tuple of positions from "below." All you need to do to keep things flowing is to yield the result from below with your own position added to the front:

```
    ...
    else:
        for pos in range(num):
            if not conflict(state, pos):
                for result in queens(num, state + (pos,)):
                    yield (pos,) + result
```

The for pos and if not conflict parts of this are identical to what you had before, so you can rewrite this a bit to simplify the code. Let's add some default arguments as well:

```
def queens(num=8, state=()):
    for pos in range(num):
        if not conflict(state, pos):
            if len(state) == num-1:
                yield (pos,)
            else:
                for result in queens(num, state + (pos,)):
                    yield (pos,) + result
```

If you find the code hard to understand, you might find it helpful to formulate what it does in your own words. (And you do remember that the comma in (pos,) is necessary to make it a tuple, and not simply a parenthesized value, right?)

The queens generator gives you all the solutions (that is, all the legal ways of placing the queens):

```
>>> list(queens(3))
[]
>>> list(queens(4))
[(1, 3, 0, 2), (2, 0, 3, 1)]
>>> for solution in queens(8):
...     print solution
...
(0, 4, 7, 5, 2, 6, 1, 3)
(0, 5, 7, 2, 6, 3, 1, 4)
...
(7, 2, 0, 5, 1, 4, 6, 3)
(7, 3, 0, 2, 5, 1, 6, 4)
>>>
```

If you run queens with eight queens, you see a lot of solutions flashing by. Let's find out how many:

```
>>> len(list(queens(8)))
92
```

## Wrapping It Up

Before leaving the queens, let's make the output a bit more understandable. Clear output is always a good thing because it makes it easier to spot bugs, among other things.

```
def prettyprint(solution):
    def line(pos, length=len(solution)):
        return '. ' * (pos) + 'X ' + '. ' * (length-pos-1)
    for pos in solution:
        print line(pos)
```

Note that I've made a little helper function inside prettyprint. I put it there because I assumed I wouldn't need it anywhere outside. In the following, I print out a random solution to satisfy myself that it is correct:

```
>>> import random
>>> prettyprint(random.choice(list(queens(8))))
. . . . . X . .
. X . . . . . .
. . . . . . X .
X . . . . . . .
. . . X . . . .
. . . . . . . X
. . . . X . . .
. . X . . . . .
```

This "drawing" corresponds to the diagram in Figure 9-2. Fun to play with Python, isn't it?

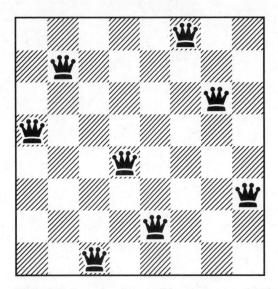

**Figure 9-2.** *One of many possible solutions to the Eight Queens problem*

# A Quick Summary

You've seen a lot of magic here. Let's take stock:

**New-style vs. old-style classes**: The way classes work in Python is changing. Recent (pre-3.0) versions of Python have two sorts of classes, with the old-style ones quickly going out of fashion. The new-style classes were introduced in version 2.2, and they provide several extra features (for example, they work with super and property, while old-style classes do not). To create a new-style class, you must subclass object, either directly or indirectly, or set the __metaclass__ property.

**Magic methods**: Several special methods (with names beginning and ending with double underscores) exist in Python. These methods differ quite a bit in function, but most of them are called automatically by Python under certain circumstances. (For example, __init__ is called after object creation.)

**Constructors**: These are common to many object-oriented languages, and you'll probably implement one for almost every class you write. Constructors are named __init__ and are automatically called immediately after an object is created.

**Overriding**: A class can override methods (or any other attributes) defined in its superclasses simply by implementing the methods. If the new method needs to call the overridden version, it can either call the unbound version from the superclass directly (old-style classes) or use the super function (new-style classes).

**Sequences and mappings**: Creating a sequence or mapping of your own requires implementing all the methods of the sequence and mapping protocols, including such magic methods as __getitem__ and __setitem__. By subclassing list (or UserList) and dict (or UserDict), you can save a lot of work.

**Iterators**: An *iterator* is simply an object that has a next method. Iterators can be used to iterate over a set of values. When there are no more values, the next method should raise a StopIteration exception. *Iterable* objects have an __iter__ method, which returns an iterator, and can be used in for loops, just like sequences. Often, an iterator is also iterable; that is, it has an __iter__ method that returns the iterator itself.

**Generators**: A *generator-function* (or method) is a function (or method) that contains the keyword yield. When called, the generator-function returns a *generator*, which is a special type of iterator. You can interact with an active generator from the outside by using the methods send, throw, and close.

**Eight Queens**: The Eight Queens problem is well known in computer science and lends itself easily to implementation with generators. The goal is to position eight queens on a chessboard so that none of the queens is in a position from which she can attack any of the others.

## New Functions in This Chapter

| Function | Description |
|---|---|
| iter(obj) | Extracts an iterator from an iterable object |
| property(fget, fset, fdel, doc) | Returns a property; all arguments are optional |
| super(class, obj) | Returns a bound instance of class's superclass |

Note that iter and super may be called with other parameters than those described here. For more information, see the standard Python documentation (http://python.org/doc).

## What Now?

Now you know most of the Python language. So why are there still so many chapters left? Well, there is still a *lot* to learn, much of it about how Python can connect to the external world in various ways. And then we have testing, extending, packaging, and the projects, so we're not done yet—not by far.

# CHAPTER 10

■■■

# Batteries Included

**Y**ou now know most of the basic Python language. While the core language is powerful in itself, Python gives you more tools to play with. A standard installation includes a set of modules called the *standard library*. You have already seen some of them (`math` and `cmath`, which contain mathematical functions for real and complex numbers, for example), but there are many more. This chapter shows you a bit about how modules work, and how to explore them and learn what they have to offer. Then the chapter offers an overview of the standard library, focusing on a few selected useful modules.

## Modules

You already know about making your own programs (or *scripts*) and executing them. You have also seen how you can fetch functions into your programs from external modules using `import`:

```
>>> import math
>>> math.sin(0)
0.0
```

Let's take a look at how you can write your own modules.

### Modules Are Programs

Any Python program can be imported as a module. Let's say you have written the program in Listing 10-1 and stored it in a file called `hello.py` (the name is important).

**Listing 10-1**. *A Simple Module*

```
# hello.py
print "Hello, world!"
```

Where you save it is also important; in the next section you learn more about that, but for now let's say you save it in the directory C:\python (Windows) or ~/python (UNIX/Mac OS X).

Then you can tell your interpreter where to look for the module by executing the following (using the Windows directory):

```
>>> import sys
>>> sys.path.append('c:/python')
```

---

■**Tip**  In UNIX, you cannot simply append the string '~/python' to sys.path. You must use the full path (such as '/home/yourusername/python') or, if you want to automate it, use sys.path.expanduser('~/python').

---

This simply tells the interpreter that it should look for modules in the directory c:\python in addition to the places it would normally look. After having done this, you can import your module (which is stored in the file c:\python\hello.py, remember?):

```
>>> import hello
Hello, world!
```

---

■**Note**  When you import a module, you may notice that a new file appears—in this case c:\python\hello.pyc. The file with the .pyc extension is a (platform-independent) processed ("compiled") Python file that has been translated to a format that Python can handle more efficiently. If you import the same module later, Python will import the .pyc file rather than the .py file, unless the .py file has changed; in that case, a new .pyc file is generated. Deleting the .pyc file does no harm (as long as there is an equivalent .py file available)—a new one is created when needed.

---

As you can see, the code in the module is executed when you import it. However, if you try to import it again, nothing happens:

```
>>> import hello
>>>
```

Why doesn't it work this time? Because modules aren't really meant to *do* things (such as printing text) when they're imported. They are mostly meant to *define* things, such as variables, functions, classes, and so on. And because you need to define things only once, importing a module several times has the same effect as importing it once.

## WHY ONLY ONCE?

The import-only-once behavior is a substantial optimization in most cases, and it can be very important in one special case: if two modules import each other.

In many cases, you may write two modules that need to access functions and classes from each other to function properly. For example, you may have created two modules—clientdb and billing—containing code for a client database and a billing system, respectively. Your client database may contain calls to your billing system (for example, automatically sending a bill to a client every month), while the billing system probably needs to access functionality from your client database to do the billing correctly.

If each module could be imported several times, you would end up with a problem here. The module clientdb would import billing, which again imports clientdb, which . . . you get the picture. You get an endless loop of imports (endless recursion, remember?). However, because nothing happens the second time you import the module, the loop is broken.

If you *insist* on reloading your module, you can use the built-in function reload. It takes a single argument (the module you want to reload) and returns the reloaded module. This may be useful if you have made changes to your module and want those changes reflected in your program while it is running. To reload the simple hello module (containing only a print statement), I would use the following:

```
>>> hello = reload(hello)
Hello, world!
```

Here, I assume that hello has already been imported (once). By assigning the result of reload to hello, I have replaced the previous version with the reloaded one. As you can see from the printed greeting, I am really importing the module here.

If you've created an object x by instantiating the class Foo from the module bar, and you then reload bar, the object x refers to will not be re-created in any way. x will still be an instance of the old version of Foo (from the old version of bar). If, instead, you want x to be based on the new Foo from the reloaded module, you will need to create it anew.

Note that the reload function has disappeared in Python 3.0. While you can achieve similar functionality using exec, the best thing in most cases is simply to stay away from module reloading.

## Modules Are Used to Define Things

So modules are executed the first time they are imported into your program. That seems sort of useful, but not very. What makes them worthwhile is that they (just like classes) keep their scope around afterward. That means that any classes or functions you define, and any variables you assign a value to, become attributes of the module. This may seem complicated, but in practice it is very simple.

## Defining a Function in a Module

Let's say you have written a module like the one in Listing 10-2 and stored it in a file called
hello2.py. Also assume that you've put it in a place where the Python interpreter can find it,
either using the sys.path trick from the previous section or the more conventional methods
from the section "Making Your Modules Available," which follows.

---

■**Tip**  If you make a program (which is meant to be executed, and not really used as a module) available in
the same manner as other modules, you can actually execute it using the -m switch to the Python interpreter.
Running the command python -m progname args will run the program progname with the command-line
arguments args, provided that the file progname.py (note the suffix) is installed along with your other modules (that is, provided you have imported progname).

---

**Listing 10-2.** *A Simple Module Containing a Function*

```
# hello2.py
def hello():
    print "Hello, world!"
```

You can then import it like this:

```
>>> import hello2
```

The module is then executed, which means that the function hello is defined in the scope
of the module, so you can access the function like this:

```
>>> hello2.hello()
Hello, world!
```

Any name defined in the global scope of the module will be available in the same manner.

Why would you want to do this? Why not just define everything in your main program?
The primary reason is *code reuse*. If you put your code in a module, you can use it in more than
one of your programs, which means that if you write a good client database and put it in a module called clientdb, you can use it when billing, when sending out spam (though I hope you
won't), and in any program that needs access to your client data. If you hadn't put this in a
separate module, you would need to rewrite the code in each one of these programs. So,
remember: to make your code reusable, make it modular! (And, yes, this is definitely related to
abstraction.)

## Adding Test Code in a Module

Modules are used to define things such as functions and classes, but every once in a while
(quite often, actually), it is useful to add some test code that checks whether things work as they

should. For example, if you wanted to make sure that the hello function worked, you might rewrite the module hello2 into a new one, hello3, defined in Listing 10-3.

**Listing 10-3.** *A Simple Module with Some Problematic Test Code*

```
# hello3.py
def hello():
    print "Hello, world!"

# A test:
hello()
```

This seems reasonable—if you run this as a normal program, you will see that it works. However, if you import it as a module, to use the hello function in another program, the test code is executed, as in the first hello module in this chapter:

```
>>> import hello3
Hello, world!
>>> hello3.hello()
Hello, world!
```

This is not what you want. The key to avoiding it is "telling" the module whether it's being run as a program on its own or being imported into another program. To do that, you need the variable __name__:

```
>>> __name__
'__main__'
>>> hello3.__name__
'hello3'
```

As you can see, in the "main program" (including the interactive prompt of the interpreter), the variable __name__ has the value '__main__'. In an imported module, it is set to the name of that module. Therefore, you can make your module's test code more well behaved by putting in an if statement, as shown in Listing 10-4.

**Listing 10-4.** *A Module with Conditional Test Code*

```
# hello4.py

def hello():
    print "Hello, world!"

def test():
    hello()

if __name__ == '__main__': test()
```

If you run this as a program, the `hello` function is executed; if you import it, it behaves like a normal module:

```
>>> import hello4
>>> hello4.hello()
Hello, world!
```

As you can see, I've wrapped up the test code in a function called `test`. I could have put the code directly into the `if` statement; however, by putting it in a separate test function, you can test the module even if you have imported it into another program:

```
>>> hello4.test()
Hello, world!
```

---

**Note** If you write more thorough test code, it might be a good idea to put it in a separate program. See Chapter 16 for more on writing tests.

---

## Making Your Modules Available

In the previous examples, I have altered `sys.path`, which contains a list of directories (as strings) in which the interpreter should look for modules. However, you don't want to do this in general. The ideal case would be for `sys.path` to contain the correct directory (the one containing your module) to begin with. There are two ways of doing this: put your module in the right place or tell the interpreter where to look. The following sections discuss these two solutions.

### Putting Your Module in the Right Place

Putting your module in the right place (or, rather *a* right place, because there may be several possibilities) is quite easy. It's just a matter of finding out where the Python interpreter looks for modules and then putting your file there.

---

**Note** If the Python interpreter on the machine you're working on has been installed by an administrator and you do not have administrator permissions, you may not be able to save your module in any of the directories used by Python. You will then need to use the alternative solution: tell the interpreter where to look.

---

As you may remember, the list of directories (the so-called search path) can be found in the path variable in the sys module:

```
>>> import sys, pprint
>>> pprint.pprint(sys.path)
```

```
['C:\\Python25\\Lib\\idlelib',
 'C:\\WINDOWS\\system32\\python25.zip',
 'C:\\Python25',
 'C:\\Python25\\DLLs',
 'C:\\Python25\\lib',
 'C:\\Python25\\lib\\plat-win',
 'C:\\Python25\\lib\\lib-tk',
 'C:\\Python25\\lib\\site-packages']
```

---

■**Tip**  If you have a data structure that is too big to fit on one line, you can use the `pprint` function from the `pprint` module instead of the normal `print` statement. `pprint` is a pretty-printing function, which makes a more intelligent printout.

---

This is a relatively standard path for a Python 2.5 installation on Windows. You may not get the exact same result. The point is that each of these strings provides a place to put modules if you want your interpreter to find them. Even though all these will work, the `site-packages` directory is the best choice because it's meant for this sort of thing. Look through your `sys.path` and find your `site-packages` directory, and save the module from Listing 10-4 in it, but give it another name, such as `another_hello.py`. Then try the following:

```
>>> import another_hello
>>> another_hello.hello()
Hello, world!
```

As long as your module is located in a place like `site-packages`, all your programs will be able to import it.

### Telling the Interpreter Where to Look

Putting your module in the correct place might not be the right solution for you for a number of reasons:

- You don't want to clutter the Python interpreter's directories with your own modules.

- You don't have permission to save files in the Python interpreter's directories.

- You would like to keep your modules somewhere else.

The bottom line is that if you place your modules somewhere else, you must tell the interpreter where to look. As you saw earlier, one way of doing this is to edit `sys.path`, but that is *not* a common way to do it. The standard method is to include your module directory (or directories) in the environment variable PYTHONPATH.

Depending on which operating system you are using, the contents of PYTHONPATH varies (see the sidebar "Environment Variables"), but basically it's just like `sys.path`—a list of directories.

## ENVIRONMENT VARIABLES

Environment variables are not part of the Python interpreter—they're part of your operating system. Basically, they are like Python variables, but they are set outside the Python interpreter. To find out how to set them, you should consult your system documentation, but here are a few pointers.

In UNIX and Mac OS X, you will probably set environment variables in some shell file that is executed every time you log in. If you use a shell such as `bash`, the file is `.bashrc`, found in your home directory. Add the following to that file to add the directory `~/python` to your PYTHONPATH:

```
export PYTHONPATH=$PYTHONPATH:~/python
```

Note that multiple directories are separated by colons. Other shells may have a different syntax for this, so you should consult the relevant documentation.

In Windows, you may be able to edit environment variables from your Control Panel (in reasonably advanced versions of Windows, such as Windows XP, 2000, NT, and Vista; on older versions such as Windows 98, this does not work, and you must edit your `autoexec.bat` file instead, as covered in the next paragraph). From the Start menu, select Start ➤ Settings ➤ Control Panel. In the Control Panel, double-click the System icon. In the dialog box that opens, select the Advanced tab and click the Environment Variables button. That brings up another dialog box with two tables: one with your user variables and one with system variables. You are interested in the user variables. If you see PYTHONPATH there already, select it, click Edit, and edit it. Otherwise, click New and use PYTHONPATH as the name; enter your directory as the value. Note that multiple directories are separated by semicolons.

If the previous tactic doesn't work, you can edit the file `autoexec.bat`, which you can find (assuming that you have a relatively standard setup) in the top directory of the C drive. Open the file in Notepad (or the IDLE text editor, for that matter) and add a line setting the PYTHONPATH. If you want to add the directory `C:\python`, type the following:

```
set PYTHONPATH=%PYTHONPATH%;C:\python
```

Note that the IDE you're using might have its own mechanisms for setting environment variables and the Python path.

---

■**Tip**  You don't need to change the `sys.path` by using PYTHONPATH. Path configuration files provide a useful shortcut to make Python do it for you. A path configuration file is a file with the file name extension `.pth` and contains directories that should be added to `sys.path`. Empty lines and lines beginning with # are ignored. Files beginning with `import` are executed. For a path configuration file to be executed, it must be placed in a directory where it can be found. For Windows, use the directory named by `sys.prefix` (probably something like `C:\Python22`); in UNIX and Mac OS X, use the `site-packages` directory. (For more information, look up the `site` module in the Python Library Reference. This module is automatically imported during initialization of the Python interpreter.)

---

## Naming Your Module

As you may have noticed, the file that contains the code of a module must be given the same name as the module, with an additional .py file name extension. In Windows, you can use the file name extension .pyw instead. You learn more about what that file name extension means in Chapter 12.

# Packages

To structure your modules, you can group them into *packages*. A package is basically just another type of module. The interesting thing about them is that they can contain other modules. While a module is stored in a file (with the file name extension .py), a package is a directory. To make Python treat it as a package, it must contain a file (module) named __init__.py. The contents of this file will be the contents of the package, if you import it as if it were a plain module. For example, if you had a package named constants, and the file constants/__init__.py contains the statement PI = 3.14, you would be able to do the following:

```
import constants
print constants.PI
```

To put modules inside a package, simply put the module files inside the package directory.

For example, if you wanted a package called drawing, which contained one module called shapes and one called colors, you would need the files and directories (UNIX pathnames) shown in Table 10-1.

**Table 10-1.** *A Simple Package Layout*

| File/Directory | Description |
| --- | --- |
| ~/python/ | Directory in PYTHONPATH |
| ~/python/drawing/ | Package directory (drawing package) |
| ~/python/drawing/__init__.py | Package code (drawing module) |
| ~/python/drawing/colors.py | colors module |
| ~/python/drawing/shapes.py | shapes module |

In Table 10-1, it is assumed that you have placed the directory ~/python in your PYTHONPATH. In Windows, simply replace ~/python with c:\python and reverse the direction of the slashes (to backslashes).

With this setup, the following statements are all legal:

```
import drawing            # (1) Imports the drawing package
import drawing.colors     # (2) Imports the colors module
from drawing import shapes # (3) Imports the shapes module
```

After the first statement, the contents of the __init__ module in drawing would be available; the shapes and colors modules, however, would not be. After the second statement, the colors module would be available, but only under its full name, drawing.colors. After the third statement, the shapes module would be available, under its short name (that is, simply shapes). Note that these statements are just examples. There is no need, for example, to import the package itself before importing one of its modules as I have done here. The second statement could very well be executed on its own, as could the third. You may nest packages inside each other.

# Exploring Modules

Before I describe some of the standard library modules, I'll show you how to explore modules on your own. This is a valuable skill because you will encounter many useful modules in your career as a Python programmer, and I couldn't possibly cover all of them here. The current standard library is large enough to warrant books all by itself (and such books have been written)—and it's growing. New modules are added with each release, and often some of the modules undergo slight changes and improvements. Also, you will most certainly find several useful modules on the Web, and being able to grok[1] them quickly and easily will make your programming much more enjoyable.

## What's in a Module?

The most direct way of probing a module is to investigate it in the Python interpreter. The first thing you need to do is to import it, of course. Let's say you've heard rumors about a standard module called copy:

```
>>> import copy
```

No exceptions are raised—so it exists. But what does it do? And what does it contain?

### Using dir

To find out what a module contains, you can use the dir function, which lists all the attributes of an object (and therefore all functions, classes, variables, and so on of a module). If you print out dir(copy), you get a long list of names. (Go ahead, try it.) Several of these names begin with an underscore—a hint (by convention) that they aren't meant to be used outside the module. So let's filter them out with a little list comprehension (check the section on list comprehension in Chapter 5 if you don't remember how this works):

```
>>> [n for n in dir(copy) if not n.startswith('_')]
['Error', 'PyStringMap', 'copy', 'deepcopy', 'dispatch_table', 'error', 'name', 't']
```

The list comprehension is the list consisting of all the names from dir(copy) that don't have an underscore as their first letter. This list is much less confusing than the full listing.

---

1. The term *grok* is hackerspeak, meaning "to understand fully," taken from Robert A. Heinlein's novel *Stranger in a Strange Land* (Ace Books, reissue 1995).

### The __all__ Variable

What I did with the little list comprehension in the previous section was to make a guess about what I was *supposed* to see in the copy module. However, you can get the correct answer directly from the module itself. In the full dir(copy) list, you may have noticed the name __all__. This is a variable containing a list similar to the one I created with list comprehension, except that this list has been set in the module itself. Let's see what it contains:

```
>>> copy.__all__
['Error', 'copy', 'deepcopy']
```

My guess wasn't all that bad. I got only a few extra names that weren't intended for my use. But where did this __all__ list come from, and why is it really there? The first question is easy to answer. It was set in the copy module, like this (copied directly from copy.py):

```
__all__ = ["Error", "copy", "deepcopy"]
```

So why is it there? It defines the public interface of the module. More specifically, it tells the interpreter what it means to import all the names from this module. So if you use this:

```
from copy import *
```

you get only the four functions listed in the __all__ variable. To import PyStringMap, for example, you would need to be explicit, by either importing copy and using copy.PyStringMap, or by using from copy import PyStringMap.

Setting __all__ like this is actually a useful technique when writing modules, too. Because you may have a lot of variables, functions, and classes in your module that other programs might not need or want, it is only polite to filter them out. If you don't set __all__, the names exported in a starred import defaults to all global names in the module that don't begin with an underscore.

## Getting Help with help

Until now, you've been using your ingenuity and knowledge of various Python functions and special attributes to explore the copy module. The interactive interpreter is a very powerful tool for this sort of exploration because your mastery of the language is the only limit to how deeply you can probe a module. However, there is one standard function that gives you all the information you would normally need. That function is called help. Let's try it on the copy function:

```
>>> help(copy.copy)
Help on function copy in module copy:

copy(x)
    Shallow copy operation on arbitrary Python objects.

    See the module's __doc__ string for more info.

>>>
```

This tells you that copy takes a single argument x, and that it is a "shallow copy operation." But it also mentions the module's __doc__ string. What's that? You may remember that I mentioned docstrings in Chapter 6. A docstring is simply a string you write at the beginning of a function to document it. That string may then be referred to by the function attribute __doc__. As you may understand from the preceding help text, modules may also have docstrings (they are written at the beginning of the module), as may classes (they are written at the beginning of the class).

Actually, the preceding help text was extracted from the copy function's docstring:

```
>>> print copy.copy.__doc__
Shallow copy operation on arbitrary Python objects.

    See the module's __doc__ string for more info.
```

The advantage of using help over just examining the docstring directly like this is that you get more information, such as the function signature (that is, the arguments it takes). Try to call help(copy) (on the module itself) and see what you get. It prints out a lot of information, including a thorough discussion of the difference between copy and deepcopy (essentially that deepcopy(x) makes copies of the values found in x as attributes and so on, while copy(x) just copies x, binding the attributes of the copy to the same values as those of x).

## Documentation

A natural source for information about a module is, of course, its documentation. I've postponed the discussion of documentation because it's often much quicker to just examine the module a bit yourself first. For example, you may wonder, "What were the arguments to range again?" Instead of searching through a Python book or the standard Python documentation for a description of range, you can just check it directly:

```
>>> print range.__doc__
range([start,] stop[, step]) -> list of integers

Return a list containing an arithmetic progression of integers.
range(i, j) returns [i, i+1, i+2,..., j-1]; start (!) defaults to 0.
When step is given, it specifies the increment (or decrement).
For example, range(4) returns [0, 1, 2, 3].  The end point is omitted!
These are exactly the valid indices for a list of 4 elements.
```

You now have a precise description of the range function, and because you probably had the Python interpreter running already (wondering about functions like this usually happens while you are programming), accessing this information took just a couple of seconds.

However, not every module and every function has a good docstring (although it should), and sometimes you may need a more thorough description of how things work. Most modules you download from the Web have some associated documentation. In my opinion, some of the most useful documentation for learning to program in Python is the Python Library Reference, which describes all of the modules in the standard library. If I want to look up some fact about Python, nine times out of ten, I find it there. The library reference is available for online browsing (at http://python.org/doc/lib) or for download, as are several other standard documents (such as the Python Tutorial and the Python Language Reference). All of the documentation is available from the Python web site at `http://python.org/doc`.

## Use the Source

The exploration techniques I've discussed so far will probably be enough for most cases. But those of you who wish to truly understand the Python language may want to know things about a module that can't be answered without actually reading the source code. Reading source code is, in fact, one of the best ways to learn Python—besides coding yourself.

Doing the actual reading shouldn't be much of a problem, but where is the source? Let's say you wanted to read the source code for the standard module copy. Where would you find it? One solution would be to examine `sys.path` again and actually look for it yourself, just like the interpreter does. A faster way is to examine the module's `__file__` property:

```
>>> print copy.__file__
C:\Python24\lib\copy.py
```

---

■**Note** If the file name ends with `.pyc`, just use the corresponding file whose name ends with `.py`.

---

There it is! You can open the copy.py file in your code editor (for example, IDLE) and start examining how it works.

---

■**Caution** When opening a standard library file in a text editor, you run the risk of accidentally modifying it. Doing so might break it, so when you close the file, make sure that you don't save any changes you might have made.

---

Note that some modules don't have any Python source you can read. They may be built into the interpreter (such as the `sys` module) or they may be written in the C programming language.[2] (See Chapter 17 for more information on extending Python using C.)

# The Standard Library: A Few Favorites

Chances are that you're beginning to wonder what the title of this chapter means. The phrase "batteries included" with reference to Python was originally coined by Frank Stajano and refers to Python's copious standard library. When you install Python, you get a lot of useful modules (the "batteries") for "free." Because there are so many ways of getting more information about these modules (as explained in the first part of this chapter), I won't include a full reference here (which would take up far too much space anyway); instead, I'll describe

---

2.  If the module was written in C, the C source code should be available.

a few of my favorite standard modules to whet your appetite for exploration. You'll encounter more standard modules in the project chapters (Chapters 20 through 29). The module descriptions are not complete but highlight some of the interesting features of each module.

## sys

The sys module gives you access to variables and functions that are closely linked to the Python interpreter. Some of these are shown in Table 10-2.

**Table 10-2.** *Some Important Functions and Variables in the sys Module*

| Function/Variable | Description |
| --- | --- |
| argv | The command-line arguments, including the script name |
| exit([arg]) | Exits the current program, optionally with a given return value or error message |
| modules | A dictionary mapping module names to loaded modules |
| path | A list of directory names where modules can be found |
| platform | A platform identifier such as sunos5 or win32 |
| stdin | Standard input stream—a file-like object |
| stdout | Standard output stream—a file-like object |
| stderr | Standard error stream—a file-like object |

The variable sys.argv contains the arguments passed to the Python interpreter, including the script name.

The function sys.exit exits the current program. (If called within a try/finally block, discussed in Chapter 8, the finally clause is still executed.) You can supply an integer to indicate whether the program succeeded—a UNIX convention. You'll probably be fine in most cases if you rely on the default (which is zero, indicating success). Alternatively, you can supply a string, which is used as an error message and can be very useful for a user trying to figure out why the program halted; then, the program exits with that error message and a code indicating failure.

The mapping sys.modules maps module names to actual modules. It applies to only currently imported modules.

The module variable sys.path was discussed earlier in this chapter. It's a list of strings, in which each string is the name of a directory where the interpreter will look for modules when an import statement is executed.

The module variable sys.platform (a string) is simply the name of the "platform" on which the interpreter is running. This may be a name indicating an operating system (such as sunos5 or win32), or it may indicate some other kind of platform, such as a Java Virtual Machine (for example, java1.4.0) if you're running Jython.

The module variables sys.stdin, sys.stdout, and sys.stderr are file-like stream objects. They represent the standard UNIX concepts of standard input, standard output, and standard error. To put it simply, sys.stdin is where Python gets its input (used in the functions input and `raw_input`, for example), and `sys.stdout` is where it prints. You learn more about files (and these three streams) in Chapter 11.

As an example, consider the problem of using printing arguments in reverse order. When you call a Python script from the command line, you may add some arguments after it—the so-called *command-line arguments*. These will then be placed in the list `sys.argv`, with the name of the Python script as `sys.argv[0]`. Printing these out in reverse order is pretty simple, as you can see in Listing 10-5.

**Listing 10-5.** *Reversing and Printing Command-Line Arguments*

```
# reverseargs.py
import sys
args = sys.argv[1:]
args.reverse()
print ' '.join(args)
```

As you can see, I make a copy of `sys.argv`. You can modify the original, but in general, it's safer not to because other parts of the program may also rely on `sys.argv` containing the original arguments. Notice also that I skip the first element of `sys.argv`—the name of the script. I reverse the list with `args.reverse()`, but I can't print the result of that operation. It is an in-place modification that returns `None`. An alternative approach would be the following:

```
print ' '.join(reversed(sys.argv[1:]))
```

Finally, to make the output prettier, I use the `join` string method. Let's try the result (assuming a UNIX shell here, but it will work equally well at an MS-DOS prompt, for example):

```
$ python reverseargs.py this is a test
test a is this
```

## os

The os module gives you access to several operating system services. The os module is extensive; only a few of the most useful functions and variables are described in Table 10-3. In addition to these, os and its submodule `os.path` contain several functions to examine, construct, and remove directories and files, as well as functions for manipulating paths (for example, `os.path.split` and `os.path.join` let you ignore `os.pathsep` most of the time). For more information about this functionality, see the standard library documentation.

**Table 10-3.** *Some Important Functions and Variables in the os Module*

| Function/Variable | Description |
| --- | --- |
| environ | Mapping with environment variables |
| system(command) | Executes an operating system command in a subshell |
| sep | Separator used in paths |
| pathsep | Separator to separate paths |

*Continued*

**Table 10-3.** *Continued*

| Function/Variable | Description |
| --- | --- |
| linesep | Line separator ('\n', '\r', or '\r\n') |
| urandom(n) | Returns n bytes of cryptographically strong random data |

The mapping os.environ contains environment variables described earlier in this chapter. For example, to access the environment variable PYTHONPATH, you would use the expression os.environ['PYTHONPATH']. This mapping can also be used to change environment variables, although not all platforms support this.

The function os.system is used to run external programs. There are other functions for executing external programs, including execv, which exits the Python interpreter, yielding control to the executed program, and popen, which creates a file-like connection to the program. For more information about these functions, consult the standard library documentation.

---

■**Tip** In current versions of Python, the subprocess module is available. It collects the functionality of the os.system, execv, and popen functions.

---

The module variable os.sep is a separator used in pathnames. The standard separator in UNIX (and the Mac OS X command-line version of Python) is /. The standard in Windows is \\ (the Python syntax for a single backslash), and in Mac OS, it is :. (On some platforms, os.altsep contains an alternate path separator, such as / in Windows.)

You use os.pathsep when grouping several paths, as in PYTHONPATH. The pathsep is used to separate the pathnames: : in UNIX (and the Mac OS X command-line version of Python), ; in Windows, and :: in Mac OS.

The module variable os.linesep is the line separator string used in text files. In UNIX (and, again, the command-line version in Mac OS X), this is a single newline character (\n), in Mac OS, it's a single carriage return character (\r); and in Windows, it's the combination of a carriage return and a newline (\r\n).

The urandom function uses a system-dependent source of "real" (or, at least, cryptographically strong) randomness. If your platform doesn't support it, you'll get a NotImplementedError.

As an example, consider the problem of starting a web browser. The system command can be used to execute any external program, which is very useful in environments such as UNIX where you can execute programs (or *commands*) from the command line to list the contents of a directory, send email, and so on. But it can be useful for starting programs with graphical user interfaces, too—such as a web browser. In UNIX, you can do the following (provided that you have a browser at /usr/ bin/firefox):

```
os.system('/usr/bin/firefox')
```

Here's a Windows version (again, use the path of a browser you have installed):

```
os.system(r'c:\"Program Files"\"Mozilla Firefox"\firefox.exe')
```

Note that I've been careful about enclosing `Program Files` and `Mozilla Firefox` in quotes; otherwise, DOS (which handles the command) balks at the whitespace. (This may be important for directories in your `PYTHONPATH` as well.) Note also that you must use backslashes here because DOS gets confused by forward slashes. If you run this, you will notice that the browser tries to open a web site named `Files"\Mozilla...`—the part of the command after the whitespace. Also, if you try to run this from IDLE, a DOS window appears, but the browser doesn't start until you close that DOS window. All in all, not exactly ideal behavior.

Another function that suits the job better is the Windows-specific function `os.startfile`:

```
os.startfile(r'c:\Program Files\Mozilla Firefox\firefox.exe')
```

As you can see, `os.startfile` accepts a plain path, even if it contains whitespace (that is, don't enclose `Program Files` in quotes as in the `os.system` example).

Note that in Windows, your Python program keeps on running after the external program has been started by `os.system` (or `os.startfile`); in UNIX, your Python program waits for the `os.system` command to finish.

## A BETTER SOLUTION: WEBBROWSER

The `os.system` function is useful for a lot of things, but for the specific task of launching a web browser, there's an even better solution: the `webbrowser` module. It contains a function called open, which lets you automatically launch a web browser to open the given URL. For example, if you want your program to open the Python web site in a web browser (either starting a new browser or using one that is already running), you simply use this:

```
import webbrowser
webbrowser.open('http://www.python.org')
```

The page should pop up. Pretty nifty, huh?

# fileinput

You learn a lot about reading from and writing to files in Chapter 11, but here is a sneak preview. The `fileinput` module enables you to easily iterate over all the lines in a series of text files. If you call your script like this (assuming a UNIX command line):

```
$ python some_script.py file1.txt file2.txt file3.txt
```

you will be able to iterate over the lines of `file1.txt` through `file3.txt` in turn. You can also iterate over lines supplied to standard input (`sys.stdin`, remember?), for example, in a UNIX pipe, using the standard UNIX command `cat`:

```
$ cat file.txt | python some_script.py
```

If you use `fileinput`, calling your script with `cat` in a UNIX pipe works just as well as supplying the file names as command-line arguments to your script. The most important functions of the `fileinput` module are described in Table 10-4.

**Table 10-4.** *Some Important Functions in the fileinput Module*

| Function | Description |
| --- | --- |
| input([files[, inplace[, backup]]]) | Facilitates iteration over lines in multiple input streams |
| filename() | Returns the name of the current file |
| lineno() | Returns the current (cumulative) line number |
| filelineno() | Returns the line number within current file |
| isfirstline() | Checks whether the current line is first in file |
| isstdin() | Checks whether the last line was from sys.stdin |
| nextfile() | Closes the current file and moves to the next |
| close() | Closes the sequence |

fileinput.input is the most important of the functions. It returns an object that you can iterate over in a for loop. If you don't want the default behavior (in which fileinput finds out which files to iterate over), you can supply one or more file names to this function (as a sequence). You can also set the inplace parameter to a true value (inplace=True) to enable in-place processing. For each line you access, you'll need to print out a replacement, which will be put back into the current input file. The optional backup argument gives a file name extension to a backup file created from the original file when you do in-place processing.

The function fileinput.filename returns the file name of the file you are currently in (that is, the file that contains the line you are currently processing).

The function fileinput.lineno returns the number of the current line. This count is cumulative so that when you are finished with one file and begin processing the next, the line number is not reset but starts at one more than the last line number in the previous file.

The function fileinput.filelineno returns the number of the current line within the current file. Each time you are finished with one file and begin processing the next, the file line number is reset, and restarts at 1.

The function fileinput.isfirstline returns a true value if the current line is the first line of the current file; otherwise, it returns a false value.

The function fileinput.isstdin returns a true value if the current file is sys.stdin; otherwise, it returns false.

The function fileinput.nextfile closes the current file and skips to the next one. The lines you skip do not count against the line count. This can be useful if you know that you are finished with the current file—for example, if each file contains words in sorted order, and you are looking for a specific word. If you have passed the word's position in the sorted order, you can safely skip to the next file.

The function fileinput.close closes the entire chain of files and finishes the iteration.

As an example of using fileinput, let's say you have written a Python script and you want to number the lines. Because you want the program to keep working after you've done this, you must add the line numbers in comments to the right of each line. To line them up, you can use string formatting. Let's allow each program line to get 40 characters maximum and add the comment after that. The program in Listing 10-6 shows a simple way of doing this with fileinput and the inplace parameter.

**Listing 10-6.** *Adding Line Numbers to a Python Script*

```
# numberlines.py

import fileinput

for line in fileinput.input(inplace=True):
    line = line.rstrip()
    num  = fileinput.lineno()
    print '%-40s # %2i' % (line, num)
```

If you run this program on itself, like this:

```
$ python numberlines.py numberlines.py
```

you end up with the program in Listing 10-7. Note that the program itself has been modified, and that if you run it like this several times, you will have multiple numbers on each line. Recall that rstrip is a string method that returns a copy of a string, where all the whitespace on the right has been removed (see the section "String Methods" in Chapter 3 and Table B-6 in Appendix B).

**Listing 10-7.** *The Line Numbering Program with Line Numbers Added*

```
# numberlines.py                          # 1
                                          # 2
import fileinput                          # 3
                                          # 4
for line in fileinput.input(inplace=1):   # 5
    line = line.rstrip()                  # 6
    num  = fileinput.lineno()             # 7
    print '%-40s # %2i' % (line, num)     # 8
```

---

■**Caution** Be careful about using the inplace parameter—it's an easy way to ruin a file. You should test your program carefully *without* setting inplace (this will simply print out the result), making sure the program works before you let it modify your files.

---

For another example using fileinput, see the section about the random module, later in this chapter.

## Sets, Heaps, and Deques

There are many useful data structures around, and Python supports some of the more common ones. Some of these, such as dictionaries (or hash tables) and lists (or dynamic arrays), are integral to the language. Others, although somewhat more peripheral, can still come in handy sometimes.

## Sets

Sets were introduced in Python 2.3, through the Set class in the sets module. Although you may come upon Set instances in existing code, there is really very little reason to use them yourself, unless you want to be backward-compatible. In Python 2.3, sets were made part of the language, through the set type. This means that you don't need to import the sets module—you can just create sets directly:

```
>>> set(range(10))
set([0, 1, 2, 3, 4, 5, 6, 7, 8, 9])
```

Sets are constructed from a sequence (or some other iterable object). Their main use is to check membership, and thus duplicates are ignored:

```
>>> set([0, 1, 2, 3, 0, 1, 2, 3, 4, 5])
set([0, 1, 2, 3, 4, 5])
```

Just as with dictionaries, the ordering of set elements is quite arbitrary and shouldn't be relied on:

```
>>> set(['fee', 'fie', 'foe'])
set(['foe', 'fee', 'fie'])
```

In addition to checking for membership, you can perform various standard set operations (which you may know from mathematics), such as union and intersection, either by using methods or by using the same operations as you would for bit operations on integers (see Appendix B). For example, you can find the union of two sets using either the union method of one of them or the bitwise OR operator, |:

```
>>> a = set([1, 2, 3])
>>> b = set([2, 3, 4])
>>> a.union(b)
set([1, 2, 3, 4])
>>> a | b
set([1, 2, 3, 4])
```

Here are some other methods and their corresponding operators; the names should make it clear what they mean:

```
>>> c = a & b
>>> c.issubset(a)
True
>>> c <= a
True
>>> c.issuperset(a)
False
>>> c >= a
False
>>> a.intersection(b)
set([2, 3])
```

```
>>> a & b
set([2, 3])
>>> a.difference(b)
set([1])
>>> a - b
set([1])
>>> a.symmetric_difference(b)
set([1, 4])
>>> a ^ b
set([1, 4])
>>> a.copy()
set([1, 2, 3])
>>> a.copy() is a
False
```

There are also various in-place operations, with corresponding methods, as well as the basic methods add and remove. For more information, see the section about set types in the Python Library Reference (http://python.org/doc/lib/types-set.html).

---

■**Tip**  If you need a function for finding, say, the union of two sets, you can simply use the unbound version of the union method, from the set type. This could be useful, for example, in concert with reduce:

```
>>> mySets = []
>>> for i in range(10):
...     mySets.append(set(range(i,i+5)))
...
>>> reduce(set.union, mySets)
set([0, 1, 2, 3, 4, 5, 6, 7, 8, 9, 10, 11, 12, 13])
```

---

Sets are mutable, and may therefore not be used, for example, as keys in dictionaries. Another problem is that sets themselves may contain only immutable (hashable) values, and thus may not contain other sets. Because sets of sets often occur in practice, this could be a problem. Luckily, there is the frozenset type, which represents *immutable* (and, therefore, hashable) sets:

```
>>> a = set()
>>> b = set()
>>> a.add(b)
Traceback (most recent call last):
  File "<stdin>", line 1, in ?
TypeError: set objects are unhashable
>>> a.add(frozenset(b))
```

The frozenset constructor creates a copy of the given set. It is useful whenever you want to use a set either as a member of another set or as the key to a dictionary.

## Heaps

Another well-known data structure is the *heap*, a kind of priority queue. A priority queue lets you add objects in an arbitrary order, and at any time (possibly in between the adding), find (and possibly remove) the smallest element. It does so much more efficiently than, say, using min on a list.

In fact, there is no separate heap type in Python—only a module with some heap-manipulating functions. The module is called heapq (the q stands for queue), and it contains six functions (see Table 10-5), the first four of which are directly related to heap manipulation. You must use a list as the heap object itself.

**Table 10-5.** *Some Important Functions in the fileinput Module*

| Function | Description |
| --- | --- |
| heappush(heap, x) | Pushes x onto the heap |
| heappop(heap) | Pops off the smallest element in the heap |
| heapify(heap) | Enforces the heap property on an arbitrary list |
| heapreplace(heap, x) | Pops off the smallest element and pushes x |
| nlargest(n, iter) | Returns the n largest elements of iter |
| nsmallest(n, iter) | Returns the n smallest elements of iter |

The heappush function is used to add an item to a heap. Note that you shouldn't use it on any old list—only one that has been built through the use of the various heap functions. The reason for this is that the order of the elements is important (even though it may look a bit haphazard; the elements aren't exactly sorted).

```
>>> from heapq import *
>>> from random import shuffle
>>> data = range(10)
>>> shuffle(data)
>>> heap = []
>>> for n in data:
...     heappush(heap, n)
>>> heap
[0, 1, 3, 6, 2, 8, 4, 7, 9, 5]
>>> heappush(heap, 0.5)
>>> heap
[0, 0.5, 3, 6, 1, 8, 4, 7, 9, 5, 2]
```

The order of the elements isn't as arbitrary as it seems. They aren't in strictly sorted order, but there is one guarantee made: the element at position i is always greater than the one in position i // 2 (or, conversely, it's smaller than the elements at positions 2*i and 2*i + 1). This is the basis for the underlying heap algorithm. This is called the *heap property*.

The heappop function pops off the smallest element, which is always found at index 0, and makes sure that the smallest of the remaining elements takes over this position (while preserving the heap property). Even though popping the first element of a list isn't terribly efficient in general, it's not a problem here, because heappop does some nifty shuffling behind the scenes:

```
>>> heappop(heap)
0
>>> heappop(heap)
0.5
>>> heappop(heap)
1
>>> heap
[2, 5, 3, 6, 9, 8, 4, 7]
```

The heapify function takes an arbitrary list and makes it a legal heap (that is, it imposes the heap property) through the least possible amount of shuffling. If you don't build your heap from scratch with heappush, this is the function to use before starting to use heappush and heappop:

```
>>> heap = [5, 8, 0, 3, 6, 7, 9, 1, 4, 2]
>>> heapify(heap)
>>> heap
[0, 1, 5, 3, 2, 7, 9, 8, 4, 6]
```

The heapreplace function is not quite as commonly used as the others. It pops the smallest element off the heap and then pushes a new element onto it. This is a bit more efficient than a heappop followed by a heappush:

```
>>> heapreplace(heap, 0.5)
0
>>> heap
[0.5, 1, 5, 3, 2, 7, 9, 8, 4, 6]
>>> heapreplace(heap, 10)
0.5
>>> heap
[1, 2, 5, 3, 6, 7, 9, 8, 4, 10]
```

The remaining two functions of the heapq module, nlargest(n, iter) and nsmallest(n, iter), are used to find the n largest or smallest elements, respectively, of any iterable object iter. You could do this by using sorting (for example, using the sorted function) and slicing, but the heap algorithm is faster and more memory-efficient (and, not to mention, easier to use).

## Deques (and Other Collections)

Double-ended queues, or *deques*, can be useful when you need to remove elements in the order in which they were added. In Python 2.4, the collections module was added, which contains the deque type.

---

■**Note**  As of Python 2.5, the `collections` module contains the `deque` type and `defaultdict`—a dictionary with a default value for nonexisting keys. Possible future additions are B-trees and Fibonacci heaps.

---

A deque is created from an iterable object (just like sets) and has several useful methods:

```
>>> from collections import deque
>>> q = deque(range(5))
>>> q.append(5)
>>> q.appendleft(6)
>>> q
deque([6, 0, 1, 2, 3, 4, 5])
>>> q.pop()
5
>>> q.popleft()
6
>>> q.rotate(3)
>>> q
deque([2, 3, 4, 0, 1])
>>> q.rotate(-1)
>>> q
deque([3, 4, 0, 1, 2])
```

The deque is useful because it allows appending and popping efficiently at the beginning (to the left), which you cannot do with lists. As a nice side effect, you can also rotate the elements (that is, shift them to the right or left, wrapping around the ends) efficiently. Deque objects also have the extend and extendleft methods, with extend working like the corresponding list method, and extendleft working analogously to appendleft. Note that the elements in the iterable object used in extendleft will appear in the deque in reverse order.

## time

The `time` module contains functions for, among other things, getting the current time, manipulating times and dates, reading dates from strings, and formatting dates as strings. Dates can be represented as either a real number (the seconds since 0 hours, January 1 in the "epoch," a platform-dependent year; for UNIX, it's 1970), or a tuple containing nine integers. These integers are explained in Table 10-6. For example, the tuple

```
(2008, 1, 21, 12, 2, 56, 0, 21, 0)
```

represents January 21, 2008, at 12:02:56, which is a Monday and the twenty-first day of the year (no daylight savings).

**Table 10-6.** *The Fields of Python Date Tuples*

| Index | Field | Value |
|-------|-------|-------|
| 0 | Year | For example, 2000, 2001, and so on |
| 1 | Month | In the range 1–12 |
| 2 | Day | In the range 1–31 |
| 3 | Hour | In the range 0–23 |
| 4 | Minute | In the range 0–59 |
| 5 | Second | In the range 0–61 |
| 6 | Weekday | In the range 0–6, where Monday is 0 |
| 7 | Julian day | In the range 1–366 |
| 8 | Daylight savings | 0, 1, or –1 |

The range for seconds is 0–61 to account for leap seconds and double-leap seconds. The daylight savings number is a Boolean value (true or false), but if you use –1, mktime (a function that converts such a tuple to a timestamp measured in seconds since the epoch) will probably get it right. Some of the most important functions in the time module are described in Table 10-7.

**Table 10-7.** *Some Important Functions in the time Module*

| Function | Description |
|----------|-------------|
| asctime([tuple]) | Converts a time tuple to a string |
| localtime([secs]) | Converts seconds to a date tuple, local time |
| mktime(tuple) | Converts a time tuple to local time |
| sleep(secs) | Sleeps (does nothing) for secs seconds |
| strptime(string[, format]) | Parses a string into a time tuple |
| time() | Current time (seconds since the epoch, UTC) |

The function time.asctime formats the current time as a string, like this:

```
>>> time.asctime()
'Fri Dec 21 05:41:27 2008'
```

You can also supply a date tuple (such as those created by localtime) if you don't want the current time. (For more elaborate formatting, you can use the strftime function, described in the standard documentation.)

The function `time.localtime` converts a real number (seconds since epoch) to a date tuple, local time. If you want universal time,[3] use gmtime instead.

The function `time.mktime` converts a date tuple to the time since epoch in seconds; it is the inverse of `localtime`.

The function `time.sleep` makes the interpreter wait for a given number of seconds.

The function `time.strptime` converts a string of the format returned by `asctime` to a date tuple. (The optional format argument follows the same rules as those for `strftime`; see the standard documentation.)

The function `time.time` returns the current (universal) time as seconds since the epoch. Even though the epoch may vary from platform to platform, you can reliably time something by keeping the result of `time` from before and after the event (such as a function call), and then computing the difference. For an example of these functions, see the next section, which covers the `random` module.

The functions shown in Table 10-7 are just a selection of those available from the `time` module. Most of the functions in this module perform tasks similar to or related to those described in this section. If you need something not covered by the functions described here, take a look at the section about the `time` module in the Python Library Reference (http://python.org/doc/lib/module-time.html); chances are you may find exactly what you are looking for.

Additionally, two more recent time-related modules are available: `datetime` (which supports date and time arithmetic) and `timeit` (which helps you time pieces of your code). You can find more information about both in the Python Library Reference, and `timeit` is also discussed briefly in Chapter 16.

## random

The `random` module contains functions that return random numbers, which can be useful for simulations or any program that generates random output.

---

■**Note** Actually, the numbers generated are pseudo-random. That means that while they appear completely random, there is a predictable system that underlies them. However, because the module is so good at pretending to be random, you probably won't ever have to worry about this (unless you want to use these numbers for strong-cryptography purposes, in which case they may not be "strong" enough to withstand a determined attack—but if you're into strong cryptography, you surely don't need me to explain such elementary issues). If you need *real* randomness, you should check out the `urandom` function of the `os` module. The class `SystemRandom` in the `random` module is based on the same kind of functionality, and gives you data that is close to real randomness.

---

Some important functions in this module are shown in Table 10-8.

---

3. For more information about universal time, see http://en.wikipedia.org/wiki/Universal_time.

**Table 10-8.** *Some Important Functions in the random Module*

| Function | Description |
| --- | --- |
| random() | Returns a random real number $n$ such that $0 \le n \le 1$ |
| getrandbits(n) | Returns $n$ random bits, in the form of a long integer |
| uniform(a, b) | Returns a random real number $n$ such that $a \le n \le b$ |
| randrange([start], stop, [step]) | Returns a random number from range(start, stop, step) |
| choice(seq) | Returns a random element from the sequence seq |
| shuffle(seq[, random]) | Shuffles the sequence seq in place |
| sample(seq, n) | Chooses n random, unique elements from the sequence seq |

The function random.random is one of the most basic random functions; it simply returns a pseudo-random number $n$ such that $0 \le n \le 1$. Unless this is exactly what you need, you should probably use one of the other functions, which offer extra functionality. The function random.getrandbits returns a given number of bits (binary digits), in the form of a long integer. This is probably mostly useful if you're really into random stuff (for example, working with cryptography).

The function random.uniform, when supplied with two numerical parameters a and b, returns a random (uniformly distributed) real number $n$ such that $a \le n \le b$. So, for example, if you want a random angle, you could use uniform(0,360).

The function random.randrange is the standard function for generating a random integer in the range you would get by calling range with the same arguments. For example, to get a random number in the range from 1 to 10 (inclusive), you would use randrange(1,11) (or, alternatively, randrange(10)+1), and if you want a random odd positive integer lower than 20, you would use randrange(1,20,2).

The function random.choice chooses (uniformly) a random element from a given sequence.

The function random.shuffle shuffles the elements of a (mutable) sequence randomly, such that every possible ordering is equally likely.

The function random.sample chooses (uniformly) a given number of elements from a given sequence, making sure that they're all different.

---

■**Note**  For the statistically inclined, there are other functions similar to uniform that return random numbers sampled according to various other distributions, such as betavariate, exponential, Gaussian, and several others.

---

Let's look at some examples using the random module. In these examples, I use several of the functions from the time module described previously. First, let's get the real numbers representing the limits of the time interval (the year 2008). You do that by expressing the date as a time tuple (using -1 for day of the week, day of the year, and daylight savings, making Python calculate that for itself) and calling `mktime` on these tuples:

```
from random import *
from time import *
date1 = (2008, 1, 1, 0, 0, 0, -1, -1, -1)
time1 = mktime(date1)
date2 = (2009, 1, 1, 0, 0, 0, -1, -1, -1)
time2 = mktime(date2)
```

Then you generate a random number uniformly in this range (the upper limit excluded):

```
>>> random_time = uniform(time1, time2)
```

Then you simply convert this number back to a legible date:

```
>>> print asctime(localtime(random_time))
Mon Jun 24 21:35:19 2008
```

For the next example, let's ask the user how many dice to throw, and how many sides each one should have. The die-throwing mechanism is implemented with `randrange` and a `for` loop:

```
from random import randrange
num   = input('How many dice? ')
sides = input('How many sides per die? ')
sum = 0
for i in range(num): sum += randrange(sides) + 1
print 'The result is', sum
```

If you put this in a script file and run it, you get an interaction something like the following:

```
How many dice? 3
How many sides per die? 6
The result is 10
```

Now assume that you have made a text file in which each line of text contains a fortune. Then you can use the `fileinput` module described earlier to put the fortunes in a list, and then select one randomly:

```
# fortune.py
import fileinput, random
fortunes = list(fileinput.input())
print random.choice(fortunes)
```

In UNIX, you could test this on the standard dictionary file /usr/dict/words to get a random word:

```
$ python fortune.py /usr/dict/words
dodge
```

As a last example, suppose that you want your program to deal you cards, one at a time, each time you press Enter on your keyboard. Also, you want to make sure that you don't get the same card more than once. First, you make a "deck of cards"—a list of strings:

```
>>> values = range(1, 11) + 'Jack Queen King'.split()
>>> suits = 'diamonds clubs hearts spades'.split()
>>> deck = ['%s of %s' % (v, s) for v in values for s in suits]
```

The deck you just created isn't very suitable for a game of cards. Let's just peek at some of the cards:

```
>>> from pprint import pprint
>>> pprint(deck[:12])
['1 of diamonds',
 '1 of clubs',
 '1 of hearts',
 '1 of spades',
 '2 of diamonds',
 '2 of clubs',
 '2 of hearts',
 '2 of spades',
 '3 of diamonds',
 '3 of clubs',
 '3 of hearts',
 '3 of spades']
```

A bit too ordered, isn't it? That's easy to fix:

```
>>> from random import shuffle
>>> shuffle(deck)
>>> pprint(deck[:12])
['3 of spades',
 '2 of diamonds',
 '5 of diamonds',
 '6 of spades',
 '8 of diamonds',
 '1 of clubs',
 '5 of hearts',
 'Queen of diamonds',
 'Queen of hearts',
 'King of hearts',
 'Jack of diamonds',
 'Queen of clubs']
```

Note that I've just printed the 12 first cards here, to save some space. Feel free to take a look at the whole deck yourself.

Finally, to get Python to deal you a card each time you press Enter on your keyboard, until there are no more cards, you simply create a little while loop. Assuming that you put the code needed to create the deck into a program file, you could simply add the following at the end:

```
while deck: raw_input(deck.pop())
```

---

■**Note**  If you try the while loop shown here in the interactive interpreter, you'll notice that an empty string is printed out every time you press Enter. This is because raw_input returns what you write (which is nothing) and that will get printed. In a normal program, this return value from raw_input is simply ignored. To have it "ignored" interactively, too, just assign the result of raw_input to some variable you won't look at again and name it something like ignore.

---

# shelve

In the next chapter, you learn how to store data in files, but if you want a really simple storage solution, the shelve module can do most of the work for you. All you need to do is supply it with a file name. The only function of interest in shelve is open. When called (with a file name) it returns a Shelf object, which you can use to store things. Just treat it as a normal dictionary (except that the keys must be strings), and when you're finished (and want things saved to disk), call its close method.

## A Potential Trap

It is important to realize that the object returned by shelve.open is not an ordinary mapping, as the following example demonstrates:

```
>>> import shelve
>>> s = shelve.open('test.dat')
>>> s['x'] = ['a', 'b', 'c']
>>> s['x'].append('d')
>>> s['x']
['a', 'b', 'c']
```

Where did the 'd' go?

The explanation is simple: when you look up an element in a shelf object, the object is reconstructed from its stored version; and when you assign an element to a key, it is stored. What happened in the preceding example was the following:

- The list ['a', 'b', 'c'] was stored in s under the key 'x'.

- The stored representation was retrieved, a new list was constructed from it, and 'd' was appended to the copy. This modified version was *not* stored!

- Finally, the original is retrieved again—without the 'd'.

To correctly modify an object that is stored using the shelve module, you must bind a temporary variable to the retrieved copy, and then store the copy again after it has been modified:[4]

```
>>> temp = s['x']
>>> temp.append('d')
>>> s['x'] = temp
>>> s['x']
['a', 'b', 'c', 'd']
```

From Python 2.4 onward, there is another way around this problem: set the writeback parameter of the open function to true. If you do, all of the data structures that you read from or assign to the shelf will be kept around in memory (cached) and written back to disk only when you close the shelf. If you're not working with a huge amount of data, and you don't want to worry about these things, setting writeback to true (and making sure you close your shelf at the end) may be a good idea.

## A Simple Database Example

Listing 10-8 shows a simple database application that uses the shelve module.

**Listing 10-8.** *A Simple Database Application*

```
# database.py
import sys, shelve

def store_person(db):
    """
    Query user for data and store it in the shelf object
    """
    pid = raw_input('Enter unique ID number: ')
    person = {}
    person['name']  = raw_input('Enter name: ')
    person['age']   = raw_input('Enter age: ')
    person['phone'] = raw_input('Enter phone number: ')

    db[pid] = person

def lookup_person(db):
    """
    Query user for ID and desired field, and fetch the corresponding data from
    the shelf object
    """
    pid = raw_input('Enter ID number: ')
    field = raw_input('What would you like to know? (name, age, phone)  ')
    field = field.strip().lower()
```

---

4. Thanks to Luther Blissett for pointing this out.

```python
        print field.capitalize() + ':', \
            db[pid][field]

def print_help():
    print 'The available commands are:'
    print 'store  : Stores information about a person'
    print 'lookup : Looks up a person from ID number'
    print 'quit   : Save changes and exit'
    print '?      : Prints this message'

def enter_command():
    cmd = raw_input('Enter command (? for help): ')
    cmd = cmd.strip().lower()
    return cmd

def main():
    database = shelve.open('C:\\database.dat') # You may want to change this name
    try:
        while True:
            cmd = enter_command()
            if   cmd == 'store':
                store_person(database)
            elif cmd == 'lookup':
                lookup_person(database)
            elif cmd == '?':
                print_help()
            elif cmd == 'quit':
                return
    finally:
        database.close()

if __name__ == '__main__': main()
```

The program shown in Listing 10-8 has several interesting features:

- Everything is wrapped in functions to make the program more structured. (A possible improvement is to group those functions as the methods of a class.)

- The main program is in the main function, which is called only if __name__ == '__main__'. That means you can import this as a module and then call the main function from another program.

- I open a database (*shelf*) in the main function, and then pass it as a parameter to the other functions that need it. I could have used a global variable, too, because this program is so small, but it's better to avoid global variables in most cases, unless you have a reason to use them.

- After reading in some values, I make a modified version by calling `strip` and `lower` on them because if a supplied key is to match one stored in the database, the two must be *exactly* alike. If you always use `strip` and `lower` on what the users enter, you can allow them to be sloppy about using uppercase or lowercase letters and additional white-space. Also, note that I've used `capitalize` when printing the field name.

- I have used `try` and `finally` to ensure that the database is closed properly. You never know when something might go wrong (and you get an exception), and if the program terminates without closing the database properly, you may end up with a corrupt database file that is essentially useless. By using `try` and `finally`, you avoid that.

So, let's take this database out for a spin. Here is a sample interaction:

```
Enter command (? for help): ?
The available commands are:
store  : Stores information about a person
lookup : Looks up a person from ID number
quit   : Save changes and exit
?      : Prints this message
Enter command (? for help): store
Enter unique ID number: 001
Enter name: Mr. Gumby
Enter age: 42
Enter phone number: 555-1234
Enter command (? for help): lookup
Enter ID number: 001
What would you like to know? (name, age, phone) phone
Phone: 555-1234
Enter command (? for help): quit
```

This interaction isn't terribly interesting. I could have done exactly the same thing with an ordinary dictionary instead of the `shelf` object. But now that I've quit the program, let's see what happens when I restart it—perhaps the following day?

```
Enter command (? for help): lookup
Enter ID number: 001
What would you like to know? (name, age, phone) name
Name: Mr. Gumby
Enter command (? for help): quit
```

As you can see, the program reads in the file I created the first time, and Mr. Gumby is still there!

Feel free to experiment with this program, and see if you can extend its functionality and improve its user-friendliness. Perhaps you can think of a version that you have use for yourself? How about a database of your record collection? Or a database to help you keep track of friends who have borrowed books from you. (I know I could use that last one.)

# re

*Some people, when confronted with a problem, think, "I know, I'll use regular expressions." Now they have two problems.*

—Jamie Zawinski

The re module contains support for *regular expressions*. If you've heard about regular expressions, you probably know how powerful they are; if you haven't, prepare to be amazed.

You should note, however, that mastering regular expressions may be a bit tricky at first. (Okay, very tricky, actually.) The key is to learn about them a little bit at a time—just look up (in the documentation) the parts you need for a specific task. There is no point in memorizing it all up front. This section describes the main features of the re module and regular expressions, and enables you to get started.

---

■**Tip**  In addition to the standard documentation, Andrew Kuchling's "Regular Expression HOWTO" (`http://amk.ca/python/howto/regex/`) is a useful source of information on regular expressions in Python.

---

## What Is a Regular Expression?

A regular expression (also called a *regex* or *regexp*) is a pattern that can match a piece of text. The simplest form of regular expression is just a plain string, which matches itself. In other words, the regular expression `'python'` matches the string `'python'`. You can use this matching behavior for such things as searching for patterns in text, replacing certain patterns with some computed values, or splitting text into pieces.

### The Wildcard

A regular expression can match more than one string, and you create such a pattern by using some special characters. For example, the period character (dot) matches any character (except a newline), so the regular expression `'.ython'` would match both the string `'python'` and the string `'jython'`. It would also match strings such as `'qython'`, `'+ython'`, or `' ython'` (in which the first letter is a single space), but not strings such as `'cpython'` or `'ython'` because the period matches a single letter, and neither two nor zero.

Because it matches "anything" (any single character except a newline), the period is called a *wildcard*.

### Escaping Special Characters

When you use special characters in regular expressions, it's important to know that you may run into problems if you try to use them as normal characters. For example, imagine you want to match the string `'python.org'`. Do you simply use the pattern `'python.org'`? You could, but that would also match `'pythonzorg'`, for example, which you probably wouldn't want. (The dot matches any character except a newline, remember?) To make a special character behave like a normal one, you *escape* it, just as I demonstrated how to escape quotes in strings in Chapter 1. You place a backslash in front of it. Thus, in this example, you would use `'python\\.org'`, which would match `'python.org'` and nothing else.

---

**▊Note**  To get a single backslash, which is required here by the `re` module, you need to write two back-slashes in the string—to escape it from the interpreter. Thus you have *two levels* of escaping here: (1) from the interpreter, and (2) from the `re` module. (Actually, in some cases you can get away with using a single backslash and have the interpreter escape it for you automatically, but don't rely on it.) If you are tired of dou-bling up backslashes, use a raw string, such as `r'python\.org'`.

---

### Character Sets

Matching any character can be useful, but sometimes you want more control. You can create a so-called *character set* by enclosing a substring in brackets. Such a character set will match any of the characters it contains. For example, `'[pj]ython'` would match both `'python'` and `'jython'`, but nothing else. You can also use ranges, such as `'[a-z]'` to match any character from *a* to *z* (alphabetically), and you can combine such ranges by putting one after another, such as `'[a-zA-Z0-9]'` to match uppercase and lowercase letters and digits. (Note that the character set will match only *one* such character, though.)

To invert the character set, put the character ^ first, as in `'[^abc]'` to match any character except *a*, *b*, or *c*.

---

#### SPECIAL CHARACTERS IN CHARACTER SETS

In general, special characters such as dots, asterisks, and question marks must be escaped with a backslash if you want them to appear as literal characters in the pattern, rather than function as regular expression oper-ators. Inside character sets, escaping these characters is generally not necessary (although perfectly legal). You should, however, keep in mind the following rules:

- You do need to escape the caret (^) if it appears at the beginning of the character set, unless you want it to function as a negation operator. (In other words, don't place it at the beginning unless you mean it.)

- Similarly, the right bracket (]) and the dash (-) must be put either at the beginning of the character set or escaped with a backslash. (Actually, the dash may also be put at the end, if you wish.)

---

### Alternatives and Subpatterns

Character sets are nice when you let each letter vary independently, but what if you want to match only the strings `'python'` and `'perl'`? You can't specify such a specific pattern with char-acter sets or wildcards. Instead, you use the special character for alternatives: the pipe character (|). So, your pattern would be `'python|perl'`.

However, sometimes you don't want to use the choice operator on the entire pattern—just a part of it. To do that, you enclose the part, or subpattern, in parentheses. The previous example could be rewritten as `'p(ython|erl)'`. (Note that the term *subpattern* can also apply to a single character.)

### Optional and Repeated Subpatterns

By adding a question mark after a subpattern, you make it optional. It may appear in the matched string, but it isn't strictly required. So, for example, this (slightly unreadable) pattern:

`r'(http://)?(www\.)?python\.org'`

would match all of the following strings (and nothing else):

```
'http://www.python.org'
'http://python.org'
'www.python.org'
'python.org'
```

A few things are worth noting here:

- I've escaped the dots, to prevent them from functioning as wildcards.

- I've used a raw string to reduce the number of backslashes needed.

- Each optional subpattern is enclosed in parentheses.

- The optional subpatterns may or may not appear , independently of each other.

The question mark means that the subpattern can appear once or not at all. A few other operators allow you to repeat a subpattern more than once:

- `(pattern)*`: pattern is repeated zero or more times.

- `(pattern)+`: pattern is repeated one or more times.

- `(pattern){m,n}`: pattern is repeated from m to n times.

So, for example, `r'w*\.python\.org'` matches `'www.python.org'`, but also `'.python.org'`, `'ww.python.org'`, and `'wwwwww.python.org'`. Similarly, `r'w+\.python\.org'` matches `'w.python.org'` but not `'.python.org'`, and `r'w{3,4}\.python\.org'` matches only `'www.python.org'` and `'wwww.python.org'`.

---

■**Note**  The term *match* is used loosely here to mean that the pattern matches the entire string. The `match` function (see Table 10-9) requires only that the pattern matches the beginning of the string.

---

### The Beginning and End of a String

Until now, you've only been looking at a pattern matching an entire string, but you can also try to find a substring that matches the pattern, such as the substring `'www'` of the string `'www.python.org'` matching the pattern `'w+'`. When you're searching for substrings like this, it can sometimes be useful to anchor this substring either at the beginning or the end of the full string. For example, you might want to match `'ht+p'` at the beginning of a string, but not anywhere else. Then you use a caret ('^') to mark the beginning. For example, '^ht+p' would match 'http://python.org' (and 'htttttp://python.org', for that matter) but not 'www.http.org'. Similarly, the end of a string may be indicated by the dollar sign ($).

---

**■Note** For a complete listing of regular expression operators, see the section "Regular Expression Syntax" in the Python Library Reference (http://python.org/doc/lib/re-syntax.html).

---

## Contents of the re Module

Knowing how to write regular expressions isn't much good if you can't use them for anything. The re module contains several useful functions for working with regular expressions. Some of the most important ones are described in Table 10-9.

**Table 10-9.** *Some Important Functions in the re Module*

| Function | Description |
|---|---|
| compile(pattern[, flags]) | Creates a pattern object from a string with a regular expression |
| search(pattern, string[, flags]) | Searches for pattern in string |
| match(pattern, string[, flags]) | Matches pattern at the beginning of string |
| split(pattern, string[, maxsplit=0]) | Splits a string by occurrences of pattern |
| findall(pattern, string) | Returns a list of all occurrences of pattern in string |
| sub(pat, repl, string[, count=0]) | Substitutes occurrences of pat in string with repl |
| escape(string) | Escapes all special regular expression characters in string |

The function re.compile transforms a regular expression (written as a string) to a pattern object, which can be used for more efficient matching. If you use regular expressions represented as strings when you call functions such as search or match, they must be transformed into regular expression objects internally anyway. By doing this once, with the compile function, this step is no longer necessary each time you use the pattern. The pattern objects have the searching/matching functions as methods, so re.search(pat, string) (where pat is a regular expression written as a string) is equivalent to pat.search(string) (where pat is a pattern object created with compile). Compiled regular expression objects can also be used in the normal re functions.

The function re.search searches a given string to find the first substring, if any, that matches the given regular expression. If one is found, a MatchObject (evaluating to true) is returned; otherwise, None (evaluating to false) is returned. Due to the nature of the return values, the function can be used in conditional statements, like this:

```
if re.search(pat, string):
    print 'Found it!'
```

However, if you need more information about the matched substring, you can examine the returned `MatchObject`. (More about `MatchObject` in the next section.)

The function `re.match` tries to match a regular expression at the beginning of a given string. So `re.match('p', 'python')` returns true (a match object), while `re.match('p', 'www.python.org')` returns false (None).

---

**Note**  The `match` function will report a match if the pattern matches the `beginning` of a string; the pattern is *not* required to match the entire string. If you want to do that, you need to add a dollar sign to the end of your pattern. The dollar sign will match the end of the string and thereby "stretch out" the match.

---

The function `re.split` splits a string by the occurrences of a pattern. This is similar to the string method `split`, except that you allow full regular expressions instead of only a fixed separator string. For example, with the string method `split`, you could split a string by the occurrences of the string `', '` but with `re.split` you can split on any sequence of space characters and commas:

```
>>> some_text = 'alpha, beta,,,,gamma    delta'
>>> re.split('[, ]+', some_text)
['alpha', 'beta', 'gamma', 'delta']
```

---

**Note**  If the pattern contains parentheses, the parenthesized groups are interspersed between the split substrings. For example, `re.split('o(o)', 'foobar')` would yield `['f', 'o', 'bar']`.

---

As you can see from this example, the return value is a list of substrings. The `maxsplit` argument indicates the maximum number of splits allowed:

```
>>> re.split('[, ]+', some_text, maxsplit=2)
['alpha', 'beta', 'gamma    delta']
>>> re.split('[, ]+', some_text, maxsplit=1)
['alpha', 'beta,,,,gamma    delta']
```

The function `re.findall` returns a list of all occurrences of the given pattern. For example, to find all words in a string, you could do the following:

```
>>> pat = '[a-zA-Z]+'
>>> text = '"Hm... Err -- are you sure?" he said, sounding insecure.'
>>> re.findall(pat, text)
['Hm', 'Err', 'are', 'you', 'sure', 'he', 'said', 'sounding', 'insecure']
```

Or you could find the punctuation:

```
>>> pat = r'[.?\-",]+'
>>> re.findall(pat, text)
['"', '...', '--', '?"', ',', '.']
```

Note that the dash (-) has been escaped so Python won't interpret it as part of a character range (such as a-z).

The function re.sub is used to substitute the leftmost, nonoverlapping occurrences of a pattern with a given replacement. Consider the following example:

```
>>> pat = '{name}'
>>> text = 'Dear {name}...'
>>> re.sub(pat, 'Mr. Gumby', text)
'Dear Mr. Gumby...'
```

See the section "Group Numbers and Functions in Substitutions" later in this chapter for information about how to use this function more effectively.

The function re.escape is a utility function used to escape all the characters in a string that might be interpreted as a regular expression operator. Use this if you have a long string with a lot of these special characters and you want to avoid typing a lot of backslashes, or if you get a string from a user (for example, through the raw_input function) and want to use it as a part of a regular expression. Here is an example of how it works:

```
>>> re.escape('www.python.org')
'www\\.python\\.org'
>>> re.escape('But where is the ambiguity?')
'But\\ where\\ is\\ the\\ ambiguity\\?'
```

---

**Note** In Table 10-9, you'll notice that some of the functions have an optional parameter called flags. This parameter can be used to change how the regular expressions are interpreted. For more information about this, see the section about the re module in the Python Library Reference (http://python.org/doc/lib/module-re.html). The flags are described in the subsection "Module Contents."

---

## Match Objects and Groups

The re functions that try to match a pattern against a section of a string all return MatchObject objects when a match is found. These objects contain information about the substring that matched the pattern. They also contain information about which parts of the pattern matched which parts of the substring. These parts are called *groups*.

A group is simply a subpattern that has been enclosed in parentheses. The groups are numbered by their left parenthesis. Group zero is the entire pattern. So, in this pattern:

```
'There (was a (wee) (cooper)) who (lived in Fyfe)'
```

the groups are as follows:

```
0  There was a wee cooper who lived in Fyfe
1  was a wee cooper
2  wee
3  cooper
4  lived in Fyfe
```

Typically, the groups contain special characters such as wildcards or repetition operators, and thus you may be interested in knowing what a given group has matched. For example, in this pattern:

```
r'www\.(.+)\.com$'
```

group 0 would contain the entire string, and group 1 would contain everything between `'www.'` and `'.com'`. By creating patterns like this, you can extract the parts of a string that interest you.

Some of the more important methods of re match objects are described in Table 10-10.

**Table 10-10.** *Some Important Methods of re Match Objects*

| Method | Description |
| --- | --- |
| group([group1, ...]) | Retrieves the occurrences of the given subpatterns (*groups*) |
| start([group]) | Returns the starting position of the occurrence of a given group |
| end([group]) | Returns the ending position (an exclusive limit, as in slices) of the occurrence of a given group |
| span([group]) | Returns both the beginning and ending positions of a group |

The method group returns the (sub)string that was matched by a given group in the pattern. If no group number is given, group 0 is assumed. If only a single group number is given (or you just use the default, 0), a single string is returned. Otherwise, a tuple of strings corresponding to the given group numbers is returned.

---

■**Note** In addition to the entire match (group 0), you can have only 99 groups, with numbers in the range 1–99.

---

The method start returns the starting index of the occurrence of the given group (which defaults to 0, the whole pattern).

The method end is similar to start, but returns the ending index plus one.

The method span returns the tuple (start, end) with the starting and ending indices of a given group (which defaults to 0, the whole pattern).

Consider the following example:

```
>>> m = re.match(r'www\.(.*)\..{3}', 'www.python.org')
>>> m.group(1)
'python'
>>> m.start(1)
4
>>> m.end(1)
10
>>> m.span(1)
(4, 10)
```

## Group Numbers and Functions in Substitutions

In the first example using `re.sub`, I simply replaced one substring with another—something I could easily have done with the `replace` string method (described in the section "String Methods" in Chapter 3). Of course, regular expressions are useful because they allow you to search in a more flexible manner, but they also allow you to perform more powerful substitutions.

The easiest way to harness the power of `re.sub` is to use group numbers in the substitution string. Any escape sequences of the form `'\\n'` in the replacement string are replaced by the string matched by group n in the pattern. For example, let's say you want to replace words of the form `'*something*'` with `'<em>something</em>'`, where the former is a normal way of expressing emphasis in plain-text documents (such as email), and the latter is the corresponding HTML code (as used in web pages). Let's first construct the regular expression:

```
>>> emphasis_pattern = r'\*([^\*]+)\*'
```

Note that regular expressions can easily become hard to read, so using meaningful variable names (and possibly a comment or two) is important if anyone (including you!) is going to view the code at some point.

---

**■Tip** One way to make your regular expressions more readable is to use the VERBOSE flag in the `re` functions. This allows you to add whitespace (space characters, tabs, newlines, and so on) to your pattern, which will be ignored by `re`—except when you put it in a character class or escape it with a backslash. You can also put comments in such verbose regular expressions. The following is a pattern object that is equivalent to the emphasis pattern, but which uses the VERBOSE flag:

```
>>> emphasis_pattern = re.compile(r'''
...          \*       # Beginning emphasis tag -- an asterisk
...          (        # Begin group for capturing phrase
...          [^\*]+   # Capture anything except asterisks
...          )        # End group
...          \*       # Ending emphasis tag
...          ''', re.VERBOSE)
...
```

---

Now that I have my pattern, I can use `re.sub` to make my substitution:

```
>>> re.sub(emphasis_pattern, r'<em>\1</em>', 'Hello, *world*!')
'Hello, <em>world</em>!'
```

As you can see, I have successfully translated the text from plain text to HTML.

But you can make your substitutions even more powerful by using a function as the replacement. This function will be supplied with the `MatchObject` as its only parameter, and the string it returns will be used as the replacement. In other words, you can do whatever you want to the matched substring, and do elaborate processing to generate its replacement. What possible use could you have for such power, you ask? Once you start experimenting with regular expressions, you will surely find countless uses for this mechanism. For one application, see the section "A Sample Template System" a little later in the chapter.

## GREEDY AND NONGREEDY PATTERNS

The repetition operators are by default *greedy*, which means that they will match as much as possible. For example, let's say I rewrote the emphasis program to use the following pattern:

```
>>> emphasis_pattern = r'\*(.+)\*'
```

This matches an asterisk, followed by one or more characters, and then another asterisk. Sounds perfect, doesn't it? But it isn't:

```
>>> re.sub(emphasis_pattern, r'<em>\1</em>', '*This* is *it*!')
'<em>This* is *it</em>!'
```

As you can see, the pattern matched everything from the first asterisk to the last—including the two asterisks between! This is what it means to be greedy: take everything you can.

In this case, you clearly don't want this overly greedy behavior. The solution presented in the preceding text (using a character set matching anything *except* an asterisk) is fine when you know that one specific letter is illegal. But let's consider another scenario. What if you used the form `'**something**'` to signify emphasis? Now it shouldn't be a problem to include single asterisks inside the emphasized phrase. But how do you avoid being too greedy?

Actually, it's quite easy—you just use a nongreedy version of the repetition operator. All the repetition operators can be made nongreedy by putting a question mark after them:

```
>>> emphasis_pattern = r'\*\*(.+?)\*\*'
>>> re.sub(emphasis_pattern, r'<em>\1</em>', '**This** is **it**!')
'<em>This</em> is <em>it</em>!'
```

Here I've used the operator `+?` instead of `+`, which means that the pattern will match one or more occurrences of the wildcard, as before. However, it will match as few as it can, because it is now nongreedy. So, it will match only the minimum needed to reach the next occurrence of `'\*\*'`, which is the end of the pattern. As you can see, it works nicely.

## Finding the Sender of an Email

Have you ever saved an email as a text file? If you have, you may have seen that it contains a lot of essentially unreadable text at the top, similar to that shown in Listing 10-9.

**Listing 10-9.** *A Set of (Fictitious) Email Headers*

```
From foo@bar.baz  Thu Dec 20 01:22:50 2008
Return-Path: <foo@bar.baz>
Received: from xyzzy42.bar.com (xyzzy.bar.baz [123.456.789.42])
        by frozz.bozz.floop (8.9.3/8.9.3) with ESMTP id BAA25436
        for <magnus@bozz.floop>; Thu, 20 Dec 2004 01:22:50 +0100 (MET)
Received: from [43.253.124.23] by bar.baz
        (InterMail vM.4.01.03.27 201-229-121-127-20010626) with ESMTP
        id <20041220002242.ADASD123.bar.baz@[43.253.124.23]>;
        Thu, 20 Dec 2004 00:22:42 +0000
User-Agent: Microsoft-Outlook-Express-Macintosh-Edition/5.02.2022
Date: Wed, 19 Dec 2008 17:22:42 -0700
Subject: Re: Spam
From: Foo Fie <foo@bar.baz>
To: Magnus Lie Hetland <magnus@bozz.floop>
CC: <Mr.Gumby@bar.baz>
Message-ID: <B8467D62.84F%foo@baz.com>
In-Reply-To: <20041219013308.A2655@bozz.floop>
Mime-version: 1.0
Content-type: text/plain; charset="US-ASCII"
Content-transfer-encoding: 7bit
Status: RO
Content-Length: 55
Lines: 6

So long, and thanks for all the spam!


Yours,

Foo Fie
```

Let's try to find out who this email is from. If you examine the text, I'm sure you can figure it out in this case (especially if you look at the signature at the bottom of the message itself, of course). But can you see a general pattern? How do you extract the name of the sender, without the email address? Or how can you list all the email addresses mentioned in the headers? Let's handle the former task first.

The line containing the sender begins with the string 'From: ' and ends with an email address enclosed in angle brackets (< and >). You want the text found between those brackets. If you use the fileinput module, this should be an easy task. A program solving the problem is shown in Listing 10-10.

---

■**Note**  You could solve this problem without using regular expressions if you wanted. You could also use the email module.

---

**Listing 10-10.** *A Program for Finding the Sender of an Email*

```
# find_sender.py
import fileinput, re
pat = re.compile('From: (.*) <.*?>$')
for line in fileinput.input():
    m = pat.match(line)
    if m: print m.group(1)
```

You can then run the program like this (assuming that the email message is in the text file message.eml):

```
$ python find_sender.py message.eml
Foo Fie
```

You should note the following about this program:

- I compile the regular expression to make the processing more efficient.

- I enclose the subpattern I want to extract in parentheses, making it a group.

- I use a nongreedy pattern to so the email address matches only the last pair of angle brackets (just in case the name contains some brackets).

- I use a dollar sign to indicate that I want the pattern to match the entire line, all the way to the end.

- I use an if statement to make sure that I did in fact match something before I try to extract the match of a specific group.

To list all the email addresses mentioned in the headers, you need to construct a regular expression that matches an email address but nothing else. You can then use the method findall to find all the occurrences in each line. To avoid duplicates, you keep the addresses in a set (described earlier in this chapter). Finally, you extract the keys, sort them, and print them out:

```
import fileinput, re
pat = re.compile(r'[a-z\-\.]+@[a-z\-\.]+', re.IGNORECASE)
addresses = set()
```

```
for line in fileinput.input():
    for address in pat.findall(line):
        addresses.add(address)
for address in sorted(addresses):
    print address
```

The resulting output when running this program (with the email message in Listing 10-9 as input) is as follows:

```
Mr.Gumby@bar.baz
foo@bar.baz
foo@baz.com
magnus@bozz.floop
```

Note that when sorting, uppercase letters come before lowercase letters.

■ **Note** I haven't adhered strictly to the problem specification here. The problem was to find the addresses in the header, but in this case the program finds all the addresses in the entire file. To avoid that, you can call `fileinput.close()` if you find an empty line, because the header can't contain empty lines. Alternatively, you can use `fileinput.nextfile()` to start processing the next file, if there is more than one.

## A Sample Template System

A *template* is a file you can put specific values into to get a finished text of some kind. For example, you may have a mail template requiring only the insertion of a recipient name. Python already has an advanced template mechanism: string formatting. However, with regular expressions, you can make the system even more advanced. Let's say you want to replace all occurrences of '[something]' (the "fields") with the result of evaluating something as an expression in Python. Thus, this string:

```
'The sum of 7 and 9 is [7 + 9].'
```

should be translated to this:

```
'The sum of 7 and 9 is 16.'
```

Also, you want to be able to perform assignments in these fields, so that this string:

```
'[name="Mr. Gumby"]Hello, [name]'
```

should be translated to this:

```
'Hello, Mr. Gumby'
```

This may sound like a complex task, but let's review the available tools:

- You can use a regular expression to match the fields and extract their contents.

- You can evaluate the expression strings with eval, supplying the dictionary containing the scope. You do this in a try/except statement. If a SyntaxError is raised, you probably have a statement (such as an assignment) on your hands and should use exec instead.

- You can execute the assignment strings (and other statements) with exec, storing the template's scope in a dictionary.

- You can use re.sub to substitute the result of the evaluation into the string being processed.

Suddenly, it doesn't look so intimidating, does it?

---

■**Tip** If a task seems daunting, it almost always helps to break it down into smaller pieces. Also, take stock of the tools at your disposal for ideas on how to solve your problem.

---

See Listing 10-11 for a sample implementation.

**Listing 10-11.** *A Template System*

```
# templates.py

import fileinput, re

# Matches fields enclosed in square brackets:
field_pat = re.compile(r'\[(.+?)\]')


# We'll collect variables in this:
scope = {}

# This is used in re.sub:
def replacement(match):
    code = match.group(1)
    try:
        # If the field can be evaluated, return it:
        return str(eval(code, scope))
    except SyntaxError:
        # Otherwise, execute the assignment in the same scope...
        exec code in scope
        # ...and return an empty string:
        return ''

# Get all the text as a single string:
```

```
# (There are other ways of doing this; see Chapter 11)
lines = []
for line in fileinput.input():
    lines.append(line)
text = ''.join(lines)

# Substitute all the occurrences of the field pattern:
print field_pat.sub(replacement, text)
```

Simply put, this program does the following:

- Define a pattern for matching fields.

- Create a dictionary to act as a scope for the template.

- Define a replacement function that does the following:

  - Grabs group 1 from the match and puts it in code.

  - Tries to evaluate code with the scope dictionary as namespace, converts the result to a string, and returns it. If this succeeds, the field was an expression and everything is fine. Otherwise (that is, a SyntaxError is raised), go to the next step.

  - Execute the field in the same namespace (the scope dictionary) used for evaluating expressions, and then returns an empty string (because the assignment doesn't evaluate to anything).

- Use fileinput to read in all available lines, put them in a list, and join them into one big string.

- Replace all occurrences of field_pat using the replacement function in re.sub, and print the result.

---

**Note** In previous versions of Python, it was much more efficient to put the lines into a list and then join them at the end than to do something like this:

```
text = ''
for line in fileinput.input():
    text += line
```

Although this looks elegant, each assignment must create a new string, which is the old string with the new one appended, which can lead to a waste of resources and make your program slow. In older versions of Python, the difference between this and using join could be huge. In more recent versions, using the += operator may, in fact, be *faster*. If performance is important to you, you could try out both solutions. And if you want a more elegant way to read in all the text of a file, take a peek at Chapter 11.

---

So, I have just created a really powerful template system in only 15 lines of code (not counting whitespace and comments). I hope you're starting to see how powerful Python becomes when you use the standard libraries. Let's finish this example by testing the template system. Try running it on the simple file shown in Listing 10-12.

**Listing 10-12.** *A Simple Template Example*

```
[x = 2]
[y = 3]
The sum of [x] and [y] is [x + y].
```

You should see this:

---

```
The sum of 2 and 3 is 5.
```

---

**Note** It may not be obvious, but there are three empty lines in the preceding output—two above and one below the text. Although the first two fields have been replaced by empty strings, the newlines following them are still there. Also, the `print` statement adds a newline, which accounts for the empty line at the end.

But wait, it gets better! Because I have used `fileinput`, I can process several files in turn. That means that I can use one file to define values for some variables, and then another file as a template where these values are inserted. For example, I might have one file with definitions as in Listing 10-13, named `magnus.txt`, and a template file as in Listing 10-14, named `template.txt`.

**Listing 10-13.** *Some Template Definitions*

```
[name     = 'Magnus Lie Hetland' ]
[email    = 'magnus@foo.bar'      ]
[language = 'python'              ]
```

**Listing 10-14.** *A Template*

```
[import time]
Dear [name],

I would like to learn how to program. I hear you use
the [language] language a lot -- is it something I
should consider?

And, by the way, is [email] your correct email address?
```

```
Fooville, [time.asctime()]
```

```
Oscar Frozzbozz
```

The import time isn't an assignment (which is the statement type I set out to handle), but because I'm not being picky and just use a simple try/except statement, my program supports any statement or expression that works with eval or exec. You can run the program like this (assuming a UNIX command line):

```
$ python templates.py magnus.txt template.txt
```

You should get some output similar to the following:

```
Dear Magnus Lie Hetland,

I would like to learn how to program. I hear you use
the python language a lot -- is it something I
should consider?

And, by the way, is magnus@foo.bar your correct email address?


Fooville, Wed Apr 24 20:34:29 2008

Oscar Frozzbozz
```

Even though this template system is capable of some quite powerful substitutions, it still has some flaws. For example, it would be nice if you could write the definition file in a more flexible manner. If it were executed with execfile, you could simply use normal Python syntax. That would also fix the problem of getting all those blank lines at the top of the output.

Can you think of other ways of improving the program? Can you think of other uses for the concepts used in this program? The best way to become really proficient in any programming language is to play with it—test its limitations and discover its strengths. See if you can rewrite this program so it works better and suits your needs.

**Note** There is, in fact, a perfectly good template system available in the standard libraries, in the string module. Just take a look at the Template class, for example.

## Other Interesting Standard Modules

Even though this chapter has covered a lot of material, I have barely scratched the surface of the standard libraries. To tempt you to dive in, I'll quickly mention a few more cool libraries:

functools: Here, you can find functionality that lets you use a function with only *some* of its parameters (partial evaluation), filling in the remaining ones at a later time. In Python 3.0, this is where you will find filter and reduce.

difflib: This library enables you to compute how similar two sequences are. It also enables you to find the sequences (from a list of possibilities) that are "most similar" to an original sequence you provide. difflib could be used to create a simple searching program, for example.

hashlib: With this module, you can compute small "signatures" (numbers) from strings. And if you compute the signatures for two different strings, you can be almost certain that the two signatures will be different. You can use this on large text files. These modules have several uses in cryptography and security.[5]

csv: CSV is short for comma-separated values, a simple format used by many applications (for example, many spreadsheets and database programs) to store tabular data. It is mainly used when exchanging data between different programs. The csv module lets you read and write CSV files easily, and it handles some of the trickier parts of the format quite transparently.

timeit, profile, and trace: The timeit module (with its accompanying command-line script) is a tool for measuring the time a piece of code takes to run. It has some tricks up its sleeve, and you probably ought to use it rather than the time module for performance measurements. The profile module (along with its companion module, pstats) can be used for a more comprehensive analysis of the efficiency of a piece of code. The trace module (and program) can give you a coverage analysis (that is, which parts of your code are executed and which are not). This can be useful when writing test code, for example.

datetime: If the time module isn't enough for your time-tracking needs, it's quite possible that datetime will be. It has support for special date and time objects, and allows you to construct and combine these in various ways. The interface is in many ways a bit more intuitive than that of the time module.

itertools: Here, you have a lot of tools for creating and combining iterators (or other iterable objects). There are functions for chaining iterables, for creating iterators that return consecutive integers forever (similar to range, but without an upper limit), to cycle through an iterable repeatedly, and other useful stuff.

logging: Simply using print statements to figure out what's going on in your program can be useful. If you want to keep track of things even without having a lot of debugging output, you might write this information to a log file. This module gives you a standard set of tools for managing one or more central logs, with several levels of priority for your log messages, among other things.

---

5. See also the md5 and sha modules.

getopt and optparse: In UNIX, command-line programs are often run with various *options* or *switches*. (The Python interpreter is a typical example.) These will all be found in sys.argv, but handling these correctly yourself is far from easy. The getopt library is a tried-and-true solution to this problem, while optparse is newer, more powerful, and much easier to use.

cmd: This module enables you to write a command-line interpreter, somewhat like the Python interactive interpreter. You can define your own commands that the user can execute at the prompt. Perhaps you could use this as the user interface to one of your programs?

# A Quick Summary

In this chapter, you've learned about modules: how to create them, how to explore them, and how to use some of those included in the standard Python libraries.

**Modules**: A module is basically a subprogram whose main function is to *define things*, such as functions, classes, and variables. If a module contains any test code, it should be placed in an if statement that checks whether __name__=='__main__'. Modules can be imported if they are in the PYTHONPATH. You import a module stored in the file foo.py with the statement import foo.

**Packages**: A package is just a module that contains other modules. Packages are implemented as directories that contain a file named __init__.py.

**Exploring modules**: After you have imported a module into the interactive interpreter, you can explore it in many ways. Among them are using dir, examining the __all__ variable, and using the help function. The documentation and the source code can also be excellent sources of information and insight.

**The standard library**: Python comes with several modules included, collectively called the standard library. Some of these were reviewed in this chapter:

- sys: A module that gives you access to several variables and functions that are tightly linked with the Python interpreter.

- os: A module that gives you access to several variables and functions that are tightly linked with the operating system.

- fileinput: A module that makes it easy to iterate over the lines of several files or streams.

- sets, heapq, and deque: Three modules that provide three useful data structures. Sets are also available in the form of the built-in type set.

- time: A module for getting the current time, and for manipulating and formatting times and dates.

- random: A module with functions for generating random numbers, choosing random elements from a sequence, and shuffling the elements of a list.

- shelve: A module for creating a persistent mapping, which stores its contents in a database with a given file name.

- re: A module with support for regular expressions.

If you are curious to find out more about modules, I again urge you to browse the Python Library Reference (http://python.org/doc/lib). It's really interesting reading.

## New Functions in This Chapter

| Function | Description |
| --- | --- |
| dir(obj) | Returns an alphabetized list of attribute names |
| help([obj]) | Provides interactive help or help about a specific object |
| reload(module) | Returns a reloaded version of a module that has already been imported. To be abolished in Python 3.0. |

## What Now?

If you have grasped at least a few of the concepts in this chapter, your Python prowess has probably taken a great leap forward. With the standard libraries at your fingertips, Python changes from powerful to extremely powerful. With what you have learned so far, you can write programs to tackle a wide range of problems. In the next chapter, you learn more about using Python to interact with the outside world of files and networks, and thereby tackle problems of greater scope.

■ ■ ■

# CHAPTER 11

# Files and Stuff

**S**o far, we've mainly been working with data structures that reside in the interpreter itself. What little interaction our programs have had with the outside world has been through input, raw_input, and print. In this chapter, we go one step further and let our programs catch a glimpse of a larger world: the world of files and streams. The functions and objects described in this chapter will enable you to store data between program invocations and to process data from other programs.

## Opening Files

You can open files with the open function, which has the following syntax:

```
open(name[, mode[, buffering]])
```

The open function takes a file name as its only mandatory argument, and returns a file object. The mode and buffering arguments are both optional and will be explained in the following sections.

Assuming that you have a text file (created with your text editor, perhaps) called somefile.txt stored in the directory C:\text (or something like ~/text in UNIX), you can open it like this:

```
>>> f = open(r'C:\text\somefile.txt')
```

If the file doesn't exist, you may see an exception traceback like this:

```
Traceback (most recent call last):
  File "<pyshell#0>", line 1, in ?
IOError: [Errno 2] No such file or directory: "C:\\text\\somefile.txt"
```

You'll see what you can do with such file objects in a little while, but first, let's take a look at the other two arguments of the open function.

### File Modes

If you use open with only a file name as a parameter, you get a file object you can read from. If you want to write to the file, you must state that explicitly, supplying a *mode*. (Be patient—I get to the actual reading and writing in a little while.) The mode argument to the open function can have several values, as summarized in Table 11-1.

**Table 11-1.** *Most Common Values for the Mode Argument of the open Function*

| Value | Description |
| --- | --- |
| 'r' | Read mode |
| 'w' | Write mode |
| 'a' | Append mode |
| 'b' | Binary mode (added to other mode) |
| '+' | Read/write mode (added to other mode) |

Explicitly specifying read mode has the same effect as not supplying a mode string at all. The write mode enables you to write to the file.

The '+' can be added to any of the other modes to indicate that both reading and writing is allowed. So, for example, 'r+' can be used when opening a text file for reading and writing. (For this to be useful, you will probably want to use seek as well; see the sidebar "Random Access" later in this chapter.)

The 'b' mode changes the way the file is handled. Generally, Python assumes that you are dealing with text files (containing characters). Typically, this is not a problem. But if you are processing some other kind of file (called a *binary* file) such as a sound clip or an image, you should add a 'b' to your mode: for example, 'rb' to read a binary file.

## WHY USE BINARY MODE?

If you use binary mode when you read (or write) a file, things won't be much different. You are still able to read a number of bytes (basically the same as characters), and perform other operations associated with text files. The main point is that when you use binary mode, Python gives you exactly the contents found in the file—and in text mode, it won't necessarily do that.

If you find it shocking that Python manipulates your text files, don't worry. The only "trick" it employs is to standardize your line endings. Generally, in Python, you end your lines with a newline character (\n), as is the norm in UNIX systems. This is not standard in Windows, however. In Windows, a line ending is marked with \r\n. To hide this from your program (so it can work seamlessly across different platforms), Python does some automatic conversion here. When you read text from a file in text mode in Windows, it converts \r\n to \n. Conversely, when you write text to a file in text mode in Windows, it converts \n to \r\n. (The Macintosh version does the same thing, but converts between \n and \r.)

The problem occurs when you work with a binary file, such as a sound clip. It may contain bytes that can be interpreted as the line-ending characters mentioned in the previous paragraph, and if you are using text mode, Python performs its automatic conversion. However, that will probably destroy your binary data. So, to avoid that, you simply use binary mode, and no conversions are made.

Note that this distinction is not important on platforms (such as UNIX) where the newline character is the standard line terminator, because no conversion is performed there anyway.

> **■Note** Files can be opened in universal newline support mode, using the mode character U together with, for example, r. In this mode, all line-ending characters/strings (\r\n, \r, or \n) are then converted to newline characters (\n), regardless of which convention is followed on the current platform.

## Buffering

The open function takes a third (optional) parameter, which controls the *buffering* of the file. If the parameter is 0 (or False), input/output (I/O) is unbuffered (all reads and writes go directly from/to the disk); if it is 1 (or True), I/O is buffered (meaning that Python may use memory instead of disk space to make things go faster, and only update when you use flush or close—see the section "Closing Files," later in this chapter). Larger numbers indicate the buffer size (in bytes), while –1 (or any negative number) sets the buffer size to the default.

# The Basic File Methods

Now you know how to open files. The next step is to do something useful with them. In this section, you learn about some basic methods of file objects (and some other file-like objects, sometimes called *streams*).

> **■Note** You will probably run into the term *file-like* repeatedly in your Python career (I've used it a few times already). A file-like object is simply one supporting a few of the same methods as a file, most notably either read or write or both. The objects returned by urllib.urlopen (see Chapter 14) are a good example of this. They support methods such as read, readline, and readlines, but not (at the time of writing) methods such as isatty, for example.

---

### THREE STANDARD STREAMS

In Chapter 10, in the section about the sys module, I mentioned three standard streams. These are actually files (or file-like objects), and you can apply most of what you learn about files to them.

A standard source of data input is sys.stdin. When a program reads from standard input, you can supply text by typing it, or you can link it with the standard output of another program, using a *pipe*, as demonstrated in the section "Piping Output." (This is a standard UNIX concept.)

The text you give to print appears in sys.stdout. The prompts for input and raw_input also go there. Data written to sys.stdout typically appears on your screen, but can be rerouted to the standard input of another program with a pipe, as mentioned.

Error messages (such as stack traces) are written to sys.stderr. In many ways, it is similar to sys.stdout.

## Reading and Writing

The most important capabilities of files (or streams) are supplying and receiving data. If you have a file-like object named f, you can write data (in the form of a string) with the method f.write, and read data (also as a string) with the method f.read.

Each time you call f.write(string), the string you supply is written to the file after those you have written previously:

```
>>> f = open('somefile.txt', 'w')
>>> f.write('Hello, ')
>>> f.write('World!')
>>> f.close()
```

Notice that I call the close method when I'm finished with the file. You learn more about it in the section "Closing Your Files" later in this chapter.

Reading is just as simple. Just remember to tell the stream how many characters (bytes) you want to read.

Here's an example (continuing where I left off):

```
>>> f = open('somefile.txt', 'r')
>>> f.read(4)
'Hell'
>>> f.read()
'o, World!'
```

First, I specify how many characters to read (4), and then I simply read the rest of the file (by not supplying a number). Note that I could have dropped the mode specification from the call to open because 'r' is the default.

## Piping Output

In a UNIX shell (such as GNU bash), you can write several commands after one another, linked together with *pipes*, as in this example (assuming GNU bash):

```
$ cat somefile.txt | python somescript.py | sort
```

---

■**Note** GNU bash is also available in Windows. For more information, visit http://www.cygwin.com. In Mac OS X, the shell is available out of the box, through the Terminal application, for example.

---

This pipeline consists of three commands:

- `cat somefile.txt`: This command simply writes the contents of the file `somefile.txt` to standard output (`sys.stdout`).

- `python somescript.py`: This command executes the Python script `somescript`. The script presumably reads from its standard input and writes the result to standard output.

- `sort`: This command reads all the text from standard input (`sys.stdin`), sorts the lines alphabetically, and writes the result to standard output.

But what is the point of these pipe characters (|), and what does `somescript.py` do?

The pipes link up the standard output of one command with the standard input of the next. Clever, eh? So you can safely guess that `somescript.py` reads data from its `sys.stdin` (which is what `cat somefile.txt` writes) and writes some result to its `sys.stdout` (which is where `sort` gets its data).

A simple script (`somescript.py`) that uses `sys.stdin` is shown in Listing 11-1. The contents of the file `somefile.txt` are shown in Listing 11-2.

**Listing 11-1.** *Simple Script That Counts the Words in sys.stdin*

```
# somescript.py
import sys
text = sys.stdin.read()
words = text.split()
wordcount = len(words)
print 'Wordcount:', wordcount
```

**Listing 11-2.** *A File Containing Some Nonsensical Text*

```
Your mother was a hamster and your
father smelled of elderberries.
```

Here are the results of `cat somefile.txt | python somescript.py`:

```
Wordcount: 11
```

## RANDOM ACCESS

In this chapter, I treat files only as streams—you can read data only from start to finish, strictly in order. In fact, you can also move around a file, accessing only the parts you are interested in (called *random access*) by using the two file-object methods seek and tell.

The method seek(offset[, whence]) moves the current position (where reading or writing is performed) to the position described by offset and whence. offset is a byte (character) count. whence defaults to 0, which means that the offset is from the beginning of the file (the offset must be nonnegative). whence may also be set to 1 (move relative to current position; the offset may be negative), or 2 (move relative to the end of the file). Consider this example:

```
>>> f = open(r'c:\text\somefile.txt', 'w')
>>> f.write('01234567890123456789')
>>> f.seek(5)
>>> f.write('Hello, World!')
>>> f.close()
>>> f = open(r'c:\text\somefile.txt')
>>> f.read()
'01234Hello, World!89'
```

The method tell() returns the current file position, as in the following example:

```
>>> f = open(r'c:\text\somefile.txt')
>>> f.read(3)
'012'
>>> f.read(2)
'34'
>>> f.tell()
5L
```

Note that the number returned from f.tell in this case was a long integer. That may not always be the case.

## Reading and Writing Lines

Actually, what I've been doing until now is a bit impractical. Usually, I could just as well be reading in the lines of a stream as reading letter by letter. You can read a single line (text from where you have come so far, up to and including the first line separator you encounter) with the method file.readline. You can either use it without any arguments (in which case a line is simply read and returned) or with a nonnegative integer, which is then the maximum number of characters (or bytes) that readline is allowed to read. So if someFile.readline() returns 'Hello, World!\n', someFile.readline(5) returns 'Hello'. To read all the lines of a file and have them returned as a list, use the readlines method.

The method `writelines` is the opposite of `readlines`: give it a list (or, in fact, any sequence or iterable object) of strings, and it writes all the strings to the file (or stream). Note that newlines are *not* added; you need to add those yourself. Also, there is no `writeline` method because you can just use `write`.

---

■**Note**  On platforms that use other line separators, substitute "carriage return" (Mac) or "carriage return and newline" (Windows) for "newline" (as determined by `os.linesep`).

---

## Closing Files

You should remember to close your files by calling their `close` method. Usually, a file object is closed automatically when you quit your program (and possibly before that), and not closing files you have been *reading* from isn't really that important. However, closing those files can't hurt, and might help to avoid keeping the file uselessly "locked" against modification in some operating systems and settings. It also avoids using up any quotas for open files your system might have.

You should always close a file you have *written* to because Python may *buffer* (keep stored temporarily somewhere, for efficiency reasons) the data you have written, and if your program crashes for some reason, the data might not be written to the file at all. The safe thing is to close your files after you're finished with them.

If you want to be certain that your file is closed, you should use a `try`/`finally` statement with the call to `close` in the `finally` clause:

```
# Open your file here
try:
    # Write data to your file
finally:
    file.close()
```

There is, in fact, a statement designed specifically for this situation (introduced in Python 2.5)—the `with` statement:

```
with open("somefile.txt") as somefile:
    do_something(somefile)
```

The `with` statement lets you open a file and assign it to a variable name (in this case, soefile). You then write data to your file (and, perhaps, do other things) in the body of the statement, and the file is automatically closed when the end of the statement is reached, even if that is caused by an exception.

In Python 2.5, the `with` statement is available only after the following import:

```
from __future__ import with_statement
```

In later versions, the statement is always available.

■**Tip**  After writing something to a file, you usually want the changes to appear in that file, so other programs reading the same file can see the changes. Well, isn't that what happens, you say? Not necessarily. As mentioned, the data may be *buffered* (stored temporarily somewhere in memory), and not written until you close the file. If you want to keep working with the file (and not close it) but still want to make sure the file on disk is updated to reflect your changes, call the file object's flush method. (Note, however, that flush might not allow other programs running at the same time to access the file, due to locking considerations that depend on your operating system and settings. Whenever you can conveniently close the file, that is preferable.)

## CONTEXT MANAGERS

The with statement is actually a quite general construct, allowing you to use so-called *context managers*. A context manager is an object that supports two methods: __enter__ and __exit__.

The __enter__ method takes no arguments. It is called when entering the with statement, and the return value is bound to the variable after the as keyword.

The __exit__ method takes three arguments: an exception type, an exception object, and an exception traceback. It is called when leaving the method (with any exception raised supplied through the parameters). If __exit__ returns false, any exceptions are suppressed.

Files may be used as context managers. Their __enter__ methods return the file objects themselves, while their __exit__ methods close the files. For more information about this powerful, yet rather advanced, feature, check out the description of context managers in the Python Reference Manual. Also see the sections on context manager types and on contextlib in the Python Library Reference.

## Using the Basic File Methods

Assume that somefile.txt contains the text in Listing 11-3. What can you do with it?

**Listing 11-3.** *A Simple Text File*

```
Welcome to this file
There is nothing here except
This stupid haiku
```

Let's try the methods you know, starting with read(n):

```
>>> f = open(r'c:\text\somefile.txt')
>>> f.read(7)
'Welcome'
>>> f.read(4)
' to '
>>> f.close()
```

Next up is read():

```
>>> f = open(r'c:\text\somefile.txt')
>>> print f.read()
Welcome to this file
There is nothing here except
This stupid haiku
>>> f.close()
```

Here's readline():

```
>>> f = open(r'c:\text\somefile.txt')
>>> for i in range(3):
        print str(i) + ': ' + f.readline(),
0: Welcome to this file
1: There is nothing here except
2: This stupid haiku
>>> f.close()
```

And here's readlines():

```
>>> import pprint
>>> pprint.pprint(open(r'c:\text\somefile.txt').readlines())
['Welcome to this file\n',
 'There is nothing here except\n',
 'This stupid haiku']
```

Note that I relied on the file object being closed automatically in this example.
Now let's try writing, beginning with write(string):

```
>>> f = open(r'c:\text\somefile.txt', 'w')
>>> f.write('this\nis no\nhaiku')
>>> f.close()
```

After running this, the file contains the text in Listing 11-4.

**Listing 11-4.** *The Modified Text File*

```
this
is no
haiku
```

Finally, here's writelines(list):

```
>>> f = open(r'c:\text\somefile.txt')
>>> lines = f.readlines()
>>> f.close()
>>> lines[1] = "isn't a\n"
>>> f = open(r'c:\text\somefile.txt', 'w')
>>> f.writelines(lines)
>>> f.close()
```

After running this, the file contains the text in Listing 11-5.

**Listing 11-5.** *The Text File, Modified Again*

```
this
isn't a
haiku
```

# Iterating over File Contents

Now you've seen some of the methods file objects present to us, and you've learned how to acquire such file objects. One of the common operations on files is to iterate over their contents, repeatedly performing some action as you go. There are many ways of doing this, and you can certainly just find your favorite and stick to that. However, others may have done it differently, and to understand their programs, you should know all the basic techniques. Some of these techniques are just applications of the methods you've already seen (read, readline, and readlines); others I'll introduce here (for example, xreadlines and file iterators).

In all the examples in this section, I use a fictitious function called process to represent the processing of each character or line. Feel free to implement it in any way you like. Here's one simple example:

```
def process(string):
    print 'Processing: ', string
```

More useful implementations could do such things as storing data in a data structure, computing a sum, replacing patterns with the re module, or perhaps adding line numbers.

Also, to try out the examples, you should set the variable filename to the name of some actual file.

## Doing It Byte by Byte

One of the most basic (but probably least common) ways of iterating over file contents is to use the read method in a while loop. For example, you might want to loop over every character (byte) in the file. You could do that as shown in Listing 11-6.

**Listing 11-6.** *Looping over Characters with read*

```
f = open(filename)
char = f.read(1)
while char:
    process(char)
    char = f.read(1)
f.close()
```

This program works because when you have reached the end of the file, the read method returns an empty string, but until then, the string always contains one character (and thus has the Boolean value true). As long as char is true, you know that you aren't finished yet.

As you can see, I have repeated the assignment char = f.read(1), and code repetition is generally considered a bad thing. (Laziness is a virtue, remember?) To avoid that, I can use the while True/break technique introduced in Chapter 5. The resulting code is shown in Listing 11-7.

**Listing 11-7.** *Writing the Loop Differently*

```
f = open(filename)
while True:
    char = f.read(1)
    if not char: break
    process(char)
f.close()
```

As mentioned in Chapter 5, you shouldn't use the break statement too often (because it tends to make the code more difficult to follow). Even so, the approach shown in Listing 11-7 is usually preferred to that in Listing 11-6, precisely because you avoid duplicated code.

## One Line at a Time

When dealing with text files, you are often interested in iterating over the *lines* in the file, not each individual character. You can do this easily in the same way as we did with characters, using the readline method (described earlier, in the section "Reading and Writing Lines"), as shown in Listing 11-8.

**Listing 11-8.** *Using readline in a while Loop*

```
f = open(filename)
while True:
    line = f.readline()
    if not line: break
    process(line)
f.close()
```

## Reading Everything

If the file isn't too large, you can just read the whole file in one go, using the read method with no parameters (to read the entire file as a string), or the readlines method (to read the file into a list of strings, in which each string is a line). Listings 11-9 and 11-10 show how easy it is to iterate over characters and lines when you read the file like this. Note that reading the contents of a file into a string or a list like this can be useful for other things besides iteration. For example, you might apply a regular expression to the string, or you might store the list of lines in some data structure for further use.

**Listing 11-9.** *Iterating over Characters with read*

```
f = open(filename)
for char in f.read():
    process(char)
f.close()
```

**Listing 11-10.** *Iterating over Lines with readlines*

```
f = open(filename)
for line in f.readlines():
    process(line)
f.close()
```

## Lazy Line Iteration with fileinput

Sometimes you need to iterate over the lines in a very large file, and readlines would use too much memory. You could use a while loop with readline, of course, but in Python, for loops are preferable when they are available. It just so happens that they are in this case. You can use a method called *lazy line iteration*—it's lazy because it reads only the parts of the file actually needed (more or less).

You have already encountered fileinput in Chapter 10. Listing 11-11 shows how you might use it. Note that the fileinput module takes care of opening the file. You just need to give it a file name.

**Listing 11-11.** *Iterating over Lines with fileinput*

```
import fileinput
for line in fileinput.input(filename):
    process(line)
```

---

■**Note** In older code, you may also see lazy line iteration performed using the xreadlines method. It works almost like readlines except that it doesn't read all the lines into a list. Instead it creates an xreadlines object. Note that xreadlines is somewhat old-fashioned, and you should instead use fileinput or file iterators (explained next) in your own code.

---

## File Iterators

It's time for the coolest (and, perhaps, the most common) technique of all. If Python had had this since the beginning, I suspect that several of the other methods (at least xreadlines) would never have appeared. So what is this cool technique? In current versions of Python (from version 2.2), files are *iterable,* which means that you can use them directly in for loops to iterate over their lines. See Listing 11-12 for an example. Pretty elegant, isn't it?

**Listing 11-12.** *Iterating over a File*

```
f = open(filename)
for line in f:
    process(line)
f.close()
```

In these iteration examples, I have explicitly closed my files. Although this is generally a good idea, it's not critical, as long as I don't write to the file. If you are willing to let Python take care of the closing, you could simplify the example even further, as shown in Listing 11-13. Here, I don't assign the opened file to a variable (like the variable f I've used in the other examples), and therefore I have no way of explicitly closing it.

**Listing 11-13.** *Iterating over a File Without Storing the File Object in a Variable*

```
for line in open(filename):
    process(line)
```

Note that sys.stdin is iterable, just like other files, so if you want to iterate over all the lines in standard input, you can use this form:

```
import sys
for line in sys.stdin:
    process(line)
```

Also, you can do all the things you can do with iterators in general, such as converting them into lists of strings (by using list(open(filename))), which would simply be equivalent to using readlines.

Consider the following example:

```
>>> f = open('somefile.txt', 'w')
>>> f.write('First line\n')
>>> f.write('Second line\n')
>>> f.write('Third line\n')
>>> f.close()
>>> lines = list(open('somefile.txt)')
>>> lines
['First line\n', 'Second line\n', 'Third line\n']
>>> first, second, third = open('somefile.txt')
>>> first
'First line\n'
>>> second
'Second line\n'
>>> third
'Third line\n'
```

In this example, it's important to note the following:

- I've used print to write to the file. This automatically adds newlines after the strings I supply.

- I use sequence unpacking on the opened file, putting each line in a separate variable. (This isn't exactly common practice because you usually won't know the number of lines in your file, but it demonstrates the "iterability" of the file object.)

- I close the file after having written to it, to ensure that the data is flushed to disk. (As you can see, I haven't closed it after reading from it. Sloppy, perhaps, but not critical.)

# A Quick Summary

In this chapter, you've seen how to interact with the environment through files and file-like objects, one of the most important techniques for I/O in Python. Here are some of the highlights from the chapter:

**File-like objects**: A file-like object is (informally) an object that supports a set of methods such as read and readline (and possibly write and writelines).

**Opening and closing files**: You open a file with the open function (in newer versions of Python, actually just an alias for file), by supplying a file name. If you want to make sure your file is closed, even if something goes wrong, you can use the with statement.

**Modes and file types**: When opening a file, you can also supply a *mode*, such as 'r' for read mode or 'w' for write mode. By appending 'b' to your mode, you can open files as binary files. (This is necessary only on platforms where Python performs line-ending conversion, such as Windows, but might be prudent elsewhere, too.)

**Standard streams**: The three standard files (stdin, stdout, and stderr, found in the sys module) are file-like objects that implement the UNIX *standard I/O* mechanism (also available in Windows).

**Reading and writing**: You read from a file or file-like object using the method read. You write with the method write.

**Reading and writing lines**: You can read lines from a file using readline, readlines, and (for efficient iteration) xreadlines. You can write files with writelines.

**Iterating over file contents**: There are many ways of iterating over file contents. It is most common to iterate over the lines of a text file, and you can do this by simply iterating over the file itself. There are other methods too, such as readlines and xreadlines, that are compatible with older versions of Python.

## New Functions in This Chapter

| Function | Description |
|---|---|
| `file(name[, mode[, buffering]])` | Opens a file and returns a file object. |
| `open(name[, mode[, buffering]])` | Alias for `file`; use `open` rather than `file` when opening a file. |

## What Now?

So now you know how to interact with the environment through files, but what about interacting with the user? So far we've used only `input`, `raw_input`, and `print`, and unless the user writes something in a file that your program can read, you don't really have any other tools for creating user interfaces. That changes in the next chapter, where I cover graphical user interfaces, with windows, buttons, and so on.

# CHAPTER 12

■ ■ ■

# Graphical User Interfaces

In this chapter, you learn how to make graphical user interfaces (GUIs) for your Python programs—you know, windows with buttons and text fields and stuff like that. Pretty cool, huh?

Plenty of so-called "GUI toolkits" are available for Python, but none of them is recognized as *the* standard GUI toolkit. This has its advantages (greater freedom of choice) and drawbacks (others can't use your programs unless they have the same GUI toolkit installed). Fortunately, there is no conflict between the various GUI toolkits available for Python, so you can install as many different GUI toolkits as you want.

This chapter gives a brief introduction to one of the most mature cross-platform GUI toolkits for Python, called wxPython. For a more thorough introduction to wxPython programming, consult the official documentation (`http://wxpython.org`). For some more information about GUI programming, see Chapter 28.

## A Plethora of Platforms

Before writing a GUI program in Python, you need to decide which GUI platform you want to use. Simply put, a platform is one specific set of graphical components, accessible through a given Python module, called a GUI toolkit. As noted earlier, many such toolkits are available for Python. Some of the most popular ones are listed in Table 12-1. For an even more detailed list, you could search the Vaults of Parnassus (`http://py.vaults.ca/`) for the keyword "GUI." An extensive list of toolkits can also be found in the Python Wiki (`http://wiki.python.org/moin/GuiProgramming`), and Guilherme Polo has written a paper comparing four major platforms.[1]

**Table 12-1.** *Some Popular GUI Toolkits Available for Python*

| Package | Description | Web Site |
|---------|-------------|----------|
| Tkinter | Uses the Tk platform. Readily available. Semistandard. | `http://wiki.python.org/moin/TkInter` |
| wxPython | Based on wxWindows. Cross-platform. Increasingly popular. | `http://wxpython.org` |

*Continued*

---

1. "PyGTK, PyQt, Tkinter and wxPython comparison," *The Python Papers*, Volume 3, Issue 1, pages 26–37. Available from `http://pythonpapers.org`.

**Table 12-1.** *Continued*

| Package | Description | Web Site |
|---------|-------------|----------|
| PythonWin | Windows only. Uses native Windows GUI capabilities. | `http://starship.python.net/crew/mhammond` |
| Java Swing | Jython only. Uses native Java GUI capabilities. | `http://java.sun.com/docs/books/tutorial/uiswing` |
| PyGTK | Uses the GTK platform. Especially popular on Linux. | `http://pygtk.org` |
| PyQt | Uses the Qt platform. Cross-platform. | `http://wiki.python.org/moin/PyQt` |

So which GUI toolkit should you use? It is largely a matter of taste, although each toolkit has its advantages and drawbacks. Tkinter is sort of a *de facto* standard because it has been used in most "official" Python GUI programs, and it is included as a part of the Windows binary distribution. On UNIX, however, you need to compile and install it yourself. I'll cover Tkinter, as well as Java Swing, in the section "But I'd Rather Use . . ." later in this chapter.

Another toolkit that is gaining in popularity is wxPython. This is a mature and feature-rich toolkit, which also happens to be the favorite of Python's creator, Guido van Rossum. We'll use wxPython for this chapter's example.

For information about PythonWin, PyGTK, and PyQt, check out the project home pages (see Table 12-1).

# Downloading and Installing wxPython

To download wxPython, simply visit the download page, `http://wxpython.org/download.php`. This page gives you detailed instructions about which version to download, as well as the prerequisites for the various versions.

If you're running Windows, you probably want a prebuilt binary. You can choose between one version with Unicode support and one without; unless you know you need Unicode, it probably won't make much of a difference which one you choose. Make sure you choose the binary that corresponds to your version of Python. A version of wxPython compiled for Python 2.3 won't work with Python 2.4, for example.

For Mac OS X, you should again choose the wxPython version that agrees with your Python version. You might also need to take the OS version into consideration. Again, you may need to choose between a version with Unicode support and one without; just take your pick. The download links and associated explanations should make it perfectly clear which version you need.

If you're using Linux, you could check to see if your package manager has wxPython. It should be present in most mainstream distributions. There are also RPM packages for various flavors of Linux. If you're running a Linux distribution with RPM, you should at least download the wxPython common and runtime packages; you probably won't need the devel package. Again, choose the version corresponding to your Python version and Linux distribution.

If none of the binaries fit your hardware or operating system (or Python version, for that matter), you can always download the source distribution. Getting this to compile might require downloading other source packages for various prerequisites. You'll find fairly detailed explanations on the wxPython download page.

Once you have wxPython itself, I strongly suggest that you download the demo distribution, which contains documentation, sample programs, and one very thorough (and instructive) demo program. This demo program exercises most of the wxPython features, and lets you see the source code for each portion in a very user-friendly manner—definitely worth a look if you want to keep learning about wxPython on your own.

Installation should be fairly automatic and painless. To install Windows binaries, simply run the downloaded executables (.exe files). In OS X, the downloaded file should appear as if it were a CD-ROM that you can open, with a .pkg you can double-click. To install using RPM, consult your RPM documentation. Both the Windows and Mac OS X versions will start an installation wizard, which should be simple to follow. Simply accept all default settings, keep clicking Continue, and, finally, click Finish.

To see whether your installation works, you could try out the wxPython demo (which must be installed separately). In Windows, it should be available in your Start menu. When installing it in OS X, you could simply drag the wxPython Demo file to Applications, and then run it from there later. Once you've finished playing with the demo (for now, anyway), you can get started writing your own program, which is, of course, much more fun.

# Building a Sample GUI Application

To demonstrate using wxPython, I will show you how to build a simple GUI application. Your task is to write a basic program that enables you to edit text files. We aren't going to write a full-fledged text editor, but instead stick to the essentials. After all, the goal is to demonstrate the basic mechanisms of GUI programming in Python.

The requirements for this minimal text editor are as follows:

- It must allow you to open text files, given their file names.

- It must allow you to edit the text files.

- It must allow you to save the text files.

- It must allow you to quit.

When writing a GUI program, it's often useful to draw a sketch of how you want it to look. Figure 12-1 shows a simple layout that satisfies the requirements for our text editor.

**Figure 12-1.** *A sketch of the text editor*

The elements of the interface can be used as follows:

- Type a file name in the text field to the left of the buttons and click Open to open a file. The text contained in the file is put in the text field at the bottom.

- You can edit the text to your heart's content in the large text field.

- If and when you want to save your changes, click the Save button, which again uses the text field containing the file name, and writes the contents of the large text field to the file.

- There is no Quit button. If you close the window, the program quits.

In some languages, writing a program like this is a daunting task, but with Python and the right GUI toolkit, it's really a piece of cake. (You may not agree with me right now, but by the end of this chapter, I hope you will.)

## Getting Started

To get started, import the wx module:

```
import wx
```

There are several ways of writing wxPython programs, but one thing you can't escape is creating an application object. The basic application class is called wx.App, and it takes care of all kinds of initialization behind the scenes. The simplest wxPython program would be something like this:

```
import wx
app = wx.App()
app.MainLoop()
```

---

**Note**  If you're having trouble getting wx.App to work, you may want to try to replace it with
wx.PySimpleApp.

---

Because there are no windows the user can interact with, the program exits immediately.

As you can see from this example, the methods in the wx package are written with an initial
uppercase character, contrary to common practice in Python. The reason for this is that the
method names mirror method names from the underlying C++ package, wxWidgets. Even
though there is no formal rule against initial cap method or function names, the norm is to
reserve such names for classes.

## Windows and Components

Windows, also known as *frames*, are simply instances of the wx.Frame class. Widgets in the wx
framework are created with their *parent* as the first argument to their constructor. If you're creating an individual window, there will be no parent to consider, so simply use None, as you see in
Listing 12-1. Also, make sure you call the window's Show method before you call app.MainLoop;
otherwise, it will remain hidden. (You could also call win.Show in an event handler, as discussed a
bit later.)

**Listing 12-1.** *Creating and Showing a Frame*

```
import wx
app = wx.App()
win = wx.Frame(None)
win.Show()
app.MainLoop()
```

If you run this program, you should see a single window appear, similar to that in Figure 12-2.

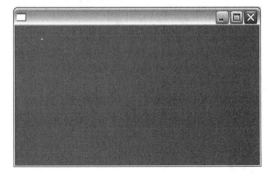

**Figure 12-2.** *A GUI program with only one window*

Adding a button to this frame is about as simple as it can be—simply instantiate wx.Button,
using win as the parent argument, as shown in Listing 12-2.

**Listing 12-2.** *Adding a Button to a Frame*

```
import wx
app = wx.App()
win = wx.Frame(None)
btn = wx.Button(win)
win.Show()
app.MainLoop()
```

This will give you a window with a single button, as shown in Figure 12-3.

**Figure 12-3.** *The program after adding a button*

This certainly is quite rough. The window has no title, the button has no label, and you probably don't want the button to cover the entire window in this way.

## Labels, Titles, and Positions

You can set the labels of widgets when you create them, by using the label argument of the constructor. Similarly, you can set the titles of frames by using the title argument. I find it most practical to use keyword arguments with the wx constructors, so I don't need to remember their order. You can see an example of this in Listing 12-3.

**Listing 12-3.** *Adding Labels and Titles with Keyword Arguments*

```
import wx

app = wx.App()
win = wx.Frame(None, title="Simple Editor")

loadButton = wx.Button(win, label='Open')

saveButton = wx.Button(win, label='Save')

win.Show()

app.MainLoop()
```

The result of running this program should be something like what you see in Figure 12-4.

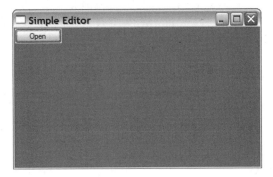

**Figure 12-4.** *A window with layout problems*

Something isn't quite right about this version of the program: one button seems to be missing! Actually, it's not missing—it's just hiding. By placing the buttons more carefully, you should be able to uncover the hidden button. A very basic (and not very practical) method is to simply set positions and size by using the pos and size arguments to the constructors, as in the code presented in Listing 12-4.

**Listing 12-4.** *Setting Button Positions*

```
import wx

app = wx.App()
win = wx.Frame(None, title="Simple Editor", size=(410, 335))
win.Show()

loadButton = wx.Button(win, label='Open',
                       pos=(225, 5), size=(80, 25))

saveButton = wx.Button(win, label='Save',
                       pos=(315, 5), size=(80, 25))

filename = wx.TextCtrl(win, pos=(5, 5), size=(210, 25))

contents = wx.TextCtrl(win, pos=(5, 35), size=(390, 260),
                       style=wx.TE_MULTILINE | wx.HSCROLL)

app.MainLoop()
```

As you can see, both position and size are pairs of numbers. The position is a pair of x and y coordinates, while the size consists of width and height.

This piece of code has a couple other new things: I've created a couple of *text controls* (wx.TextCtrl objects) and given one of them a custom *style*. The default text control is a *text field*, with a single line of editable text, and no scroll bar. In order to create a *text area*, you can simply tweak the style with the style parameter. The style is actually a single integer, but you don't need to specify it directly. Instead, you use bitwise OR (the pipe) to combine various style facets that are available under special names from the wx module. In this case, I've combined wx.TE_MULTILINE, to get a multiline text area (which, by default, has a vertical scroll bar), and wx.HSCROLL, to get a horizontal scroll bar. The result of running this program is shown in Figure 12-5.

**Figure 12-5.** *Properly positioned components*

## More Intelligent Layout

Although specifying the geometry of each component is easy to understand, it can be a bit tedious. Doodling a bit on graph paper may help in getting the coordinates right, but there are more serious drawbacks to this approach than having to play around with numbers. If you run the program and try to resize the window, you'll notice that the geometries of the components don't change. This is no disaster, but it does look a bit odd. When you resize a window, you assume that its contents will be resized and relocated as well.

If you consider how I did the layout, this behavior shouldn't really come as a surprise. I explicitly set the position and size of each component, but didn't say anything about how they should behave when the window was resized. There are many ways of specifying this. One of the easiest ways of doing layout in wx is using *sizers*, and the easiest one to use is wx.BoxSizer.

A sizer manages the size of contents. You simply add widgets to a sizer, together with a few layout parameters, and then give this sizer the job of managing the layout of the parent component. In our case, we'll add a background component (a wx.Panel), create some nested wx.BoxSizers, and then set the sizer of the panel with its SetSizer method, as shown in Listing 12-5.

**Listing 12-5.** *Using a Sizer*

```
import wx

app = wx.App()
win = wx.Frame(None, title="Simple Editor", size=(410, 335))
```

```
bkg = wx.Panel(win)

loadButton = wx.Button(bkg, label='Open')
saveButton = wx.Button(bkg, label='Save')
filename = wx.TextCtrl(bkg)
contents = wx.TextCtrl(bkg, style=wx.TE_MULTILINE | wx.HSCROLL)

hbox = wx.BoxSizer()
hbox.Add(filename, proportion=1, flag=wx.EXPAND)
hbox.Add(loadButton, proportion=0, flag=wx.LEFT, border=5)
hbox.Add(saveButton, proportion=0, flag=wx.LEFT, border=5)

vbox = wx.BoxSizer(wx.VERTICAL)
vbox.Add(hbox, proportion=0, flag=wx.EXPAND | wx.ALL, border=5)
vbox.Add(contents, proportion=1,
         flag=wx.EXPAND | wx.LEFT | wx.BOTTOM | wx.RIGHT, border=5)

bkg.SetSizer(vbox)
win.Show()

app.MainLoop()
```

This code gives the same result as the previous program, but instead of using lots of absolute coordinates, I am now placing things in relation to one another.

The constructor of the wx.BoxSizer takes an argument determining whether it's horizontal or vertical (wx.HORIZONTAL or wx.VERTICAL), with horizontal being the default. The Add method takes several arguments. The proportion argument sets the proportions according to which space is allocated when the window is resized. For example, in the horizontal box sizer (the first one), the filename widget gets all of the extra space when resizing. If each of the three had its proportion set to 1, each would get an equal share. You can set the proportion to any number.

The flag argument is similar to the style argument of the constructor. You construct it by using bitwise OR between symbolic constants (integers that have special names). The wx.EXPAND flag makes sure the component will expand into the allotted space. The wx.LEFT, wx.RIGHT, wx.TOP, wx.BOTTOM, and wx.ALL flags determine on which sides the border argument applies, and the border arguments gives the width of the border (spacing).

And that's it. I've got the layout I wanted. One crucial thing is lacking, however. If you click the buttons, nothing happens.

---

**■Tip** For more information about sizers, or anything else related to wxPython, check out the wxPython demo. It has sample code for anything you might want to know about, and then some. If that seems daunting, check out the wxPython web site, http://wxpython.org.

---

## Event Handling

In GUI lingo, the actions performed by the user (such as clicking a button) are called *events*. You need to make your program notice these events somehow, and then react to them. You accomplish this by binding a function to the widget where the event in question might occur. When the event does occur (if ever), that function will then be called. You link the event handler to a given event with a widget method called Bind.

Let's assume that you have written a function responsible for opening a file, and you've called it load. Then you can use that as an event handler for loadButton as follows:

```
loadButton.Bind(wx.EVT_BUTTON, load)
```

This is pretty intuitive, isn't it? I've linked a function to the button—when the button is clicked, the function is called. The symbolic constant wx.EVT_BUTTON signifies a *button event*. The wx framework has such event constants for all kinds of events, from mouse motion to keyboard presses and more.

---

■**Note**  There is nothing magical about my choice to use loadButton and load as the button and handler names, even though the button text says "Open." It's just that if I had called the button openButton, open would have been the natural name for the handler, and that would have made the built-in file-opening function open unavailable. While there are ways of dealing with this, I found it easier to use a different name.

---

## The Finished Program

Let's fill in the remaining blanks. All you need now are the two event handlers, load and save. When an event handler is called, it receives a single event object as its only parameter, which holds information about what happened. But let's ignore that here, because you're only interested in the fact that a click occurred.

Even though the event handlers are the meat of the program, they are surprisingly simple. Let's take a look at the load function first. It looks like this:

```
def load(event):
    file = open(filename.GetValue())
    contents.SetValue(file.read())
    file.close()
```

The file opening/reading part should be familiar from Chapter 11. As you can see, the file name is found by using filename's GetValue method (where filename is the small text field, remember?). Similarly, to put the text into the text area, you simply use contents.SetValue.

The save function is just as simple. It's the exact same as load, except that it has a 'w' and a write for the file-handling part, and GetValue for the text area:

```
def save(event):
    file = open(filename.GetValue(), 'w')
    file.write(contents.GetValue())
    file.close()
```

And that's it. Now I simply bind these to their respective buttons, and the program is ready to run. See Listing 12-6 for the final program.

**Listing 12-6.** *The Final GUI Program*

```
import wx
def load(event):
    file = open(filename.GetValue())
    contents.SetValue(file.read())
    file.close()

def save(event):
    file = open(filename.GetValue(), 'w')
    file.write(contents.GetValue())
    file.close()

app = wx.App()
win = wx.Frame(None, title="Simple Editor", size=(410, 335))

bkg = wx.Panel(win)

loadButton = wx.Button(bkg, label='Open')
loadButton.Bind(wx.EVT_BUTTON, load)

saveButton = wx.Button(bkg, label='Save')
saveButton.Bind(wx.EVT_BUTTON, save)

filename = wx.TextCtrl(bkg)
contents = wx.TextCtrl(bkg, style=wx.TE_MULTILINE | wx.HSCROLL)

hbox = wx.BoxSizer()
hbox.Add(filename, proportion=1, flag=wx.EXPAND)
hbox.Add(loadButton, proportion=0, flag=wx.LEFT, border=5)
hbox.Add(saveButton, proportion=0, flag=wx.LEFT, border=5)

vbox = wx.BoxSizer(wx.VERTICAL)
vbox.Add(hbox, proportion=0, flag=wx.EXPAND | wx.ALL, border=5)
vbox.Add(contents, proportion=1,
        flag=wx.EXPAND | wx.LEFT | wx.BOTTOM | wx.RIGHT, border=5)

bkg.SetSizer(vbox)
win.Show()

app.MainLoop()
```

You can try out the editor using the following steps:

1.  Run the program. You should get a window like the one in the previous runs.

2.  Type something in the large text area (for example, "Hello, world!").

3.  Type a file name in the small text field (for example, `hello.txt`). Make sure that this file does not already exist or it will be overwritten.

4.  Click the Save button.

5.  Close the editor window (just for fun).

6.  Restart the program.

7.  Type the same file name in the little text field.

8.  Click the Open button. The text of the file should reappear in the large text area.

9.  Edit the file to your heart's content, and save it again.

Now you can keep opening, editing, and saving until you grow tired of that. Then you can start thinking of improvements. How about allowing your program to download files with the `urllib` module, for example?

You might also consider using more object-oriented design in your programs, of course. For example, you may want to manage the main application as an instance of a custom application class (a subclass of `wx.App`, perhaps?), and instead of setting up your layout at the top level of your program, you could make a separate window class (a subclass of `wx.Frame`?). See Chapter 28 for some examples.

### HEY! WHAT ABOUT PYW?

In Windows, you could save your GUI programs with a `.pyw` ending. In Chapter 1, I asked you to give your file this ending and double-click it (in Windows). Nothing happened then, and I promised to explain it later. In Chapter 10, I mentioned it again, and said I would explain it in this chapter. So I will.

It's no big deal, really. It's just that when you double-click an ordinary Python script in Windows, a DOS window appears with a Python prompt in it. That's fine if you use `print` and `raw_input` as the basis of your interface, but now that you know how to make GUIs, this DOS window will only be in your way. The truth behind the `.pyw` window is that it will run Python without the DOS window, which is just perfect for GUI programs.

## But I'd Rather Use . . .

As you've learned, you can choose from many GUI toolkits for Python. Here, I will give you some examples from a couple of the more popular ones: Tkinter and Jython/Swing.

To illustrate these toolkits, I've created a simple example—simpler, even, than the editor example you just completed. It's just a single window containing a single button with the label

"Hello" filling the window. When you click the button, it prints out the words "Hello, world!" In the interest of simplicity, I'm not using any fancy layout features here. Here is a simple wxPython version:

```
import wx

def hello(event):
    print "Hello, world!"

app = wx.App()

win = wx.Frame(None, title="Hello, wxPython!",
               size=(200, 100))
button = wx.Button(win, label="Hello")
button.Bind(wx.EVT_BUTTON, hello)

win.Show()
app.MainLoop()
```

The resulting window is shown in Figure 12-6.

**Figure 12-6.** *A simple GUI example*

## Using Tkinter

Tkinter is an old-timer in the Python GUI business. It is a wrapper around the Tk GUI toolkit (associated with the programming language Tcl). It is included by default in the Windows and Mac OS distributions. The following URLs may be useful:

- http://www.ibm.com/developerworks/linux/library/l-tkprg

- http://www.nmt.edu/tcc/help/lang/python/tkinter.pdf

Here is the GUI example implemented with Tkinter:

```
from Tkinter import *
def hello(): print 'Hello, world'
win = Tk() # Tkinter's 'main window'
win.title('Hello, Tkinter! ')
win.geometry('200x100') # Size 200, 100

btn = Button(win, text='Hello ', command=hello)
btn.pack(expand=YES, fill=BOTH)

mainloop()
```

## Using Jython and Swing

If you're using Jython (the Java implementation of Python), packages such as wxPython and Tkinter aren't available. The only GUI toolkits that are readily available are the Java standard library packages Abstract Window Toolkit (AWT) and Swing (Swing is the most recent and considered the standard Java GUI toolkit). The good news is that both of these are automatically available so you don't need to install them separately. For more information, visit the Jython web site and look into the Swing documentation written for Java:

- http://www.jython.org

- http://java.sun.com/docs/books/tutorial/uiswing

Here is the GUI example implemented with Jython and Swing:

```
from javax.swing import *
import sys

def hello(event): print 'Hello, world! '
btn = JButton('Hello')
btn.actionPerformed = hello

win = JFrame('Hello, Swing!')
win.contentPane.add(btn)

def closeHandler(event): sys.exit()
win.windowClosing = closeHandler

btn.size = win.size = 200, 100
win.show()
```

Note that one additional event handler has been added here (closeHandler) because the Close button doesn't have any useful default behavior in Java Swing. Also note that you don't need to explicitly enter the main event loop because it's running in parallel with the program (in a separate thread).

## Using Something Else

The basics of most GUI toolkits are the same. Unfortunately, however, when learning how to use a new package, it takes time to find your way through all the details that enable you to do exactly what you want. So you should take your time before deciding which package you want to work with (the section "A Plethora of Platforms" earlier in this chapter should give you some idea of where to start), and then immerse yourself in its documentation and start writing code. I hope this chapter has provided the basic concepts you need to make sense of that documentation.

# A Quick Summary

Once again, let's review what we've covered in this chapter:

**Graphical user interfaces (GUIs)**: GUIs are useful in making your programs more user friendly. Not all programs need them, but whenever your program interacts with a user, a GUI is probably helpful.

**GUI platforms for Python**: Many GUI platforms are available to the Python programmer. Although this richness is definitely a boon, choosing between them can sometimes be difficult.

**wxPython**: wxPython is a mature and feature-rich cross-platform GUI toolkit for Python.

**Layout**: You can position components quite simply by specifying their geometry directly. However, to make them behave properly when their containing window is resized, you will need to use some sort of layout manager. One common layout mechanism in wxPython is *sizers*.

**Event handling**: Actions performed by the user trigger *events* in the GUI toolkit. To be of any use, your program will probably be set up to react to some of these events; otherwise, the user won't be able to interact with it. In wxPython, event handlers are added to components with the Bind method.

## What Now?

That's it. You now know how to write programs that can interact with the outside world through files and GUIs. In the next chapter, you learn about another important component of many program systems: databases.

# CHAPTER 13

■ ■ ■

# Database Support

**U**sing simple, plain-text files can get you only so far. Yes, they *can* get you *very* far, but at some point, you may need some extra functionality. You may want some automated serialization, and you can turn to shelve (see Chapter 10) and pickle (a close relative of shelve). But you may want features that go beyond even this. For example, you might want to have automated support for concurrent access to your data; that is, to allow several users to read from and write to your disk-based data without causing any corrupted files or the like. Or you may want to be able to perform complex searches using many data fields or properties at the same time, rather than the simple single-key lookup of shelve. There are plenty of solutions to choose from, but if you want this to scale to large amounts of data and you want the solution to be easily understandable by other programmers, choosing a relatively standard form of *database* is probably a good idea.

This chapter discusses the Python Database API, a standardized way of connecting to SQL databases, and demonstrates how to execute some basic SQL using this API. The last section also discusses some alternative database technology.

I won't be giving you a tutorial on relational databases or the SQL language. The documentation for most databases (such as PostgreSQL or MySQL, or, the one used in this chapter, SQLite) should cover what you need to know. If you haven't used relational databases before, you might want to check out http://www.sqlcourse.com (or just do a Web search on the subject) or *Beginning SQL Queries* by Clare Churcher (Apress, 2008).

The simple database used throughout this chapter (SQLite) is, of course, not the only choice—by far. There are several popular commercial choices (such as Oracle or Microsoft SQL Server), as well as some solid and widespread open source databases (such as MySQL, PostgreSQL, and Firebird). Chapter 26 uses PostgreSQL and has some instructions for MySQL and SQLite. For a list of some other databases supported by Python packages, check out http://www.python.org/topics/database/ or visit the Database category of Vaults of Parnassus (http://www.vex.net/parnassus).

Relational (SQL) databases aren't the only kind around, of course. There are object databases such as the Zope Object Database (ZODB, http://wiki.zope.org/ZODB), compact table-based ones such as Metakit (http://www.equi4.com/metakit/python.html), or even simpler *key-value* databases, such as BSD DB (http://docs.python.org/lib/module-bsddb.html).

While this chapter focuses on rather low-level database interaction, you can find several high-level libraries to help you abstract away some of the grind (see, for example, http://www.sqlalchemy.org or http://www.sqlobject.org, or search the Web for other so-called object-relational mappers for Python).

# The Python Database API

As I've mentioned, you can choose from various SQL databases, and many of them have corresponding client modules in Python (some databases even have several). Most of the basic functionality of all the databases is the same, so a program written to use one of them might easily—in theory—be used with another. The problem with switching between different modules that provide the same functionality (more or less) is usually that their interfaces (APIs) are different. In order to solve this problem for database modules in Python, a standard Database API (DB API) has been agreed upon. The current version of the API (2.0) is defined in PEP 249, Python Database API Specification v2.0 (available from `http://python.org/peps/pep-0249.html`).

This section gives you an overview of the basics. I won't cover the optional parts of the API, because they don't apply to all databases. You can find more information in the PEP mentioned, or in the database programming guide in the official Python Wiki (available from `http://wiki.python.org/moin/DatabaseProgramming`). If you're not really interested in all the API details, you can skip this section.

## Global Variables

Any compliant database module (compliant, that is, with the DB API, version 2.0) must have three global variables, which describe the peculiarities of the module. The reason for this is that the API is designed to be very flexible and to work with several different underlying mechanisms without too much wrapping. If you want your program to work with several different databases, this can be a nuisance, because you need to cover many different possibilities. A more realistic course of action, in many cases, would be to simply check these variables to see that a given database module is acceptable to your program. If it isn't, you could simply exit with an appropriate error message, for example, or raise some exception. The global variables are summarized in Table 13-1.

**Table 13-1.** *The Module Properties of the Python DB API*

| Variable Name | Use |
| --- | --- |
| apilevel | The version of the Python DB API in use |
| threadsafety | How thread-safe the module is |
| paramstyle | Which parameter style is used in the SQL queries |

The API level (apilevel) is simply a string constant, giving the API version in use. According to the DB API version 2.0, it may either have the value '1.0' or the value '2.0'. If the variable isn't there, the module is not 2.0-compliant, and you should (according to the API) assume that the DB API version 1.0 is in effect. It also probably wouldn't hurt to write your code to allow other values here (who knows when, say, version 3.0 of the DB API will come out?).

The thread-safety level (threadsafety) is an integer ranging from 0 to 3, inclusive. 0 means that threads may not share the module at all, and 3 means that the module is completely thread-safe. A value of 1 means that threads may share the module itself, but not connections (see "Connections and Cursors," later in this chapter), and 2 means that threads may share modules and connections, but not cursors. If you don't use threads (which, most of the time, you probably won't), you don't have to worry about this variable at all.

The parameter style (`paramstyle`) indicates how parameters are spliced into SQL queries when you make the database perform multiple similar queries. The value `'format'` indicates standard string formatting (using basic format codes), so you insert `%s` where you want to splice in parameters, for example. The value `'pyformat'` indicates extended format codes, as used with dictionary splicing, such as `%(foo)s`. In addition to these Pythonic styles, there are three ways of writing the splicing fields: `'qmark'` means that question marks are used, `'numeric'` means fields of the form `:1` or `:2` (where the numbers are the numbers of the parameters), and `'named'` means fields like `:foobar`, where `foobar` is a parameter name. If parameter styles seem confusing, don't worry. For basic programs, you won't need them, and if you need to understand how a specific database interface deals with parameters, the relevant documentation will probably explain it.

## Exceptions

The API defines several exceptions, to make fine-grained error handling possible. However, they're defined in a hierarchy, so you can also catch several types of exceptions with a single except block. (Of course, if you expect everything to work nicely, and you don't mind having your program shut down in the unlikely event of something going wrong, you can just ignore the exceptions altogether.)

The exception hierarchy is shown in Table 13-2. The exceptions should be available globally in the given database module. For more in-depth descriptions of these exceptions, see the API specification (the PEP mentioned previously).

**Table 13-2.** *Exceptions Specified in the Python DB API*

| Exception | Superclass | Description |
| --- | --- | --- |
| StandardError | | Generic superclass of all exceptions |
| Warning | StandardError | Raised if a nonfatal problem occurs |
| Error | StandardError | Generic superclass of all error conditions |
| InterfaceError | Error | Errors relating to the interface, not the database |
| DatabaseError | Error | Superclass for errors relating to the database |
| DataError | DatabaseError | Problems related to the data; e.g., values out of range |
| OperationalError | DatabaseError | Errors internal to the operation of the database |
| IntegrityError | DatabaseError | Relational integrity compromised; e.g., key check fails |
| InternalError | DatabaseError | Internal errors in the database; e.g., invalid cursor |
| ProgrammingError | DatabaseError | User programming error; e.g., table not found |
| NotSupportedError | DatabaseError | An unsupported feature (e.g., rollback) requested |

# Connections and Cursors

In order to use the underlying database system, you must first *connect* to it. For this you use the aptly named function connect. It takes several parameters; exactly which depends on the database. The API defines the parameters in Table 13-3 as a guideline. It recommends that they be usable as keyword arguments, and that they follow the order given in the table. The arguments should all be strings.

**Table 13-3.** *Common Parameters of the connect Function*

| Parameter Name | Description | Optional? |
|---|---|---|
| dsn | Data source name. Specific meaning database dependent. | No |
| user | User name | Yes |
| password | User password | Yes |
| host | Host name | Yes |
| database | Database name | Yes |

You'll see specific examples of using the connect function in the section "Getting Started" later in this chapter, as well as in Chapter 26.

The connect function returns a connection object. This represents your current session with the database. Connection objects support the methods shown in Table 13-4.

**Table 13-4.** *Connection Object Methods*

| Method Name | Description |
|---|---|
| close() | Closes the connection. Connection object and its cursors are now unusable. |
| commit() | Commits pending transactions, if supported; otherwise does nothing. |
| rollback() | Rolls back pending transactions (may not be available). |
| cursor() | Returns a cursor object for the connection. |

The rollback method may not be available, because not all databases support transactions. (*Transactions* are just sequences of actions.) If it exists, it will "undo" any transactions that have not been committed.

The commit method is always available, but if the database doesn't support transactions, it doesn't actually do anything. If you close a connection and there are still transactions that have not been committed, they will implicitly be rolled back—but only if the database supports rollbacks! So if you don't want to rely on this, you should always commit before you close your connection. If you commit, you probably don't need to worry too much about closing your connection; it's automatically closed when it's garbage-collected. If you want to be on the safe side, though, a call to close won't cost you that many keystrokes.

The cursor method leads us to another topic: cursor objects. You use cursors to execute SQL queries and to examine the results. Cursors support more methods than connections, and probably will be quite a bit more prominent in your programs. Table 13-5 gives an overview of the cursor methods, and Table 13-6 gives an overview of the attributes.

**Table 13-5.** *Cursor Object Methods*

| Name | Description |
|---|---|
| callproc(name[, params]) | Calls a named database procedure with given name and parameters (optional). |
| close() | Closes the cursor. Cursor is now unusable. |
| execute(oper[, params]) | Executes a SQL operation, possibly with parameters. |
| executemany(oper, pseq) | Executes a SQL operation for each parameter set in a sequence. |
| fetchone() | Fetches the next row of a query result set as a sequence, or None. |
| fetchmany([size]) | Fetches several rows of a query result set. Default size is arraysize. |
| fetchall() | Fetches all (remaining) rows as a sequence of sequences. |
| nextset() | Skips to the next available result set (optional). |
| setinputsizes(sizes) | Used to predefine memory areas for parameters. |
| setoutputsize(size[, col]) | Sets a buffer size for fetching big data values. |

**Table 13-6.** *Cursor Object Attributes*

| Name | Description |
|---|---|
| description | Sequence of result column descriptions. Read-only. |
| rowcount | The number of rows in the result. Read-only. |
| arraysize | How many rows to return in fetchmany. Default is 1. |

Some of these methods will be explained in more detail in the upcoming text, while some (such as setinputsizes and setoutputsizes) will not be discussed. Consult the PEP for more details.

# Types

In order to interoperate properly with the underlying SQL databases, which may place various requirements on the values inserted into columns of certain types, the DB API defines certain constructors and constants (singletons) used for special types and values. For example, if you want to add a date to a database, it should be constructed with (for example) the Date constructor of the corresponding database connectivity module. That allows the connectivity module to perform any necessary transformations behind the scenes. Each module is required to implement the constructors and special values shown in Table 13-7. Some modules may not be entirely compliant. For example, the sqlite3 module (discussed next) does not export the special values (STRING through ROWID) in Table 13-7.

**Table 13-7.** *DB API Constructors and Special Values*

| Name | Description |
|---|---|
| Date(year, month, day) | Creates an object holding a date value |
| Time(hour, minute, second) | Creates an object holding a time value |
| Timestamp(y, mon, d, h, min, s) | Creates an object holding a timestamp value |
| DateFromTicks(ticks) | Creates an object holding a date value from ticks since epoch |
| TimeFromTicks(ticks) | Creates an object holding a time value from ticks |
| TimestampFromTicks(ticks) | Creates an object holding a timestamp value from ticks |
| Binary(string) | Creates an object holding a binary string value |
| STRING | Describes string-based column types (such as CHAR) |
| BINARY | Describes binary columns (such as LONG or RAW) |
| NUMBER | Describes numeric columns |
| DATETIME | Describes date/time columns |
| ROWID | Describes row ID columns |

# SQLite and PySQLite

As mentioned previously, many SQL database engines are available, with corresponding Python modules. Most of these database engines are meant to be run as server programs, and require administrator privileges even to install them. In order to lower the threshold for playing around with the Python DB API, I've chosen to use a tiny database engine called SQLite, which doesn't need to be run as a stand-alone server, and which can work directly on local files, instead of with some centralized database storage mechanism.

In recent Python versions (from 2.5) SQLite has the advantage that a wrapper for it (PySQLite) is included in the standard library. Unless you're compiling Python from source yourself, chances are that the database itself is also included. You might want to just try the program snippets in the section "Getting Started." If they work, you don't need to bother with installing PySQLite and SQLite separately.

---

■**Note** If you're not using the standard library version of PySQLite, you may need to modify the `import` statement. Refer to the relevant documentation for more information.

---

## GETTING PYSQLITE

If you are using an older version of Python, you will need to install PySQLite before you can use the SQLite database. You can download it from the official web page, `http://pysqlite.org`.

For Linux systems with package manager systems, chances are you can get PySQLite and SQLite directly from the package manager.

The Windows binaries for PySQLite actually *include* the database engine itself (that is, SQLite), so all you need to do is to download the PySQLite installer corresponding to your Python version, run it, and you're all set.

If you're not using Windows, and your operating system does not have a package manager where you can find PySQLite and SQLite, you will need to get the source packages for PySQLite and SQLite and compile them yourself.

If you're using a recent version of Python, you will most certainly have PySQLite. If anything is missing, it will be the database itself, SQLite (but again, that will probably be available as well). You can get the sources from the SQLite web page, `http://sqlite.org`. (Make sure you get one of the source packages where automatic code generation has already been performed.) Compiling SQLite is basically a matter of following the instructions in the included README file. When subsequently compiling PySQLite, you need to make sure that the compilation process can access the SQLite libraries and include files. If you've installed SQLite in some standard location, it may well be that the setup script in the PySQLite distribution can find it on its own. In that case, you simply need to execute the following commands:

```
python setup.py build
python setup.py install
```

You could simply use the latter command, which will perform the build automatically. If this gives you heaps of error messages, chances are the installation script didn't find the required files. Make sure you know where the include files and libraries are installed, and supply them explicitly to the install script. Let's say I compiled SQLite in place in a directory called /home/mlh/sqlite/current; then the header files could be found in /home/mlh/sqlite/current/ src and the library in /home/mlh/sqlite/current/build/lib. In order to let the installation process use these paths, edit the setup script, setup.py. In this file you'll want to set the variables include_dirs and library_dirs:

```
include_dirs = ['/home/mlh/sqlite/current/src']
library_dirs = ['/home/mlh/sqlite/current/build/lib']
```

After rebinding these variables, the install procedure described earlier should work without errors.

## Getting Started

You can import SQLite as a module, under the name `sqlite3` (if you are using the one in the Python standard library). You can then create a connection directly to a database file—which will be created if it does not exist—by supplying a file name (which can be a relative or absolute path to the file):

```
>>> import sqlite3
>>> conn = sqlite3.connect('somedatabase.db')
```

You can then get a cursor from this connection:

```
>>> curs = conn.cursor()
```

This cursor can then be used to execute SQL queries. Once you're finished, if you've made any changes, make sure you commit them, so they're actually saved to the file:

```
>>> conn.commit()
```

You can (and should) commit each time you've modified the database, not just when you're ready to close it. When you *are* ready to close it, just use the `close` method:

```
>>> conn.close()
```

## A Sample Database Application

As an example, I'll demonstrate how to construct a little nutrient database, based on data from the United States Department of Agriculture (USDA) Nutrient Data Laboratory (`http://www.ars.usda.gov/nutrientdata`). On their web page, follow the link to the USDA National Nutrient Database for Standard Reference. There, you should find a lot of different data files in plain-text (ASCII) format, just the way we like it. Follow the Download link, and download the zip file referenced by the ASCII link under the heading "Abbreviated." You should now get a zip file containing a text file named `ABBREV.txt`, along with a PDF file describing its contents.[1] If you have trouble finding this particular file, any old data will do. Just modify the source code to suit.

The data in the `ABBREV.txt` file has one data record per line, with the fields separated by caret (^) characters. The numeric fields contain numbers directly, while the textual fields have their string values "quoted" with a tilde (~) on each side. Here is a sample line, with parts deleted for brevity:

```
~07276~^~HORMEL SPAM ... PORK W/ HAM  MINCED  CND~^ ... ^~1 serving~^^~~^0
```

Parsing such a line into individual fields is a simple as using `line.split('^')`. If a field starts with a tilde, you know it's a string and can use `field.strip('~')` to get its contents. For the other (numeric) fields, `float(field)` should do the trick, except, of course, when the field is empty. The program developed in the following sections will transfer the data in this ASCII file into your SQL database, and let you perform some (semi-)interesting queries on them.

---

1. At the time of writing, you can get this file from `http://www.nal.usda.gov/fnic/foodcomp/Data/SR20/dnload/sr20abbr.zip`.

■**Note**  This sample program is intentionally simple. For a slightly more advanced example of database use in Python, see Chapter 26.

## Creating and Populating Tables

To actually create the tables of the database and populate them, writing a completely separate one-shot program is probably the easiest solution. You can run this program once, and then forget about both it and the original data source (the ABBREV.txt file), although keeping them around is probably a good idea.

The program shown in Listing 13-1 creates a table called food with some appropriate fields, reads the file ABBREV.txt, parses it (by splitting the lines and converting the individual fields using a utility function, convert), and inserts values read from the text field into the database using a SQL INSERT statement in a call to curs.execute.

■**Note**  It would have been possible to use curs.executemany, supplying a list of all the rows extracted from the data file. This would have given a minor speedup in this case, but might have given a more substantial speedup if a networked client/server SQL system were used.

**Listing 13-1.** *Importing Data into the Database (importdata.py)*

```python
import sqlite3

def convert(value):
    if value.startswith('~'):
        return value.strip('~')
    if not value:
        value = '0'
    return float(value)

conn = sqlite3.connect('food.db')
curs = conn.cursor()

curs.execute('''
CREATE TABLE food (
    id          TEXT        PRIMARY KEY,
    desc        TEXT,
    water       FLOAT,
    kcal        FLOAT,
    protein     FLOAT,
    fat         FLOAT,
    ash         FLOAT,
    carbs       FLOAT,
```

```
    fiber       FLOAT,
    sugar       FLOAT
)
''')

query = 'INSERT INTO food VALUES (?,?,?,?,?,?,?,?,?,?)'

for line in open('ABBREV.txt'):
    fields = line.split('^')
    vals = [convert(f) for f in fields[:field_count]]
    curs.execute(query, vals)

conn.commit()
conn.close()
```

---

**■Note**  In Listing 13-1, I use the "qmark" version of `paramstyle`; that is, a question mark as a field marker. If you're using an older version of PySQLite, you may need to use % characters instead.

---

When you run this program (with `ABBREV.txt` in the same directory), it will create a new file called `food.db`, containing all the data of the database.

I encourage you to play around with this example, using other inputs, adding `print` statements, and the like.

## Searching and Dealing with Results

Using the database is really simple. Again, you create a connection and get a cursor from that connection. Execute the SQL query with the execute method and extract the results with, for example, the `fetchall` method. Listing 13-2 shows a tiny program that takes a SQL `SELECT` condition as a command-line argument and prints out the returned rows in a record format. You could try it out with a command line like the following:

```
$ python food_query.py "kcal <= 100 AND fiber >= 10 ORDER BY sugar"
```

You may notice a problem when you run this. The first row, raw orange peel, seems to have no sugar at all. That's because the field is missing in the data file. You could improve the import script to detect this condition, and insert None instead of a real value, to indicate missing data. Then you could use a condition such as the following:

```
"kcal <= 100 AND fiber >= 10 AND sugar ORDER BY sugar"
```

requiring the sugar field to have real data in any returned rows. As it happens, this strategy will work with the current database, as well, where this condition will discard rows where the sugar level is zero.

■**Caution**  You might want to try a condition that searches for a specific food item, using an ID, such as 08323 for Cocoa Pebbles. The problem is that SQLite handles its values in a rather nonstandard fashion. Internally, all values are, in fact, strings, and some conversion and checking goes on between the database and the Python API. Usually, this works just fine, but this is an example of where you might run into trouble. If you supply the value 08323, it will be interpreted as the number 8323, and subsequently converted into the string "8323"—an ID that doesn't exist. One might have expected an error message here, rather than this surprising and rather unhelpful behavior, but if you are careful, and use the string "08323" in the first place, you'll be fine.

**Listing 13-2.** *Food Database Query Program (food_query.py)*

```
import sqlite3, sys

conn = sqlite3.connect('food.db')
curs = conn.cursor()

query = 'SELECT * FROM food WHERE %s' % sys.argv[1]
print query
curs.execute(query)
names = [f[0] for f in curs.description]
for row in curs.fetchall():
    for pair in zip(names, row):
        print '%s: %s' % pair
    print
```

# A Quick Summary

This chapter has given a rather brief introduction to making Python programs interact with relational databases. It's brief because, if you master Python and SQL, the coupling between the two, in the form of the Python DB API, is quite easy to master. Here are some of the concepts covered in this chapter:

**The Python DB API**: This API provides a simple, standardized interface to which database wrapper modules should conform, to make it easier to write programs that will work with several different databases.

**Connections**: A connection object represents the communication link with the SQL database. From it, you can get individual cursors, using the cursor method. You also use the connection object to commit or roll back transactions. After you're finished with the database, the connection can be closed.

**Cursors**: A cursor is used to execute queries and to examine the results. Resulting rows can be retrieved one by one, or many (or all) at once.

**Types and special values**: The DB API specifies the names of a set of constructors and special values. The constructors deal with date and time objects, as well as binary data objects. The special values represent the types of the relational database, such as STRING, NUMBER, and DATETIME.

**SQLite**: This is a small, embedded SQL database, whose Python wrapper is called PySQLite. It's fast and simple to use, and does not require a separate server to be set up.

## New Functions in This Chapter

| Function | Description |
| --- | --- |
| connect(...) | Connect to a database and return a connection object[2] |

## What Now?

Persistence and database handling are important parts of many, if not most, big program systems. Another component shared by a great number of such systems is a network, which is dealt with in the next chapter.

---

2. The parameters to the connect function are database dependent.

■ ■ ■

# CHAPTER 14

# Network Programming

In this chapter, I give you a sample of the various ways in which Python can help you write programs that use a network, such as the Internet, as an important component. Python is a very powerful tool for network programming. Many libraries for common network protocols and for various layers of abstractions on top of them are available, so you can concentrate on the logic of your program, rather than on shuffling bits across wires. Also, it's easy to write code for handling various protocol formats that may *not* have existing code, because Python's really good at tackling patterns in byte streams (you've already seen this in dealing with text files in various ways).

Because Python has such an abundance of network tools available for you to use, I can only give you a brief peek at its networking capabilities here. You can find some other examples elsewhere in this book. Chapter 15 includes a discussion of web-oriented network programming, and several of the projects in later chapters use networking modules to get the job done. If you want to know even *more* about network programming in Python, I can heartily recommend John Goerzen's *Foundations of Python Network Programming* (Apress, 2004), which deals with the subject very thoroughly.

In this chapter, I give you an overview of some of the networking modules available in the Python standard library. Then comes a discussion of the SocketServer class and its friends, followed by a brief look at the various ways in which you can handle several connections at once. Finally, I give you a look at the Twisted framework, a rich and mature framework for writing networked applications in Python.

---

**Note** If you have a strict firewall in place, it will probably warn you once you start running your own network programs and stop them from connecting to the network. You should either configure your firewall to let your Python do its work, or, if the firewall has an interactive interface (such as the Windows XP firewall), simply allow the connections when asked. Note, though, that any software connected to a network is a potential security risk, even if (or especially if) you wrote the software yourself.

---

## A Handful of Networking Modules

You can find plenty of networking modules in the standard library, and many more elsewhere. In addition to those that clearly deal mainly with networking, several modules (such as those that deal with various forms of data encoding for network transport) may be seen as network related. I've been fairly restrictive in my selection of modules here.

## The socket Module

A basic component in network programming is the *socket*. A socket is basically an "information channel" with a program on both ends. The programs may be on different computers (connected through a network) and may send information to each other through the socket. Most network programming in Python hides the basic workings of the socket module and doesn't interact with the sockets directly.

Sockets come in two varieties: server sockets and client sockets. After you create a server socket, you tell it to wait for connections. It will then listen at a certain network address (a combination of an IP address and a port number) until a client socket connects. The two can then communicate.

Dealing with client sockets is usually quite a bit easier than dealing with the server side, because the server must be ready to deal with clients whenever they connect, and it must deal with multiple connections, while the client simply connects, does its thing, and disconnects. Later in this chapter, I discuss server programming through the SocketServer class family and the Twisted framework.

A socket is an instance of the socket class from the socket module. It is instantiated with up to three parameters: an address family (defaulting to socket.AF_INET), whether it's a stream (socket.SOCK_STREAM, the default) or a datagram (socket.SOCK_DGRAM) socket, and a protocol (defaulting to 0, which should be okay). For a plain-vanilla socket, you don't really need to supply any arguments.

A server socket uses its bind method followed by a call to listen to listen to a given address. A client socket can then connect to the server by using its connect method with the same address as used in bind. (On the server side, you can, for example, get the name of the current machine using the function socket.gethostname.) In this case, an address is just a tuple of the form (host, port), where host is a host name (such as www.example.com) and port is a port number (an integer). The listen method takes a single argument, which is the length of its backlog (the number of connections allowed to queue up, waiting for acceptance, before connections start being disallowed).

Once a server socket is listening, it can start accepting clients. This is done using the accept method. This method will block (wait) until a client connects, and then it will return a tuple of the form (client, address), where client is a client socket and address is an address, as explained earlier. The server can deal with the client as it sees fit, and then start waiting for new connections, with another call to accept. This is usually done in an infinite loop.

---

■**Note**   The form of server programming discussed here is called *blocking* or *synchronous* network programming. In the section "Multiple Connections" later in this chapter, you'll see examples of nonblocking or asynchronous network programming, as well as using threads to be able to deal with several clients at once.

---

For transmitting data, sockets have two methods: send and recv (for "receive"). You can call send with a string argument to send data, and recv with a desired (maximum) number of bytes to receive data. If you're not sure which number to use, 1024 is as good a choice as any.

Listings 14-1 and 14-2 show an example client/server pair that is about as simple as it gets. If you run them on the same machine (starting the server first), the server should print out a message about getting a connection, and the client should then print out a message it has received from the server. You can run several clients while the server is still running. By replacing the call to gethostname in the client with the actual host name of the machine where the server is running, you can have the two programs connect across a network from one machine to another.

---

**Note**  The port numbers you use are normally restricted. In a Linux or UNIX system, you need administrator privileges to use a port below 1024. These low-numbered ports are used for standard services, such as port 80 for your web server (if you have one). Also, if you stop a server with Ctrl+C, for example, you might need to wait for a bit before using the same port number again (you may get an "Address already in use" error).

---

**Listing 14-1.** *A Minimal Server*

```
import socket

s = socket.socket()

host = socket.gethostname()
port = 1234
s.bind((host, port))

s.listen(5)
while True:
    c, addr = s.accept()
    print 'Got connection from', addr
    c.send('Thank you for connecting')
    c.close()
```

**Listing 14-2.** *A Minimal Client*

```
import socket

s = socket.socket()

host = socket.gethostname()
port = 1234

s.connect((host, port))
print s.recv(1024)
```

You can find more information about the socket module in the Python Library Reference (http://python.org/doc/lib/module-socket.html) and in Gordon McMillan's Socket Programming HOWTO (http://docs.python.org/dev/howto/sockets.html).

# The urllib and urllib2 Modules

Of the networking libraries available, the ones that probably give you the most bang for the buck are urllib and urllib2. They enable you to access files across a network, just as if they were located on your computer. Through a simple function call, virtually anything you can refer to with a Uniform Resource Locator (URL) can be used as input to your program. Just imagine the possibilities you get if you combine this with the re module: you can download web pages, extract information, and create automatic reports of your findings.

The two modules do more or less the same job, with urllib2 being a bit more "fancy." For simple downloads, urllib is quite all right. If you need HTTP authentication or cookies, or you want to write extensions to handle your own protocols, then urllib2 might be the right choice for you.

## Opening Remote Files

You can open remote files almost exactly as you do local files; the difference is that you can use only read mode, and instead of open (or file), you use urlopen from the urllib module:

```
>>> from urllib import urlopen
>>> webpage = urlopen('http://www.python.org')
```

If you are online, the variable webpage should now contain a file-like object linked to the Python web page at http://www.python.org.

---

■**Note** If you want to experiment with urllib but aren't currently online, you can access local files with URLs that start with file:, such as file:c:\text\somefile.txt. (Remember to escape your backslashes.)

---

The file-like object that is returned from urlopen supports (among others) the close, read, readline, and readlines methods, as well as iteration.

Let's say you want to extract the (relative) URL of the "About" link on the Python page you just opened. You could do that with regular expressions (for more information about regular expressions, see the section about the re module in Chapter 10):

```
>>> import re
>>> text = webpage.read()
>>> m = re.search('<a href="([^"]+)" .*?>about</a>', text, re.IGNORECASE)
>>> m.group(1)
'/about/'
```

---

■**Note**  You may need to modify the regular expression if the web page has changed since the time of writing, of course.

---

## Retrieving Remote Files

The urlopen function gives you a file-like object you can read from. If you would rather have urllib take care of downloading the file for you, storing a copy in a local file, you can use urlretrieve instead. Rather than returning a file-like object, it returns a tuple (filename, headers), where filename is the name of the local file (this name is created automatically by urllib), and headers contains some information about the remote file. (I'll ignore headers here; look up urlretrieve in the standard library documentation of urllib if you want to know more about it.) If you want to specify a file name for the downloaded copy, you can supply that as a second parameter:

```
urlretrieve('http://www.python.org', 'C:\\python_webpage.html')
```

This retrieves the Python home page and stores it in the file C:\python_webpage.html. If you don't specify a file name, the file is put in some temporary location, available for you to open (with the open function), but when you're finished with it, you may want to have it removed so that it doesn't take up space on your hard drive. To clean up such temporary files, you can call the function urlcleanup without any arguments, and it takes care of things for you.

---

### SOME UTILITIES

In addition to reading and downloading files through URLs, urllib also offers some functions for manipulating the URLs themselves. (The following assumes some knowledge of URLs and CGI.) The following functions are available:

- quote(string[, safe]): Returns a string in which all special characters (characters that have special significance in URLs) have been replaced by URL-friendly versions (such as %7E instead of ~). This can be useful if you have a string that might contain such special characters and you want to use it as a URL. The safe string includes characters that should not be coded like this. The default is '/'.

- quote_plus(string[, safe]): Works like quote, but also replaces spaces with plus signs.

- unquote(string): The reverse of quote.

- unquote_plus(string): The reverse of quote_plus.

- urlencode(query[, doseq]): Converts a mapping (such as a dictionary) or a sequence of two-element tuples—of the form (key, value)—into a "URL-encoded" string, which can be used in CGI queries. (Check the Python documentation for more information.)

## Other Modules

As mentioned, beyond the modules explicitly discussed in this chapter, there are hordes of network-related modules in the Python library and elsewhere. Table 14-1 lists some network-related modules from the Python standard library. As noted in the table, some of these modules are discussed elsewhere in the book.

**Table 14-1.** *Some Network-Related Modules in the Standard Library*

| Module | Description |
| --- | --- |
| asynchat | Additional functionality for asyncore (see Chapter 24) |
| asyncore | Asynchronous socket handler (see Chapter 24) |
| cgi | Basic CGI support (see Chapter 15) |
| Cookie | Cookie object manipulation, mainly for servers |
| cookielib | Client-side cookie support |
| email | Support for e-mail messages (including MIME) |
| ftplib | FTP client module |
| gopherlib | Gopher client module |
| httplib | HTTP client module |
| imaplib | IMAP4 client module |
| mailbox | Reads several mailbox formats |
| mailcap | Access to MIME configuration through mailcap files |
| mhlib | Access to MH mailboxes |
| nntplib | NNTP client module (see Chapter 23) |
| poplib | POP client module |
| robotparser | Support for parsing web server robot files |
| SimpleXMLRPCServer | A simple XML-RPC server (see Chapter 27) |
| smtpd | SMTP server module |
| smtplib | SMTP client module |
| telnetlib | Telnet client module |
| urlparse | Support for interpreting URLs |
| xmlrpclib | Client support for XML-RPC (see Chapter 27) |

# SocketServer and Friends

As you saw in the section about the socket module earlier, writing a simple socket server isn't really hard. If you want to go beyond the basics, however, getting some help can be nice. The SocketServer module is the basis for a framework of several servers in the standard library, including BaseHTTPServer, SimpleHTTPServer, CGIHTTPServer, SimpleXMLRPCServer, and DocXMLRPCServer, all of which add various specific functionality to the basic server.

SocketServer contains four basic classes: TCPServer, for TCP socket streams; UDPServer, for UDP datagram sockets; and the more obscure UnixStreamServer and UnixDatagramServer. You probably won't need the last three.

To write a server using the SocketServer framework, you put most of your code in a request handler. Each time the server gets a request (a connection from a client), a request handler is instantiated, and various handler methods are called on it to deal with the request. Exactly which methods are called depends on the specific server and handler class used, and you can subclass them to make the server call a custom set of handlers. The basic BaseRequestHandler class places all of the action in a single method on the handler, called handle, which is called by the server. This method then has access to the client socket in the attribute self.request. If you're working with a stream (which you probably are, if you use TCPServer), you can use the class StreamRequestHandler, which sets up two other attributes, self.rfile (for reading) and self.wfile (for writing). You can then use these file-like objects to communicate with the client.

The various other classes in the SocketServer framework implement basic support for HTTP servers, including running CGI scripts, as well as support for XML-RPC (discussed in Chapter 27).

Listing 14-3 gives you a SocketServer version of the minimal server from Listing 14-1. It can be used with the client in Listing 14-2. Note that the StreamRequestHandler takes care of closing the connection when it has been handled. Also note that giving ' ' as the host name means that you're referring to the machine where the server is running.

**Listing 14-3.** *A SocketServer-Based Minimal Server*

```
from SocketServer import TCPServer, StreamRequestHandler

class Handler(StreamRequestHandler):

    def handle(self):
        addr = self.request.getpeername()
        print 'Got connection from', addr
        self.wfile.write('Thank you for connecting')

server = TCPServer(('', 1234), Handler)
server.serve_forever()
```

You can find more information about the SocketServer framework in the Python Library Reference (http://python.org/doc/lib/module-SocketServer.html) and in John Goerzen's *Foundations of Python Network Programming* (Apress, 2004).

# Multiple Connections

The server solutions discussed so far have been *synchronous*: only one client can connect and get its request handled at a time. If one request takes a bit of time, such as, for example, a complete chat session, it's important that more than one connection can be dealt with simultaneously.

You can deal with multiple connections in three main ways: forking, threading, and asynchronous I/O. Forking and threading can be dealt with very simply, by using mix-in classes with any of the `SocketServer` servers (see Listings 14-4 and 14-5). Even if you want to implement them yourself, these methods are quite easy to work with. They do have their drawbacks, however. Forking takes up resources, and may not scale well if you have many clients (although, for a reasonable number of clients, on modern UNIX or Linux systems, forking is quite efficient, and can be even more so if you have a multi-CPU system). Threading can lead to synchronization problems. I won't go into these problems in any detail here (nor will I discuss multithreading in depth), but I'll show you how to use the techniques in the following sections.

### FORKS? THREADS? WHAT'S ALL THIS, THEN?

Just in case you don't know about forking or threads, here is a little clarification. *Forking* is a UNIX term. When you fork a process (a running program), you basically duplicate it, and both resulting processes keep running from the current point of execution, each with its own copy of the memory (variables and such). One process (the original one) will be the *parent* process, while the other (the copy) will be the *child*. If you're a science fiction fan, you might think of parallel universes; the forking operation creates a fork in the timeline, and you end up with two universes (the two processes) existing independently. Luckily, the processes are able to determine whether they are the original or the child (by looking at the return value of the `fork` function), so they can act differently. (If they couldn't, what would be the point, really? Both processes would do the same job, and you would just bog down your computer.)

In a forking server, a child is forked off for every client connection. The parent process keeps listening for new connections, while the child deals with the client. When the client is satisfied, the child process simply exits. Because the forked processes run in parallel, the clients don't need to wait for each other.

Because forking can be a bit resource intensive (each forked process needs its own memory), an alternative exists: threading. *Threads* are lightweight processes, or subprocesses, all of them existing within the same (real) process, sharing the same memory. This reduction in resource consumption comes with a downside, though. Because threads share memory, you must make sure they don't interfere with the variables for each other, or try to modify the same things at the same time, creating a mess. These issues fall under the heading of "synchronization." With modern operating systems (except Microsoft Windows, which doesn't support forking), forking is actually quite fast, and modern hardware can deal with the resource consumption much better than before. If you don't want to bother with synchronization issues, then forking may be a good alternative.

The best thing may, however, be to avoid this sort of parallelism altogether. In this chapter, you find other solutions, based on the `select` function. Another way to avoid threads and forks is to switch to Stackless Python (http://stackless.com), a version of Python designed to be able to switch between different contexts quickly and painlessly. It supports a form of thread-like parallelism called *microthreads*, which scale much better than real threads. For example, Stackless Python microthreads have been used in EVE Online (http://www.eve-online.com) to serve thousands of users.

Asynchronous I/O is a bit more difficult to implement at a low level. The basic mechanism is the `select` function of the `select` module (described in the section "Asynchronous I/O with select and poll"), which is quite hard to deal with. Luckily, frameworks exist that work with asynchronous I/O on a higher level, giving you a simple, abstract interface to a very powerful and scalable mechanism. A basic framework of this kind, which is included in the standard library, consists of the asyncore and asynchat modules, discussed in Chapter 24. Twisted (which is discussed last in this chapter) is a very powerful asynchronous network programming framework.

## Forking and Threading with SocketServer

Creating a forking or threading server with the SocketServer framework is so simple it hardly needs any explanation. Listings 14-4 and 14-5 show you how to make the server from Listing 14-3 forking and threading, respectively. The forking or threading behavior is useful only if the handle method takes a long time to finish. Note that forking doesn't work in Windows.

**Listing 14-4.** *A Forking Server*

```
from SocketServer import TCPServer, ForkingMixIn, StreamRequestHandler

class Server(ForkingMixIn, TCPServer): pass

class Handler(StreamRequestHandler):

    def handle(self):
        addr = self.request.getpeername()
        print 'Got connection from', addr
        self.wfile.write('Thank you for connecting')

server = Server(('', 1234), Handler)
server.serve_forever()
```

**Listing 14-5.** *A Threading Server*

```
from SocketServer import TCPServer, ThreadingMixIn, StreamRequestHandler

class Server(ThreadingMixIn, TCPServer): pass

class Handler(StreamRequestHandler):

    def handle(self):
        addr = self.request.getpeername()
        print 'Got connection from', addr
        self.wfile.write('Thank you for connecting')

server = Server(('', 1234), Handler)
server.serve_forever()
```

## Asynchronous I/O with select and poll

When a server communicates with a client, the data it receives from the client may come in fits and spurts. If you're using forking and threading, that's not a problem. While one parallel waits for data, other parallels may continue dealing with their own clients. Another way to go, however, is to deal only with the clients that actually have something to say at a given moment. You don't even have to hear them out—you just hear (or, rather, *read*) a little, and then put it back in line with the others.

This is the approach taken by the frameworks asyncore/asynchat (see Chapter 24) and Twisted (see the following section). The basis for this kind of functionality is the select function, or, where available, the poll function, both from the select module. Of the two, poll is more scalable, but it is available only in UNIX systems (that is, not in Windows).

The select function takes three sequences as its mandatory arguments, with an optional timeout in seconds as its fourth argument. The sequences are file descriptor integers (or objects with a fileno method that return such an integer). These are the connections that we're waiting for. The three sequences are for input, output, and exceptional conditions (errors and the like). If no timeout is given, select blocks (that is, waits) until one of the file descriptors is ready for action. If a timeout is given, select blocks for at most that many seconds, with zero giving a straight poll (that is, no blocking). select returns three sequences (a triple—that is, a tuple of length three), each representing an active subset of the corresponding parameter. For example, the first sequence returned will be a sequence of input file descriptors where there is something to read.

The sequences can, for example, contain file objects (not in Windows) or sockets. Listing 14-6 shows a server using select to serve several connections. (Note that the server socket itself is supplied to select, so that it can signal when there are new connections ready to be accepted.) The server is a simple logger that prints out (locally) all data received from its clients. You can test it by connecting to it using telnet (or by writing a simple socket-based client that feeds it some data). Try connecting with multiple telnet connections to see that it can serve more than one client at once (although its log will then be a mixture of the input from the two).

**Listing 14-6.** *A Simple Server Using select*

```python
import socket, select

s = socket.socket()

host = socket.gethostname()
port = 1234
s.bind((host, port))

s.listen(5)
inputs = [s]
while True:
    rs, ws, es = select.select(inputs, [], [])
    for r in rs:
        if r is s:
            c, addr = s.accept()
            print 'Got connection from', addr
            inputs.append(c)
```

```
        else:
            try:
                data = r.recv(1024)
                disconnected = not data
            except socket.error:
                disconnected = True

            if disconnected:
                print r.getpeername(), 'disconnected'
                inputs.remove(r)
            else:
                print data
```

The poll method is easier to use than select. When you call poll, you get a poll object. You can then register file descriptors (or objects with a fileno method) with the poll object, using its register method. You can later remove such objects again, using the unregister method. Once you've registered some objects (for example, sockets), you can call the poll method (with an optional timeout argument) and get a list (possibly empty) of pairs of the form (fd, event), where fd is the file descriptor and event tells you what happened. It's a bitmask, meaning that it's an integer where the individual bits correspond to various events. The various events are constants of the select module, and are explained in Table 14-2. To check whether a given bit is set (that is, if a given event occurred), you use the bitwise and operator (&), like this:

```
if event & select.POLLIN: ...
```

**Table 14-2.** *Polling Event Constants in the select Module*

| Event Name | Description |
| --- | --- |
| POLLIN | There is data to read available from the file descriptor. |
| POLLPRI | There is urgent data to read from the file descriptor. |
| POLLOUT | The file descriptor is ready for data, and will not block if written to. |
| POLLERR | Some error condition is associated with the file descriptor. |
| POLLHUP | Hung up. The connection has been lost. |
| POLLNVAL | Invalid request. The connection is not open. |

The program in Listing 14-7 is a rewrite of the server from Listing 14-6, now using poll instead of select. Note that I've added a map (fdmap) from file descriptors (ints) to socket objects.

**Listing 14-7.** *A Simple Server Using poll*

```
import socket, select

s = socket.socket()
```

```
host = socket.gethostname()
port = 1234
s.bind((host, port))

fdmap = {s.fileno(): s}


s.listen(5)
p = select.poll()
p.register(s)
while True:
    events = p.poll()
    for fd, event in events:
        if fd in fdmap:
            c, addr = s.accept()
            print 'Got connection from', addr
            p.register(c)
            fdmap[c.fileno()] = c
        elif event & select.POLLIN:
            data = fdmap[fd].recv(1024)
            if not data: # No data -- connection closed
                print fdmap[fd].getpeername(), 'disconnected'
                p.unregister(fd)
                del fdmap[fd]
            else:
                print data
```

You can find more information about select and poll in the Python Library Reference (http://python.org/doc/lib/module-select.html). Also, reading the source code of the standard library modules asyncore and asynchat (found in the asyncore.py and asynchat.py files in your Python installation) can be enlightening.

# Twisted

Twisted, from Twisted Matrix Laboratories (http://twistedmatrix.com), is an *event-driven* networking framework for Python, originally developed for network games but now used by all kinds of network software. In Twisted, you implement event handlers, much like you would in a GUI toolkit (see Chapter 12). In fact, Twisted works quite nicely together with several common GUI toolkits (Tk, GTK, Qt, and wxWidgets). In this section, I'll cover some of the basic concepts and show you how to do some relatively simple network programming using Twisted. Once you grasp the basic concepts, you can check out the Twisted documentation (available on the Twisted web site, along with quite a bit of other information) to do some more serious network programming. Twisted is a *very* rich framework and supports, among other things, web servers and clients, SSH2, SMTP, POP3, IMAP4, AIM, ICQ, IRC, MSN, Jabber, NNTP, DNS, and more!

# Downloading and Installing Twisted

Installing Twisted is quite easy. First, go to the Twisted Matrix web site (`http://twistedmatrix.com`) and, from there, follow one of the download links. If you're using Windows, download the Windows installer for your version of Python. If you're using some other system, download a source archive. (If you're using a package manager such as Portage, RPM, APT, Fink, or MacPorts, you can probably get it to download and install Twisted directly.) The Windows installer is a self-explanatory step-by-step wizard. It may take some time compiling and unpacking things, but all you have to do is wait. To install the source archive, you first unpack it (using `tar` and then either `gunzip` or `bunzip2`, depending on which type of archive you downloaded), and then run the Distutils script:

```
python setup.py install
```

You should then be able to use Twisted.

# Writing a Twisted Server

The basic socket servers written earlier in this chapter are very explicit. Some of them have an explicit event loop, looking for new connections and new data. `SocketServer`-based servers have an implicit loop where the server looks for connections and creates a handler for each connection, but the handlers still must be explicit about trying to read data. Twisted (like the `asyncore/asynchat` framework, discussed in Chapter 24) uses an even more event-based approach. To write a basic server, you implement event handlers that deal with situations such as a new client connecting, new data arriving, and a client disconnecting (as well as many other events). Specialized classes can build more refined events from the basic ones, such as wrapping "data arrived" events, collecting the data until a newline is found, and then dispatching a "line of data arrived" event.

---

**■Note** One thing I have not dealt with in this section, but which is somewhat characteristic of Twisted, is the concept of *deferreds* and deferred execution. See the Twisted documentation for more information (see, for example, the tutorial called "Deferreds are beautiful," available from the HOWTO page of the Twisted documentation).

---

Your event handlers are defined in a protocol. You also need a factory that can construct such protocol objects when a new connection arrives. If you just want to create instances of a custom protocol class, you can use the factory that comes with Twisted, the `Factory` class in the module `twisted.internet.protocol`. When you write your protocol, use the `Protocol` from the same module as your superclass. When you get a connection, the event handler `connectionMade` is called. When you lose a connection, `connectionLost` is called. Data is received from the client through the handler `dataReceived`. Of course, you can't use the event-handling strategy to send data back to the client—for that you use the object `self.transport`, which has a `write` method. It also has a `client` attribute, which contains the client address (host name and port).

Listing 14-8 contains a Twisted version of the server from Listings 14-6 and 14-7. I hope you agree that the Twisted version is quite a bit simpler and more readable. There is a little bit of setup involved; you need to instantiate `Factory` and set its `protocol` attribute so it knows which protocol to use when communicating with clients (that is, your custom protocol). Then you start listening at a given port with that factory standing by to handle connections by instantiating protocol objects. You do this using the `listenTCP` function from the `reactor` module. Finally, you start the server by calling the `run` function from the same module.

**Listing 14-8.** *A Simple Server Using Twisted*

```
from twisted.internet import reactor
from twisted.internet.protocol import Protocol, Factory

class SimpleLogger(Protocol):

    def connectionMade(self):
        print 'Got connection from', self.transport.client

    def connectionLost(self, reason):
        print self.transport.client, 'disconnected'

    def dataReceived(self, data):
        print data

factory = Factory()
factory.protocol = SimpleLogger

reactor.listenTCP(1234, factory)
reactor.run()
```

If you connected to this server using telnet to test it, you may have gotten a single character on each line of output, depending on buffering and the like. You could simply use `sys.sout.write` instead of `print`, but in many cases, you might like to get a single line at a time, rather than just arbitrary data. Writing a custom protocol that handles this for you would be quite easy, but there is, in fact, such a class available already. The module `twisted.protocols.basic` contains a couple of useful predefined protocols, among them `LineReceiver`. It implements `dataReceived` and calls the event handler `lineReceived` whenever a full line is received.

---

■**Tip** If you need to do something when you receive data in *addition* to using `lineReceived`, which depends on the `LineReceiver` implementation of `dataReceived`, you can use the new event handler defined by `LineReceiver` called `rawDataReceived`.

---

Switching the protocol requires only a minimum of work. Listing 14-9 shows the result. If you look at the resulting output when running this server, you'll see that the newlines are stripped; in other words, using `print` won't give you double newlines anymore.

**Listing 14-9.** *An Improved Logging Server, Using the LineReceiver Protocol*

```
from twisted.internet import reactor
from twisted.internet.protocol import Factory
from twisted.protocols.basic import LineReceiver


class SimpleLogger(LineReceiver):

    def connectionMade(self):
        print 'Got connection from', self.transport.client

    def connectionLost(self, reason):
        print self.transport.client, 'disconnected'

    def lineReceived(self, line):
        print line

factory = Factory()
factory.protocol = SimpleLogger

reactor.listenTCP(1234, factory)
reactor.run()
```

As noted earlier, there is a lot more to the Twisted framework than what I've shown you here. If you're interested in learning more, you should check out the online documentation, available at the Twisted web site (`http://twistedmatrix.com`).

# A Quick Summary

This chapter has given you a taste of several approaches to network programming in Python. Which approach you choose will depend on your specific needs and preferences. Once you've chosen, you will, most likely, need to learn more about the specific method. Here are some of the topics this chapter touched upon:

**Sockets and the** `socket` **module**: Sockets are information channels that let programs (processes) communicate, possibly across a network. The `socket` module gives you low-level access to both client and server sockets. Server sockets listen at a given address for client connections, while clients simply connect directly.

`urllib` **and** `urllib2`: These modules let you read and download data from various servers, given a URL to the data source. The `urllib` module is a simpler implementation, while `urllib2` is very extensible and quite powerful. Both work through straightforward functions such as `urlopen`.

**The** `SocketServer` **framework**: This is a network of synchronous server base classes, found in the standard library, which lets you write servers quite easily. There is even support for simple web (HTTP) servers with CGI. If you want to handle several connections simultaneously, you need to use a *forking* or *threading* mix-in class.

select **and** poll: These two functions let you consider a set of connections and find out which ones are ready for reading and writing. This means that you can serve several connections piecemeal, in a round-robin fashion. This gives the illusion of handling several connections at the same time, and, although superficially a bit more complicated to code, is a much more scalable and efficient solution than threading or forking.

**Twisted**: This framework, from Twisted Matrix Laboratories, is very rich and complex, with support for most major network protocols. Even though it is large, and some of the idioms used may seem a bit foreign, basic usage is very simple and intuitive. The Twisted framework is also asynchronous, so it's very efficient and scalable. If you have Twisted available, it may very well be the best choice for many custom network applications.

## New Functions in This Chapter

| Function | Description |
| --- | --- |
| urllib.urlopen(url[, data[, proxies]]) | Opens a file-like object from a URL |
| urllib.urlretrieve(url[, fname[, hook[, data]]]) | Downloads a file from a URL |
| urllib.quote(string[, safe]) | Quotes special URL characters |
| urllib.quote_plus(string[, safe]) | The same as quote, but quotes spaces as + |
| urllib.unquote(string) | The reverse of quote |
| urllib.unquote_plus(string) | The reverse of quote_plus |
| urllib.urlencode(query[, doseq]) | Encodes mapping for use in CGI queries |
| select.select(iseq, oseq, eseq[, timeout]) | Finds sockets ready for reading/writing |
| select.poll() | Creates a poll object, for polling sockets |
| reactor.listenTCP(port, factory) | Twisted function; listens for connections |
| reactor.run() | Twisted function; main server loop |

## What Now?

You thought we were finished with network stuff now, huh? Not a chance. The next chapter deals with a quite specialized and much publicized entity in the world of networking: the Web.

# CHAPTER 15

■ ■ ■

# Python and the Web

This chapter tackles some aspects of web programming with Python. This is a really vast area, but I've selected three main topics for your amusement: screen scraping, CGI, and mod_python. In addition, I give you some pointers for finding the proper toolkits for more advanced web application and web service development. For extended examples using CGI, see Chapters 25 and 26. For an example of using the specific web service protocol XML-RPC, see Chapter 27.

## Screen Scraping

Screen scraping is a process whereby your program downloads web pages and extracts information from them. This is a useful technique that pops up every time there is a page online that has information you want to use in your program. It is *especially* useful, of course, if the web page in question is dynamic; that is, if it changes over time. Otherwise, you could just download it once and extract the information manually. (The *ideal* situation is, of course, one where the information is available through *web services*, as discussed later in this chapter.)

Conceptually, the technique is very simple. You download the data and analyze it. You could, for example, simply use urllib, get the web page's HTML source, and then use regular expressions (see Chapter 10) or another technique to extract the information. Let's say, for example, that you wanted to extract the various employer names and web sites from the Python Job Board, at http://python.org/community/jobs. You browse the source and see that the names and URLs can be found as links in h3 elements, like this (except on one, unbroken line):

```
<h3><a name="google-mountain-view-ca-usa"><a class="reference"
href="http://www.google.com">Google</a> ...
```

Listing 15-1 shows a sample program that uses urllib and re to extract the required information.

**Listing 15-1.** *A Simple Screen-Scraping Program*

```
from urllib import urlopen
import re
p = re.compile('<h3><a .*?><a .*? href="(.*?)">(.*?)</a>')
text = urlopen('http://python.org/community/jobs').read()
for url, name in p.findall(text):
    print '%s (%s)' % (name, url)
```

The code could certainly be improved (for example, by filtering out duplicates), but it does its job pretty well. There are, however, at least three weaknesses with this approach:

- The regular expression isn't exactly readable. For more complex HTML code and more complex queries, the expressions can become even more hairy and unmaintainable.

- It doesn't deal with HTML peculiarities like CDATA sections and character entities (such as &amp;). If you encounter such beasts, the program will, most likely, fail.

- The regular expression is tied to details in the HTML source code, rather than some more abstract structure. This means that small changes in how the web page is structured can break the program. (By the time you're reading this, it may already be broken.)

The following sections deal with two possible solutions for the problems posed by the regular expression-based approach. The first is to use a program called Tidy (as a Python library) together with XHTML parsing. The second is to use a library called Beautiful Soup, specifically designed for screen scraping.

---

**■Note** There are other tools for screen scraping with Python. You might, for example, want to check out Ka-Ping Yee's `scrape.py` (found at `http://zesty.ca/python`).

---

## Tidy and XHTML Parsing

The Python standard library has plenty of support for parsing structured formats such as HTML and XML (see the Python Library Reference, Section 8, "Structured Markup Processing Tools," at `http://python.org/doc/lib/markup.html`). I discuss XML and XML parsing in more depth in Chapter 22. In this section, I just give you the tools needed to deal with XHTML, the most up-to-date dialect of HTML, which just happens to be a form of XML.

If every web page consisted of correct and valid XHTML, the job of parsing it would be quite simple. The problem is that older HTML dialects are a bit more sloppy, and some people don't even care about the strictures of those sloppier dialects. The reason for this is, probably, that most web browsers are quite forgiving, and will try to render even the most jumbled and meaningless HTML as best they can. If this happens to look acceptable to the page authors, they may be satisfied. This does make the job of screen scraping quite a bit harder, though.

The general approach for parsing HTML in the standard library is event-based; you write event handlers that are called as the parser moves along the data. The standard library modules `sgmllib` and `htmllib` will let you parse really sloppy HTML in this manner, but if you want to extract data based on document structure (such as the first item after the second level-two heading), you'll need to do some heavy guessing if there are missing tags, for example. You are certainly welcome to do this, if you like, but there is another way: Tidy.

### What's Tidy?

Tidy (`http://tidy.sf.net`) is a tool for fixing ill-formed and sloppy HTML. It can fix a range of common errors in a rather intelligent manner, doing a lot of work that you would probably rather not do yourself. It's also quite configurable, letting you turn various corrections on or off.

Here is an example of an HTML file filled with errors, some of them just Old Skool HTML, and some of them plain wrong (can you spot all the problems?):

```
<h1>Pet Shop
<h2>Complaints</h3>

<p>There is <b>no <i>way</b> at all</i> we can accept returned
parrots.

<h1><i>Dead Pets</h1>

<p>Our pets may tend to rest at times, but rarely die within the
warranty period.

<i><h2>News</h2></i>

<p>We have just received <b>a really nice parrot.

<p>It's really nice.</b>

<h3><hr>The Norwegian Blue</h3>

<h4>Plumage and <hr>pining behavior</h4>
<a href="#norwegian-blue">More information<a>

<p>Features:
<body>
<li>Beautiful plumage
```

Here is the version that is fixed by Tidy:

```
<!DOCTYPE html PUBLIC "-//W3C//DTD HTML 4.01 Transitional//EN">
<html>
<head>
<title></title>
</head>
<body>
<h1>Pet Shop</h1>
<h2>Complaints</h2>
<p>There is <b>no <i>way</i> at all</b> we can accept returned
parrots.</p>
<h1><i>Dead Pets</i></h1>
<p>Our pets may tend to rest at times, but rarely die within the
warranty period.</p>
<h2><i>News</i></h2>
<p>We have just received <b>a really nice parrot.</b></p>
<p><b>It's really nice.</b></p>
<hr>
```

```
<h3>The Norwegian Blue</h3>
<h4>Plumage and</h4>
<hr>
<h4>pining behavior</h4>
<a href="#norwegian-blue">More information</a>
<p>Features:</p>
<ul class="noindent">
<li>Beautiful plumage</li>
</ul>
</body>
</html>
```

Of course, Tidy can't fix all problems with an HTML file, but it does make sure it's well-formed (that is, all elements nest properly), which makes it much easier for you to parse it.

### Getting a Tidy Library

You can get Tidy and the library version of Tidy, Tidylib, from `http://tidy.sf.net`. You should also get a Python wrapper. You can get µTidyLib from `http://utidylib.berlios.de`, or mxTidy from `http://egenix.com/products/python/mxExperimental/mxTidy`.

At the time of writing, µTidyLib seems to be the most up-to-date of the two, but mxTidy is a bit easier to install. In Windows, simply download the installer for mxTidy, run it, and you have the module `mx.Tidy` at your fingertips. There are also RPM packages available. If you want to install the source package (presumably in a UNIX or Linux environment), you can simply run the Distutils script, using `python setup.py install`.

### Using Command-Line Tidy in Python

You don't *have* to install either of the libraries, though. If you're running a UNIX or Linux machine of some sort, it's quite possible that you have the command-line version of Tidy available. And no matter what operating system you're using, you can probably get an executable binary from the TidyLib web site (`http://tidy.sf.net`).

Once you have the binary version, you can use the `subprocess` module (or some of the popen functions) to run the Tidy program. Assuming, for example, that you have a messy HTML file called `messy.html`, the following program will run Tidy on it and print the result.

```
from subprocess import Popen, PIPE

text = open('messy.html').read()
tidy = Popen('tidy', stdin=PIPE, stdout=PIPE, stderr=PIPE)

tidy.stdin.write(text)
tidy.stdin.close()

print tidy.stdout.read()
```

In practice, instead of printing the result, you would, most likely, extract some useful information from it, as demonstrated in the following sections.

## But Why XHTML?

The main difference between XHTML and older forms of HTML (at least for our current purposes) is that XHTML is quite strict about closing all elements explicitly. So in HTML you might end one paragraph simply by beginning another (with a `<p>` tag), but in XHTML, you first need to close the paragraph explicitly (with a `</p>` tag). This makes XHTML much easier to parse, because you can tell directly when you enter or leave the various elements. Another advantage of XHTML (which I won't really capitalize on in this chapter) is that it is an XML dialect, so you can use all kinds of nifty XML tools on it, such as XPath. For example, the links to the forms extracted by the program in Listing 15-1 could also be extracted by the XPath expression `//h3/a/@href`. (For more about XML, see Chapter 22; for more about the uses of XPath, see, for example, `http://www.w3schools.com/xpath`.)

A very simple way of parsing the kind of well-behaved XHTML you get from Tidy is using the standard library module (and class) `HTMLParser`.[1]

## Using HTMLParser

Using `HTMLParser` simply means subclassing it and overriding various event-handling methods such as `handle_starttag` and `handle_data`. Table 15-1 summarizes the relevant methods and when they're called (automatically) by the parser.

**Table 15-1.** *The HTMLParser Callback Methods*

| Callback Method | When Is It Called? |
|---|---|
| `handle_starttag(tag, attrs)` | When a start tag is found, `attrs` is a sequence of (`name`, `value`) pairs. |
| `handle_startendtag(tag, attrs)` | For empty tags; default handles start and end separately. |
| `handle_endtag(tag)` | When an end tag is found. |
| `handle_data(data)` | For textual data. |
| `handle_charref(ref)` | For character references of the form `&#ref;`. |
| `handle_entityref(name)` | For entity references of the form `&name;`. |
| `handle_comment(data)` | For comments; called with only the comment contents. |
| `handle_decl(decl)` | For declarations of the form `<!…>`. |
| `handle_pi(data)` | For processing instructions. |

For screen-scraping purposes, you usually won't need to implement all the parser callbacks (the event handlers), and you probably won't need to construct some abstract representation of the entire document (such as a document tree) to find what you want. If you just keep track of the minimum of information needed to find what you're looking for, you're in business. (See Chapter 22 for more about this topic, in the context of XML parsing with SAX.) Listing 15-2 shows a program that solves the same problem as Listing 15-1, but this time using `HTMLParser`.

---

1. This is not to be confused with the class `HTMLParser` from the `htmllib` module, which you can also use, of course, if you're so inclined. It's more liberal in accepting ill-formed input.

**Listing 15-2.** *A Screen-Scraping Program Using the HTMLParser Module*

```
from urllib import urlopen
from HTMLParser import HTMLParser

class Scraper(HTMLParser):

    in_h3 = False
    in_link = False

    def handle_starttag(self, tag, attrs):
        attrs = dict(attrs)
        if tag == 'h3':
            self.in_h3 = True

        if tag == 'a' and 'href' in attrs:
            self.in_link = True
            self.chunks = []
            self.url = attrs['href']

    def handle_data(self, data):
        if self.in_link:
            self.chunks.append(data)

    def handle_endtag(self, tag):
        if tag == 'h3':
            self.in_h3 = False
        if tag == 'a':
            if self.in_h3 and self.in_link:
                print '%s (%s)' % (''.join(self.chunks), self.url)
            self.in_link = False

text = urlopen('http://python.org/community/jobs').read()
parser = Scraper()
parser.feed(text)
parser.close()
```

A few things are worth noting. First of all, I've dropped the use of Tidy here, because the HTML in the web page is well behaved enough. If you're lucky, you may find that you don't need to use Tidy either. Also note that I've used a couple of Boolean *state variables* (attributes) to keep track of whether I'm inside h3 elements and links. I check and update these in the event handlers. The attrs argument to handle_starttag is a list of (key, value) tuples, so I've used dict to turn them into a dictionary, which I find to be more manageable.

The handle_data method (and the chunks attribute) may need some explanation. It uses a technique that is quite common in event-based parsing of structured markup such as HTML and XML. Instead of assuming that I'll get all the text I need in a single call to handle_data, I assume that I may get several chunks of it, spread over more than one call. This may happen for several reasons—buffering, character entities, markup that I've ignored, and so on—and I just need to make sure I get all the text. Then, when I'm ready to present my result (in the handle_endtag method), I simply join all the chunks together. To actually run the parser, I call its feed method with the text, and then call its close method.

This solution is, most likely, more robust to any changes in the input data than the version using regular expressions (Listing 15-1). Still, you may object that it is too verbose (it's *certainly* more verbose than the XPath expression, for example) and perhaps almost as hard to understand as the regular expression. For a more complex extraction task, the arguments in favor of this sort of parsing might seem more convincing, but one is still left with the feeling that there must be a better way. And, if you don't mind installing another module, there is . . .

## Beautiful Soup

Beautiful Soup is a spiffy little module for parsing and dissecting the kind of HTML you often find on the Web—the sloppy and ill-formed kind. To quote the Beautiful Soup web site (http://crummy.com/software/BeautifulSoup):

> You didn't write that awful page. You're just trying to get some data out of it. Right now, you don't really care what HTML is supposed to look like.
>
> Neither does this parser.

Downloading and installing Beautiful Soup is a breeze. Download the file BeautifulSoup.py and put it in your Python path (for example, in the site-packages directory of your Python installation). If you want, you can instead download a tar archive with installer scripts and tests. With Beautiful Soup installed, the running example of extracting Python jobs from the Python Job Board becomes really, really simple *and* readable, as shown in Listing 15-3.

**Listing 15-3.** *A Screen-Scraping Program Using Beautiful Soup*

```
from urllib import urlopen
from BeautifulSoup import BeautifulSoup

text = urlopen('http://python.org/community/jobs').read()
soup = BeautifulSoup(text)

jobs = set()
for header in soup('h3'):
    links = header('a', 'reference')
    if not links: continue
    link = links[0]
    jobs.add('%s (%s)' % (link.string, link['href']))

print '\n'.join(sorted(jobs, key=lambda s: s.lower()))
```

I simply instantiate the BeautifulSoup class with the HTML text I want to scrape, and then use various mechanisms to extract parts of the resulting parse tree. For example, I call soup('h3') to get a list of all h3 elements. I iterate over these, binding the header variable to each one in turn, and call header('a', 'reference') to get a list of a child elements of the reference class (I'm talking CSS classes here). I could also have followed the strategy from previous examples, of retrieving the a elements that have href attributes; in Beautiful Soup, using class attributes like this is easier.

As I'm sure you noticed, I added the use of set and sorted (with a key function set to ignore case differences) in Listing 15-3. This has nothing to do with Beautiful Soup; it was just to make the program more useful, by eliminating duplicates and printing the names in sorted order.

If you want to use your scrapings for an RSS feed (discussed later in this chapter), you can use another tool related to Beautiful Soup, called Scrape 'N' Feed (at http://crummy.com/software/ScrapeNFeed).

# Dynamic Web Pages with CGI

While the first part of this chapter dealt with client-side technology, now we switch gears and tackle the server side. This section deals with a basic web programming technology: the Common Gateway Interface (CGI). CGI is a standard mechanism by which a web server can pass your queries (typically supplied through a web form) to a dedicated program (for example, your Python program) and display the result as a web page. It is a simple way of creating web applications without writing your own special-purpose application server. For more information about CGI programming in Python, see the Web Programming topic guide on the Python web site (http://wiki.python.org/moin/WebProgramming).

The key tool in Python CGI programming is the cgi module. You can find a thorough description of it in the Python Library Reference (http://python.org/doc/lib/module-cgi.html). Another module that can be very useful during the development of CGI scripts is cgitb—more about that later, in the section "Debugging with cgitb."

Before you can make your CGI scripts accessible (and runnable) through the Web, you need to put them where a web server can access them, add a *pound bang* line, and set the proper file permissions. These three steps are explained in the following sections.

## Step 1. Preparing the Web Server

I'm assuming that you have access to a web server—in other words, that you can put stuff on the Web. Usually, that is a matter of putting your web pages, images, and so on in a particular directory (in UNIX, typically called public_html). If you don't know how to do this, you should ask your Internet service provider (ISP) or system administrator.

---

■**Tip**  If you are running Mac OS X, you have the Apache web server as part of your operating system installation. It can be switched on through the Sharing preference pane of System Preferences, by checking the Web Sharing option.

---

Your CGI programs must also be put in a directory where they can be accessed via the Web. In addition, they must somehow be identified as CGI scripts, so the web server doesn't just serve the plain source code as a web page. There are two typical ways of doing this:

- Put the script in a subdirectory called `cgi-bin`.

- Give your script the file name extension `.cgi`.

Exactly how this works varies from server to server—again, check with your ISP or system administrator if you're in doubt. (For example, if you're using Apache, you may need to turn on the `ExecCGI` option for the directory in question.)

## Step 2. Adding the Pound Bang Line

When you've put the script in the right place (and possibly given it a specific file name extension), you must add a pound bang line to the beginning of the script. I mentioned this in Chapter 1 as a way of executing your scripts without needing to explicitly execute the Python interpreter. Usually, this is just convenient, but for CGI scripts, it's crucial—without it, the web server won't know how to execute your script. (For all it knows, the script could be written in some other programming language such as Perl or Ruby.) In general, simply adding the following line to the beginning of your script will do:

```
#!/usr/bin/env python
```

Note that it must be the very first line. (No empty lines before it.) If that doesn't work, you need to find out exactly where the Python executable is and use the full path in the pound bang line, as in the following:

```
#!/usr/bin/python
```

If this doesn't work, it may be that there is something wrong that you cannot see, namely that the line ends in \r\n instead of simply \n, and your web server gets confused. Make sure you're saving the file as a plain UNIX-style text file.

In Windows, you use the full path to your Python binary, as in this example:

```
#!C:\Python22\python.exe
```

## Step 3. Setting the File Permissions

The final thing you need to do (at least if your web server is running on a UNIX or Linux machine) is to set the proper file permissions. You must make sure that everyone is allowed to *read* and *execute* your script file (otherwise the web server wouldn't be able to run it), but also make sure that only *you* are allowed to *write* to it (so no one can change your script).

---

■**Tip**  Sometimes, if you edit a script in Windows and it's stored on a UNIX disk server (you may be accessing it through Samba or FTP, for example), the file permissions may be fouled up after you've made a change to your script. So if your script won't run, make sure that the permissions are still correct.

---

The UNIX command for changing file permissions (or file *mode*) is chmod. Simply run the following command (if your script is called `somescript.cgi`), using your normal user account, or perhaps one set up specifically for such web tasks:

```
chmod 755 somescript.cgi
```

After having performed all these preparations, you should be able to open the script as if it were a web page and have it executed.

---

■**Note**  You shouldn't open the script in your browser as a local file. You must open it with a full http URL so that you actually fetch it via the Web (through your web server).

---

Your CGI script won't normally be allowed to modify any files on your computer. If you want to allow it to change a file, you must explicitly give it permission to do so. You have two options. If you have root (system administrator) privileges, you may create a specific user account for your script and change ownership of the files that need to be modified. If you don't have root access, you can set the file permissions for the file so all users on the system (including that used by the web server to run your CGI scripts) are allowed to write to the file. You can set the file permissions with this command:

```
chmod 666 editable_file.txt
```

---

■**Caution**  Using file mode 666 is a potential security risk. Unless you know what you're doing, it's best avoided.

---

## CGI Security Risks

Some security issues are associated with using CGI programs. If you allow your CGI script to write to files on your server, that ability may be used to destroy data unless you code your program carefully. Similarly, if you evaluate data supplied by a user as if it were Python code (for example, with exec or eval) or as a shell command (for example, with os.system or using the subprocess module), you risk performing arbitrary commands, which is a *huge* (as in *humongous*) risk.

For a relatively comprehensive source of information about web security, see the World Wide Web Consortium's security FAQ (http://www.w3.org/Security/Faq). See also the security note on the subject in the Python Library Reference (http://python.org/doc/lib/cgi-security.html).

## A Simple CGI Script

The simplest possible CGI script looks something like Listing 15-4.

**Listing 15-4.** *A Simple CGI Script*

```
#!/usr/bin/env python

print 'Content-type: text/plain'
print # Prints an empty line, to end the headers

print 'Hello, world!'
```

If you save this in a file called simple1.cgi and open it through your web server, you should see a web page containing only the words "Hello, world!" in plain text. To be able to open this file through a web server, you must put it where the web server can access it. In a typical UNIX environment, putting it in a directory called public_html in your home directory would enable you to open it with the URL http://localhost/~username/simple1.cgi (substitute your user name for username). Ask your ISP or system administrator for details.

As you can see, everything the program writes to standard output (for example, with print) ends up in the resulting web page—at least almost everything. The fact is that the first things you print are HTTP headers, which are lines of information *about* the page. The only header I concern myself with here is Content-type. As you can see, the phrase Content-type is followed by a colon, a space, and the type name text/plain. This indicates that the page is plain text. To indicate HTML, this line should instead be as follows:

```
print 'Content-type: text/html'
```

After all the headers have been printed, a single empty line is printed to signal that the document itself is about to begin. And, as you can see, in this case the document is simply the string 'Hello, world!'.

## Debugging with cgitb

Sometimes a programming error makes your program terminate with a stack trace due to an uncaught exception. When running the program through CGI, this will most likely result in an unhelpful error message from the web server. In Python 2.2, a module called cgitb (for CGI traceback) was added to the standard library. By importing it and calling its enable function, you can get a quite helpful web page with information about what went wrong. Listing 15-5 gives an example of how you might use the cgitb module.

**Listing 15-5.** *A CGI Script That Invokes a Traceback (faulty.cgi)*

```
#!/usr/bin/env python

import cgitb; cgitb.enable()

print 'Content-type: text/html'

print

print 1/0

print 'Hello, world!'
```

The result of accessing this script in a browser (through a web server) is shown in Figure 15-1.

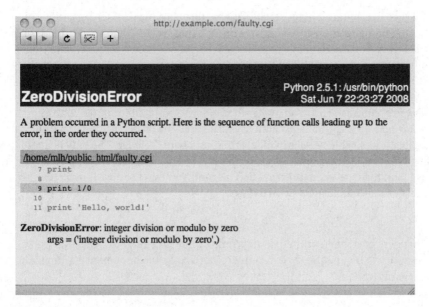

**Figure 15-1.** *A CGI traceback from the cgitb module*

Note that you might want to turn off the cgitb functionality after developing the program, since the traceback page isn't meant for the casual user of your program.[2]

---

2. An alternative is to turn off the display and log the errors to files instead. See the Python Library Reference for more information.

## Using the cgi Module

So far, the programs have only produced output; they haven't used any form of input. Input is supplied to the CGI script from an HTML form (described in the next section) as key-value pairs, or *fields*. You can retrieve these fields in your CGI script using the FieldStorage class from the cgi module. When you create your FieldStorage instance (you should create only one), it fetches the input variables (or fields) from the request and presents them to your program through a dictionary-like interface. The values of the FieldStorage can be accessed through ordinary key lookup, but due to some technicalities (related to file uploads, which we won't be dealing with here), the elements of the FieldStorage aren't really the values you're after. For example, if you knew the request contained a value named name, you couldn't simply do this:

```
form = cgi.FieldStorage()
name = form['name']
```

You would need to do this:

```
form = cgi.FieldStorage()
name = form['name'].value
```

A simpler way of fetching the values is the getvalue method, which is similar to the dictionary method get, except that it returns the value of the value attribute of the item. Here is an example:

```
form = cgi.FieldStorage()
name = form.getvalue('name', 'Unknown')
```

In the preceding example, I supplied a default value ('Unknown'). If you don't supply one, None will be the default. The default is used if the field is not filled in.

Listing 15-6 contains a simple example that uses cgi.FieldStorage.

**Listing 15-6.** *A CGI Script That Retrieves a Single Value from a FieldStorage (simple2.cgi)*

```
#!/usr/bin/env python

import cgi
form = cgi.FieldStorage()

name = form.getvalue('name', 'world')

print 'Content-type: text/plain'
print

print 'Hello, %s!' % name
```

### INVOKING CGI SCRIPTS WITHOUT FORMS

Input to CGI scripts generally comes from web forms that have been submitted, but it is also possible to call the CGI program with parameters directly. You do this by adding a question mark after the URL to your script, and then adding key-value pairs separated by ampersands (&). For example, if the URL to the script in Listing 15-6 were `http://www.someserver.com/simple2.cgi`, you could call it with name=Gumby and age=42 with the URL `http://www.someserver.com/simple2.cgi?name=Gumby&age=42`. If you try that, you should get the message "Hello, Gumby!" instead of "Hello, world!" from your CGI script. (Note that the age parameter isn't used.) You can use the `urlencode` method of the `urllib` module to create this kind of URL query:

```
>>> urllib.urlencode({'name': 'Gumby', 'age': '42'})
'age=42&name=Gumby'
```

You can use this strategy in your own programs, together with `urllib`, to create a screen-scraping program that can actually interact with a CGI script. However, if you're writing both ends (that is, both server and client side) of such a contraption, you would, most likely, be better off using some form of web service (as described in the section "Web Services: Scraping Done Right" in this chapter).

## A Simple Form

Now you have the tools for handling a user request; it's time to create a form that the user can submit. That form can be a separate page, but I'll just put it all in the same script.

To find out more about writing HTML forms (or HTML in general), you should perhaps get a good book on HTML (your local bookstore probably has several). You can also find plenty of information on the subject online. Here are some resources:

- `http://www.webreference.com/htmlform`

- `http://www.htmlhelp.com/faq/html/forms.html`

- `http://www.cs.tut.fi/~jkorpela/forms`

- `http://www.w3schools.com/html/html_forms.asp`

- `http://www.htmlgoodies.com/tutors/fm.html`

Also, if you find some page that you think looks like a good example for what you would like to do, you can inspect its source in your browser by choosing View Source or something similar (depending on which browser you have) from one of the menus.

■**Note** There are two main ways of getting information from a CGI script: the GET method and the POST method. For the purposes of this chapter, the difference between the two isn't really important. Basically, GET is for retrieving things, and encodes its query in the URL; POST can be used for any kind of query, but encodes the query a bit differently. For more information about GET and POST, see the forms tutorials in the preceding list.

Let's return to our script. An extended version can be found in Listing 15-7.

**Listing 15-7.** *A Greeting Script with an HTML Form (simple3.cgi)*

```python
#!/usr/bin/env python

import cgi
form = cgi.FieldStorage()

name = form.getvalue('name', 'world')

print """Content-type: text/html

<html>
  <head>
    <title>Greeting Page</title>
  </head>
  <body>
    <h1>Hello, %s!</h1>


    <form action='simple3.cgi'>
    Change name <input type='text' name='name' />
    <input type='submit' />
    </form>
  </body>
</html>
""" % name
```

In the beginning of this script, the CGI parameter name is retrieved, as before, with the default 'world'. If you just open the script in your browser without submitting anything, the default is used.

Then a simple HTML page is printed, containing name as a part of the headline. In addition, this page contains an HTML form whose action attribute is set to the name of the script itself (simple3.cgi). That means that if the form is submitted, you are taken back to the same script. The only input element in the form is a text field called name. Thus, if you submit the field with a new name, the headline should change because the name parameter now has a value.

Figure 15-2 shows the result of accessing the script in Listing 15-7 through a web server.

**Figure 15-2.** *The result of executing the CGI script in Listing 15-7*

# One Step Up: mod_python

If you like CGI, you will probably *love* mod_python. It's an extension (module) for the Apache web server, and you can get it from the mod_python web site (http://modpython.org). It makes the Python interpreter directly available as a part of Apache, which makes a whole host of different cool stuff possible. At the core, it gives you the ability to write Apache *handlers* in Python, as opposed to in C, which is the norm. The mod_python handler framework gives you access to a rich API, uncovering Apache internals and more.

In addition to the basic functionality, mod_python comes with several handlers that can make web development a more pleasant task:

- The CGI handler, which lets you run CGI scripts using the mod_python interpreter, *considerably* speeding up their execution

- The PSP handler, which lets you mix HTML and Python code to create *executable web pages*, or Python Server Pages

- The publisher handler, which lets you call Python functions using URLs

In this section, I will focus on these three standard handlers; if you want to write your own custom handlers, you should check out the mod_python documentation.

# Installing mod_python

Installing mod_python and getting it to work is, perhaps, a bit more difficult than doing so for many of the other packages I've discussed so far. If nothing else, you need to make it cooperate with Apache. So, if you plan to install mod_python yourself, you should either use some form of package manager system (which will install it automatically) or make sure you know a bit about running and maintaining the Apache web server. (You can find more information about Apache at http://httpd.apache.org.) If you're lucky, you may already have access to a machine where mod_python is installed; if you're uncertain, just try to use it, as described here, and see if your code runs properly. (Of course, you could also bug your ISP or administrator to install it for you.)

If you *do* want to install it yourself, you can get the information you need in the mod_python documentation, available online or for download at the mod_python web site (http://modpython.org). You can probably also get some assistance on the mod_python mailing list (with subscription available from the same web site). The process is slightly different depending on whether you use UNIX or Windows.

## Installing on UNIX

Assuming you have already compiled your Apache web server and you have the Apache source code available, here are the highlights of compiling and installing mod_python.

First, download the mod_python source code. Unpack the archive and enter the directory. Then, run the configure script of mod_python:

```
$ ./configure --with-apxs=/usr/local/apache/bin/apxs
```

Modify the path to the apxs program if this is not where it is found. On my Gentoo system, for example, I would use /usr/sbin/apxs2. (Or, rather, I would install mod_python automatically with the Portage package system, but that's beside the point.)

Make a note of any useful messages, such as any messages about LoadModule.

Once this configuration is done, compile everything:

```
$ make
```

Once everything has been compiled, install mod_python:

```
$ make install
```

You may need to run this with root privileges (or give a --prefix option to configure).

---

■**Note**  On a Mac OS X system, you can use MacPorts to install mod_python.

---

## Installing on Windows

You can download the mod_python installer from http://www.apache.org/dist/httpd/modpython/win/ (get the newest version) and double-click it. The installation is straightforward and will take you through the steps of finding your Python and Apache installations.

You may get an error at the end of the process if you did not install Tcl/Tk with Python, though the installer tells you how to finish the installation manually. To do this, copy mod_python_so.pyd from Python's Lib\site-packages folder to the modules directory under your Apache root folder.

## Configuring Apache

Assuming everything went well (if not, check out the sources of information given earlier), you now must configure Apache to use mod_python. Find the Apache configuration file that is used for specifying modules. This file it is usually called httpd.conf or apache.conf, although it may have a different name in your distribution (consult the relevant documentation, if needed). Add the line that corresponds to your operating system:

```
# UNIX
LoadModule python_module libexec/mod_python.so

# Windows
LoadModule python_module modules/mod_python.so
```

There may be slight variations in how to write this (for example, the exact path to mod_python.so), though the correct version for UNIX should have been reported as a result of running configure, earlier.

Now Apache knows where to find mod_python, but it has no reason to use it—you need to tell it when to do so. To do that, you must add some lines to your Apache configuration, either in some main configuration file (possibly commonapache2.conf, depending on your installation) or in a file called .htaccess in the directory where you place your scripts for web access. (The latter option is only available if it has been allowed in the main configuration of the server using the AllowOverride directive.) In the following, I assume that you're using the .htaccess method; otherwise, you need to wrap the directives like this (remember to use quotes around the path if you are a Windows user):

```
<Directory /path/to/your/directory>
    (Add the directives here)
</Directory>
```

The specific directives to use are described in the following sections.

---

■**Note**  If the procedure described here fails for you, see the Apache and mod_python web sites for more detailed information about installation.

---

# CGI Handler

The CGI handler simulates the environment your program runs in when you actually use CGI. This means that you're really using mod_python to run your program, but you can still (mostly) write it as if it were a CGI script, using the cgi and cgitb modules, for example. (There are some limitations; see the documentation for details.)

The main reason for using the CGI handler as opposed to plain CGI is performance. According to a simple test in the mod_python documentation, you can increase your performance by about one order of magnitude (a factor of about 10) or even more. The publisher (described later) is faster than this, and writing your own handler is *even* faster, possibly tripling the speed of the CGI handler. If you want *only* speed, the CGI handler may be an easy option. If you're writing new code, though, and want some extra functionality and flexibility, using one of the other solutions (described in the following sections) is probably a better idea. The CGI handler doesn't really tap into the great potential of mod_python and is best used with legacy code.

To use the CGI handler, put the following in an .htaccess file in the directory where you keep your CGI scripts:

```
SetHandler mod_python
PythonHandler mod_python.cgihandler
```

---

■**Note** Make sure you don't have conflicting definitions in your global Apache configuration, as the .htaccess file won't override it.

---

For debugging information (which can be useful when something goes wrong, as it usually will), you can add the following:

```
PythonDebug On
```

You should remove this directive when you're finished developing; there's no point in exposing the innards of your program to the (potentially malevolent) public.

Once you've set things up properly, you should be able to run your CGI scripts just as before.

---

■**Note** In order to run your CGI script, you might need to give your script a .py ending, even if you access it with a URL ending in .cgi. mod_python converts the .cgi to a .py when it looks for a file to fulfill the request.

---

## PSP

If you've used PHP (the PHP: Hypertext Preprocessor, originally known as Personal Home Page Tools, or PHP Tools), Microsoft Active Server Pages (ASP), JavaServer Pages (JSP), or something similar, the concepts underlying Python Server Pages (PSP), should be familiar. PSP documents are a mix of HTML (or, for that matter, some other form of document) and Python code, with the Python code enclosed in special-purpose tags. Any HTML (or other plain data) will be converted to calls to an output function.

Setting up Apache to serve your PSP pages is as simple as putting the following in your .htaccess file:

```
AddHandler mod_python .psp
PythonHandler mod_python.psp
```

This will treat files with the .psp file extension as PSP files.

---

■**Caution**  While developing your PSP pages, using the directive PythonDebug On can be useful. You should *not*, though, keep it on when the system is used for real, because any error in the PSP page will result in an exception traceback *including the source code being served to the user*. Letting a potentially hostile user see the source code of your program is something that should not be done lightly. If you publish the code deliberately, others may help you find security flaws, and this can definitely be one of the strong sides to open source software development. However, simply letting users glimpse your code through error messages is probably not useful, and it's potentially a security risk.

---

There are two main sets of PSP tags: one for *statements* and another for *expressions*. The values of expressions in expression tags are put directly into the output document. Listing 15-8 is a simple PSP example, which first performs some setup code (statements) and then outputs some random data as part of the web page, using an expression tag.

**Listing 15-8.** *A Slightly Stochastic PSP Example*

```
<%
from random import choice
adjectives = ['beautiful', 'cruel']
%>
<html>
  <head>
    <title>Hello</title>
  </head>
  <body>
  <p>Hello, <%=choice(adjectives)%> world. My name is Mr. Gumby.</p>
  </body>
</html>
```

You can mix plain output, statements, and expressions in any way you like. You can write comments (which will not be part of the output) <%- like this -%>.

There is really very little to PSP programming beyond these basics. You need to be aware of one issue, though: if code in a statement tag starts an indented block, the block will persist, with the following HTML being put *inside* the block. One way to close such a block is to insert a comment, as in the following:

```
A <%
for i in range(3):
%> merry, <%
# End the for loop
%> merry christmas time.
```

In general, if you've used PHP, JSP, or the like, you will probably notice that PSP is more picky about newlines and indentation—a feature inherited from Python itself.

---

■**Note**  Many other systems somewhat resemble mod_python's PSP. Some are almost identical, such as the Webware PSP system (`http://webwareforpython.org`). Some are similarly named, but with a rather different syntax, such as the Spyce PSP (`http://spyce.sf.net`). The web development system Zope (`http://zope.org`) has its own template languages (such as ZPT). The rather innovative template system Clearsilver (`http://clearsilver.net`) has Python bindings, and could be an interesting alternative for the curious. A visit to the Vaults of Parnassus Web category (`http://py.vaults.ca/apyllo.py?i=127386987`) or a web search for "python template system" (or something similar) should point you toward several other interesting systems.

---

## The Publisher

This is where mod_python *really* comes into its own: it lets you write Python programs that have a much more interesting environment than CGI scripts. To use the publisher handler, put the following in your `.htaccess` file (again, optionally adding `PythonDebug On` while you're developing):

```
AddHandler mod_python .py
PythonHandler mod_python.publisher
```

This will run any file with a name ending in `.py` as a Python script, using the publisher handler.

The first thing to know about the publisher is that it exposes functions to the Web as if they were documents. For example, if you have a script called `script.py` available from `http://example.com/script.py` that contains a function called `func`, the URL `http://example.com/script.py/func` will make the publisher first run the function (with a special *request object* as the only parameter), and then display whatever is returned as the document displayed to the user. As is the custom with ordinary web documents, the default "document" (that is, function) is called `index`, so the URL `http://example.com/script.py` will call the function by that name. In other words, something like the following is sufficient to make use of the publisher handler:

```
def index(req):
    return "Hello, world!"
```

The request object lets you access several pieces of information about the request received, as well as setting custom HTTP headers and the like. Consult the mod_python documentation for instructions on how to use the request object. If you don't care about it, you can just drop it, like this:

```
def index():
    return "Hello, world!"
```

The publisher actually checks how many arguments the given function takes as well as what they're called and supplies only what it can accept.

---

■**Tip** You can do the same sort of magic checking as the publisher, if that interests you. The technique is not necessarily portable across Python implementations (for example, to Jython), but if you're sticking to CPython, you can use the inspect module to poke at such corners of functions (and other objects) to see how many arguments they take and what the arguments are called.

---

You can give your function *more* (or just *other*) arguments than the request object, too:

```
def greet(name='world'):
    return 'Hello, %s!' % name
```

Note that the dispatcher uses the *names* of the arguments, so when there is no argument called req, you won't receive the request object. You can now access this function and supply it with an argument using a URL such as http://example.com/script.py/greet?name=Gumby. The resulting web page should now contain the greeting "Hello, Gumby!".

Note that the default argument is quite useful. If the user (or the calling program) doesn't supply all parameters, it's better to display a default page of some sort than to confront the user with a rather obscure "internal server error" message. Also, it would be problematic if supplying extra arguments (not used by the function) would lead to an error condition. Luckily, that won't happen, because the dispatcher uses only the arguments it needs.

One nice thing about the dispatcher is that access control and authorization are very easy to implement. The path given in the URL (after the script name) is actually a series of attribute lookups. For each step in the series of lookups, mod_python also looks for the attributes __auth__ and __access__ in the same object (or module) as the attribute itself. If you have defined the __auth__ attribute, and it is callable (for example, a function or method), the user is queried for a user name and password, and __auth__ is called with the request object, the user name, and the password. If the return value is true, the user is authenticated. If __auth__ is a dictionary, the user name will be looked up, and the password will be matched against the corresponding key. The __auth__ attribute can also be some constant value. If it is false, the user is never authorized. (You can use the __auth_realm__ attribute to give the realm name, usually used in the login query dialog box.)

Once a user has been authenticated, it is time to check whether that user should be granted access to a given object (for example, the module or script itself). For this check, you use the __access__ attribute. If you have defined __access__ and it is callable, it is called with the request object and the user name, and, again, the truth value returned determines whether the user is granted access (with a true value granting access). If __access__ is a list, then the user is granted access if the user name is found in the list. Just like __auth__, __access__ can be a Boolean constant.

Listing 15-9 gives a simple example of a script with authentication and access control.

**Listing 15-9.** *Simple Authentication with the mod_python Publisher*

```
from sha import sha

__auth_realm__ = "A simple test"

def __auth__(req, user, pswd):
    return user == "gumby" and sha(pswd).hexdigest() == \
    '17a15a277d43d3d9514ff731a7b5fa92dfd37aff'

def __access__(req, user):
    return True

def index(req, name="world"):
    return "<html>Hello, %s!</html>" % name
```

Note that the script in Listing 15-9 uses the sha module to avoid storing the password (which is goop, by the way) in plain text. Instead, a digest of the correct password is compared with a digest of the password supplied by the user. This doesn't give a great increase in security, but it's better than nothing.

The __access__ function doesn't really do anything useful in the example in Listing 15-9. In a real application, you might have a common authentication function, to check that the users really are who they claim to be (that is, verify that the passwords fit the user names), and then use specialized __access__ functions (or lists) in different objects to restrict access to a subset of the users. For more information about how objects are published, see the section "The Publishing Algorithm" in the mod_python documentation.

---

■**Note** The __auth__ mechanism uses HTTP authentication, as opposed to the cookie-based authentication used by some systems (where your session, or logged-in status, is stored in a cookie).

---

# Web Application Frameworks

The CGI mechanism and the mod_python toolkit are, in many ways, very basic building blocks for web application development. If you wish to develop more complex systems, you will probably want to use a web application framework. Four safe choices are Zope (often used along with the content management system Plone), Django, Pylons, and TurboGears.[3] These are systems that include support for mapping from URLs to method calls (like mod_python),

---

3. Maybe you've heard of Ruby on Rails. Frameworks such as Django, Pylon, and TurboGears are, in some ways, Python parallels.

object-relational mapping for persistent storage (for example, in SQL databases), templating for dynamic web page generation, and much more. Twisted (described in Chapter 14) is also relevant here.

Much documentation (including books) is available for these frameworks. For a quick start, check out their web pages. For even more hints, check out the Web Programming topic guide in the Python Wiki (`http://wiki.python.org/moin/WebProgramming`). Table 15-2 lists the URLs for the frameworks mentioned, as well as some other frameworks that might be of interest.

**Table 15-2.** *Python Web Application Frameworks*

| Name | Web Site |
|------|----------|
| Albatross | `http://object-craft.com.au/projects/albatross` |
| CherryPy | `http://cherrypy.org` |
| Django | `http://djangoproject.com` |
| Plone | `http://plone.org` |
| Pylons | `http://pylonshq.com` |
| Quixote | `http://quixote.ca` |
| Spyce | `http://spyce.sf.net` |
| TurboGears | `http://turbogears.org` |
| web.py | `http://webpy.org` |
| Webware | `http://webwareforpython.org` |
| Zope | `http://zope.org` |

# Web Services: Scraping Done Right

Web services are a bit like computer-friendly web pages. They are based on standards and protocols that enable programs to exchange information across the network, usually with one program, the client or *service requester*, asking for some information or service, and the other program, the server or *service provider*, providing this information or service. Yes, this is glaringly obvious stuff, and it also seems very similar to the network programming discussed in Chapter 14, but there are differences.

Web services often work on a rather high level of abstraction. They use HTTP (the "Web protocol") as the underlying protocol. On top of this, they use more content-oriented protocols, such as some XML format to encode requests and responses. This means that a web server can be the platform for web services. As the title of this section indicates, it's web scraping taken to another level. You could see the web service as a dynamic web page designed for a computerized client, rather than for human consumption.

There are standards for web services that go really far in capturing all kinds of complexity, but you can get a lot done with utter simplicity as well. In this section, I give only a brief introduction to the subject, with some pointers to where you can find the tools and information you might need.

■**Note** As there are many ways of implementing web services, including a multitude of protocols, and each web service system may provide several services, it can sometimes be necessary to describe a service in a manner that can be interpreted automatically by a client—a *meta*service, so to speak. The standard for this sort of description is the Web Service Description Language (WSDL). WSDL is an XML format that describes such things as which methods are available through a service, along with their arguments and return values. Many, if not most, web service toolkits will include support for WSDL in addition to the actual service protocols, such as SOAP.

## RSS and Friends

RSS, which stands for either Rich Site Summary, RDF Site Summary, or Really Simple Syndication (depending on the version number), is, in its simplest form, a format for listing news items in XML. What makes RSS documents (or *feeds*) more of a service than simply a static document is that they're expected to be updated regularly (or irregularly). They may even be computed dynamically, representing, for example, the most recent additions to a blog or the like. A newer format used for the same thing is Atom. For information about RSS and its relative Resource Description Framework (RDF), see `http://www.w3.org/RDF`. For a specification of Atom, see `http://tools.ietf.org/html/rfc4287`.

Plenty of RSS readers are out there, and often they can also handle other formats such as Atom. Because the RSS format is so easy to deal with, developers keep coming up with new applications for it. For example, some browsers (such as Mozilla Firefox) will let you bookmark an RSS feed, and will then give you a dynamic bookmark submenu with the individual news items as menu items. RSS is also the backbone of podcasting (web-based "broadcasting" of sound or video files).

The problem is that if you want to write a client program that handles feeds from several sites, you must be prepared to parse several different formats, and you may even need to parse HTML fragments found in the individual entries of the feed. Even though you could use `BeautifulSoup` (more specifically, the XML-oriented `BeautifulStoneSoup` class) to tackle this, it's probably a better idea to use Mark Pilgrim's Universal Feed Parser (`http://feedparser.org`), which handles several feed formats (including RSS and Atom, along with some extensions) and has support for some degree of content cleanup. Pilgrim has also written a useful article, "Parsing RSS At All Costs" (`http://xml.com/pub/a/2003/01/22/dive-into-xml.html`), in case you want to deal with some of the cleanup yourself.

## Remote Procedure Calls with XML-RPC

Beyond the simple *download-and-parse* mechanic of RSS lies the remote procedure call. A remote procedure call is an abstraction of a basic network interaction. Your client program asks the server program to perform some computation and return the result, but it is all camouflaged as a simple procedure (or function or method) call. In the client code, it looks like an ordinary method is called, but the object on which it is called actually resides on a different machine entirely. Probably the simplest mechanism for this sort of procedure call is XML-RPC, which implements the network communication with HTTP and XML. Because there is nothing language-specific about the protocol, it is easy for client programs written in one language to call functions on a server program written in another.

■**Tip** For Python-specific alternatives to XML-RPC, check out the remote procedure call mechanisms of Pyro (http://pyro.sf.net) and Twisted (http://twistedmatrix.com).

The Python standard library includes support for both client-side and server-side XML-RPC programming. For examples of using XML-RPC, see Chapters 27 and 28.

---

**RPC AND REST**

Even though the two mechanisms are rather different, remote procedure calls may be compared to the so-called representational state transfer style of network programming, usually called REST. REST-based (or RESTful) programs also allow clients to access the servers programmatically, but the server program is assumed not to have any hidden state. Returned data is uniquely determined by the given URL (or, in the case of HTTP POST, additional data supplied by the client).

More information about REST is readily available online. For example, you could start with the Wikipedia article on it, at http://en.wikipedia.org/wiki/Representational_State_Transfer. A simple and elegant protocol that is used quite a bit in RESTful programming is JavaScript Object Notation, or JSON (http://www.json.org), which allows you to represent complex objects in a plain-text format. A comparison of JSON modules for Python can be found at http://deron.meranda.us/python/comparing_json_modules.

---

## SOAP

SOAP[4] is also a protocol for exchanging messages, with XML and HTTP as underlying technologies. Like XML-RPC, SOAP supports remote procedure calls, but the SOAP specification is much more complex than that of XML-RPC. SOAP is asynchronous, supports metarequests about routing, and has a complex typing system (as opposed to XML-RPC's simple set of fixed types).

There is no single standard SOAP toolkit for Python. You might want to consider Twisted (http://twistedmatrix.com), ZSI (http://pywebsvcs.sf.net), or SOAPy (http://soapy.sf.net). For more information about the SOAP format itself, see http://www.w3.org/TR/soap.

# A Quick Summary

Here is a summary of the topics covered in this chapter:

**Screen scraping**: This is the practice of downloading web pages automatically, and extracting information from them. The Tidy program and its library version are useful tools for fixing ill-formed HTML before using an HTML parser. Another option is to use Beautiful Soup, which is very forgiving of messy input.

---

4. While the name once stood for Simple Object Access Protocol, this is no longer true. Now it's just SOAP.

**CGI**: The Common Gateway Interface is a way of creating dynamic web pages, by making a web server run and communicate with your programs, and display the results. The `cgi` and `cgitb` modules are useful for writing CGI scripts. CGI scripts are usually invoked from HTML forms.

**mod_python**: The mod_python handler framework makes it possible to write Apache handlers in Python. It includes three useful standard handlers: the CGI handler, the PSP handler, and the publisher handler.

**Web application frameworks and servers**: For developing large, complex web applications in Python, a web application framework is almost a must. Zope, Django, Pylon, and TurboGears are some good Python framework choices.

**Web services**: Web services are to programs what (dynamic) web pages are to people. You may see them as a way of making it possible to do network programming at a higher level of abstraction. Common web service standards are RSS (and its relatives, RDF and Atom), XML-RPC, and SOAP.

## New Functions in This Chapter

| Function | Description |
| --- | --- |
| `cgitb.enable()` | Enables tracebacks in CGI script |

## What Now?

I'm sure you've tested the programs you've written so far by running them. In the next chapter, you will learn how you can *really* test them—thoroughly and methodically, maybe even obsessively (if you're lucky).

# CHAPTER 16

▪ ▪ ▪

# Testing, 1-2-3

**H**ow do you know that your program works? Can you rely on yourself to write flawless code all the time? Meaning no disrespect, I would guess that's unlikely. It's quite easy to write correct code in Python most of the time, certainly, but chances are your code will have bugs.[1] Debugging is a fact of life for programmers—an integral part of the craft of programming. However, the only way to get started debugging is to *run your program*. Right? And simply running your program might not be enough. If you have written a program that processes files in some way, for example, you will need some files to run it on. Or if you have written a utility library with mathematical functions, you will need to supply those functions with parameters in order to get your code to run.

Programmers do this kind of thing all the time. In compiled languages, the cycle goes something like "edit, compile, run," around and around. In some cases, even getting the program to compile may be a problem, so the programmer simply switches between editing and compiling. In Python, the compilation step isn't there—you simply edit and run. Running your program is what testing is all about.

In this chapter, I discuss the basics of testing. I give you some notes on how to let testing become one of your programming habits and show you some useful tools for writing your tests. In addition to the testing and profiling tools of the standard library, I show you how to use the code analyzers PyChecker and PyLint.

For more on programming practice and philosophy, see Chapter 19. There, I also mention logging, which is somewhat related to testing.

## Test First, Code Later

To plan for change and flexibility, which is crucial if your code is going to survive even to the end of your own development process, it's important to set up tests for the various parts of your program (so-called *unit tests*). It's also a very practical and pragmatic part of designing your application. Rather than the intuitive "code a little, test a little" practice, the Extreme Programming crowd (a relatively new movement in software design and development) has introduced the highly useful, but somewhat counterintuitive, dictum "test a little, code a little."

---

1. Did you know that the original computer bug was, in fact, a moth? It was found stuck in a relay in the Mark II computer at Harvard in 1945. The term *bug* for a computer glitch and the related word *debugging* are credited to Grace Hopper, who taped the original bug into her logbook. The logbook—with the bug—is on display at the US Naval Surface Weapons Center in Dahlgren, Virginia. (See http://en.wikipedia.org/wiki/Software_bug for more information.)

In other words, test first and code later. This is also known as *test-driven programming*. While this may be unfamiliar at first, it can have many advantages, and it does grow on you over time. Eventually, once you've used test-driven programming for a while, writing code without having tests in place will seem really backwards.

## Precise Requirement Specification

When developing a piece of software, you must first know what problem the software will solve—what objectives it will meet. You can clarify your goals for the program by writing a *requirement specification*, a document (or just some quick notes) describing requirements the program must satisfy. It is then easy to check at some later time whether the requirements are indeed satisfied. But many programmers dislike writing reports and in general prefer to have their computer do as much of their work as possible. Here's good news: you can specify the requirements in Python and have the interpreter check whether they are satisfied!

---

**Note**   There are many types of requirements, including such vague concepts as client satisfaction. In this section, I focus on *functional* requirements—that is, what is required of the program's functionality.

---

The idea is to start by writing a test program, and *then* write a program that passes the tests. The test program is your requirement specification and helps you stick to those requirements while developing the program.

Let's take a simple example. Suppose you want to write a module with a single function that will compute the area of a rectangle with a given height and a given width. Before you start coding, you write a unit test with some examples for which you know the answers. Your test program might look like the one in Listing 16-1.

**Listing 16-1.** *A Simple Test Program*

```
from area import rect_area
height = 3
width = 4
correct_answer = 12
answer = rect_area(height, width)
if answer == correct_answer:
    print 'Test passed '
else:
    print 'Test failed '
```

In this example, I call the function rect_area (which I haven't written yet) on the height 3 and width 4, and compare the answer with the correct one, which is 12.[2]

---

2.  Of course, testing only one case like this won't give you much confidence in the correctness of the code. A real test program would probably be a lot more thorough.

If you then carelessly implement `rect_area` (in the file `area.py`) as follows, and try to run the test program, you would get an error message:

```
def rect_area(height, width):
    return height * height # This is wrong...
```

You could then examine the code to see what was wrong, and replace the returned expression with `height * width`.

Writing a test before you write your code isn't just a preparation for finding bugs—it's much more profound than that. It's a preparation for seeing whether your code works at all. It's a bit like the old Zen koan: "Does a tree falling in the forest make a sound if no one is there to hear it?" Well, of course it does (sorry, Zen monks), but the sound doesn't have any impact on you or anyone else. With your code, the question is, "Until you test it, does it actually *do* anything?" Philosophy aside, it can be useful to adopt the attitude that a feature doesn't really exist (or isn't really a feature) until you have a test for it. Then you can clearly demonstrate that it's there and is doing what it's supposed to do. This isn't only useful while developing the program initially, but also when you later extend and maintain the code.

## Planning for Change

In addition to helping a great deal as you write the program, automated tests help you avoid accumulating errors when you introduce changes. As discussed in Chapter 19, you should be prepared to change your code, rather than clinging frantically to what you have, but change has its dangers. When you change some piece of your code, you very often introduce an unforeseen bug or two. If you have designed your program well (with a lot of abstraction and encapsulation), the effects of a change should be local, and affect only a small piece of the code. That means that debugging is easier *if you spot the bug*.

---

### CODE COVERAGE

The concept of *coverage* is an important part of testing lore. When you run your tests, chances are you won't run all parts of your code, even though that would be the ideal situation. (Actually, the *ideal* situation would be to run through every possible state of your program, using every possible input, but that's really not going to happen.) One of the goals of a good test suite is to get good coverage, and one way of ensuring that is to use a coverage tool, which measures the percentage of your code that was actually run during the testing. At the time of writing, there is no really standardized coverage tool for Python, but a web search for something like "test coverage python" should turn up a few options. One option is the (currently undocumented) program `trace.py`, which comes with the Python distribution. You can run it as a program on the command line (possibly using the -m switch, saving you the trouble of finding the file), or you can import it as a module. For help on how to use it, you can either run the program with the --help switch or import the module and execute `help(trace)` in the interpreter.

At times, you may feel overwhelmed by the requirement to test everything extensively. Don't worry—you don't have to test hundreds of combinations of inputs and state variables, at least not to begin with. The most important part of test-driven programming is that you actually run your method (or function or script) repeatedly while coding, to get continual feedback on how you're doing. If you want to increase your confidence in the correctness of the code (as well as the coverage), you can always add more tests later.

The point is that if you don't have a thorough set of tests handy, you may not even discover that you have introduced a bug until later, when you no longer know how the error was introduced. And without a good suite of tests, it is much harder to pinpoint exactly what is wrong. You can't roll with the punches unless you see them coming. One way of making sure that you get good *test coverage* (that is, that your tests exercise much, if not most, of your code) is, in fact, to follow the tenets of test-driven programming. If you make sure that you have written the tests *before* you write the function, you can be certain that every function is tested.

## The 1-2-3 (and 4) of Testing

Before we get into the nitty-gritty of writing tests, here's a breakdown of the test-driven development process (or one variation of it):

1. Figure out the new feature you want. Possibly document it, and then write a test for it.

2. Write some skeleton code for the feature, so that your program runs without any syntax errors or the like, but your test fails. It is important to see your test fail, so you are sure that it actually *can* fail. If there is something wrong with the test, and it always succeeds no matter what (this has happened to me many times), you aren't really testing anything. This bears repeating: see your test *fail* before you try to make it *succeed*.

3. Write dummy code for your skeleton, just to appease the test. This doesn't have to accurately implement the functionality; it just needs to make the test pass. This way, you can have all your tests pass all the time when developing (except the first time you run the test, remember?), even while initially implementing the functionality.

4. Rewrite (or *refactor*) the code so that it actually does what it's supposed to, all the while making sure that your test keeps succeeding.

You should keep your code in a healthy state when you leave it—don't leave it with any tests failing. Well, that's what they say. I find that I sometimes leave it with *one* test failing, which is the point at which I'm currently working, as a sort of "to-do" or "continue here" for myself. This is really bad form if you're developing together with others, though. You should never check failing code into the common code repository.

# Tools for Testing

You may think that writing a lot of tests to make sure that every detail of your program works correctly sounds like a chore. Well, I have good news for you: there is help in the standard libraries (isn't there always?). Two brilliant modules are available to automate the testing process for you:

- unittest: A generic testing framework.

- doctest: A simpler module, designed for checking documentation, but excellent for writing unit tests as well.

Let's begin with a look at doctest, which is a great starting point.

# doctest

Throughout this book, I use examples taken directly from the interactive interpreter. I find that this is an effective way to show how things work, and when you have such an example, it's easy to test it for yourself. In fact, interactive interpreter sessions can be a useful form of documentation to put in docstrings. For instance, let's say I write a function for squaring a number, and add an example to its docstring:

```
def square(x):
    '''
    Squares a number and returns the result.

    >>> square(2)
    4
    >>> square(3)
    9
    '''
    return x*x
```

As you can see, I've included some text in the docstring, too. What does this have to do with testing? Let's say the square function is defined in the module my_math (that is, a file called my_math.py). Then you could add the following code at the bottom:

```
if __name__=='__main__':
    import doctest, my_math
    doctest.testmod(my_math)
```

That's not a lot, is it? You simply import doctest and the my_math module itself, and then run the testmod (for "test module") function from doctest. What does this do? Let's try it:

```
$ python my_math.py
$
```

Nothing seems to have happened, but that's a good thing. The doctest.testmod function reads all the docstrings of a module and seeks out any text that looks like an example from the interactive interpreter. Then it checks whether the example represents reality.

---

**▨Note**  If I were writing a real function here, I would (or should, according to the rules I laid down earlier) first write the docstring, run the script with doctest to see the test fail, add a dummy version (for example using if statements to deal with the specific inputs in the docstring) so that the test succeeds, and *then* start working on getting the implementation right. On the other hand, if you're going to do full-out "test-first, code-later" programming, the unittest framework (discussed later) might suit your needs better.

---

To get some more input, you can just give the -v (for "verbose") switch to your script:

```
$ python my_math.py -v
```

This command would result in the following output:

```
Running my_math.__doc__
0 of 0 examples failed in my_math.__doc__
Running my_math.square.__doc__
Trying: square(2)
Expecting: 4
ok

Trying: square(3)
Expecting: 9
ok
0 of 2 examples failed in my_math.square.__doc__
1 items had no tests:
    test
1 items passed all tests:
   2 tests in my_math.square
2 tests in 2 items.
2 passed and 0 failed.
Test passed.
```

As you can see, a lot happened behind the scenes. The testmod function checks both the module docstring (which, as you can see, contains no tests) and the function docstring (which contains two tests, both of which succeed).

With this in place, you can safely change your code. Let's say that you want to use the Python exponentiation operator instead of plain multiplication, and use x**2 instead of x*x. You edit the code, but accidentally forget to enter the number 2, ending up with x**x. Try it, and then run the script to test the code. What happens? This is the output you get:

```
**************************************************************
Failure in example: square(3)
from line #5 of my_math.square
Expected: 9
Got: 27
**************************************************************
1 items had failures:
   1 of   2 in my_math.square
***Test Failed*** 1 failures.
```

So the bug was caught, and you get a very clear description of what is wrong. Fixing the problem shouldn't be difficult now.

■**Caution**  Don't trust your tests blindly, and be sure to test enough cases. As you can see, the test using square(2) does *not* catch the bug because for x==2, x**2 and x**x are the same thing!

For more information about the doctest module, you should again check out the library reference (http://python.org/doc/lib/module-doctest.html).

## unittest

While doctest is very easy to use, unittest (based on the popular test framework JUnit, for Java) is more flexible and powerful. unittest may have a steeper learning curve than doctest, but I suggest that you take a look at this module, because it allows you to write very large and thorough test sets in a more structured manner.

I will give you just a gentle introduction here. unittest includes some features that you probably won't need for most of your testing. For complete details, see the Python Library Reference (http://python.org/doc/lib/module-unittest.html).

■**Tip**  A couple of interesting alternatives to the unit test tools in the standard library are py.test (http://codespeak.net/py/dist/test.html) and nose (http://code.google.com/p/python-nose).

Again, let's take a look at a simple example. You're going to write a module called my_math containing a function for calculating products, called product. So where do you begin? With a test, of course (in a file called test_my_math.py), using the TestCase class from the unittest module (see Listing 16-2).

**Listing 16-2.** *A Simple Test Using the unittest Framework*

```
import unittest, my_math

class ProductTestCase(unittest.TestCase):

    def testIntegers(self):
        for x in xrange(-10, 10):
            for y in xrange(-10, 10):
                p = my_math.product(x, y)
                self.failUnless(p == x*y, 'Integer multiplication failed')

    def testFloats(self):
        for x in xrange(-10, 10):
```

```
            for y in xrange(-10, 10):
                x = x/10.0
                y = y/10.0
                p = my_math.product(x, y)
                self.failUnless(p == x*y, 'Float multiplication failed')

if __name__ == '__main__': unittest.main()
```

The function unittest.main takes care of running the tests for you. It will instantiate all subclasses of TestCase and run all methods whose names start with test.

___

■**Tip** If you define methods called setUp and tearDown, they will be executed before and after each of the test methods. You can use these methods to provide common initialization and cleanup code for all the tests, a so-called *test fixture*.

___

Running this test script will, of course, simply give you an exception about the module my_math not existing. Methods such as failUnless check a condition to determine whether the given test succeeds or fails. The module has many other methods, such as failIf, failUnlessEqual, and failIfEqual. See Table 16-1 for a brief overview. (Again, refer to the Python Library Reference, http://python.org/doc/lib/testcase-objects.html, for complete information.)

**Table 16-1.** *Some Useful TestCase Methods*

| Method | Description |
| --- | --- |
| assert_(expr[, msg]) | Fail if the expression is false, optionally giving a message. (Note the underscore.) |
| failUnless(expr[, msg]) | Same as assert_. |
| assertEqual(x, y[, msg]) | Fail if two values are different, printing both values in traceback. |
| failUnlessEqual(x, y[, msg]) | Same as assertEqual. |
| assertNotEqual(x, y[, msg]) | The opposite of assertEqual. |
| failIfEqual(x, y[, msg]) | The same as assertNotEqual. |
| assertAlmostEqual(x, y[, places[, msg]]) | Similar to assertEqual, but with some leeway for float values. |
| failUnlessAlmostEqual(x, y[, places[, msg]]) | The same as assertAlmostEqual. |
| assertNotAlmostEqual(x, y[, places[, msg]]) | The opposite of assertAlmostEqual. |
| failIfAlmostEqual(x, y[, msg]) | The same as assertNotAlmostEqual. |
| assertRaises(exc, callable, ...) | Fail unless the callable raises exc when called (with optional arguments). |

| Method | Description |
|--------|-------------|
| failUnlessRaises(exc, callable, ...) | Same as assertRaises. |
| failIf(expr[, msg]) | Opposite of assert_. |
| fail([msg]) | Unconditional failure, with an optional message, as for the other methods. |

The unittest module distinguishes between *errors*, where an exception is raised, and *failures*, which result from calls to failUnless and the like. The next step is to write skeleton code, so we don't get errors—only failures. This simply means to create a module called my_math (that is, a file called my_math.py) containing the following:

```
def product(x, y):
    pass
```

All filler, no fun. If you run the test now, you should get two FAIL messages, like this:

```
FF
======================================================================
FAIL: testFloats (__main__.ProductTestCase)
----------------------------------------------------------------------
Traceback (most recent call last):
  File "test_my_math.py", line 17, in testFloats
    self.failUnless(p == x*y, 'Float multiplication failed')
AssertionError: Float multiplication failed


======================================================================
FAIL: testIntegers (__main__.ProductTestCase)
----------------------------------------------------------------------
Traceback (most recent call last):
  File "test_my_math.py", line 9, in testIntegers
    self.failUnless(p == x*y, 'Integer multiplication failed')
AssertionError: Integer multiplication failed


----------------------------------------------------------------------
Ran 2 tests in 0.001s

FAILED (failures=2)
```

This was all expected, so don't worry too much. Now, at least, you know that the tests are really linked to the code—the code was wrong, and the tests failed. Wonderful.

The next step is to make it work. In this case, there isn't much to it, of course:

```
def product(x, y):
    return x * y
```

Now the output is simply as follows:

```
..
-----------------------------------------------------------------------
Ran 2 tests in 0.015s

OK
```

The two dots at the top are the tests. If you look closely at the jumbled output from the failed version, you'll see two characters on the top there as well: two Fs, indicating two failures.

Just for fun, change the product function so that it fails for the specific parameters 7 and 9:

```python
def product(x, y):
    if x == 7 and y == 9:
        return 'An insidious bug has surfaced!'
    else:
        return x * y
```

If you run the test script again, you should get a single failure:

```
.F
=======================================================================
FAIL: testIntegers (__main__.ProductTestCase)
-----------------------------------------------------------------------
Traceback (most recent call last):
  File "test_my_math.py", line 9, in testIntegers
    self.failUnless(p == x*y, 'Integer multiplication failed')
AssertionError: Integer multiplication failed


-----------------------------------------------------------------------
Ran 2 tests in 0.005s

FAILED (failures=1)
```

■**Tip**  There is also a GUI for unittest. See the PyUnit (another name for unittest) web page, http://pyunit.sf.net, for more information.

# Beyond Unit Tests

Tests are clearly important, and for any somewhat complex project, they are absolutely vital. Even if you don't want to bother with structured suites of unit tests, you really must have some way of running your program to see whether it works. Having this capability in place *before* you do any significant amount of coding can save you a bundle of work (and pain) later on.

There are other ways of probulating (what, you don't watch *Futurama*?) your program, and here I'll show you several tools for doing just that: source code checking and profiling. Source code checking is a way of looking for common mistakes or problems in your code (a bit like what compilers can do for statically typed languages, but going far beyond that). Profiling is a way of finding out how fast your program really is. I discuss the topics in this order to honor the good old rule, "Make it work, make it better, make it faster." The unit testing helped make it work; source code checking can help make it better; and, finally, profiling can help make it faster.

## Source Code Checking with PyChecker and PyLint

For quite some time, PyChecker (`http://pychecker.sf.net`) was the only tool for checking Python source code, looking for mistakes such as supplying arguments that won't work with a given function and so forth. (All right, there was `tabnanny`, in the standard library, but that isn't all that powerful, since it just checks your indentation.) Then along came PyLint (`http://www.logilab.org/projects/pylint`), which supports most of the features of PyChecker and quite a few more (such as whether your variable names fit a given naming convention, whether you're adhering to your own coding standards, and the like).

Installing the tools is simple. They are both available from several package manager systems (such as Debian APT and Gentoo Portage), and may also be downloaded directly from their respective web sites. You install using Distutils, with the standard command:

```
python setup.py install
```

PyLint also requires the Logilab Common libraries to work. Download that package, called `logilab-common`, available from the PyLint web site, and install it the same way as PyLint.

Once this is done, the tools should be available as command-line scripts (`pychecker` and `pylint` for PyChecker and PyLint, respectively) and as Python modules (with the same names).

---

■ **Note** In Windows, the two tools use the batch files `pychecker.bat` and `pylint.bat` as command-line tools. You may need to add these to your `PATH` environment variable to have the `pychecker` and `pylint` commands available on the command line.

---

To check files with PyChecker, you run the script with the file names as arguments, like this:

```
pychecker file1.py file2.py ...
```

With PyLint, you use the *module* (or package) names:

```
pylint module
```

You can get more information about both tools by running them with the `-h` command-line switch. When you run either of these commands, you will probably get quite a bit of output (most likely more output from `pylint` than from `pychecker`). Both tools are quite configurable with respect to which warnings you want to get (or suppress); see their respective documentation for more information.

Before leaving the checkers, let's see how you can combine them with unit tests. After all, it would be very pleasant to have them (or just one of them) run automatically as a test in your test suite, and to silently succeed if nothing is wrong. Then you could actually have a test suite that doesn't just test functionality, but code quality as well.

Both PyChecker and PyLint can be imported as modules (`pychecker.checker` and `pylint.lint`, respectively), but they aren't really designed to be used programmatically. When you import `pychecker.checker`, it will check the code that comes later (including imported modules), printing warnings to standard output. The `pylint.lint` module has an undocumented function called Run, which is used in the `pylint` script itself. This also prints out warnings rather than returning them in some way. Instead of grappling with these issues, I suggest using PyChecker and PyLint in the way they're meant to be used: as command-line tools. And the way of using command-line tools in Python is the `subprocess` module (or one of its older relatives; see the Python Library Reference for more information). Listing 16-3 is an example of the earlier test script, now with two code-checking tests.

**Listing 16-3.** *Calling External Checkers Using the subprocess Module*

```
import unittest, my_math
from subprocess import Popen, PIPE

class ProductTestCase(unittest.TestCase):

    # Insert previous tests here

    def testWithPyChecker(self):
        cmd = 'pychecker', '-Q', my_math.__file__.rstrip('c')
        pychecker = Popen(cmd, stdout=PIPE, stderr=PIPE)
        self.assertEqual(pychecker.stdout.read(), '')

    def testWithPyLint(self):
        cmd = 'pylint', '-rn', 'my_math'
        pylint = Popen(cmd, stdout=PIPE, stderr=PIPE)
        self.assertEqual(pylint.stdout.read(), '')

if __name__ == '__main__': unittest.main()
```

I've given some command-line switches to the checker programs, to avoid extraneous output that would interfere with the tests. For pychecker, I have supplied the -Q (quiet) switch. For pylint, I have supplied -rn (with n standing for "no") to turn off reports, meaning that it will display only warnings and errors. I have used assertEqual (instead of, for example, failIf) in order to have the actual output read from the stdout attribute displayed in the failure messages of unittest (this is, in fact, the main reason for using assertEqual instead of failUnless together with == in general).

The pylint command runs directly with a module name supplied, so that's pretty straightforward. To get pychecker to work properly, we need to get a file name. To get that, I've used the __file__ property of the my_math module, rstriping away any c that may be found at the end of the file name (because the module may actually come from a .pyc file).

In order to appease PyLint (rather than configuring it to shut up about things such as short variable names, missing revisions, and docstrings), I have rewritten the my_math module slightly:

```
"""
A simple math module.
"""

__revision__ = '0.1'

def product(factor1, factor2):
    'The product of two numbers'
    return factor1 * factor2
```

If you run the tests now, you should not get any errors. Try to play around with the code and see if you can get any of the checkers to report errors while the functionality tests still work. (Feel free to drop either PyChecker or PyLint—one is probably enough.) For example, try to rename the parameters back to x and y, and PyLint should complain about short variable names. Or add print 'Hello, world!' after the return statement, and both checkers, quite reasonably, will complain (possibly giving different reasons for the complaint).

## THE LIMITS OF AUTOMATIC CHECKING: WILL IT EVER END?

It should be obvious that there are limits to the capabilities of an automatic checker such as PyChecker or PyLint. While they are quite impressive in the breadth of errors and problems they can uncover, they can't know what your program is ultimately intended to do; hence, the need for custom-tailored unit tests. But beyond this obvious barrier, automatic checkers have other limits. If you like slightly theoretical oddities, you might be interested in a result from the exotic world of computation theory known as *the halting theorem*. Let's consider a hypothetical checker program that we could run like this:

```
halts.py myprog.py data.txt
```

As you can probably guess, the checker should check the behavior of myprog.py when run on the input data.txt. We want to check for only *one* thing: infinite loops (or infinite recursion, so *two* things, actually). In other words, the program halts.py should determine whether myprog.py would ever stop (halt) when run on data.txt. Given that existing checker programs can analyze the code and figure out which types the various variables must be for things to work, detecting such a simple thing as an infinite loop would seem like a breeze, right? Sorry, but no, not in the general case, anyway. According to the halting problem, it simply can't be done.

Don't take my word for it—the reasoning is actually quite simple. Assume that we *have* a working halting-checker, and assume (for simplicity) that it's written as a Python module. Now, let's assume that we write the following little insidious program, named trouble.py:

```
import halts, sys
name = sys.argv[1]
if halts.check(name, name):
    while True: pass
```

It uses the functionality of the `halts` module to check whether a program given as the first command-line argument will ever halt *if supplied with itself as input*. It could be run like this, for example:

```
trouble.py myprog.py
```

This would determine whether `myprog.py` would ever halt if supplied with `myprog.py` (that is, itself) as input. If the determination is that it *would* halt, `trouble.py` will enter an infinite loop. Otherwise, it will simply finish (that is, halt).

With me so far? Good. (If not, try rereading the previous stuff a couple of times; that usually helps.) Now consider the following slightly mind-bending scenario:

```
halts.py trouble.py trouble.py
```

Ta-da! What, it doesn't seem mind-bending to you? It just checks whether `trouble.py` would halt with `trouble.py` (that is, itself) as input. Sure, that's not so mind-bending in itself. But what would the result be? Consider the two alternatives: if `halts.py` says "yes"—that is, `trouble.py trouble.py` will halt—then `trouble.py trouble.py` is defined *not* to halt. We run into the same (converse) problem if we get a "no." Either way, `halts.py` is destined to get it wrong, and there is no way to fix it. We began the story by assuming that the checker actually worked, and now we have reached a contradiction, which means our assumption was wrong.

This doesn't mean that we can't detect *any* kinds of infinite looping, of course. Seeing a `while True` without a `break`, `raise`, or `return` would be a strong clue, for example. It's just not possible to detect this *in general*. Sadly, many other similar properties can't be automatically analyzed in general.[3] So even with such nifty tools as PyChecker and PyLint, we'll need to rely on manual debugging rooted in our knowledge of the special circumstances of our program. And, perhaps, we should try to avoid intentionally writing tricky programs such as `trouble.py`.

## Profiling

Now that you've made your code work, and possibly made it better than the initial version, it may be time to make it faster. Then, again, it may not. One very important rule (along with such principles as KISS = Keep It Small and Simple, or YAGNI = You Ain't Gonna Need It) that you should heed when tempted to fiddle with your code to speed it up:

> *Premature optimization is the root of all evil.*
>
> —Donald Knuth, paraphrasing C. A. R. Hoare

Another way of stating this, in the words of Ken Thompson, co-inventor of UNIX, is "When in doubt, use brute force." In other words, don't worry about fancy algorithms or clever optimization tricks if you don't really, really need them. If the program is fast enough, chances are that the value of clean, simple, understandable code is much higher than that of a slightly faster program. After all, in a few months, faster hardware will probably be available anyway.

---

3. Check out *Computers Ltd: What They Really Can't Do* by David Harel (Oxford University Press, 2000) for a lot of interesting material on the subject.

But if you *do* need to optimize your program, because it simply isn't fast enough for your requirements, you absolutely should profile it before doing anything else. That is because it's really hard to guess where the bottlenecks are, unless your program is really simple. And if you don't know what's slowing down your program, chances are you'll be optimizing the wrong thing.

The standard library includes a nice profiler module called profile (and a faster drop-in C version, called hotshot). Using the profiler is straightforward. Just call its run method with a string argument.

```
>>> import profile
>>> from my_math import product
>>> profile.run('product(1, 2)')
```

■**Note**  In some Linux distributions, you may need to install a separate package in order to get the profile module to work. If it works, fine. If not, you might want to check out the relevant documentation to see if this is the problem.

This will give you a printout with information about how many times various functions and methods were called and how much time was spent in the various functions. If you supply a file name, for example, 'my_math.profile', as the second argument to run, the results will be saved to a file. You can then later use the pstats module to examine the profile:

```
>>> import pstats
>>> p = pstats.Stats('my_math.profile')
```

Using this Stats object, you can examine the results programmatically. (For details on the API, consult the standard library documentation.)

■**Tip**  The standard library also contains a module called timeit, which is a simple way of timing small snippets of Python code. The timeit module isn't really useful for detailed profiling, but it can be a nice tool when all you want to do is figure out how much time a piece of code takes to execute. Trying to do this yourself can often lead to inaccurate measurements (unless you know what you're doing). Using timeit is usually a better choice (unless you opt for a full profiling, of course). You can find more information about timeit in the Python Library Reference (http://python.org/doc/lib/module-timeit.html).

Now, if you're really worried about the speed of your program, you *could* add a unit test that profiles your program and enforces certain constraints (such as failing if the program takes more than a second to finish). It might be a fun thing to do, but it's not something I recommend. Obsessive profiling can easily take your attention away from things that really matter, such as clean, understandable code. If the program is *really* slow, you'll notice that anyway, because your tests will take forever to finish.

# A Quick Summary

Here are the main topics covered in the chapter:

**Test-driven programming**: Basically, test-driven programming means to test first, code later. Tests let you rewrite your code with confidence, making your development and maintenance more flexible.

**The** doctest **and** unittest **modules**: These are indispensable tools if you want to do unit testing in Python. The doctest module is designed to check examples in docstrings, but can easily be used to design test suites. For more flexibility and structure in your suites, the unittest framework is very useful.

**PyChecker and PyLint**: These two tools read source code and point out potential (and actual) problems. They check everything from short variable names to unreachable pieces of code. With a little coding you can make them (or one of them) part of your test suite, to make sure all of your rewrites and refactorings conform to your coding standards.

**Profiling**: If you really care about speed and want to optimize your program (only do this if it's absolutely necessary), you should profile it first. Use the profile (or hotshot) module to find bottlenecks in your code.

## New Functions in This Chapter

| Function | Description |
| --- | --- |
| doctest.testmod(module) | Checks docstring examples. (Takes many more arguments.) |
| unittest.main() | Runs the unit tests in the current module. |
| profile.run(stmt[, filename]) | Executes and profiles statement. Optionally, saves results to filename. |

## What Now?

Now you've seen all kinds of things you can do with the Python language and the standard libraries. You've seen how to probe and tweak your code until it screams (if you got serious about profiling, despite my warnings). If you *still* aren't getting the oomph you require, it's time to reach for heavier weapons. In the words of Neo in *The Matrix*. "We need guns. Lots of guns." In less metaphorical terms, it's time to pop the cover and tweak the engine with some low-level tools. (Wait, that was still metaphorical, wasn't it?)

# CHAPTER 17

■ ■ ■

# Extending Python

**Y**ou can implement anything in Python, really; it's a powerful language, but sometimes it can get a bit too slow. For example, if you're writing a scientific simulation of some form of nuclear reaction, or you're rendering the graphics for the next *Star Wars* movie (wait—there won't be any more now, will there?), writing the high-performance code in Python will probably not be a good choice. Python is meant to be easy to work with and to help make the development fast. The flexibility needed for this comes with a hefty price in terms of efficiency. It's certainly fast enough for most common programming tasks, but if you need real speed, languages such as C, C++, and Java can usually beat it by several orders of magnitude.

## The Best of Both Worlds

Now, I don't want to encourage the speed freaks among you to start developing exclusively in C. Although this may speed up the program itself, it will most certainly slow down your programming. So you need to consider what is most important: getting the program done quickly, or eventually (in the distant future) getting a program that runs *really, really* fast. If Python is *fast enough*, the extra pain involved will make using a low-level language such as C something of a meaningless choice (unless you have other requirements, such as running on an embedded device that doesn't have room for Python, or something like that).

This chapter deals with the cases where you *do* need extra speed. The best solution then probably isn't to switch entirely to C (or some other low- or mid-level language); instead, I recommend the following approach, which has worked for plenty of industrial-strength speed freaks out there (in one form or another):

1. Develop a prototype in Python. (See Chapter 19 for some material on prototyping.)

2. Profile your program and determine the bottlenecks. (See Chapter 16 for some material on testing.)

3. Rewrite the bottlenecks as a C (or C++, C#, Java, Fortran,[1] and so on) extension.

---

1. Fortran was the first "real" programming language (originally developed in 1954). In some areas, Fortran is still the language of choice for high-performance computing. If you want to (or, perhaps more likely, have to) use Fortran for your extensions, you should check out Pyfort (http://pyfortran.sf.net) and F2PY (http://cens.ioc.ee/projects/f2py2e).

The resulting architecture—a Python framework with one or more C components—is a very powerful one, because it combines the best of two worlds. It's a matter of choosing the right tools for each job. It affords you the benefits of developing a complex system in a high-level language (Python), and it lets you develop your smaller (and presumably simpler) speed-critical components in a low-level language (C).

---

■**Note**  There are other reasons for reaching for C. For example, if you want to write low-level code for interfacing with a strange piece of hardware, you really have no alternative.

---

If you have some knowledge of what the bottlenecks of your system will be even before you begin, you can (and probably should) design your prototype so that replacing the critical parts is easy. I think I might as well state this in the form of a tip:

---

■**Tip**  Encapsulate potential bottlenecks.

---

You may find that you don't need to replace the bottlenecks with C extensions (perhaps you suddenly got hold of a faster computer), but at least the option is there.

There is another situation that is a common use case for extensions as well: legacy code. You may want to use some code that exists only in, say, C. You can then "wrap" this code (write a small C library that gives you a proper interface) and create a Python extension library from your wrapper.

In the following sections, I give you some starting points for extending both the classic C implementation of Python, either by writing all the code yourself or by using a tool called SWIG, and for extending two other implementations: Jython and IronPython. You will also find some hints about other options for accessing external code. Read on . . .

## THE OTHER WAY AROUND

In this chapter, I focus on writing extensions to your Python programs in a compiled language. But turning this on its head—writing a program in a compiled language and embedding a Python interpreter for minor scripting and extensions—can have its uses. In that case, what you're after when embedding Python isn't speed—it's flexibility. In many ways, it's the same "best of both worlds" argument that is used for writing compiled extensions; it's just that the focus is shifted.

The embedding approach is used in many real-world systems. For example, many computer games (which are almost invariably written in compiled languages, with a code base primarily developed for maximum speed) use dynamic languages such as Python for describing high-level behavior (such as the "intelligence" of the characters in the game), while the main code engine takes care of graphics and the like.

The documentation referenced in the main text (for CPython, Jython, and IronPython) also discusses the embedding option, in case you wish to go that route.

# The Really Easy Way: Jython and IronPython

If you happen to be running Jython or IronPython (both mentioned in Chapter 1), extending Python with native modules is quite easy. The reason for this is that Jython and IronPython give you direct access to modules and classes from the underlying languages (Java for Jython, and C# and other .NET languages for IronPython), so you don't need to conform to some specific API (as you must when extending CPython). You simply implement the functionality you need, and, as if by magic, it will work in Python. As a case in point, you can access the Java standard libraries directly in Jython and the C# standard libraries directly in IronPython.

Listing 17-1 shows a simple Java class.

**Listing 17-1.** *A Simple Java Class (JythonTest.java)*

```java
public class JythonTest {

    public void greeting() {
        System.out.println("Hello, world!");
    }

}
```

You can compile this with some Java compiler, such as javac (freely downloadable from http://java.sun.com):

```
$ javac JythonTest.java
```

---

■**Tip**  If you're working with Java, you can also use the command jythonc to compile your Python classes into Java classes, which can then be imported into your Java programs.

---

Once you have compiled the class, you fire up Jython (and put the .class file either in your current directory or somewhere in your Java CLASSPATH):

```
$ CLASSPATH=JythonTest.class jython
```

You can then import the class directly:

```
>>> import JythonTest
>>> test = JythonTest()
>>> test.greeting()
Hello, world!
```

See? There's nothing to it.

## JYTHON PROPERTY MAGIC

Jython has several nifty tricks up its sleeve when it comes to interacting with Java classes. One of the most obviously useful is that it gives you access to so-called JavaBean properties through ordinary attribute access. In Java, you use accessor methods to read or modify these. What this means is that if the Java instance foo has a method called setBar, you can simply use foo.bar = baz instead of foo.setBar(baz). Similarly, if the instance has a method called either getBar or isBar (for Boolean properties), you can access the value using foo.bar. Using an example from the Jython documentation, instead of this:

```
b = awt.Button()
b.setEnabled(False)
```

you could use this:

```
b = awt.Button()
b.enabled = False
```

In fact, all properties can be set through keyword arguments in constructors as well. So you could, in fact, simply write this:

```
b = awt.Button(enabled=False)
```

This works with tuples for multiple arguments and even function arguments for Java idioms such as event listeners:

```
def exit(event):
    java.lang.System.exit(0)
b = awt.Button("Close Me!", actionPerformed=exit)
```

In Java, you would need to implement a separate class with the proper actionPerformed method, and then add that using b.addActionListener.

Listing 17-2 shows a similar class in C#.

**Listing 17-2.** *A Simple C# Class (IronPythonTest.cs)*

```
using System;
namespace FePyTest {
   public class IronPythonTest {

      public void greeting() {
         Console.WriteLine("Hello, world!");
      }

   }
}
```

Compile this with your compiler of choice (free software is available from `http://www.mono-project.com`). For Microsoft .NET, the command is as follows:

```
csc.exe /t:library IronPythonTest.cs
```

One way of using this in IronPython would be to compile the class to a dynamic link library (DLL; see the documentation for your C# installation for details) and update the relevant environment variables (such as PATH) as needed. Then you should be able to use it as in the following (using the IronPython interactive interpreter):

```
>>> import clr
>>> clr.AddReferenceToFile("IronPythonTest.dll")
>>> import FePyTest
>>> f = FePyTest.IronPythonTest()
>>> f.greeting()
```

For more details on these implementations of Python, visit the Jython web site (`http://www.jython.org`) and the IronPython web site (`http://www.codeplex.com/Wiki/View.aspx?ProjectName=IronPython`).

# Writing C Extensions

This is what it's all about, really. Extending Python normally means extending CPython, the standard version of Python, implemented in the programming language C.

---

**■Tip** For a basic introduction and some background material, see the Wikipedia article on C, `http://en.wikipedia.org/wiki/C_programming_language`. For more information, check out Ivor Horton's book *Beginning C: From Novice to Professional, Fourth Edition* (Apress, 2006). A really authoritative source of information is the all-time classic by Brian Kernighan and Dennis Ritchie, the inventors of the language: *C Programming Language, Second Edition* (Prentice-Hall, 1988).

---

C isn't quite as dynamic as Java or C#, and it's not as easy for Python to figure out things for itself if you just supply it with your compiled C code. Therefore, you need to adhere to a strict API when writing C extensions for Python. I discuss this API a bit later, in the section "Hacking It on Your Own." Several projects try to make the process of writing C extensions easier, though, and one of the better-known projects is SWIG, which I discuss in the following section. (See the sidebar "Other Approaches" for some . . . well . . . other approaches.)

## OTHER APPROACHES

If you're using CPython, plenty of tools are available to help you speed up your programs, either by generating and using C libraries or by actually speeding up your Python code. Here is an overview of some options:

- **Psyco** (`http://psyco.sf.net`): A specialized just-in-time compiler for Python, which can speed up certain kinds of code (especially low-level code dealing with lists of numbers) by an order of magnitude or more. It won't help in all cases, and does need quite a bit of memory to do its job well. It's very easy to use. In the simplest case, just import it and call `psyco.full()`. One of the interesting things about Psyco is that it actually analyzes what goes on while the program is running, so it may, in fact, speed up some Python code beyond what you could achieve by writing a C extension! (Perhaps it's worth a try, before you dive into the nearest C textbook?)

- **Pyrex** (`http://www.cosc.canterbury.ac.nz/~greg/python/Pyrex`): A Python "dialect"—sort of. It's a language specifically designed for writing extension modules for Python. The Pyrex language combines Python (or a subset of it) with optional static typing as in C. Once you've written a module in Pyrex, you can translate it into C code using the `pyrexc` program. The resulting C code will have been constructed to conform to the Python C API, so after compiling it (as described in the main text), you should be able to use it in your Python program without problems. Pyrex can certainly take much of the drudgery out of writing C extensions, while still letting you control the details you might care about, such as the exact C data types for some of your variables.

- **PyPy** (`http://codespeak.net/pypy`): This is an ambitious and forward-looking implementation of Python—*in Python*. While this might sound super-slow, the hope is that eventually, through quite advanced code analysis and compilation, it will outperform CPython. According to the web site, "Rumors have it that the secret goal is being faster-than-C, which is nonsense, isn't it?" At the core of PyPy lies RPython, which is a restricted dialect of Python. RPython is suited for automated type inference and the like, permitting translation into static languages or native machine code, or to other dynamic languages (such as JavaScript), for that matter.

- **Weave** (`http://www.scipy.org/Weave`). Part of the SciPy distribution, but also available separately, Weave is a tool for including C or C++ code directly in your Python code (as strings) and having the code compiled and executed seamlessly. If you have certain mathematical expressions you want to compute quickly, for example, then this might be the way to go. Weave can also speed up expressions using numeric arrays (see the next item).

- **NumPy** (`http://numeric.scipy.org`): NumPy gives you access to numeric arrays, which are very useful for analyzing many forms of numeric data (from stock values to astronomical images). One advantage is the simple interface, which relieves the need to explicitly specify many low-level operations. The main advantage, however, is speed. Performing many common operations on every element in a numeric array is much, much faster than doing something equivalent with lists and `for` loops, because the implicit loops are implemented directly in C. Numeric arrays work well with both Pyrex and Weave.

- **ctypes** (`http://python.net/crew/theller/ctypes`): The ctypes library takes a very direct approach—it simply lets you import existing (shared) C libraries. While there are some restrictions, this is, perhaps, one of the simplest ways of accessing C code. There is no need for wrappers or special APIs. You just import the library and use it. As of Python 2.5, ctypes is part of the Python standard library.

- **subprocess** (http://docs.python.org/lib/module-subprocess.html): Okay, this one is a bit different. The subprocess module can be found in the standard library, along with the older modules and functions with similar functionality. It allows you to have Python run external programs, and communicate with them through command-line arguments and the standard input, output, and error streams. If your speed-critical code can do much of its work in a few long-running batch jobs, little time will be lost starting the program and communicating with it. In that case, simply placing your C code in a completely separate program and running it as a subprocess could well be the cleanest solution of all.

- **modulator**: Found in the Tools directory of your Python distribution, this script can be used to generate some of the boilerplate code needed for C extensions.

- **PyCXX** (http://cxx.sourceforge.net): Previously known as CXX, or CXX/Objects, this is a set of C++ facilities for writing Python extensions. For example, it includes a good deal of support for reference counting, to reduce the chances of making errors.

- **SIP** (http://www.riverbankcomputing.co.uk/software/sip): SIP (a pun on SWIG?) was originally created as a tool for the development of the GUI package PyQt and consists of a code generator and a Python module. It uses specification files in a manner similar to SWIG.

- **Boost.Python** (http://www.boost.org/libs/python/doc): Boost.Python is designed to enable seamless interoperability between Python and C++, and can give you great help with issues such as reference counting and manipulating Python objects in C++. One of the main ways of using it is to write C++ code in a rather Python-like style (enabled by Boost.Python's macros), and then compile that directly into Python extensions using your favorite C++ compiler. As a rather different yet very solid alternative to SWIG, this might certainly be worth a look.

# A Swig of . . . SWIG

SWIG (http://www.swig.org), short for Simple Wrapper and Interface Generator, is a tool that works with several languages. On the one hand, it lets you write your extension code in C or C++; on the other hand, it automatically wraps these so that you can use them in several high-level languages such as Tcl, Python, Perl, Ruby, and Java. This means that if you decide to write some of your system as a C extension, rather than implement it directly in Python, the C extension library can also be made available (using SWIG) to a host of *other* languages. This can be very useful if you want several subsystems written in different languages to work together; your C (or C++) extension can then become a hub for the cooperation.

Installing SWIG follows the same pattern as installing other Python tools:

- You can get SWIG from the web site, http://www.swig.org.

- Many UNIX/Linux distributions come with SWIG. Many package managers will let you install it directly.

- There is a binary installer for Windows.

- Compiling the sources yourself is again simply a matter of calling configure and make install.

If you have problems installing SWIG, you should be able to find helpful information on the web site.

## What Does It Do?

Using SWIG is a simple process, provided that you have some C code:

1. Write an *interface file* for your code. This is quite similar to C header files (and, for simple cases, you can use your header file directly).

2. Run SWIG on the interface file, in order to automatically produce some more C code (*wrapper code*).

3. Compile the original C code together with the generated wrapper code in order to generate a shared library.

In the following, I discuss each of these steps, starting with a bit of C code.

## I Prefer Pi

A palindrome (such as the title of this section) is a sentence that is the same when read backwards, if you ignore spaces and punctuation and the like. Let's say you want to recognize huge palindromes, without the allowance for whitespace and friends. (Perhaps you need it for analyzing a protein sequence or something.) Of course, the string would have to be really big for this to be a problem for a pure Python program, but let's say the strings are really big, and that you need to do a whole lot of these checks. You decide to write a piece of C code to deal with it (or perhaps you find some finished code—as mentioned, using existing C code in Python is one of the main uses of SWIG). Listing 17-3 shows a possible implementation.

**Listing 17-3.** *A Simple C Function for Detecting a Palindrome (palindrome.c)*

```c
#include <string.h>

int is_palindrome(char *text) {
  int i, n=strlen(text);
  for (i=0; i<=n/2; ++i) {
    if (text[i] != text[n-i-1]) return 0;
  }
  return 1;
}
```

Just for reference, an equivalent pure Python function is shown in Listing 17-4.

**Listing 17-4.** *Detecting Palindromes in Python*

```python
def is_palindrome(text):
    n = len(text)
    for i in range(len(text)//2):
```

```
    if text[i] != text[n-i-1]:
        return False
return True
```

You'll see how to compile and use the C code in a bit.

## The Interface File

Assuming that you put the code from Listing 17-3 in a file called `palindrome.c`, you should now put an interface description in a file called `palindrome.i`. In many cases, if you define a header file (that is, `palindrome.h`), SWIG may be able to get the information it needs from that. So if you have a header file, feel free to try to use it. One of the reasons for explicitly writing an interface file is that you can tweak how SWIG actually wraps the code; the most important tweak is excluding things. For example, if you're wrapping a huge C library, perhaps you just want to export a couple of functions to Python. In that case, you put only the functions you want to export in the interface file.

In the interface file, you simply declare all the functions (and variables) you want to export, just like in a header file. In addition, there is a section at the top (delimited by %{ and %}) where you specify included header files (such as `string.h` in our case) and before even that, a %module declaration, giving the name of the module. (Some of this is optional, and there is a lot more you can do with interface files; see the SWIG documentation for more information.) Listing 17-5 shows this interface file.

**Listing 17-5.** *Interface to the Palindrome Library (palindrome.i)*

```
%module palindrome

%{
#include <string.h>
%}

extern int is_palindrome(char *text);
```

## Running SWIG

Running SWIG is probably the easiest part of the process. Although many command-line switches are available (try running `swig -help` for a list of options), the only one needed is the `-python` option, to make sure SWIG wraps your C code so you can use it in Python. Another option you may find useful is `-c++`, which you use if you're wrapping a C++ library. You run SWIG with the interface file (or, if you prefer, a header file) like this:

```
$ swig -python palindrome.i
```

After this, you should have two new files: one called `palindrome_wrap.c` and one called `palindrome.py`.

## Compiling, Linking, and Using

Compiling is, perhaps, the trickiest part (at least I think so). In order to compile things properly, you need to know where you keep the source code of your Python distribution (or, at least, the header files called pyconfig.h and Python.h; you will probably find these in the root directory of your Python installation, and in the Include subdirectory, respectively). You also need to figure out the correct switches to compile your code into a shared library with your C compiler of choice. If you're having trouble finding the right combination of arguments and switches, take a look at the next section "A Shortcut Through the Magic Forest of Compilers."

Here is an example for Solaris using the cc compiler, assuming that $PYTHON_HOME points to the root of Python installation:

```
$ cc -c palindrome.c
$ cc -I$PYTHON_HOME -I$PYTHON_HOME/Include -c palindrome_wrap.c
$ cc -G palindrome.o palindrome_wrap.o -o _palindrome.so
```

Here is the sequence for using the gcc compiler in Linux:

```
$ gcc -c palindrome.c
$ gcc -I$PYTHON_HOME -I$PYTHON_HOME/Include -c palindrome_wrap.c
$ gcc -shared palindrome.o palindrome_wrap.o -o _palindrome.so
```

It may be that all the necessary include files are found in one place, such as /usr/include/python2.5 (update the version number as needed). In this case, the following should do the trick:

```
$ gcc -c palindrome.c
$ gcc -I/usr/include/python2.5 -c palindrome_wrap.c
$ gcc -shared palindrome.o palindrome_wrap.o -o _palindrome.so
```

In Windows (again assuming that you're using gcc on the command line), you could use the following command as the last one, for creating the shared library:

```
$ gcc -shared palindrome.o palindrome_wrap.o C:/Python25/libs/libpython25.a -o
 _palindrome.dll
```

In Mac OS X, you could do something like the following (where PYTHON_HOME would be /Library/Frameworks/Python.framework/Versions/Current if you're using the official Python installation):

```
$ gcc -dynamic -I$PYTHON_HOME/include/python2.5 -c palindrome.c
$ gcc -dynamic -I$PYTHON_HOME/include/python2.5 -c palindrome_wrap.c
$ gcc -dynamiclib palindrome_wrap.o palindrome.o -o _palindrome.so -Wl, -undefined,
 dynamic_lookup
```

---

■**Note** If you use gcc on Solaris, add the flag -fPIC to the first two command lines (right after the command gcc). Otherwise, the compiler will become mighty confused when you try to link the files in the last command. Also, if you're using a package manager (as is common in many Linux platforms), you may need to install a separate package (called something like python-dev) to get the header files needed to compile your extensions.

---

After these darkly magical incantations, you should end up with a highly useful file called
_palindrome.so. This is your *shared library*, which can be imported directly into Python (if it's
put somewhere in your PYTHONPATH, such as in the current directory):

```
>>> import _palindrome
>>> dir(_palindrome)
['__doc__', '__file__', '__name__', 'is_palindrome']
>>> _palindrome.is_palindrome('ipreferpi')
1
>>> _palindrome.is_palindrome('notlob')
0
```

In older versions of SWIG, that would have been all there was to it. Recent versions of
SWIG, however, generate some wrapping code in Python as well (the file palindrome.py,
remember?). This wrapper code imports the _palindrome module and takes care of a bit of
checking. If you would rather skip that, you could just remove the palindrome.py file and link
your library directly into a file named palindrome.so.

Using the wrapper code works just as well as using the shared library:

```
>>> import palindrome
>>> from palindrome import is_palindrome
>>> if is_palindrome('abba'):
...     print 'Wow -- that never occurred to me...'
...
Wow -- that never occurred to me...
```

### A Shortcut Through the Magic Forest of Compilers

If you think the compilation process can be a bit arcane, you're not alone. If you automate the
compilation (say, using a makefile), users will need to configure the setup by specifying where
their Python installation is, which specific options to use with their compiler, and, not the least,
which compiler to use. You can avoid this elegantly by using Distutils. In fact, it has direct support for SWIG, so you don't even need to run that manually. You just write the code and the
interface file, and run your Distutils script. For more information about this magic, see the
section "Compiling Extensions" in Chapter 18.

## Hacking It on Your Own

SWIG does quite a bit of magic behind the scenes, but not all of it is strictly necessary. If you
want to get close to the metal and grind your teeth on the processor, so to speak, you can certainly write your wrapper code yourself, or simply write your C code so that it uses the Python
C API directly.

The Python C API is described in the documents "Extending and Embedding the Python
Interpreter" (a tutorial) and "Python/C API Reference Manual" (a reference), both by Guido
van Rossum and available from http://python.org/doc. There is quite a bit of information to
swallow in these documents, but if you know some C programming, the tutorial includes a

fairly gentle introduction. I'll try to be even gentler (and briefer) here. If you're curious about what I'm leaving out (which is rather a lot), you should take a look at the documents on the Python site.

## Reference Counting

If you haven't worked with it before, reference counting will probably be one of the most foreign concepts you'll encounter in this section, although it's not really all that complicated. In Python, memory used is dealt with automatically—you just create objects, and they disappear when you no longer use them. In C, this isn't the case. You must explicitly *deallocate* objects (or, rather, chunks of memory) that you're no longer using. If you don't, your program may start hogging more and more memory, and you have what's called a *memory leak*.

When writing Python extensions, you have access to the same tools Python uses "under the hood" to manage memory, one of which is reference counting. The idea is that as long as some parts of your code have references to an object (that is, in C-speak, pointers pointing to it), it should not be deallocated. However, once the number of references to an object hits zero, the number can no longer increase—there is no code that can create new references to it, and it's just "free floating" in memory. At this point, it's safe to deallocate it. Reference counting automates this process. You follow a set of rules where you increment or decrement the reference count for an object under various circumstances (through a part of the Python API), and if the count ever goes to zero, the object is automatically deallocated. This means that no single piece of code has the sole responsibility for managing an object. You can create an object, return it from a function, and forget about it, safe in the knowledge that it will disappear when it is no longer needed.

You use two macros, called `Py_INCREF` and `Py_DECREF`, to increment and decrement the reference count of an object, respectively. You can find detailed information about how to use these in the Python documentation (`http://python.org/doc/ext/refcounts.html`). Here is the gist of it:

- You can't *own* an object, but you can own a *reference* to it. The reference count of an object is the number of owned references to that object.

- If you own a reference, you are responsible for calling `Py_DECREF` when you no longer need the reference.

- If you *borrow* a reference temporarily, you should *not* call `Py_DECREF` when you're finished with the object; that's the responsibility of the owner.

---

■**Caution**   You should certainly *never* use a borrowed reference after the owner has disposed of it. See the "Thin Ice" sections in the documentation for some more advice on staying safe.

---

- You can turn a borrowed reference into an owned reference by calling Py_INCREF. This creates a *new* owned reference; the original owner still owns the original reference.

- When you receive an object as a parameter, it's up to you whether you want the ownership of its reference transferred (for example, if you're going to store it somewhere) or you simply want to borrow it. This should be documented clearly. If your function is called from Python, it's safe to simply borrow—the object will live for the duration of the function call. If, however, your function is called from C, this cannot be guaranteed, and you might want to create an owned reference, and then release it when you're finished.

Hopefully, this will all seem clearer when we get down to a concrete example in a little while.

---

### MORE GARBAGE COLLECTION

Reference counting is a form of *garbage collection*, where the term *garbage* refers to objects that are no longer of use to the program. Python also uses a more sophisticated algorithm to detect *cyclic* garbage; that is, objects that refer only to each other (and thus have nonzero reference counts), but have no other objects referring to them.

You can access the Python garbage collector in your Python programs, through the gc module. You can find more information about it in the Python Library Reference (`http://python.org/doc/lib/module-gc.html`).

---

## A Framework for Extensions

Quite a lot of cookie-cutter code is needed to write a Python C extension, which is why tools such as SWIG, Pyrex, and modulator are so nice. Automating cookie-cutter code is the way to go. Doing it by hand can be a great learning experience, though. You do have quite some leeway in how you structure your code, really. I'll just show you a way that works.

The first thing to remember is that the Python.h header file must be included *first*, before other standard header files. That is because it may, on some platforms, perform some redefinitions that should be used by the other headers. So, for simplicity, just place this:

```
#include <Python.h>
```

as the first line of your code.

Your function can be called anything you want. It should be static, return a pointer (an owned reference) to an object of the PyObject type, and take two arguments, both also pointers to PyObject. The objects are conventionally called self and args (with self being the self-object, or NULL, and args being a tuple of arguments). In other words, the function should look something like this:

```
static PyObject *somename(PyObject *self, PyObject *args) {
    PyObject *result;
```

```
    /* Do something here, including allocating result. */

    Py_INCREF(result); /* Only if needed! */
    return result;
}
```

The self argument is actually used only in bound methods. In other functions, it will simply be a NULL pointer.

Note that the call to Py_INCREF may not be needed. If the object is created in the function (for example, using a utility function such as Py_BuildValue), the function will *already* own a reference to it, and can simply return it. If, however, you wish to return None from your function, you should use the existing object Py_None. In this case, however, the function does *not* own a reference to Py_None, and so should call Py_INCREF(Py_None) before returning it.

The args parameter contains all the arguments to your function (except, if present, the self argument). In order to extract the objects, you use the function PyArg_ParseTuple (for positional arguments) and PyArg_ParseTupleAndKeywords (for positional and keyword arguments). I'll stick to positional arguments here.

The function PyArg_ParseTuple has the following signature:

```
int PyArg_ParseTuple(PyObject *args, char *format, ...);
```

The format string describes the arguments you're expecting, and then you supply the addresses of the variables you want populated at the end. The return value is a Boolean value. If it's true, everything went well; otherwise, there was an error. If there was an error, the proper preparations for raising an exception will have been made (you can learn more about that in the documentation), and all you need to do is to return NULL to set it off. So, if you're not expecting any arguments (an empty format string), the following is a useful way of handling arguments:

```
    if (!PyArg_ParseTuple(args, "")) {
        return NULL;
    }
```

If the code proceeds beyond this statement, you know you have your arguments (in this case, no arguments). Format strings can look like "s" for a string, "i" for an integer, "o" for a Python object, with possible combinations such as "iis" for two integers and a string. There are many more format string codes. A full reference of how to write format strings can be found in the Python/C API Reference Manual (http://python.org/doc/api/arg-parsing.html).

---

**Note**  You can create your own built-in types and classes in extension modules, too. It's not too hard, really, but still a rather involved subject. If you mainly need to factor out some bottleneck code into C, using functions will probably be enough for most of your needs anyway. If you want to learn how to create types and classes, the Python documentation is a good source of information.

---

Once you have your function in place, some extra wrapping is still needed to make your C code act as a module. But let's get back to that once we have a real example to work with, shall we?

## Palindromes, Detartrated[2] for Your Pleasure

Without further ado, I give you the hand-coded Python C API version of the palindrome module (with some interesting new stuff added) in Listing 17-6.

**Listing 17-6.** *Palindrome Checking Again (palindrome2.c)*

```
#include <Python.h>

static PyObject *is_palindrome(PyObject *self, PyObject *args) {
    int i, n;
    const char *text;
    int result;
    /* "s" means a single string: */
    if (!PyArg_ParseTuple(args, "s", &text)) {
        return NULL;
    }
    /* The old code, more or less: */
    n=strlen(text);
    result = 1;
    for (i=0; i<=n/2; ++i) {
        if (text[i] != text[n-i-1]) {
            result = 0;
            break;
        }
    }
    /* "i" means a single integer: */
    return Py_BuildValue("i", result);
}

/* A listing of our methods/functions: */
static PyMethodDef PalindromeMethods[] = {
    /* name, function, argument type, docstring */
    {"is_palindrome", is_palindrome, METH_VARARGS, "Detect palindromes"},
    /* An end-of-listing sentinel: */
    {NULL, NULL, 0, NULL}
};


/* An initialization function for the module (the name is
   significant): */
PyMODINIT_FUNC initpalindrome() {
    Py_InitModule("palindrome", PalindromeMethods);
}
```

---

2. That is, the tartrates have been removed. Okay, so the word is totally irrelevant to the code (and more relevant to fruit juices), but at least it's a palindrome.

Most of the added stuff in Listing 17-6 is total boilerplate. Where you see `palindrome`, you could insert the name of your module. Where you see `is_palindrome`, insert the name of your function. If you have more functions, simply list them all in the `PyMethodDef` array. One thing is worth noting, though: the name of the initialization function must be `initmodule`, where `module` is the name of your module; otherwise, Python won't find it.

So, let's compile! You do this just as described in the section on SWIG, except that there is only one file to deal with now. Here is an example using `gcc` (remember to add `-fPIC` in Solaris):

```
$ gcc -I$PYTHON_HOME -I$PYTHON_HOME/Include -shared palindrome2.c -o palindrome.so
```

Again, you should have a file called `palindrome.so`, ready for your use. Put it somewhere in your `PYTHONPATH` (such as the current directory) and away we go:

```
>>> from palindrome import is_palindrome
>>> is_palindrome('foobar')
0
>>> is_palindrome('deified')
1
```

And that's it. Now go play. (But be careful; remember the Waldi Ravens quote from this book's Introduction.)

# A Quick Summary

Extending Python is a huge subject. The tiny glimpse provided by this chapter included the following:

**Extension philosophy**: Python extensions are useful mainly for two things: for using existing (legacy) code or for speeding up bottlenecks. If you're writing your own code from scratch, try to prototype it in Python, find the bottlenecks, and factor them out as extensions *if needed*. Encapsulating potential bottlenecks beforehand can be useful.

**Jython and IronPython**: Extending these implementations of Python is quite easy. You simply implement your extension as a library in the underlying implementation (Java for Jython and C# or some other .NET language for IronPython) and the code is immediately usable from Python.

**Extension approaches**: Plenty of tools are available for extending or speeding up your code. You can find tools for making the incorporation of C code into your Python program easier, for speeding up common operations such as numeric array manipulation, and for speeding up Python itself. Such tools include SWIG, Psyco, Pyrex, Weave, NumPy, ctypes, subprocess, and modulator.

**SWIG**: SWIG is a tool for automatically generating wrapper code for your C libraries. The wrapper code takes care of the Python C API so you don't have to deal with it. SWIG is one of the easiest and most popular ways of extending Python.

**Using the Python/C API**: You can write C code yourself that can be imported directly into Python as shared libraries. To do this, you must adhere to the Python/C API. Things you need to take care of for each function include reference counting, extracting arguments, and building return values. There is also a certain amount of code needed to make a C library work as a module, including listing the functions in the module and creating a module initialization function.

## New Functions in This Chapter

| Function | Description |
| --- | --- |
| Py_INCREF(obj) | Increments reference count of obj |
| Py_DECREF(obj) | Decrements reference count of obj |
| PyArg_ParseTuple(args, fmt, ...) | Extracts positional arguments |
| PyArg_ParseTupleAndKeywords(args, kws, fmt, kwlist) | Extracts positional *and* keyword arguments |
| PyBuildValue(fmt, value) | Builds a PyObject from a C value |

## What Now?

Now you should either have some really cool programs or at least some really cool program ideas. Once you have something you want to share with the world (and you *do* want to share your code with the world, don't you?), the next chapter can be your next step.

# CHAPTER 18

■ ■ ■

# Packaging Your Programs

**O**nce your program is ready for release, you will probably want to package it properly before distributing it. If it consists of a single .py file, this might not be much of an issue. If you're dealing with nonprogrammer users, however, even placing a simple Python library in the right place or fiddling with the PYTHONPATH may be more than they want to deal with. Users normally want to simply double-click an installation program, follow some installation wizard, and then have your program ready to run.

Lately, Python programmers have also become used to a similar convenience, although with a slightly more low-level interface. The Distutils toolkit for distributing Python packages makes it easy to write install scripts in Python. You can use these scripts to build archive files for distribution, which the programmer (user) can then use for compiling and installing your libraries.

In this chapter, I focus on Distutils, because it is an essential tool in every Python programmer's toolkit. And Distutils actually goes beyond the script-based installation of Python libraries. Using Distutils, you can build simple Windows installers and, with the extension py2exe, you can also build stand-alone Windows executable programs. And if you want a self-installing archive for your binaries, I provide a few pointers for achieving that as well.

## Distutils Basics

Distutils is documented thoroughly in the two documents "Distributing Python Modules" and "Installing Python Modules," both available from the Python Library Reference (http://python.org/doc/lib/module-distutils.html). You can use Distutils to do all manner of useful things by writing a script as simple as the one shown in Listing 18-1.

**Listing 18-1.** *Simple Distutils Setup Script (setup.py)*

```python
from distutils.core import setup

setup(name='Hello',
      version='1.0',
      description='A simple example',
      author='Magnus Lie Hetland',
      py_modules=['hello'])
```

You don't really *have* to supply all of this information in the setup function (you don't actually need to supply any arguments at all), and you certainly can supply more (such as author_email or url). The names should be self-explanatory.

---

■**Tip**  The setuptools project (http://peak.telecommunity.com/DevCenter/setuptools) is based on Distutils, but includes several enhancements. For example, setuptools lets you create so-called "Python eggs," which are portable, single-file bundles designed for distributing Python packages. It also provides quite a bit of automatic interaction with the Python Package Index (http://pypi.python.org), a centralized index of Python packages.

---

Save the script in Listing 18-1 as setup.py (this is a universal convention for Distutils setup scripts), and make sure that you have a simple module called hello.py in the same directory.

---

■**Caution**  The setup script will create new files and subdirectories in the current directory when you run it, so you should probably experiment with it in a fresh directory to avoid having old files being overwritten.

---

Now let's see how you can put this simple script to use. Execute it as follows:

```
python setup.py
```

You should get some output like the following:

```
usage: setup.py [global_opts] cmd1 [cmd1_opts] [cmd2 [cmd2_opts] ...]
   or: setup.py --help [cmd1 cmd2 ...]
   or: setup.py --help-commands
   or: setup.py cmd --help

error: no commands supplied
```

As you can see, you can get more information using the --help or --help-commands switches. Try issuing the build command, just to see Distutils in action:

```
python setup.py build
```

You should now see output like the following:

```
running build
running build_py
creating build
creating build/lib
copying hello.py -> build/lib
```

Distutils has created a subdirectory called build, with yet another subdirectory named lib, and placed a copy of hello.py in build/lib. The build subdirectory is a sort of working area where Distutils assembles a package (and compiles extension libraries, for example). You don't really need to run the build command when installing, because it will be run automatically, if needed, when you run the install command.

**Note** In this example, the install command will copy the hello.py module to some system-specific directory in your PYTHONPATH. This should not pose a risk, but if you don't want to clutter your system, you might want to remove it afterward. Make a note of the specific location where it is placed, as output by setup.py. You could also use the -n switch to do a dry run. At the time of writing, there is no standard uninstall command (although you can find custom uninstallation implementations online), so you'll need to uninstall the module by hand.

Speaking of which . . . let's try to install the module:

```
python setup.py install
```

Now you should see something like the following:

```
running install
running build
running build_py
running install_lib
copying build/lib/hello.py -> /path/to/python/lib/python2.5/site-packages
byte-compiling /path/to/python/lib/python2.5/site-packages/hello.py to hello.pyc
```

> **Note** If you're running a version of Python that you didn't install yourself, and don't have the proper priv-ileges, you may not be allowed to install the module as shown, because you don't have write permissions to the correct directory.

This is the standard mechanism used to install Python modules, packages, and extensions. All you need to do is provide the little setup script.

The sample script uses only the Distutils directive py_modules. If you want to install entire packages, you can use the directive packages in an equivalent manner (just list the package names). You can set many other options (some of which are covered in the section "Compiling Extensions," later in this chapter). You can also create configuration files for Distutils to set var-ious properties (see the section "Distutils Configuration Files" in "Installing Python Modules," `http://python.org/doc/inst/config-syntax.html`).

The various ways of providing options (command-line switches, keyword arguments to setup, and Distutils configuration files) let you specify such things as *what* to install and *where* to install it. And these options can be used for more than one thing. The following section shows you how to wrap the modules you specified for installation as an archive file, ready for distribution.

# Wrapping Things Up

Once you've written a setup.py script that will let the user install your modules, you can use it yourself to build an archive file, a Windows installer, or an RPM package.

## Building an Archive File

You do this with the sdist (for "source distribution") command:

```
python setup.py sdist
```

If you run this, you will probably get quite a bit of output, including some warnings. The warnings I get include a complaint about a missing author_email option, a missing MANIFEST.in file, and a missing README file. You can safely ignore all of these (although feel free to add an author_email option to your setup.py script, similar to the author option, a README or README.txt text file, and an empty file called MANIFEST.in in the current directory).

After the warnings you should see output like the following:

```
writing manifest file 'MANIFEST'
creating Hello-1.0
making hard links in Hello-1.0...
hard linking hello.py -> Hello-1.0
hard linking setup.py -> Hello-1.0
tar -cf dist/Hello-1.0.tar Hello-1.0
gzip -f9 dist/Hello-1.0.tar
removing 'Hello-1.0' (and everything under it)
```

As you can see, when you create a source distribution, a file called MANIFEST is created. This file contains a list of all your files. The MANIFEST.in file is a template for the manifest, and it is used when figuring out what to install. You can include lines like the following to specify files that you want to have included, if Distutils hasn't figured it out by itself, using your setup.py script (and default includes, such as README):

```
include somedirectory/somefile.txt
```

```
include somedirectory/*
```

---

**Note** If you've run the sdist command before, and you have a file called MANIFEST already, you will see the word reading instead of writing at the beginning. If you've restructured your package and want to repackage it, deleting the MANIFEST file can be a good idea, in order to start afresh.

---

Now, in addition to the build subdirectory, you should have one called dist. Inside it, you will find a gzip'ed tar archive called Hello-1.0.tar.gz. This can now be distributed to others, and they can unpack it and install it using the included setup.py script. If you don't want a .tar.gz file, plenty of other distribution formats are available, and you can set them all through the command-line switch --formats. (As the plural name indicates, you can supply more than one format, separated by commas, to create more archive files in one go.) The format names available in Python 2.5 (accessible through the --help-formats switch to the sdist command) are bztar (for bzip2'ed tar files), gztar (the default, for gzip'ed tar files), tar (for uncompressed tar files), zip (for ZIP files), and ztar (for compressed tar files, using the UNIX command compress).

## Creating a Windows Installer or an RPM Package

Using the command bdist, you can create simple Windows installers and Linux RPM files. (You normally use this to create *binary* distributions, where extensions have been compiled for a particular architecture. See the following section for information about compiling extensions.) The formats available for bdist (in addition to the ones available for sdist) are rpm (for RPM packages) and wininst (for Windows executable installer).

One interesting twist is that you can, in fact, build Windows installers for your package in non-Windows systems, provided that you don't have any extensions you need to compile. If you have access to both, say, a Linux machine and a Windows box, you could try running the following on a Linux machine:

```
python setup.py bdist --formats=wininst
```

Then (after ignoring a few warnings about compiler settings) copy the file dist/Hello-1.0.win32.exe to your Windows machine and run it. You should be presented with a rudimentary installer wizard. (You can cancel the process before actually installing the module.)

### USING A *REAL* INSTALLER

The installer you get with the `wininst` format in Distutils is very basic. As with normal Distutils installation, it will not let you uninstall your packages, for example. This may be acceptable in some situations, but sometimes you may want a more professional look, especially if you're creating an executable using py2exe (as described in this chapter). In this case, you might want to consider using some standard installer such as Inno Setup (`http://jrsoftware.org/isinfo.php`), which works very well with executables created with py2exe. This type of installer will install your program in a more normal Windows fashion and give you functionality such as the ability to uninstall the program.

A more Python-centric (but, at present, unmaintained) option is the McMillan installer (a web search should give you an updated download location), which can also work as an alternative to py2exe when building executable programs. Other options include InstallShield (`http://installshield.com`), Wise installer (`http://wise.com`), Installer VISE (`http://www.mindvision.com`), Nullsoft Scriptable Install System (`http://nsis.sf.net`), Youseful Windows Installer (`http://youseful.com`), and Ghost Installer (`http://ethalone.com`). A web search will probably turn up several other solutions.

For more information about Windows installer technology, see Phil Wilson's *The Definitive Guide to Windows Installer* (Apress, 2004).

## Compiling Extensions

In Chapter 17, you saw how to write extensions for Python. You may agree that compiling these extensions could be a bit cumbersome at times. Luckily, you can use Distutils for this as well. You may want to refer back to Chapter 17 for the source code to the program `palindrome` (in Listing 17-6). Assuming that you have the source file `palindrome2.c` in the current (empty) directory, the following `setup.py` script could be used to compile (and install) it:

```
from distutils.core import setup, Extension

setup(name='palindrome',
      version='1.0',
      ext_modules = [
          Extension('palindrome', ['palindrome2.c'])
      ])
```

If you run the `install` command with this `setup.py` script, the `palindrome` extension module should be compiled automatically before it is installed. As you can see, instead of specifying a list of module names, you give the `ext_modules` argument a list of `Extension` instances. The constructor takes a name and a list of related files; this is where you would specify header (`.h`) files, for example.

If you would rather just compile the extension in place (resulting in a file called `palindrome.so` in the current directory for most UNIX systems), you can use the following command:

```
python setup.py build_ext --inplace
```

Now we get to a real juicy bit. If you have SWIG installed (see Chapter 17), you can have Distutils use it directly!

Take a look at the source for the original palindrome.c (without all the wrapping code) in Listing 17-3. It's certainly much simpler than the wrapped-up version. Being able to compile it directly as a Python extension, having Distutils use SWIG for you, can be very convenient. It's all very simple, really—you just add the name of the interface (.i) file (see Listing 17-5) to the list of files in the Extension instance:

```
from distutils.core import setup, Extension

setup(name='palindrome',
      version='1.0',
      ext_modules = [
          Extension('palindrome', ['palindrome.c',
                                   'palindrome.i'])
      ])
```

If you run this script using the same command as before (build_ext, possibly with the --inplace switch), you should end up with a palindrome.so file again, but this time without needing to write all the wrapper code yourself.

# Creating Executable Programs with py2exe

The py2exe extension to Distutils (available from http://www.py2exe.org) allows you to build executable Windows programs (.exe files), which can be useful if you don't want to burden your users with having to install a Python interpreter separately.

---

■**Tip** After creating your executable program, you may want to use an installer, such as Inno Setup (http://jrsoftware.org/isinfo.php), to distribute the executable program and the accompanying files created by py2exe. See the "Using a Real Installer" sidebar.

---

The py2exe package can be used to create executables with GUIs (such as wx, as described in Chapter 12). Let's use a very simple example here (it uses the raw_input trick first discussed in the section "What About Double-Clicking?" in Chapter 1):

```
print 'Hello, world!'
raw_input('Press <enter>')
```

Again, starting in an empty directory containing only this file, called hello.py, create a setup.py file like this:

```
from distutils.core import setup
import py2exe

setup(console=['hello.py'])
```

You can run this script like this:

```
python setup.py py2exe
```

This will create a console application (called hello.exe) along with a couple of other files in the dist subdirectory. You can either run it from the command line or double-click it.

For more information about how py2exe works, and how you can use it in more advanced ways, visit the py2exe web site (http://www.py2exe.org).

---

■**Tip**  If you're using Mac OS, you might want to check out Bob Ippolito's py2app (http://undefined.org/python/py2app.html).

---

## LETTING THE WORLD KNOW

You have a choice of many places to announce your new software, such as Freshmeat (http://freshmeat.net). There is, however, a standard, centralized index of Python packages called, fittingly, the Python Package Index, or simply PyPI. Visit the PyPI web site (http://pypi.python.org) to look for new packages or new versions of old packages, or to publish your own packages.

In addition to the packages themselves, you can register a lot of useful metadata (possibly with the aid of Distutils or its relation setuptools), such as author, license, platform, categories, and descriptive keywords. The register command in Distutils will do most of the work for you.

## A Quick Summary

Finally, you now know how to create shiny, professional-looking software with fancy GUI installers—or how to automate the generation of those precious .tar.gz files. Here is a summary of the specific concepts covered:

**Distutils**: The Distutils toolkit lets you write installer scripts, conventionally called setup.py. With these scripts, you can install modules, packages, and extensions. You can also build distributable archives and simple Windows installers.

**Distutils commands**: You can run your setup.py script with several commands, such as build, build_ext, install, sdist, and bdist.

**Installers**: Many installer generators are available. Using an installer to install your Python program makes the process easier for your users.

**Compiling extensions**: You can use Distutils to have your C extensions compiled automatically, with Distutils automatically locating your Python installation and figuring out which compiler to use. You can even have it run SWIG automatically.

**Executable binaries**: The py2exe extension to Distutils can be used to create executable binaries from your Python programs. Along with a couple of extra files (which can be conveniently installed with an installer), these `.exe` files can be run without installing a Python interpreter separately.

## New Functions in This Chapter

| Function | Description |
| --- | --- |
| `distutils.core.setup(...)` | Configures Distutils with keyword arguments in your `setup.py` script |

## What Now?

That's it for the technical stuff—sort of. In the next chapter, you get some programming methodology and philosophy, and then come the projects. Enjoy!

CHAPTER 19

■■■

# Playful Programming

At this point, you should have a clearer picture of how Python works than when you started. Now the rubber hits the road, so to speak, and in the next ten chapters you put your newfound skills to work. Each chapter contains a single do-it-yourself project with a lot of room for experimentation, while at the same time giving you the necessary tools to implement a solution.

In this chapter, I give you some general guidelines for programming in Python.

## Why Playful?

I think one of the strengths of Python is that it makes programming fun—for me, anyway. It's much easier to be productive when you're having fun; and one of the fun things about Python is that it allows you to be very productive. It's a positive feedback loop, and you get far too few of those in life.

The expression *Playful Programming* is one I invented as a less extreme version of *Extreme Programming*, or XP.[1] I like many of the ideas of the XP movement but have been too lazy to commit completely to their principles. Instead, I've picked up a few things, and combined them with what I feel is a natural way of developing programs in Python.

## The Jujitsu of Programming

You have perhaps heard of *jujitsu?* It's a Japanese martial art, which, like its descendants *judo* and *aikido*,[2] focuses on flexibility of response, or "bending instead of breaking." Instead of trying to impose your preplanned moves on an opponent, you go with the flow, using your opponent's movements against him. This way (in theory), you can beat an opponent who is bigger, meaner, and stronger than you.

How does this apply to programming? The key is the syllable "ju," which may be (very roughly) translated as flexibility. When you run into trouble while programming (as you invariably will), instead of trying to cling stiffly to your initial designs and ideas, be flexible. Roll with the punches. Be prepared to change and adapt. Don't treat unforeseen events as frustrating

---

1. Extreme Programming is an approach to software development that, arguably, has been in use by programmers for years, but that was first named and documented by Kent Beck. For more information, see http://www.extremeprogramming.org.
2. Or, for that matter, its Chinese relatives, such as *taijiquan* or *baguazhang*.

interruptions; treat them as stimulating starting points for creative exploration of new options and possibilities.

The point is that when you sit down and plan how your program should be, you don't have any real experience with that specific program. How could you? After all, it doesn't exist yet. By working on the implementation, you gradually learn new things that could have been useful when you did the original design. Instead of ignoring these lessons you pick up along the way, you should use them to redesign (or *refactor*) your software. I'm not saying that you should just start hacking away with no idea of where you are headed, but that you should prepare for change, and accept that your initial design *will* need to be revised. It's like the old writer's saying: "Writing is rewriting."

This practice of flexibility has many aspects; here I'll touch upon two of them:

**Prototyping**: One of the nice things about Python is that you can write programs quickly. Writing a prototype program is an excellent way to learn more about your problem.

**Configuration**: Flexibility comes in many forms. The purpose of configuration is to make it easy to change certain parts of your program, both for you and your users.

A third aspect, automated testing, is absolutely essential if you want to be able to change your program easily. With tests in place, you can be sure that your program still works after introducing a modification. Prototyping and configuration are discussed in the following sections. For information about testing, see Chapter 16.

# Prototyping

In general, if you wonder how something works in Python, just try it. You don't need to do extensive preprocessing, such as compiling or linking, which is necessary in many other languages. You can just run your code directly. And not only that, you can run it piecemeal in the interactive interpreter, prodding at every corner until you thoroughly understand its behavior.

This kind of exploration doesn't cover only language features and built-in functions. Sure, it's useful to be able to find out exactly how, say, the `iter` function works, but even more important is the ability to easily create a prototype of the program you are about to write, just to see how *that* works.

---

**Note**  In this context, the word *prototype* means a tentative implementation, a mock-up that implements the main functionality of the final program, but which may need to be completely rewritten at some later stage—or not. Quite often, what started out as a prototype can be turned into a working program.

---

After you have put some thought into the structure of your program (such as which classes and functions you need), I suggest implementing a simple version of it, possibly with very limited functionality. You'll quickly notice how much easier the process becomes when you have a running program to play with. You can add features, change things you don't like, and so on. You can really see how it works, instead of just thinking about it or drawing diagrams on paper.

You can use prototyping in any programming language, but the strength of Python is that writing a mock-up is a very small investment, so you're not committed to using it. If you find that your design wasn't as clever as it could have been, you can simply toss out your prototype and start from scratch. The process might take a few hours, or a day or two. If you were programming in C++, for example, much more work would probably be involved in getting something up and running, and discarding it would be a major decision. By committing to one version, you lose flexibility; you get locked in by early decisions that may prove wrong in light of the real-world experience you get from actually implementing it.

In the projects that follow this chapter, I consistently use prototyping instead of detailed analysis and design up front. Every project is divided into two implementations. The first is a fumbling experiment in which I've thrown together a program that solves the problem (or possibly only a part of the problem) in order to learn about the components needed and what's required of a good solution. The greatest lesson will probably be seeing all the flaws of the program in action. By building on this newfound knowledge, I take another, hopefully more informed, whack at it. Of course, you should feel free to revise the code, or even start afresh a third time. Usually, starting from scratch doesn't take as much time as you might think. If you have already thought through the practicalities of the program, the typing shouldn't take too long.

## THE CASE AGAINST REWRITING

Although I'm advocating the use of prototypes here, there is reason to be a bit cautious about restarting your project from scratch at any point, especially if you've invested some time and effort into the prototype. It is probably better to refactor and modify that prototype into a more functional system, for several reasons.

One common problem that can occur is "second system syndrome." This is the tendency to try to make the second version so clever or perfect that it's never finished.

The "continual rewriting syndrome," quite prevalent in fiction writing, is the tendency to keep fiddling with your program, perhaps starting from scratch again and again. At some point, leaving well enough alone may be the best strategy—just get something that *works*.

Then there is "code fatigue." You grow tired of your code. It seems ugly and clunky to you after you've worked with it for a long time. Sadly, one of the reasons it may seem hacky and clunky is that it has grown to accommodate a range of special cases, and to incorporate several forms of error handling and the like. These are features you would need to reintroduce in a new version anyway, and they have probably cost you quite a bit of effort (not the least in the form of debugging) to implement in the first place.

In other words, if you think your prototype could be turned into a workable system, by all means, keep hacking at it, rather than restarting. In the project chapters that follow, I have separated the development cleanly into two versions: the prototype and the final program. This is partly for clarity and partly to highlight the experience and insight one can get by writing the first version of a piece of software. In the real world, I might very well have started with the prototype and "refactored myself" in the direction of the final system.

For more on the horrors of restarting from scratch, take a look at Joel Spolsky's article "Things You Should Never Do, Part I" (found on his web site, `http://joelonsoftware.com`). According to Spolsky, rewriting the code from scratch is the single worst strategic mistake that any software company can make.

# Configuration

In this section, I return to the ever important principle of abstraction. In Chapters 6 and 7, I showed you how to abstract away code by putting it in functions and methods, and hiding larger structures inside classes. Let's take a look at another, much simpler, way of introducing abstraction in your program: extracting *symbolic constants* from your code.

## Extracting Constants

By *constants*, I mean built-in literal values such as numbers, strings, and lists. Instead of writing these repeatedly in your program, you can gather them in global variables. I know I've been warning you about those, but problems with global variables occur primarily when you start changing them, because it can be difficult to keep track of which part of your code is responsible for which change. I'll leave these variables alone, however, and use them as if they were constant (hence the term *symbolic constants*). To signal that a variable is to be treated as a symbolic constant, you can use a special naming convention, using only capital letters in their variable names and separating words with underscores.

Let's take a look at an example. In a program that calculates the area and circumference of circles, you could keep writing 3.14 every time you needed the value π. But what if you, at some later time, wanted a more exact value, say 3.14159? You would need to search through the code and replace the old value with the new. This isn't very hard, and in most good text editors, it could be done automatically. However, what if you had started out with the value 3? Would you later want to replace every occurrence of the number 3 with 3.14159? Hardly. A much better way of handling this would be to start the program with the line `PI = 3.14`, and then use the name `PI` instead of the number itself. That way, you could simply change this single line to get a more exact value at some later time. Just keep this in the back of your mind: whenever you write a constant (such as the number 42 or the string "Hello, world!") more than once, consider placing it in a global variable instead.

---

■**Note**    Actually, the value of $\pi$ is found in the `math` module, under the name `math.pi`:

```
>> from math import pi
>> pi
3.1415926535897931
```

---

This may seem agonizingly obvious to you. But the real point of all this comes in the next section, where I talk about configuration files.

## Configuration Files

Extracting constants for your own benefit is one thing, but some constants can even be exposed to your users. For example, if they don't like the background color of your GUI program, perhaps you should let them use another color. Or perhaps you could let users decide what greeting message they would like to get when they start your exciting arcade game or the default starting page of the new web browser you just implemented.

Instead of putting these configuration variables at the top of one of your modules, you can put them in a separate file. The simplest way of doing this is to have a separate module for configuration. For example, if PI is set in the module file config.py, you can (in your main program) do the following:

```
from config import PI
```

Then, if the user wants a different value for PI, she can simply edit config.py without having to wade through your code.

---

■**Caution**  There is a trade-off with the use of configuration files. On the one hand, configuration is useful, but using a central, shared repository of variables for an entire project can make it less modular and more monolithic. Make sure you're not breaking abstractions (such as encapsulation).

---

Another possibility is to use the standard library module ConfigParser, which will allow you to use a reasonably standard format for configuration files. It allows both standard Python assignment syntax, such as this:

```
greeting = 'Hello, world!'
```

(although this would give you two extraneous quotes in your string) and another configuration format used in many programs:

```
greeting: Hello, world!
```

You must divide the configuration file into *sections*, using headers such as [files] or [colors]. The names can be anything, but you need to enclose them in brackets. A sample configuration file is shown in Listing 19-1, and a program using it is shown in Listing 19-2. For more information about the features of the ConfigParser module, consult the library documentation (http://python.org/doc/lib/module-ConfigParser.html).

**Listing 19-1.** *A Simple Configuration File*

```
[numbers]

pi: 3.1415926535897931

[messages]

greeting: Welcome to the area calculation program!
question: Please enter the radius:
result_message: The area is
```

**Listing 19-2.** *A Program Using ConfigParser*

```
from ConfigParser import ConfigParser

CONFIGFILE = "python.txt"

config = ConfigParser()
# Read the configuration file:
config.read(CONFIGFILE)

# Print out an initial greeting;
# 'messages' is the section to look in:
print config.get('messages', 'greeting')

# Read in the radius, using a question from the config file:
radius = input(config.get('messages', 'question') + ' ')

# Print a result message from the config file;
# end with a comma to stay on same line:
print config.get('messages', 'result_message'),

# getfloat() converts the config value to a float:
print config.getfloat('numbers', 'pi') * radius**2
```

I won't go into much detail about configuration in the following projects, but I suggest you think about making your programs highly configurable. That way, users can adapt the program to their tastes, which can make using it more pleasurable. After all, one of the main frustrations of using software is that you can't make it behave the way you want it to.

## LEVELS OF CONFIGURATION

Configurability is an integral part of the UNIX tradition of programming. In Chapter 10 of his excellent book, *The Art of UNIX Programming* (Addison-Wesley, 2003), Eric S. Raymond describes the following three sources of configuration or control information, which (if included) should probably be consulted *in this order*,[3] so the later sources override the earlier ones:

- **Configuration files**: See the "Configuration Files" section in this chapter.

- **Environment variables**: These can be fetched using the dictionary os.environ.

- **Switches and arguments passed to the program on the command line**: For handling command-line arguments, you can use sys.argv directly. If you want to deal with switches (options), you should check out the optparse module (or perhaps getopt), as mentioned in Chapter 10.

---

3.  Actually, global configuration files and system-set environment variables come before these. See the book for more details.

# Logging

Somewhat related to testing (discussed in Chapter 16), and quite useful when furiously rework-ing the innards of a program, logging can certainly help you discover problems and bugs. Logging is basically collecting data about your program as it runs, so you can examine it after-ward (or as the data accumulates, for that matter). A very simple form of logging can be done with the print statement. Just put a statement like this at the beginning of your program:

```
log = open('logfile.txt', 'w')
```

You can then later put any interesting information about the state of your program into this file, as follows:

```
print >> log, ('Downloading file from URL %s' % url)
text = urllib.urlopen(url).read()
print >> log, 'File successfully downloaded'
```

This approach won't work well if your program crashes during the download. It would be safer if you opened and closed your file for every log statement (or, at least, flushed the file after writing). Then, if your program crashed, you could see that the last line in your log file said "Downloading file from . . ." and you would know that the download wasn't successful.

The way to go, actually, is using the logging module in the standard library. Basic usage is pretty straightforward, as demonstrated by the program in Listing 19-3.

**Listing 19-3.** *A Program Using the logging Module*

```
import logging

logging.basicConfig(level=logging.INFO, filename='mylog.log')

logging.info('Starting program')

logging.info('Trying to divide 1 by 0')

print 1 / 0

logging.info('The division succeeded')

logging.info('Ending program')
```

Running that program would result in the following log file (called mylog.log):

```
INFO:root:Starting program
INFO:root:Trying to divide 1 by 0
```

As you can see, nothing is logged after trying to divide 1 by 0 because this error effectively kills the program. Because this is such a simple error, you can tell what is wrong by the excep-tion traceback that prints as the program crashes. The most difficult type of bug to track down is one that doesn't stop your program, but simply makes it behave strangely. Examining a detailed log file may help you find out what's going on.

The log file in this example isn't very detailed, but by configuring the `logging` module properly, you can set up just how you want your logging to work. Here are a few examples:

- Log entries of different types (information, debug info, warnings, custom types, and so on). By default, only warnings are let through (which is why I explicitly set the level to `logging.INFO` in Listing 19-3).

- Log just items that relate to certain parts of your program.

- Log information about time, date, and so forth.

- Log to different locations, such as sockets.

- Configure the logger to filter out some or most of the logging, so you get only what you need at any one time, without rewriting the program.

The `logging` module is quite sophisticated, and there is much to be learned in the documentation (`http://python.org/doc/lib/module-logging.html`).

## If You Can't Be Bothered

"All this is well and good," you may think, "but there's no way I'm going to put that much effort into writing a simple little program. Configuration, testing, logging—it sounds really boring."

Well, that's fine. You may not need it for simple programs. And even if you're working on a larger project, you may not really *need* all of this at the beginning. I would say that the minimum is that you have some way of testing your program (as discussed in Chapter 16), even if it's not based on automatic unit tests. For example, if you're writing a program that automatically makes you coffee, you should have a coffee pot around, to see if it works.

In the project chapters that follow, I don't write full test suites, intricate logging facilities, and so forth. I present you with some simple test cases to demonstrate that the programs work, and that's it. If you find the core idea of a project interesting, you should take it further—try to enhance and expand it. And in the process, you should consider the issues you read about in this chapter. Perhaps a configuration mechanism would be a good idea? Or a more extensive test suite? It's up to you.

## If You Want to Learn More

Just in case you want more information about the art, craft, and philosophy of programming, here are some books that discuss these things more in depth:

- *The Pragmatic Programmer*, by Andrew Hunt and David Thomas (Addison-Wesley, 1999)

- *Refactoring*, by Kent Beck et al. (Addison-Wesley, 1999)

- *Design Patterns*, by the "Gang of Four," Erich Gamma, Richard Helm, Ralph Johnson, John Vlissides (Addison-Wesley, 1994)

- *Test-Driven Development: By Example*, by Kent Beck (Addison-Wesley, 2002)

- *The Art of UNIX Programming*, by Eric S. Raymond (Addison-Wesley, 2003)[4]

- *Introduction to Algorithms*, *Second Edition*, by Thomas H. Cormen et al. (MIT Press, 2001)

- *The Art of Computer Programming*, Volumes 1–3, by Donald Knuth (Addison-Wesley, 1998)

- *Concepts, Techniques, and Models of Computer Programming*, by Peter Van Roy and Seif Haridi (MIT Press, 2004)

Even if you don't read every page of every book (I know I haven't), just browsing through a few of these can give you quite a lot of insight.

# A Quick Summary

In this chapter, I described some general principles and techniques for programming in Python, conveniently lumped under the heading "Playful Programming." Here are the highlights:

**Flexibility**: When designing and programming, you should aim for flexibility. Instead of clinging to your initial ideas, you should be willing to—and even prepared to—revise and change every aspect of your program as you gain insight into the problem at hand.

**Prototyping**: One important technique for learning about a problem and possible implementations is to write a simple version of your program to see how it works. In Python, this is so easy that you can write several prototypes in the time it takes to write a single version in many other languages. Still, you should be wary of rewriting your code from scratch if you don't have to—refactoring is usually a better solution.

**Configuration**: Extracting constants from your program makes it easier to change them at some later point. Putting them in a configuration file makes it possible for your users to configure the program to behave as they would like. Employing environment variables and command-line options can make your program even more configurable.

**Logging**: Logging can be quite useful for uncovering problems with your program—or just to monitor its ordinary behavior. You can implement simple logging yourself, using the `print` statement, but the safest bet is to use the `logging` module from the standard library.

## What Now?

Indeed, what now? Now is the time to take the plunge and really start programming. It's time for the projects.

All ten project chapters have a similar structure, with the following sections:

**What's the Problem?**: In this section, the main goals of the project are outlined, including some background information.

**Useful Tools**: Here, I describe modules, classes, functions, and so on that might be useful for the project.

---

4. Also available online at Raymond's web site (`http://catb.org/~esr/writings/taoup`).

**Preparations**: This section covers any preparations necessary before starting to program. This may include setting up the necessary framework for testing the implementation.

**First Implementation**: This is the first whack—a tentative implementation to learn more about the problem.

**Second Implementation**: After the first implementation, you will probably have a better understanding of things, which will enable you to create a new and improved version.

**Further Exploration**: Finally, I give pointers for further experimentation and exploration.

Let's get started with the first project, which is to create a program that automatically marks up files for HTML.

■ ■ ■

# CHAPTER 20

# Project 1: Instant Markup

In this project, you see how to use Python's excellent text-processing capabilities, including the capability to use regular expressions to change a plain-text file into one marked up in a language such as HTML or XML. You need such skills if you want to use text written by people who don't know these languages in a system that requires the contents to be marked up.

Don't speak fluent XML? Don't worry about that—if you have only a passing acquaintance with HTML, you'll do fine in this chapter. If you need an introduction to HTML, I suggest you take a look at Dave Raggett's excellent guide "Getting Started with HTML" at the World Wide Web Consortium's site (http://www.w3.org/MarkUp/Guide). For an example of XML use, see Chapter 22.

Let's start by implementing a simple prototype that does the basic processing, and then extend that program to make the markup system more flexible.

## What's the Problem?

You want to add some formatting to a plain-text file. Let's say you've been handed the file from someone who can't be bothered with writing in HTML, and you need to use the document as a web page. Instead of adding all the necessary tags manually, you want your program to do it automatically.

---

**Note** In recent years, this sort of "plain-text markup" has, in fact, become quite common, probably mainly because of the explosion of wiki and blog software with plain-text interfaces. See the section "Further Exploration" at the end of this chapter for more information.

---

Your task is basically to classify various text elements, such as headlines and emphasized text, and then clearly mark them. In the specific problem addressed here, you add HTML markup to the text, so the resulting document can be displayed in a web browser and used as a web page. However, once you have built your basic engine, there is no reason why you can't add other kinds of markup (such as various forms of XML or perhaps LaTeX codes). After analyzing a text file, you can even perform other tasks, such as extracting all the headlines to make a table of contents.

**Note** LaTeX is another markup system (based on the TeX typesetting program) for creating various types of technical documents. I mention it here only as an example of other uses for your program. If you want to know more, you can visit the TeX Users Group web site at http://www.tug.org.

The text you're given may contain some clues (such as emphasized text being marked *like this*), but you'll probably need some ingenuity in making your program guess how the document is structured.

Before starting to write your prototype, let's define some goals:

- The input shouldn't be required to contain artificial codes or tags.

- You should be able to deal with both different blocks, such as headings, paragraphs, and list items, and in-line text, such as emphasized text or URLs.

- Although this implementation deals with HTML, it should be easy to extend it to other markup languages.

You may not be able to reach these goals fully in the first version of your program, but that's the point of the prototype, You write the prototype to find flaws in your original ideas and to learn more about how to write a program that solves your problem.

**Tip** If you can, it's probably a good idea to modify your original program incrementally rather than beginning from scratch. In the interest of clarity, I give you two completely separate versions of the program here.

## Useful Tools

Consider what tools might be needed in writing this program:

- You certainly need to read from and write to files (see Chapter 11), or at least read from standard input (sys.stdin) and output with print.

- You probably need to iterate over the lines of the input (see Chapter 11).

- You need a few string methods (see Chapter 3).

- Perhaps you'll use a generator or two (see Chapter 9).

- You probably need the re module (see Chapter 10).

If any of these concepts seem unfamiliar to you, you should perhaps take a moment to refresh your memory.

# Preparations

Before you start coding, you need some way of assessing your progress; you need a test suite. In this project, a single test may suffice: a test *document* (in plain text). Listing 20-1 contains sample text that you want to mark up automatically.

**Listing 20-1.** *A Sample Plain-Text Document (test_input.txt)*

```
Welcome to World Wide Spam, Inc.


These are the corporate web pages of *World Wide Spam*, Inc. We hope
you find your stay enjoyable, and that you will sample many of our
products.

A short history of the company

World Wide Spam was started in the summer of 2000. The business
concept was to ride the dot-com wave and to make money both through
bulk email and by selling canned meat online.

After receiving several complaints from customers who weren't
satisfied by their bulk email, World Wide Spam altered their profile,
and focused 100% on canned goods. Today, they rank as the world's
13,892nd online supplier of SPAM.

Destinations

From this page you may visit several of our interesting web pages:

  - What is SPAM? (http://wwspam.fu/whatisspam)

  - How do they make it? (http://wwspam.fu/howtomakeit)

  - Why should I eat it? (http://wwspam.fu/whyeatit)

How to get in touch with us

You can get in touch with us in *many* ways: By phone (555-1234), by
email (wwspam@wwspam.fu) or by visiting our customer feedback page
(http://wwspam.fu/feedback).
```

To test your implementation, just use this document as input and view the results in a web browser, or perhaps examine the added tags directly.

---

**■Note**  It is usually better to have an automated test suite than to check your test results manually. (Do you see any way of automating this test?)

---

# First Implementation

One of the first things you need to do is split the text into paragraphs. It's obvious from Listing 20-1 that the paragraphs are separated by one or more empty lines. A better word than *paragraph* might be *block*, because this name can apply to headlines and list items as well.

## Finding Blocks of Text

A simple way to find these blocks is to collect all the lines you encounter until you find an empty line, and then return the lines you have collected so far. That would be one block. Then, you could start all over again. You don't need to bother collecting empty lines, and you won't return empty blocks (where you have encountered more than one empty line). Also, you should make sure that the last line of the file is empty; otherwise, you won't know when the last block is finished. (There are other ways of finding out, of course.)

Listing 20-2 shows an implementation of this approach.

**Listing 20-2.** *A Text Block Generator (util.py)*

```
def lines(file):
    for line in file: yield line
    yield '\n'

def blocks(file):
    block = []
    for line in lines(file):
        if line.strip():
            block.append(line)
        elif block:
            yield ''.join(block).strip()
            block = []
```

The lines generator is just a little utility that tacks an empty line onto the end of the file. The blocks generator implements the approach described. When a block is yielded, its lines are joined, and the resulting string is stripped, giving you a single string representing the block, with excessive whitespace at either end (such as list indentations or newlines) removed. (If you don't like this way of finding paragraphs, I'm sure you can figure out several other approaches. It might even be fun to see how many you can invent.)

■**Note** In older versions of Python (prior to 2.3), you needed to add `from __future__ import generators` as the first line of this module. See also the section "Simulating Generators" in Chapter 9.

I've put the code in the file `util.py`, which means that you can import the utility genera-tors in your program later.

## Adding Some Markup

With the basic functionality from Listing 20-2, you can create a simple markup script. The basic steps of this program are as follows:

1. Print some beginning markup.

2. For each block, print the block enclosed in paragraph tags.

3. Print some ending markup.

This isn't very difficult, but it's not extremely useful either. Let's say that instead of enclos-ing the first block in paragraph tags, you enclose it in top heading tags (h1). Also, you replace any text enclosed in asterisks with emphasized text (using em tags). At least that's a *bit* more useful. Given the blocks function, and using `re.sub`, the code is very simple. See Listing 20-3.

**Listing 20-3.** *A Simple Markup Program (simple_markup.py)*

```
import sys, re
from util import *

print '<html><head><title>...</title><body>'

title = True
for block in blocks(sys.stdin):
    block = re.sub(r'\*(.+?)\*', r'<em>\1</em>', block)
    if title:
        print '<h1>'
        print block
        print '</h1>'
        title = False
    else:
        print '<p>'
        print block
        print '</p>'

print '</body></html>'
```

This program can be executed on the sample input as follows:

```
$ python simple_markup.py < test_input.txt > test_output.html
```

The file test_output.html will then contain the generated HTML code. Figure 20-1 shows how this HTML code looks in a web browser.

**Figure 20-1.** *The first attempt at generating a web page*

Although not very impressive, this prototype does perform some important tasks. It divides the text into blocks that can be handled separately, and it applies a filter (consisting of a call to re.sub) to each block in turn. This seems like a good approach to use in your final program.

Now what would happen if you tried to extend this prototype? You would probably add checks inside the for loop to see whether the block was a heading, a list item, or something else. You would add more regular expressions. It could quickly grow into a mess. Even more important, it would be very difficult to make it output anything other than HTML; and one of the goals of this project is to make it easy to add other output formats. Let's assume you want to refactor your program and structure it a bit differently.

# Second Implementation

So, what did you learn from this first implementation? To make it more extensible, you need to make your program more *modular* (divide the functionality into independent components). One way of achieving modularity is through object-oriented design (see Chapter 7). You need to find some abstractions to make your program more manageable as its complexity grows. Let's begin by listing some possible components:

- **A parser**: Add an object that reads the text and manages the other classes.

- **Rules**: You can make one rule for each type of block. The rule should be able to detect the applicable block type and to format it appropriately.

- **Filters**: Use filters to wrap up some regular expressions to deal with in-line elements.

- **Handlers**: The parser uses handlers to generate output. Each handler can produce a different kind of markup.

Although this isn't a very detailed design, at least it gives you some ideas about how to divide your code into smaller parts and make each part manageable.

## Handlers

Let's begin with the handlers. A handler is responsible for generating the resulting marked-up text, but it receives detailed instructions from the parser. Let's say it has a pair of methods for each block type: one for starting the block and one for ending it. For example, it might have the methods start_paragraph and end_paragraph to deal with paragraph blocks. For HTML, these could be implemented as follows:

```
class HTMLRenderer:
    def start_paragraph(self):
        print '<p>'
    def end_paragraph(self):
        print '</p>'
```

Of course, you'll need similar methods for other block types. (For the full code of the HTMLRenderer class, see Listing 20-4 later in this chapter.) This seems flexible enough. If you wanted some other type of markup, you would just make another handler (or renderer) with other implementations of the start and end methods.

---

■**Note**  The term *handler* (as opposed to *renderer*, for example) was chosen to indicate that it handles the method calls generated by the parser (see also the following section, "A Handler Superclass"). It doesn't *have* to render the text in some markup language, as HTMLRenderer does. A similar handler mechanism is used in the XML parsing scheme called SAX, which is explained in Chapter 22.

---

How do you deal with regular expressions? As you may recall, the re.sub function can take a function as its second argument (the replacement). This function is called with the match object, and its return value is inserted into the text. This fits nicely with the handler philosophy discussed previously—you just let the handlers implement the replacement methods. For example, emphasis can be handled like this:

```
def sub_emphasis(self, match):
    return '<em>%s</em>' % match.group(1)
```

If you don't understand what the group method does, perhaps you should take another look at the re module, described in Chapter 10.

In addition to the start, end, and sub methods, you'll have a method called feed, which you use to feed actual text to the handler. In your simple HTML renderer, you'll just implement it like this:

```
def feed(self, data):
    print data
```

## A Handler Superclass

In the interest of flexibility, let's add a Handler class, which will be the superclass of your handlers and will take care of some administrative details. Instead of needing to call the methods by their full name (for example, start_paragraph), it may at times be useful to handle the block types as strings (for example, 'paragraph') and supply the handler with those. You can do this by adding some generic methods called start(type), end(type), and sub(type). In addition, you can make start, end, and sub check whether the corresponding methods (such as start_paragraph for start('paragraph')) are really implemented, and do nothing if no such method is found. An implementation of this Handler class follows. (This code is taken from the module handlers shown later in Listing 20-4.)

```
class Handler:
    def callback(self, prefix, name, *args):
        method = getattr(self, prefix+name, None)
        if callable(method): return method(*args)
    def start(self, name):
        self.callback('start_', name)
    def end(self, name):
        self.callback('end_', name)
    def sub(self, name):
        def substitution(match):
            result = self.callback('sub_', name, match)
            if result is None: result = match.group(0)
            return result
        return substitution
```

---

**■Note**  This code requires nested scopes, which are not available prior to Python 2.1. If, for some reason, you're using Python 2.1, you need to add the line from __future__ import nested_scopes at the top of the handlers module. (To some degree, nested scopes can be simulated with default arguments. See the sidebar "Nested Scopes" in Chapter 6.) Also, callable is not available in Python 3.0. To get around that, you could simply use a try/except statement to see if you're able to call it.

---

Several things in this code warrant some explanation:

- The `callback` method is responsible for finding the correct method (such as `start_paragraph`), given a prefix (such as `'start_'`) and a name (such as `'paragraph'`). It performs its task by using `getattr` with `None` as the default value. If the object returned from `getattr` is callable, it is called with any additional arguments supplied. So, for example, calling `handler.callback('start_', 'paragraph')` calls the method `handler.start_paragraph` with no arguments, given that it exists.

- The `start` and `end` methods are just helper methods that call `callback` with the respective prefixes `start_` and `end_`.

- The `sub` method is a bit different. It doesn't call `callback` directly, but returns a new function, which is used as the replacement function in `re.sub` (which is why it takes a match object as its only argument).

Let's consider an example. Say `HTMLRenderer` is a subclass of `Handler` and it implements the method `sub_emphasis` as described in the previous section (see Listing 20-4 for the actual code of `handlers.py`). Let's say you have an `HTMLRenderer` instance in the variable handler:

```
>>> from handlers import HTMLRenderer
>>> handler = HTMLRenderer()
```

What then will `handler.sub('emphasis')` do?

```
>>> handler.sub('emphasis')
<function substitution at 0x168cf8>
```

It returns a function (`substitution`) that basically calls the `handler.sub_emphasis` method when you call it. That means that you can use this function in a `re.sub` statement:

```
>>> import re
>>> re.sub(r'\*(.+?)\*', handler.sub('emphasis'), 'This *is* a test')
'This <em>is</em> a test'
```

Magic! (The regular expression matches occurrences of text bracketed by asterisks, which I'll discuss shortly.) But why go to such lengths? Why not just use `r'<em>\1</em>'`, as in the simple version? Because then you would be committed to using the `em` tag, but you want the handler to be able to decide which markup to use. If your handler were a (hypothetical) `LaTeXRenderer`, for example, you might get another result altogether:

```
>> re.sub(r'\*(.+?)\*', handler.sub('emphasis'), 'This *is* a test')
'This \emph{is} a test'
```

The markup has changed, but the code has not.

We also have a backup, in case no substitution is implemented. The `callback` method tries to find a suitable `sub_something` method, but if it doesn't find one, it returns `None`. Because your function is a `re.sub` replacement function, you *don't* want it to return `None`. Instead, if you do not find a substitution method, you just return the original match without any modifications. If the callback returns `None`, `substitution` (inside `sub`) returns the original matched text (`match.group(0)`) instead.

# Rules

Now that you've made the handlers quite extensible and flexible, it's time to turn to the parsing (interpretation of the original text). Instead of making one big if statement with various conditions and actions, such as in the simple markup program, let's make the rules a separate kind of object.

The rules are used by the main program (the parser), which must determine which rules are applicable for a given block, and then make each rule do what is needed to transform the block. In other words, a rule must be able to do the following:

- Recognize blocks where it applies (the *condition*).

- Transform blocks (the *action*).

So each rule object must have two methods: condition and action.

The condition method needs only one argument: the block in question. It should return a Boolean value indicating whether the rule is applicable to the given block.

---

**■Tip**   For complex rule parsing, you might want to give the rule object access to some state variables as well, so it knows more about what has happened so far, or which other rules have or have not been applied.

---

The action method also needs the block as an argument, but to be able to affect the output, it must also have access to the handler object.

In many circumstances, only one rule may be applicable; that is, if you find that a headline rule is used (indicating that the block is a headline), you should *not* attempt to use the paragraph rule. A simple implementation of this would be to have the parser try the rules one by one, and stop the processing of the block once one of the rules is triggered. This would be fine in general, but as you'll see, sometimes a rule may not preclude the execution of other rules. Therefore, you add another piece of functionality to your action method: it returns a Boolean value indicating whether the rule processing for the current block should stop. (You could also use an exception for this, similarly to the StopIteration mechanism of iterators.)

Pseudocode for the headline rule might be as follows:

```
class HeadlineRule:
    def condition(self, block):
        if the block fits the definition of a headline, return True;
        otherwise, return False.
    def action(self, block, handler):
        call methods such as handler.start('headline'), handler.feed(block) and
        handler.end('headline').
        because we don't want to attempt to use any other rules,
        return True, which will end the rule processing for this block.
```

## A Rule Superclass

Although you don't strictly need a common superclass for your rules, several of them may share the same general action—calling the start, feed, and end methods of the handler with the appropriate type string argument, and then returning True (to stop the rule processing). Assuming that all the subclasses have an attribute called type containing this type name as a string, you can implement your superclass as shown in the code that follows. (The Rule class is found in the rules module; the full code is shown later in Listing 20-5.)

```
class Rule:
    def action(self, block, handler):
        handler.start(self.type)
        handler.feed(block)
        handler.end(self.type)
        return True
```

The condition method is the responsibility of each subclass. The Rule class and its subclasses are put in the rules module.

## Filters

You won't need a separate class for your filters. Given the sub method of your Handler class, each filter can be represented by a regular expression and a name (such as emphasis or url). You see how in the next section, when I show you how to deal with the parser.

## The Parser

We've come to the heart of the application: the Parser class. It uses a handler and a set of rules and filters to transform a plain-text file into a marked-up file—in this specific case, an HTML file. Which methods does it need? It needs a constructor to set things up, a method to add rules, a method to add filters, and a method to parse a given file.

The following is the code for the Parser class (from Listing 20-6, later in this chapter, which details markup.py).

```
class Parser:
    """
    A Parser reads a text file, applying rules and controlling a
    handler.
    """
    def __init__(self, handler):
        self.handler = handler
        self.rules = []
        self.filters = []
    def addRule(self, rule):
        self.rules.append(rule)
```

```
def addFilter(self, pattern, name):
    def filter(block, handler):
        return re.sub(pattern, handler.sub(name), block)
    self.filters.append(filter)
def parse(self, file):
    self.handler.start('document')
    for block in blocks(file):
        for filter in self.filters:
            block = filter(block, self.handler)
        for rule in self.rules:
            if rule.condition(block):
                last = rule.action(block, self.handler)
                if last: break
    self.handler.end('document')
```

Although there is quite a lot to digest in this class, most of it isn't very complicated. The constructor simply assigns the supplied handler to an instance variable (attribute) and then initializes two lists: one of rules and one of filters. The addRule method adds a rule to the rule list. The addFilter method, however, does a bit more work. Like addRule, it adds a filter to the filter list, but before doing so, it creates that filter. The filter is simply a function that applies re.sub with the appropriate regular expression (pattern) and uses a replacement from the handler, accessed with handler.sub(name).

The parse method, although it might look a bit complicated, is perhaps the easiest method to implement because it merely does what you've been planning to do all along. It begins by calling start('document') on the handler, and ends by calling end('document'). Between these calls, it iterates over all the blocks in the text file. For each block, it applies both the filters and the rules. Applying a filter is simply a matter of calling the filter function with the block and handler as arguments, and rebinding the block variable to the result, as follows:

```
block = filter(block, self.handler)
```

This enables each of the filters to do its work, which is replacing parts of the text with marked-up text (such as replacing *this* with this).

There is a bit more logic in the rule loop. For each rule, there is an if statement, checking whether the rule applies by calling rule.condition(block). If the rule applies, rule.action is called with the block and handler as arguments. Remember that the action method returns a Boolean value indicating whether to finish the rule application for this block. Finishing the rule application is done by setting the variable last to the return value of action, and then conditionally breaking out of the for loop:

```
if last: break
```

■**Note** You can collapse these two statements into one, eliminating the `last` variable:

```
if rule.action(block, self.handler): break
```

Whether or not to do so is largely a matter of taste. Removing the temporary variable makes the code simpler, but leaving it in clearly labels the return value.

## Constructing the Rules and Filters

Now you have all the tools you need, but you haven't created any specific rules or filters yet. The motivation behind much of the code you've written so far is to make the rules and filters as flexible as the handlers. You can write several independent rules and filters and add them to your parser through the `addRule` and `addFilter` methods, making sure to implement the appropriate methods in your handlers.

A complicated rule set makes it possible to deal with complicated documents. However, let's keep it simple for now. Let's create one rule for the title, one rule for other headings, and one for list items. Because list items should be treated collectively as a list, you'll create a separate list rule, which deals with the entire list. Lastly, you can create a default rule for paragraphs, which covers all blocks not dealt with by the previous rules.

We can specify the rules in informal terms as follows:

- A heading is a block that consists of only one line, which has a length of at most 70 characters. If the block ends with a colon, it is not a heading.

- The title is the first block in the document, provided that it is a heading.

- A list item is a block that begins with a hyphen (-).

- A list begins between a block that is not a list item and a following list item and ends between a list item and a following block that is not a list item.

These rules follow some of my intuitions about how a text document is structured. Your opinions on this (and your text documents) may differ. Also, the rules have weaknesses (for example, what happens if the document ends with a list item?). Feel free to improve on them.

The complete source code for the rules is shown later in Listing 20-5 (`rules.py`, which also contains the basic `Rule` class).

Let's begin with the heading rule:

```
class HeadingRule(Rule):
    """
    A heading is a single line that is at most 70 characters and
    that doesn't end with a colon.
    """
    type = 'heading'
    def condition(self, block):
        return not '\n' in block and len(block) <= 70 and not block[-1] == ':'
```

The attribute type has been set to the string 'heading', which is used by the action method inherited from Rule. The condition simply checks that the block does not contain a newline (\n) character, that its length is at most 70, and that the last character is not a colon.

The title rule is similar, but only works once, for the first block. After that, it ignores all blocks because its attribute first has been set to a *false* value.

```
class TitleRule(HeadingRule):
    """
    The title is the first block in the document, provided that it is
    a heading.
    """
    type = 'title'
    first = True

    def condition(self, block):
        if not self.first: return False
        self.first = False
        return HeadingRule.condition(self, block)
```

The list item rule condition is a direct implementation of the preceding specification.

```
class ListItemRule(Rule):
    """
    A list item is a paragraph that begins with a hyphen. As part of
    the formatting, the hyphen is removed.
    """
    type = 'listitem'
    def condition(self, block):
        return block[0] == '-'
    def action(self, block, handler):
        handler.start(self.type)
        handler.feed(block[1:].strip())
        handler.end(self.type)
        return True
```

Its action is a reimplementation of that found in Rule. The only difference is that it removes the first character from the block (the hyphen) and strips away excessive whitespace from the remaining text. The markup provides its own "list bullet," so you won't need the hyphen anymore.

All the rule actions so far have returned True. The list rule does not, because it is triggered when you encounter a list item after a nonlist item or when you encounter a nonlist item after a list item. Because it doesn't actually mark up these blocks but merely indicates the beginning and end of a list (a group of list items) you don't want to halt the rule processing—so it returns False.

```python
class ListRule(ListItemRule):
    """
    A list begins between a block that is not a list item and a
    subsequent list item. It ends after the last consecutive list
    item.
    """
    type = 'list'
    inside = False
    def condition(self, block):
        return True
    def action(self, block, handler):
        if not self.inside and ListItemRule.condition(self, block):
            handler.start(self.type)
            self.inside = True
        elif self.inside and not ListItemRule.condition(self, block):
            handler.end(self.type)
            self.inside = False
        return False
```

The list rule might require some further explanation. Its condition is always true because you want to examine all blocks. In the action method, you have two alternatives that may lead to action:

- If the attribute inside (indicating whether the parser is currently inside the list) is false (as it is initially), and the condition from the list item rule is true, you have just entered a list. Call the appropriate start method of the handler, and set the inside attribute to True.

- Conversely, if inside is true, and the list item rule condition is false, you have just left a list. Call the appropriate end method of the handler, and set the inside attribute to False.

After this processing, the function returns False to let the rule handling continue. (This means, of course, that the order of the rules is critical.)

The final rule is ParagraphRule. Its condition is always true because it is the "default" rule. It is added as the last element of the rule list, and handles all blocks that aren't dealt with by any other rule.

```python
class ParagraphRule(Rule):
    """
    A paragraph is simply a block that isn't covered by any of the
    other rules.
    """
    type = 'paragraph'
    def condition(self, block):
        return True
```

The filters are simply regular expressions. Let's add three filters: one for emphasis, one for URLs, and one for email addresses. Let's use the following three regular expressions:

```
r'\*(.+?)\*'
r'(http://[\.a-zA-Z/]+)'
r'([\.a-zA-Z]+@[\.a-zA-Z]+[a-zA-Z]+)'
```

The first pattern (emphasis) matches an asterisk followed by one or more arbitrary characters (matching as few as possible, hence the question mark), followed by another asterisk. The second pattern (URLs) matches the string 'http://' (here, you could add more protocols) followed by one or more characters that are dots, letters, or slashes. (This pattern will not match all legal URLs—feel free to improve it.) Finally, the email pattern matches a sequence of letters and dots followed by an at sign (@), followed by more letters and dots, finally followed by a sequence of letters, ensuring that you don't end with a dot. (Again—feel free to improve this.)

## Putting It All Together

You now just need to create a Parser object and add the relevant rules and filters. Let's do that by creating a subclass of Parser that does the initialization in its constructor. Then let's use that to parse sys.stdin. The final program is shown in Listings 20-4 through 20-6. (These listings depend on the utility code in Listing 20-2.) The final program may be run just like the prototype:

```
$ python markup.py < test_input.txt > test_output.html
```

**Listing 20-4.** *The Handlers (handlers.py)*

```python
class Handler:
    """
    An object that handles method calls from the Parser.

    The Parser will call the start() and end() methods at the
    beginning of each block, with the proper block name as a
    parameter. The sub() method will be used in regular expression
    substitution. When called with a name such as 'emphasis', it will
    return a proper substitution function.
    """
    def callback(self, prefix, name, *args):
        method = getattr(self, prefix+name, None)
        if callable(method): return method(*args)
    def start(self, name):
        self.callback('start_', name)
    def end(self, name):
        self.callback('end_', name)
    def sub(self, name):
        def substitution(match):
            result = self.callback('sub_', name, match)
            if result is None: result = match.group(0)
            return result
        return substitution
```

```python
class HTMLRenderer(Handler):
    """
    A specific handler used for rendering HTML.

    The methods in HTMLRenderer are accessed from the superclass
    Handler's start(), end(), and sub() methods. They implement basic
    markup as used in HTML documents.
    """
    def start_document(self):
        print '<html><head><title>...</title></head><body>'
    def end_document(self):
        print '</body></html>'
    def start_paragraph(self):
        print '<p>'
    def end_paragraph(self):
        print '</p>'
    def start_heading(self):
        print '<h2>'
    def end_heading(self):
        print '</h2>'
    def start_list(self):
        print '<ul>'
    def end_list(self):
        print '</ul>'
    def start_listitem(self):
        print '<li>'
    def end_listitem(self):
        print '</li>'
    def start_title(self):
        print '<h1>'
    def end_title(self):
        print '</h1>'
    def sub_emphasis(self, match):
        return '<em>%s</em>' % match.group(1)
    def sub_url(self, match):
        return '<a href="%s">%s</a>' % (match.group(1), match.group(1))
    def sub_mail(self, match):
        return '<a href="mailto:%s">%s</a>' % (match.group(1), match.group(1))
    def feed(self, data):
        print data
```

**Listing 20-5.** *The Rules (rules.py)*

```python
class Rule:
    """
    Base class for all rules.
    """
```

```python
    def action(self, block, handler):
        handler.start(self.type)
        handler.feed(block)
        handler.end(self.type)
        return True

class HeadingRule(Rule):
    """
    A heading is a single line that is at most 70 characters and
    that doesn't end with a colon.
    """
    type = 'heading'
    def condition(self, block):
        return not '\n' in block and len(block) <= 70 and not block[-1] == ':'

class TitleRule(HeadingRule):
    """
    The title is the first block in the document, provided that it is
    a heading.
    """
    type = 'title'
    first = True

    def condition(self, block):
        if not self.first: return False
        self.first = False
        return HeadingRule.condition(self, block)

class ListItemRule(Rule):
    """
    A list item is a paragraph that begins with a hyphen. As part of
    the formatting, the hyphen is removed.
    """
    type = 'listitem'
    def condition(self, block):
        return block[0] == '-'
    def action(self, block, handler):
        handler.start(self.type)
        handler.feed(block[1:].strip())
        handler.end(self.type)
        return True

class ListRule(ListItemRule):
    """
    A list begins between a block that is not a list item and a
    subsequent list item. It ends after the last consecutive list
    item.
```

```
    """
    type = 'list'
    inside = False
    def condition(self, block):
        return True
    def action(self, block, handler):
        if not self.inside and ListItemRule.condition(self, block):
            handler.start(self.type)
            self.inside = True
        elif self.inside and not ListItemRule.condition(self, block):
            handler.end(self.type)
            self.inside = False
        return False

class ParagraphRule(Rule):
    """
    A paragraph is simply a block that isn't covered by any of the
    other rules.
    """
    type = 'paragraph'
    def condition(self, block):
        return True
```

**Listing 20-6.** *The Main Program (markup.py)*

```
import sys, re
from handlers import *
from util import *
from rules import *

class Parser:
    """
    A Parser reads a text file, applying rules and controlling a
    handler.
    """
    def __init__(self, handler):
        self.handler = handler
        self.rules = []
        self.filters = []
    def addRule(self, rule):
        self.rules.append(rule)
    def addFilter(self, pattern, name):
        def filter(block, handler):
            return re.sub(pattern, handler.sub(name), block)
        self.filters.append(filter)
```

```python
    def parse(self, file):
        self.handler.start('document')
        for block in blocks(file):
            for filter in self.filters:
                block = filter(block, self.handler)
            for rule in self.rules:
                if rule.condition(block):
                    last = rule.action(block, self.handler)
                    if last: break
        self.handler.end('document')

class BasicTextParser(Parser):
    """
    A specific Parser that adds rules and filters in its
    constructor.
    """
    def __init__(self, handler):
        Parser.__init__(self, handler)
        self.addRule(ListRule())
        self.addRule(ListItemRule())
        self.addRule(TitleRule())
        self.addRule(HeadingRule())
        self.addRule(ParagraphRule())

        self.addFilter(r'\*(.+?)\*', 'emphasis')
        self.addFilter(r'(http://[\.a-zA-Z/]+)', 'url')
        self.addFilter(r'([\.a-zA-Z]+@[\.a-zA-Z]+[a-zA-Z]+)', 'mail')

handler = HTMLRenderer()
parser = BasicTextParser(handler)

parser.parse(sys.stdin)
```

You can see the result of running the program on the sample text in Figure 20-2.

The second implementation is clearly more complicated and extensive than the first version. The added complexity is well worth the effort because the resulting program is much more flexible and extensible. Adapting it to new input and output formats is merely a matter of subclassing and initializing the existing classes, rather than rewriting everything from scratch, as you would have had to do in the first prototype.

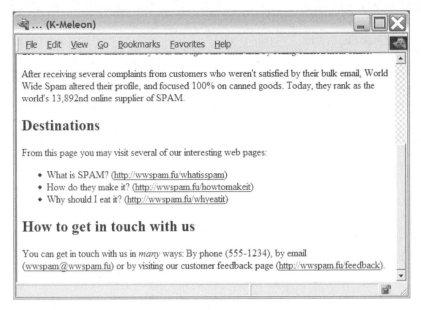

**Figure 20-2.** *The second attempt at generating a web page*

# Further Exploration

Several expansions are possible for this program. Here are some possibilities:

- Add support for tables. Find all aligning left word borders and split the block into columns.

- Add support for interpreting all uppercase words as emphasis. (To do this properly, you will need to take into account acronyms, punctuations, names, and other capitalized words.)

- Add support for LaTeX output.

- Write a handler that does something other than markup. Perhaps write a handler that analyzes the document in some way.

- Create a script that automatically converts all text files in a directory to HTML files.

- Check out some existing plain-text formats (such as various forms of wiki markup). See Table 20-1 for some ideas. A web search (or a look at some wiki or blog systems) will probably turn up more results.

**Table 20-1.** *Some Plain-Text and Wiki-Style Markup Systems*

| Markup System | Web Site |
| --- | --- |
| Atox | http://atox.sf.net |
| atx | http://www.aaronsw.com/2002/atx |
| BBCode | http://www.bbcode.org |
| Epytext | http://epydoc.sourceforge.net/epytext.html |
| EtText | http://ettext.taint.org |
| Grutatxt | http://www.triptico.com/software/grutatxt.html |
| Markdown | http://daringfireball.net/projects/markdown |
| reStructuredText | http://docutils.sourceforge.net/rst.html |
| Setext | http://www.valdemar.net/~erik/setext |
| SmartASCII | http://www.gnosis.cx/TPiP |
| Textile | http://www.textism.com/tools/textile |
| txt2html | http://txt2html.sourceforge.net |
| WikiCreole | http://www.wikicreole.org |
| WikiMarkupStandard | http://www.usemod.com/cgi-bin/mb.pl?WikiMarkupStandard |
| Wikitext | http://en.wikipedia.org/wiki/Wikitext |
| YAML | http://www.yaml.org |

## What Now?

Phew! After this strenuous (but useful, I hope) project, it's time for some lighter material. In the next chapter, you create some graphics based on data that is automatically downloaded from the Internet. Piece of cake.

# CHAPTER 21

■■■

# Project 2: Painting a Pretty Picture

In this project, you learn how you can create graphics in Python. More specifically, you create a PDF file with graphics helping you visualize data that you read from a text file. While you could get such functionality from a regular spreadsheet, Python gives you much more power, as you'll see when you get to the second implementation and automatically download your data from the Internet.

In the previous chapter, we looked at HTML and XML—and here is another acronym, which I guess you're probably familiar with: PDF, short for Portable Document Format. PDF is a format created by Adobe that can represent any kind of document with graphics and text. The PDF file is not really editable (as, say, a Microsoft Word file would be), but there is reader software freely available for most platforms, and the PDF file should look the same no matter which reader you use or which platform you are on (as opposed to HTML, with which the correct fonts may not be available, you would normally have to ship pictures as separate files, and so on). If you don't already have a PDF reader, Adobe's own Acrobat Reader is freely available from the Adobe web site (`http://adobe.com/products/acrobat/readstep.html`).

## What's the Problem?

Python is excellent for analyzing data. With its file-handling and string-processing facilities, it's probably easier to create some form of report from a data file than to create something similar in your average spreadsheet, especially if what you want to do requires some complicated programming logic.

You have seen (in Chapter 3) how you can use string formatting to get pretty output—for example, if you want to print numbers in columns. However, sometimes plain text just isn't enough. (As they say, a picture is worth a thousand words.) In this project, you learn the basics of the ReportLab package, which enables you to create graphics and documents in the PDF format (and a few other formats) almost as easily as you created plain text earlier.

As you play with the concepts in this project, I encourage you to find some application that is interesting to you. I have chosen to use data about sunspots (from the Space Weather Prediction Center, a part of the US National Oceanic and Atmospheric Administration) and to create a line diagram from this data.

The program should be able to do the following:

- Download a data file from the Internet.

- Parse the data file and extract the interesting parts.

- Create PDF graphics based on the data.

As in the previous project, these goals might not be fully met by the first prototype.

## Useful Tools

The crucial tool in this project is the graphics-generating package. Quite a few such packages are available. If you visit the Vaults of Parnassus site (http://www.vex.net/parnassus), you will find a separate category for graphics. I have chosen ReportLab because it is easy to use and has extensive functionality for both graphics and document generation in PDF. If you want to go beyond the basics, you might also want to consider the PYX graphics package (http://pyx.sf.net), which is really powerful and has support for TEX-based typography.

To get the ReportLab package, go to the official web site at http://www.reportlab.org. There you will find the software, documentation, and samples. The software should be available at http://www.reportlab.org/downloads.html. Simply download the ReportLab toolkit, uncompress the archive (ReportLab_x.zip, where x is a version number), and put the reportlab directory inside the uncompressed directory in your Python path.

When you have done this, you should be able to import the reportlab module, as follows:

```
>>> import reportlab
>>>
```

> **Note** Although I show you how some ReportLab features work in this project, much more functionality is available. To learn more, I suggest you obtain the user guide and the (separate) graphics guide, made available on the ReportLab web site (on the documentation page). They are quite readable and are much more comprehensive than this one chapter could possibly be.

## Preparations

Before you start programming, you need some data with which to test your program. I have chosen (quite arbitrarily) to use data about sunspots, available from the web site of the Space Weather Prediction Center (http://www.swpc.noaa.gov). You can find the data I use in my examples at http://www.swpc.noaa.gov/ftpdir/weekly/Predict.txt.

This data file is updated weekly and contains information about sunspots and radio flux. (Don't ask me what that means.) Once you have this file, you're ready to start playing with the problem.

Here is a part of the file to give you an idea of how the data looks:

```
#          Predicted Sunspot Number And Radio Flux Values
#                    With Expected Ranges
#
#          -----Sunspot Number------  ----10.7 cm Radio Flux----
# YR MO    PREDICTED   HIGH    LOW   PREDICTED   HIGH    LOW
#-----------------------------------------------------------
2007 12       4.8      5.0     4.7     67.6      70.4    64.7
2008 01       4.3      4.4     4.2     66.7      69.5    63.8
2008 02       4.0      4.1     3.9     66.1      68.9    63.2
2008 03       4.2      4.3     4.0     65.7      68.6    62.8
2008 04       4.6      4.8     4.4     65.7      68.6    62.7
2008 05       5.2      5.6     4.9     65.6      68.7    62.5
2008 06       5.8      6.3     5.2     65.2      68.5    62.0
2008 07       6.3      7.1     5.5     64.9      68.4    61.4
2008 08       7.4      8.6     6.3     65.1      68.9    61.2
2008 09       8.6     10.2     7.0     65.4      69.6    61.2
```

# First Implementation

In this first implementation, let's just put the data into our source code, as a list of tuples. That way, it's easily accessible. Here is an example of how you can do it:

```
data = [
#    Year  Month  Predicted  High    Low
(2007, 12,     4.8,        5.0,    4.7),
(2008,  1,     4.3,        4.4,    4.2),
    # Add more data here
    ]
```

With that out of the way, let's see how you can turn the data into graphics.

## Drawing with ReportLab

ReportLab consists of many parts and enables you to create output in several ways. The most basic module for generating PDFs is pdfgen. It contains a Canvas class with several low-level methods for drawing. To draw a line on a Canvas called c, you call the c.line method, for example.

You'll use the more high-level graphics framework (in the package reportlab.graphics and its submodules), which will enable you to create various shape objects and to add them to a Drawing object that you can later output to a file in PDF format.

Listing 21-1 shows a sample program that draws the string "Hello, world!" in the middle of a 100 × 100-point PDF figure. (You can see the result in Figure 21-1.) The basic structure is as follows: you create a drawing of a given size, you create graphical elements (in this case, a

String object) with certain properties, and then you add the elements to the drawing. Finally, the drawing is rendered into PDF format and saved to a file.

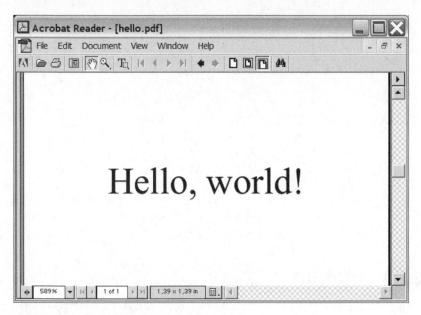

**Figure 21-1.** *A simple ReportLab figure*

**Listing 21-1.** *A Simple ReportLab Program (hello_report.py)*

```
from reportlab.graphics.shapes import Drawing, String
from reportlab.graphics import renderPDF

d = Drawing(100, 100)
s = String(50, 50, 'Hello, world!', textAnchor='middle')

d.add(s)

renderPDF.drawToFile(d, 'hello.pdf', 'A simple PDF file')
```

The call to renderPDF.drawToFile saves your PDF file to a file called hello.pdf in the current directory.

The main arguments to the String constructor are its x and y coordinates and its text. In addition, you can supply various attributes (such as font size, color, and so on). In this case, I've supplied a textAnchor, which is the part of the string that should be placed at the point given by the coordinates.

**Note**  When you run this program, you may get two warnings: one saying that the Python Imaging Library is not available, and the other that `zlib` is not available. (If you have installed either of these, that warning will, of course, not appear.) You won't need either of these libraries for the code in this project, so you can simply ignore the warnings. And if you don't get the warning, that's not a problem, of course.

## Constructing Some PolyLines

To create a line diagram (a graph) of the sunspot data, you need to create some lines. In fact, you need to create several lines that are linked. ReportLab has a special class for this: `PolyLine`.

A `PolyLine` is created with a list of coordinates as its first argument. This list is of the form `[(x0, y0), (x1, y1), ...]`, with each pair of x and y coordinates making one point on the `PolyLine`. See Figure 21-2 for a simple `PolyLine`.

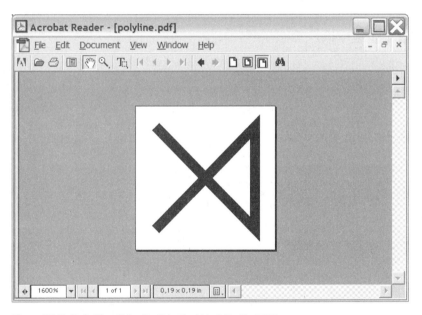

**Figure 21-2.** *PolyLine([(0, 0), (10, 0), (10, 10), (0, 10)])*

To make a line diagram, one polyline must be created for each column in the data set. Each point in these polylines will consist of a time (constructed from the year and month) and a value (which is the number of sunspots, taken from the relevant column). To get one of the columns (the values), list comprehensions can be useful:

```
pred = [row[2] for row in data]
```

Here, pred (for "predicted") will be a list of all the values in the third column of the data. You can use a similar strategy for the other columns. (The time for each row would need to be calculated from both the year and month; for example, *year + month*/12.)

Once you have the values and the timestamps, you can add your polylines to the drawing like this:

```
drawing.add(PolyLine(zip(times, pred), strokeColor=colors.blue))
```

It isn't necessary to set the stroke color, of course, but it makes it easier to tell the lines apart. (Note how zip is used to combine the times and values into a list of tuples.)

## Writing the Prototype

You now have what you need to write your first version of the program. The source code is shown in Listing 21-2.

**Listing 21-2.** *The First Prototype for the Sunspot Graph Program (sunspots_proto.py)*

```
from reportlab.lib import colors
from reportlab.graphics.shapes import *
from reportlab.graphics import renderPDF

data = [
#    Year  Month  Predicted  High  Low
    (2007,  8,    113.2,     114.2, 112.2),
    (2007,  9,    112.8,     115.8, 109.8),
    (2007, 10,    111.0,     116.0, 106.0),
    (2007, 11,    109.8,     116.8, 102.8),
    (2007, 12,    107.3,     115.3,  99.3),
    (2008,  1,    105.2,     114.2,  96.2),
    (2008,  2,    104.1,     114.1,  94.1),
    (2008,  3,     99.9,     110.9,  88.9),
    (2008,  4,     94.8,     106.8,  82.8),
    (2008,  5,     91.2,     104.2,  78.2),
    ]

drawing = Drawing(200, 150)

pred = [row[2]-40 for row in data]
high = [row[3]-40 for row in data]
low = [row[4]-40 for row in data]
times = [200*((row[0] + row[1]/12.0) - 2007)-110 for row in data]

drawing.add(PolyLine(zip(times, pred), strokeColor=colors.blue))
drawing.add(PolyLine(zip(times, high), strokeColor=colors.red))
drawing.add(PolyLine(zip(times, low),  strokeColor=colors.green))
```

```
drawing.add(String(65, 115, 'Sunspots', fontSize=18, fillColor=colors.red))

renderPDF.drawToFile(drawing, 'report1.pdf', 'Sunspots')
```

As you can see, I have adjusted the values and timestamps to get the positioning right. The resulting drawing is shown in Figure 21-3.

**Figure 21-3.** *A simple sunspot graph*

Although it is pleasing to have made a program that works, there is clearly still room for improvement.

## Second Implementation

So, what did you learn from your prototype? You have figured out the basics of how to draw stuff with ReportLab. You have also seen how you can extract the data in a way that works well for drawing your graph. However, there are some weaknesses in the program. To position things properly, I had to add some ad hoc modifications to the values and timestamps. And the program doesn't actually get the data from anywhere (or, rather, it "gets" the data from a list inside the program itself, rather than reading it from an outside source).

Unlike Project 1 (in Chapter 20), the second implementation won't be much larger or more complicated than the first. It will be an incremental improvement that uses some more appropriate features from ReportLab and actually fetches its data from the Internet.

## Getting the Data

As you saw in Chapter 14, you can fetch files across the Internet with the standard module urllib. Its function urlopen works in a manner quite similar to open, but takes a URL instead of a file name as its argument. When you have opened the file and read its contents, you need to filter out what you don't need. The file contains empty lines (consisting of only whitespace) and lines beginning with some special characters (# and :). The program should ignore these. (See the sample file fragment in the section "Preparations" earlier in this chapter.)

Assuming that the URL is kept in a variable called URL, and that the variable COMMENT_CHARS has been set to the string '#:', you can get a list of rows (as in our original program) like this:

```
data = []
for line in urlopen(URL).readlines():
    if not line.isspace() and not line[0] in COMMENT_CHARS:
        data.append([float(n) for n in line.split()])
```

The preceding code will include all the columns in the data list, although you aren't particularly interested in the ones pertaining to radio flux. However, those columns will be filtered out when you extract the columns you really need (as you did in the original program).

---

■**Note** If you are using a data source of your own (or if, by the time you read this, the data format of the sunspot file has changed), you will, of course, need to modify this code accordingly.

---

## Using the LinePlot Class

If you thought getting the data was surprisingly simple, drawing a prettier line plot isn't much of a challenge either. In a situation like this, it's best to thumb through the documentation (in this case, the ReportLab docs) to see if a feature that can do what you need already exists, so you don't need to implement it all yourself. Luckily, there is just such a thing: the LinePlot class from the module reportlab.graphics.charts.lineplots. Of course, you could have looked for this to begin with, but in the spirit of rapid prototyping, you just used what was at hand to see what you could do. Now it's time to go one step further.

The LinePlot is instantiated without any arguments, and then you set its attributes before adding it to the Drawing. The main attributes you need to set are x, y, height, width, and data. The first four should be self-explanatory; the latter is simply a list of point-lists, where a point-list is a list of tuples, like the one you used in your PolyLines.

To top it off, let's set the stroke color of each line. The final code is shown in Listing 21-3. The resulting figure (which will, of course, look quite a bit different with different input data) is shown in Figure 21-4.

**Listing 21-3.** *The Final Sunspot Program (sunspots.py)*

```
from urllib import urlopen
from reportlab.graphics.shapes import *
from reportlab.graphics.charts.lineplots import LinePlot
from reportlab.graphics.charts.textlabels import Label
from reportlab.graphics import renderPDF

URL = 'http://www.swpc.noaa.gov/ftpdir/weekly/Predict.txt'
COMMENT_CHARS = '#:'


drawing = Drawing(400, 200)
data = []
for line in urlopen(URL).readlines():
    if not line.isspace() and not line[0] in COMMENT_CHARS:
        data.append([float(n) for n in line.split()])

pred = [row[2] for row in data]
high = [row[3] for row in data]
low = [row[4] for row in data]
times = [row[0] + row[1]/12.0 for row in data]

lp = LinePlot()
lp.x = 50
lp.y = 50
lp.height = 125
lp.width = 300
lp.data = [zip(times, pred), zip(times, high), zip(times, low)]
lp.lines[0].strokeColor = colors.blue
lp.lines[1].strokeColor = colors.red
lp.lines[2].strokeColor = colors.green

drawing.add(lp)

drawing.add(String(250, 150, 'Sunspots',
            fontSize=14, fillColor=colors.red))


renderPDF.drawToFile(drawing, 'report2.pdf', 'Sunspots')
```

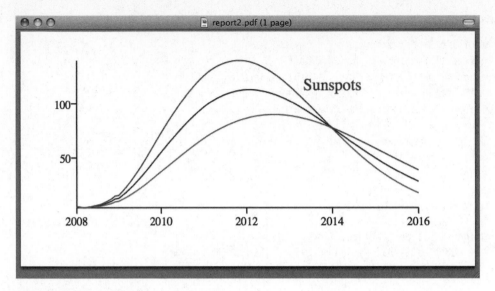

**Figure 21-4.** *The final sunspot graph*

# Further Exploration

Many graphics and plotting packages are available for Python. One good alternative to ReportLab is PyX, which I mentioned earlier in this chapter. It is also possible to use wxPython (discussed in Chapter 12) to create vector graphics files of different kinds.

Using either ReportLab or PyX (or some other package), you could try to incorporate automatically generated graphics into a document (perhaps generating parts of that as well). You could use some of the techniques from Chapter 20 to add markup to the text. If you want to create a PDF document, Platypus, a part of ReportLab, is useful for that. (You could also integrate the PDF graphics with some typesetting system such as LaTeX.) If you want to create web pages, there are ways of creating pixmap graphics (such as GIF or PNG) using Python as well—just do a web search on the topic.

If your primary goal is to plot data (which is what we did in this project), you have many alternatives to ReportLab and PyX. One good option is Matplotlib/pylab (`http://matplotlib.sf.net`), but a lot of other (similar) packages are available.

## What Now?

In the first project, you learned how to add markup to a plain-text file by creating an extensible parser. In the next project, you learn about analyzing marked-up text (in XML) by using parser mechanisms that already exist in the Python standard library. The goal of the project is to use a single XML file to specify an entire web site, which will then be generated automatically (with files, directories, added headers, and footers) by your program. The techniques you learn in the next project will be applicable to XML parsing in general, and with XML being used in an increasing number of different settings, that can't hurt.

■■■

# CHAPTER 22

# Project 3: XML for All Occasions

I mentioned XML briefly in Project 1. Now it's time to examine it in more detail. In this project, you see how XML can be used to represent many kinds of data, and how XML files can be processed with the Simple API for XML, or SAX. The goal of this project is to generate a full web site from a single XML file that describes the various web pages and directories.

In this chapter, I assume that you know what XML is and how to write it. If you know some HTML, you're already familiar with the basics. XML isn't really a specific language (such as HTML); it's more like a set of rules that define a *class* of languages. Basically, you still write tags the same way as in HTML, but in XML you can invent tag names yourself. Such specific sets of tag names and their structural relationships can be described in *Document Type Definitions* or *XML Schema*—I won't be discussing those here.

For a concise description of what XML is, see the World Wide Web Consortium's (W3C's) "XML in 10 points" (`http://www.w3.org/XML/1999/XML-in-10-points`). A more thorough tutorial can be found on the W3Schools web site (`http://www.w3schools.com/xml`). For more information about SAX, see the official SAX web site (`http://www.saxproject.org`).

## What's the Problem?

The general problem you'll be attacking in this project is to parse (read and process) XML files. Because you can use XML to represent practically anything, and you can do whatever you want with the data when you parse it, the applications are boundless (as the title of this chapter indicates).

The specific problem tackled in this chapter is to generate a complete web site from a single XML file that contains the structure of the site and the basic contents of each page.

Before you proceed with this project, I suggest that you take a few moments to read a bit about XML and to check out its applications. That might give you a better understanding of when it might be a useful file format and when it would just be overkill. (After all, plain-text files can be just fine when they're all you need.)

### ANYTHING, YOU SAY?

You may be skeptical about what you can really represent with XML. Well, let me give you just a few examples of the uses of XML:

- To mark up text for ordinary document processing—for example, in the form of XHTML (http://www.w3.org/TR/xhtml1) or DocBook XML (http://www.docbook.org)

- To represent music (http://musicxml.org)

- To represent human moods, emotions, and character traits (http://xml.coverpages.org/humanML.html)

- To describe any physical object (http://xml.coverpages.org/pml-ons.html)

- To call Python methods across a network (using XML-RPC, demonstrated in Chapter 27)

A sampling of existing applications of XML may be found on the XML Cover Pages (http://xml.coverpages.org/xml.html#applications) and at CBEL (http://www.cbel.com/xml_markup_languages).

Let's define the specific goals for the project:

- The entire web site should be described by a single XML file, which should include information about individual web pages and directories.

- The program should create the directories and web pages as needed.

- It should be easy to change the general design of the entire web site and regenerate all the pages with the new design.

This last point is perhaps enough to make it all worthwhile, but there are other benefits. By placing all your contents in a single XML file, you could easily write other programs that use the same XML processing techniques to extract various kinds of information, such as tables of contents, indices for custom search engines, and so on. And even if you don't use this for your web site, you could use it to create HTML-based slide shows (or, by using something like ReportLab, discussed in the previous chapter, you could even create PDF slide shows).

## Useful Tools

Python has some built-in XML support, but if you're using an old version, you may need to install some extras yourself. In this project, you'll need a functioning SAX parser. To see if you have a usable SAX parser, try to execute the following:

```
>>> from xml.sax import make_parser
>>> parser = make_parser()
```

In all likelihood, no exceptions will be raised when you do this. In that case, you're all set and can continue to the "Preparations" section.

---

**■Tip**  Plenty of XML tools for Python are out there. One very interesting alternative to the "standard" PyXML framework is Fredrik Lundh's ElementTree (and the C implementation, cElementTree), which is also included in recent versions of the Python standard library, in the package `xml.etree`. If you have an older Python version, you can get ElementTree from `http://effbot.org/zone`. It's quite powerful and easy to use, and may well be worth a look if you're serious about using XML in Python.

---

If you do get an exception (which may be the case for older Python versions), you must install PyXML. First, download the PyXML package from `http://sf.net/projects/pyxml`. There you can find RPM packages for Linux, binary installers for Windows, and source distributions for other platforms. The RPMs are installed with `rpm --install`, and the binary Windows distribution is installed simply by executing it. The source distribution is installed through the standard Python installation mechanism, Distutils. Simply unpack the `tar.gz` file, change to the unpacked directory, and execute the following:

```
$ python setup.py install
```

You should now be able to use the XML tools.

# Preparations

Before you can write the program that processes your XML files, you must design your XML format. What tags do you need, what attributes should they have, and which tags should go where? To find out, let's first consider what it is you want your XML to describe.

The main concepts are web site, directory, page, name, title, and contents:

- You won't be storing any information about the web site itself, so the *web site* is just the top-level element enclosing all the files and directories.

- A *directory* is mainly a container for files and other directories.

- A *page* is a single web page.

- Both directories and web pages need *names*. These will be used as directory names and file names, as they will appear in the file system and the corresponding URLs.

- Each web page should have a *title* (not the same as its file name).

- Each web page will also have some *contents*. You'll just use plain XHTML to represent the contents here. That way, you can simply pass it through to the final web pages and let the browsers interpret it.

In short, your document will consist of a single `website` element, containing several `directory` and `page` elements, each of the directory elements optionally containing more pages and directories. The `directory` and `page` elements will have an attribute called `name`, which will contain their name. In addition, the page tag has a `title` attribute. The page element contains XHTML code (of the type found inside the XHTML body tag). A sample file is shown in Listing 22-1.

**Listing 22-1.** *A Simple Web Site Represented As an XML File (website.xml)*

```
<website>
  <page name="index" title="Home Page">
    <h1>Welcome to My Home Page</h1>

    <p>Hi, there. My name is Mr. Gumby, and this is my home page. Here
    are some of my interests:</p>

    <ul>
      <li><a href="interests/shouting.html">Shouting</a></li>
      <li><a href="interests/sleeping.html">Sleeping</a></li>
      <li><a href="interests/eating.html">Eating</a></li>
    </ul>
  </page>
  <directory name="interests">
    <page name="shouting" title="Shouting">
      <h1>Mr. Gumby's Shouting Page</h1>

      <p>...</p>
    </page>
    <page name="sleeping" title="Sleeping">
      <h1>Mr. Gumby's Sleeping Page</h1>

      <p>...</p>
    </page>
    <page name="eating" title="Eating">
      <h1>Mr. Gumby's Eating Page</h1>

      <p>...</p>
    </page>
  </directory>
</website>
```

# First Implementation

At this point, we haven't yet looked at how XML parsing works. The approach we are using here (called SAX) consists of writing a set of event handlers (just as in GUI programming) and then letting an existing XML parser call these handlers as it reads the XML document.

## WHAT ABOUT DOM?

There are two common ways of dealing with XML in Python (and other programming languages, for that matter): SAX and the Document Object Model (DOM). A SAX parser reads through the XML file and tells you what it sees (text, tags, and attributes), storing only small parts of the document at a time. This makes SAX simple, fast, and memory-efficient, which is why I have chosen to use it in this chapter. DOM takes another approach: it constructs a data structure (the *document tree*), which represents the entire document. This is slower and requires more memory, but can be useful if you want to manipulate the structure of your document, for example.

For information about using DOM in Python, check out the Python Library Reference (`http://www.python.org/doc/current/lib/module-xml.dom.html`). In addition to the standard DOM handling, the standard library contains two other modules: `xml.dom.minidom` (a simplified DOM) and `xml.dom.pulldom` (a cross between SAX and DOM, which reduces memory requirements).

A very fast and simple XML parser (which doesn't really use DOM, but creates a complete document tree from your XML document) is pyRXP (`http://www.reportlab.org/pyrxp.html`). And then there is ElementTree, which is flexible and easy to use.

## Creating a Simple Content Handler

Several event types are available when parsing with SAX, but let's restrict ourselves to three: the beginning of an element (the occurrence of an opening tag), the end of an element (the occurrence of a closing tag), and plain text (characters). To parse the XML file, let's use the parse function from the xml.sax module. This function takes care of reading the file and generating the events, but as it generates these events, it needs some event handlers to call. These event handlers will be implemented as methods of a *content handler* object. You'll subclass the ContentHandler class from xml.sax.handler because it implements all the necessary event handlers (as dummy operations that have no effect), and you can override only the ones you need.

Let's begin with a minimal XML parser (assuming that your XML file is called website.xml):

```
from xml.sax.handler import ContentHandler
from xml.sax import parse

class TestHandler(ContentHandler): pass
parse('website.xml', TestHandler())
```

If you execute this program, seemingly nothing happens, but you shouldn't get any error messages either. Behind the scenes, the XML file is parsed, and the default event handlers are called, but because they don't do anything, you won't see any output.

Let's try a simple extension. Add the following method to the TestHandler class:

```
def startElement(self, name, attrs):
    print name, attrs.keys()
```

This overrides the default startElement event handler. The parameters are the relevant tag name and its attributes (kept in a dictionary-like object). If you run the program again (using website.xml from Listing 22-1), you see the following output:

---

```
website []
page [u'name', u'title']
h1 []
p []
ul []
li []
a [u'href']
li []
a [u'href']
li []
a [u'href']
directory [u'name']
page [u'name', u'title']
h1 []
p []
page [u'name', u'title']
h1 []
p []
page [u'name', u'title']
h1 []
p []
```

---

How this works should be pretty clear. In addition to startElement, you'll use endElement (which takes only a tag name as its argument) and characters (which takes a string as its argument).

The following is an example that uses all these three methods to build a list of the headlines (the h1 elements) of the web site file:

```
from xml.sax.handler import ContentHandler
from xml.sax import parse

class HeadlineHandler(ContentHandler):

    in_headline = False
```

```
    def __init__(self, headlines):
        ContentHandler.__init__(self)
        self.headlines = headlines
        self.data = []


    def startElement(self, name, attrs):
        if name == 'h1':
            self.in_headline = True

    def endElement(self, name):
        if name == 'h1':
            text = ''.join(self.data)
            self.data = []
            self.headlines.append(text)
            self.in_headline = False

    def characters(self, string):
        if self.in_headline:
            self.data.append(string)

headlines = []
parse('website.xml', HeadlineHandler(headlines))

print 'The following <h1> elements were found:'
for h in headlines:
    print h
```

Note that the HeadlineHandler keeps track of whether it's currently parsing text that is inside a pair of h1 tags. This is done by setting self.in_headline to True when startElement finds an h1 tag, and setting self.in_headline to False when endElement finds an h1 tag. The characters method is automatically called when the parser finds some text. As long as the parser is between two h1 tags (self.in_headline is True), characters will append the string (which may be just a part of the text between the tags) to self.data, which is a list of strings. The task of joining these text fragments, appending them to self.headlines (as a single string), and resetting self.data to an empty list also befalls endElement. This general approach (of using Boolean variables to indicate whether you are currently "inside" a given tag type) is quite common in SAX programming.

Running this program (again, with the website.xml file from Listing 22-1), you get the following output:

```
The following <h1> elements were found:
Welcome to My Home Page
Mr. Gumby's Shouting Page
Mr. Gumby's Sleeping Page
Mr. Gumby's Eating Page
```

## Creating HTML Pages

Now you're ready to make the prototype. For now, let's ignore the directories and concentrate on creating HTML pages. You need to create a slightly embellished event handler that does the following:

- At the start of each page element, opens a new file with the given name, and writes a suitable HTML header to it, including the given title

- At the end of each page element, writes a suitable HTML footer to the file, and closes it

- While inside the page element, passes through all tags and characters without modifying them (writes them to the file as they are)

- While not inside a page element, ignores all tags (such as website and directory)

   Most of this is pretty straightforward (at least if you know a bit about how HTML documents are constructed). There are two problems, however, which may not be completely obvious:

- You can't simply "pass through" tags (write them directly to the HTML file you're building) because you are given their names only (and possibly some attributes). You must reconstruct the tags (with angle brackets and so forth) yourself.

- SAX itself gives you no way of knowing whether you are currently "inside" a page element. You must keep track of that sort of thing yourself (as you did in the HeadlineHandler example). For this project, you're interested only in whether or not to pass through tags and characters, so you'll use a Boolean variable called passthrough, which you'll update as you enter and leave the pages.

   See Listing 22-2 for the code for the simple program.

**Listing 22-2.** *A Simple Page Maker Script (pagemaker.py)*

```
from xml.sax.handler import ContentHandler
from xml.sax import parse

class PageMaker(ContentHandler):
    passthrough = False
    def startElement(self, name, attrs):
        if name == 'page':
            self.passthrough = True
            self.out = open(attrs['name'] + '.html', 'w')
            self.out.write('<html><head>\n')
            self.out.write('<title>%s</title>\n' % attrs['title'])
            self.out.write('</head><body>\n')
```

```
        elif self.passthrough:
            self.out.write('<' + name)
            for key, val in attrs.items():
                self.out.write(' %s="%s"' % (key, val))
            self.out.write('>')


    def endElement(self, name):
        if name == 'page':
            self.passthrough = False
            self.out.write('\n</body></html>\n')
            self.out.close()
        elif self.passthrough:
            self.out.write('</%s>' % name)
    def characters(self, chars):
        if self.passthrough: self.out.write(chars)

parse('website.xml', PageMaker ())
```

You should execute this in the directory in which you want your files to appear. Note that even if two pages are in two different directory elements, they will end up in the same real directory. (That will be fixed in our second implementation.)

Again, using the file website.xml from Listing 22-1, you get four HTML files. The file called index.html contains the following:

```
<html><head>
<title>Home Page</title>
</head><body>

    <h1>Welcome to My Home Page</h1>

    <p>Hi, there. My name is Mr. Gumby, and this is my home page. Here
    are some of my interests:</p>

    <ul>
      <li><a href="interests/shouting.html">Shouting</a></li>
      <li><a href="interests/sleeping.html">Sleeping</a></li>
      <li><a href="interests/eating.html">Eating</a></li>
    </ul>

</body></html>
```

Figure 22-1 shows how this page looks when viewed in a browser.

Looking at the code, two main weaknesses should be obvious:

- It uses if statements to handle the various event types. If you need to handle many such event types, your if statements will get large and unreadable.

- The HTML code is hard-wired. It should be easy to replace.

Both of these weaknesses will be addressed in the second implementation.

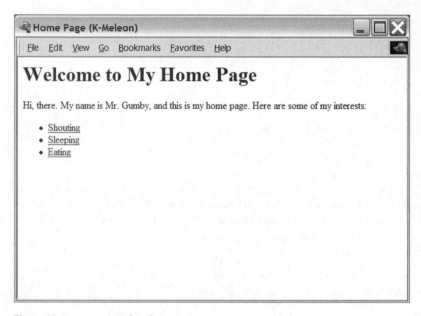

**Figure 22-1.** *A generated web page*

# Second Implementation

Because the SAX mechanism is so low level and basic, you may often find it useful to write a mix-in class that handles some administrative details such as gathering character data, managing Boolean state variables (such as passthrough), or dispatching the events to your own custom event handlers. The state and data handling are pretty simple in this project, so let's focus on the handler dispatch.

## A Dispatcher Mix-In Class

Rather than needing to write large if statements in the standard generic event handlers (such as startElement), it would be nice to just write your own specific ones (such as startPage) and have them called automatically. You can implement that functionality in a mix-in class, and then subclass the mix-in along with ContentHandler.

■**Note**  As mentioned in Chapter 7, a *mix-in* is a class with limited functionality that is meant to be sub-classed along with some other more substantial class.

You want the following functionality in your program:

- When startElement is called with a name such as 'foo', it should attempt to find an event handler called startFoo and call it with the given attributes.

- Similarly, if endElement is called with 'foo', it should try to call endFoo.

- If, in any of these methods, the given handler is not found, a method called defaultStart (or defaultEnd, respectively) will be called, if present. If the default handler isn't present either, nothing should be done.

In addition, some care should be taken with the parameters. The custom handlers (for example, startFoo) do not need the tag name as a parameter, while the custom default handlers (for example, defaultStart) do. Also, only the start handlers need the attributes.

Confused? Let's begin by writing the simplest parts of the class:

```
class Dispatcher:

    # ...

    def startElement(self, name, attrs):
        self.dispatch('start', name, attrs)
    def endElement(self, name):
        self.dispatch('end', name)
```

Here, the basic event handlers are implemented, and they simply call a method called dispatch, which takes care of finding the appropriate handler, constructing the argument tuple, and then calling the handler with those arguments. Here is the code for the dispatch method:

```
def dispatch(self, prefix, name, attrs=None):
    mname = prefix + name.capitalize()
    dname = 'default' + prefix.capitalize()
    method = getattr(self, mname, None)
    if callable(method): args = ()
    else:
        method = getattr(self, dname, None)
        args = name,
    if prefix == 'start': args += attrs,
    if callable(method): method(*args)
```

The following is what happens:

1. From a prefix (either 'start' or 'end') and a tag name (for example, 'page'), construct the method name of the handler (for example, 'startPage').

2. Using the same prefix, construct the name of the default handler (for example, 'defaultStart').

3. Try to get the handler with getattr, using None as the default value.

4. If the result is callable, assign an empty tuple to args.

5. Otherwise, try to get the default handler with getattr, again using None as the default value. Also, set args to a tuple containing only the tag name (because the default handler needs that).

6. If you are dealing with a start handler, add the attributes to the argument tuple (args).

7. If your handler is callable (that is, it is either a viable specific handler or a viable default handler), call it with the correct arguments.

Got that? This basically means that you can now write content handlers like this:

```
class TestHandler(Dispatcher, ContentHandler):
    def startPage(self, attrs):
        print 'Beginning page', attrs['name']
    def endPage(self):
        print 'Ending page'
```

Because the dispatcher mix-in takes care of most of the plumbing, the content handler is fairly simple and readable. (Of course, you'll add more functionality in a little while.)

## Factoring Out the Header, Footer, and Default Handling

This section is much easier than the previous one. Instead of doing the calls to self.out.write directly in the event handler, you'll create separate methods for writing the header and footer. That way, you can easily override these methods by subclassing the event handler. Let's make the default header and footer really simple:

```
def writeHeader(self, title):
    self.out.write("<html>\n  <head>\n    <title>")
    self.out.write(title)
    self.out.write("</title>\n  </head>\n  <body>\n")

def writeFooter(self):
    self.out.write("\n  </body>\n</html>\n")
```

Handling of the XHTML contents was also linked a bit too intimately with the original handlers. The XHTML will now be handled by defaultStart and defaultEnd:

```
def defaultStart(self, name, attrs):
    if self.passthrough:
        self.out.write('<' + name)
        for key, val in attrs.items():
            self.out.write(' %s="%s"' % (key, val))
        self.out.write('>')

def defaultEnd(self, name):
    if self.passthrough:
        self.out.write('</%s>' % name)
```

This works just like before, except that I've moved the code to separate methods (which is usually a good thing). Now, on to the last piece of the puzzle.

## Support for Directories

To create the necessary directories, you need a couple of useful functions from the os and os.path modules. One of these functions is os.makedirs, which makes all the necessary directories in a given path. For example, os.makedirs('foo/bar/baz') creates the directory foo in the current directory, then creates bar in foo, and finally, baz in bar. If foo already exists, only bar and baz are created, and similarly, if bar also exists, only baz is created. However, if baz exists as well, an exception is raised.

To avoid this exception, you need the function os.path.isdir, which checks whether a given path is a directory (that is, whether it exists already). Another useful function is os.path.join, which joins several paths with the correct separator (for example, / in UNIX and so forth).

At all times during the processing, keep the current directory path as a list of directory names, referenced by the variable directory. When you enter a directory, append its name; when you leave it, pop the name off. Assuming that directory is set up properly, you can define a function for ensuring that the current directory exists:

```
def ensureDirectory(self):
    path = os.path.join(*self.directory)
    if not os.path.isdir(path): os.makedirs(path)
```

Notice how I've used argument splicing (with the star operator, *) on the directory list when supplying it to os.path.join.

The base directory of our web site (for example, public_html) can be given as an argument to the constructor, which then looks like this:

```
def __init__(self, directory):
    self.directory = [directory]
    self.ensureDirectory()
```

# The Event Handlers

Finally we've come to the event handlers. You need four of them: two for dealing with directories, and two for pages. The directory handlers simply use the directory list and the ensureDirectory method:

```
def startDirectory(self, attrs):
    self.directory.append(attrs['name'])
    self.ensureDirectory()

def endDirectory(self):
    self.directory.pop()
```

The page handlers use the writeHeader and writeFooter methods. In addition, they set the passthrough variable (to pass through the XHTML), and—perhaps most important—they open and close the file associated with the page:

```
def startPage(self, attrs):
    filename = os.path.join(*self.directory+[attrs['name']+'.html'])
    self.out = open(filename, 'w')
    self.writeHeader(attrs['title'])
    self.passthrough = True


def endPage(self):
    self.passthrough = False
    self.writeFooter()
    self.out.close()
```

The first line of startPage may look a little intimidating, but it is more or less the same as the first line of ensureDirectory, except that you add the file name (and give it an .html suffix). The full source code of the program is shown in Listing 22-3.

**Listing 22-3.** *The Web Site Constructor (website.py)*

```
from xml.sax.handler import ContentHandler
from xml.sax import parse
import os

class Dispatcher:

    def dispatch(self, prefix, name, attrs=None):
        mname = prefix + name.capitalize()
        dname = 'default' + prefix.capitalize()
        method = getattr(self, mname, None)
        if callable(method): args = ()
```

```
        else:
            method = getattr(self, dname, None)
            args = name,
        if prefix == 'start': args += attrs,
        if callable(method): method(*args)

    def startElement(self, name, attrs):
        self.dispatch('start', name, attrs)

    def endElement(self, name):
        self.dispatch('end', name)

class WebsiteConstructor(Dispatcher, ContentHandler):

    passthrough = False

    def __init__(self, directory):
        self.directory = [directory]
        self.ensureDirectory()

    def ensureDirectory(self):
        path = os.path.join(*self.directory)
        if not os.path.isdir(path): os.makedirs(path)


    def characters(self, chars):
        if self.passthrough: self.out.write(chars)

    def defaultStart(self, name, attrs):
        if self.passthrough:
            self.out.write('<' + name)
            for key, val in attrs.items():
                self.out.write(' %s="%s"' % (key, val))
            self.out.write('>')

    def defaultEnd(self, name):
        if self.passthrough:
            self.out.write('</%s>' % name)

    def startDirectory(self, attrs):
        self.directory.append(attrs['name'])
        self.ensureDirectory()

    def endDirectory(self):
        self.directory.pop()
```

```python
    def startPage(self, attrs):
        filename = os.path.join(*self.directory+[attrs['name']+'.html'])
        self.out = open(filename, 'w')
        self.writeHeader(attrs['title'])
        self.passthrough = True

    def endPage(self):
        self.passthrough = False
        self.writeFooter()
        self.out.close()

    def writeHeader(self, title):
        self.out.write('<html>\n  <head>\n    <title>')
        self.out.write(title)
        self.out.write('</title>\n  </head>\n  <body>\n')

    def writeFooter(self):
        self.out.write('\n  </body>\n</html>\n')

parse('website.xml', WebsiteConstructor('public_html'))
```

Listing 22-3 generates the following files and directories:

- public_html/

- public_html/index.html

- public_html/interests

- public_html/interests/shouting.html

- public_html/interests/sleeping.html

- public_html/interests/eating.html

## ENCODING BLUES

If your XML file contains special characters (those with ordinal numbers above 127), you may be in trouble. The XML parser uses Unicode strings during its processing, and returns those to you (for example, in the `characters` event handler). Unicode handles the special characters just fine. However, if you want to convert this Unicode string to an ordinary string (which is what happens when you print it, for example), an exception is raised (assuming that your default encoding is ASCII):

```python
>>> some_string = u'Möööse'
>>> some_string
u'M\xf6\xf6\xf6se'
>>> print some_string
```

```
Traceback (most recent call last):
  File "<stdin>", line 1, in ?
UnicodeError: ASCII encoding error: ordinal not in range(128)
```

As you can see, the error message is "ASCII encoding error," which actually means that Python has tried to *encode* the Unicode string with the ASCII encoding, which isn't possible when it contains special characters like this. (You can find the default encoding of your installation using the `sys.getdefaultencoding` function. You can also change it with the `sys.setdefaultencoding`, but only in the site-wide customization file called `site.py`.) Encoding is done with the `encode` method:

```
>>> some_string.encode('ascii')
Traceback (most recent call last):
  File "<stdin>", line 1, in ?
UnicodeError: ASCII encoding error: ordinal not in range(128)
```

To solve this problem, you need to use another encoding, such as ISO8859-1 (which is fine for most European languages):

```
>>> print some_string.encode('iso8859-1')
Möööse
```

(The actual appearance of the output will depend on your terminal emulator.)

Note that if you're using non-ASCII characters directly in your source code, you need to mark that, so that the interpreter knows what to do with the file. For Latin 1 (another name for ISO8859-1), you could simply put the following comment into your file (directly after the pound bang line):

```
# -*- coding: latin-1 -*-
```

You can find more information about such encodings at the W3C web site (`http://www.w3.org/International/O-charset.html`).

# Further Exploration

Now you have the basic program. What can you do with it? Here are some suggestions:

- Create a new `ContentHandler` for generating a table of contents or a menu (with links) for the web site.

- Add navigational aids to the web pages that tell the users where (in which directory) they are.

- Create a subclass of `WebsiteConstructor` that overrides `writeHeader` and `writeFooter` to provide customized design.

- Create another `ContentHandler` that constructs a single web page from the XML file.

- Create a `ContentHandler` that summarizes your web site somehow, for example in RSS.

- Check out other tools for transforming XML, especially XML Transformations (XSLT).

- Create one or more PDF documents based on the XML file, using a tool such as ReportLab's Platypus (`http://www.reportlab.org`).

- Make it possible to edit the XML file through a web interface (see Chapter 25).

## What Now?

After this foray into the world of XML parsing, let's do some more network programming. In the next chapter, you create a program that can gather news items from various network sources (such as web pages and Usenet groups) and generate custom news reports for you.

■ ■ ■

# CHAPTER 23

# Project 4: In the News

In this project, you see how you go from a simple prototype without any form of abstraction (no functions, no classes) to a generic system in which some important abstractions have been added. Also, you get a brief introduction to the `nntplib` library, which lets you interact with Network News Transfer Protocol (NNTP) servers.

NNTP is a standard network protocol for managing messages posted on Usenet discussion groups. NNTP servers form a global network that collectively manages these newsgroups, and through an NNTP client (also called a *newsreader*) you can post and read messages. Most recent web browsers include NNTP clients, and separate clients exist as well.

The main network of NNTP servers, called Usenet, was established in 1980 (although the NNTP protocol wasn't used until 1985). Compared to current Web 2.0 trends, this is quite "old school," but most of the Internet is based (to some degree) on such old-school technologies,[1] and it probably doesn't hurt to play around with the low-level stuff a bit. Also, you could always replace the NNTP stuff in this chapter with some news-gathering module of your own (perhaps using the web API of some social networking site like Facebook or MySpace).

## What's the Problem?

The program you write in this project will be an information-gathering agent, a program that can gather information (more specifically, news) and compile a report for you. Given the network functionality you have already encountered, that might not seem very difficult—and it isn't, really. But in this project you go a bit beyond the simple "download a file with `urllib`" approach. You use another network library that is a bit more difficult to use than `urllib`, namely `nntplib`. In addition, you get to refactor the program to allow many types of news sources and various types of destinations, making a clear separation between the front end and the back end, with the main engine in the middle.

---

1. Did you know, for example, that the discussion groups at `http://groups.google.com`, such as `sci.math` and `rec.arts.sf.written`, are really Usenet groups under the hood?

The main goals for the final program are as follows:

- The program should be able to gather news from many different sources.

- It should be easy to add new news sources (and even new kinds of sources).

- The program should be able to dispatch its compiled news report to many different destinations, in many different formats.

- It should be easy to add new destinations (and even new kinds of destinations).

## Useful Tools

For this project, you don't need to install separate software. However, you do need some standard library modules, including one that you haven't seen before, nntplib, which deals with NNTP servers. Instead of explaining all the details of that module, let's examine it through some prototyping.

You will also be using the time module (covered in Chapter 10).

## Preparations

To be able to use nntplib, you need to have access to an NNTP server. If you're not sure whether you do, you could ask your ISP or system administrator for details. In the code examples in this chapter, I use the newsgroup comp.lang.python.announce, so you should make sure that your news (NNTP) server has that group, or you should find some other group you would like to use. It is important that the NNTP server support the NEWNEWS command. If it doesn't, the programs in this chapter won't work. (If you don't know whether your server supports this command, simply try to execute the programs and see what happens.)

If you don't have access to an NNTP server, or your server's NEWNEWS command is disabled, several open servers are available for anyone to use. A quick web search for "free nntp server" should give you some servers to choose from, or you could check out http://www.newzbot.com as a starting point.

Assuming that your news server is news.foo.bar (this is not a real server name, and won't work), you can test your NNTP server like this:

```
>>> from nntplib import NNTP
>>> server = NNTP('news.foo.bar')
>>> server.group('comp.lang.python.announce')[0]
```

---

**■Note**  To connect to some servers, you may need to supply additional parameters for authentication. Consult the Python Library Reference (http://docs.python.org/lib/module-nntplib.html) for details on the optional parameters of the NNTP constructor.

---

The result of the last line should be a string beginning with `'211'` (basically meaning that the server has the group you asked for) or `'411'` (which means that the server doesn't have the group). It might look something like this:

```
'211 51 1876 1926 comp.lang.python.announce'
```

If the returned string starts with `'411'`, you should use a newsreader to look for another group you might want to use. (You may also get an exception with an equivalent error message.) If an exception is raised, perhaps you got the server name wrong. Another possibility is that you were "timed out" between the time you created the server object and the time you called the group method—the server may allow you to stay connected for only a short period of time (such as 10 seconds). If you're having trouble typing that fast, simply put the code in a script and execute it (with an added `print`) or put the server object creation and method call on the same line (separated by a semicolon).

# First Implementation

In the spirit of prototyping, let's just tackle the problem head on. The first thing you want to do is download the most recent messages from a newsgroup on an NNTP server. To keep things simple, just print out the result to standard output (with `print`).

Before looking at the details of the implementation, you might want to browse the source code in Listing 23-1 later in this section, and perhaps even execute the program to see how it works.

The program logic isn't very complicated, but you need to figure out how to use `nntplib`. You'll be using one single object of the NNTP class. As you saw in the previous section, this class is instantiated with a single constructor argument—the name of an NNTP server. You need to call three methods on this instance:

- `newnews`, which returns a list of articles posted after a certain date and time

- `head`, which gives you various information about the articles (most notably their subjects)

- `body`, which gives you the main text of the articles

The `newnews` method requires a date string (in the form *yymmdd*) and an hour string (in the form *hhmmss*) in addition to the group name. To construct these, you need some functions from the `time` module: `time`, `localtime`, and `strftime`. (See Chapter 10 for more information about the `time` module.)

Let's say you want to download all new messages since yesterday. To do this, you need to construct a date and time 24 hours before the current time. The current time (in seconds) is found with the `time` function. To find the time yesterday, all you need to do is subtract 24 hours (in seconds). To be able to use this time with `strftime`, it must be converted to a time tuple (see Chapter 10) with the `localtime` function. The code for finding "yesterday" then becomes as follows:

```
from time import time, localtime
day = 24 * 60 * 60 # Number of seconds in one day
yesterday = localtime(time() - day)
```

The next step is to format the time correctly, as two strings. For that, you use `strftime`, as in the following example:

```
>>> from time import strftime
>>> strftime('%y%m%d')
'020409'
>>> strftime('%H%M%S')
'141625'
```

The string argument to `strftime` is a *format string*, which specifies the format to use for the time. Most characters are used directly in the resulting time string, but those preceded by a percent sign are replaced with various time-related values. For instance, `%y` is replaced with the last two digits of the year, `%m` with the month (as a two-digit number), and so on. For a full list of these codes, consult the Python Library Reference (`http://docs.python.org/lib/module-time.html`). When supplied only with a format string, `strftime` uses the current time. Optionally, you may supply a time tuple as a second argument:

```
from time import strftime
date = strftime('%y%m%d', yesterday)
hour = strftime('%H%M%S', yesterday)
```

---

■**Tip**  The `datetime` module gives you a more object-oriented way of dealing with dates and times. Check out the standard library documentation at `http://docs.python.org/lib/module-datetime.html`.

---

Now that you have the date and time in the correct format for the `newnews` method, you just need to instantiate a server and call the method. Using the same fictitious server name as earlier, the code becomes as follows:

```
servername = 'news.foo.bar'
group = 'comp.lang.python.announce'
server = NNTP(servername)

ids = server.newnews(group, date, hour)[1]
```

Note that I've extracted the second argument of the tuple that is returned from `newnews`. It's sufficient for this example's purposes: a list of *article IDs* of the articles that were posted after the given date and hour.

---

■**Note**  The `newnews` method sends a `NEWNEWS` command to the NNTP server. As described in the "Preparations" section, this command may not be understood or supported by the server, giving you the error code 500 or 501, respectively, or disabled by the administrator, giving the error code 502. In such cases, you should find another server.

---

You need the article IDs when you call the head and body methods later, to tell the server which article you're talking about.

So, you're all set to start using head and body (for each of the IDs) and printing out the results. Just like newnews, head and body return tuples with various information (such as whether or not the command succeeded), but you care only about the returned data itself, which is the fourth element—a list of strings. The body of the article with a given ID can be fetched like this:

```
body = server.body(id)[3]
```

From the head (a list of lines containing various information about the article, such as the subject, the date it was posted, and so on), you want only the subject. The subject line is in the form "Subject: Hello, world!", so you need to find the line that starts with "Subject:" and extract the rest of the line. Because (according to the NNTP standard) "subject" can also be spelled as all lowercase, all uppercase, or any kind of combination of uppercase and lowercase letters, you simply call the lower method on the line and compare it to "subject". Here is the loop that finds the subject within the data returned by the call to head:

```
head = server.head(id)[3]
for line in head:
    if line.lower().startswith('subject:'):
        subject = line[9:]
        break
```

The break isn't strictly necessary, but when you've found the subject, there's no need to iterate over the rest of the lines.

After having extracted the subject and body of an article, you just print it, for instance, like this:

```
print subject
print '-'*len(subject)
print '\n'.join(body)
```

After printing all the articles, you call server.quit(), and that's it. In a UNIX shell such as bash, you could run this program like this:

```
$ python newsagent1.py | less
```

The use of less is useful for reading the articles one at a time. If you have no such pager program available, you could rewrite the print part of the program to store the resulting text in a file, which you'll also be doing in the second implementation (see Chapter 11 for more information about file handling). If you don't get any output, try looking further back than yesterday. The source code for the simple news-gathering agent is shown in Listing 23-1.

**Listing 23-1.** *A Simple News-Gathering Agent (newsagent1.py)*

```
from nntplib import NNTP
from time import strftime, time, localtime
```

```
day = 24 * 60 * 60 # Number of seconds in one day

yesterday = localtime(time() - day)
date = strftime('%y%m%d', yesterday)
hour = strftime('%H%M%S', yesterday)

servername = 'news.foo.bar'
group = 'comp.lang.python.announce'
server = NNTP(servername)

ids = server.newnews(group, date, hour)[1]


for id in ids:
    head = server.head(id)[3]
    for line in head:
        if line.lower().startswith('subject:'):
            subject = line[9:]
            break

    body = server.body(id)[3]

    print subject
    print '-'*len(subject)
    print '\n'.join(body)

server.quit()
```

# Second Implementation

The first implementation worked, but was quite inflexible in that it let you retrieve news only from Usenet discussion groups. In the second implementation, you fix that by refactoring the code a bit. You add structure and abstraction by creating some classes and methods to represent the various parts of the code. Once you've done that, some of the parts may be replaced by other classes much more easily than you could replace parts of the code in the original program.

Again, before immersing yourself in the details of the second implementation, you might want to skim (and perhaps execute) the code in Listing 23-2, later in this chapter.

---

■**Note** You need to set the `clpa_server` variable to a usable server before the code in Listing 23-2 will work.

---

So, what classes do you need? Let's just do a quick review of the important nouns in the problem description, as suggested in Chapter 7: information, agent, news, report, network, news source, destination, front end, back end, and main engine. This list of nouns suggests the following main classes (or kinds of classes): NewsAgent, NewsItem, Source, and Destination. The various sources will constitute the front end, and the destinations will constitute the back end, with the news agent sitting in the middle.

The easiest of these is NewsItem. It represents only a piece of data, consisting of a title and a body (a short text), and can be implemented as follows:

```
class NewsItem:

    def __init__(self, title, body):
        self.title = title
        self.body = body
```

To find out exactly what is needed from the news sources and the news destinations, it could be a good idea to start by writing the agent itself. The agent must maintain two lists: one of sources and one of destinations. Adding sources and destinations can be done through the methods addSource and addDestination:

```
class NewsAgent:

    def __init__(self):
        self.sources = []
        self.destinations = []

    def addSource(self, source):
        self.sources.append(source)

    def addDestination(self, dest):
        self.destinations.append(dest)
```

The only thing missing now is a method to distribute the news items from the sources to the destinations. During distribution, each destination must have a method that returns all its news items, and each source needs a method for receiving all the news items that are being distributed. Let's call these methods getItems and receiveItems. In the interest of flexibility, let's just require getItems to return an arbitrary iterator of NewsItems. To make the destinations easier to implement, however, let's assume that receiveItems is callable with a sequence argument (which can be iterated over more than once, to make a table of contents before listing the news items, for example). After this has been decided, the distribute method of NewsAgent simply becomes as follows:

```
    def distribute(self):
        items = []
        for source in self.sources:
            items.extend(source.getItems())
        for dest in self.destinations:
            dest.receiveItems(items)
```

This iterates through all the sources, building a list of news items. Then it iterates through all the destinations and supplies each of them with the full list of news items.

Now, all you need is a couple of sources and destinations. To begin testing, you can simply create a destination that works like the printing in the first prototype:

```
class PlainDestination:

    def receiveItems(self, items):
        for item in items:
            print item.title
            print '-'*len(item.title)
            print item.body
```

The formatting is the same; the difference is that you have *encapsulated* the formatting. It is now one of several alternative destinations, rather than a hard-coded part of the program. A slightly more complicated destination (HTMLDestination, which produces HTML) can be seen in Listing 23-2, later in this chapter. It builds on the approach of PlainDestination with a few extra features:

- The text it produces is HTML.

- It writes the text to a specific file, rather than standard output.

- It creates a table of contents in addition to the main list of items.

And that's it, really. The table of contents is created using hyperlinks that link to parts of the page. You accomplish this by using links of the form <a  href="#nn">...</a> (where nn is some number), which leads to the headline with the enclosing anchor tag <a  name="nn">...</a> (where nn should be the same number as in the table of contents). The table of contents and the main listing of news items are built in two different for loops. You can see a sample result (using the upcoming NNTPSource) in Figure 23-1.

When thinking about the design, I considered using a generic superclass to represent news sources and one to represent news destinations. As it turns out, the sources and destinations don't really share any behavior, so there is no point in using a common superclass. As long as they implement the necessary methods (getItems and receiveItems) correctly, the NewsAgent will be happy. (This is an example of using a *protocol*, as described in Chapter 9, rather than requiring a specific, common superclass.)

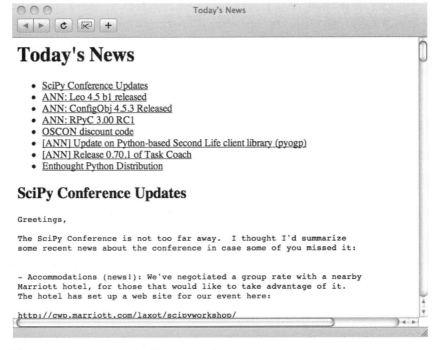

**Figure 23-1.** *An automatically generated news page*

When creating an NNTPSource, much of the code can be snipped from the original proto-type. As you will see in Listing 23-2, the main differences from the original are the following:

- The code has been encapsulated in the getItems method. The servername and group variables are now arguments to the constructor. Also a window (a time window) is added, instead of assuming that you want the news since yesterday (which is equivalent to set-ting window to 1).

- To extract the subject, a Message object from the email module is used (constructed with the message_from_string function). This is the sort of thing you might add to later ver-sions of your program as you thumb through the documentation (to see if features that can do what you need already exist).

- Instead of printing each news item directly, a NewsItem object is yielded (making getItems a generator).

To show the flexibility of the design, let's add another news source—one that can extract news items from web pages (using regular expressions; see Chapter 10 for more information). SimpleWebSource (see Listing 23-2) takes a URL and two regular expressions (one representing titles and one representing bodies) as its constructor arguments. In getItems, it uses the regular expression methods findall to find all the occurrences (titles and bodies) and zip to combine these. It then iterates over the list of (title, body) pairs, yielding a NewsItem for each. As you can see, adding new kinds of sources (or destinations, for that matter) isn't very difficult.

To put the code to work, let's instantiate an agent, some sources, and some destinations. In the function runDefaultSetup (which is called if the module is run as a program), several such objects are instantiated:

- A SimpleWebSource for the BBC News web site, which uses two simple regular expressions to extract the information it needs

---

■**Note**   The layout of the HTML on the BBC News pages might change, in which case you need to rewrite the regular expressions. This also applies if you are using some other page. Just view the HTML source and try to find a pattern that applies.

---

- An NNTPSource for comp.lang.python, with the time window set to 1, so it works just like the first prototype

- A PlainDestination, which prints all the news gathered

- An HTMLDestination, which generates a news page called news.html

When all of these objects have been created and added to the NewsAgent, the distribute method is called.

You can run the program like this:

```
$ python newsagent2.py
```

The resulting news.html page is shown in Figure 23-2.

The full source code of the second implementation is found in Listing 23-2.

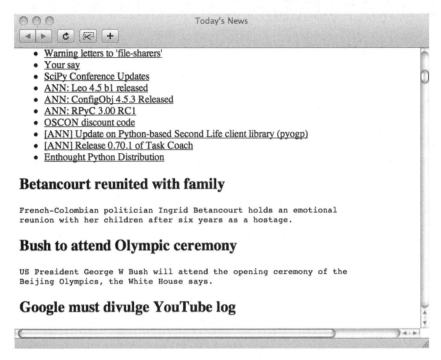

**Figure 23-2.** *A news page with more than one source*

**Listing 23-2.** *A More Flexible News-Gathering Agent (newsagent2.py)*

```python
from nntplib import NNTP
from time import strftime, time, localtime
from email import message_from_string
from urllib import urlopen
import textwrap
import re

day = 24 * 60 * 60 # Number of seconds in one day

def wrap(string, max=70):
    """
    Wraps a string to a maximum line width.
    """
```

```
        return '\n'.join(textwrap.wrap(string)) + '\n'

class NewsAgent:
    """
    An object that can distribute news items from news
    sources to news destinations.
    """
    def __init__(self):
        self.sources = []
        self.destinations = []

    def addSource(self, source):
        self.sources.append(source)

    def addDestination(self, dest):
        self.destinations.append(dest)

    def distribute(self):
        """
        Retrieve all news items from all sources, and
        Distribute them to all destinations.
        """
        items = []
        for source in self.sources:
            items.extend(source.getItems())
        for dest in self.destinations:
            dest.receiveItems(items)

class NewsItem:
    """
    A simple news item consisting of a title and body text.
    """
    def __init__(self, title, body):
        self.title = title
        self.body = body

class NNTPSource:
    """
    A news source that retrieves news items from an NNTP group.
    """
    def __init__(self, servername, group, window):
        self.servername = servername
        self.group = group
        self.window = window

    def getItems(self):
```

```
        start = localtime(time() - self.window*day)
        date = strftime('%y%m%d', start)
        hour = strftime('%H%M%S', start)

        server = NNTP(self.servername)


        ids = server.newnews(self.group, date, hour)[1]

        for id in ids:
            lines = server.article(id)[3]
            message = message_from_string('\n'.join(lines))

            title = message['subject']
            body = message.get_payload()
            if message.is_multipart():
                body = body[0]

            yield NewsItem(title, body)

        server.quit()

class SimpleWebSource:
    """
    A news source that extracts news items from a web page using
    regular expressions.
    """
    def __init__(self, url, titlePattern, bodyPattern):
        self.url = url
        self.titlePattern = re.compile(titlePattern)
        self.bodyPattern = re.compile(bodyPattern)

    def getItems(self):
        text = urlopen(self.url).read()
        titles = self.titlePattern.findall(text)
        bodies = self.bodyPattern.findall(text)
        for title, body in zip(titles, bodies):
            yield NewsItem(title, wrap(body))

class PlainDestination:
    """
    A news destination that formats all its news items as
    plain text.
    """
    def receiveItems(self, items):
        for item in items:
            print item.title
```

```
            print '-'*len(item.title)
            print item.body


class HTMLDestination:
    """
    A news destination that formats all its news items
    as HTML.
    """
    def __init__(self, filename):
        self.filename = filename

    def receiveItems(self, items):

        out = open(self.filename, 'w')
        print >> out, """
        <html>
          <head>
            <title>Today's News</title>
          </head>
          <body>
          <h1>Today's News</h1>
        """

        print >> out, '<ul>'
        id = 0
        for item in items:
            id += 1
            print >> out, '  <li><a href="#%i">%s</a></li>' % (id, item.title)
        print >> out, '</ul>'

        id = 0
        for item in items:
            id += 1
            print >> out, '<h2><a name="%i">%s</a></h2>' % (id, item.title)
            print >> out, '<pre>%s</pre>' % item.body

        print >> out, """
          </body>
        </html>
        """
```

```python
def runDefaultSetup():
    """
    A default setup of sources and destination. Modify to taste.
    """
    agent = NewsAgent()


    # A SimpleWebSource that retrieves news from the
    # BBC News site:
    bbc_url = 'http://news.bbc.co.uk/text_only.stm'
    bbc_title = r'(?s)a href="[^"]*">\s*<b>\s*(.*?)\s*</b>'
    bbc_body = r'(?s)</a>\s*<br />\s*(.*?)\s*<'
    bbc = SimpleWebSource(bbc_url, bbc_title, bbc_body)

    agent.addSource(bbc)

    # An NNTPSource that retrieves news from comp.lang.python.announce:
    clpa_server = 'news.foo.bar' # Insert real server name
    clpa_group = 'comp.lang.python.announce'
    clpa_window = 1
    clpa = NNTPSource(clpa_server, clpa_group, clpa_window)

    agent.addSource(clpa)

    # Add plain-text destination and an HTML destination:
    agent.addDestination(PlainDestination())
    agent.addDestination(HTMLDestination('news.html'))

    # Distribute the news items:
    agent.distribute()

if __name__ == '__main__': runDefaultSetup()
```

# Further Exploration

Because of its extensible nature, this project invites much further exploration. Here are some ideas:

- Create a more ambitious WebSource, using the screen-scraping techniques discussed in Chapter 15.

- Create an RSSSource, which parses RSS, also discussed briefly in Chapter 15.

- Improve the layout for the HTMLDestination.

- Create a page monitor that gives you a news item if a given web page has changed since the last time you examined it. (Just download a copy when it has changed and compare that later. Take a look at the standard library module `filecmp` for comparing files.)

- Create a CGI version of the news script (see Chapter 15).

- Create an `EmailDestination`, which sends you an email message with news items. (See the standard library module `smtplib` for sending email.)

- Add command-line switches to decide which news formats you want. (See the standard library modules `getopt` and `optparse` for some techniques.)

- Give the information about where the news comes from, to allow a fancier layout.

- Try to categorize your news items (by searching for keywords, perhaps).

- Create an `XMLDestination`, which produces XML files suitable for the site builder in Project 3 (Chapter 22). *Voilà*—you have a news web site.

## What Now?

You've done a lot of file creation and file handling (including downloading the required files), and although that is very useful for a lot of things, it isn't very interactive. In the next project, you create a chat server, where you can chat with your friends online. You can even extend it to create your own virtual (textual) environment.

# CHAPTER 24

■ ■ ■

# Project 5: A Virtual Tea Party

In this project, you do some serious network programming. You'll write a chat server—a program that lets several people connect via the Internet and chat with each other in real time. There are many ways to create such a beast in Python. A simple and natural approach might be to use the Twisted framework (discussed in Chapter 14), for example, with the LineReceiver class taking center stage. In this chapter, I stick to the standard libraries, basing the program on the modules asyncore and asynchat. If you like, you could try out some of the alternative methods (such as forking or threading) discussed in Chapter 14.

## What's the Problem?

Online chatting is quite common. Many chat services of various kinds (IRC, instant messaging services, and so forth) are available all over the Internet. Some of these are even full-fledged text-based virtual worlds (see http://www.mudconnect.com for a long list). If you want to set up a chat server, you can just download and install one of the many free server programs. However, writing a chat server yourself is useful for two reasons:

- You learn about network programming.

- You can customize it as much as you want.

The second point suggests that you can start with a simple chat server and develop it into basically any kind of server (including a virtual world), with all the power of Python at your fingertips. Pretty awesome, isn't it?

For now, the chat server project has the following requirements:

- The server should be able to receive multiple connections from different users.

- It should let the users act *in parallel*.

- It should be able to interpret commands such as say or logout.

- The server should be easily extensible.

The two things that will require special tools are the network connections and the asynchronous nature of the program.

# Useful Tools

The only new tools you need in this project are the asyncore module from the standard library and its relative asynchat. I'll describe the basics of how these work. You can find more details about them in the Python Library Reference (http://python.org/doc/lib/module-asyncore.html and http://python.org/doc/lib/module-asynchat.html).

As discussed in Chapter 14, the basic component in a network program is the *socket*. Sockets can be created directly by importing the socket module and using the functions there. So what do you need asyncore for?

The asyncore framework enables you to juggle several users who are connected simultaneously. Imagine a scenario in which you have no special tools for handling this. When you start up the server, it waits for users to connect. When one user is connected, it starts reading data from that user and supplying results through a socket. But what happens if another user is already connected? The second user to connect must wait until the first one has finished. In some cases, that will work just fine, but when you're writing a chat server, the whole point is that more than one user can be connected—how else could users chat with one another?

The asyncore framework is based on an underlying mechanism (the select function from the select module, as discussed in Chapter 14) that allows the server to serve all the connected users in a piecemeal fashion. Instead of reading *all* the available data from one user before going on to the next, only *some* data is read. Also, the server reads only from the sockets where there *is* data to be read. This is done again and again, in a loop. Writing is handled similarly. You could implement this yourself using just the modules socket and select, but asyncore and asynchat provide a very useful framework that takes care of the details for you. (For alternative ways of implementing parallel user connections, see the section "Multiple Connections" in Chapter 14.)

# Preparations

The first thing you need is a computer that's connected to a network (such as the Internet); otherwise, others won't be able to connect to your chat server. (It is possible to connect to the chat server from your own machine, but that's not much fun in the long run, is it?) To be able to connect, the user must know the address of your machine (a machine name such as foo.bar.baz.com or an IP address). In addition, the user must know the *port number* used by your server. You can set this in your program; in the code in this chapter, I use the (rather arbitrary) port number 5005.

---

**■Note** As mentioned in Chapter 14, certain port numbers are restricted and require administrator privileges. In general, numbers greater than 1023 are okay.

---

To test your server, you need a *client*—the program on the user side of the interaction. A simple program for this sort of thing is telnet (which basically lets you connect to any socket server). In UNIX, you probably have this program available on the command line:

```
$ telnet some.host.name 5005
```

The preceding command connects to the machine some.host.name on port 5005. To connect to the same machine on which you're running the telnet command, simply use the machine name localhost. (You might want to supply an escape character through the -e switch to make sure you can quit telnet easily. See the man page for more details.)

In Windows, you can use either the standard telnet command (in a command-prompt window) or a terminal emulator with telnet functionality, such as PuTTY (software and more information available at http://www.chiark.greenend.org.uk/~sgtatham/putty). However, if you are installing new software, you might as well get a client program tailored to chatting. MUD (or MUSH or MOO or some other related acronym) clients[1] are quite suitable for this sort of thing. My client of choice is TinyFugue (software and more information available at http://tinyfugue.sf.net). It is mainly designed for use in UNIX. (Several clients are available for Windows as well; just do a web search for "mud client" or something similar.)

# First Implementation

Let's break things down a bit. We need to create two main classes: one representing the chat server and one representing each of the chat sessions (the connected users).

## The ChatServer Class

To create the basic ChatServer, you subclass the dispatcher class from asyncore. The dispatcher is basically just a socket object, but with some extra event-handling features, which you'll be using in a minute.

See Listing 24-1 for a basic chat server program (that does very little).

**Listing 24-1.** *A Minimal Server Program*

```
from asyncore import dispatcher
import asyncore

class ChatServer(dispatcher): pass

s = ChatServer()
asyncore.loop()
```

If you run this program, nothing happens. To make the server do anything interesting, you should call its create_socket method to create a socket, and its bind and listen methods to bind the socket to a specific port number and to tell it to listen for incoming connections. (That is what servers do, after all.) In addition, you'll override the handle_accept event-handling method to actually do something when the server accepts a client connection. The resulting program is shown in Listing 24-2.

---

1. MUD stands for Multi-User Dungeon/Domain/Dimension. MUSH stands for Multi-User Shared Hallucination. MOO means MUD, object-oriented. See, for example, Wikipedia (http://en.wikipedia.org/wiki/MUD) for more information.

**Listing 24-2.** *A Server That Accepts Connections*

```
from asyncore import dispatcher
import socket, asyncore

class ChatServer(dispatcher):

    def handle_accept(self):
        conn, addr = self.accept()
        print 'Connection attempt from', addr[0]

s = ChatServer()
s.create_socket(socket.AF_INET, socket.SOCK_STREAM)
s.bind(('', 5005))
s.listen(5)
asyncore.loop()
```

The handle_accept method calls self.accept, which lets the client connect. This returns a connection (a socket that is specific for this client) and an address (information about which machine is connecting). Instead of doing anything useful with this connection, the handle_accept method simply prints that a connection attempt was made. addr[0] is the IP address of the client.

The server initialization calls create_socket with two arguments that specify the type of socket you want. You could use different types, but those shown here are what you usually want. The call to the bind method simply binds the server to a specific address (host name and port). The host name is empty (an empty string, essentially meaning localhost, or, more technically, "all interfaces on this machine") and the port number is 5005. The call to listen tells the server to listen for connections; it also specifies a backlog of five connections. The final call to asyncore.loop starts the server's listening loop as before.

This server actually works. Try to run it and then connect to it with your client. The client should immediately be disconnected, and the server should print out the following:

```
Connection attempt from 127.0.0.1
```

The IP address will be different if you don't connect from the same machine as your server.

To stop the server, simply use a keyboard interrupt: Ctrl+C in UNIX or Ctrl+Break in Windows.

Shutting down the server with a keyboard interrupt results in a stack trace. To avoid that, you can wrap the loop in a try/except statement. With some other cleanups, the basic server ends up as shown in Listing 24-3.

**Listing 24-3.** *The Basic Server with Some Cleanups*

```
from asyncore import dispatcher
import socket, asyncore

PORT = 5005
```

```
class ChatServer(dispatcher):

    def __init__(self, port):
        dispatcher.__init__(self)
        self.create_socket(socket.AF_INET, socket.SOCK_STREAM)
        self.set_reuse_addr()
        self.bind(('', port))
        self.listen(5)

    def handle_accept(self):
        conn, addr = self.accept()
        print 'Connection attempt from', addr[0]

if __name__ == '__main__':
    s = ChatServer(PORT)
    try: asyncore.loop()
    except KeyboardInterrupt: pass
```

The added call to set_reuse_addr lets you reuse the same address (specifically, the port number) even if the server isn't shut down properly. (Without this call, you may need to wait for a while before the server can be started again, or change the port number each time the server crashes, because your program may not be able to properly notify your operating system that it's finished with the port.)

## The ChatSession Class

The basic ChatServer isn't very useful. Instead of ignoring the connection attempts, a new dispatcher object should be created for each connection. However, these objects will behave differently from the one used as the main server. They won't be listening on a port for incoming connections; they already *are* connected to a client. Their main task is collecting data (text) coming from the client and responding to it. You could implement this functionality yourself by subclassing dispatcher and overriding various methods, but, luckily, there is a module that already does most of the work: asynchat.

Despite the name, asynchat isn't specifically designed for the type of streaming (continuous) chat application that we're working on. (The chat in the name refers to "chat-style" or command-response protocols.) The good thing about the async_chat class (found in the asynchat module) is that it hides the most basic socket reading and writing operations, which can be a bit difficult to get right. All that's needed to make it work is to override two methods: collect_incoming_data and found_terminator. The former is called each time a bit of text has been read from the socket, and the latter is called when a *terminator* is read. The terminator (in this case) is just a line break. (You'll need to tell the async_chat object about that by calling set_terminator as part of the initialization.)

An updated program, now with a ChatSession class, is shown in Listing 24-4.

**Listing 24-4.** *Server Program with ChatSession Class*

```python
from asyncore import dispatcher
from asynchat import async_chat
import socket, asyncore

PORT = 5005

class ChatSession(async_chat):

    def __init__(self, sock):
        async_chat.__init__(self, sock)
        self.set_terminator("\r\n")
        self.data = []

    def collect_incoming_data(self, data):
        self.data.append(data)

    def found_terminator(self):
        line = ''.join(self.data)
        self.data = []
        # Do something with the line...
        print line

class ChatServer(dispatcher):

    def __init__(self, port):
        dispatcher.__init__(self)
        self.create_socket(socket.AF_INET, socket.SOCK_STREAM)
        self.set_reuse_addr()
        self.bind(('', port))
        self.listen(5)
        self.sessions = []


    def handle_accept(self):
        conn, addr = self.accept()
        self.sessions.append(ChatSession(conn))

if __name__ == '__main__':
    s = ChatServer(PORT)
    try: asyncore.loop()
    except KeyboardInterrupt: print
```

Several things are worth noting in this new version:

- The set_terminator method is used to set the line terminator to "\r\n", which is the commonly used line terminator in network protocols.

- The ChatSession object keeps the data it has read so far as a list of strings called data. When more data is read, collect_incoming_data is called automatically, and it simply appends the data to the list. Using a list of strings and later joining them (with the join string method) is a common idiom (and historically more efficient than incrementally adding strings). Feel free to use += with strings instead.

- The found_terminator method is called when a terminator is found. The current implementation creates a line by joining the current data items, and resets self.data to an empty list. However, because you don't have anything useful to do with the line yet, it is simply printed.

- The ChatServer keeps a list of sessions.

- The handle_accept method of the ChatServer now creates a new ChatSession object and appends it to the list of sessions.

Try running the server and connecting with two (or more) clients simultaneously. Every line you type in a client should be printed in the terminal where your server is running. That means the server is now capable of handling several simultaneous connections. Now all that's missing is the capability for the clients to see what the others are saying!

## Putting It Together

Before the prototype can be considered a fully functional (albeit simple) chat server, one main piece of functionality is lacking: what the users say (each line they type) should be broadcast to the others. That functionality can be implemented by a simple for loop in the server, which loops over the list of sessions and writes the line to each of them. To write data to an async_chat object, you use the push method.

This broadcasting behavior also adds another problem: you must make sure that connections are removed from the list when the clients disconnect. You can do that by overriding the event-handling method handle_close. The final version of the first prototype can be seen in Listing 24-5.

**Listing 24-5.** *A Simple Chat Server (simple_chat.py)*

```
from asyncore import dispatcher
from asynchat import async_chat
import socket, asyncore

PORT = 5005
NAME = 'TestChat'
```

```python
class ChatSession(async_chat):
    """
    A class that takes care of a connection between the server
    and a single user.
    """
    def __init__(self, server, sock):
        # Standard setup tasks:
        async_chat.__init__(self, sock)
        self.server = server
        self.set_terminator("\r\n")
        self.data = []
        # Greet the user:
        self.push('Welcome to %s\r\n' % self.server.name)

    def collect_incoming_data(self, data):
        self.data.append(data)

    def found_terminator(self):
        """
        If a terminator is found, that means that a full
        line has been read. Broadcast it to everyone.
        """
        line = ''.join(self.data)
        self.data = []
        self.server.broadcast(line)

    def handle_close(self):
        async_chat.handle_close(self)
        self.server.disconnect(self)

class ChatServer(dispatcher):
    """
    A class that receives connections and spawns individual
    sessions. It also handles broadcasts to these sessions.
    """
    def __init__(self, port, name):
        # Standard setup tasks
        dispatcher.__init__(self)
        self.create_socket(socket.AF_INET, socket.SOCK_STREAM)
        self.set_reuse_addr()
        self.bind(('', port))
        self.listen(5)
        self.name = name
        self.sessions = []
```

```
    def disconnect(self, session):
        self.sessions.remove(session)

    def broadcast(self, line):
        for session in self.sessions:
            session.push(line + '\r\n')

    def handle_accept(self):
        conn, addr = self.accept()
        self.sessions.append(ChatSession(self, conn))

if __name__ == '__main__':
    s = ChatServer(PORT, NAME)
    try: asyncore.loop()
    except KeyboardInterrupt: print
```

# Second Implementation

The first prototype may be a fully functioning chat server, but its functionality is quite limited. The most obvious limitation is that you can't discern who is saying what. Also, it does not interpret commands (such as say or logout), which the original specification requires. So, you need to add support for identity (one unique name per user) and command interpretation, and you must make the behavior of each session depend on the state it's in (just connected, logged in, and so on)—all of this in a manner that lends itself easily to extension.

## Basic Command Interpretation

I'll show you how to model the command interpretation on the Cmd class of the cmd module in the standard library. (Unfortunately, you can't use this class directly because it can be used only with sys.stdin and sys.stdout, and you're working with several streams.) What you need is a function or method that can handle a single line of text (as typed by the user). It should split off the first word (the command) and call an appropriate method based on it. For example, this line:

```
say Hello, world!
```

might result in the following call:

```
do_say('Hello, world!')
```

possibly with the session itself as an added argument (so do_say would know who did the talking).

Here is a simple implementation, with an added method to express that a command is unknown:

```
class CommandHandler:
    """
    Simple command handler similar to cmd.Cmd from the standard
    library.
    """
```

```
def unknown(self, session, cmd):
    session.push('Unknown command: %s\r\n' % cmd)

def handle(self, session, line):
    if not line.strip(): return
    parts = line.split(' ', 1)
    cmd = parts[0]
    try: line = parts[1].strip()
    except IndexError: line = ''
    meth = getattr(self, 'do_'+cmd, None)
    try:
        meth(session, line)
    except TypeError:
        self.unknown(session, cmd)
```

The use of getattr in this class is similar to that in the markup project in Chapter 20.

With the basic command handling out of the way, you need to define some actual commands. And which commands are available (and what they do) should depend on the current state of the session. How do you represent that state?

## Rooms

Each state can be represented by a custom command handler. This is easily combined with the standard notion of chat rooms (or locations in a MUD). Each room is a CommandHandler with its own specialized commands. In addition, it should keep track of which users (sessions) are currently inside it. Here is a generic superclass for all your rooms:

```
class EndSession(Exception): pass

class Room(CommandHandler):
    """
    A generic environment which may contain one or more users
    (sessions). It takes care of basic command handling and
    broadcasting.
    """

    def __init__(self, server):
        self.server = server
        self.sessions = []

    def add(self, session):
        self.sessions.append(session)
```

```
def remove(self, session):
    self.sessions.remove(session)

def broadcast(self, line):
    for session in self.sessions:
        session.push(line)

def do_logout(self, session, line):
    raise EndSession
```

In addition to the basic add and remove methods, a broadcast method simply calls push on all of the users (sessions) in the room. There is also a single command defined—logout (in the form of the do_logout method). It raises an exception (EndSession), which is dealt with at a higher level of the processing (in found_terminator).

## Login and Logout Rooms

In addition to representing normal chat rooms (this project includes only one such chat room), the Room subclasses can represent other states, which was indeed the intention. For example, when a user connects to the server, he is put in a dedicated LoginRoom (with no other users in it). The LoginRoom prints a welcome message when the user enters (in the add method). It also overrides the unknown method to tell the user to log in; the only command it responds to is the login command, which checks whether the name is acceptable (not an empty string, and not already used by another user).

The LogoutRoom is much simpler. Its only job is to delete the user's name from the server (which has a dictionary called users where the sessions are stored). If the name isn't there (because the user never logged in), the resulting KeyError is ignored.

For the source code of these two classes, see Listing 24-6 later in this chapter.

---

■**Note**  Even though the server's users dictionary keeps references to all the sessions, no session is ever retrieved from it. The users dictionary is used only to keep track of which names are in use. However, instead of using some arbitrary value (such as True), I decided to let each user name refer to the corresponding session. Even though there is no immediate use for it, it may be useful in some later version of the program (for example, if one user wants to send a message privately to another). An alternative would have been to simply keep a set or list of sessions.

---

## The Main Chat Room

The main chat room also overrides the add and remove methods. In add, it broadcasts a message about the user who is entering, and it adds the user's name to the users dictionary in the server. The remove method broadcasts a message about the user who is leaving.

In addition to these methods, the ChatRoom class implements three commands:

- The say command (implemented by do_say) broadcasts a single line, prefixed with the name of the user who spoke.

- The look command (implemented by do_look) tells the user which users are currently in the room.

- The who command (implemented by do_who) tells the user which users are currently logged in. In this simple server, look and who are equivalent, but if you extend it to contain more than one room, their functionality will differ.

For the source code, see Listing 24-6 later in this chapter.

## The New Server

I've now described most of the functionality. The main additions to ChatSession and ChatServer are as follows:

- ChatSession has a method called enter, which is used to enter a new room.

- The ChatSession constructor uses LoginRoom.

- The handle_close method uses LogoutRoom.

- The ChatServer constructor adds the dictionary users and the ChatRoom called main_room to its attributes.

Notice also how handle_accept no longer adds the new ChatSession to a list of sessions because the sessions are now managed by the rooms.

---

■**Note** In general, if you simply instantiate an object, like the ChatSession in handle_accept, without binding a name to it or adding it to a container, it will be lost, and may be garbage-collected (which means that it will disappear completely). Because all dispatchers are handled (referenced) by asyncore (and async_chat is a subclass of dispatcher), this is not a problem here.

---

The final version of the chat server is shown in Listing 24-6. For your convenience, I've listed the available commands in Table 24-1.

**Listing 24-6.** *A Slightly More Complicated Chat Server (chatserver.py)*

```
from asyncore import dispatcher
from asynchat import async_chat
import socket, asyncore


PORT = 5005
NAME = 'TestChat'
```

```python
class EndSession(Exception): pass

class CommandHandler:
    """
    Simple command handler similar to cmd.Cmd from the standard
    library.
    """


    def unknown(self, session, cmd):
        'Respond to an unknown command'
        session.push('Unknown command: %s\r\n' % cmd)

    def handle(self, session, line):
        'Handle a received line from a given session'
        if not line.strip(): return
        # Split off the command:
        parts = line.split(' ', 1)
        cmd = parts[0]
        try: line = parts[1].strip()
        except IndexError: line = ''
        # Try to find a handler:
        meth = getattr(self, 'do_'+cmd, None)
        try:
            # Assume it's callable:
            meth(session, line)
        except TypeError:
            # If it isn't, respond to the unknown command:
            self.unknown(session, cmd)

class Room(CommandHandler):
    """
    A generic environment that may contain one or more users
    (sessions). It takes care of basic command handling and
    broadcasting.
    """

    def __init__(self, server):
        self.server = server
        self.sessions = []

    def add(self, session):
        'A session (user) has entered the room'
        self.sessions.append(session)
```

```python
    def remove(self, session):
        'A session (user) has left the room'
        self.sessions.remove(session)

    def broadcast(self, line):
        'Send a line to all sessions in the room'
        for session in self.sessions:
            session.push(line)


    def do_logout(self, session, line):
        'Respond to the logout command'
        raise EndSession

class LoginRoom(Room):
    """
    A room meant for a single person who has just connected.
    """

    def add(self, session):
        Room.add(self, session)
        # When a user enters, greet him/her:
        self.broadcast('Welcome to %s\r\n' % self.server.name)

    def unknown(self, session, cmd):
        # All unknown commands (anything except login or logout)
        # results in a prodding:
        session.push('Please log in\nUse "login <nick>"\r\n')

    def do_login(self, session, line):
        name = line.strip()
        # Make sure the user has entered a name:
        if not name:
            session.push('Please enter a name\r\n')
        # Make sure that the name isn't in use:
        elif name in self.server.users:
            session.push('The name "%s" is taken.\r\n' % name)
            session.push('Please try again.\r\n')
        else:
            # The name is OK, so it is stored in the session, and
            # the user is moved into the main room.
            session.name = name
            session.enter(self.server.main_room)
```

```python
class ChatRoom(Room):
    """
    A room meant for multiple users who can chat with the others in
    the room.
    """

    def add(self, session):
        # Notify everyone that a new user has entered:
        self.broadcast(session.name + ' has entered the room.\r\n')
        self.server.users[session.name] = session
        Room.add(self, session)


    def remove(self, session):
        Room.remove(self, session)
        # Notify everyone that a user has left:
        self.broadcast(session.name + ' has left the room.\r\n')

    def do_say(self, session, line):
        self.broadcast(session.name+': '+line+'\r\n')

    def do_look(self, session, line):
        'Handles the look command, used to see who is in a room'
        session.push('The following are in this room:\r\n')
        for other in self.sessions:
            session.push(other.name + '\r\n')

    def do_who(self, session, line):
        'Handles the who command, used to see who is logged in'
        session.push('The following are logged in:\r\n')
        for name in self.server.users:
            session.push(name + '\r\n')

class LogoutRoom(Room):
    """
    A simple room for a single user. Its sole purpose is to remove
    the user's name from the server.
    """

    def add(self, session):
        # When a session (user) enters the LogoutRoom it is deleted
        try: del self.server.users[session.name]
        except KeyError: pass
```

```
class ChatSession(async_chat):
    """
    A single session, which takes care of the communication with a
    single user.
    """

    def __init__(self, server, sock):
        async_chat.__init__(self, sock)
        self.server = server
        self.set_terminator("\r\n")
        self.data = []
        self.name = None
        # All sessions begin in a separate LoginRoom:
        self.enter(LoginRoom(server))


    def enter(self, room):
        # Remove self from current room and add self to
        # next room...
        try: cur = self.room
        except AttributeError: pass
        else: cur.remove(self)
        self.room = room
        room.add(self)

    def collect_incoming_data(self, data):
        self.data.append(data)

    def found_terminator(self):
        line = ''.join(self.data)
        self.data = []
        try: self.room.handle(self, line)
        except EndSession:
            self.handle_close()

    def handle_close(self):
        async_chat.handle_close(self)
        self.enter(LogoutRoom(self.server))

class ChatServer(dispatcher):
    """
    A chat server with a single room.
    """
```

```
    def __init__(self, port, name):
        dispatcher.__init__(self)
        self.create_socket(socket.AF_INET, socket.SOCK_STREAM)
        self.set_reuse_addr()
        self.bind(('', port))
        self.listen(5)
        self.name = name
        self.users = {}
        self.main_room = ChatRoom(self)

    def handle_accept(self):
        conn, addr = self.accept()
        ChatSession(self, conn)

if __name__ == '__main__':
    s = ChatServer(PORT, NAME)
    try: asyncore.loop()
    except KeyboardInterrupt: print
```

**Table 24-1.** *Commands Available in the Chat Server*

| Command | Available In | Description |
|---|---|---|
| login name | Login room | Used to log into the server |
| logout | All rooms | Used to log out of the server |
| say statement | Chat room(s) | Used to say something |
| look | Chat room(s) | Used to find out who is in the same room |
| who | Chat room(s) | Used to find out who is logged on to the server |

An example of a chat session is shown in Figure 24-1. The server in that example was started with the this command:

```
python chatserver.py
```

and the user dilbert connected to the server using this command:

```
telnet localhost 5005
```

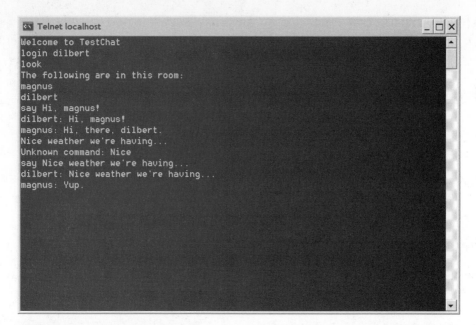

**Figure 24-1.** *A sample chat session*

# Further Exploration

You can do a lot to extend and enhance the basic server presented in this chapter:

- You could make a version with multiple chat rooms, and you could extend the command set to make it behave in any way you want.

- You might want to make the program recognize only certain commands (such as login or logout) and treat all other text entered as general chatting, thereby avoiding the need for a say command.

- You could prefix all commands with a special character (for example, a slash, giving commands like /login and /logout) and treat everything that doesn't start with the specified character as general chatting.

- You might want to create your own GUI client, but that's a bit trickier than it might seem. The GUI toolkit has one event loop, and the communication with the server may require another. To make them cooperate, you may need to use threading. (For an example of how this can be done in simple cases where the various threads don't directly access each other's data, see Chapter 28.)

## What Now?

Now you have your very own chat server. In the next project, you tackle a different type of network programming: CGI, the mechanism underlying most web applications (as discussed in Chapter 15). The specific application of this technology in the next project is *remote editing*, which enables several users to collaborate on developing the same document. You may even use it to edit your own web pages remotely.

■ ■ ■

# CHAPTER 25

# Project 6: Remote Editing
# with CGI

This chapter's project uses CGI, which is discussed in more detail in Chapter 15. The specific application is *remote editing*—editing a document on another machine via the Web. This can be useful in collaboration systems (groupware), for example, where several people may be working on the same document. It can also be useful for updating your web pages.

## What's the Problem?

You have a document stored on one machine and want to be able to edit it from another machine via the Web. This enables you to have a shared document edited by several collaborating authors. You won't need to use FTP or similar file-transfer technologies, and you won't need to worry about synchronizing multiple copies. To edit the file, all you need is a web browser.

---

**Note** This sort of remote editing is one of the core mechanisms of *wikis* (see, for example, `http://en.wikipedia.org/wiki/Wiki`).

---

Specifically, the system should meet the following requirements:

- It should be able to display the document as a normal web page.

- It should be able to display the document in a text area in a web form.

- You should be able to save the text from the form.

- The program should protect the document with a password.

- The program should be easily extensible to support editing more than one document.

As you'll see, all of this is quite easy to do with the standard Python library module `cgi` and some plain Python coding. However, the techniques used in this application can be used for creating web interfaces to all of your Python programs, so it's pretty useful.

# Useful Tools

The main tool when writing CGI programs is, as discussed in Chapter 15, the cgi module, along with the cgitb module for debugging. See Chapter 15 for more information.

# Preparations

The steps needed for making your CGI script accessible through the Web are described in detail in Chapter 15 in the section "Dynamic Web Pages with CGI." Just follow those steps, and you should be fine.

# First Implementation

The first implementation is based on the basic structure of the greeting script shown in Listing 15-7 (Chapter 15). All that's needed for the first prototype is some file handling.

For the script to be useful, it must store the edited text between invocations. Also, the form should be made a bit bigger than in the greeting script (simple3.cgi from Listing 15-7 in Chapter 15), and the text field should be changed into a text area. You should also use the POST CGI method instead of the default GET method. (Using POST is normally the thing to do if you are submitting large amounts of data.)

The general logic of the program is as follows:

1. Get the CGI parameter text with the current value of the data file as the default.

2. Save the text to the data file.

3. Print out the form, with the text in the textarea.

In order for the script to be allowed to write to your data file, you must first create such a file (for example, simple_edit.dat). It can be empty or perhaps contain the initial document (a plain text file, possibly containing some form of markup such as XML or HTML). Then you must set the permissions so that it is universally writable, as described in Chapter 15. The resulting code is shown in Listing 25-1.

**Listing 25-1.** *A Simple Web Editor (simple_edit.cgi)*

```
#!/usr/bin/env python

import cgi
form = cgi.FieldStorage()


text = form.getvalue('text', open('simple_edit.dat').read())
f = open('simple_edit.dat', 'w')
f.write(text)
f.close()
```

```
print """Content-type: text/html

<html>
  <head>
    <title>A Simple Editor</title>
  </head>
  <body>
    <form action='simple_edit.cgi' method='POST'>
    <textarea rows='10' cols='20' name='text'>%s</textarea><br />
    <input type='submit' />
    </form>
  </body>
</html>
""" % text
```

When accessed through a web server, the CGI script checks for an input value called text. If such a value is submitted, the text is written to the file simple_edit.dat. The default value is the file's current contents. Finally, a web page (containing the field for editing and submitting the text) is displayed, as shown in Figure 25-1.

**Figure 25-1.** *The simple_edit.cgi script in action*

# Second Implementation

Now that you have the first prototype on the road, what's missing? The system should be able to edit more than one file, and it should use password protection. (Because the document can be viewed by opening it directly in a browser, you won't be paying much attention to the viewing part of the system.)

The main difference from the first prototype is that you'll split it into two separate CGI scripts (one for each "action" your system should be able to perform). The files of the new prototypes are as follows:

`index.html`: A plain web page with a form where you can enter a file name. It also has an Open button, which triggers `edit.cgi`.

`edit.cgi`: A script that displays a given file in a text area. It has a text field for password entry and a Save button, which triggers `save.cgi`.

`save.cgi`: A script that saves the text it receives to a given file and displays a simple message (for example, "The file has been saved"). This script should also take care of the password checking.

Let's tackle these one by one.

## Creating the File Name Form

`index.html` is an HTML file that contains the form used to enter a file name:

```
<html>
  <head>
    <title>File Editor</title>
  </head>
  <body>
    <form action='edit.cgi' method='POST'>
      <b>File name:</b><br />
      <input type='text' name='filename' />
      <input type='submit' value='Open' />
  </body>
</html>
```

Notice how the text field is named `filename`. That ensures its contents will be supplied as the CGI parameter `filename` to the `edit.cgi` script (which is the `action` attribute of the `form` tag). If you open this file in a browser, enter a file name in the text field, and click Open, the `edit.cgi` script will be run.

## Writing the Editor Script

The page displayed by the `edit.cgi` script should include a text area containing the current text of the file you're editing, and a text field for entering a password. The only input needed is the file name, which the script receives from the form in `index.html`. Note, however, that it is possible to open the `edit.cgi` script directly, without submitting the form in `index.html`. In that case, you have no guarantee that the `filename` field of `cgi.FieldStorage` is set. So you need to add a check to ensure that there *is* a file name. If there is, the file will be opened from a directory that contains the files that may be edited. Let's call the directory `data`. (You will, of course, have to create this directory.)

**■Caution** Note that by supplying a file name that contains path elements such as .. (two dots), it may be possible to access files outside this directory. To make sure that the files accessed are within the given directory, you should perform some extra checking, such as listing all the files in the directory (using the glob module, for example) and checking that the supplied file name is one of the candidate files (making sure you use full, absolute path names all around). See the section "Validating File Names" in Chapter 27 for another approach.

The code, then, becomes something like Listing 25-2.

**Listing 25-2.** *The Editor Script (edit.cgi)*

```python
#!/usr/bin/env python

print 'Content-type: text/html\n'

from os.path import join, abspath
import cgi, sys

BASE_DIR = abspath('data')

form = cgi.FieldStorage()
filename = form.getvalue('filename')
if not filename:
    print 'Please enter a file name'
    sys.exit()
text = open(join(BASE_DIR, filename)).read()

print """
<html>
  <head>
    <title>Editing...</title>
  </head>
  <body>
    <form action='save.cgi' method='POST'>
      <b>File:</b> %s<br />
      <input type='hidden' value='%s' name='filename' />
      <b>Password:</b><br />
      <input name='password' type='password' /><br />
      <b>Text:</b><br />
      <textarea name='text' cols='40' rows='20'>%s</textarea><br />
      <input type='submit' value='Save' />
    </form>
  </body>
```

```
</html>
""" % (filename, filename, text)
```

Note that the `abspath` function has been used to get the absolute path of the `data` directory. Also note that the file name has been stored in a `hidden` form element so that it will be relayed to the next script (`save.cgi`) without giving the user an opportunity to change it. (You have no guarantees of that, of course, because users may write their own forms, put them on another machine, and have those forms call your CGI scripts with custom values.)

For password handling, the sample code uses an input element of type `password` rather than `text`, which means that the characters entered will be displayed as asterisks.

---

■**Note**  This script is based on the assumption that the file name given refers to an existing file. Feel free to extend it so that it can handle other cases as well.

---

## Writing the Save Script

The script that performs the saving is the last component of this simple system. It receives a file name, a password, and some text. It checks that the password is correct, and if it is, the program stores the text in the file with the given file name. (The file should have its permissions set properly; see the discussion of setting file permissions in Chapter 15.)

Just for fun, you'll use the `sha` module in the password handling. The Secure Hash Algorithm (SHA) is a way of extracting an essentially meaningless string of seemingly random data (a *digest*) from an input string. The idea behind the algorithm is that it is almost impossible to construct a string that has a given digest, so if you know the digest of a password (for example), there is no (easy) way you can reconstruct the password or invent one that will reproduce the digest. This means that you can safely compare the digest of a supplied password with a stored digest (of the correct password) instead of comparing the passwords themselves. By using this approach, you don't need to store the password itself in the source code, and someone reading the code would be none the wiser about what the password actually *was*.

---

■**Caution**  As I said, this "security" feature is mainly for fun. Unless you are using a secure connection with SSL or some similar technology (which is beyond the scope of this project), it is still possible to pick up the password being submitted over the network.

---

Here is an example of how you can use sha:

```
>>> from sha import sha
>>> sha('foobar').hexdigest()
'8843d7f92416211de9ebb963ff4ce28125932878'
>>> sha('foobaz').hexdigest()
'21eb6533733a5e4763acacd1d45a60c2e0e404e1'
```

As you can see, a small change in the password gives you a completely different digest. You can see the code for save.cgi in Listing 25-3.

**Listing 25-3.** *The Saving Script (save.cgi)*

```python
#!/usr/bin/env python

print 'Content-type: text/html\n'

from os.path import join, abspath
import cgi, sha, sys

BASE_DIR = abspath('data')

form = cgi.FieldStorage()

text = form.getvalue('text')
filename = form.getvalue('filename')
password = form.getvalue('password')

if not (filename and text and password):
    print 'Invalid parameters.'
    sys.exit()

if sha.sha(password).hexdigest() != '8843d7f92416211de9ebb963ff4ce28125932878':
    print 'Invalid password'
    sys.exit()

f = open(join(BASE_DIR,filename), 'w')
f.write(text)
f.close()

print 'The file has been saved.'
```

## Running the Editor

Follow these steps to use the editor:

1. Open the page index.html in a web browser. Be sure to open it through a web server (by using a URL of the form http://www.someserver.com/index.html) and not as a local file. The result is shown in Figure 25-2.

2. Enter a file name of a file that your CGI editor is permitted to modify, and then click Open. Your browser should then contain the output of the edit.cgi script, as shown in Figure 25-3.

3. Edit the file to taste, enter the password (one you've set yourself, or the one used in the example, which is foobar), and click Save. Your browser should then contain the output of the save.cgi script, which is simply the message "The file has been saved."

4. If you want to verify that the file has been modified, repeat the process of opening the file (steps 1 and 2).

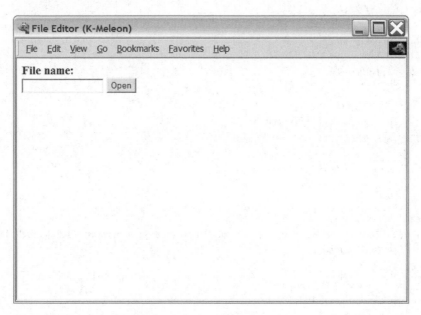

**Figure 25-2.** *The opening page of the CGI editor*

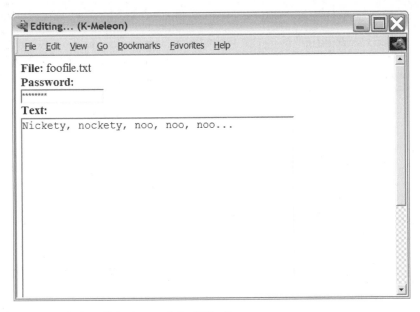

**Figure 25-3.** *The editing page of the CGI editor*

# Further Exploration

With the techniques shown in this project, you can develop all kinds of web systems. Some possible additions to the existing system are as follows:

- Add version control. Save old copies of the edited file so you can "undo" your changes.

- Add support for user names so you know who changed what.

- Add file locking (for example, with the `fcntl` module) so two users can't edit the file at the same time.

- Add a `view.cgi` script that automatically adds markup to the files (like the one in Chapter 20).

- Make the scripts more robust by checking their input more thoroughly and adding more user-friendly error messages.

- Avoid printing a confirmation message like "The file has been saved." You can either add some more useful output or redirect the user to another page/script. Redirection can be done with the `Location` header, which works like `Content-type`. Just add `Location:` followed by a space and a URL to the header section of the output (*before* the first empty line).

In addition to expanding the capabilities of this CGI system, you might want to check out some more complex web environments for Python (as discussed in Chapter 15).

## What Now?

Now you've tried your hand at writing CGI scripts. In the next project, you expand on that by using a SQL database for storage. With that powerful combination, you'll implement a fully functional web-based bulletin board.

■ ■ ■

# CHAPTER 26

# Project 7: Your Own Bulletin Board

**M**any kinds of software enable you to communicate with other people over the Internet. You've seen a few already (for example, the Usenet groups in Chapter 23 and the chat server in Chapter 24). In this chapter, you will implement another such system: a web-based discussion forum.

## What's the Problem?

In this project, you create a simple system for posting and responding to messages via the Web. This has utility in itself, as a discussion forum. One famous example of such a forum is Slashdot (`http://slashdot.org`). The system developed in this chapter is quite simple, but the basic functionality is there, and it should be capable of handling quite a large number of postings.

However, the material covered in this chapter has uses beyond developing stand-alone discussion forums. It could be used to implement a more general system for collaboration, for example, or an issue-tracking system, a blog with commenting functionality, or something completely different. The combination of CGI (or similar technologies) and a solid database (in this case, a SQL database) is quite powerful and versatile.

---

■**Tip** Even though it's fun and educational to write your own software, in many cases, it's more cost-effective to search for existing software. In the case of discussion forums and the like, chances are that you can find quite a few well-developed systems freely available. Also, most web application frameworks, such as Django, Zope, and TurboGears (mentioned in Chapter 15), have built-in support for this sort of functionality.

---

Specifically, the final system should meet the following requirements:

- It should display the subjects of all current messages.

- It should support message threading (displaying replies indented under the message they reply to).

- You should be able to view existing messages.

- You should be able to reply to existing messages.

In addition to these functional requirements, it would be nice if the system were reasonably stable, could handle a large number of messages, and avoided such problems as two users writing to the same file at the same time. The desired robustness can be achieved by using a database server of some sort, instead of writing the file-handling code yourself.

## Useful Tools

In addition to the CGI stuff from Chapter 15, you'll need a SQL database, as discussed in Chapter 13. You could either use the stand-alone database SQLite, which is used in that chapter, or you could use some other system, such as either of the following two excellent, freely available databases:

- PostgreSQL (http://www.postgresql.org)

- MySQL (http://www.mysql.org)

In this chapter, I use PostgreSQL for the examples, but the code should work with most SQL databases (including MySQL or SQLite) with few edits.

Before moving on, you should make sure that you have access to a SQL database server (or a stand-alone SQL database, such as SQLite) and check its documentation for instructions on how to manage it.

In addition to the database server itself, you'll need a Python module that can interface with the server (and hide the details from you). Most such modules support the Python DB API, which is discussed in more detail in Chapter 13. In this chapter, I use psycopg (http://initd.org/Software/psycopg), a robust front end for PostgreSQL. If you're using MySQL, the MySQLdb module (http://sourceforge.net/projects/mysql-python) is a good choice.

After you have installed your database module, you should be able to import it (for example, with import psycopg or import MySQLdb) without raising any exceptions.

## Preparations

Before your program can start using your database, you must actually create the database. That is done using SQL (see Chapter 13 for some pointers).

The database structure is intimately linked with the problem and can be a bit tricky to change once you've created it and populated it with data (messages). Let's keep it simple.

You'll have only one table, which will contain one row for each message. Each message will have a unique ID (an integer), a subject, a sender (or poster), and some text (the body).

In addition, because you want to be able to display the messages hierarchically (threading), each message should store a reference to the message it is a reply to. The resulting CREATE TABLE SQL command is shown in Listing 26-1.

**Listing 26-1.** *Creating the Database in PostgreSQL*

```
CREATE TABLE messages (
    id          SERIAL PRIMARY KEY,
    subject     TEXT NOT NULL,
    sender      TEXT NOT NULL,
    reply_to    INTEGER REFERENCES messages,
    text        TEXT NOT NULL
);
```

Note that this command uses some PostgreSQL-specific features (SERIAL, which ensures that each message automatically receives a unique ID; the TEXT data type; and REFERENCES, which makes sure that reply_to contains a valid message ID). A more MySQL-friendly version is shown in Listing 26-2.

**Listing 26-2.** *Creating the Database in MySQL*

```
CREATE TABLE messages (
    id          INT NOT NULL AUTO_INCREMENT,
    subject     VARCHAR(100) NOT NULL,
    sender      VARCHAR(15) NOT NULL,
    reply_to    INT,
    text        MEDIUMTEXT NOT NULL,
    PRIMARY KEY(id)
);
```

Finally, for those of you using SQLite, there's a schema in Listing 26-3.

**Listing 26-3.** *Creating the Database in SQLite*

```
create table messages (
    id          integer primary key autoincrement,
    subject     text not null,
    sender      text not null,
    reply_to    int,
    text        text not null
);
```

I've kept these code snippets simple (a SQL guru would certainly find ways to improve them) because the focus of this chapter is, after all, the Python code. The SQL statements create a new table with the following five fields (columns):

id: Used to identify the individual messages. Each message automatically receives a unique ID by the database manager, so you don't need to worry about assigning those from your Python code.

subject: A string that contains the subject of the message.

sender: A string that contains the sender's name or email address or something like that.

reply_to: If the message is a reply to another message, this field contains the id of the other message. (Otherwise, the field won't contain anything.)

text: A string that contains the body of the message.

When you've created this database and set the permissions on it so that your web server is allowed to read its contents and insert new rows, you're ready to start coding the CGI.

# First Implementation

In this project, the first prototype will be very limited. It will be a single script that uses the database functionality so that you can get a feel for how it works. Once you have that pegged, writing the other necessary scripts won't be very hard. In many ways, this is just a short reminder of the material covered in Chapter 13.

The CGI part of the code is very similar to that in Chapter 25. If you haven't read that chapter yet, you might want to take a look at it. You should also be sure to review the section "CGI Security Risks" in Chapter 15.

---

■**Caution** In the CGI scripts in this chapter, I've imported and enabled the cgitb module. This is very useful to uncover flaws in your code, but you should probably remove the call to cgitb.enable before deploying the software—you probably wouldn't want an ordinary user to face a full cgitb traceback.

---

The first thing you need to know is how the Python DB API works. If you haven't read Chapter 13, you probably should at least skim through it now. If you would rather just press on, here is the core functionality again (replace db with the name of your database module—for example, psycopg or MySQLdb):

conn = db.connect('user=foo dbname=bar'): Connects to the database named bar as user foo and assigns the returned connection object to conn. (Note that the parameter to connect is a string.)

---

■**Caution** In this project, I assume that you have a dedicated machine on which the database and web server run. The given user (foo) should be allowed to connect only from that machine to avoid unwanted access. If you have other users on your machine, you should probably protect your database with a password, which may also be supplied in the parameter string to connect. To find out more about this, consult the documentation for your database (and your Python database module).

---

curs = conn.cursor(): Gets a *cursor* object from the connection object. The cursor is used to actually execute SQL statements and fetch the results.

conn.commit(): Commits the changes caused by the SQL statements since the last commit.

conn.close(): Closes the connection.

curs.execute(sql_string): Executes a SQL statement.

curs.fetchone(): Fetches one result row as a sequence—for example, a tuple.

curs.dictfetchone(): Fetches one result row as a dictionary. (Not part of the standard, and therefore not available in all modules.)

curs.fetchall(): Fetches all result rows as a sequence of sequences—for example, a list of tuples.

curs.dictfetchall(): Fetches all result rows as a sequence (for example, a list) of dictionaries. (Not part of the standard, and therefore not available in all modules.)

Here is a simple test (assuming psycopg)—retrieving all the messages in the database (which is currently empty, so you won't get any):

```
>>> import psycopg
>>> conn = psycopg.connect('user=foo dbname=bar')
>>> curs = conn.cursor()
>>> curs.execute('SELECT * FROM messages')
>>> curs.fetchall()
[]
```

Because you haven't implemented the web interface yet, you must enter messages manually if you want to test the database. You can do that either through an administrative tool (such as mysql for MySQL or psql for PostgreSQL), or you can use the Python interpreter with your database module.

Here is a useful piece of code you can use for testing purposes:

```
#!/usr/bin/env python
# addmessage.py
```

```
import psycopg
conn = psycopg.connect('user=foo dbname=bar')
curs = conn.cursor()

reply_to = raw_input('Reply to: ')
subject = raw_input('Subject: ')
sender = raw_input('Sender: ')
text = raw_input('Text: ')

if reply_to:
    query = """
    INSERT INTO messages(reply_to, sender, subject, text)
    VALUES(%s, '%s', '%s', '%s')""" % (reply_to, sender, subject, text)
else:
    query = """
    INSERT INTO messages(sender, subject, text)
    VALUES('%s', '%s', '%s')""" % (sender, subject, text)

curs.execute(query)
conn.commit()
```

Note that this code is a bit crude. It doesn't keep track of IDs for you (you'll have to make sure that what you enter as reply_to, if anything, is a valid ID), and it doesn't deal properly with text containing single quotes (this can be problematic because single quotes are used as string delimiters in SQL). These issues will be dealt with in the final system, of course.

Try to add a few messages and examine the database at the interactive Python prompt. If everything seems okay, it's time to write a CGI script that accesses the database.

Now that you have the database-handling code figured out and some ready-made CGI code you can pinch from Chapter 25, writing a script for viewing the message subjects (a simple version of the "main page" of the forum) shouldn't be too hard. You must do the standard CGI setup (in this case, mainly printing the Content-type string), do the standard database setup (get a connection and a cursor), execute a simple SQL select command to get all the messages, and then retrieve the resulting rows with curs.fetchall or curs.dictfetchall.

Listing 26-4 shows a script that does these things. The only really new stuff in the listing is the formatting code, which is used to get the threaded look where replies are displayed below and to the right of the messages they are replies to.

It basically works like this:

- For each message, get the reply_to field. If it is None (not a reply), add the message to the list of top-level messages. Otherwise, append the message to the list of children kept in children[parent_id].

- For each top-level message, call format. The format function prints the subject of the message. Also, if the message has any children, it opens a blockquote element (HTML), calls format (recursively) for each child, and ends the blockquote element.

If you open the script in your web browser (see Chapter 15 for information about how to run CGI scripts), you should see a threaded view of all the messages you've added (or their subjects, anyway).

For an idea of what the bulletin board looks like, see Figure 26-1 later in this chapter.

---

**■Note** If you're using SQLite, you can't use `dictfetchall`, as in Listing 26-4. The line `rows = curs.dictfetchall()` can be replaced with the following snippet:

```
names = [d[0] for d in curs.description]
rows = [dict(zip(names, row)) for row in curs.fetchall()]
```

---

**Listing 26-4.** *The Main Bulletin Board (simple_main.cgi)*

```python
#!/usr/bin/python

print 'Content-type: text/html\n'

import cgitb; cgitb.enable()

import psycopg
conn = psycopg.connect('dbname=foo user=bar')
curs = conn.cursor()

print """
<html>
  <head>
    <title>The FooBar Bulletin Board</title>
  </head>
  <body>
    <h1>The FooBar Bulletin Board</h1>
    """


curs.execute('SELECT * FROM messages')
rows = curs.dictfetchall()

toplevel = []
children = {}

for row in rows:
    parent_id = row['reply_to']
    if parent_id is None:
        toplevel.append(row)
    else:
        children.setdefault(parent_id,[]).append(row)
```

```
def format(row):
    print row['subject']
    try: kids = children[row['id']]
    except KeyError: pass
    else:
        print '<blockquote>'
        for kid in kids:
            format(kid)
        print '</blockquote>'

print '<p>'

for row in toplevel:
    format(row)

print """
    </p>
  </body>
</html>
"""
```

---

■**Note** If, for some reason, you can't get the program to work, it may be that you haven't set up your database properly. Consult the documentation for your database to see what is needed in order to let a given user connect and to modify the database. You may, for example, need to list the IP address of the connecting machine explicitly.

---

# Second Implementation

The first implementation was quite limited in that it didn't even allow users to post messages. In this section, you expand on the simple system in the first prototype, which contains the basic structure for the final version. Some measures will be added to check the supplied parameters (such as checking whether reply_to is really a number and whether the required parameters are really supplied), but you should note that making a system like this robust and user-friendly is a tough task. If you intend to use the system (or, I hope, an improved version of your own), you should be prepared to work quite a bit on these issues.

But before you can even think of improving stability, you need something that works, right? So, where do you begin? How do you structure the system?

A simple way of structuring web programs (using technologies such as CGI) is to have one script per action performed by the user. In the case of this system, that would mean the following scripts:

main.cgi: Displays the subjects of all messages (threaded) with links to the articles themselves.

view.cgi: Displays a single article and contains a link that will let you reply to it.

`edit.cgi`: Displays a single article in editable form (with text fields and text areas, just as in Chapter 25). Its Submit button is linked to the save script.

`save.cgi`: Receives information about an article (from `edit.cgi`) and saves it by inserting a new row into the database table.

Let's deal with these separately.

## Writing the Main Script

The `main.cgi` script is very similar to the `simple_main.cgi` script from the first prototype. The main difference is the addition of links. Each subject will be a link to a given message (to `view.cgi`), and at the bottom of the page, you'll add a link that allows the user to post a new message (a link to `edit.cgi`).

Take a look at the code in Listing 26-5. The line containing the link to each article (part of the `format` function) looks like this:

```
print '<p><a href="view.cgi?id=%(id)i">%(subject)s</a></p>' % row
```

Basically, it creates a link to `view.cgi?id=someid` where `someid` is the `id` of the given row. This syntax (the question mark and key=val) is simply a way of passing parameters to a CGI script. That means if users click this link, they are taken to `view.cgi` with the `id` parameter properly set. The "Post message" link is just a link to `edit.cgi`.

**Listing 26-5.** *The Main Bulletin Board (main.cgi)*

```
#!/usr/bin/python

print 'Content-type: text/html\n'

import cgitb; cgitb.enable()

import psycopg
conn = psycopg.connect('dbname=foo user=bar')
curs = conn.cursor()

print """
<html>
  <head>
    <title>The FooBar Bulletin Board</title>
  </head>
  <body>
    <h1>The FooBar Bulletin Board</h1>
    """

curs.execute('SELECT * FROM messages')
rows = curs.dictfetchall()
```

```
toplevel = []
children = {}

for row in rows:
    parent_id = row['reply_to']
    if parent_id is None:
        toplevel.append(row)
    else:
        children.setdefault(parent_id,[]).append(row)

def format(row):
    print '<p><a href="view.cgi?id=%(id)i">%(subject)s</a></p>' % row
    try: kids = children[row['id']]
    except KeyError: pass
    else:
        print '<blockquote>'
        for kid in kids:
            format(kid)
        print '</blockquote>'

print '<p>'

for row in toplevel:
    format(row)

print """
    </p>
    <hr />
    <p><a href="edit.cgi">Post message</a></p>
  </body>
</html>
"""
```

So, let's see how `view.cgi` handles the `id` parameter.

## Writing the View Script

The `view.cgi` script uses the supplied CGI parameter `id` to retrieve a single message from the database. It then formats a simple HTML page with the resulting values. This page also contains a link back to the main page (`main.cgi`) and, perhaps more interestingly, to `edit.cgi`, but this time with the `reply_to` parameter set to `id` to ensure that the new message will be a reply to the current one. See Listing 26-6 for the code of `view.cgi`.

**Listing 26-6.** *The Message Viewer (view.cgi)*

```python
#!/usr/bin/python

print 'Content-type: text/html\n'

import cgitb; cgitb.enable()

import psycopg
conn = psycopg.connect('dbname=foo user=bar')
curs = conn.cursor()

import cgi, sys
form = cgi.FieldStorage()
id = form.getvalue('id')

print """
<html>
  <head>
    <title>View Message</title>
  </head>
  <body>
    <h1>View Message</h1>
    """

try: id = int(id)
except:
    print 'Invalid message ID'
    sys.exit()

curs.execute('SELECT * FROM messages WHERE id = %i' % id)
rows = curs.dictfetchall()

if not rows:
    print 'Unknown message ID'
    sys.exit()

row = rows[0]

print """
    <p><b>Subject:</b> %(subject)s<br />
    <b>Sender:</b> %(sender)s<br />
    <pre>%(text)s</pre>
    </p>
```

```
        <hr />
        <a href='main.cgi'>Back to the main page</a>
        | <a href="edit.cgi?reply_to=%(id)s">Reply</a>
    </body>
</html>
""" % row
```

## Writing the Edit Script

The edit.cgi script actually performs a dual function: it is used to edit new messages and also to edit replies. The difference isn't all that great: if a reply_to is supplied in the CGI request, it is kept in a *hidden input* in the edit form. Also, the subject is set to "Re: parentsubject" by default (unless the subject already begins with "Re:"—you don't want to keep adding those). Here is the code snippet that takes care of these details:

```
subject = ''
if reply_to is not None:
    print '<input type="hidden" name="reply_to" value="%s"/>' % reply_to
    curs.execute('SELECT subject FROM messages WHERE id = %s' % reply_to)
    subject = curs.fetchone()[0]
    if not subject.startswith('Re: '):
        subject = 'Re: ' + subject
```

---

■**Note** Hidden inputs are used to temporarily store information in a web form. They don't show up to the user as text areas and the like do, but their value is still passed to the CGI script that is the action of the form. That way, the script that generates the form can pass information to the script that will eventually process the same form.

---

Listing 26-7 shows the source code for the edit.cgi script.

**Listing 26-7.** *The Message Editor (edit.cgi)*

```
#!/usr/bin/python

print 'Content-type: text/html\n'

import cgitb; cgitb.enable()


import psycopg
conn = psycopg.connect('dbname=foo user=bar')
curs = conn.cursor()
```

```
import cgi, sys
form = cgi.FieldStorage()
reply_to = form.getvalue('reply_to')

print """
<html>
  <head>
    <title>Compose Message</title>
  </head>
  <body>
    <h1>Compose Message</h1>

    <form action='save.cgi' method='POST'>
    """

subject = ''
if reply_to is not None:
    print '<input type="hidden" name="reply_to" value="%s"/>' % reply_to
    curs.execute('SELECT subject FROM messages WHERE id = %s' % reply_to)
    subject = curs.fetchone()[0]
    if not subject.startswith('Re: '):
        subject = 'Re: ' + subject

print """
    <b>Subject:</b><br />
    <input type='text' size='40' name='subject' value='%s' /><br />
    <b>Sender:</b><br />
    <input type='text' size='40' name='sender' /><br />
    <b>Message:</b><br />
    <textarea name='text' cols='40' rows='20'></textarea><br />
    <input type='submit' value='Save'/>
    </form>
    <hr />
    <a href='main.cgi'>Back to the main page</a>'
  </body>
</html>
""" % subject
```

## Writing the Save Script

Now let's move on to the final script. The save.cgi script will receive information about a message (from the form generated by edit.cgi) and will store it in the database. That means using a SQL INSERT command, and because the database has been modified, conn.commit must be called so the changes aren't lost when the script terminates.

Listing 26-8 shows the source code for the save.cgi script.

**Listing 26-8.** *The Save Script (save.cgi)*

```
#!/usr/bin/python

print 'Content-type: text/html\n'

import cgitb; cgitb.enable()

def quote(string):
    if string:
        return string.replace("'", "\\'")
    else:
        return string

import psycopg
conn = psycopg.connect('dbname=foo user=bar')
curs = conn.cursor()

import cgi, sys
form = cgi.FieldStorage()

sender = quote(form.getvalue('sender'))
subject = quote(form.getvalue('subject'))
text = quote(form.getvalue('text'))
reply_to = form.getvalue('reply_to')

if not (sender and subject and text):
    print 'Please supply sender, subject, and text'
    sys.exit()

if reply_to is not None:
    query = """
    INSERT INTO messages(reply_to, sender, subject, text)
    VALUES(%i, '%s', '%s', '%s')""" % (int(reply_to), sender, subject, text)
else:
    query = """
    INSERT INTO messages(sender, subject, text)
    VALUES('%s', '%s', '%s')""" % (sender, subject, text)

curs.execute(query)
conn.commit()


print """
<html>
```

```
<head>
  <title>Message Saved</title>
</head>
<body>
  <h1>Message Saved</h1>
  <hr />
  <a href='main.cgi'>Back to the main page</a>
</body>
</html>s
"""
```

## Trying It Out

To test this system, start by opening `main.cgi`. From there, click the Post message link. That should take you to `edit.cgi`. Enter some values in all the fields and click the Save link. That should take you to `save.cgi`, which will display the message Message Saved. Click the Back to the main page link to get back to `main.cgi`. The listing should now include your new message.

To view your message, simply click its subject. You should go to `view.cgi` with the correct ID. From there, try to click the Reply link, which should take you to `edit.cgi` once again, but this time with `reply_to` set (in a hidden input tag) and with a default subject. Once again, enter some text, click Save, and go back to the main page. It should now show your reply, displayed under the original subject. (If it's not showing, try to reload the page.)

The main page is shown in Figure 26-1, the message viewer in Figure 26-2, and the message composer in Figure 26-3.

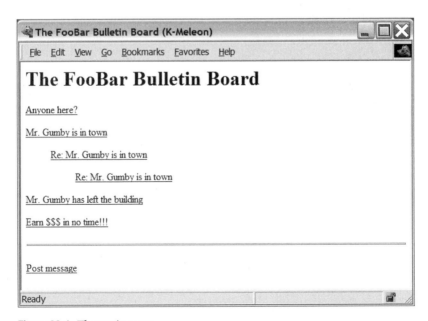

**Figure 26-1.** *The main page*

**Figure 26-2.** *The message viewer*

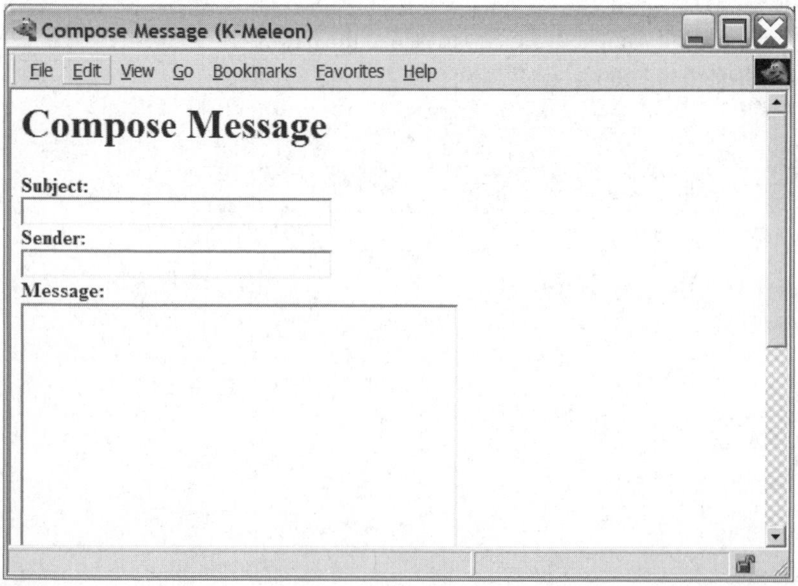

**Figure 26-3.** *The message composer*

# Further Exploration

Now that you have the power to develop huge and powerful web applications with reliable and efficient storage, there are many things you can sink your teeth into:

- How about making a web front end to a database of your favorite Monty Python sketches?

- If you're interested in improving the system in this chapter, you should think about abstraction. How about creating a utility module with a function to print a standard header and another to print a standard footer? That way, you wouldn't need to write the same HTML stuff in each script. Also, it might be useful to add a user database with some password handling or abstract away the code for creating a connection.

- If you would like a storage solution that doesn't require a dedicated server, you could use SQLite (which is used in Chapter 13), or you might want to check out Metakit, a really neat little database package that also lets you store an entire database in a single file (http://equi4.com/metakit/python.html).

- Yet another alternative is the Berkeley DB (http://www.sleepycat.com), which is quite simple but can handle astonishing amounts of data very efficiently. (The Berkeley DB is accessible, when installed, through the standard library modules bsddb, dbhash, and anydbm.)

## What Now?

If you think writing your own discussion forum software is cool, how about writing your own peer-to-peer file sharing program, like BitTorrent (or, at least, its lobotomized half brother)? Well, in the next project, that's exactly what you'll do. And the good news is that it will be easier than most of the network programming you've done so far, thanks to the wonder of remote procedure calls.

## CHAPTER 27

■■■■

# Project 8: File Sharing with XML-RPC

This chapter's project is a simple file sharing application. You may be familiar with the concept of file sharing from such applications as the (in)famous Napster (no longer downloadable in its original form), Gnutella (see `http://www.gnutellaforums.com` for discussions about available clients), BitTorrent (available from `http://www.bittorrent.com`), and many others. What you'll be writing is in many ways similar to these, although quite a bit simpler.

The main technology you'll use is XML-RPC. As mentioned in Chapter 15, this is a protocol for calling procedures (functions) remotely, possibly across a network. If you want, you can quite easily use plain socket programming (possibly employing some of the techniques described in Chapters 14 and 24) to implement the functionality of this project. That might even give you better performance, because the XML-RPC protocol does come with a certain overhead. However, XML-RPC is very easy to use and will most likely simplify your code considerably.

## What's the Problem?

You want to create a peer-to-peer file sharing program. *File sharing* basically means exchanging files (everything from text files to sound or video clips) between programs running on different machines. *Peer-to-peer* is a term that describes a type of interaction between computer programs that is somewhat different from the common *client-server* interaction (where a client may connect to a server but not vice versa). In a peer-to-peer interaction, any peer may connect to any other. In such a (virtual) network of peers, there is no central authority (as represented by the server in a client/server architecture), which makes the network more robust. It won't collapse unless you shut down most of the peers.

---

■**Tip**  If you're interested in learning more about peer-to-peer systems, try a web search on the phrase "peer-to-peer."

---

Many issues are involved in constructing a peer-to-peer system. In a system such as the old-school Gnutella, a peer may disseminate a query to all of its neighbors (the other peers it knows about), and they may subsequently disseminate the query further. Any peer that responds to the query can then send a reply back through the chain of peers to the initial one. The peers work individually and in parallel. More recent systems, such as BitTorrent, use even more clever techniques, such as requiring that you upload files in order to be allowed to download files. To simplify things, this project's system will contact each neighbor in turn, waiting for its response before moving on. This is not quite as efficient as the parallel approach of Gnutella, but good enough for your purposes.

Also, most peer-to-peer systems have clever ways of organizing their structure—that is, which peers are "next to" which—and how this structure evolves over time, as peers connect and disconnect. We'll keep that very simple in this project, but leave things open for improvements.

The following are the requirements that the file sharing program must satisfy:

- Each node must keep track of a set of known nodes, from which it can ask for help. It must be possible for a node to introduce itself to another node (and thereby be included in this set).

- It must be possible to ask a node for a file (by supplying a file name). If the node has the file in question, it should return it; otherwise, it should ask each of its neighbors in turn for the same file (and they, in turn, may ask *their* neighbors). If one of these nodes has the file, it is returned.

- To avoid loops (A asking B, which in turn asks A) and to avoid overly long chains of neighbors asking neighbors (A asking B asking C . . . asking Z), it must be possible to supply a *history* when querying a node. This history is just a list of which nodes have participated in the query up until this point. By not asking nodes already in the history, you avoid loops, and by limiting the length of the history, you avoid overly long query chains.

- There must be some way of connecting to a node and identifying yourself as a trusted party. By doing so, you should be given access to functionality that is not available to untrusted parties (such as other nodes in the peer-to-peer network). This functionality may include asking the node to download and store a file from the other peers in the network (through a query).

- You must have some user interface that lets you connect to a node (as a trusted party) and make it download files. It should be easy to extend and, for that matter, replace this interface.

All of this may seem a bit steep, but as you'll see, implementing it isn't all that hard. And you'll probably find that once you have this in place, adding functionality won't be all that difficult either.

## Useful Tools

In this project, you'll use quite a few standard library modules.

The main modules you'll be using are xmlrpclib and its close friend SimpleXMLRPCServer. The use of xmlrpclib is quite straightforward. You simply create a ServerProxy object with a URL to the server, and you immediately have access to the remote procedures. Using `SimpleXMLRPCServer` is a tad more involved, as you'll learn as you work through the project in this chapter.

For the interface to the file sharing program, you'll be using a module from the standard library called `cmd`. To get some (very limited) parallelism, you'll use the `threading` module, and to extract the components of a URL, you'll use the `urlparse` module. These modules are explained later in the chapter.

Other modules you might want to brush up on are `random`, `string`, `time`, and `os.path`. See Chapter 10, as well as the Python Library Reference, for additional details.

# Preparations

The libraries used in this project don't require much preparation. If you have a fairly recent version of Python, all of the necessary libraries should be available out of the box.

You don't strictly *have* to be connected to a network to use the software in this project, but it will make things more interesting. If you have access to two (or more) separate machines that are connected (for example, both connected to the Internet), you can run the software on each of these machines and have them communicate with each other (although you may need to make changes to any firewall rules you're running). For testing purposes, it is also possible to run multiple file sharing nodes on the same machine.

# First Implementation

Before you can write a first prototype of the Node class (a single node or peer in the system), you need to know a bit about how the `SimpleXMLRPCServer` class works. It is instantiated with a tuple of the form (`servername, port`). The server name is the name of the machine on which the server will run. (You can use an empty string here to indicate localhost, the machine where you're actually executing the program.) The port number can be any port you have access to, typically 1024 and above.

After you have instantiated the server, you may register an instance that implements its "remote methods," with the `register_instance` method. Alternatively, you can register individual functions with the `register_function` method. When you're ready to run the server (so that it can respond to requests from outside), you call its method `serve_forever`. You can easily try this out. Start two interactive Python interpreters. In the first one, enter the following code:

```
>>> from SimpleXMLRPCServer import SimpleXMLRPCServer
>>> s = SimpleXMLRPCServer(("", 4242)) # Localhost at port 4242
>>> def twice(x): # Example function
...     return x*2
...
>>> s.register_function(twice) # Add functionality to the server
>>> s.serve_forever() # Start the server
```

After executing the last statement, the interpreter should seem to "hang." Actually, it's waiting for RPC requests.

To make such a request, switch to the other interpreter and execute the following:

```
>>> from xmlrpclib import ServerProxy # ... or simply Server, if you prefer
>>> s = ServerProxy('http://localhost:4242') # Localhost again...
>>> s.twice(2)
4
```

Pretty impressive, eh? Especially considering that the client part (using xmlrpclib) could be run on a different machine. (In that case, you would need to use the actual name of the server machine instead of simply localhost.) As you can see, to access the remote procedures implemented by the server, all that is required is to instantiate a ServerProxy with the correct URL. It really couldn't be much easier.

## Implementing a Simple Node

Now that we've covered the XML-RPC technicalities, it's time to get started with the coding. (The full source code of the first prototype is found in Listing 27-1, at the end of this section.)

To find out where to begin, it might be a good idea to review your requirements from earlier in this chapter. You're mainly interested in two things: what information must your Node hold (attributes) and what actions must it be able to perform (methods)?

The Node must have at least the following attributes:

- A directory name, so it knows where to find/store its files.

- A "secret" (or password) that can be used by others to identify themselves (as trusted parties).

- A set of known peers (URLs).

- A URL, which may be added to the query history or possibly supplied to other Nodes. (This project won't implement the latter.)

The Node constructor will simply set these four attributes. In addition, you'll need a method for querying the Node, a method for making it fetch and store a file, and a method to introduce another Node to it. Let's call these methods query, fetch, and hello. The following is a sketch of the class, written as pseudocode:

```
class Node:

    def __init__(self, url, dirname, secret):
        self.url = url
        self.dirname = dirname
        self.secret = secret
        self.known = set()

    def query(self, query):
        Look for a file (possibly asking neighbors), and return it as
        a string
```

```
def fetch(self, query, secret):
    If the secret is correct, perform a regular query and store
    the file. In other words, make the Node find the file and download it.

def hello(self, other):
    Add the other Node to the known peers
```

Assuming that the set of known URLs is called known, the hello method is very simple. It just adds other to self.known, where other is the only parameter (a URL). However, XML-RPC requires all methods to return a value; None is not accepted. So, let's define two result "codes" that indicate success or failure:

```
OK = 1
FAIL = 2
```

Then the hello method can be implemented as follows:

```
def hello(self, other):
    self.known.add(other)
    return OK
```

When the Node is registered with a SimpleXMLRPCServer, it will be possible to call this method from the "outside."

The query and fetch methods are a bit more tricky. Let's begin with fetch because it's the simpler of the two. It must take two parameters: the query and the "secret," which is required so that your Node can't be arbitrarily manipulated by anyone. Note that calling fetch causes the Node to download a file. Access to this method should therefore be more restricted than, for example, query, which simply passes the file through.

If the supplied secret is not equal to self.secret (the one supplied at startup), fetch simply returns FAIL. Otherwise, it calls query to get the file corresponding to the given query (a file name). But what does query return? When you call query, you would like to know whether the query succeeded, and you would like to have the contents of the relevant file returned if it did. So, let's define the return value of query as the pair (tuple) code, data, where code is either OK or FAIL, and data is the sought-after file (if code equals OK) stored in a string, or an arbitrary value (for example, an empty string) otherwise.

In fetch, the code and the data are retrieved. If the code is FAIL, then fetch simply returns FAIL as well. Otherwise, it opens a new file (in write mode) whose name is the same as the query and which is found in the directory self.dirname (you use os.path.join to join the two). The data is written to the file, the file is closed, and OK is returned. See Listing 27-1 later in this section for the relatively straightforward implementation.

Now, turn your attention to query. It receives a query as a parameter, but it should also accept a history (which contains URLs that should not be queried because they are already waiting for a response to the same query). Because this history is empty in the first call to query, you can use an empty list as a default value.

If you take a look at the code in Listing 27-1, you'll see that it abstracts away part of the behavior of query by creating two utility methods called _handle and _broadcast. Note that their names begin with underscores, which means that they won't be accessible through

XML-RPC. (This is part of the behavior of SimpleXMLRPCServer, not a part of XML-RPC itself.) That is useful because these methods aren't meant to provide separate functionality to an outside party, but are there to structure the code.

For now, let's just assume that _handle takes care of the internal handling of a query (checks whether the file exists at this specific Node, fetches the data, and so forth) and that it returns a code and some data, just as query itself is supposed to. As you can see from the listing, if code == OK, then code, data is returned immediately—the file was found. However, what should query do if the code returned from _handle is FAIL? Then it must ask all other known Nodes for help. The first step in this process is to add self.url to history.

---

■**Note**  Neither the += operator nor the append list method has been used when updating the history because both of these modify lists in place, and you don't want to modify the default value itself.

---

If the new history is too long, query returns FAIL (along with an empty string). The maximum length is arbitrarily set to 6 and kept in the global constant MAX_HISTORY_LENGTH.

## WHY IS MAX_HISTORY_LENGTH SET TO 6?

The idea is that any peer in the network should be able to reach another in, at most, six steps. This, of course, depends on the structure of the network (which peers know which), but is supported by the hypothesis of "six degrees of separation," which applies to people and who they know. For a description of this hypothesis, see, for example, Wikipedia's article on six degrees of separation (http://en.wikipedia.org/wiki/Six_degrees_of_separation).

Using this number in your program may not be very scientific, but at least it seems like a good guess. On the other hand, in a large network with many nodes, the sequential nature of your program may lead to bad performance for large values of MAX_HISTORY_LENGTH, so you might want to reduce it if things get slow.

If history isn't too long, the next step is to broadcast the query to all known peers, which is done with the _broadcast method. The _broadcast method isn't very complicated (see Listing 27-1). It iterates over a copy of self.known. If a peer is found in history, the loop continues to the next peer (using the continue statement). Otherwise, a ServerProxy is constructed, and the query method is called on it. If the query succeeds, its return value is used as the return value from _broadcast. Exceptions may occur, due to network problems, a faulty URL, or the fact that the peer doesn't support the query method. If such an exception occurs, the peer's URL is removed from self.known (in the except clause of the try statement enclosing the query). Finally, if control reaches the end of the function (nothing has been returned yet), FAIL is returned, along with an empty string.

---

■**Note**  You shouldn't simply iterate over `self.known` because the set may be modified during the iteration. Using a copy is safer.

---

The `_start` method creates a `SimpleXMLRPCServer` (using the little utility function `getPort`, which extracts the port number from a URL), with `logRequests` set to false (you don't want to keep a log). It then registers `self` with `register_instance` and calls the server's `serve_forever` method.

Finally, the `main` method of the module extracts a URL, a directory, and a secret (password) from the command line; creates a `Node`; and calls its `_start` method.

For the full code of the prototype, see Listing 27-1.

**Listing 27-1.** *A Simple Node Implementation (simple_node.py)*

```
from xmlrpclib import ServerProxy
from os.path import join, isfile
from SimpleXMLRPCServer import SimpleXMLRPCServer
from urlparse import urlparse
import sys

MAX_HISTORY_LENGTH = 6

OK = 1
FAIL = 2
EMPTY = ''

def getPort(url):
    'Extracts the port from a URL'
    name = urlparse(url)[1]
    parts = name.split(':')
    return int(parts[-1])


class Node:
    """
    A node in a peer-to-peer network.
    """
    def __init__(self, url, dirname, secret):
        self.url = url
        self.dirname = dirname
        self.secret = secret
        self.known = set()
```

```python
    def query(self, query, history=[]):
        """
        Performs a query for a file, possibly asking other known Nodes for
        help. Returns the file as a string.
        """
        code, data = self._handle(query)
        if code == OK:
            return code, data
        else:
            history = history + [self.url]
            if len(history) >= MAX_HISTORY_LENGTH:
                return FAIL, EMPTY
            return self._broadcast(query, history)

    def hello(self, other):
        """
        Used to introduce the Node to other Nodes.
        """
        self.known.add(other)
        return OK

    def fetch(self, query, secret):
        """
        Used to make the Node find a file and download it.
        """
        if secret != self.secret: return FAIL
        code, data = self.query(query)
        if code == OK:
            f = open(join(self.dirname, query), 'w')
            f.write(data)
            f.close()
            return OK
        else:
            return FAIL


    def _start(self):
        """
        Used internally to start the XML-RPC server.
        """
        s = SimpleXMLRPCServer(("", getPort(self.url)), logRequests=False)
        s.register_instance(self)
        s.serve_forever()
```

```
    def _handle(self, query):
        """
        Used internally to handle queries.
        """
        dir = self.dirname
        name = join(dir, query)
        if not isfile(name): return FAIL, EMPTY
        return OK, open(name).read()

    def _broadcast(self, query, history):
        """
        Used internally to broadcast a query to all known Nodes.
        """
        for other in self.known.copy():
            if other in history: continue
            try:
                s = ServerProxy(other)
                code, data = s.query(query, history)
                if code == OK:
                    return code, data
            except:
                self.known.remove(other)
        return FAIL, EMPTY

def main():
    url, directory, secret = sys.argv[1:]
    n = Node(url, directory, secret)
    n._start()

if __name__ == '__main__': main()
```

Now let's take a look at a simple example of how this program may be used.

## Trying Out the First Implementation

Make sure you have several terminals (xterm, DOS window, or equivalent) open. Let's say you want to run two peers (both on the same machine). Create a directory for each of them, such as files1 and files2. Put a file (for example, test.txt) into the files2 directory. Then, in one terminal, run the following command:

```
python simple_node.py http://localhost:4242 files1 secret1
```

In a real application, you would use the full machine name instead of localhost, and you would probably use a secret that is a bit more cryptic than secret1.

This is your first peer. Now create another one. In a different terminal, run the following command:

```
python simple_node.py http://localhost:4243 files2 secret2
```

As you can see, this peer serves files from a different directory, uses another port number (4243), and has another secret. If you have followed these instructions, you should have two peers running (each in a separate terminal window). Let's start up an interactive Python interpreter and try to connect to one of them:

```
>>> from xmlrpclib import *
>>> mypeer = ServerProxy('http://localhost:4242') # The first peer
>>> code, data = mypeer.query('test.txt')
>>> code
2
```

As you can see, the first peer fails when asked for the file test.txt. (The return code 2 represents failure, remember?) Let's try the same thing with the second peer:

```
>>> otherpeer = ServerProxy('http://localhost:4243') # The second peer
>>> code, data = otherpeer.query('test.txt')
>>> code
1
```

This time, the query succeeds because the file test.txt is found in the second peer's file directory. If your test file doesn't contain too much text, you can display the contents of the data variable to make sure that the contents of the file have been transferred properly:

```
>>> data
'This is a test\n'
```

So far, so good. How about introducing the first peer to the second one?

```
>>> mypeer.hello('http://localhost:4243') # Introducing mypeer to otherpeer
```

Now the first peer knows the URL of the second, and thus may ask it for help. Let's try querying the first peer again. This time, the query should succeed:

```
>>> mypeer.query('test.txt')
[1, 'This is a test\n']
```

Bingo!

Now there is only one thing left to test: can you make the first node actually download and store the file from the second one?

```
>>> mypeer.fetch('test.txt', 'secret1')
1
```

Well, the return value (1) indicates success. And if you look in the files1 directory, you should see that the file test.txt has miraculously appeared. Cool, eh? Feel free to start several peers (on different machines, if you want to), and introduce them to each other. When you grow tired of playing, proceed to the next implementation.

# Second Implementation

The first implementation has plenty of flaws and shortcomings. I won't address all of them (some possible improvements are discussed in the section "Further Exploration," at the end of this chapter), but here are some of the more important ones:

- If you try to stop a Node and then restart it, you will probably get some error message about the port being in use already.

- You should have a more user-friendly interface than xmlrpclib in an interactive Python interpreter.

- The return codes are inconvenient. A more natural and Pythonic solution would be to use a custom exception if the file can't be found.

- The Node doesn't check whether the file it returns is actually inside the file directory. By using paths such as '../somesecretfile.txt', a sneaky cracker may get unlawful access to any of your other files.

The first problem is easy to solve. You simply set the allow_reuse_address attribute of the SimpleXMLRPCServer to true:

```
SimpleXMLRPCServer.allow_reuse_address = 1
```

If you don't want to modify this class directly, you can create your own subclass. The other changes are a bit more involved, and are discussed in the following sections. The source code is shown in Listings 27-2 and 27-3 later in this chapter. (You might want to take a quick look at these listings before reading on.)

## Creating the Client Interface

The client interface uses the Cmd class from the cmd module. For details about how this works, see the Python Library Reference. Simply put, you subclass Cmd to create a command-line interface, and implement a method called do_foo for each command foo you want it to be able to handle. This method will receive the rest of the command line as its only argument (as a string). For example, if you type this in the command-line interface:

```
say hello
```

the method do_say is called with the string 'hello' as its only argument. The prompt of the Cmd subclass is determined by the prompt attribute.

The only commands implemented in your interface will be fetch (to download a file) and exit (to exit the program). The fetch command simply calls the fetch method of the server, printing an error message if the file could not be found. The exit commands prints an empty line (for aesthetic reasons only) and calls sys.exit. (The EOF command corresponds to "end of file," which occurs when the user presses Ctrl+D in UNIX.)

But what is all the stuff going on in the constructor? Well, you want each client to be associated with a peer of its own. You *could* simply create a Node object and call its _start method, but then your Client couldn't do anything until the _start method returned, which makes the Client completely useless. To fix this, the Node is started in a separate *thread*. Normally, using threads involves a lot of safeguarding and synchronization with locks and the like. However, because a Client interacts with its Node only through XML-RPC, you don't need any of this. To run the _start method in a separate thread, you just need to put the following code into your program at some suitable place:

```
from threading import Thread
n = Node(url, dirname, self.secret)
t = Thread(target=n._start)
t.start()
```

---

■**Caution**  You should be careful when rewriting the code of this project. The minute your Client starts interacting directly with the Node object or vice versa, you may easily run into trouble, because of the threading. Make sure you fully understand threading before you do this.

---

To make sure that the server is fully started before you start connecting to it with XML-RPC, you'll give it a head start, and wait for a moment with time.sleep.

Afterward, you'll go through all the lines in a file of URLs and introduce your server to them with the hello method.

You don't really want to be bothered with coming up with a clever secret password. Instead, you can use the utility function randomString (in Listing 27-3, shown later in this chapter), which generates a random secret string that is shared between the Client and the Node.

## Raising Exceptions

Instead of returning a code indicating success or failure, you'll just assume success and raise an exception in the case of failure. In XML-RPC, exceptions (or *faults*) are identified by numbers. For this project, I have (arbitrarily) chosen the numbers 100 and 200 for ordinary failure (an unhandled request) and a request refusal (access denied), respectively.

```
UNHANDLED      = 100
ACCESS_DENIED = 200


class UnhandledQuery(Fault):
    """
    An exception that represents an unhandled query.
    """
    def __init__(self, message="Couldn't handle the query"):
        Fault.__init__(self, UNHANDLED, message)
```

```
class AccessDenied(Fault):
    """
    An exception that is raised if a user tries to access a
    resource for which he or she is not authorized.
    """
    def __init__(self, message="Access denied"):
        Fault.__init__(self, ACCESS_DENIED, message)
```

The exceptions are subclasses of `xmlrpclib.Fault`. When they are raised in the server, they are passed on to the client with the same `faultCode`. If an ordinary exception (such as `IOException`) is raised in the server, an instance of the `Fault` class is still created, so you can't simply use arbitrary exceptions here. (Make sure you have a recent version of `SimpleXMLRPCServer`, so it handles exceptions properly.)

As you can see from the source code, the logic is still basically the same, but instead of using `if` statements for checking returned codes, the program now uses exceptions. (Because you can use only `Fault` objects, you need to check the `faultCodes`. If you weren't using XML-RPC, you would have used different exception classes instead, of course.)

## Validating File Names

The last issue to deal with is to check whether a given file name is found within a given directory. There are several ways to do this, but to keep things platform-independent (so it works in Windows, in UNIX, and in Mac OS, for example), you should use the module `os.path`.

The simple approach taken here is to create an absolute path from the directory name and the file name (so that, for example, `'/foo/bar/../baz'` is converted to `'/foo/baz'`), the directory name is joined with an empty file name (using `os.path.join`) to ensure that it ends with a file separator (such as `'/'`), and then you check that the absolute file name begins with the absolute directory name. If it does, the file is actually inside the directory.

The full source code for the second implementation is shown Listings 27-2 and 27-3.

**Listing 27-2.** *A New Node Implementation (server.py)*

```
from xmlrpclib import ServerProxy, Fault
from os.path import join, abspath, isfile
from SimpleXMLRPCServer import SimpleXMLRPCServer
from urlparse import urlparse
import sys

SimpleXMLRPCServer.allow_reuse_address = 1

MAX_HISTORY_LENGTH = 6

UNHANDLED     = 100
ACCESS_DENIED = 200
```

```
class UnhandledQuery(Fault):
    """
    An exception that represents an unhandled query.
    """

    def __init__(self, message="Couldn't handle the query"):
        Fault.__init__(self, UNHANDLED, message)


class AccessDenied(Fault):
    """
    An exception that is raised if a user tries to access a
    resource for which he or she is not authorized.
    """

    def __init__(self, message="Access denied"):
        Fault.__init__(self, ACCESS_DENIED, message)

def inside(dir, name):
    """
    Checks whether a given file name lies within a given directory.
    """

    dir = abspath(dir)
    name = abspath(name)
    return name.startswith(join(dir, ''))

def getPort(url):
    """
    Extracts the port number from a URL.
    """

    name = urlparse(url)[1]
    parts = name.split(':')
    return int(parts[-1])

class Node:
    """
    A node in a peer-to-peer network.
    """

    def __init__(self, url, dirname, secret):
        self.url = url
        self.dirname = dirname
        self.secret = secret
        self.known = set()

    def query(self, query, history=[]):
        """
        Performs a query for a file, possibly asking other known Nodes for
        help. Returns the file as a string.
```

```
    """
    try:
        return self._handle(query)
    except UnhandledQuery:
        history = history + [self.url]
        if len(history) >= MAX_HISTORY_LENGTH: raise
        return self._broadcast(query, history)


def hello(self, other):
    """
    Used to introduce the Node to other Nodes.
    """
    self.known.add(other)
    return 0

def fetch(self, query, secret):
    """
    Used to make the Node find a file and download it.
    """
    if secret != self.secret: raise AccessDenied
    result = self.query(query)
    f = open(join(self.dirname, query), 'w')
    f.write(result)
    f.close()
    return 0

def _start(self):
    """
    Used internally to start the XML-RPC server.
    """
    s = SimpleXMLRPCServer(("", getPort(self.url)), logRequests=False)
    s.register_instance(self)
    s.serve_forever()

def _handle(self, query):
    """
    Used internally to handle queries.
    """
    dir = self.dirname
    name = join(dir, query)
    if not isfile(name): raise UnhandledQuery
    if not inside(dir, name): raise AccessDenied
    return open(name).read()
```

```python
    def _broadcast(self, query, history):
        """
        Used internally to broadcast a query to all known Nodes.
        """
        for other in self.known.copy():
            if other in history: continue
            try:
                s = ServerProxy(other)
                return s.query(query, history)

            except Fault, f:
                if f.faultCode == UNHANDLED: pass
                else: self.known.remove(other)
            except:
                self.known.remove(other)
        raise UnhandledQuery

def main():
    url, directory, secret = sys.argv[1:]
    n = Node(url, directory, secret)
    n._start()

if __name__ == '__main__': main()
```

**Listing 27-3.** *A Node Controller Interface (client.py)*

```python
from xmlrpclib import ServerProxy, Fault
from cmd import Cmd
from random import choice
from string import lowercase
from server import Node, UNHANDLED
from threading import Thread
from time import sleep
import sys

HEAD_START = 0.1 # Seconds
SECRET_LENGTH = 100

def randomString(length):
    """
    Returns a random string of letters with the given length.
    """
    chars = []
    letters = lowercase[:26]
```

```python
        while length > 0:
            length -= 1
            chars.append(choice(letters))
        return ''.join(chars)

class Client(Cmd):
    """
    A simple text-based interface to the Node class.
    """

    prompt = '> '


    def __init__(self, url, dirname, urlfile):
        """
        Sets the url, dirname, and urlfile, and starts the Node
        Server in a separate thread.
        """
        Cmd.__init__(self)
        self.secret = randomString(SECRET_LENGTH)
        n = Node(url, dirname, self.secret)
        t = Thread(target=n._start)
        t.setDaemon(1)
        t.start()
        # Give the server a head start:
        sleep(HEAD_START)
        self.server = ServerProxy(url)
        for line in open(urlfile):
            line = line.strip()
            self.server.hello(line)

    def do_fetch(self, arg):
        "Call the fetch method of the Server."
        try:
            self.server.fetch(arg, self.secret)
        except Fault, f:
            if f.faultCode != UNHANDLED: raise
            print "Couldn't find the file", arg

    def do_exit(self, arg):
        "Exit the program."
        print
        sys.exit()

    do_EOF = do_exit # End-Of-File is synonymous with 'exit'
```

```
def main():
    urlfile, directory, url = sys.argv[1:]
    client = Client(url, directory, urlfile)
    client.cmdloop()

if __name__ == '__main__': main()
```

### Trying Out the Second Implementation

Let's see how the program is used. Start it like this:

```
python client.py urls.txt directory http://servername.com:4242
```

The file urls.txt should contain one URL per line—the URLs of all the other peers you know. The directory given as the second argument should contain the files you want to share (and will be the location where new files are downloaded). The last argument is the URL to the peer. When you run this command, you should get a prompt like this:

```
>
```

Try fetching a nonexistent file:

```
> fetch fooo
Couldn't find the file fooo
```

By starting several nodes (either on the same machine using different ports or on different machines) that know about each other (just put all the URLs in the URL files), you can try these out as you did with the first prototype. When you get bored with this, move on to the next section.

# Further Exploration

You can probably think of several ways to improve and extend the system described in this chapter. Here are some ideas:

- Add caching. If your node relays a file through a call to query, why not store the file at the same time? That way, you can respond more quickly the next time someone asks for the same file. You could perhaps set a maximum size for the cache, remove old files, and so on.

- Use a threaded or asynchronous server (a bit difficult). That way, you can ask several other nodes for help without waiting for their replies, and they can later give you the reply by calling a reply method.

- Allow more advanced queries, such as querying on the contents of text files.

- Use the hello method more extensively. When you discover a new peer (through a call to hello), why not introduce it to all the peers you know? Perhaps you can think of more clever ways of discovering new peers?

- Read up on the representational state transfer (REST) philosophy of distributed systems. REST is an emerging alternative to web service technologies such as XML-RPC. (See, for example, `http://en.wikipedia.org/wiki/REST`.)

- Use `xmlrpclib.Binary` to wrap the files, to make the transfer safer for nontext files.

- Read the `SimpleXMLRPCServer` code. Check out the `DocXMLRPCServer` class and the multi-call extension in `libxmlrpc`.

## What Now?

Now that you have a peer-to-peer file sharing system working, how about making it more user friendly? In the next chapter, you learn how to add a GUI as an alternative to the current `cmd`-based interface.

■■■

# CHAPTER 28

# Project 9: File Sharing II—Now with GUI!

**T**his is a relatively short project because much of the functionality you need has already been written—in Chapter 27. In this chapter, you see how easy it can be to add a GUI to an existing Python program.

## What's the Problem?

In this project, you expand the file sharing system developed in Chapter 27, with a GUI client. This will make the program much easier to use, which means that more people might choose to use it (and, of course, multiple users sharing files is the whole point of the program). A secondary goal of this project is to show that a program that has a sufficiently modular design can be quite easy to extend (one of the arguments for using object-oriented programming).

The GUI client should satisfy the following requirements:

- It should allow you to enter a file name and submit it to the server's fetch method.

- It should list the files currently available in the server's file directory.

That's it. Because you already have much of the system working, the GUI part is a relatively simple extension.

## Useful Tools

In addition to the tools used in Chapter 27, you will need the wxPython toolkit. For more information about (and installation instructions for) wxPython, see Chapter 12. The code in this chapter was developed using wxPython version 2.6, but will work with the latest version.

If you want to use another GUI toolkit, feel free to do so. The example in this chapter will give you the general idea of how you can build your own implementation, with your favorite tools. (Chapter 12 describes several GUI toolkits.)

# Preparations

Before you begin this project, you should have Project 8 (from Chapter 27) in place, and a usable GUI toolkit installed, as mentioned in the previous section. Beyond that, no significant preparations are necessary for this project.

# First Implementation

If you want to take a peek at the full source code for the first implementation, it can be found in Listing 28-1 later in this section. Much of the functionality is quite similar to that of the project in the preceding chapter. The client presents an interface (the fetch method) through which the user may access the functionality of the server. Let's review the GUI-specific parts of the code.

The client in Chapter 27 was a subclass of cmd.Cmd; the Client described in this chapter subclasses wx.App. While you're not required to subclass wx.App (you could create a completely separate Client class), it can be a natural way of organizing your code. The GUI-related setup is placed in a separate method, called OnInit, which is called automatically after the App object has been created. It performs the following steps:

1. It creates a window with the title "File Sharing Client."

2. It creates a text field and assigns that text field to the attribute self.input (and, for convenience, to the local variable input). It also creates a button with the text "Fetch." It sets the size of the button and binds an event handler to it. Both the text field and the button have the panel bkg as their parent.

3. It adds the text field and button to the window, laying them out using box sizers. (Feel free to use another layout mechanism.)

4. It shows the window, and returns True, to indicate that OnInit was successful.

The event handler is quite similar to the handler do_fetch from Chapter 27. It retrieves the query from self.input (the text field). It then calls self.server.fetch inside a try/except statement. Note that the event handler receives an event object as its only argument.

The source code for the first implementation is shown in Listing 28-1.

**Listing 28-1.** *A Simple GUI Client (simple_guiclient.py)*

```
from xmlrpclib import ServerProxy, Fault
from server import Node, UNHANDLED
from client import randomString
from threading import Thread
from time import sleep
from os import listdir
import sys
import wx
```

```python
HEAD_START = 0.1 # Seconds
SECRET_LENGTH = 100

class Client(wx.App):
    """
    The main client class, which takes care of setting up the GUI and
    starts a Node for serving files.
    """
    def __init__(self, url, dirname, urlfile):
        """
        Creates a random secret, instantiates a Node with that secret,
        starts a Thread with the Node's _start method (making sure the
        Thread is a daemon so it will quit when the application quits),
        reads all the URLs from the URL file and introduces the Node to
        them.
        """
        super(Client, self).__init__()
        self.secret = randomString(SECRET_LENGTH)
        n = Node(url, dirname, self.secret)
        t = Thread(target=n._start)
        t.setDaemon(1)
        t.start()
        # Give the server a head start:
        sleep(HEAD_START)
        self.server = ServerProxy(url)
        for line in open(urlfile):
            line = line.strip()
            self.server.hello(line)


    def OnInit(self):
        """
        Sets up the GUI. Creates a window, a text field, and a button, and
        lays them out. Binds the submit button to self.fetchHandler.
        """

        win = wx.Frame(None, title="File Sharing Client", size=(400, 45))

        bkg = wx.Panel(win)

        self.input = input = wx.TextCtrl(bkg);

        submit = wx.Button(bkg, label="Fetch", size=(80, 25))
        submit.Bind(wx.EVT_BUTTON, self.fetchHandler)

        hbox = wx.BoxSizer()
```

```
            hbox.Add(input, proportion=1, flag=wx.ALL | wx.EXPAND, border=10)
            hbox.Add(submit, flag=wx.TOP | wx.BOTTOM | wx.RIGHT, border=10)

            vbox = wx.BoxSizer(wx.VERTICAL)
            vbox.Add(hbox, proportion=0, flag=wx.EXPAND)

            bkg.SetSizer(vbox)

            win.Show()

            return True

    def fetchHandler(self, event):
        """
        Called when the user clicks the 'Fetch' button. Reads the
        query from the text field, and calls the fetch method of the
        server Node. If the query is not handled, an error message is
        printed.
        """

        query = self.input.GetValue()
        try:
            self.server.fetch(query, self.secret)
        except Fault, f:
            if f.faultCode != UNHANDLED: raise
            print "Couldn't find the file", query


def main():
    urlfile, directory, url = sys.argv[1:]
    client = Client(url, directory, urlfile)
    client.MainLoop()

if __name__ == "__main__": main()
```

Except for the relatively simple code explained previously, the GUI client works just like the text-based client in Chapter 27. You can run it in the same manner, too. To run this program, you need a URL file, a directory of files to share, and a URL for your Node. Here is a sample run:

```
$ python simple_guiclient.py urlfile.txt files/ http://localhost:8080
```

Note that the file urlfile.txt must contain the URLs of some other Nodes for the program to be of any use. You can either start several programs on the same machine (with different port numbers) for testing purposes, or run them on different machines. Figure 28-1 shows the GUI of the client.

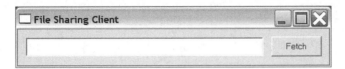

**Figure 28-1.** *The simple GUI client*

This implementation works, but it performs only part of its job. It should also list the files available in the server's file directory. To do that, the server (Node) itself must be extended.

# Second Implementation

The first prototype was very simple. It did its job as a file sharing system, but wasn't very user friendly. It would help a lot if users could see which files they had available (either located in the file directory when the program starts or subsequently downloaded from another Node). The second implementation will address this file listing issue. The full source code can be found in Listing 28-2.

To get a listing from a Node, you must add a method. You could protect it with a password as you have done with fetch, but making it publicly available may be useful, and it doesn't represent any real security risk. Extending an object is really easy: you can do it through sub-classing. You simply construct a subclass of Node called ListableNode, with a single additional method, list, which uses the method os.listdir, which returns a list of all the files in a directory:

```
class ListableNode(Node):

    def list(self):
        return listdir(self.dirname)
```

To access this server method, the method updateList is added to the client:

```
def updateList(self):
    self.files.Set(self.server.list())
```

The attribute self.files refers to a list box, which has been added in the OnInit method. The updateList method is called in OnInit at the point where the list box is created, and again each time fetchHandler is called (because calling fetchHandler may potentially alter the list of files).

**Listing 28-2.** *The Finished GUI Client (guiclient.py)*

```
from xmlrpclib import ServerProxy, Fault
from server import Node, UNHANDLED
from client import randomString
from threading import Thread
```

```
from time import sleep
from os import listdir
import sys
import wx

HEAD_START = 0.1 # Seconds
SECRET_LENGTH = 100


class ListableNode(Node):
    """
    An extended version of Node, which can list the files
    in its file directory.
    """
    def list(self):
        return listdir(self.dirname)

class Client(wx.App):
    """
    The main client class, which takes care of setting up the GUI and
    starts a Node for serving files.
    """
    def __init__(self, url, dirname, urlfile):
        """
        Creates a random secret, instantiates a ListableNode with that secret,
        starts a Thread with the ListableNode's _start method (making sure the
        Thread is a daemon so it will quit when the application quits),
        reads all the URLs from the URL file and introduces the Node to
        them. Finally, sets up the GUI.
        """
        self.secret = randomString(SECRET_LENGTH)
        n = ListableNode(url, dirname, self.secret)
        t = Thread(target=n._start)
        t.setDaemon(1)
        t.start()
        # Give the server a head start:
        sleep(HEAD_START)
        self.server = ServerProxy(url)
        for line in open(urlfile):
            line = line.strip()
            self.server.hello(line)
        # Get the GUI going:
        super(Client, self).__init__()
```

```python
def updateList(self):
    """
    Updates the list box with the names of the files available
    from the server Node.
    """
    self.files.Set(self.server.list())


def OnInit(self):
    """
    Sets up the GUI. Creates a window, a text field, a button, and
    a list box, and lays them out. Binds the submit button to
    self.fetchHandler.
    """

    win = wx.Frame(None, title="File Sharing Client", size=(400, 300))

    bkg = wx.Panel(win)

    self.input = input = wx.TextCtrl(bkg);

    submit = wx.Button(bkg, label="Fetch", size=(80, 25))
    submit.Bind(wx.EVT_BUTTON, self.fetchHandler)

    hbox = wx.BoxSizer()

    hbox.Add(input, proportion=1, flag=wx.ALL | wx.EXPAND, border=10)
    hbox.Add(submit, flag=wx.TOP | wx.BOTTOM | wx.RIGHT, border=10)

    self.files = files = wx.ListBox(bkg)
    self.updateList()

    vbox = wx.BoxSizer(wx.VERTICAL)
    vbox.Add(hbox, proportion=0, flag=wx.EXPAND)
    vbox.Add(files, proportion=1,
             flag=wx.EXPAND | wx.LEFT | wx.RIGHT | wx.BOTTOM, border=10)

    bkg.SetSizer(vbox)

    win.Show()

    return True
```

```
    def fetchHandler(self, event):
        """
        Called when the user clicks the 'Fetch' button. Reads the
        query from the text field, and calls the fetch method of the
        server Node. After handling the query, updateList is called.
        If the query is not handled, an error message is printed.
        """
        query = self.input.GetValue()
        try:
            self.server.fetch(query, self.secret)
            self.updateList()

        except Fault, f:
            if f.faultCode != UNHANDLED: raise
            print "Couldn't find the file", query

def main():
    urlfile, directory, url = sys.argv[1:]
    client = Client(url, directory, urlfile)
    client.MainLoop()

if __name__ == '__main__': main()
```

And that's it. You now have a GUI-enabled peer-to-peer file sharing program, which can
be run with this command:

```
$ python guiclient.py urlfile.txt files/ http://localhost:8080
```

Figure 28-2 shows the finished GUI client.

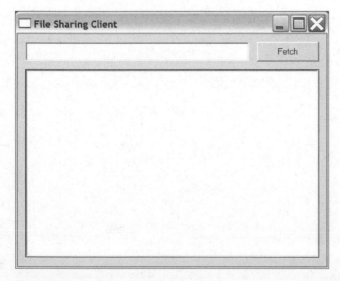

**Figure 28-2.** *The finished GUI client*

Of course, there are plenty of ways to expand the program. For some ideas, see the next section. Beyond that, just let your imagination go wild.

# Further Exploration

Some ideas for extending the file sharing system are given in Chapter 27. Here are some more:

- Add a status bar that displays such messages as "Downloading" or "Couldn't find file foo.txt."

- Figure out ways for Nodes to share their "friends." For example, when one Node is introduced to another, each of them could introduce the other to the Nodes it already knows. Also, before a Node shuts down, it might tell all its current neighbors about all the Nodes it knows.

- Add a list of known Nodes (URLs) to the GUI. Make it possible to add new URLs and save them in a URL file.

## What Now?

You've written a full-fledged GUI-enabled peer-to-peer file sharing system. Although that sounds pretty challenging, it wasn't all that hard, was it? Now it's time to face the last and greatest challenge: writing your own arcade game.

# CHAPTER 29

■■■

# Project 10: Do-It-Yourself Arcade Game

**W**elcome to the final project. Now that you've sampled several of Python's many capabilities, it's time to go out with a bang. In this chapter, you learn how to use Pygame, an extension that enables you to write full-fledged, full-screen arcade games in Python. Although easy to use, Pygame is quite powerful and consists of several components that are thoroughly documented in the Pygame documentation (available on the Pygame web site, `http://pygame.org`). This project introduces you to some of the main Pygame concepts, but because this chapter is only meant as a starting point, I've skipped several interesting features, such as sound and video handling. I recommend that you investigate the other features yourself, once you've familiarized yourself with the basics. You might also want to take a look at *Beginning Game Development with Python and Pygame* by Will McGugan (Apress, 2007).

## What's the Problem?

So, how do you write a computer game? The basic design process is similar to the one you use when writing any other program, but before you can develop an object model, you need to design the game itself. What are its characters, its setting, and its objectives?

I'll keep things reasonably simple here, so as not to clutter the presentation of the basic Pygame concepts. Feel free to create a much more elaborate game if you like.

The game you'll create will be based on the well-known Monty Python sketch "Self-Defense Against Fresh Fruit." In this sketch, a Sergeant Major (John Cleese) is instructing his soldiers in self-defense techniques against attackers, wielding fresh fruit such as pomegranates, mangoes in syrup, greengages, and bananas. The defense techniques include using a gun, unleashing a tiger, and dropping a 16-ton weight on top of the attacker. In this game, you'll turn things around—the player controls a banana that desperately tries to survive a course in self-defense, avoiding a barrage of 16-ton weights dropping from above. I guess a fitting name for the game might be Squish.

---

■**Note** If you would like to try your hand at a game of your own as you follow this chapter, feel free to do so. If you just want to change the look and feel of the game, simply replace the graphics (a couple of GIF or PNG images) and some of the descriptive text.

---

The specific goals of this project revolve around the game design. The game should behave as it was designed (the banana should be movable, and the 16-ton weight should drop from above). In addition, the code should be modular and easily extensible (as always). A useful requirement might be that game states (such as the game introduction, the various game levels, and the "game over" state) should be part of the design, and that new states should be easy to add.

# Useful Tools

The only new tool you need in this project is Pygame, which you can download from the Pygame web site (`http://pygame.org`). To get Pygame to work in UNIX, you may need to install some extra software, but it's all documented in the Pygame installation instructions (also available from the Pygame web site). The Windows binary installer is very easy to use—simply execute the installer and follow the instructions.

---

■**Note**  The Pygame distribution does not include NumPy (`http://numpy.scipy.org`), which may be useful for manipulating sounds and images. Although it's not needed for this project, you might want to check it out. The Pygame documentation thoroughly describes how to use NumPy with Pygame.

---

The Pygame distribution consists of several modules, most of which you won't need in this project. The following sections describe the modules you do need. (Only the specific functions or classes you'll need are discussed here.) In addition to the functions described in the following sections, the various objects used (such as surfaces, groups, and sprites) have several useful methods, which I'll discuss as they are used in the implementation sections.

---

■**Tip**  You can find a nice introduction to Pygame in the "Line-by-Line Chimp" tutorial on the Pygame web site (`http://pygame.org/docs/tut/chimp/ChimpLineByLine.html`). It addresses a few issues not discussed here, such as playing sound clips.

---

## pygame

The pygame module automatically imports all the other Pygame modules, so if you place `import pygame` at the top of your program, you can automatically access the other modules, such as `pygame.display` and `pygame.font`.

The pygame module contains (among other things) the `Surface` function, which returns a new surface object. Surface objects are simply blank images of a given size that you can use for drawing and blitting. To blit (calling a surface object's blit method) simply means to transfer the contents of one surface to another. (The word *blit* is derived from the technical term *block transfer*, which is abbreviated BLT.)

The init function is central to any Pygame game. It must be called before your game enters its main event loop. This function automatically initializes all the other modules (such as font and image).

You need the error class when you want to catch Pygame-specific errors.

## pygame.locals

The pygame.locals module contains names (variables) you might want in your own module's scope. It contains names for event types, keys, video modes, and more. It is designed to be safe to use when you import everything (from pygame.locals import *), although if you know what you need, you may want to be more specific (for example, from pygame.locals import FULLSCREEN).

## pygame.display

The pygame.display module contains functions for dealing with the Pygame display, which either may be contained in a normal window or occupy the entire screen. In this project, you need the following functions:

flip: Updates the display. In general, when you modify the current screen, you do that in two steps. First, you perform all the necessary modifications to the surface object returned from the get_surface function, and then you call pygame.display.flip to update the display to reflect your changes.

update: Used instead of flip when you want to update only a part of the screen. It can be used with the list of rectangles returned from the draw method of the RenderUpdates class (described in the upcoming discussion of the pygame.sprite module) as its only parameter.

set_mode: Sets the display size and the type of display. Several variations are possible, but here you'll restrict yourself to the FULLSCREEN version, and the default "display in a window" version.

set_caption: Sets a caption for the Pygame program. The set_caption function is primarily useful when you run your game in a window (as opposed to full screen) because the caption is used as the window title.

get_surface: Returns a surface object on which you can draw your graphics before calling pygame.display.flip or pygame.display.blit. The only surface method used for drawing in this project is blit, which transfers the graphics found in one surface object onto another one, at a given location. (In addition, the draw method of a Group object will be used to draw Sprite objects onto the display surface.)

# pygame.font

The pygame.font module contains the Font function. Font objects are used to represent different typefaces. They can be used to render text as images that may then be used as normal graphics in Pygame.

# pygame.sprite

The pygame.sprite module contains two very important classes: Sprite and Group.

The Sprite class is the base class for all visible game objects—in the case of this project, the banana and the 16-ton weight. To implement your own game objects, you subclass Sprite, override its constructor to set its image and rect properties (which determine how the Sprite looks and where it is placed), and override its update method, which is called whenever the sprite might need updating.

Instances of the Group class (and its subclasses) are used as containers for Sprites. In general, using groups is A Good Thing. In simple games (such as in this project), just create a group called sprites or allsprites or something similar, and add all your Sprites to it. When you call the Group object's update method, the update methods of all your Sprite objects will then be called automatically. Also, the Group object's clear method is used to erase all the Sprite objects it contains (using a callback to do the erasing), and the draw method can be used to draw all the Sprites.

In this project, you'll use the RenderUpdates subclass of Group, whose draw method returns a list of rectangles that have been affected. These may then be passed to pygame.display.update to update only the parts of the display that need to be updated. This can potentially improve the performance of the game quite a bit.

# pygame.mouse

In Squish, you'll use the pygame.mouse module for just two things: hiding the mouse cursor and getting the mouse position. You hide the mouse with pygame.mouse.set_visible(False), and you get the position with pygame.mouse.get_pos().

# pygame.event

The pygame.event module keeps track of various events such as mouse clicks, mouse motion, keys that are pressed or released, and so on. To get a list of the most recent events, use the function pygame.event.get.

---

■**Note** If you rely only on state information such as the mouse position returned by pygame.mouse. get_pos, you don't need to use pygame.event.get. However, you need to keep the Pygame updated ("in sync"), which you can do by calling the function pygame.event.pump regularly.

---

## pygame.image

The pygame.image module is used to deal with images such as those stored in GIF, PNG, JPEG, and several other file formats. In this project, you need only the load function, which reads an image file and creates a surface object containing the image.

# Preparations

Now that you know a bit about what some of the different Pygame modules do, it's almost time to start hacking away at the first prototype game. There are, however, a couple of preparations you need to make before you can get the prototype up and running. First of all, you should make sure that you have Pygame installed, including the image and font modules. (You might want to import both of these in an interactive Python interpreter to make sure they are available.)

You also need a couple of images (for example, from a web site like http://www.openclipart.org or found through Google's image search). If you want to stick to the theme of the game as presented in this chapter, you need one image depicting a 16-ton weight and one depicting a banana, both of which are shown in Figure 29-1. Their exact sizes aren't all that important, but you might want to keep them in the range of 100 × 100 through 200 × 200 pixels. You should have these two images available in a common image file format such as GIF, PNG, or JPEG.

---

■**Note**  You might also want a separate image for the *splash screen,* the first screen that greets the user of your game. In this project, I simply used the weight symbol for that as well.

---

**Figure 29-1.** *The weight and banana graphics used in my version of the game*

# First Implementation

When you use a new tool such as Pygame, it often pays off to keep the first prototype as simple as possible and to focus on learning the basics of the new tool, rather than the intricacies of the program itself. Let's restrict the first version of Squish to an animation of 16-ton weights falling from above. The steps needed for this are as follows:

1. Initialize Pygame, using `pygame.init`, `pygame.display.set_mode`, and `pygame.mouse.set_visible`. Get the screen surface with `pygame.display.get_surface`. Fill the screen surface with a solid white color (with the `fill` method) and call `pygame.display.flip` to display this change.

2. Load the weight image.

3. Create an instance of a custom `Weight` class (a subclass of `Sprite`) using the image. Add this object to a `RenderUpdates` group called (for example) `sprites`. (This will be particularly useful when dealing with multiple sprites.)

4. Get all recent events with `pygame.event.get`. Check all the events in turn. If an event of type `QUIT` is found, or if an event of type `KEYDOWN` representing the escape key (`K_ESCAPE`) is found, exit the program. (The event types and keys are kept in the attributes `type` and `key` in the event object. Constants such as `QUIT`, `KEYDOWN`, and `K_ESCAPE` can be imported from the module `pygame.locals`.)

5. Call the `clear` and `update` methods of the `sprites` group. The `clear` method uses the callback to clear all the sprites (in this case, the weight), and the `update` method calls the `update` method of the `Weight` instance. (You must implement the latter method yourself.)

6. Call `sprites.draw` with the screen surface as the argument to draw the `Weight` sprite at its current position. (This position changes each time `update` is called.)

7. Call `pygame.display.update` with the rectangle list returned from `sprites.draw` to update the display only in the right places. (If you don't need the performance, you can use `pygame.display.flip` here to update the entire display.)

8. Repeat steps 4 through 7.

See Listing 29-1 for code that implements these steps. The `QUIT` event would occur if the user quit the game—for example, by closing the window.

**Listing 29-1.** *A Simple "Falling Weights" Animation (weights.py)*

```
import sys, pygame
from pygame.locals import *
from random import randrange

class Weight(pygame.sprite.Sprite):

    def __init__(self):
        pygame.sprite.Sprite.__init__(self)
        # image and rect used when drawing sprite:
        self.image = weight_image
        self.rect = self.image.get_rect()
        self.reset()
```

```python
    def reset(self):
        """
        Move the weight to a random position at the top of the screen.
        """
        self.rect.top = -self.rect.height
        self.rect.centerx = randrange(screen_size[0])

    def update(self):
        """
        Update the weight for display in the next frame.
        """
        self.rect.top += 1

        if self.rect.top > screen_size[1]:
            self.reset()

# Initialize things
pygame.init()
screen_size = 800, 600
pygame.display.set_mode(screen_size, FULLSCREEN)
pygame.mouse.set_visible(0)

# Load the weight image
weight_image = pygame.image.load('weight.png')
weight_image = weight_image.convert() # ... to match the display

# Create a sprite group and add a Weight
sprites = pygame.sprite.RenderUpdates()
sprites.add(Weight())

# Get the screen surface and fill it
screen = pygame.display.get_surface()
bg = (255, 255, 255) # White
screen.fill(bg)
pygame.display.flip()

# Used to erase the sprites:
def clear_callback(surf, rect):
    surf.fill(bg, rect)

while True:
    # Check for quit events:
    for event in pygame.event.get():
        if event.type == QUIT:
            sys.exit()
        if event.type == KEYDOWN and event.key == K_ESCAPE:
            sys.exit()
```

```
# Erase previous positions:
sprites.clear(screen, clear_callback)
# Update all sprites:
sprites.update()
# Draw all sprites:
updates = sprites.draw(screen)
# Update the necessary parts of the display:
pygame.display.update(updates)
```

You can run this program with the following command:

```
$ python weights.py
```

You should make sure that both `weights.py` and `weight.png` (the weight image) are in the current directory when you execute this command.

---

■**Note**  I have used a PNG image with transparency here, but a GIF image might work just as well. JPEG images aren't really well suited for transparency.

---

Figure 29-2 shows a screenshot of the program created in Listing 29-1.

Most of the code should speak for itself. However, a few points need some explanation:

- All sprite objects should have two attributes called `image` and `rect`. The former should contain a surface object (an image), and the latter should contain a rectangle object (just use `self.image.get_rect()` to initialize it). These two attributes will be used when drawing the sprites. By modifying `self.rect`, you can move the sprite around.

- Surface objects have a method called `convert`, which can be used to create a copy with a different color model. You don't need to worry about the details, but using `convert` without any arguments creates a surface that is tailored for the current display, and displaying it will be as fast as possible.

- Colors are specified through RGB triples (red-green-blue, with each value being 0–255), so the tuple (255, 255, 255) represents white.

**Figure 29-2.** *A simple animation of falling weights*

You modify a rectangle (such as self.rect in this case) by assigning to its attributes (top, bottom, left, right, topleft, topright, bottomleft, bottomright, size, width, height, center, centerx, centery, midleft, midright, midtop, and midbottom) or calling methods such as inflate or move. (These are all described in the Pygame documentation at http://pygame.org/docs/ref/rect.html.)

Now that the Pygame technicalities are in place, it's time to extend and refactor your game logic a bit.

# Second Implementation

In this section, instead of walking you through the design and implementation step by step, I have added copious comments and docstrings to the source code, shown in Listings 29-2 through 29-4. You can examine the source ("use the source," remember?) to see how it works, but here is a short rundown of the essentials (and some not-quite-intuitive particulars):

- The game consists of five files: config.py, which contains various configuration variables; objects.py, which contains the implementations of the game objects; squish.py, which contains the main Game class and the various game state classes; and weight.png and banana.png, the two images used in the game.

- The rectangle method clamp ensures that a rectangle is placed within another rectangle, moving it if necessary. This is used to ensure that the banana doesn't move off-screen.

- The rectangle method inflate resizes (inflates) a rectangle by a given number of pixels in the horizontal and vertical direction. This is used to shrink the banana boundary, to allow some overlap between the banana and the weight before a hit (or "squish") is registered.

- The game itself consists of a game object and various game states. The game object only has one state at a time, and the state is responsible for handling events and displaying itself on the screen. A state may also tell the game to switch to another state. (A Level state may, for example, tell the game to switch to a GameOver state.)

That's it. You can run the game by executing the squish.py file, as follows:

```
$ python squish.py
```

You should make sure that the other files are in the same directory. In Windows, you can simply double-click the squish.py file.

---

**Tip** If you rename squish.py to squish.pyw, double-clicking it in Windows won't pop up a gratuitous terminal window. If you want to put the game on your desktop (or somewhere else) without moving all the modules and image files along with it, simply create a shortcut to the squish.pyw file. See Chapter 18 for details on packaging your game.

---

**Listing 29-2.** *The Squish Configuration File (config.py)*

```
# Configuration file for Squish
# ----------------------------


# Feel free to modify the configuration variables below to taste.
# If the game is too fast or too slow, try to modify the speed
# variables.
```

```
# Change these to use other images in the game:
banana_image = 'banana.png'
weight_image = 'weight.png'
splash_image = 'weight.png'

# Change these to affect the general appearance:
screen_size = 800, 600
background_color = 255, 255, 255
margin = 30
full_screen = 1
font_size = 48

# These affect the behavior of the game:
drop_speed = 5
banana_speed = 10
speed_increase = 1
weights_per_level = 10
banana_pad_top = 40
banana_pad_side = 20
```

**Listing 29-3.** *The Squish Game Objects (objects.py)*

```
import pygame, config, os
from random import randrange

"This module contains the game objects of the Squish game."

class SquishSprite(pygame.sprite.Sprite):

    """
    Generic superclass for all sprites in Squish.  The constructor
    takes care of loading an image, setting up the sprite rect, and
    the area within which it is allowed to move. That area is governed
    by the screen size and the margin.
    """

    def __init__(self, image):
        pygame.sprite.Sprite.__init__(self)
        self.image = pygame.image.load(image).convert()
        self.rect = self.image.get_rect()
        screen = pygame.display.get_surface()
        shrink = -config.margin * 2
        self.area = screen.get_rect().inflate(shrink, shrink)
```

```
class Weight(SquishSprite):

    """
    A falling weight. It uses the SquishSprite constructor to set up
    its weight image, and will fall with a speed given as a parameter
    to its constructor.
    """

    def __init__(self, speed):
        SquishSprite.__init__(self, config.weight_image)
        self.speed = speed
        self.reset()

    def reset(self):
        """
        Move the weight to the top of the screen (just out of sight)
        and place it at a random horizontal position.
        """
        x = randrange(self.area.left, self.area.right)
        self.rect.midbottom = x, 0

    def update(self):
        """
        Move the weight vertically (downwards) a distance
        corresponding to its speed. Also set the landed attribute
        according to whether it has reached the bottom of the screen.
        """
        self.rect.top += self.speed
        self.landed = self.rect.top >= self.area.bottom


class Banana(SquishSprite):

    """
    A desperate banana. It uses the SquishSprite constructor to set up
    its banana image, and will stay near the bottom of the screen,
    with its horizontal position governed by the current mouse
    position (within certain limits).
    """

    def __init__(self):
        SquishSprite.__init__(self, config.banana_image)
        self.rect.bottom = self.area.bottom
```

```
        # These paddings represent parts of the image where there is
        # no banana. If a weight moves into these areas, it doesn't
        # constitute a hit (or, rather, a squish):
        self.pad_top = config.banana_pad_top
        self.pad_side = config.banana_pad_side

    def update(self):
        """
        Set the Banana's center x-coordinate to the current mouse
        x-coordinate, and then use the rect method clamp to ensure
        that the Banana stays within its allowed range of motion.
        """
        self.rect.centerx = pygame.mouse.get_pos()[0]
        self.rect = self.rect.clamp(self.area)

    def touches(self, other):
        """
        Determines whether the banana touches another sprite (e.g., a
        Weight). Instead of just using the rect method colliderect, a
        new rectangle is first calculated (using the rect method
        inflate with the side and top paddings) that does not include
        the 'empty' areas on the top and sides of the banana.
        """
        # Deflate the bounds with the proper padding:
        bounds = self.rect.inflate(-self.pad_side, -self.pad_top)
        # Move the bounds so they are placed at the bottom of the Banana:
        bounds.bottom = self.rect.bottom
        # Check whether the bounds intersect with the other object's rect:
        return bounds.colliderect(other.rect)
```

**Listing 29-4.** *The Main Game Module (squish.py)*

```
import os, sys, pygame
from pygame.locals import *
import objects, config

"This module contains the main game logic of the Squish game."

class State:

    """
    A generic game state class that can handle events and display
    itself on a given surface.
    """
```

```
    def handle(self, event):
        """
        Default event handling only deals with quitting.
        """
        if event.type == QUIT:
            sys.exit()
        if event.type == KEYDOWN and event.key == K_ESCAPE:
            sys.exit()

    def firstDisplay(self, screen):
        """
        Used to display the State for the first time. Fills the screen
        with the background color.
        """
        screen.fill(config.background_color)
        # Remember to call flip, to make the changes visible:
        pygame.display.flip()

    def display(self, screen):
        """
        Used to display the State after it has already been displayed
        once. The default behavior is to do nothing.
        """
        pass


class Level(State):

    """
    A game level. Takes care of counting how many weights have been
    dropped, moving the sprites around, and other tasks relating to
    game logic.
    """

    def __init__(self, number=1):
        self.number = number
        # How many weights remain to dodge in this level?
        self.remaining = config.weights_per_level

        speed = config.drop_speed
        # One speed_increase added for each level above 1:
        speed += (self.number-1) * config.speed_increase
```

```python
        # Create the weight and banana:
        self.weight = objects.Weight(speed)
        self.banana = objects.Banana()
        both = self.weight, self.banana # This could contain more sprites...
        self.sprites = pygame.sprite.RenderUpdates(both)

    def update(self, game):
        "Updates the game state from the previous frame."
        # Update all sprites:
        self.sprites.update()
        # If the banana touches the weight, tell the game to switch to
        # a GameOver state:
        if self.banana.touches(self.weight):
            game.nextState = GameOver()
        # Otherwise, if the weight has landed, reset it. If all the
        # weights of this level have been dodged, tell the game to
        # switch to a LevelCleared state:
        elif self.weight.landed:
            self.weight.reset()
            self.remaining -= 1
            if self.remaining == 0:
                game.nextState = LevelCleared(self.number)

    def display(self, screen):
        """
        Displays the state after the first display (which simply wipes
        the screen). As opposed to firstDisplay, this method uses
        pygame.display.update with a list of rectangles that need to
        be updated, supplied from self.sprites.draw.
        """
        screen.fill(config.background_color)
        updates = self.sprites.draw(screen)
        pygame.display.update(updates)


class Paused(State):

    """
    A simple, paused game state, which may be broken out of by pressing
    either a keyboard key or the mouse button.
    """

    finished = 0   # Has the user ended the pause?
    image = None   # Set this to a file name if you want an image
    text = ''      # Set this to some informative text
```

```
def handle(self, event):
    """
    Handles events by delegating to State (which handles quitting
    in general) and by reacting to key presses and mouse
    clicks. If a key is pressed or the mouse is clicked,
    self.finished is set to true.
    """
    State.handle(self, event)
    if event.type in [MOUSEBUTTONDOWN, KEYDOWN]:
        self.finished = 1

def update(self, game):
    """
    Update the level. If a key has been pressed or the mouse has
    been clicked (i.e., self.finished is true), tell the game to
    move to the state represented by self.nextState() (should be
    implemented by subclasses).
    """
    if self.finished:
        game.nextState = self.nextState()

def firstDisplay(self, screen):
    """
    The first time the Paused state is displayed, draw the image
    (if any) and render the text.
    """
    # First, clear the screen by filling it with the background color:
    screen.fill(config.background_color)

    # Create a Font object with the default appearance, and specified size:
    font = pygame.font.Font(None, config.font_size)

    # Get the lines of text in self.text, ignoring empty lines at
    # the top or bottom:
    lines = self.text.strip().splitlines()

    # Calculate the height of the text (using font.get_linesize()
    # to get the height of each line of text):
    height = len(lines) * font.get_linesize()

    # Calculate the placement of the text (centered on the screen):
    center, top = screen.get_rect().center
    top -= height // 2
```

```
        # If there is an image to display...
        if self.image:
            # load it:
            image = pygame.image.load(self.image).convert()
            # get its rect:
            r = image.get_rect()
            # move the text down by half the image height:
            top += r.height // 2
            # place the image 20 pixels above the text:
            r.midbottom = center, top - 20
            # blit the image to the screen:
            screen.blit(image, r)

        antialias = 1    # Smooth the text
        black = 0, 0, 0  # Render it as black

        # Render all the lines, starting at the calculated top, and
        # move down font.get_linesize() pixels for each line:
        for line in lines:
            text = font.render(line.strip(), antialias, black)
            r = text.get_rect()
            r.midtop = center, top
            screen.blit(text, r)
            top += font.get_linesize()

        # Display all the changes:
        pygame.display.flip()


class Info(Paused):

    """
    A simple paused state that displays some information about the
    game. It is followed by a Level state (the first level).
    """

    nextState = Level
    text = '''
In this game you are a banana,
trying to survive a course in
self-defense against fruit, where the
participants will "defend" themselves
against you with a 16 ton weight.'''
```

```
class StartUp(Paused):

    """
    A paused state that displays a splash image and a welcome
    message. It is followed by an Info state.
    """

    nextState = Info
    image = config.splash_image
    text = '''
Welcome to Squish,
the game of Fruit Self-Defense'''


class LevelCleared(Paused):

    """
    A paused state that informs the user that he or she has cleared a
    given level.  It is followed by the next level state.
    """

    def __init__(self, number):
        self.number = number
        self.text = '''Level %i cleared
Click to start next level''' % self.number


    def nextState(self):
        return Level(self.number+1)


class GameOver(Paused):

    """
    A state that informs the user that he or she has lost the
    game. It is followed by the first level.
    """

    nextState = Level
    text = '''
Game Over
Click to Restart, Esc to Quit'''
```

```
class Game:

    """
    A game object that takes care of the main event loop, including
    changing between the different game states.
    """

    def __init__(self, *args):
        # Get the directory where the game and the images are located:
        path = os.path.abspath(args[0])
        dir = os.path.split(path)[0]
        # Move to that directory (so that the image files may be
        # opened later on):
        os.chdir(dir)
        # Start with no state:
        self.state = None
        # Move to StartUp in the first event loop iteration:
        self.nextState = StartUp()

    def run(self):
        """
        This method sets things in motion. It performs some vital
        initialization tasks, and enters the main event loop.
        """
        pygame.init() # This is needed to initialize all the pygame modules

        # Decide whether to display the game in a window or to use the
        # full screen:
        flag = 0                        # Default (window) mode

        if config.full_screen:
            flag = FULLSCREEN       # Full screen mode
        screen_size = config.screen_size
        screen = pygame.display.set_mode(screen_size, flag)

        pygame.display.set_caption('Fruit Self Defense')
        pygame.mouse.set_visible(False)

        # The main loop:
        while True:
            # (1) If nextState has been changed, move to the new state, and
            #     display it (for the first time):
            if self.state != self.nextState:
                self.state = self.nextState
                self.state.firstDisplay(screen)
```

```
        # (2) Delegate the event handling to the current state:
        for event in pygame.event.get():
            self.state.handle(event)
        # (3) Update the current state:
        self.state.update(self)
        # (4) Display the current state:
        self.state.display(screen)


if __name__ == '__main__':
    game = Game(*sys.argv)
    game.run()
```

Some screenshots of the game are shown in Figures 29-3 through 29-6.

**Figure 29-3.** *The Squish opening screen*

**Figure 29-4.** *A banana about to be squished*

**Level 42 cleared**
**Click to start next level**

**Figure 29-5.** *The "level cleared" screen*

**Game Over**
**Click to Restart, Esc to Quit**

**Figure 29-6.** *The "game over" screen*

# Further Exploration

Here are some ideas for how you can improve the game:

- Add sounds to it.

- Keep track of the score. Each weight dodged could be worth 16 points, for example. How about keeping a high-score file? Or even an online high-score server (using asyncore or XML-RPC, as discussed in Chapters 24 and 27, respectively)?

- Make more objects fall simultaneously.

- Give the player more than one "life."

- Create a stand-alone executable of your game (using py2exe, for example) and package it with an installer. (See Chapter 18 for details.)

For a much more elaborate (and extremely entertaining) example of Pygame programming, check out the SolarWolf game by Pete Shinners, the Pygame maintainer (http://www.pygame.org/shredwheat/solarwolf). You can find plenty of information and several other games at the Pygame web site. If playing with Pygame gets you hooked on game development, you might want to check out web sites like http://www.gamedev.net and http://www.flipcode.com. A web search should give you plenty of other similar sites.

## What Now?

Well, this is it. You have finished the last project. If you take stock of what you have accomplished (assuming that you have followed all the projects), you should be rightfully impressed with yourself. The breadth of the topics presented has given you a taste of the possibilities that await you in the world of Python programming. I hope you have enjoyed the trip this far, and I wish you good luck on your continued journey as a Python programmer.

# APPENDIX A

■ ■ ■

# The Short Version

This is a minimal introduction to Python, based on my popular web tutorial, "Instant Python" (http://hetland.org/writing/instant-python.html). It targets programmers who already know a language or two, but who want to get up to speed with Python. For information on downloading and executing the Python interpreter, see Chapter 1.

## The Basics

To get a basic feel for the Python language, think of it as pseudocode, because that's pretty close to the truth. Variables don't have types, so you don't need to declare them. They appear when you assign to them, and disappear when you don't use them anymore. Assignment is done with the = operator, like this:

```
x = 42
```

Note that equality is tested by the == operator.

You can assign several variables at once, like this:

```
x,y,z = 1,2,3
first, second = second, first
a = b = 123
```

Blocks are indicated through indentation, and *only* through indentation. (No begin/end or braces.) The following are some common control structures:

```
if x < 5 or (x > 10 and x < 20):
    print "The value is OK."

if x < 5 or 10 < x < 20:
    print "The value is OK."

for i in [1,2,3,4,5]:
    print "This is iteration number", i

x = 10
while x >= 0:
    print "x is still not negative."
    x = x-1
```

The first two examples are equivalent.

The index variable given in the for loop iterates through the elements of a list[1] (written with brackets, as in the example). To make an "ordinary" for loop (that is, a counting loop), use the built-in function range:

```
# Print out the values from 0 to 99, inclusive
for value in range(100):
    print value
```

The line beginning with # is a comment and is ignored by the interpreter.

Now you know enough (in theory) to implement any algorithm in Python. Let's add some *basic* user interaction. To get input from the user (from a text prompt), use the built-in function input:

```
x = input("Please enter a number: ")
print "The square of that number is", x*x
```

The input function displays the (optional) prompt given and lets the user enter any valid Python value. In this case, we were expecting a number. If something else (such as a string) is entered, the program would halt with an error message. To avoid that, you would need to add some error checking. I won't go into that here; suffice it to say that if you want the user input returned *verbatim* as a string (so that *anything* can be entered), use the function raw_input instead. If you wanted to convert an input string s to an integer, you could then use int(s).

---

■**Note** If you want to input a string with input, the user must write the quotes explicitly. In Python, strings can be enclosed in either single or double quotes. In Python 3.0, the original input disappears, and raw_input is renamed input. See Appendix D for more on Python 3.0.

---

So, you have control structures, input, and output covered—now you need some snazzy data structures. The most important ones are *lists* and *dictionaries*. Lists are written with brackets, and can (naturally) be nested:

```
name = ["Cleese", "John"]
x = [[1,2,3],[y,z],[[[]]]]
```

One of the nice things about lists is that you can access their elements separately or in groups, through *indexing* and *slicing*. Indexing is done (as in many other languages) by writing the index in brackets after the list. (Note that the first element has index 0.)

```
print name[1], name[0] # Prints "John Cleese"
name[0] = "Smith"
```

---

1. Or any other iterable object, actually.

Slicing is almost like indexing, except that you indicate both the start and stop index of the result, with a colon (:) separating them:

```
x = ["SPAM","SPAM","SPAM","SPAM","SPAM","eggs","and","SPAM"]
print x[5:7] # Prints the list ["eggs","and"]
```

Notice that the end is noninclusive. If one of the indices is dropped, it is assumed that you want everything in that direction. In other words, the slice x[:3] means "every element from the beginning of x up to element 3, noninclusive" (well, element 3 is actually the fourth element, because the counting starts at 0). The slice x[3:] would, on the other hand, mean "every element in x, starting at element 3 (inclusive) up to, and including, the last one." For really interesting results, you can use negative numbers, too: x[-3] is the third element from the end of the list.

Now then, what about dictionaries? To put it simply, they are like lists, except that their contents aren't ordered. How do you index them then? Well, every element has a *key*, or a *name*, which is used to look up the element, just as in a real dictionary. The following example demonstrates the syntax used to create dictionaries:

```
phone = { "Alice" : 23452532, "Boris" : 252336,
          "Clarice" : 2352525, "Doris" : 23624643 }

person = { 'first name': "Robin", 'last name': "Hood",
           'occupation': "Scoundrel" }
```

Now, to get person's occupation, you use the expression person["occupation"]. If you wanted to change the person's last name, you could write this:

```
person['last name'] = "of Locksley"
```

Simple, isn't it? Like lists, dictionaries can hold other dictionaries, or lists, for that matter. And naturally, lists can hold dictionaries, too. That way, you can easily make some quite advanced data structures.

# Functions

Our next step is abstraction. You want to give a name to a piece of code and call it with a couple of parameters. In other words, you want to define a *function* (also called a *procedure*). That's easy. Use the keyword def, as follows:

```
def square(x):
    return x*x

print square(2) # Prints out 4
```

The return statement is used to return a value from the function.

When you pass a parameter to a function, you bind the parameter to the value, thus creating a new reference. This means that you can modify the original value directly inside the function, but if you make the parameter name refer to something else (rebind it), that change won't affect the original. This works just like in Java, for example. Let's take a look at an example:

```
def change(x):
    x[1] = 4

y = [1,2,3]
change(y)
print y # Prints out [1,4,3]
```

As you can see, the original list is passed in, and if the function modifies it, these modifications carry over to the place where the function was called. Note the behavior in the following example, however, where the function body *rebinds* the parameter:

```
def nochange(x):
    x = 0

y = 1
nochange(y)
print y # Prints out 1
```

Why doesn't y change now? Because you *don't change the value*! The value that is passed in is the number 1, and you can't change a number in the same way that you change a list. The number 1 is (and will always be) the number 1. What the example *does* change is what the parameter x *refers to*, and this does *not* carry over to the calling environment.

Python has all kinds of nifty things such as *named arguments* and *default arguments*, and can handle a variable number of arguments to a single function. For more information about this, see Chapter 6.

If you know how to use functions in general, what I've told you so far is basically what you need to know about them in Python.

It might be useful to know, however, that functions are *values* in Python. So if you have a function such as square, you could do something like the following:

```
queeble = square
print queeble(2) # Prints out 4
```

To call a function without arguments, you must remember to write doit() and not doit. The latter, as shown, only returns the function itself, as a value. This goes for methods in objects, too. Methods are described in the next section.

# Objects and Stuff . . .

I assume you know how object-oriented programming works. Otherwise, this section might not make much sense. No problem—start playing without the objects, or check out Chapter 7.

In Python, you define classes with the (surprise!) `class` keyword, as follows:

```
class Basket:

    # Always remember the *self* argument
    def __init__(self, contents=None):
        self.contents = contents or []

    def add(self, element):
        self.contents.append(element)

    def print_me(self):
        result = ""
        for element in self.contents:
            result = result + " " + repr(element)
        print "Contains:" + result
```

Several things are worth noting in this example:

- Methods are called like this: `object.method(arg1, arg2)`.

- Some arguments can be *optional* and given a default value (as mentioned in the previous section on functions). This is done by writing the definition like this:

  ```
  def spam(age=32): ...
  ```

- Here, `spam` can be called with one or zero parameters. If it's called without any parameters, age will have the default value of 32.

- `repr` converts an object to its string representation. (So if `element` contains the number 1, then `repr(element)` is the same as `"1"`, whereas `'element'` is a literal string.)

No methods or member variables (attributes) are protected (or private or the like) in Python. Encapsulation is pretty much a matter of programming style. (If you *really* need it, there are naming conventions that will allow some privacy, such as prefixing a name with a single or double underscore.)

Now, about that short-circuit logic . . .

All values in Python can be used as logic values. Some of the more empty ones (such as `False`, `[]`, `0`, `""`, and `None`) represent logical falsity; most other values (such as `True`, `[0]`, `1`, and `"Hello, world"`) represent logical truth.

Logical expressions such as `a and b` are evaluated like this:

- Check if a is true.

- If it is *not*, then simply return it.

- If it *is*, then simply return b (which will represent the truth value of the expression).

The corresponding logic for `a or b` is this:

- If a is true, then return it.

- If it isn't, then return b.

This short-circuit mechanism enables you to use and and or like the Boolean operators they are supposed to implement, but it also enables you to write short and sweet little conditional expressions. For example, this statement:

```
if a:
    print a
else:
    print b
```

could instead be written like this:

```
print a or b
```

Actually, this is somewhat of a Python idiom, so you might as well get used to it.

---

■**Note**  In Python 2.5, actual conditional expressions were introduced, so you could, in fact, write this:

```
print a if a else b
```

---

The Basket constructor (Basket.__init__) in the previous example uses this strategy in handling default parameters. The argument contents has a default value of None (which is, among other things, false); therefore, to check if it had a value, you could write this:

```
if contents:
    self.contents = contents
else:
    self.contents = []
```

Instead, the constructor uses this simple statement:

```
self.contents = contents or []
```

Why don't you give it the default value of [ ] in the first place? Because of the way Python works, this would give all the Basket instances the same empty list as default contents. As soon as one of them started to fill up, they all would contain the same elements, and the default would not be empty anymore. To learn more about this, see the discussion about the difference between *identity* and *equality* in Chapter 5.

---

■**Note**  When using None as a placeholder as done in the Basket.__init__ method, using contents is None as the condition is safer than simply checking the argument's Boolean value. This will allow you to pass in a false value such as an empty list of your own (to which you could keep a reference outside the object).

---

If you would like to use an empty list as the default value, you can avoid the problem of sharing this among instances by doing the following:

```
def __init__(self, contents=[]):
    self.contents = contents[:]
```

Can you guess how this works? Instead of using the same empty list everywhere, you use the expression contents[:] to make a copy. (You simply slice the entire thing.)

So, to actually make a Basket and to use it (to call some methods on it), you would do something like this:

```
b = Basket(['apple','orange'])
b.add("lemon")
b.print_me()
```

This would print out the contents of the Basket: an apple, an orange, and a lemon.

There are magic methods other than __init__. One such method is __str__, which defines how the object wants to look if it is treated like a string. You could use this in the basket instead of print_me:

```
def __str__(self):
    result = ""
    for element in self.contents:
        result = result + " " + repr(element)
    return "Contains:" + result
```

Now, if you wanted to print the basket b, you could just use this:

```
print b
```

Cool, huh?

Subclassing works like this:

```
class SpamBasket(Basket):
    # ...
```

Python allows multiple inheritance, so you can have several superclasses in the parentheses, separated by commas. Classes are instantiated like this: x = Basket(). Constructors are, as I said, made by defining the special member function __init__. Let's say that SpamBasket had a constructor __init__(self, type). Then you could make a spam basket like this: y = SpamBasket("apples").

If in the constructor of SpamBasket, you needed to call the constructor of one or more superclasses, you could call it like this: Basket.__init__(self). Note that in addition to supplying the ordinary parameters, you must explicitly supply self, because the superclass __init__ doesn't know which instance it is dealing with.

For more about the wonders of object-oriented programming in Python, see Chapter 7.

# Some Loose Ends

Here, I'll quickly review a few other useful things before ending this appendix. Most useful functions and classes are put in *modules*, which are really text files with the file name extension .py that contain Python code. You can import these and use them in your own programs. For example, to use the function sqrt from the standard module math, you can do either this:

```
import math
x = math.sqrt(y)
```

or this:

```
from math import sqrt
x = sqrt(y)
```

For more information on the standard library modules, see Chapter 10.

All the code in the module/script is run when it is imported. If you want your program to be both an importable module and a runnable program, you might want to add something like this at the end of it:

```
if __name__ == "__main__": main()
```

This is a magic way of saying that if this module is run as an executable script (that is, it is not being imported into another script), then the function main should be called. Of course, you could do anything after the colon there.

And for those of you who want to make an executable script in UNIX, use the following first line to make it run by itself:

```
#!/usr/bin/env python
```

Finally, a brief mention of an important concept: *exceptions*. Some operations (such as dividing something by zero or reading from a nonexistent file) produce an error condition or *exception*. You can even make your own exceptions and raise them at the appropriate times.

If nothing is done about the exception, your program ends and prints out an error message. You can avoid this with a try/except statement, as in this example:

```
def safe_division(a, b):
    try:
        return a/b
    except ZeroDivisionError: pass
```

ZeroDivisionError is a standard exception. In this case, you *could* have checked if b was zero, but in many cases, that strategy is not feasible. And besides, if you removed the try/except statement in safe_division, thereby making it a risky function to call (called something like unsafe_division), you could still do the following:

```
try:
    unsafe_division(a, b)
except ZeroDivisionError:
    print "Something was divided by zero in unsafe_division"
```

In cases in which you *typically* would not have a specific problem, but it *might* occur, using exceptions enables you to avoid costly testing and so forth.

Well, that's it. Hope you learned something. Now go and play. And remember the Python motto of learning: use the source (which basically means read all the code you can get your hands on).

■■■

# Python Reference

This is not a full Python reference by far—you can find that in the standard Python documentation (`http://python.org/doc/ref`). Rather, this is a handy "cheat sheet" that can be useful for refreshing your memory as you start out programming in Python. See Appendix D for changes in the language that are introduced in version 3.0.

## Expressions

This section summarizes Python expressions. Table B-1 lists the most important basic (literal) values in Python; Table B-2 lists the Python operators, along with their precedence (those with high precedence are evaluated before those with low precedence); Table B-3 describes some of the most important built-in functions; Tables B-4 through B-6 describe the list methods, dictionary methods, and string methods, respectively.

**Table B-1.** *Basic (Literal) Values*

| Type | Description | Syntax Samples |
|------|-------------|----------------|
| Integer | Numbers without a fractional part | `42` |
| Long integer | Large integer numbers | `42L` |
| Float | Numbers with a fractional part | `42.5, 42.5e-2` |
| Complex | Sum of a real (integer or float) and imaginary number | `38 + 4j, 42j` |
| String | An immutable sequence of characters | `'foo', "bar", """baz""", r'\n'` |
| Unicode | An immutable sequence of Unicode characters | `u'foo', u"bar", u"""baz"""` |

**Table B-2.** *Operators*

| Operator | Description | Precedence |
|----------|-------------|------------|
| `lambda` | Lambda expression | 1 |
| `or` | Logical or | 2 |
| `and` | Logical and | 3 |

*Continued*

**Table B-2.** *Continued*

| Operator | Description | Precedence |
| --- | --- | --- |
| not | Logical negation | 4 |
| in | Membership test | 5 |
| not in | Negative membership test | 5 |
| is | Identity test | 6 |
| is not | Negative identity test | 6 |
| < | Less than | 7 |
| > | Greater than | 7 |
| <= | Less than or equal to | 7 |
| >= | Greater than or equal to | 7 |
| == | Equal to | 7 |
| != | Not equal to | 7 |
| \| | Bitwise or | 8 |
| ^ | Bitwise exclusive or | 9 |
| & | Bitwise and | 10 |
| << | Left shift | 11 |
| >> | Right shift | 11 |
| + | Addition | 12 |
| - | Subtraction | 12 |
| * | Multiplication | 13 |
| / | Division | 13 |
| % | Remainder | 13 |
| + | Unary identity | 14 |
| - | Unary negation | 14 |
| ~ | Bitwise complement | 15 |
| ** | Exponentiation | 16 |
| x.attribute | Attribute reference | 17 |
| x[index] | Item access | 18 |
| x[index1:index2[:index3]] | Slicing | 19 |
| f(args...) | Function call | 20 |
| (...) | Parenthesized expression or tuple display | 21 |

| Operator | Description | Precedence |
|---|---|---|
| `[...]` | List display | 22 |
| `{key:value, ...}` | Dictionary display | 23 |
| `` `expressions...` `` | String conversion | 24 |

**Table B-3.** *Some Important Built-in Functions*

| Function | Description |
|---|---|
| `abs(number)` | Returns the absolute value of a number. |
| `apply(function[, args[, kwds]])` | Calls a given function, optionally with parameters. |
| `all(iterable)` | Returns `True` if all the elements of `iterable` are true; otherwise, it returns `False`. |
| `any(iterable)` | Returns `True` if any of the elements of `iterable` are true; otherwise, it returns `False`. |
| `basestring()` | An abstract superclass for `str` and `unicode`, usable for type checking. |
| `bool(object)` | Returns `True` or `False`, depending on the Boolean value of `object`. |
| `callable(object)` | Checks whether an object is callable. |
| `chr(number)` | Returns a character whose ASCII code is the given number. |
| `classmethod(func)` | Creates a class method from an instance method (see Chapter 7). |
| `cmp(x, y)` | Compares x and y. If x < y, it returns a negative number; if x > y, it returns a positive number; and if x == y, it returns zero. |
| `complex(real[, imag])` | Returns a complex number with the given real (and, optionally, imaginary) component. |
| `delattr(object, name)` | Deletes the given attribute from the given object. |
| `dict([mapping-or-sequence])` | Constructs a dictionary, optionally from another mapping or a list of (key, value) pairs. May also be called with keyword arguments. |
| `dir([object])` | Lists (most of) the names in the currently visible scopes, or optionally (most of) the attributes of the given object. |
| `divmod(a, b)` | Returns (a//b, a%b) (with some special rules for floats). |

*Continued*

**Table B-3.** *Continued*

| Function | Description |
|----------|-------------|
| enumerate(iterable) | Iterates over (index, item) pairs, for all items in iterable. |
| eval(string[, globals[, locals]]) | Evaluates a string containing an expression, optionally in a given global and local scope. |
| execfile(file[, globals[, locals]]) | Executes a Python file, optionally in a given global and local scope. |
| file(filename[, mode[, bufsize]]) | Creates a file object with a given file name, optionally with a given mode and buffer size. |
| filter(function, sequence) | Returns a list of the elements from the given sequence for which function returns true. |
| float(object) | Converts a string or number to a float. |
| frozenset([iterable]) | Creates a set that is immutable, which means it can be added to other sets. |
| getattr(object, name[, default]) | Returns the value of the named attribute of the given object, optionally with a given default value. |
| globals() | Returns a dictionary representing the current global scope. |
| hasattr(object, name) | Checks whether the given object has the named attribute. |
| help([object]) | Invokes the built-in help system, or prints a help message about the given object. |
| hex(number) | Converts a number to a hexadecimal string. |
| id(object) | Returns the unique ID for the given object. |
| input([prompt]) | Equivalent to eval(raw_input(prompt)). |
| int(object[, radix]) | Converts a string or number (optionally with a given radix) or number to an integer. |
| isinstance(object, classinfo) | Checks whether the given object is an instance of the given classinfo value, which may be a class object, a type object, or a tuple of class and type objects. |
| issubclass(class1, class2) | Checks whether class1 is a subclass of class2 (every class is a subclass of itself). |
| iter(object[, sentinel]) | Returns an iterator object, which is object.__iter__(), an iterator constructed for iterating a sequence (if object supports __getitem__), or, if sentinel is supplied, an iterator that keeps calling object in each iteration until sentinel is returned. |
| len(object) | Returns the length (number of items) of the given object. |

| Function | Description |
| --- | --- |
| list([sequence]) | Constructs a list, optionally with the same items as the supplied sequence. |
| locals() | Returns a dictionary representing the current local scope (do not modify this dictionary). |
| long(object[, radix]) | Converts a string (optionally with a given radix) or number to a long integer. |
| map(function, sequence, ...) | Creates a list consisting of the values returned by the given function when applying it to the items of the supplied sequence(s). |
| max(object1, [object2, ...]) | If object1 is a nonempty sequence, the largest element is returned; otherwise, the largest of the supplied arguments (object1, object2, . . .) is returned. |
| min(object1, [object2, ...]) | If object1 is a nonempty sequence, the smallest element is returned; otherwise, the smallest of the supplied arguments (object1, object2, . . .) is returned. |
| object() | Returns an instance of object, the base class for all new style classes. |
| oct(number) | Converts an integer number to an octal string. |
| open(filename[, mode[, bufsize]]) | An alias for file (use open, not file, when opening files). |
| ord(char) | Returns the ASCII value of a single character (a string or Unicode string of length 1). |
| pow(x, y[, z]) | Returns x to the power of y, optionally modulo z. |
| property([fget[, fset[, fdel[, doc]]]]) | Creates a property from a set of accessors (see Chapter 9). |
| range([start, ]stop[, step]) | Returns a numeric range (as a list) with the given start (inclusive, default 0), stop (exclusive), and step (default 1). |
| raw_input([prompt]) | Returns data input by the user as a string, optionally using a given prompt. |
| reduce(function, sequence[, initializer]) | Applies the given function cumulatively to the items of the sequence, using the cumulative result as the first argument and the items as the second argument, optionally with a start value (initializer). |
| reload(module) | Reloads an already loaded module and returns it. |
| repr(object) | Returns a string representation of the object, often usable as an argument to eval. |
| reversed(sequence) | Returns a reverse iterator over the sequence. |

*Continued*

**Table B-3.** *Continued*

| Function | Description |
| --- | --- |
| round(float[, n]) | Rounds off the given float to n digits after the decimal point (default zero). |
| set([iterable]) | Returns a set whose elements are taken from iterable (if given). |
| setattr(object, name, value) | Sets the named attribute of the given object to the given value. |
| sorted(iterable[, cmp][, key][, reverse]) | Returns a new sorted list from the items in iterable. Optional parameters are the same as for the list method sort. |
| staticmethod(func) | Creates a static (class) method from an instance method (see Chapter 7). |
| str(object) | Returns a nicely formatted string representation of the given object. |
| sum(seq[, start]) | Returns the sum of a sequence of numbers, added to the optional parameter start (default 0). |
| super(type[, obj/type]) | Returns the superclass of the given type (optionally instantiated). |
| tuple([sequence]) | Constructs a tuple, optionally with the same items as the supplied sequence. |
| type(object) | Returns the type of the given object. |
| type(name, bases, dict) | Returns a new type object with the given name, bases, and scope. |
| unichr(number) | The Unicode version of chr. |
| unicode(object[, encoding[, errors]]) | Returns a Unicode encoding of the given object, possibly with a given encoding, and a given mode for handling errors ('strict', 'replace', or 'ignore'; 'strict' is the default). |
| vars([object]) | Returns a dictionary representing the local scope, or a dictionary corresponding to the attributes of the given object (do not modify the returned dictionary, as the result of such a modification is not defined by the language reference). |
| xrange([start, ]stop[, step]) | Similar to range, but the returned object uses less memory, and should be used only for iteration. |
| zip(sequence1, ...) | Returns a list of tuples, where each tuple contains an item from each of the supplied sequences. The returned list has the same length as the shortest of the supplied sequences. |

**Table B-4.** *List Methods*

| Method | Description |
|--------|-------------|
| aList.append(obj) | Equivalent to aList[len(aList):len(aList)] = [obj]. |
| aList.count(obj) | Returns the number of indices i for which alist[i] == obj. |
| aList.extend(sequence) | Equivalent to aList[len(aList):len(aList)] = sequence. |
| aList.index(obj) | Returns the smallest i for which aList[i] == obj (or raises a ValueError if no such i exists). |
| aList.insert(index, obj) | Equivalent to aList[index:index] = [obj] if index >= 0; if index < 0, object is prepended to the list. |
| aList.pop([index]) | Removes and returns the item with the given index (default –1). |
| aList.remove(obj) | Equivalent to del aList[aList.index(obj)]. |
| aList.reverse() | Reverses the items of aList in place. |
| aList.sort([cmp][, key][, reverse]) | Sorts the items of aList in place (stable sorting). Can be customized by supplying a comparison function, cmp; a key function, key, which will create the keys for the sorting); and a reverse flag (a Boolean value). |

**Table B-5.** *Dictionary Methods*

| Method | Description |
|--------|-------------|
| aDict.clear() | Removes all the items of aDict. |
| aDict.copy() | Returns a copy of aDict. |
| aDict.fromkeys(seq[, val]) | Returns a dictionary with keys from seq and values set to val (default None). May be called directly on the dictionary type, dict, as a class method. |
| aDict.get(key[, default]) | Returns aDict[key] if it exists; otherwise, it returns the given default value (default None). |
| aDict.has_key(key) | Checks whether aDict has the given key. |
| aDict.items() | Returns a list of (key, value) pairs representing the items of aDict. |
| aDict.iteritems() | Returns an iterable object over the same (key, value) pairs as returned by aDict.items. |
| aDict.iterkeys() | Returns an iterable object over the keys of aDict. |
| aDict.itervalues() | Returns an iterable object over the values of aDict. |
| aDict.keys() | Returns a list of the keys of aDict. |

*Continued*

**Table B-5.** *Continued*

| Method | Description |
| --- | --- |
| aDict.pop(key[, d]) | Removes and returns the value corresponding to the given key, or the given default, d. |
| aDict.popitem() | Removes an arbitrary item from aDict and returns it as a (key, value) pair. |
| aDict.setdefault(key[, default]) | Returns aDict[key] if it exists; otherwise, it returns the given default value (default None) and binds aDict[key] to it. |
| aDict.update(other) | For each item in other, adds the item to aDict (possibly overwriting existing items). Can also be called with arguments similar to the dictionary constructor, aDict. |
| aDict.values() | Returns a list of the values in aDict (possibly containing duplicates). |

**Table B-6.** *String Methods*

| Method | Description |
| --- | --- |
| string.capitalize() | Returns a copy of the string in which the first character is capitalized. |
| string.center(width[, fillchar]) | Returns a string of length max(len(string), width) in which a copy of string is centered, padded with fillchar (the default is space characters). |
| string.count(sub[, start[, end]]) | Counts the occurrences of the substring sub, optionally restricting the search to string[start:end]. |
| string.decode([encoding[, errors]]) | Returns decoded version of the string using the given encoding, handling errors as specified by errors ('strict', 'ignore', or 'replace'). |
| string.encode([encoding[, errors]]) | Returns the encoded version of the string using the given encoding, handling errors as specified by errors ('strict', 'ignore', or 'replace'). |
| string.endswith(suffix[, start[, end]]) | Checks whether string ends with suffix, optionally restricting the matching with the given indices start and end. |
| string.expandtabs([tabsize]) | Returns a copy of the string in which tab characters have been expanded using spaces, optionally using the given tabsize (default 8). |
| string.find(sub[, start[, end]]) | Returns the first index where the substring sub is found, or –1 if no such index exists, optionally restricting the search to string[start:end]. |

| Method | Description |
|---|---|
| string.index(sub[, start[, end]]) | Returns the first index where the substring sub is found, or raises a ValueError if no such index exists, optionally restricting the search to string[start:end]. |
| string.isalnum() | Checks whether the string consists of alpha-numeric characters. |
| string.isalpha() | Checks whether the string consists of alpha-betic characters. |
| string.isdigit() | Checks whether the string consists of digits. |
| string.islower() | Checks whether all the case-based characters (letters) of the string are lowercase. |
| string.isspace() | Checks whether the string consists of whitespace. |
| string.istitle() | Checks whether all the case-based characters in the string following non-case–based letters are uppercase and all other case-based characters are lowercase. |
| string.isupper() | Checks whether all the case-based characters of the string are uppercase. |
| string.join(sequence) | Returns a string in which the string elements of sequence have been joined by string. |
| string.ljust(width[, fillchar]) | Returns a string of length max(len(string), width) in which a copy of string is left-justified, padded with fillchar (the default is space characters). |
| string.lower() | Returns a copy of the string in which all case-based characters have been lowercased. |
| string.lstrip([chars]) | Returns a copy of the string in which all chars have been stripped from the beginning of the string (the default is all whitespace characters, such as spaces, tabs, and newlines). |
| string.partition(sep) | Searches for sep in the string and returns (head, sep, tail). |
| string.replace(old, new[, max]) | Returns a copy of the string in which the occurrences of old have been replaced with new, optionally restricting the number of replacements to max. |
| string.rfind(sub[, start[, end]]) | Returns the last index where the substring sub is found, or –1 if no such index exists, optionally restricting the search to string[start:end]. |
| string.rindex(sub[, start[, end]]) | Returns the last index where the substring sub is found, or raises a ValueError if no such index exists, optionally restricting the search to string[start:end]. |

*Continued*

**Table B-6.** *Continued*

| Method | Description |
| --- | --- |
| string.rjust(width[, fillchar]) | Returns a string of length max(len(string), width) in which a copy of string is right-justified, padded with fillchar (the default is space characters). |
| string.rpartition(sep) | Same as partition, but searches from the right. |
| string.rstrip([chars]) | Returns a copy of the string in which all chars have been stripped from the end of the string (the default is all whitespace characters, such as spaces, tabs, and newlines). |
| string.rsplit([sep[, maxsplit]]) | Same as split, but when using maxsplit, counts from right to left. |
| string.split([sep[, maxsplit]]) | Returns a list of all the words in the string, using sep as the separator (splits on all whitespace if left unspecified), optionally limiting the number of splits to maxsplit. |
| string.splitlines([keepends]) | Returns a list with all the lines in string, optionally including the line breaks (if keepends is supplied and is true). |
| string.startswith(prefix[, start[, end]]) | Checks whether string starts with prefix, optionally restricting the matching with the given indices start and end. |
| string.strip([chars]) | Returns a copy of the string in which all chars have been stripped from the beginning and the end of the string (the default is all whitespace characters, such as spaces, tabs, and newlines). |
| string.swapcase() | Returns a copy of the string in which all the case-based characters have had their case swapped. |
| string.title() | Returns a copy of the string in which all the words are capitalized. |
| string.translate(table[, deletechars]) | Returns a copy of the string in which all characters have been translated using table (constructed with the maketrans function in the string module), optionally deleting all characters found in the string deletechars. |
| string.upper() | Returns a copy of the string in which all the case-based characters have been uppercased. |
| string.zfill(width) | Pads string on the left with zeros to fill width. |

# Statements

This section gives you a quick summary of each of the statement types in Python.

## Simple Statements

Simple statements consist of a single (logical) line.

### Expression Statements

Expressions can be statements on their own. This is especially useful if the expression is a function call or a documentation string.

Example:

```
"This module contains SPAM-related functions."
```

### Assert Statements

Assert statements check whether a condition is true and raise an `AssertionError` (optionally with a supplied error message) if it isn't.

Example:

```
assert age >= 12, 'Children under the age of 12 are not allowed'
```

### Assignment Statements

Assignment statements bind variables to values. Multiple variables may be assigned to simultaneously (through sequence unpacking) and assignments may be chained.

Examples:

```
x = 42                    # Simple assignment
name, age = 'Gumby', 60   # Sequence unpacking
x = y = z = 10            # Chained assignments
```

### Augmented Assignment Statements

Assignments may be augmented by operators. The operator will then be applied to the existing value of the variable and the new value, and the variable will be rebound to the result. If the original value is mutable, it may be modified instead (with the variable staying bound to the original).

Examples:

```
x *= 2                    # Doubles x
x += 5                    # Adds 5 to x
```

## The pass Statement

The pass statement is a "no-op," which does nothing. It is useful as a placeholder, or as the only statement in syntactically required blocks where you want no action to be performed.

Example:

```
try: x.name
except AttributeError: pass
else: print 'Hello', x.name
```

## The del Statement

The del statement unbinds variables and attributes, and removes parts (positions, slices, or slots) from data structures (mappings or sequences). It cannot be used to delete values directly, because values are only deleted through garbage collection.

Examples:

```
del x                  # Unbinds a variable
del seq[42]            # Deletes a sequence element
del seq[42:]           # Deletes a sequence slice
del map['foo']         # Deletes a mapping item
```

## The print Statement

The print statement writes one or more values (automatically formatted with str, separated by single spaces) to a given stream, with sys.stdout being the default. It adds a line break to the end of the written string unless the print statement ends with a comma.

Examples:

```
print 'Hello, world!'    # Writes 'Hello, world\n' to sys.stdout
print 1, 2, 3            # Writes '1 2 3\n' to sys.stdout
print >> somefile, 'xyz' # Writes 'xyz' to somefile
print 42,                # Writes '42 ' to sys.stdout
```

## The return Statement

The return statement halts the execution of a function and returns a value. If no value is supplied, None is returned.

Examples:

```
return                 # Returns None from the current function
return 42              # Returns 42 from the current function
return 1, 2, 3         # Returns (1, 2, 3) from the current function
```

## The yield Statement

The yield statement temporarily halts the execution of a generator and yields a value. A generator is a form of iterator and can be used in for loops, among other things.

Example:

```
yield 42               # Returns 42 from the current function
```

## The raise Statement

The raise statement raises an exception. It may be used without any arguments (inside an except clause, to re-raise the currently caught exception), with a subclass of Exception and an optional argument (in which case, an instance is constructed), or with an instance of a subclass of Exception.

Examples:

```
raise                      # May only be used inside except clauses
raise IndexError
raise IndexError, 'index out of bounds'
raise IndexError('index out of bounds')
```

## The break Statement

The break statement ends the immediately enclosing loop statement (for or while) and continues execution immediately after that loop statement.

Example:

```
while True:
    line = file.readline()
    if not line: break
    print line
```

## The continue Statement

The continue statement is similar to the break statement in that it halts the current iteration of the immediately enclosing loop, but instead of ending the loop completely, it continues execution at the beginning of the next iteration.

Example:

```
while True:
    line = file.readline()
    if not line: break
    if line.isspace(): continue
    print line
```

## The import Statement

The import statement is used to import names (variables bound to functions, classes, or other values) from an external module. This also covers from __future__ import ... statements for features that will become standard in future versions of Python.

Examples:

```
import math
from math import sqrt
from math import sqrt as squareroot
from math import *
```

### The global Statement

The global statement is used to mark a variable as global. It is used in functions to allow statements in the function body to rebind global variables. Using the global statement is generally considered poor style and should be avoided whenever possible.

Example:

```
count = 1
def inc():
    global count
    count += 1
```

### The exec Statement

The exec statement is used to execute strings containing Python statements, optionally with a given global and local namespace (dictionaries).

Examples:

```
exec 'print "Hello, world!"'
exec 'x = 2' in myglobals, mylocals # ... where myglobals and mylocals are dicts
```

## Compound Statements

Compound statements contain groups (blocks) of other statements.

### The if Statement

The if statement is used for conditional execution, and it may include elif and else clauses.

Example:

```
if x < 10:
    print 'Less than ten'
elif 10 <= x < 20:
    print 'Less than twenty'
else:
    print 'Twenty or more'
```

### The while Statement

The while statement is used for repeated execution (looping) while a given condition is true. It may include an else clause (which is executed if the loop finishes normally, without any break or return statements, for instance).

Example:

```
x = 1
while x < 100:
    x *= 2
print x
```

## The for Statement

The for statement is used for repeated execution (looping) over the elements of sequences or other iterable objects (objects having an __iter__ method that returns an iterator). It may include an else clause (which is executed if the loop finishes normally, without any break or return statements, for instance).

Example:

```
for i in range(10, 0, -1):
    print i
print 'Ignition!'
```

## The try Statement

The try statement is used to enclose pieces of code where one or more known exceptions may occur, and enables your program to trap these exceptions and perform exception-handling code if an exception is trapped. The try statement can combine several except clauses (handling exceptional circumstances) and finally clauses (executed no matter what; useful for cleanup).

Example:

```
try:
    1/0
except ZeroDivisionError:
    print "Can't divide anything by zero."
finally:
    print "Done trying to calculate 1/0"
```

## The with Statement

The with statement is used to wrap a block of code using a so-called context manager, allowing the context manager to perform some setup and cleanup actions. For example, files can be used as context managers, and they will close themselves as part of the cleanup.

---

■**Note** In Python 2.5, you need from __future__ import with_statement for the with statement to work as described.

---

Example:

```
with open("somefile.txt") as myfile:
    dosomething(myfile)
# The file will have been closed here
```

## Function Definitions

Function definitions are used to create function objects and to bind global or local variables to these function objects.

Example:

```python
def double(x):
    return x*2
```

## Class Definitions

Class definitions are used to create class objects and to bind global or local variables to these class objects.

Example:

```python
class Doubler:
    def __init__(self, value):
        self.value = value
    def double(self):
        self.value *= 2
```

# APPENDIX C

■■■

# Online Resources

**A**s you learn Python, the Internet will serve as an invaluable resource. This appendix describes some of the web sites that may be of interest to you as you are starting out. If you are looking for something Python-related that isn't described here, I suggest that you first check the official Python web site (`http://python.org`), and then use your favorite web search engine, or the other way around. There is a lot of information about Python online; chances are you'll find something. If you don't, you can always try `comp.lang.python` (described in this appendix). If you're an IRC user (see `http://irchelp.org` for information), you might want to check out the #python channel on `irc.freenode.net`.

## Python Distributions

Several Python distributions are available. Here are some of the more prominent ones:

**Official Python distribution** (`http://python.org/download`): This comes with a default integrated development environment called IDLE (for more information, see `http://docs.python.org/lib/idle.html`).

**ActivePython** (`http://activestate.com`): This is ActiveState's Python distribution, which includes several nonstandard packages in addition to the official distribution. This is also the home of Visual Python, a Python plug-in for Visual Studio .NET.

**Jython** (`http://www.jython.org`): Jython is the Java implementation of Python.

**IronPython** (`http://www.codeplex.com/Wiki/View.aspx?ProjectName=IronPython`): IronPython is the C# implementation of Python.

**MacPython** (`http://homepages.cwi.nl/~jack/macpython/index.html`): MacPython is the Macintosh port of Python for older versions of Mac OS. The new Mac version can be found on the main Python site (`http://python.org`). You can also get Python through MacPorts (`http://macports.org`).

**pywin32** (`http://sf.net/projects/pywin32/`): These are the Python for Windows extensions. If you have ActivePython installed, you already have all these extensions.

# Python Documentation

Answers to most of your Python questions are most likely somewhere on the python.org web site. The documentation can be found at http://python.org/doc, with the following subdivisions:

**Python Tutorial** (http://python.org/doc/tut): This is a relatively simple introduction to the language.

**Python Reference Manual** (http://python.org/doc/ref): This document contains a precise definition of the Python language. It may not be the place to start when learning Python, but it contains precise answers to most questions you might have about the language.

**Python Library Reference** (http://python.org/doc/lib): This is probably the most useful piece of Python documentation you'll ever find. It describes all (or most) of the modules in the standard Python library. If you are wondering how to solve a problem in Python, this should be the first place you look—perhaps the solution already exists in the libraries.

**Extending and Embedding the Python Interpreter** (http://python.org/doc/ext): This is a document that describes how to write Python extension modules in the C language, and how to use the Python interpreter as a part of larger C programs. (Python itself is implemented in C.)

**Macintosh Library Modules** (http://python.org/doc/mac): This document describes functionality specific to the Macintosh port of Python.

**Python/C API Reference Manual** (http://python.org/doc/api): This is a rather technical document describing the details of the Python/C application programming interface (API), which enables C programs to interface with the Python interpreter.

Two other useful documentation resources are Python Documentation Online (http://pydoc.org) and pyhelp.cgi (http://starship.python.net/crew/theller/pyhelp.cgi), which allow you to search the standard Python documentation. If you want some "recipes" and solutions provided by the Python community, the Python Cookbook (http://aspn.activestate.com/ASPN/Python/Cookbook) is a good place to look.

The future of Python is decided by the language's Benevolent Dictator For Life (BDFL), Guido van Rossum, but his decisions are guided and informed by so-called Python Enhancement Proposals, which may be accessed at http://python.org/dev/peps. Various HOWTO documents (relatively specific tutorials) can be found at http://python.org/doc/howto.

# Useful Toolkits and Modules

One source for finding software implemented in Python (including useful toolkits and modules you can use in your own programs) is the Vaults of Parnassus (http://www.vex.net/parnassus); another is the Python Package Index (http://pypi.python.org/pypi). If you can't find what you're looking for on either of these sites, try a standard web search, or perhaps take a look at freshmeat (http://freshmeat.net) or SourceForge (http://sf.net).

Table C-1 lists the URLs of some of the most well-known GUI toolkits available for Python. For a more thorough description, see Chapter 12. Table C-2 lists the URLs of the third-party packages used in the ten projects (Chapters 20–29).

**Table C-1.** *Some Well-Known GUI Toolkits for Python*

| Toolkit | URL |
| --- | --- |
| Tkinter | `http://python.org/topics/tkinter/doc.html` |
| wxPython | `http://www.wxpython.org` |
| PythonWin | `http://sf.net/projects/pywin32/` |
| Java Swing | `http://java.sun.com/docs/books/tutorial/uiswing` |
| PyGTK | `http://www.pygtk.org` |
| PyQt | `http://www.thekompany.com/projects/pykde` |

**Table C-2.** *The Third-Party Modules Used in This Book's Ten Projects*

| Package | URL |
| --- | --- |
| Psycopg | `http://initd.org/pub/software/psycopg/` |
| MySQLdb | `http://sourceforge.net/projects/mysql-python` |
| Pygame | `http://www.pygame.org` |
| PyXML | `http://sourceforge.net/projects/pyxml` |
| ReportLab | `http://www.reportlab.org` |

# Newsgroups, Mailing Lists, and Blogs

An important forum for Python discussion is the Usenet group `comp.lang.python`. If you're serious about Python, skimming this group regularly can be quite useful. Its companion group, `comp.lang.python.announce`, contains announcements about new Python software (including new Python distributions, Python extensions, and software written using Python).

Several official mailing lists are available. For instance, the `comp.lang.python` group is mirrored in the `python-list@python.org` mailing list. If you have a Python problem and need help, simply send an email to `help@python.org` (assuming that you've exhausted all other options, of course). For learning about programming in Python, the tutor list (`tutor@python.org`) may be useful. For information about how to join these (and other) mailing lists, see `http://mail.python.org/mailman/listinfo`.

A couple of useful blogs are Unofficial Planet Python (`http://planetpython.org`) and The Daily Python-URL (`http://pythonware.com/daily`).

■■■

# Python 3.0

This book describes mainly the language defined by Python version 2.5. Python version 3.0 (and its companion "transition" release, 2.6) isn't all that different. Most things work just as they did before, but the language cleanups introduced mean that some existing code will break.

If you're transitioning from older code to Python 3.0, a couple of tools can come in quite handy. First, Python 2.6 comes with optional warnings about 3.0 incompatibilities (run Python with the -3 flag). If you first make sure your code runs without errors in 2.6 (which is largely backward-compatible), you can refactor away any incompatibility warnings. (Needless to say, you should have solid unit tests in place before you do this; see Chapter 16 for more advice on testing.) Second, Python 3.0 ships with an automatic refactoring tool called 2to3, which can automatically upgrade your source files. (Be sure to back up or check in your files before performing any large-scale transformations.) If you wish to have both 2.6 and 3.0 code available, you could keep working on the 2.6 code (with the proper warnings turned on), and generate 3.0 code when it's time for releasing.

Throughout the book, you'll find notes about things that change in Python 3.0. This appendix gives a more comprehensive set of pointers for moving to the world of 3.0. I'll describe some of the more noticeable changes, but not everything that is new in Python 3.0. There are many changes, both major and minor. Table D-1 (which is based on the document *What's New in Python 3.0?*, by Guido van Rossum), at the end of this appendix, lists quite a few more changes and also refers to relevant PEP documents, when applicable (available from http://python.org/dev/peps). Table D-2 lists some other sources of further information.

## Strings and I/O

The following sections deal with new features related to text. Strings are no longer simply byte sequences (although such sequences are still available), the input/print pair has been revamped slightly, and string formatting has had a major facelift.

### Strings, Bytes, and Encodings

The distinction between text and byte sequences is significantly cleaned up in Python 3.0. Strings in previous versions were based on the somewhat outmoded (yet still prevalent) notion that text characters can easily be represented as single bytes. While this is true for English and most western languages, it fails to account for ideographic scripts, such as Chinese.

The Unicode standard was created to encompass all written languages, and it admits about 100,000 different characters, each of which has a unique numeric code. In Python 3.0, str is, in fact, the unicode type from earlier versions, which is a sequence of Unicode characters. As there is no unique way of encoding these into byte sequences (which you need to do in order to perform disk I/O, for example), you must supply an encoding (with UTF-8 as the default in most cases). So, text files are now assumed to be encoded versions of Unicode, rather than simply arbitrary sequences of bytes. (Binary files are still just byte sequences, though.) As a consequence of this, constants such as string.letters have been given the prefix ascii_ (for example, string.ascii_letters) to make the link to a specific encoding clear.

To avoid losing the old functionality of the previous str class, there is a new class called bytes, which represents immutable sequences of bytes (as well as bytearray, which is its mutable sibling).

## Console I/O

There is little reason to single out console printing to the degree that it has its own statement. Therefore, the print statement is changed into a function. It still works in a manner very similar to the original statement (for example, you can print several arguments by separating them with commas), but the stream redirection functionality is now a keyword argument. In other words, instead of writing this:

```
print >> sys.stderr, "fatal error:", error
```

you would write this:

```
print("fatal error:", error, file=sys.stderr)
```

Also, the behavior of the original input no longer has its own function. The name input is now used for what used to be raw_input, and you need to explicitly say eval(input()) to get the old functionality.

## New String Formatting

Strings now have a new method, called format, which allows you to perform rather advanced string formatting. The fields in the string where values are to be spliced in are enclosed in braces, rather than prefaced with a % (and braces are escaped by using double braces). The replacement fields refer to the arguments of the format method, either by numbers (for positional arguments) or names (for keyword arguments):

```
>>> "{0}, {1}, {x}".format("a", 1, x=42)
'a 1 42'
```

In addition, the replacement fields can access attributes and elements of the values to be replaced, such as in "{foo.bar}" or "{foo[bar]}", and can be modified by format specifiers similar to those in the current system. This new mechanism is quite flexible, and because it allows classes to specify their own format string behavior (through the magic __format__ method), you will be able to write much more elegant output formatting code.

# Classes and Functions

Although none of the changes are quite as fundamental as the introduction of new-style classes, Python 3 has some goodies in store in the abstraction department: functions can now be annotated with information about parameters and return values, there is a framework for abstract base classes, metaclasses have a more convenient syntax, and you can have keyword-only parameters and nonlocal (but not global) variables.

## Function Annotation

The new function annotation system is something of a wildcard. It allows you to annotate the arguments and the return type of a function (or method) with the values of arbitrary expressions, and then to retrieve these values later. However, what this system is to be used for is not specified. It is motivated by several practical applications (such as more fine-grained docstring functionality, type specifications and checking, generic functions, and more), but you can basically use it for anything you like.

A function is annotated as follows:

```
def frozzbozz(x: foo, y: bar = 42) -> baz:
    pass
```

Here, foo, bar, and baz are annotations for the positional argument x, the keyword argument y, and the return value of frozzbozz, respectively. These can be retrieved from the dictionary frozzbozz.func_annotations, with the parameter names (or "return" for the return value) as keys.

## Abstract Base Classes

Sometimes you might want to implement only *parts* of a class. For example, you may have functionality that is to be shared among several classes, so you put it in a superclass. However, the superclass isn't really complete and shouldn't be instantiated by itself—it's only there for others to inherit. This is called an *abstract base class* (or simply an *abstract class*). It's quite common for such abstract classes to define nonfunctional methods that the subclasses need to override. In this way, the base class also acts as an interface definition, in a way.

You can certainly simulate this with older Python versions (for example, by raising NotImplementedError), but now there is a more complete framework for abstract base classes. This framework includes a new metaclass (ABCMeta), and the decorators @abstractmethod and @abstractproperty for defining abstract (that is, unimplemented) methods and properties, respectively. There's also a separate module (abc) that serves as a "support framework" for abstract base classes.

## Class Decorators and New Metaclass Syntax

Class decorators work in a manner similar to function decorators. Simply put, instead of the following:

```
class A:
    pass
A = foo(A)
```

you could write this:

```
@foo
class A:
    pass
```

In other words, this lets you do some processing on the newly created class object. In fact, it may let you do many of the things you might have used a metaclass for in the past. But in case you need a metaclass, there is even a new syntax for those. Instead of this:

```
class A:
    __metaclass__ = foo
```

you can now write this:

```
class A(metaclass=foo):
    pass
```

For more information about class decorators, see PEP 3129 (http://python.org/dev/peps/pep-3129), and for more on the new metaclass syntax, see PEP 3115 (http://python.org/dev/peps/pep-3115).

## Keyword-Only Parameters

It's now possible to define parameters that must be supplied as keywords (if at all). In previous versions, any keyword parameter could also be supplied as a positional parameter, unless you used a function definition such as def foo(**kwds): and processed the kwds dictionary yourself. If a keyword argument was required, you needed to raise an exception explicitly when it was missing.

The new functionality is simple, logical, and elegant. You can now put parameters after a varargs argument:

```
def foo(*args, my_param=42): ...
```

The parameter my_param will never be filled by a positional argument, as they are all eaten by args. If it is to be supplied, it must be supplied as a keyword argument. Interestingly, you do not even need to give these keyword-only parameters a default. If you don't, they become *required* keyword-only parameters (that is, not supplying them would be an error). If you don't want the varargs argument (args), you could use the new syntactical form, where the varargs operator (*) is used without a variable:

```
def foo(x, y, *, z): ...
```

Here, x and y are required positional parameters, and z is a required keyword parameter.

## Nonlocal Variables

When nested (static) scopes were introduced in Python, they were *read-only*, and they have been ever since; that is, you can access the local variables of outer scopes, but you can't rebind them. There's a special case for the global scope, of course. If you declare a variable to be global (with the `global` keyword), you can rebind it globally. Now you can do the same for outer, non-global scopes, using the `nonlocal` keyword.

# Iterables, Comprehensions, and Views

Some other new features include being able to collect excess elements when unpacking iterables, constructing dictionaries and sets in a manner similar to list comprehension, and creating dynamically updatable views of a dictionary. The use of iterable objects has also extended to the return values of several built-in functions.

## Extended Iterable Unpacking

Iterable unpacking (such as `x, y, z = iterable`) has previously required that you know the exact number of items in the iterable object to be unpacked. Now you can use the * operator, just for parameters, to gather up extra items as a list. This operator can be used on any one of the variables on the left-hand side of the assignment, and that variable will gather up any items that are left over when the other variables have received their items:

```
>>> a, *b, c, d = [1, 2, 3, 4, 5]
>>> a, b, c, d
(1, [2, 3], 4, 5)
```

## Dictionary and Set Comprehension

It is now possible to construct dictionaries and sets using virtually the same comprehension syntax as for list comprehensions and generator expressions:

```
>>> {i:i for i in range(5)}
{0: 0, 1: 1, 2: 2, 3: 3, 4: 4}
>>> {i for i in range(10)}
{0, 1, 2, 3, 4, 5, 6, 7, 8, 9}
```

The last result also demonstrates the new syntax for sets (see the section "Some Minor Issues," later in this appendix).

## Dictionary Views

You can now access different *views* on dictionaries. These views are collection-like objects that change automatically to reflect updates to the dictionary itself. The views returned by `dict.keys` and `dict.items` are set-like, and cannot include duplicates, while the views returned by `dict.values` can. The set-like views permit set operations.

## Iterator Return Values

Several functions and methods that used to return lists now return more lazy iterable objects instead. Examples include `range`, `zip`, `map`, and `filter`.

# Things That Have Gone

Some functions will simply disappear in Python 3.0. For example, you can no longer use apply. Then again, with the * and ** operators for argument splicing, you don't really need it. Another notable example is callable. With it gone, you now have two main options for finding out whether an object is callable: you can check whether it has the magic method __callable__, or you can simply try to call it (using try/except). Other examples include execfile (use exec instead), reload (use exec here, too), reduce (it's now in the functools module), coerce (not needed with the new numeric type hierarchy), and file (use open to open files).

# Some Minor Issues

The following are some minor issues that might trip you up:

- The old (and deprecated) form of the inequality operator, <>, is no longer allowed. You should write != instead (which is common practice already).

- Backquotes won't work anymore. You should use repr instead.

- Comparison operators (<, <=, and the like) won't allow you to compare incompatible types. For example, you can no longer check whether 4 is greater than "5" (this is consistent with the existing rules for addition).

- There is a new syntax for sets: {1, 2, 3} is the same as set([1, 2, 3]). However, {} is still an empty dictionary. Use set() to get an empty set.

- Division is now real division! In other words, 1/2 will give you 0.5, not 0. For integer division, use 1//2. Because this is a "silent error" (you won't get any error messages if you try to use / for integer division), it can be insidious.

# The Standard Library

The standard library is reorganized quite a bit in Python 3.0. A thorough discussion can be found in PEP 3108 (http://www.python.org/dev/peps/pep-3108). Here are some examples:

- Several modules are removed. This includes previously deprecated modules (such as mimetools and md5), platform-specific ones (for IRIX, Mac OS, and Solaris), and some that are hardly used (such as mutex) or obsolete (such as bsddb185). Important functionality is generally preserved through other modules.

- Several modules are renamed, to conform to PEP 8: Style Guide for Python Code (http://www.python.org/dev/peps/pep-0008), among other things. For example, copy_reg is now copyreg, ConfigParser is configparser, cStringIO is dropped, and StringIO is added to the io module.

- Several modules have been grouped into packages. For example, the various HTTP-related modules (such as httplib, BaseHTTPServer, and Cookie) are now collected in the new http packages (as http.client, http.server, and http.cookies).

The idea behind these changes is, of course, to tidy things up a bit.

# Other Stuff

As I mentioned at the beginning of this appendix, Python 3.0 has a lot of new features. Table D-1 lists many of them, including some I haven't discussed in this appendix. If there's something specific that's tripping you up, you might want to take a look at the official documentation or play around with the `help` function. See also Table D-2 for some sources of further information.

**Table D-1.** *Important New Features in Python 3.0*

| Feature | Related PEP |
|---|---|
| `print` is a function. | PEP 3105 |
| Text files enforce an encoding. | |
| `zip`, `map`, and `filter` return iterators. | |
| `dict.keys()`, `dict.values()`, and `dict.items()` return views, not lists. | |
| The `cmp` argument is gone from `sorted` and `list.sort`. Use `key` instead. | PEP 3100 |
| Division is now true division: `1/2 == 0.5`. | PEP 238 |
| There is only one string type, `str`, and it's equivalent to the Python 2.*x* unicode type. | |
| The `basestring` class is removed. | |
| The new `bytes` type is used for representing binary data and encoded text. | PEP 3137 |
| `bytes` literals are written as `b"abc"`. | PEP 3137 |
| UTF-8 is the default Python source encoding. Non-ASCII identifiers are permitted. | PEP 3120 |
| `StringIO` and `cStringIO` are superseded by `io.StringIO` and `io.BytesIO`. | PEP 0364 |
| New built-in string formatting replaces the % operator. | PEP 3101 |
| Functions can have their parameters and return type annotated. | PEP 3107 |
| Use `raise Exception(args)`, not `raise Exception, args`. | PEP 3109 |
| Use `except MyException as identifier:`, not `except MyException, identifier:`. | PEP 3110 |
| Classic/old-style classes are gone. | |
| Set metaclass with class `Foo(Base, metaclass=Meta):`. | PEP 3115 |
| Abstract classes, `@abstractmethod`, and `@abstractproperty` are added. | PEP 3119 |
| Class decorators, similar to function decorators, are added. | PEP 3129 |
| Backquotes are gone. Use `repr`. | |
| `<>` is gone. Use `!=`. | |
| `True`, `False`, `None`, `as`, and `with` are keywords (they can't be used as names). | |
| `long` is renamed to `int`, and is now the only integer type, but without the `L`. | PEP 237 |
| `sys.maxint` is gone, as there is no longer a maximum. | PEP 237 |

*Continued*

**Table D-1.** *Continued*

| Feature | Related PEP |
|---|---|
| x < y is now an error if x and y are of incompatible types. | |
| __getslice__ and friends are gone. Instead, __getitem__ is called with a slice. | |
| Parameters can be specified as *keyword-only*. | PEP 3102 |
| After nonlocal x, you can assign to x in an outer (nonglobal) scope. | PEP 3104 |
| raw_input is renamed to input. For the old input behavior, use eval(input()). | PEP 3111 |
| xrange is renamed to range. | |
| Tuple parameter unpacking is removed. def foo(a, (b, c)): won't work. | PEP 3113 |
| next in iterators is renamed x.__next__. next(x) calls x.__next__. | PEP 3114 |
| There are new octal literals. Instead of 0666, write 0o666. | PEP 3127 |
| There are new binary literals. 0b1010 == 10. bin() is the binary equivalent to hex() and oct(). | PEP 3127 |
| Starred iterable unpacking is added, as for parameters: a, b, *rest = seq or *rest, a = seq. | PEP 3132 |
| super may now be invoked without arguments, and will do the right thing. | PEP 3135 |
| string.letters and friends are gone. Use string.ascii_letters. | |
| apply is gone. Replace apply(f, x) with f(*x). | |
| callable is gone. Replace callable(f) with hasattr(f, "__call__"). | |
| coerce is gone. | |
| execfile is gone. Use exec instead. | |
| file is gone. | |
| reduce is moved to the functools module. | |
| reload is gone. Use exec instead. | |
| dict.has_key is gone. Replace d.has_key(k) with k in d. | |
| exec is now a function. | |

**Table D-2.** *Sources of Information for Python 2.6 and 3.0*

| Name | URL |
|---|---|
| Python v3.0 Documentation | http://docs.python.org/dev/3.0 |
| What's New in Python 3.0? | http://docs.python.org/dev/3.0/whatsnew/3.0.html |
| PEP 3000: Python 3000 | http://www.python.org/dev/peps/pep-3000 |
| Python 3000 and You | http://www.artima.com/weblogs/viewpost.jsp?thread=227041 |

# Index

## ■Symbols and Numerics

!= (not equal to) operator, 580

\# sign, comments, 116

\#! character sequence, 21, 22

    adding pound bang line, 329

% character, string formatting, 53, 54, 56

    changes in Python 3.0, 600, 605

% (remainder) operator, 580

& (bitwise and) operator, 580

\* (multiplication) operator, 580

\* (parameter splicing) operator, 126, 127, 129

    Python 3.0, 602, 603, 604, 606

\*\* (exponential) operator, 580

\*\* (keyword splicing) operator, 128, 129, 604

+ (unary plus) operator, 580

+= operator, 522

- (unary minus) operator, 580

/ (division) operator, 580

== (equality) operator, 15, 93, 569, 580

^ (bitwise exclusive or) operator, 580

__(double underscores), 151

| (bitwise or) operator, 580

~ (bitwise negation) operator, 580

<, <= (less than) operators, 580

<< (left shift) operator, 580

>, >= (greater than) operators, 580

>> (right shift) operator, 580

2to3 (automatic refactoring tool), 599

## ■A

ABBREV.txt file, 300, 301, 302

ABCMeta metaclass, 601

abs function, 16, 30, 581

abspath function, 494

abstract classes, Python 3.0, 601, 605

abstraction, 139, 571

    *see also* OOP (object-oriented programming)

    changes in Python 3.0, 601

    classes, 147–156

    creating functions, 115–117

    documenting functions, 116

    encapsulation, 145–147

    Fibonacci numbers program, 113–114

    inheritance, 147

    interfaces, 156–157

    making code reusable, 212

    parameters, 117–130

    polymorphism, 142–145

    program structure, 114

    recursion, 133–139

    scoping, 131–133

    value of abstraction, 121

accept method, socket class, 306

access attribute

    publisher handler, mod_python, 342, 343

accessor methods, 187

    as attributes of property function, 188

    private attributes, 151

Acrobat Reader, getting, 425

action method, rule objects

    instant markup project, 412, 414

ActivePython, 6, 595

actual parameters *see* arguments

add function, operator module, 144

add method

    chat server project, 479

    set type, 229

    wx.BoxSizer class, 285

addDestination method, NewsAgent class, 459

addFilter method, Parser class, 414, 415

adding, sequences, 37

addition operator (+), 37

address family, stream socket, 306

addRule method, Parser class, 414, 415

addSource method, NewsAgent class, 459

Adobe Acrobat Reader, getting, 425

Albatross, 344

algorithms, 9, 29

alignment, string formatting, 56, 58

all function, 581

all variable, 219
allow_reuse_address attribute
    SimpleXMLRPCServer class, 527
altsep variable, os module, 224
and operator
    Boolean operators, 96
        short-circuit logic, 574
    operator precedence, 579
Anjuta environment, 6
announcements
    comp.lang.python.announce group, 597
any function, 581
Apache web server
    configuring to use, 338
    conflicting configuration definitions, 339
    dynamic web pages with CGI, 328
    mod_python, 336–343
apilevel property, Python DB API, 294
APIs
    Python Database API, 294–298
    Python/C API, 375–380, 596
App class, wx module *see* wx.App class
append method, lists, 43, 522, 585
append mode, open function (files), 262
appending to dictionaries, 71, 79
appendleft method, deque type, 232
application frameworks
    web application frameworks, 343
apply function, 140, 581
    changes in Python 3.0, 604, 606
Arachno Python environment, 6
arcade game project, 547–567
    banana about to be squished, 566
    Banana class, 558
    banana.png file, 556
    config.py file, 556
    further exploration, 567
    Game class, 565
    game states, 556
    GameOver class, 564
    goals, 548
    Info class, 563
    implementations, 551–556
    Level class, 560
    LevelCleared class, 564
    objects.py file, 556, 557
    Paused class, 561

    preparations, 551
    pygame module, 548
    Pygame, 548–551
    pygame.display module, 549
    pygame.event module, 550
    pygame.font module, 550
    pygame.image module, 551
    pygame.locals module, 549
    pygame.mouse module, 550
    pygame.sprite module, 550
    Squish opening screen, 566
    squish.py file, 556, 559
    SquishSprite class, 557
    StartUp class, 564
    State class, 559
    tools, 548–551
    Weight class, 558
    weight.png file, 554, 556
    weight.pny file, 554
archive files
    wrapping modules as, 386–387
args parameter/object, 377, 378
argument splicing, Python 3.0, 604
arguments
    calling functions without, 572
    command-line arguments, 223
        levels of configuration, 398
    default arguments, 572
    function parameters and, 118
    methods, 573
    named arguments, 572
    printing arguments, using in reverse order, 223
argv variable, sys module, 222, 223
    levels of configuration, 398
arithmetic operators, 9
    precedence, 580
arithmetic sequence, 184
arraysize attribute, cursors, 297
as clause
    changes in Python 3.0, 605
    import statement, 85
ascii constants, string module, 60
ASCII encoding error
    handling special characters, 451
asctime function, time module, 233
assert method, TestCase class, 356
assert statements, 97, 118, 589

assertAlmostEqual method, TestCase class, 356
assertEqual method, TestCase class, 356
   using instead of failUnless, 360
AssertionError class, 589
assertions, 97, 111
assertNotAlmostEqual method, TestCase class, 356
assertNotEqual method, TestCase class, 356
assertRaises method, TestCase class, 356
assignment (=) operator, 569
assignments, 15, 85–88, 589
   augmented assignments, 87, 589
   chained assignments, 87
   changing lists, 41
   description, 13, 111
   sequence unpacking, 85–87
   slice assignments, lists, 42
asterisk width specifier, 59
async_chat class
   chat server project, 473
   collect_incoming_data method, 473, 475
   found_terminator method, 473, 475
   handle_close method, 475
   push method, 475
   set_terminator method, 473, 475
asynchat module, 310
   async_chat class, 473
   chat server project, 470, 473
asynchronous I/O
   multiple connections, 312
   Twisted framework, 316–319
   with select and poll, 313–316
asyncore module, 310
   chat server project, 470
   dispatcher class, 471
   loop method, 472
   tools for chat server project, 470
Atom, 345
Atox, 424
attribute methods, 191–192
   see individual method names
attribute reference precedence, 580
AttributeError class, 162
   checking if object has specific attribute, 172
   __getattr__ method, 192
attributes, 146, 573
   accessing attributes of objects, 150–152
   accessor methods defining, 187–188
   binding to functions, 150
   checking if object has specific attribute, 172
   double underscores in attribute name, 116
   encapsulation, 146
   magic attributes, 116
   object-oriented design, 157
   private attributes, 151
   screen scraping using HTMLParser, 326
   special attributes, 116
attrs argument, handle_starttag, 326
atx, 424
augmented assignments, 87, 589
auth/auth_realm attributes
   publisher handler, mod_python, 342, 343
autoexec.bat file, 98, 216
automated tests, 351
automatic checkers
   limits to capabilities of, 361
   PyChecker/PyLint tools, 359–362, 364
automatic refactoring tool (2to3), 599
AWT (Abstract Window Toolkit), 290

**B**

backquotes, Python 3.0, 604, 605
backslash character (\)
   escaping quotes, 23
   escaping, regular expressions, 243
   raw strings, 27, 28
backticks
   representing strings, 25
backtracking, generators
   solving Eight Queens problem, 200–201
backup parameter, input function, 226
BaseRequestHandler class
   SocketServer module, 311
bases attribute, 155
   issubclass method, 154
basestring class, Python 3.0, 605
basestring function, 581
BasicTextParser class, 422
"batteries included" phrase, 221
BBCode, 424
bdist command, Distutils, 387
   formats switch, 387
   rpm format, 387
   wininst format, 387, 388
Beautiful Soup module, 327–328
Berkeley DB, 515

Binary constructor, Python DB API, 298

binary literals, Python 3.0, 606

binary mode, open function (files), 262

binary search

  recursive function for, 136–138

BINARY value, Python DB API, 298

bind method, socket class, 306

  chat server project, 471, 472

Bind method, widgets, 286, 291

binding parameters, 572

BitTorrent, 517, 518

bitwise operators, 580

BlackAdder environment, 6

blit function, 549

blitting, 549

blocking, 306

blockquote element, bulletin board project, 504

blocks, 88, 111, 569

  finding blocks of text, 406–407

blocks generator

  instant markup project, 406

blogs, 597

Boa Constructor environment, 6

body method, NNTP class, 455, 457

bool function, 581

Boole, George, 89

Boolean operators, 38, 95–96

  short-circuit logic, 96

Boolean values, 89–90

Boost.Python, 371

bottlenecks

  extending Python, 365, 380

bound methods, 150

  calling unbound superclass constructor, 180

BoxSizer class, wx module *see* wx.BoxSizer class

break statements, 102, 591

  else clause, try/except statement, 168

  extracting subject of an article, 457

  infinite recursion, 134

  using with for and while loops, 105

  while True/break idiom, 104–105, 271

broadcast method, Node class

  chat server project, 479

  XML-RPC file sharing project, 521, 522, 525, 532

browsers

  open function, webbrowser module, 225

buffering argument, open function (files), 263

buffers

  closing files after writing, 267

  updating files after writing, 268

bugs *see* debugging

build command, Distutils, 384, 385

build subdirectory, Distutils, 385

build_ext command, Distutils, 389

built-in functions, 16, 581–584

built-in string formatting, Python 3.0, 605

bulletin board project, 499–515

  creating database, 501

  cursor object, 503–504

  database password, 503

  edit.cgi script, 507, 510–511

  further exploration, 515

  hidden inputs, 510

  implementations, 502–514

  main page, 513

  main.cgi script, 506, 507–508

  message composer, 514

  message viewer, 514

  preparations, 500–502

  requirements, 500

  save.cgi script, 507, 511–513

  simple.main.cgi script, 505

  testing, 513

  tools, 500

  view.cgi script, 506, 508–510

Button class, wx module *see* wx.Button class

buttons

  adding button to frame, 281

  Bind method, widgets, 286

  event handling, 286

  setting button label, 282

  setting button size/position, 283

  wx.EVT_BUTTON symbolic constant, 286

bytearray class, Python 3.0, 600

bytes class, Python 3.0, 600

bytes literals, Python 3.0, 605

bytes type, Python 3.0, 599, 605

BytesIO, Python 3.0, 605

■C

c (%c) conversion specifier, 57

C extensions, 371

  extending Python, 369–380

C programming

  deallocating objects, 376

extending Python for improved speed, 365–366

importing existing (shared) C libraries, 370

including C/C++ directly in Python code, 370

Python/C API, 375

   reference manual, 596

C# class

IronPython extending Python, 368

C++

enabling interoperability Python/C++, 371

including C/C++ directly in Python code, 370

caching

XML-RPC file sharing project, 534

callable function, 115, 157, 159, 581

Python 3.0, 604, 606

callback method, Handler class, 411

callback methods, HTMLParser, 325

callproc method, cursors, 297

Canvas class, pdfgen module, 427

capitalize method, strings, 586

capwords function, string module, 63, 66

cat command, files, 265

catching exceptions, 163–170

catching all exceptions, 167, 169

catching exception object, 166

catching many exceptions in one block, 166

description, 173

raising exceptions again, 164–165

try/except statement, 163–169

using more than one except clause, 165–166

ceil function, 17, 30

cElementTree, 437

center method, strings, 586

CGI (Common Gateway Interface)

bulletin board project, 502, 506

   edit.cgi script, 507, 510–511

   main.cgi script, 506, 507

   save.cgi script, 507, 511–513

   simple_main.cgi script, 505

   view.cgi script, 506, 508–510

CGI handler, mod_python, 336, 338–339

CGI script, 331

debugging with cgitb, 331–332

description, 347

dynamic web pages with, 328–336

   adding the pound bang (#!) line, 329

   preparing web server, 328–329

   setting file permissions, 329–330

getting information from CGI script, 335

HTML form, 334–336

input to CGI script, 333

invoking CGI scripts without forms, 334

performance using CGI handler, 339

remote editing with CGI project, 489–498

running CGI script, 339

security risks, 330

using cgi module, 333

cgi file name extension, 329, 339

cgi module

description, 310

dynamic web pages with CGI, 328, 333

FieldStorage class, 333

remote editing with CGI project, 489, 490

cgi-bin subdirectory, 329

cgitb module

debugging with, 331–332

enable function, 331, 347

remote editing with CGI project, 490

tracebacks, 502

chained assignments, 87

chained comparison operators, 93

character sets, 243

characters event handler

XML parsing project, 440, 441

chat server project, 469–487

advantages of writing, 469

asynchat module, 473

asyncore module, 471

ChatServer class, 471–473

ChatSession class, 473–475

collecting data (text) coming from client, 473

command interpretation, 477–478

further enhancement, 486

implementations, 471–485

listening on port for incoming connections, 471

new server, 480–485

preparations, 470–471

requirements, 469

rooms, 478–480

tools, 470

chat services, 469

ChatRoom class, 479, 483

look command, 480, 485

say command, 480, 485

who command, 480, 485

ChatServer class, 480, 484, 471–473

ChatSession class, 480, 484, 473–475

    enter method, 480

checkIndex function, 185

CherryPy, 344

chmod command, UNIX, 330

choice function, random module, 144, 159, 235

chr function, 95, 112, 581

chunks attribute

    screen scraping using HTMLParser, 326

clamp method, rectangles, 556

class attribute

    finding out class of an object, 155

class decorators, Python 3.0, 601, 605

class definition statement, 594

class keyword, 573

class methods, 189–191

    cls parameter, 190

    self parameter, 189

class namespace, 152–153

class scope variable, 153

class statement, 149

    self parameter, 149

    superclasses, 153

classes, 147–148, 158, 573

    abstract classes, 601

    accessing attributes of objects, 150–152

    accessor methods, 151

    built-in exception classes, 162

    changes in Python 3.0, 605

    class decorators, 601

    class namespace, 152–153

    class statement, 149

    classes and types, 147

    creating, 148–149

        new-style classes, 206

    custom exception classes, 163

    defining, 573

    distinguishing methods from functions, 150

    exception classes, 162, 163

    inheritance, 141, 147–155, 159

    instances, 147

        isinstance method, 155

    interfaces, 156–157

    metaclasses, 176

    method definitions, 149

    mix-in classes, 444–446

    naming conventions, 148

    new-style/old-style classes, 149, 175, 206

        implementing properties with old-style classes, 191

        Python version, 3.0, 176

    object-oriented design, 157, 158

    objects and, 147, 155

    OOP, 147–156

    overriding methods, 206

    property function, 189

    specifying superclasses, 153–154

    subclasses, 147, 148

        subclassing built-in classes, 175

    superclasses, 147

        multiple superclasses, 155–156

classmethod function, 581

clear method, dictionaries, 74–75, 585

clear method, Group class

    arcade game project, 550, 552

Clearsilver, 341

Client class

    GUI client project, 539, 542

        fetchHandler, 538, 540, 541, 544

        OnInit method, 538, 539, 541, 543

    XML-RPC file sharing project, 528, 533

clients

    chat server project, 470, 471

    GUI client project, 537–545

    XML-RPC file sharing project, 527–528

close function, fileinput module, 226

    finding sender of e-mail, 253

close method, connections, 296, 300

    bulletin board project, 503

close method, cursors, 297

close method, files, 264, 267

close method, generators, 199

closeHandler, Java Swing, 290

closing files, 267–268

clpa_server variable, 458

cls parameter, class methods, 190

cmath module, 18

Cmd class, cmd module, 527

    modeling command interpretation on, 477

cmd module, 259

    Cmd class, 477, 527

    XML-RPC file sharing project, 519

cmp argument, sort method, 605

cmp function, 52, 581
  making comparisons, 93
code
  making code reusable, 212
  reading source code to explore modules, 221
  source code checking, 359
code coverage, testing, 351
Code Crusader environment, 6
code fatigue, 395
Code Forge environment, 6
code reuse, 212
coerce function, Python 3.0, 604, 606
collect_incoming_data method
  chat server project, 473, 475
collections
  *see also* mappings; sequences
  collections module, 231
combine function, 132
command interpretation
  chat server project, 477–478
  modeling on Cmd class, 477
command prompt
  running scripts from, 20
CommandHandler class
  chat server project, 478, 481
command-line arguments, 223
  levels of configuration, 398
command-line switches, 398
command-line tools
  using with subprocess module, 360
commands
  cat command, 265
  import command, 17
  pipe characters linking, 265
  python command, 265
  sort command, 265
commas
  separating print statements with, 83–84
comments, 22, 570
  documenting functions, 116
commit method, connections, 296, 300
  bulletin board project, 503
    save.cgi script, 511
Common Gateway Interface *see* CGI
comp.lang.python group, 597
comparison operators, 92–95
  chaining, 93

comparing incompatible types, 92
comparing sequences, 95
comparing strings, 94
equality operator, 93
identity operator, 93–94
in operator, 94
is operator, 93–94
membership operator, 94
Python 3.0, 604, 606
compile function, re module, 245
compiling extensions, Distutils, 388–389, 390
complex function, 581
complex numbers, 18
Complex type, 579
components *see* widgets
comprehensions, 603
computer games
  arcade game project, 547–567
concatenating strings, 24
condition method, rule objects, 412, 413, 414
conditional operator, 96
conditional statements, 88–97
  assertions, 97
  Boolean operators, 95–96
  comparison operators, 92–95
  conditional execution, 90
  conditions, 92–96
  description, 111
  elif clauses, 91
  else clauses, 90
  if statements, 90
  nesting blocks, 91
  short-circuit logic, Boolean operators, 574
config.py file, 397
  arcade game project, 556
configparser module, 397, 398
  renamed modules in Python 3.0, 604
configuration, 396–398
  description, 394, 401
  levels of, 398
configuration files, 396–398
  dividing into sections, 397
conflict function, Eight Queens problem, 202
connect function, Python DB API, 300, 304
  parameters, 296
connect method, socket class, 306

connection object, 296, 303
  bulletin board project, 503, 511
connectionLost event handler, 317
connectionMade event handler, 317
connections
  bulletin board project, 502
  chat server project, 471, 472
  network programming, 311–316
  Python DB API, 296, 303
console I/O, Python 3.0, 600
constants, 396
  string module, 60
  symbolic constants, 396
constructors, 176–181, 575
  creating, 177
  default parameters, 574
  description, 206
  init method, 177, 575
  overriding, 177–179
    using super function, 180, 181
  Python DB API, 297
  unbound superclass constructor, 179–180
containers, 32
content handlers
  creating, 439, 441
  dispatcher mix-in classes, 446
ContentHandler class
  XML parsing project, 451
  xml.sax.handler module, 439
Content-type header
  dynamic web pages with CGI, 331
context managers, 268
continual rewriting syndrome, 395
continue statements, 103, 591
  using with for and while loops, 105
control structures, 569
conversion flags, 56
conversion specifiers, 56
  % character, 56
  dictionaries, 73
  field width, 56, 59
  minimum field width, 57
  precision, 54, 56, 57
  string formatting, 54–59
  tuples, 56
  types, 56, 57
conversion types, string formatting, 56, 57

conversions
  between numbers and strings, SQLite, 303
convert function, 301
convert method, surface objects, 554
Cookie module, 310
cookie-cutter code
  automating, 377
cookielib module, 310
copy function, copy module, 220
copy method, dictionaries, 75, 585
count method, lists, 43, 585
count method, strings, 586
CounterList class, 186, 187
coverage
  code coverage, 351
  test coverage, 351, 352
CPython, extending, 367, 369–371
cracking, vs. hacking , 1
CREATE TABLE command
  bulletin board project, 501
create_socket method
  chat server project, 471, 472
cStringIO, Python 3.0, 605
csv module, 258
ctypes library, 370
cursor method, connections, 296, 300
cursor objects, 296
  in bulletin board project, 503—505
cursors, Python DB API, 296–297, 303
  attributes, 297
  bulletin board project, 503
  methods, 296
custom exception classes, 163, 173
CXX see PyCXX
cyclic garbage, 377

▪D

%d conversion specifier, 56
Daily Python-URL blog, 597
Dalke, Andrew
  Sorting Mini-HOWTO, 49
data
  analyzing many forms of numeric data, 370
  fetching data from Internet, 432
data structures, 31, 570
  containers, 32
  deques, 231–232
  heaps, 230–231

lists, 40–49
mappings and dictionary type, 69
sequences, 31–40
sets, 228–229
stacks, 45
tuples, 49–51
Database API *see* Python Database API
database parameter
    connect function, Python DB API, 296
DatabaseError exception, Python DB API, 295
databases
    compact table-based databases, 293
    food database application, 300–303
    importing data into, 301
    key-value databases, 293
    object databases, 293
    popular commercial choices, 293
    Python Database API, 294–298
    relational databases, 293
    supported by Python packages, 293
DataError exception, Python DB API, 295
datagram socket, 306
dataReceived event handler, 317
Date constructor, Python DB API, 298
DateFromTicks constructor, Python DB API, 298
dates
    fields of Python date tuples, 233
datetime module, 234, 258, 456
DATETIME value, Python DB API, 298
DB API *see* Python Database API
deallocating objects, 376
Debian Linux, installing Python, 4
debugging
    anticipating code changes, 351
    cgitb module, 331–332
    PythonDebug directive, 339, 340
    remote editing with CGI project, 490
decode method, strings, 586
decorators
    abstract classes, Python 3.0, 601
    changes in Python 3.0, 605
    class decorators, Python 3.0, 601
    description, 190
deep copy, dictionaries, 76
deepcopy function, copy module, 76, 220
def statements, 115, 571
    class namespace, 152

documenting functions, 116
    generator-function component, 198
default arguments, 572
default values, parameters, 124
    using empty lists as, 575
defaultdict dictionary, 232
defaultStart/defaultEnd methods
    XML parsing project, 445, 447
deferred execution, Twisted, 317
definitions
    class definitions, 594
    function definitions, 594
del method, 177
del operation, dictionaries, 71
del statements, 107–108, 590
    deleting elements from lists, 41
    description, 112
    using for cleanup operation, 170
delattr function, 581
__delattr__ method, 191
delitem method, 182, 184
deque module, 259
deque type, 231–232
    collections module, 231
deques, 231–232
description attribute, cursors, 297
descriptor protocol, 189
design
    object-oriented design, 157–158
destructors
    __del__ method, 177
__dict__ attribute
    avoiding endless looping, 192
    __getattribute__ method trap, 192
    seeing all values stored in objects, 157
dict function, 71, 81, 581
dictfetchall method, cursor object
    bulletin board project, 503, 504
        SQLite alternative, 505
dictfetchone method, cursor object
    bulletin board project, 503
dictionaries, 571
    ** operator, 127, 128
    accessing dictionary items, 76
    adding items to, 71, 72
    assigning value to new key, 71
    checking if key exists, 78

dictionaries *(continued)*
    constructing from other mappings, 71
    conversion specifiers, 73
    creating, 70
    creating with values of None, 76
    deep copy of, 76
    defaultdict, 232
    empty dictionary, 604
    globals function, 132
    iterating over, 100
    keys, 121
    keys and values, 70
    locals function, 132
    membership, 71, 72
    modules mapping, 222
    overwriting same key items from another, 80
    precedence, 581
    removing all items from, 74
    removing arbitrary value from, 79
    returning all items of, 78
    returning list of keys, 78
    returning list of values, 80
    returning value of specified key, 79
    shallow copy of, 75
    string formatting with, 73, 81
    subclassing dict type, 185–187
    uses, 69
dictionary comprehension, Python 3.0, 603
dictionary methods, 74–80, 585–586
    clear, 74–75, 585
    copy, 75, 585
    fromkeys, 76, 585
    get, 76–78, 585
    has_key, 78, 585, 606
    items, 78, 585
    iteritems, 78, 585
    iterkeys, 78, 585
    itervalues, 80, 585
    keys, 78, 585
    pop, 79, 586
    popitem, 79, 586
    setdefault, 79, 106, 586
    update, 80, 586
    values, 80, 586
dictionary type
    deepcopy function, 76
    in operation, 71

key related operators, 71
mappings and, 69
operations, 71–73
purpose of, 69–70
syntax, 70
types for keys, 72
uniqueness of values, 70
using, 70
dictionary views, Python 3.0, 603
difflib library, 258
digests, passwords, 494
digits constant, string module, 60
dir function, 260, 581
    exploring modules, 218
directory element
    XML parsing project, 437
directory list
    XML parsing project, 448
discussion forum
    bulletin board project, 499–515
dispatch method
    XML parsing project, 445
Dispatcher class
    bind method, 471, 472
    chat server project, 471
    create_socket method, 471
    garbage collection, 480
    handle_accept method, 471, 472, 475, 480
    listen method, 471, 472
    set_reuse_addr method, 473
    XML parsing project, 445, 448
display method, Level class, 561
display method, State class, 560
display module, pygame, 549
dist subdirectory, Distutils, 387
distribute method, NewsAgent class, 459, 462
distributing operators, 128–129, 604
distribution formats, 387
distributions
    ActivePython, 595
    alternative Python distributions, 5–7
    distributing Python packages, 383
    IronPython, 595
    Jython, 595
    MacPython, 595
    Official Python Distribution, 595

Python distributions, 595
pywin32, 595
Distutils toolkit, 383–386
bdist command, 387
build command, 384, 385
build subdirectory, 385
build_ext command, 389
compiling extensions, 388–389
description, 383, 390
dist subdirectory, 387
install command, 385
installing, 384
lib subdirectory, 385
py_modules directive, 386
py2exe extension, 389–390
register command, 390
sdist command, 386, 387
setup function, 384, 391
setup.py script, 383, 384, 385, 387, 390
setuptools project, 384
SWIG, 375, 389
uninstall command, 385, 388
wrapping modules as archive file, 386–387
division, 9, 10
division (/) operator, 580
double slash (//) operator, 10
integer division, Python 3.0, 604, 605
rounding, 16
divmod function, 581
Django, 343, 344
do_exit method, Client class
XML-RPC file sharing project, 533
do_fetch method, Client class
GUI client project, 538
XML-RPC file sharing project, 533
do_logout method, chat server project, 479
do_look method, chat server project, 480
do_say method
chat server project, 480
XML-RPC file sharing project, 527
do_who method, chat server project, 480
doc attribute
exploring modules, 220
function attributes, 116
doc parameter, property function, 189
docstrings, 116, 220
exploring modules, 220

doctest module, 352, 353–355, 364
testmod function, 353, 354, 364
Document Object Model (DOM), 439
documentation
creating graphics and documents in PDF, 425
exploring modules, 220–221
Macintosh library modules, 596
Python, 596
DOM (Document Object Model), 439
DOS, handling whitespace for, 225
double slash operator, 10
double underscores (__)
making method or attribute private, 151
double-clicking, 21
double-ended queues (deques), 231–232
draw method, 549, 550, 552
drawToFile method, renderPDF class, 428
dsn parameter
connect function, Python DB API, 296
duck typing, 145
dynamic web pages
screen scraping, 321
dynamic web pages with CGI, 328–336

### E

%E, %e conversion specifiers, 57
Eclipse environment, 6
edit.cgi script
bulletin board project, 510, 511
description, 507
link from main.cgi, 507
link from view.cgi, 508
testing, 513
remote editing with CGI project, 492–494, 496
editing
remote editing with CGI project, 489–498
eggs, Python, 384
Eight Queens problem, 200–206
ElementTree, 437
dealing with XML in Python, 439
elif clauses, if statements, 91, 592
else clauses
if statements, 90, 592
try/except statement, 168–169
combining try/except/finally/else, 170
description, 173
using in loops, 105
email, finding sender of, 251–253

email addresses filter
    instant markup project, 418
email module, 310
EmailDestination class
    news gathering project, 468
empty dictionary, 604
empty lists, 37
    using as default value, 575
empty set, 604
enable function, cgitb module, 331, 347
encapsulation, 145–147, 573
    accessing attributes of objects, 150–152
    accessor methods, 187
    attributes, 146
    description, 141, 158
    extending Python, 366
    state, 147
encode method, strings, 586
encoding, Python 3.0, 599, 605
end method
    MatchObjects, re module, 248
end method, Handler class
    instant markup project, 410, 411
endElement event handler
    XML parsing project, 440, 441, 445
endless loop trap
    setattr method, 192
EndSession exception
    chat server project, 479
endswith method, strings, 586
ensureDirectory method
    XML parsing project, 447, 448
enter method
    context managers, 268
enter method, ChatSession class, 480
enumerate function, 102, 112, 582
environ mapping, os module, 223, 224
environment variables
    description, 216
    environ mapping, os module, 224
    levels of configuration, 398
    PYTHONPATH, 215
    setting in UNIX and Mac OS X, 216
    setting in Windows, 216
EOF command, 527
Epytext
    markup systems and web sites, 424

equality (==) operator, 15, 93, 569, 580
eric environment, 6
Error exception, Python DB API, 295
error handling
    exceptions, Python DB API, 295
error messages *see* tracebacks
errors
    *see also* exceptions
    AttributeError class, 162
    catching Pygame-specific errors, 549
    distinguishing from failures in unittest, 357
    inappropriate type used, 183
    index outside range, 183
    IndexError class, 162
    IOError class, 162
    KeyError class, 162
    NameError class, 162
    NotImplementedError exception, 224
    stderr stream, sys module, 222
    SyntaxError class, 163, 254
    TypeError class, 163
    ValueError class, 163
    ZeroDivisionError class, 161, 163
escape function, re module, 245, 247
escaping quotes, 23–24
escaping special characters
    regular expressions, 242
EtText, 424
eval function, 112, 582
    sample template system, 254
eval statements, 110
    description, 112
    scope, 111
event handling
    Bind method, widgets, 286
    button events, 286
    chat server project, 471
    closeHandler, Java Swing, 290
    connectionLost event handler, 317
    connectionMade event handler, 317
    dataReceived event handler, 317
    description, 291
    HTMLParser callback methods, 325
    load function, 286
    rawDataReceived event handler, 318
    save function, 286
    screen scraping using HTMLParser, 326

when event handler is called, 286
writing Twisted server, 317
wx.EVT_BUTTON symbolic constant, 286
wxPython GUI toolkit, 286
XML parsing project, 439–441, 448–450
event module, pygame, 550
event-driven networking framework, 316
writing Twisted server, 317
events, 286
polling event constants in select module, 315
XML parsing project, 439–441
except block
Python 3.0, 605
Python DB API, 295
except clause, try statement, 593
*see also* try/except statements
catching all exceptions, 167
catching exception object, 166
catching many exceptions in one block, 166
description, 173
trapping KeyError exception, 172
using more than one except clause, 165–166
Exception class, 162
catching all exceptions, 169
raise statement, 162
exception objects, 161, 173
catching, 166
exceptions, 161, 576
*see also* errors
built-in exception classes, 162, 163
catching exceptions, 163–170
catching all exceptions, 167, 169
catching exception object, 166
catching many exceptions in one block, 166
danger of catching all exceptions, 167
description, 173
raising exceptions again, 164–165
try/except statement, 163–169
connecting to NNTP servers, 455
custom exception classes, 163, 173
doing something after exceptions, 169–170
EndSession exception, 479
exception hierarchy, 295
exception objects, 161, 173
functions and, 164, 170–171, 173
GeneratorExit exception, 199
indicating everything worked, 168–169

NotImplementedError exception, 224
Python DB API, 295
raise statement, 162–163
raising exceptions, 161–163, 173
StopIteration exception, 192
SyntaxError exception, 254
try/except statement, 163–169
using more than one except clause, 165–166
warnings, 173
XML-RPC file sharing project, 528–529
Zen of, 171–173
exec statements, 109–110, 592
changes in Python 3.0, 606
description, 112
replacing reload function functionality using, 211
sample template system, 254
scope, 111
execfile function, 582
Python 3.0, 604, 606
executable binaries, 390
executable Windows programs
creating with py2exe, 389–390
execute method, cursors, 297, 301, 302
bulletin board project, 503
executemany method, cursors, 297, 301
executing programs, 19–20
execv function, 224
exit command
XML-RPC file sharing project, 527
exit function, sys module, 222
exit method
context managers, 268
expandtabs method, strings, 586
exponentiation operator (**), 11
compared to pow function, 16
precedence, 580
expression statements, 589
expressions, 9–12, 579–588
compared to statements, 13
description, 29
evaluating expression strings, 254
logical expressions, 573
precedence, 580
extend method
deque type, 232
lists, 44, 585

extending Python, 365–366
  architecture, 366
  CPython, 367
  encapsulation, 366
  extending CPython, 369–371
  extension approaches, 380
  identifying bottlenecks, 365
  IronPython, 367–369
  Jython, 367–369
  Python extensions, 380
  SWIG, 371–375
  using Python/C API, 380, 375–380
    framework for extensions, 377–378
    hand-coded palindrome module, 379–380
    reference counting, 376–377
  wrapping legacy code, 366
  writing C extensions, 369–380
extendleft method
  deque type, 232
extensions
  compiling extensions, 388–389, 390
  framework for, 377–378
  py2exe extension, Distutils, 389–390
Extreme Programming, 349, 393

■F

%F conversion specifier, 57
%f conversion specifier, 54, 57
factorial function, 135
factorials
  recursive function to calculate, 134
Factory class
  twisted.internet.protocol module, 317
fail method, TestCase class, 357
failIf method, TestCase class, 357
failIfAlmostEqual method, TestCase class, 356
failIfEqual method, TestCase class, 356
failUnless method, TestCase class, 356
  using assertEqual instead of, 360
failUnlessAlmostEqual method, TestCase class, 356
failUnlessEqual method, TestCase class, 356
failUnlessRaises method, TestCase class, 357
failures
  distinguishing from errors in unittest, 357
False value (Boolean), 89
  changes in Python 3.0, 605
Fault class, xmlrpclib module, 528, 529

feed method
  instant markup project, 410
feeds see RSS feeds
fetch command
  XML-RPC file sharing project, 527
fetch method, Node class
  XML-RPC file sharing project, 520, 521, 524,
    526, 527, 531
fetchall method, cursors, 297, 302
  bulletin board project, 503, 504
fetchHandler, Client class
  GUI client project, 538, 540, 541, 544
fetchmany method, cursors, 297
fetchone method, cursors, 297
  bulletin board project, 503
fget/fset/fdel parameters, property function, 189
Fibonacci numbers program, 113
field width, string formatting, 56, 57, 59
FieldStorage class, cgi module, 333
file function, 275, 582
  Python 3.0, 604, 606
file iterators, 272–274
file locking
  remote editing with CGI project, 497
file methods, 263–270
  close method, 264, 267
  examples using, 268–270
  flush method, 268
  read method, 264
  readline method, 266
  readlines method, 266
  seek method, 266
  tell method, 266
  write method, 264
  writelines method, 267
  xreadlines method, 272
file permissions
  dynamic web pages with CGI, 329–330
file property, modules
  exploring modules via source code, 221
file sharing, 517
  adding GUI client to Python program, 537–545
  XML-RPC file sharing project, 517–535
filecmp module
  news gathering project, 468
fileinput module, 225–227
  description, 259

finding sender of e-mail, 252
    functions, 225
    lazy line iteration with fileinput, 272
    sample template system, 255, 256
filelineno function, fileinput module, 226
filename function, fileinput module, 226
files
    closing files, 267–268, 274
    file types, 274
    file-like objects, 263, 274
    finding file name, wxPython, 286
    iterating over file contents, 270–274
        byte by byte, 270–271
        description, 274
        file iterators, 272–274
        iterating over lines in very large file, 272
        lazy line iteration with fileinput, 272
        one line at a time, 271
        reading everything first, 271
        without storing file object in variable, 273
    modes, 261–263, 274
    opening files, 261–263
        buffering, 263
        changes to file in text mode, 262
        description, 274
    piping output, 264–265
    random access, 266
    read/write/append/binary modes, 261
    reading and writing, 264
        closing files after, 267
    reading files, 274
    reading lines, 266, 274
    streams, 274
    universal newline support mode, 263
    using as context managers, 268
    validating file names, XML-RPC, 529–534
    writing files, 274
        updating files after writing, 268
    writing lines, 266, 274
Filter class, 154
filter function, 138, 139, 140, 582
    changes in Python 3.0, 605
    instant markup project, 414
filters
    fetching data from Internet, 432
    instant markup project, 409, 413, 418
filterwarnings function, 174

finally clause, try statement, 169–170, 173, 593
    combining try/except/finally/else, 170
find method, strings, 60, 586
findall function, re module, 245, 246
    finding sender of e-mail, 252
findall method, regular expressions
    news gathering project, 462
firewalls, network programming and, 305
firstDisplay method
    arcade game project, 560, 562
flag argument, wx.BoxSizer class, 285
flags
    conversion specifiers, 56
flags parameter, 247
flip function, arcade game project, 549, 552
float function, 30, 582
    food database application, 300
Float type, 579
floating-point numbers, 10
floats, 10
floor function, 16, 30
flush method, files, 268
Font function, arcade game project, 550
font module, pygame, 550
food database application, 300–303
    creating and populating tables, 301–302
    food_query.py, 303
    importdata.py, 301
    searching and dealing with results, 302–303
footers
    writeFooter method, 446
for loops, 99, 570
    Fibonacci numbers program, 113
    generators
    iter method, 193
    iterable files, 272
    list comprehension, 105–106
    recursive generators, 196
for statements, 593
forking, 312
    chat server project, options for, 469
    multiple connections, 312
    SocketServer module, 313
form tag, action attribute, 492
formal parameters, 118
format function, bulletin board project, 504, 507

format method, strings
    changes in Python 3.0, 600
format strings, Python/C API, 378
formats switch
    bdist/sdist commands, Distutils, 387
formatting strings
    changes in Python 3.0, 600
    conversion specifiers, 54–59
    string formatting operator, 53
forms
    invoking CGI scripts without, 334
    writing HTML forms, 334–336
forums, online Python resources, 597
found_terminator method
    chat server project, 473, 475, 479
Frame class, wx module *see* wx.Frame class
frames
    adding button to frame, 281
    setting frame size, 283
    setting frame title, 282
    wx.Frame class, 281
    wxPython GUI toolkit creating, 281
frameworks
    event-driven networking framework, 316
    framework for extensions, 377–378
    SocketServer framework, 310–311, 319
    Twisted framework, 316–319, 320
    web application frameworks, 343
freshmeat.net, 596
from module import statement, 17
    reasons not to use, 18
fromkeys method, dictionaries, 76, 585
frozenset function, 582
frozenset type
    immutability, 229
ftplib module, 310
function annotation, Python 3.0, 601
function attributes
    doc attribute, 116
function call precedence, 580
function definition statement, 115, 594
functional programming, 138–139, 140
functional requirements
    requirement specification, 350
functions, 29, 571–572
    *see* individual function names
    as values in Python, 572

binding attributes to, 150
built-in functions, 16, 581–584
calling functions without arguments, 572
containing yield statement, 195
creating, 115–117
defining functions in modules, 212
    testing modules, 212–214
distinguishing methods from, 150
documenting, 116
ending functions, 117
exceptions and, 164, 170–171, 173
extinct functions in Python 3.0, 604
flags parameter, 247
formal parameters, 118
from module import statement, 17
function definition, 139
functions without return values, 117
generator-function, 198, 207
local naming, 120
methods compared, 43
nested scopes, 133
number of scopes/namespaces, 131
object-oriented design, 157
parameter/return type annotation, 601, 605
parameters, 16, 117–130, 139
    changing, 118–120
    collecting parameters, 125–128
    distributing operators, 128–129, 604
    examples using, 129–130
    gathering operators, 125–128, 602, 603, 604, 606
    immutability, 123
    keyword parameters, 123–125
    keyword-only parameters, 602, 606
    passing parameters to functions, 572
    reasons for changing, 120–122
    values, 118
parts of recursive function, 134
recursion, 133–139, 140
recursive functions, 134
return value, 16
    caution using if statements, 117
    return value is None, 117
type objects, 17
functools module, 258
future module, 10, 19

## G

%G, %g conversion specifiers, 57

games, arcade game project, 547–567

  Game class, 565

  game states, 556

  GameOver class, 564

garbage collection

  cyclic garbage, 377

  del method, 177

  gc module, 377

  reference counting, 377

  unbound objects, 480

gathering operators, 125–128, 602, 603, 604, 606

gc module, 377

generator comprehension, 196

GeneratorExit exception

  close method, generators, 199

generators, 194–200

  backtracking and, 200–201

  close method, 199

  components of, 198

  description, 207

  generator-function, 198, 207

  generator-iterator, 198

  making generators, 195

  methods, 198–199

  recursive generators, 196–197

  return statement, 195, 198

  send method, 198

  simulating, 199

  solving Eight Queens problem, 200–206

  throw method, 199

  yield expression, 198, 199

  yield statement, 195, 198

Gentoo Linux

  installing Python, 4

get function, arcade game project, 550, 552

GET method

  getting information from CGI script, 335

get method, dictionaries, 76–78, 585

get_surface function, arcade game project, 549, 552

__getattr method__, 191, 192

  raising AttributeError, 192

getattr function, 157, 159, 582

  chat server project, 478

  checking whether object has specific attribute, 173

  working with getattr method, 192

__getattribute__ method, 191

  accessing dict attribute, 192

getdefaultencoding function, sys module, 451

gethostname function, socket class, 306, 307

getitem method, 182

  changes in Python 3.0, 606

  overriding, 186

  simulating slicing, sequences, 185

  subclassing list type, 186

getItems method, NewsAgent class

  news gathering project, 459, 461, 462

getName accessor method

  private attributes, 151

getopt module, 259

  news gathering project, 468

getPort function

  XML-RPC file sharing project, 523, 530

getrandbits function, random module, 235

getslice method, Python 3.0, 606

GetValue method

  load event, wxPython, 286

  save event, wxPython, 286

getvalue method, FieldStorage class

  input to CGI script, 333

global keyword, 133, 603

global scope, 131

  exceptions and functions, 170

  rebinding variables in outer scopes, 133

global statements, 592

global variables

  avoiding, 240

  bugs when referencing, 132

  constants, 396

  object-oriented design, 157

  Python DB API, 294–295

  rebinding, 132

  shadowing, 132

  treating objects as abstract, 146

globals function, 132, 582

gmtime function, time module, 234

Gnutella, 517

gopherlib module, 310

Graphical User Interfaces *see* GUIs

graphics

  creating graphics in PDF/Python, 425

graphics creation project, 425–434
    constructing PolyLine objects, 429–430
    drawing with ReportLab, 427–429
    fetching data from Internet, 432
    further exploration, 434
    implementations, 427–434
    preparations, 426
    prototype for sunspots_proto.py, 430–431
    ReportLab package, 425
    tools, 426
    using LinePlot Class, 432–434
graphics package, reportlab module, 427
graphics-generating package
    graphics creation project, 426
graphs
    definitions and further information, 201
greater than operators, 580
greedy patterns, 250
    finding sender of e-mail, 252
grokking, 218
Group class, arcade game project, 550
    clear method, 552
    update method, 552
group method
    connecting to NNTP servers, 455
    MatchObjects, re module, 248
group numbers, regular expressions
    using in substitution string, 249
groups
    re module, 247–249
    Usenet groups, 597
Grutatxt, 424
GTK platform
    PyGTK GUI toolkit, 278
GUI client project, 537–545
    Client class, 539, 542
    further exploration, 545
    implementations, 538–545
    ListableNode class, 541
    preparations, 538
    requirements, 537
    tools, 537
GUI platforms, 291, 277
GUI toolkits
    chat server project, 486
    choosing between, 278
    description, 277
    for Jython, 290
    list of GUI toolkits for Python, 597
    popular GUI Toolkits for Python, 277
    Swing, 290
    Tk/Tkinter, 289
    wxPython, building text editor, 278–288
GUIs (Graphical User Interfaces), 291

■H
hacking
    cracking compared, 1
halting theorem, 361
halts module, 362
handle method
    arcade game project, 560, 562
    forking and threading, 313
handle method, Node class
    XML-RPC file sharing project, 521, 522, 525, 531
handle_accept method
    chat server project, 471, 472, 475, 480
handle_charref method, HTMLParser, 325
handle_close method
    chat server project, 475, 480
handle_comment method, HTMLParser, 325
handle_data method, HTMLParser, 325, 326
handle_decl method, HTMLParser, 325
handle_endtag method, HTMLParser, 325, 327
handle_entityref method, HTMLParser, 325
handle_pi method, HTMLParser, 325
handle_startendtag method, HTMLParser, 325
handle_starttag method, HTMLParser, 325, 326
Handler class, instant markup project, 410–411, 418
    callback/start/end/sub methods, 410, 411
handler module, xml.sax, 439
handlers
    CGI handler, mod_python, 336, 338–339
    creating content handler, 439–441
    instant markup project, 409–411
    mod_python handler framework, 336
    PSP handler, mod_python, 336, 339–341
    publisher handler, mod_python, 336, 341–343
handlers.py, instant markup project, 418
has_key method, dictionaries, 78, 585, 606
hasattr function, 157, 159, 582
    replacing callable function, 115
    working with getattr method, 192
hashlib module, 258

head method, NNTP class, 455, 457

header file

    framework for extensions, 377

    SWIG, 372, 373

headers

    writeHeader method, 446

heading rules

    instant markup project, 415

HeadingRule class

    instant markup project, 416, 420

HeadlineHandler class

    XML parsing project, 441

heapify function, 230, 231

heappop function, 230, 231

heappush function, 230

heapq module, 230–231, 259

heapreplace function, 230, 231

heaps, 230–231

hello method, Node class

    XML-RPC file sharing project, 520, 521, 524,
       526, 528, 531, 534

help function, 116, 582

    description, 30, 260

    exploring modules, 219–220

help switch, Distutils, 384

hex function, 582

hexadecimal numbers, 12

hidden form elements

    remote editing with CGI project, 494

hidden inputs, 510

    bulletin board project, 513

host parameter, connect function, 296

hotshot module, 363

htaccess file, 338, 339, 341

HTML

    automatically marking up plain-text file, 403

    creating HTML pages, 442–444

    fixing ill-formed HTML, 322

    index.html file, 492

    introduction to, 403

    parsing, 322

    writing HTML forms, 334–336

    XHTML advantages over, 325

HTMLDestination class

    news gathering project, 460, 462

htmllib module

    parsing HTML, 322

HTMLParser class, 325–327

    callback methods, 325

    event-handling methods, 325

    screen scraping using, 326

HTMLRenderer class

    instant markup project, 409, 411, 419

httplib module, 310

■

%i conversion specifier, 56

id column, messages table

    bulletin board project, 502

    view.cgi script, 508

id function, 582

identity operator, 93–94

IDEs for Python, 6

IDLE interactive Python shell, 2

    IDEs for Python, 6

    saving and executing programs, 19

if statements, 15, 90, 569, 592

    catching exceptions, 164

    caution when return value is None, 117

    try/except statement compared, 171, 173

I/O, Python 3.0, 600, 605

image attribute, Sprite class, 554

image module, pygame, 551

imaginary numbers, 18

imaplib module, 310

immutability

    frozenset type, 229

    lists, 119

    parameters, 123

    set type, 229

    strings/numbers/tuples, 119

    using is operator with immutable values, 94

implementation of projects

    structure of projects in this book, 402

import command, 17

    from module import statement, 17

import statements, 591

    as clause, 85

    description, 111

    fetching functions from external modules, 209

    importing something as something else, 84–85

    open function, 85

importdata.py, 301

importing modules, 259

import-only-once behavior, modules, 211

in operation, 71

in operator, 38, 39, 94

    operator precedence, 580

include_dirs variable, 299

incompatibility warnings

    transitioning to Python 3.0, 599

indentation, 569

    blocks, 88

index method, lists, 44, 138, 585

index method, strings, 587

index, sequences

    checkIndex function, 185

    description, 31

    illegal type of index used, 184

index.html file

    remote editing with CGI project, 492, 496

IndexError class, 162

    index outside range, 183, 184

indexing, lists, 570

indexing, sequences, 32–34

inequality operator

    Python 3.0, 604, 605

infinite recursion, 134

inflate method, rectangles, 555, 556

Info class, arcade game project, 563

information-gathering agent

    news gathering project, 453

inheritance, 147–155

    description, 141, 159

    multiple inheritance, 156, 575

    multiple superclasses, 155–156

    object-oriented design, 157

    overriding methods and constructors, 177, 178

    specifying superclasses, 153–154

    subclassing list/dict/str types, 185

init file

    making Python recognize packages, 217

init function, pygame module, 549, 552

__init__ method, 575

    calling unbound superclass constructor, 180

    making init magic, 177

    using super function, 180

initialization functions

    naming conventions, 380

initializing methods *see* constructors

inner scope *see* local scope

Inno Setup installer, 388

inplace parameter, input function, 226, 227

input

    compared to raw_input, 26

    fileinput module, 225–227

    getting input from users, 14–15

    hidden inputs, 510

    stdin stream, sys module, 222

input function, 14, 30, 570, 582

    changes in Python 3.0, 600

input function, fileinput module, 226

    backup parameter, 226

    inplace parameter, 226, 227

insert method, lists, 45, 585

inside attribute, ListRule class

    instant markup project, 417

inside function

    XML-RPC file sharing project, 530

inspect module

    publisher handler, mod_python, 342

    seeing all values stored in objects, 157

install command, Distutils, 385

    compiling extensions, 388

installations, Python, 1–7

    on Linux/UNIX, 3–5

    on Macintosh, 5

    on Windows, 1–3

installers

    alternative installers, 388

    creating Windows installer, 387

    Inno Setup, 388

    introduction, 390

    McMillan installer, 388

    Windows installer technology, 388

    writing install scripts with Distutils, 383–386

instances of classes, 147

    isinstance method, 155

instant markup project, 403–424

    adding markup, 407–408

    components, 409

    filters, 413, 418

    final program, 418–422

    finding blocks of text, 406–407

    further exploration, 423–424

    goals, 404

    Handler class, 410–411

    handlers, 409–411

    implementations, 406–422

Parser class, 413–415
parsers, 413–415
preparations, 405–406
Rule class, 413
rules, 412–413, 415–418
tools, 404
int function, 30, 113, 570, 582
integer type, 579
integers
    integer division, 9
    large integers, 11–12
    long integers, 11–12
    numbers containing leading zeros, 70
IntegrityError exception, Python DB API, 295
interactive interpreter, 7–9
    saving programs, 19
interface file, SWIG, 372, 373
InterfaceError exception, 295
interfaces, 156–157, 159
InternalError exception, 295
interoperability
    enabling, Python/C++, 371
interpreter, interactive, 7–9
I/O, asynchronous I/O with select and poll,
        313–316
IOError class, 162
IRC, 595
IronPython, 595
    alternative Python distributions, 6, 7
    description, 380
    extending Python, 367–369
is not operator, 580
is operator, 93–94
    operator precedence, 580
isalnum method, strings, 587
isalpha method, strings, 587
isdigit method, strings, 587
isdir function, os.path module
    XML parsing project, 447
isfirstline function, fileinput module, 226
isinstance function, 142, 159, 582
    using in checkIndex function, 185
isinstance method, 155
islower method, strings, 587
isspace method, strings, 587
isstdin function, fileinput module, 226
issubclass function, 159, 582

issubclass method, 154
istitle method, strings, 587
isupper method, strings, 587
item access, 182–187
    sequence and mapping protocol, 182–185
    subclassing list/dict/str types, 185–187
item access precedence, 580
items method, dictionaries, 78, 100, 585
    changes in Python 3.0, 605
__iter__ method, 192–194, 207
    for loops, 193
iter function, 194, 207, 582
iterable unpacking, Python 3.0, 603, 606
iteration
    definition, 192
    for loops, 99
    iterable object, 99
    iterating over dictionaries, 100
    iterating over file contents, 270–274
        byte by byte, 270–271
        file iterators, 272–274
        iterating over lines in large file, 272
        lazy line iteration with fileinput, 272
        one line at a time, 271
        reading everything first, 271
        without storing file object in variable, 273
    iterating over sequences, 32
    iterating over string-like objects, 197
    looping, 99
    numbered iteration, 101
    parallel iteration, 100–101
    reversed iteration, 102
    sorted iteration, 102
    StopIteration exception, 192
    utilities, 100–102
    while loops, 98
iterator protocol, 192–194
iterator return values, Python 3.0, 603
iterators, 192–194
    changes in Python 3.0, 605
    description, 207
    file iterators, 272–274
    generators and, 195
    introduction, 175
    iterator protocol, 192–194
    making sequences from, 194
    returning, 197

iteritems method, dictionaries, 78, 585
iterkeys method, dictionaries, 78, 585
itertools module, 258
itervalues method, dictionaries, 80, 585

## ■J

Java class, Jython extending Python, 367
Java Swing *see* Swing GUI toolkit
JavaBean properties
    Jython extending Python, 368
JavaScript Object Notation (JSON), 346
join function, os.path module
    XML parsing project, 447
join method, strings, 61, 587
    example using, 223
    performance, 255
JSON (JavaScript Object Notation), 346
just-in-time compiler for Python, 370
Jython, 595
    alternative Python distributions, 6, 7
    description, 380
    extending Python, 367–369
    GUI toolkits for, 290
    JavaBean properties, 368
jythonc command, 367

## ■K

KDevelop environment, 6
key argument of sort method, lists, 48
    changes in Python 3.0, 605
key related operations, dictionaries, 71
key types, dictionaries, 71
KeyError exception, 162
    trapping with except clause, 172
keys
    inappropriate type used, 183
    sequence key is negative integer, 183
keys method, dictionaries, 78, 100, 585
    changes in Python 3.0, 605
keys, dictionaries, 121
    checking if key exists, 78
    types for keys, 72
keyword arguments/parameters, 123–125
    ** (keyword splicing) operator, 126
    combining with positional parameters, 124
    keyword-only parameters, 602, 606

sort method, lists, 48
    using with wx constructors, 282
Komodo environment, 6

## ■L

label argument, wx.Button constructor, 282
lambda expressions, 139
lambda operator, 579
languages
    object-oriented languages, 141
large integers, 11–12
LaTeX
    markup system, 404
    typesetting system, 434
layout mechanisms, 291
lazy evaluation, Boolean operators, 96
lazy line iteration, 272
left shift operator, 580
len function, 40, 52, 582
__len__ method, 182, 184
len operation, dictionaries, 71
less command, UNIX, 457
less than operators, 580
letters constant, string module, 60
    changes in Python 3.0, 606
Level class, arcade game project, 560
LevelCleared class, arcade game project, 564
lib subdirectory, Distutils, 385
libraries
    ctypes library, 370
    difflib library, 258
    importing existing (shared) C libraries, 370
    Macintosh library modules, 596
    Python library reference, 596
    standard library modules, 259
    Tidylib, 324
library_dirs variable, 299
line method, Canvas class, 427
line numbers
    adding to Python script, 227
line separators *see* newline character
lineno function, fileinput module, 226
LinePlot Class
    graphics creation project, 432–434
LineReceiver class, Twisted framework
    chat server project, options for, 469

LineReceiver protocol
twisted.protocols.basic module, 318
lines
constructing PolyLine objects, 429–430
lines generator
instant markup project, 406
linesep variable, os module, 224
Linux
installing Python on Linux/UNIX, 3–5
list comprehension, 105–106, 112
exploring modules, 218
generator comprehension and, 196
using, 139
list constructor
making lists from iterators, 194
list function, 40, 52, 583
list item rules
instant markup project, 415
list method, ListableNode class
GUI client project, 541, 542
list methods, 43–49, 585
append method, 43, 585
count method, 43, 585
extend method, 44, 585
index method, 44, 585
insert method, 45, 585
pop method, 45–46, 585
remove method, 46, 585
reverse method, 46, 585
sort method, 47–49, 585
list rules
instant markup project, 415
ListableNode class, GUI client project, 541
list method, 541, 542
listen method
chat server project, 471, 472
socket class, 306
listenTCP function, reactor module, 318, 320
ListItemRule class
instant markup project, 416, 420
ListRule class
instant markup project, 417, 420
lists, 40–49, 570
adding items compared to dictionaries, 72
appending object to end of, 43
appending values to end of, 44
assigning to slices, 42

assigning values to, 41
changing lists, 41
copying entire list, 47
counting occurrences of elements in, 43
deleting elements from, 41
deleting slices, 42
empty lists, 37
finding first occurrence of a value, 44
immutability, 119
indexing, 570
initialization, 37
inserting elements, 42
inserting object into, 45
making lists from iterators, 194
making lists from other lists, 105
multiple references to same list, 47
operations on, 41–42
precedence, 581
removing an element from, 45
removing first occurrence of value, 46
reversed function, 47
reversing elements in, 46
selecting all elements, 35
selecting elements from start/end, 35
slicing, 119, 571
sorted function, 48
sorting into new list, 47
sorting original list, 47
subclassing list type, 185–187
tuples compared, 31
literal values, 579
ljust method, strings, 587
load function
arcade game project, 551
event handler, 286
local scope, 131
parameters, 118
locals function, 132, 583
locals module, pygame, 549, 552
localtime function, 233, 234, 455
logging, 399, 400, 401
logging module, 258, 399–400
logical expressions, 573
short-circuit logic, 574
logical operators *see* Boolean operators
login command, chat server project, 479, 485, 486
LoginRoom class, chat server project, 479, 480, 482

logout command, chat server project, 479, 485, 486

LogoutRoom class, chat server project, 479, 480, 483

logRequests value

    XML-RPC file sharing project, 523

long function, 30, 583

long integer type, 579

long integers, 11–12

    changes in Python 3.0, 605

long strings, 26–27

look command, chat server project, 480, 485

lookup function, 121

loop method, chat server project, 472

loops, 97–105

    breaking out of, 102–105

        while True/break idiom, 104, 105

    description, 112

    __dict__ attribute avoiding endless looping, 192

    for loops, 99

    iterating over dictionaries, 100

    iteration utilities, 100–102

        numbered iteration, 101

        parallel iteration, 100, 101

        reversed iteration, 102

        sorted iteration, 102

    list comprehension, 105–106

    using else clauses in, 105

    while loops, 98

lower method, strings, 62, 95, 241, 457, 587

lowercase constant, string module, 60

lstrip method, strings, 587

## ■M

-m switch

    making programs available as modules, 212

Mac OS X

    setting environment variables, 216

Macintosh

    installing Python on, 5

Macintosh library modules, 596

MacPython, 595

magic attributes

    __dict attribute__, 192

magic methods, 575

    advanced use of, 187

    constructors, 176–181

    __del__ method, 177

    __delattr__ method, 191

    __delitem__ method, 182, 184

    __getattr__ method, 191, 192

    __getattribute__ method, 191, 192

    __getitem__ method, 182

    __init__ method, 177

    introduction, 175, 206

    item access, 182–187

    __iter__ method, 192–194

    iterator protocol, 192–194

    __len__ method, 182, 184

    modules, 576

    __next__ method, 192

    __nonzero__ method, 182

    overriding methods and constructors, 177–179

        calling unbound superclass constructor, 179–180

        using super function, 180–181

    property function, 189

    sequence and mapping protocol, 182–185

    __setattr__ method, 191, 192

    __setitem__ method, 182

    subclassing list/dict/str types, 185–187

mailbox module, 310

mailcap module, 310

mailing lists, 597

main chat room, chat server project, 479

main function

    calling from another function, 240

    unittest module, 356, 364

main page, bulletin board project, 513

main value

    testing modules, 213

main.cgi script, bulletin board project, 506, 507–508

    link to edit.cgi, 507

    link to view.cgi, 507, 508

    testing, 513

MainLoop method, wx.App class, 281

makedirs function, os module

    XML parsing project, 447

maketrans function, string module, 60, 65, 66

MANIFEST.in file, 387

map function, 138, 140, 583

    changes in Python 3.0, 605

mappings

    constructing dictionaries from, 71

    deleting element associated with key, 182

    description, 32, 81, 182, 206

    dictionaries and, 69

environ mapping, 223, 224

modules mapping, 222

returning number of key-value pairs contained in, 182

returning value of key, 182

sequence and mapping protocol, 182–185

storing value for key, 182

Markdown

markup systems and web sites, 424

markup

instant markup project, 403–424

markup systems, 424

markup.py program, instant markup project, 421

Martelli, Alex, 106

Python Cookbook, 96

match function, re module, 245, 246

MatchObjects class, re module, 247–249

methods, 248

Matplotlib/pylab, 434

max function, 40, 52, 583

MAX_HISTORY_LENGTH constant

peer-to-peer file sharing, 522

maxint value, sys

changes in Python 3.0, 605

maxsplit argument

split function, re module, 246

McMillan installer, 388

membership, 51

checking membership with sets, 228

dictionaries, 71, 72

sequences, 38–39

membership operator, 94

memory leaks, 376

message composer, bulletin board project, 514

Message object, email module

news gathering project, 461

message viewer, bulletin board project, 514

message_from_string function

news gathering project, 461

messages table, bulletin board project

columns described, 502

creating, 501

__metaclass__ attribute

creating new-style classes, 206

finding out class of an object, 155

new-style/old-style classes, 175

old-style and new-style classes, 149

property function, 188

metaclass syntax, Python 3.0, 602, 605

metaclasses, 176

Metakit, 515

method resolution order (MRO), 156

methods, 51, 573

see individual method names

accessor methods, 151, 187

arguments, 573

bound methods, 150

calling, 43, 573

calling overridden version, 206

class methods, 189–191

constructors, 176–181

dictionaries, 585–586

distinguishing methods from functions, 150

functions compared, 43

generator methods, 198–199

list methods, 43–49

lists, 585

magic methods see magic methods

making method or attribute private, 151

MatchObjects, re module, 248

method definitions, 149

object-oriented design, 157, 158

overriding, 177–179

overriding in subclasses, 148, 156

polymorphism and, 143

static methods, 189–191

string methods, 60–66

strings, 586–588

methods, files, 263–270

mhlib module, 310

microthreads, 312

min function, 40, 52, 583

minimum field width, string formatting, 56, 57, 59

mix-in classes, 159

dispatcher mix-in classes, 444–446

mktime function, time module, 233, 234

mod_python framework, 336–343, 347

CGI handler, 336, 338–339

configuring Apache, 338

installing, 337

PSP handler, 336, 339–341

publisher handler, 336, 341–343

mode argument, open function (files), 261–263

modes, files, 261–263, 274

modulator tool, 371

modules, 29, 209–221, 259, 576

  *see* individual module names

  __all__ variable, 219

  "batteries included" phrase, 221

  checking if module exists, 218

  creating and locating, 209–210

  defining functions in, 212–214

  dir function, 218

  documentation, 220, 221

  exploring, 218–221

  extinct modules in Python 3.0, 604

  help function, 219–220

  import statement, 209

  importing, 17, 209, 210, 259

  import-only-once behavior, 211

  magic methods, 576

  main purpose of, 210

  making code reusable, 212

  making modules available, 214–216

  making programs available as, 212

  mapping, sys module, 222

  modifying sys.path to specify location, 210, 214

  naming file containing module code, 217

  networking, 305–310

  newly released third-party modules, 7

  packages, 259

  packaging in packages, 217

  packaging in Python 3.0, 604

  permissions affecting save location, 214

  programming, 17–19

  putting modules in existing sys.path, 214–215

    reasons for not doing, 215

  py_modules directive, Distutils, 386

  pyc file extension, 210

  pygame modules, 548–551

  reading source code, 221

  reloading, 211

  renamed modules in Python 3.0, 604

  specifying module location in PYTHONPATH, 215–216

  standard library modules, 221–259

  switching between database modules, 294

  test code contained in, 259

  testing, 212–214

  third-party modules, 597

  twisted modules, 317, 318

  wrapping modules as archive file, 386–387

  writing extension modules for Python, 370

modulo operator

  list comprehension, 105

  string formatting, 66

modulus operator, 11

mouse cursor

  pygame.mouse module, 550

mouse module, pygame, 550

move method, rectangles, 555

MRO (method resolution order), 156

μTidyLib, 324

multiple connections

  network programming, 311–316

multiple inheritance, 156, 575

multiple superclasses, 155–156

multiplication operator, 37, 580

multiplying, sequences, 37–38

mutable objects *see* immutability

mxTidy, 324

MySQL database

  bulletin board project, 500, 501

MySQLdb module, 597

  bulletin board project, 500

## ■N

name variable, testing modules, 213

name argument, open function (files), 261

named arguments, 572

named value, Python DB API, 295

NameError class, 162

namespaces

  *see also* scopes

  class namespace, 152–153

  class statement, 149

  number of namespaces, 131

  using exec and eval, 109, 111

naming conventions

  classes, 148

    making method or attribute private, 152

  initialization functions, 380

  object-oriented design, 158

  symbolic constants, 396

  variables, 13

  wx module methods, 281

nan value, 18

negative numbers

  sqrt function, 18

nested scopes, 133
    instant markup project, 410
nesting blocks, if statements, 91
Network News Transfer Protocol *see* NNTP
network programming
    asynchronous I/O with select and poll, 313–316
    chat server project, 469
    event-driven networking framework, 316
    firewalls, 305
    forking and threading with SocketServer, 313
    introduction, 305
    multiple connections, 311–316
    opening remote files, 308
    port numbers, 307
    retrieving remote files, 309
    sockets, 470
    synchronous network programming, 306
    Twisted framework, 316–319
networking modules, 305–310
newline character
    changes on opening in text mode, 262
    platforms using other line separators, 267
NEWNEWS command
    NNTP server supporting, 454, 456
newnews method, NNTP class, 455, 456
news gathering project, 453–468
    automatically generated news page, 461
    downloading messages from newsgroups, 455
    flexible news-gathering agent, 463
    further exploration, 467
    goals, 454
    implementations, 455–467
    NewsAgent class, 459
    news page with more than one source, 463
    preparations, 454–455
    tools, 454
newsgroups
    downloading messages from, 455
    online resources, 597
NewsItem class
    news gathering project, 459
newsreaders *see* NNTP clients
__next__ method, 192
    changes in Python 3.0, 606
    iter method returning iterator, 192, 207
    object implementing, 193

nextfile function, fileinput module, 226
    finding sender of e-mail, 253
nextset method, cursors, 297
nextState method, LevelCleared class
    arcade game project, 564
nlargest function, heapq module, 230, 231
NNTP (Network News Transfer Protocol), 453
NNTP class
    body method, 455, 457
    head method, 455, 457
    instantiating, 455
    newnews method, 455, 456
NNTP clients, 453
NNTP constructor
    connecting to servers, 454
NNTP servers
    '211' string beginning, 455
    '411' string beginning, 455
    connecting to servers, 454
    description, 453
    downloading messages from newsgroups, 455
    main network of, 453
    news gathering project, 454
nntplib library
    news gathering project, 453, 454, 455
nntplib module, 310
NNTPSource class
    news gathering project, 461, 462
Node class, GUI client project, 541
    updateList method, 541, 543
Node class, XML-RPC file sharing project, 520, 530
    broadcast method, 521, 522, 525, 532
    constructor, 520
    fetch method, 520, 521, 524, 531
    handle method, 521, 522, 525, 531
    hello method, 520, 521, 524, 531
    implementing, 520–525
    query method, 520, 521, 522, 524, 530
    start method, 523, 524, 531
    stopping and restarting node, 527
None value, 37
    changes in Python 3.0, 605
    return value, functions, 117
    using None as placeholder, 574
None value, Boolean values, 89
nongreedy patterns *see* greedy patterns

nonlocal keyword, 133
    Python 3.0, 602, 606
nonzero method, 182
nose
    alternatives to unit test tools, 355
not equal to operator, 580
not in operator, 580
not operator, 96, 580
NotImplementedError exception, 224
NotSupportedError exception, 295
nsmallest function, heapq module, 230, 231
NUMBER value, Python DB API, 298
numbered iteration, 101
numbers, 9–12
    complex numbers, 18
    floating-point numbers, 10
    hexadecimal numbers, 12
    imaginary numbers, 18
    immutability, 119
    nan value, 18
    numbers containing leading zeros, 70
    octal numbers, 12
numeric arrays
    analyzing many forms of numeric data, 370
numeric value, Python DB API, 295
NumPy, 370, 548

■O

%o conversion specifier, 56
object function, 583
object-oriented design, 157–158, 159
object-oriented languages, 141
    Smalltalk, 151
object-oriented programming see OOP
objects, 572–575
    accessing attributes of objects, 150–152
    checking if object has specific attribute, 172
    classes, 147–156
    classes and objects, 147
    deleting, 107
    description, 141, 158
    encapsulation, 573, 145–147
    exception objects, 161
    finding out class of an object, 155
    file-like objects, 263, 274
    inheritance, 575, 147–154, 155
    MatchObjects, re module, 247

    methods, 573
    object-oriented design, 157
    polymorphism, 142–145
        forms of, 144
        methods and, 143
    private attributes, 151
    referencing not owning, 376
    referring to the object itself, 149
    seeing all values stored in objects, 157
    treating objects as abstract, 146
objects.py file, arcade game project, 556, 557
oct function, 583
octal literals, Python 3.0, 606
octal numbers, 12
Official Python Distribution, 595
offset parameter
    seek method, files, 266
OnInit method, Client class
    GUI client project, 538, 539, 541, 543
online chatting see chat server project
online resources, 595–597
OOP (object-oriented programming)
    classes, 147–156, 158
    distinction between types and classes, 148
    encapsulation, 141, 145–147, 158
    inheritance, 141, 147–154, 155, 159
    interfaces, 156–157, 159
    objects, 141, 158
    polymorphism, 141, 142–145, 158
        forms of, 144
    summary of key concepts, 158–159
open function, files, 261–263, 275
    binary mode, 262
    buffering argument, 263
    mode argument, 261–263
    name argument, 261
open function, import statement, 85
open function, shelve module, 238
open function, webbrowser module, 225
opening files, 261–263
opent function, 583
operating systems
    os module, 223–225
OperationalError exception, 295
operations
    dictionaries, 71–73
    lists, 41–42

sequences, 32–40
  adding, 37
  checking membership, 38–39
  indexing, 32–34
  multiplying, 37–38
  slicing, 34–37
  strings, 53
  tuples, 50
operator module
  add function, 144
operators
  * (parameter splicing) operator, 126, 127
  ** (keyword splicing) operator, 128
  += operator, 522
  adding sequences, 37
  arithmetic operators, 9
  assignment operator, 13, 15
  Boolean operators, 38, 95–96
  comparison operators, 92–95
  conditional operator, 96
  distributing operators, 128–129, 604
  double slash operator, 10
  equality operator, 15, 93
  exponentiation operator (**), 11
  gathering operators, 125–128, 602, 603, 604, 606
  identity operator, 93–94
  in operator, 38, 39, 94
  is operator, 93–94
  logical operators, 96
  membership operator, 94
  modulo operator, 66
  modulus operator, 11
  multiplying sequences, 37
  parameter operators, 125–129
  precedence, 579–581
  repetition operators, 250
  splicing operators, 129
  string formatting operator, 53
  ternary operator, 96
optimization
  extending Python for speed, 365–366
  profiling, 362–363
optparse module, 259
  levels of configuration, 398
  news gathering project, 468

or operator
  Boolean operators, 96
    short-circuit logic, 574
  operator precedence, 579
  finding union of two sets, 228
ord function, 95, 112, 583
os module, 223–225, 259
  functions and variables, 223
  makedirs function, 447
os.path module, XML parsing project, 447
outer scope *see* global scope
output
  piping output, 264–265
  stdout stream, sys module, 222
overriding
  description, 206
  getitem method, 186
  methods and constructors, 177–179
    calling unbound superclass constructor, 179–180
    using super function, 180–181
  methods in subclasses, 148, 156

## ■P

package manager
  installing Python on Linux/UNIX, 4
packages, Python, 217–218
  announcing/publishing, 390
  centralized index of, 390
  description, 259
  distributing, 383
  files and directories layout, 217
  graphics-generating package, 426
  grouping modules in, 217
  making Python recognize, 217
  module packaging in Python 3.0, 604
  Python Package Index, 384
packaging programs
  creating Linux RPM packages, 387
  creating Windows installer, 387
  distribution formats, 387
  Distutils, 383–386
  introduction, 383
  wrapping modules as archive file, 386–387
page element, XML parsing project, 437, 442
painting pretty picture project *see* graphics creation project

palindrome module
 hand-coded using Python/C API, 379–380
palindromes, 372
 program to recognize, 372–375
Panel class, wx module *see* wx.Panel class
ParagraphRule class
 instant markup project, 417, 421
parallel iteration, 100–101
parameter operators, 125–129
 Python 3.0, 602, 603, 604, 606
parameters, functions, 16, 117–130
 actual parameters, 118
 annotation, 601, 605
 arguments, 118
 changing, 118–120
 collecting parameters, 125–128
 combining positional/keyword parameters, 124
 default values, 124
 description, 139
 distributing operators, 128–129, 604
 examples using parameters, 129–130
 formal parameters, 118
 gathering operators, 125–128, 602, 603, 604, 606
 immutability, 123
 keyword parameters, 123–125, 602, 606
 keyword-only parameters, 602, 606
 local naming, 120
 local scope, 118
 modifying parameters, 123
 parameter operators, 125–128
 passing parameters to functions, 572
 positional parameters, 123
  default values, 124
 reasons for changing, 120–122
 rebinding parameters, 123, 572
 self parameter, 150
 values, 118
paramstyle property, Python DB API, 294, 295
parent argument, wx constructors, 281
parse function, xml.sax module, 439
parse method, instant markup project, 414
Parser class, instant markup project, 413–415, 421
 addFilter method, 414, 415
 addRule method, 414, 415
 parse method, 414
parsers, instant markup project, 409, 413–415
parsing XML project *see* XML parsing project

parsing, HTML, 322
 HTMLParser class/module, 325–327
partition method, strings, 587
pass statements, 107, 112, 590
passthrough variable
 XML parsing project, 448
password handling, 494
password parameter
 connect function, Python DB API, 296
passwords
 bulletin board project, 503
path configuration files, 216
path submodule, os module, 223, 447
path variable, sys module, 222
 modifying to specify module location, 210, 214
 putting modules in existing sys.path, 214–215
  reasons for not doing, 215
 search path (list of directories), 214
 using PYTHONPATH alongside, 216
pathsep variable, os module, 223, 224
patterns
 greedy patterns, 250
 re module functions, 245
Paused class, arcade game project, 561
PDF (Portable Document Format) files
 editing, 425
 getting PDF reader, 425
 graphics creation project, 425
pdfgen module, ReportLab package, 427
PDFs, drawing with ReportLab, 427
peer-to-peer file sharing
 GUI client project, 544
 MAX_HISTORY_LENGTH constant, 522
 XML-RPC file sharing project, 517–535
peer-to-peer systems, 517
performance
 join method, strings, 255
 using CGI handler, 339
period (dot) character
 regular expression wildcards, 242
permissions
 dynamic web pages with CGI, 329–330
 saving modules, 214
Pilgrim, Mark, 345
pipe characters, 265
piping output, files, 264–265

placeholders
    using None as placeholder, 574
PlainDestination class
    news gathering project, 460, 462
plain-text markup, 403
    markup systems, 424
platform variable, sys module, 222
platforms, GUI, 277
Platypus, ReportLab package, 434
playful programming, 393
Plone, 344
poll function, select module, 320
    asynchronous I/O with, 315–316
poll object
    register/unregister methods, 315
POLLXYZ events
    polling event constants in select module, 315
PolyLine class
    constructing PolyLine objects, 429
polymorphism, 142–145
    description, 141, 158, 182
    duck typing, 145
    forms of, 144
    interfaces, 156
    isinstance function or, 155
    methods and, 143
    repr function, 145
    subclassing list/dict/str types, 185
    types, 145
    use of isinstance function, 185
pop functions
    heappop function, 230, 231
pop method, dictionaries, 79, 586
pop method, lists, 45–46, 585
popen function, 224
    running Tidy, 324
popitem method, 79, 586
    sequence unpacking, 86
poplib module, 310
port numbers
    chat server project, 470, 471, 473
    network programming, 307
    numbers requiring administrator privileges, 470
pos argument, wx.Button constructor, 283
positional parameters
    combining with keyword parameters, 124

default values, 124
description, 123
gathering operators, 125–128, 602, 603, 604, 606
keyword-only parameters, 602, 606
POST method
    getting information from CGI script, 335
    remote editing with CGI project, 490
PostgreSQL database
    bulletin board project, 500, 501
pound bang (#!), 21, 22
    dynamic web pages with CGI, 329
pow function, 16, 30, 583
power (exponential) operator, 11
power function, 135
powers
    recursive function to calculate, 135
pprint function, 215
precedence, operators, 579–581
precision, string formatting, 54, 56, 57
preparations for projects
    structure of projects in this book, 402
print function, Python 3.0, 605
print statement
    changes in Python 3.0, 600
print statements, 14, 111, 590
    separating with commas, 83–84
printable constant, string module, 60
printing
    pretty-printing function, 215
    using arguments in reverse order, 223
priority queues
    heaps, 230–231
private attributes, 151
problem descriptions for projects
    structure of projects in this book, 401
procedures
    functions without return values, 117
    remote procedure calls
        REST and RPC, 346
        SOAP, 346
        with Pyro, 346
        XML-RPC, 345
profile module, 258, 363
    run method, 363, 364
profiling, 359, 362–363, 364
    hotshot/profile/timeit modules, 363

programming
  *see also* OOP (object-oriented programming)
  algorithms, 9
  books about programming, 400–401
  built-in functions, 16, 581–584
  comments, 22
  configuration, 394, 396–398, 401
  configuration files, 396–398
  dictionary methods, 74–80, 585–586
  expressions, 9–12, 579–588
  flexibility in, 393–394, 401
  functional programming, 138–139, 140
  functions, 16
  input, 14–15
  list methods, 43–49, 585
  literal values, 579
  logging, 399–400, 401
  making scripts behave like programs, 20–22
  minimum requirements, 400
  modules, 17–19
  operator precedence, 579–581
  playful programming, 393
  prototyping, 394–395, 401
  pseudocode, 136
  Python reference, 579–594
  Python tutorial, 569–577
  requirement specification, 350–351
  saving and executing programs, 19–20
  statements, 13–14, 589–594
  string methods, 60–66, 586–588
  strings, 22–29
  symbolic constants, 396
  test-driven programming, 349–352, 364
  testing, 394
  text editor, 19
  variables, 13
ProgrammingError exception, Python DB API, 295
programs
  abstraction and program structure, 114
  building Windows executable programs, 383
  creating executables with py2exe, 389–390
  description, 29
  importing programs as modules, 209
  making programs available as modules, 212
  packaging, 383
    Distutils, 383–386

projects
  arcade game project, 547–567
  bulletin board project, 499–515
  chat server project, 469–487
  graphics creation project, 425–434
  GUI client project, 537–545
  instant markup project, 403–424
  news gathering project, 453–468
  remote editing with CGI project, 489–498
  structure of projects in this book, 401
  XML parsing project, 435–452
  XML-RPC file sharing project, 517–535
properties
  accessor methods defining attributes, 187–188
  creating properties, 188
    __getattr__/__setattr__ methods, 191–192
    property function, 188–189
  implementing with old-style classes, 191
  introduction, 175
  new-style/old-style classes, 175
property function, 188–189, 207, 583
  calling with arguments, 189
  descriptor protocol, 189
  __get__/__set__ methods as attributes of, 188
  magic methods, 189
  new-style/old-style classes, 206
proportion argument
  Add method, wx.BoxSizer class, 285
protocol attribute, Factory class
  writing Twisted server, 317
protocol module, 317
protocols, 182
  descriptor protocol, 189
  iterator protocol, 192–194
  sequence and mapping protocol, 182–185
prototyping, 394–395, 401
  case against rewriting, 395
  extending Python for improved speed, 365
pseudocode, 136, 569
PSP (Python Server Pages), 339
  PSP tags, 340
psp file name extension, 340
PSP handler, mod_python, 336, 339–341
Psyco, 370
psycopg module, 597
  bulletin board project, 500
pth file extension, 216

publisher handler, mod_python, 336, 341–343

pump function, arcade game project, 550

punctuation constant, string module, 60

push functions

    heappush function, 230

push method, chat server project, 475, 479

PuTTY software, 471

py file extension, 576

    naming file containing module code, 217

    running CGI script, 339

py.test

    alternatives to unit test tools, 355

Py_BuildValue function, 378, 381

Py_DECREF macro, 376, 381

Py_INCREF macro, 376, 378, 381

py_modules directive, Distutils, 386

Py_None object, 378

py2exe extension

    building Windows executable programs, 383

    Distutils, 389–390

    Inno Setup installer, 388

PyArg_ParseTuple function, 378, 381

PyArg_ParseTupleAndKeywords function, 378, 381

pyc file extension, 210

pychecker/pylint commands, 360

PyChecker/PyLint tools, 359–362, 364

PyCXX, 371

pyformat value, Python DB API, 295

Pygame documentation, 547

pygame module, 548, 597

pygame modules, functions of

    blit, 549

    flip, 549, 552

    Font, 550

    get, 550, 552

    get_surface, 549, 552

    init, 549, 552

    load, 551

    pump, 550

    set_caption, 549

    set_mode, 549, 552

    set_visible, 552

    Surface, 548

    update, 549, 552

Pygame tool, arcade game project, 548–551

    catching Pygame-specific errors, 549

pygame.display module, 549, 552

pygame.event module, 550, 552

pygame.font module, 550

pygame.image module, 551

pygame.locals module, 549

    importing constants from, 552

pygame.mouse module, 550, 552

pygame.sprite module, 550

PyGTK GUI toolkit, 278, 597

pylab, Matplotlib, 434

Pylons, 343, 344

PyObject type, 377

PyPI (Python Package Index), 384, 390, 596

PyPy, 370

PyQt GUI toolkit, 278, 597

    SIP tool, 371

Pyrex, 370

Pyro

    remote procedure calls with, 346

pyRXP

    dealing with XML in Python, 439

PySimpleApp class, wx module *see*
        wx.PySimpleApp class

PySQLite, 298, 304

    downloading and installing, 299

Python

    *see also* programming

    adding line numbers to script, 227

    alternative distributions, 5–7

    built-in functions, 16, 581–584

    cmath module, 18

    comments, 22

    compiling from sources, 4–5

    converting values to strings, 24

    creator of, 19

    dictionary methods, 74–80, 585–586

    distinction between types and classes, 148

    enabling interoperability Python/C++, 371

    expressions, 9–12, 579–588

    extending, 365–366

        extension approaches, 380

        IronPython, 367–369, 380

        Jython, 367–369, 380

        Python/C API, 375–380

        SWIG, 371–375, 380

        writing C extensions, 369–380

    functional programming, 140

    functions, 117

Python *(continued)*
GUI platforms for, 291
GUI toolkits, 597
IDEs for Python, 6
IDLE interactive Python shell, 2
including C/C++ directly in Python code, 370
installing on Windows, 1–3
installing Python on Linux/UNIX, 3–5
installing Python on Macintosh, 5
interactive interpreter, 7–9
interpreter, 9
just-in-time compiler for, 370
large integers, 12
list methods, 43–49, 585
literal values, 579
making scripts behave like normal programs, 20–22
mod_python, 336–343
modules, 17–19
operator precedence, 579–581
popular GUI Toolkits for, 277
private attributes, 151
release information, 7
RPython, 370
running scripts from command prompt, 20
Stackless Python, 312
statements, 13–14, 589–594
string methods, 60–66, 586–588
strings, 22–29
third-party modules, 597
web application frameworks, 343
web tutorial, 569
writing extension modules for, 370
Python 3.0, 599–606
abstract classes, 601
argument splicing, 604
automatic refactoring tool (2to3), 599
class decorators, 601
comparing incompatible types, 604
console I/O, 600
dictionary comprehension, 603
dictionary views, 603
extinct functions, 604
extinct modules in, 604
function annotation, 601
inequality operator, 604
integer division, 604

iterable unpacking, 603
iterator return values, 603
keyword-only parameters, 602, 606
metaclass syntax, 602
module packaging in, 604
new features in, 605
nonlocal variables, 602
renamed modules in, 604
set comprehension, 603
set syntax, 604
sources of information for, 606
standard library, 604
string formatting, 600
strings/bytes/encodings, 599
transitioning from older code to, 599
Python/C API
creating built-in types and classes, 378
deallocating objects, 376
extending Python using, 375–380
format strings, 378
framework for extensions, 377–378
hand-coded palindrome module, 379–380
reference counting, 376–377
writing extension modules for Python, 370
python command, 3, 265
Python Cookbook, 596
Alex Martelli, 96
Python Database API (Python DB API), 294–298
apilevel property, 294
bulletin board project, 502, 503
connections, 296, 502
constructors and special values, 297
cursors, 296–297, 503
description, 293, 303
exceptions, 295
global variables, 294–295
paramstyle property, 294, 295
switching between database modules, 294
threadsafety property, 294
types, 297–298
Python distributions online, 595
Python documentation online, 596
Python eggs, 384
Python Enhancement Proposals, 596
Python extensions, 380
Python help (pyhelp.cgi), 596
"Python Imaging Library not available" warning, 429

Python interpreter
    extending and embedding, 596
Python library reference, 596
Python Package Index *see* PyPI
Python reference, 579–594
Python reference manual, 596
Python Server Pages *see* PSP
Python web site, 595
PythonDebug directive, 339, 340
Python/C API reference manual, 596
PYTHONPATH environment variable, 215–216,
    224, 225
Pythonwin environment, 6
PythonWin GUI toolkit, 278, 597
pyw file extension, 217, 288
pywin32, 595
PyX package, 426, 434
PyXML module, 597
    installing, 437

## ■Q

qmark value, Python DB API, 295
    importing data into databases, 302
-Qnew command-line switch, 10
Qt platform, PyQt GUI toolkit, 278
query method, Node class
    XML-RPC file sharing project, 520, 521, 522,
        524, 526, 530
queues
    deques, 231–232
    heaps, 230–231
QUIT event
    arcade game project, 552
quit function, servers, 457
Quixote, 344
quote/quote_plus functions, urllib module, 309, 320
quotes
    escaping quotes, 23–24
    single-quoted strings, 23–24

## ■R

%r conversion specifier, 57
raise statement, exceptions, 162–163, 173, 591
    changes in Python 3.0, 605
raising exceptions, 161–163, 173
    raising exceptions again, 164–165
random access, files, 266

random data
    urandom function, 224
random function, random module, 235
random library
    choice function, 144
random module, 234–238, 260
    choice function, 159
randomString function
    XML-RPC file sharing project, 528, 532
randrange function, random module, 235, 236
range function, 99, 100, 101, 112, 583
raw strings, 27–28
raw_input
    compared to input, 26
raw_input function, 30, 570, 583
    changes in Python 3.0, 600, 606
    ignoring return value, 238
    reading strings, 113
rawDataReceived event handler, 318
RDF (Resource Description Framework), 345
RDF Site Summary, 345
re module, 242–257, 260
    *see also* regular expressions
    compile function, 245
    escape function, 245, 247
    findall function, 245, 246, 252
    finding sender of e-mail, 251–253
    flags parameter, 247
    functions, 245
        VERBOSE flag, 249
    groups, 247–249
    match function, 245, 246
    MatchObjects, 247–249
    sample template system, 253–257
    screen scraping, 321
    search function, 245
    split function, 245, 246
    sub function, 245, 247, 249, 250
    using group numbers in substitution string, 249
reactor module
    listenTCP function, 318
read method, files, 264
    examples using file methods, 268
    iterating over file contents with, 270
    reading entire file before iterating, 271
read mode, open function (files), 262

reading files, 264, 274
  closing files after reading, 267
reading lines, files, 266, 274
readline method, files, 266
  examples using file methods, 269
  iterating over file contents with, 271
readlines method, files, 266
  examples using file methods, 269
  reading entire file before iterating, 271
  xreadlines method and, 272
rebinding
  global variables, 132
  local and global scopes, 131, 132
  variables in outer scopes, 133
receiveItems method, NewsAgent class, 459
rect attribute, Sprite class, 554
rectangle objects
  clamp method, 556
  inflate method, 555, 556
  move method, 555
recursion, 133–139
  infinite recursion, 134
  parts of recursive function, 134
  recursive definitions, 134
  recursive functions, 134, 140
    binary search example, 136–138
    calculating factorials example, 134
    calculating powers example, 135
  value of, 136
recursive generators, 196, 197
recv method, socket class, 307
reduce function, 139, 140, 583
  Python 3.0, 604, 606
reduce method, set type, 229
refactoring
  2to3 (automatic refactoring tool), 599
  news gathering project, 453
reference counting
  borrowed references, 376, 377
  deallocating objects, 376
  decrementing reference count, 376
  extending Python using Python/C API, 376–377
  garbage collection, 377
  incrementing reference count, 376
references
  Python library reference, 596
  Python reference, 579–594

Python reference manual, 596
Python/C API reference manual, 596
REFERENCES keyword, PostgreSQL
  CREATE TABLE command, 501
register command, Distutils, 390
register method, poll object, 315
register_function method
  SimpleXMLRPCServer class, 519
register_instance method
  SimpleXMLRPCServer class, 519, 523
regular expressions
  see also re module
  character sets, 243
  denoting beginning/end of string, 244
  description, 242
  escaping special characters, 242
  findall method, news gathering project, 462
  finding sender of e-mail, 252
  instant markup project, 409, 411
  making readable, 249
  re module, 242–257, 260
  repeating patterns, 244
  sample template system, 253–257
  screen scraping, 322
  specifying alternative matches, 243
  subpatterns, 243–244
  transforming into pattern object, 245
  wildcards, 242
relational databases
  tutorial/reading on, 293
release information, 7
reload function, 260, 583
  modules, 211
  Python 3.0, 604, 606
  replacing functionality using exec, 211
remainder operator, 580
remote editing with CGI project, 489–498
  controlling file access, 493
  debugging, 490
  edit.cgi script, 492–494, 496
  further exploration, 497
  index.html file, 492, 496
  implementations, 490–496
  preparations, 490
  requirements, 489
  running the editor, 496
  save.cgi script, 492, 494–495, 496

tools, 490
view.cgi script, 497
remote procedure calls *see* RPC
remove method, chat server project, 479
remove method, lists, 46, 585
remove method, set type, 229
renderPDF class
  drawToFile method, 428
RenderUpdates class
  draw method, 549, 550
repetition operators, 250
replace method, strings, 63, 587
reply_to column, messages table
  bulletin board project, 502, 504, 506
    edit.cgi script, 510
    testing, 513
    view.cgi script, 508
reportlab module, 597
  graphics package, 427
  importing, 426
ReportLab package
  constructing PolyLine objects, 429–430
  description, 425
  documentation for, 426
  downloading, 426
  drawing with, 427–429
  first prototype for sunspots_proto.py, 430–431
  LinePlot class, 432–434
  pdfgen module, 427
  Platypus, 434
  reasons for choosing, 426
repr function, 25, 30, 573, 583
  polymorphism, 145
representational state transfer (REST), 346
requirement specification
  functional requirements, 350
  test-driven programming, 350–351
reset method, Weight class
  arcade game project, 558
Resource Description Framework (RDF), 345
resources
  online resources, 595
  Python 3.0, 606
REST (representational state transfer), 346, 535
reStructuredText, 424
return statement, 116, 572, 590
  ending functions, 117

generators, 195, 198
infinite recursion, 134
return value, functions, 16
  annotation, 601, 605
  functions without return values, 117
  iterator return values, Python 3.0, 603
  return value is None, 117
    caution using if statements, 117
reverse argument of sort method, lists, 49
reverse function, 223
reverse method, lists, 46, 585
reversed function, 47, 52, 102, 112, 223, 583
reversed iteration, 102
rewriting
  case against rewriting, 395
rfind method, strings, 587
Rich Site Summary, 345
right shift operator, 580
rindex method, strings, 587
rjust method, strings, 588
robotparser module, 310
rollback method, connections, 296
Room class, chat server project, 481
rooms, chat server project, 478–480
  LoginRoom class, 479
  LogoutRoom class, 479
  main chat room, 479
Rossum, Guido van, 278
round function, 16, 30, 584
rounding, division, 16
rowcount attribute, cursors, 297
ROWID value, Python DB API, 298
rpartition method, strings, 588
RPC (remote procedure calls)
  REST and RPC, 346
  SOAP, 346
  XML-RPC, 345
rpm format
  bdist command, Distutils, 387
RPMs
  creating Linux RPM packages, 387
  XML parsing project, 437
RPython, 370
rsplit method, strings, 588
RSS (Really Simple Syndication), 345
RSS feeds, 345
  client program handling feeds, 345

RSS feeds *(continued)*
    Scrape 'N' Feed, 328
    Universal Feed Parser, 345
rstrip method, strings, 227, 588
Rule class/object, instant markup project, 413, 419
    condition/action methods, 412, 414
rules, instant markup project, 409, 412–413, 415–418
run function, reactor module, 318, 320
run method, Game class
    arcade game project, 565
run method, profile module, 363, 364
runDefaultSetup function
    news gathering project, 462

## ■S

%s conversion specifier, 54
safe_substitute method, 55
sample function, random module, 235
save function, event handler, 286
save.cgi script
    bulletin board project, 507, 511–513
    remote editing with CGI project, 492, 494–495, 496
saving programs, 19–20
SAX (Simple API for XML), 435
    dealing with XML in Python, 439
    XML parsing project, 435, 438, 442
sax module, xml
    parse function, 439
SAX parser
    XML parsing project, 436
say command, chat server project, 480, 485
scope, 131–133
    *see also* namespaces
    class scope variable, 153
    description, 140
    global scope, 131
    local scope, 131
        parameters, 118
    nested scopes, 133
        instant markup project, 410
    number of scopes, 131
    rebinding global variables, 132
    using exec and eval, 109, 111
Scrape 'N' Feed, 328
scraping *see* screen scraping
screen scraping, 321–328, 346
    Beautiful Soup module, 327–328
    HTMLParser callback methods, 325

Tidy, 322–324
    using HTMLParser module, 325–327
    web services, 344–346
    XHTML, 325
scripts
    adding line numbers to, 227
    behaving like normal programs, 20–22
    running from command prompt, 20
    saving and executing programs, 19–20
scroll bars, text controls, 284
sdist command, Distutils, 386, 387
    formats switch, 387
search function, re module, 245
second implementations of projects
    structure of projects in this book, 402
second system syndrome
    case against rewriting, 395
security
    CGI security risks, 330
    password digests, 494
    PythonDebug directive, 340
    using exec and eval, 109
seek method, files, 266
select function, select module
    asynchronous I/O, 312, 314–315
    avoiding forking and threading, 312
    description, 320
    select module, poll function
        asynchronous I/O, 315–316
        polling event constants in select module, 315
self parameter
    calling unbound superclass constructor, 180
    class methods, 189
    class statement, 149
    distinguishing methods from functions, 150
    framework for extensions, 377, 378
    static methods, 189
send method, generators, 198
send method, socket class, 307
sender column, messages table
    bulletin board project, 502
sep variable, os module, 223, 224
separators
    altsep variable, 224
    linesep variable, 224
    pathsep variable, 223, 224
    sep variable, 223, 224

sequence unpacking
  assignment statements, 85–87
  file iterators, 274
  popitem method, 86
sequences, 31–40, 51, 182, 206
  accessing individual elements, 32
  accessing ranges/slices of elements, 34
  adding, 37
  arithmetic sequence, 184
  built-in sequence types, 31
  checking membership, 38–39
  close function, 226
  comparing, 95
  concatenating, 37
  creating infinite sequence, 183
  deleting element associated with key, 182
  empty lists, 37
  finding number of elements in, 40
  finding smallest/largest elements in, 40
  immutable sequences, 49
  indexing, 31, 32–34
    illegal type of index used, 184
  initialization, 37
  iterating over, 32
  key is negative integer, 183
  lists, 40–49
  making from iterators, 194
  mapping protocol and, 182–185
  multiplying, 37–38
  operations, 32–40
  returning number of elements contained in,
    182
  returning value of key, 182
  slicing, 34–37, 119
    simulating, 185
    specifying step length between elements, 36
  storing value for key, 182
  tuples, 49–51
SERIAL keyword, PostgreSQL
  CREATE TABLE command, 501
serve_forever method
  SimpleXMLRPCServer class, 519, 523
server sockets, 319
ServerProxy class
  XML-RPC file sharing project, 520
servers
  connecting to, 454

forking server, 313
  SocketServer module, 310–311
  SocketServer-based servers, 317
  threading server, 313
  writing Twisted server, 317–319
service provider, web services, 344
service requester, web services, 344
set attr method, 191, 192
Set class instances, 228
set comprehension, Python 3.0, 603
set function, 584
set methods, 187, 188
set type
  add method, 229
  frozenset type and, 229
  immutability, 229
  reduce method, 229
  remove method, 229
  sets module and, 228
  union method, 228, 229
set_caption function, arcade game project, 549
set_mode function, arcade game project, 549, 552
set_reuse_addr method, chat server project, 473
set_terminator method, chat server project, 473,
    475
set_visible function, arcade game project, 552
__setattr__ method, 191, 192
setattr function, 157, 159, 584
setdefault method, dictionaries, 79, 106, 586
setdefaultencoding function, sys module, 451
Setext, 424
setinputsizes method, cursors, 297
__setitem__ method, 182
setName method, private attributes, 151
setoutputsize method, cursors, 297
sets, 228–229
  empty set, 604
  new syntax in Python 3.0, 604
sets module, 228–229, 259
SetSizer method, wx.Panel class, 284
setup function, Distutils, 384, 391
setup script, Distutils, 383, 384
setup.py script, Distutils, 384, 385, 387
  commands to run setup.py, 390
setuptools project, 384
SetValue method
  load event, wxPython, 286

sgmllib module, 322

sha module, 343

    remote editing with CGI project, 494

shadowing

    locals function, 132

shallow copy, dictionaries, 75

shebang, 21

shelve module, 238–241, 260

    modifying objects, 239

    open function, 238

shift operator precedence, 580

short-circuit logic, Boolean operators, 96, 574

Show method, wx.Frame class, 281

shuffle function, random module, 235

signs (+/-), string formatting, 58

Simple API for XML *see* SAX

simple generators *see* generators

Simple Wrapper and Interface Generator *see* SWIG

simple_main.cgi script

    bulletin board project, 505

SimpleWebSource class

    news gathering project, 462

SimpleXMLRPCServer class, 519

    allow_reuse_address attribute, 527

    register_function method, 519

    register_instance method, 519, 523

    registering Node with, 521

    serve_forever method, 519, 523

SimpleXMLRPCServer module, 310, 518

single-quoted strings, 23–24

SIP tool, 371

site-packages directory

    executing path configuration files, 216

    putting modules in existing sys.path, 215

size argument, setting button positions using, 283

sizers, 284–285

    BoxSizer class, 284

    layout mechanisms, 291

    using relative coordinates, 284

Slashdot, 499

sleep function, time module, 233, 234

slice function, sequences, 185

slicing

    lists, 42, 571

    precedence, 580

    sequences, 34–37

simulating, 185

Smalltalk, 151

SmartASCII, 424

smtpd/smtplib modules, 310

SOAP/SOAPy, 346

socket class, socket module, 306

    accept method, 306

    bind method, 306

    connect method, 306

    gethostname function, 306, 307

    listen method, 306

    recv method, 307

    send method, 307

socket module, 306–308, 319

    socket class, 306

    tools for chat server project, 470

socket server

    connecting to, 470

sockets

    chat server project

        bind method, 471

        create_socket method, 471, 472

    datagram socket, 306

    description, 319

    network programming, 470

    stream socket, 306

    types of, 306

SocketServer framework, 319

SocketServer module, 310–311

    BaseRequestHandler class, 311

    classes, 311

    forking and threading with, 313

    SocketServer-based servers, 317

    StreamRequestHandler class, 311

sort command, files, 265

sort method, lists, 47–49, 585

    cmp built-in function, 48

    key argument, 48

    keyword arguments, 48

    reverse argument, 49

sorted function, 48, 52, 102, 112, 584

    keyword arguments, 49

sorted iteration, 102

Sorting Mini-HOWTO, 49

    Andrew Dalke, 49

source code
    encoding in Python 3.0, 605
    exploring modules, 221
source code checking, 359
    PyChecker/PyLint tools, 359–362, 364
SourceForge, 596
span method
    MatchObjects, re module, 248
special attributes *see* magic attributes
special characters
    character sets, regular expressions, 243
    escaping, regular expressions, 242
special methods *see* magic methods
special values, Python DB API, 297, 304
speed
    extending Python to improve, 365–366
splicing operators, 129
    argument splicing, Python 3.0, 604
split function, re module, 245, 246
split method, strings, 63, 588
    food database application, 300
splitlines method, strings, 588
Sprite class, pygame.sprite module
    arcade game project, 550
    image attribute, 554
    rect attribute, 554
sprite module, pygame, 550
Spyce, 341, 344
SQL
    tutorial/reading on, 293
SQLite, 298, 304
    bulletin board project, 500
        creating database in, 501
    conversions between numbers and strings, 303
sqrt function, 18, 30
stack trace
    catching exceptions, 167
    exceptions and functions, 170
Stackless Python, 312
    alternative Python distributions, 6, 7
stacks, 45
standard library modules, 221–259
    *see* individual modules
    opening/closing standard library files, 221
    Python 3.0, 604
StandardError exception, Python DB API, 295
starred iterable unpacking, 603, 606

start method
    MatchObjects class, 248
    Handler class, 410, 411
    Node class, 523, 524, 528, 531
startElement event handler
    XML parsing project, 440, 441, 445
startfile function, os module, 225
startPage method
    XML parsing project, 448
startswith method, strings, 588
StartUp class, arcade game project, 564
startUp method, test fixture, 356
state, encapsulation, 147
State class, arcade game project, 559
state variables
    screen scraping using HTMLParser, 326
statements, 13–14, 589–594
    assert statements, 97, 589
    assertions, 111
    assignment statements, 85–88, 111, 589
    blocks, 88, 111
    break statement, 102, 591
    class statement, 149, 594
    compared to expressions, 13
    conditional statements, 88–97, 111
        assertions, 97
        Boolean operators, 95–96
        comparison operators, 92–95
        elif clause, 91
        else clause, 90
        if statement, 90
        nesting blocks, 91
    continue statement, 103, 591
    def statement, 115, 116
    del statement, 41, 107–108, 112, 590
    deleting objects, 107
    description, 29
    doing nothing, 107
    eval statement, 110, 112
    exec statement, 109–110, 112, 592
    expression statements, 589
    for statement, 593
    function definition statement, 115, 594
    global statements, 592
    if statement, 15, 592
    import statements, 84–85, 111, 591

statements *(continued)*
  loops, 97–105, 112
    breaking out of, 102–105
    for loop, 99
    iteration, 100–102
    using else clause in, 105
    while loop, 98
  pass statement, 107, 112, 590
  print statement, 111, 590
    separating with commas, 83–84
  raise statement, 162–163, 591
  return statement, 116, 590
  try statements, 593
  while statement, 592
  while True/break idiom, 104–105
  with statement, 267, 593
  yield statement, 590
static methods, 189–191
  self parameter, 189
staticmethod function, 584
stderr stream, sys module, 222, 263
stdin stream, sys module, 222, 263
  file iterators, 273
  script counting words in, 265
stdout class
  write method, 318
stdout stream, sys module, 222, 263
StopIteration exception, 192
store function, 122
str function, 25, 30, 584
str type, Python 3.0, 600, 605
stream redirection functionality
  changes in Python 3.0, 600
stream socket, 306
StreamRequestHandler class, 311
streams, chat server project, 477
streams, files, 263, 274
strftime function, time module, 233, 455, 456
String constructor
  drawing with ReportLab, 428
string formatting
  % character, 53, 54, 56
  changes in Python 3.0, 600, 605
  dictionaries, 73, 81
string methods, 60–66, 586–588
  capitalize, 586
  center, 586

count, 586
decode, 586
encode, 586
endswith, 586
expandtabs, 586
find, 60, 586
index, 587
isalnum/isalpha/isdigit, 587
islower/isspace, 587
join, 61, 223, 255, 587
ljust, 587
lower, 62, 95, 241, 457, 587
lstrip, 587
partition, 587
replace, 63, 587
rfind, 587
rindex, 587
rjust, 588
rpartition, 588
rsplit, 588
rstrip, 227, 588
safe_substitute, 55
split, 63, 300, 588
splitlines, 588
startswith, 588
strip, 64, 241, 300, 588
substitute, 55
swapcase, 588
title, 63, 588
translate, 60, 64–66, 588
upper, 95, 588
zfill, 588
string module, 55
  capwords function, 63, 66
  constants, 60
  letters constant, 60, 606
  maketrans function, 65, 66
String type, 579
STRING value, Python DB API, 298
StringIO, Python 3.0, 605
strings, 22–29
  changing to lowercase, 62
  comparing, 94
  concatenating, 24
  converting values to, 24
  escaping quotes, 23–24
  evaluating expression strings, 254

executing/evaluating on the fly, 108

finding substrings, 60

formatting, 53–59

    conversion specifiers, 54–59

    conversion types, 56, 57

    precision specifiers, 54

    Python 3.0, 600

    signs/alignment/zero-padding, 58

    string formatting operator, 53

    width and precision, 57

immutability, 53, 119

input compared to raw_input, 26

long strings, 26–27

modulo operator, 66

non-english strings, 66

numbers containing leading zeros, 70

operations, 53

precedence, 581

Python 3.0, 599

raw strings, 27–28

removing whitespace, 64

repr function, 25

representing, 24–25

single-quoted strings, 23–24

subclassing str type, 185–187

template strings, 55

Unicode strings, 28–29

using group numbers in substitution string, 249

strip method, strings, 64, 241, 588

    food database application, 300

strptime function, time module, 233, 234

style parameter

    wx.BoxSizer constructor, 285

    wx.TextCtrl constructor, 283

sub function, re module, 245, 247

    instant markup project, 407, 408, 409, 411

    sample template system, 254

    using group numbers in substitution string, 249, 250

sub method, Handler class

    instant markup project, 410, 411

subclasses, 147, 148

    inheritance, 154–155

    issubclass method, 154

    overriding methods, 148, 156, 177

subclassing

    list/dict/str types, 185–187

subject column, messages table

    bulletin board project, 502

subpatterns

    finding sender of e-mail, 252

    groups, re module, 247

subpatterns, regular expressions, 243–244

subprocess module, 224, 371

    running Tidy, 324

    using command-line tools, 360

substitute method, 55

substitutions

    using group numbers in substitution string, 249

sum function, 140, 584

sunspots example

    fetching data from Internet, 432

    final sunspot program (sunspots.py), 433

    first implementation, 431

    first prototype, 430

    implementations, 427–434

    introduction, 425

    preparations, 426

    second implementation, 434

    using LinePlot class, 432, 434

super function, 180–181, 207, 584

    changes in Python 3.0, 606

    new-style/old-style classes, 175, 176, 206

    subclassing list type, 186

    using when multiple superclasses, 181

superclasses

    calling unbound superclass constructor, 179–180

    description, 147

    multiple inheritance, 156

    multiple superclasses, 155–156

    overriding methods and constructors, 177

    overriding methods in subclasses, 156

    specifying, 153–154

Surface function, arcade game project, 548

surface objects, 548

    convert method, 554

swapcase method, strings, 588

SWIG (Simple Wrapper and Interface Generator), 371–375, 380

    automating compilation, 375

    -c++ option, 373

    compiling, 373

    Distutils using, 389

    header file, 373

SWIG (Simple Wrapper and Interface Generator) *(continued)*
    installing, 371
    interface file, 373
    linking, 374
    program to recognize palindromes, 372–375
    -python option, 373
    running, 373
    using Distutils, 375
    using SWIG, 372
    wrapping code, 375
Swing GUI toolkit, 278, 597
    example illustrating, 288
    Jython and, 290
switches
    command-line switches, 398
symbolic constants, 396
synchronous network programming, 306
SyntaxError exception, 163
    sample template system, 254
sys module, 222–223, 259
    functions and variables, 222
    getdefaultencoding function, 451
    path variable
        modifying to specify module location, 210, 214
        putting modules in existing sys.path, 214–215
        search path (list of directories), 214
        using PYTHONPATH alongside, 216
    setdefaultencoding function, 451
sys.maxint, Python 3.0, 605
system function, os module, 223, 224
SystemRandom class, 234

■T

tab characters, indenting with, 88
tables
    CREATE TABLE command, 501
tags
    HTMLParser callback methods, 325
tar command
    compiling Python from sources, 4
tar files
    sdist command, Distutils, 387
TCPServer class, SocketServer module, 311
tearDown method, test fixture, 356
tell method, files, 266
telnet command, chat server project, 470

telnetlib module, 310
Template class, string module, 55, 74
template strings, 55
templates, 253–257
terminator, chat server project, 473
ternary operator, 96
test code, modules, 259
test coverage, 351, 352
test fixture, 356
TestCase class, unittest module, 355
    instantiating all subclasses of, 356
    methods, 356–357
test-driven programming, 349–352, 364
    anticipating code changes, 351
    automated tests, 351
    key steps in process, 352
    making code fail test, 352
    requirement specification, 350–351
    simple test program, 350
    unittest module, 353
testing
    alternatives to unit test tools, 355
    anticipating code changes, 351
    automated testing, 394
    beyond unit testing, 358–363
    bulletin board project, 513
    code coverage, 351
    doctest module, 352, 353–355, 364
    minimum requirements, 400
    modules, 212–214
    profiling, 359, 362–363, 364
    PyChecker/PyLint tools, 359–362, 364
    requirement specification, 350–351
    source code checking, 359
    test-driven programming, 349–352, 364
    tools for testing, 352–358
    unit testing, 349
    unittest module, 352, 355–358, 364
testmod function, doctest module, 353, 354, 364
TeX typesetting program, 404, 426
text
    finding blocks of, 406–407
text column, messages table
    bulletin board project, 502
text controls
    creating, 283
    creating text area, 283

horizontal scroll bar, 284

multiline text area, 284

text editor

selecting for programming, 19

wxPython GUI toolkit building, 279–288

creating application object, 280

creating frames (windows), 281

creating widgets (components), 281

event handling, 286

finding file name, 286

importing wx module, 280

improving layout, 284–285

interface elements, 280

minimal requirements for text editor, 279

positions and sizes, 283

putting text into text area, 286

titles and labels, 282

text files

changes in Python 3.0, 600

changes on opening in text mode, 262

text parameter, CGI, 490

textAnchor argument, String constructor, 428

TextCtrl class, wx module *see* wx.TextCtrl class

Textile, 424

threading, 312

chat server project, options for, 469

microthreads, 312

multiple connections, 312

SocketServer module, 313

XML-RPC file sharing project, 528, 534

threading module

XML-RPC file sharing project, 519

threading server, 313

threadsafety property, Python DB API, 294

throw method, generators, 199

Tidy, 322–324

getting Tidy library, 324

μTidyLib, 324

mxTidy, 324

using command-line Tidy, 324

using HTMLParser, 325

Tidylib, 324

Time constructor, Python DB API, 298

time function, time module, 233, 234, 455

time module, 232–234, 259, 454

functions, 233, 455

TimeFromTicks constructor, Python DB API, 298

timeit module, 234, 258, 363

Timestamp constructor, Python DB API, 298

TimestampFromTicks constructor, Python DB API, 298

TinyFugue, chat server project, 471

title argument, wx.Frame constructor, 282

title method, strings, 63, 588

title rules, instant markup project, 415

TitleRule class, instant markup project, 416, 420

Tk GUI toolkit, 289

Tk platform, Tkinter GUI toolkit, 277

Tkinter GUI toolkit, 277, 289, 597

choosing between GUI toolkits, 278

example illustrating, 288

toolkits *see* GUI toolkits

tools for projects

Pygame tool, 548–551

structure of projects in this book, 401

trace module, 258

trace.py program, 351

tracebacks, 161

cgitb module, 502

transactions, 296

translate method, strings, 60, 64–66, 588

translation tables, 65

trapping exceptions *see* catching exceptions

trees, 201

True value

Boolean values, 89

changes in Python 3.0, 605

while True/break idiom, 104–105

truth, Boolean values, 89

try statements, 593

try/except statements, 163–169, 576

catching all exceptions, 169

danger of, 167

catching exception object, 166

catching many exceptions in one block, 166

checking whether object has specific attribute, 172

combining try/except/finally/else, 170

else clause, 168–169, 173

finally clause, 170

if/else compared, 171, 173

trapping KeyError exception, 172

using more than one except clause, 165–166

try/finally statement, 169, 173
    calling exit function in, 222
    closing database, 241
    closing files, 267
tuple function, 50, 52, 584
tuple parameter unpacking, Python 3.0, 606
tuples, 49–51
    conversion specifiers, 56
    distributing operator, 128, 604
    empty tuple, 49
    fields of Python date tuples, 233
    finding out if object is tuple, 142
    gathering operator, 126, 604
    immutability, 119
    lists compared, 31
    tuple operations, 50
    uses of, 51
    writing tuple with single value, 50
TurboGears, 343, 344
tutorial, Python, 569–577, 596
Twisted framework, 316–319, 320
    chat server project, options for, 469
    deferred execution, 317
    downloading and installing, 317
    remote procedure calls with, 346
    SOAP toolkit, 346
    web application frameworks, 344
    writing Twisted server, 317–319
twisted.internet.protocol module
    Factory class, 317
twisted.protocols.basic module
    LineReceiver protocol, 318
txt2html, 424
type function, 159, 584
type objects, 17
TypeError class, 163
    inappropriate key type used, 183, 184
    recursive generators, 196, 197
types, 569
    *see also* classes
    bool type, 90
    classes and, 147, 148
    conversion specifiers, 57
    deque type, 231–232
    dictionary type, 69
    duck typing, 145
    polymorphism, 145

Python DB API, 297–298, 304
    string formatting, 56, 57

## ■U

%u conversion specifier, 56
UDPServer class, SocketServer module, 311
unary operators, 580
unbound methods
    calling unbound superclass constructor, 180
underscores
    magic methods, 575
    making method or attribute private, 151, 573
UnhandledQuery class
    XML-RPC file sharing project, 528, 530
unichr function, 584
unicode function, 584
Unicode strings, 28–29
Unicode type, 579
    changes in Python 3.0, 600, 605
uniform function, random module, 235
uninstall command, Distutils, 385, 388
union method, set type, 228, 229
unit testing, 349
    alternatives to unit test tools, 355
unittest module, 352, 355–358, 364
    distinguishing errors and failures, 357
    main function, 356, 364
    TestCase class, 355, 356
    test-first, code-later programming, 353
Universal Feed Parser, 345
universal newline support mode, files, 263
UNIX
    installing mod_python on, 337
    installing Python on, 3–5
    levels of configuration, 398
    making executable script in, 576
    setting environment variables, 216
UnixDatagramServer class, 311
UnixStreamServer class, 311
unknown method, chat server project, 479
Unofficial Planet Python blog, 597
unpacking
    iterable unpacking, Python 3.0, 603
    sequence unpacking, 85–87
    starred iterable unpacking, 603, 606
    tuple parameter unpacking, 606
unquote function, urllib module, 309, 320
unquote_plus function, urllib module, 309, 320

unregister method, poll object, 315
update method, dictionaries, 80, 586
upper method, strings, 95, 588
uppercase constant, string module, 60
urandom function, os module, 224
urlcleanup function, urllib module, 309
urlencode function, urllib module, 309, 320, 334
urlfile.txt file, GUI client project, 540
urllib module, 308–309, 319
    news gathering project, 453
    quote function, 309
    quote_plus function, 309
    screen scraping, 321
        invoking CGI scripts without forms, 334
    unquote function, 309
    unquote_plus function, 309
    urlcleanup function, 309
    urlencode function, 309
    urlopen function, 308, 309, 432
    urlretrieve function, 309
urllib2 module, 308–309, 319
urlopen function, urllib module, 308, 309, 320
    graphics creation project, 432
urlparse module, 310
    XML-RPC file sharing project, 519
urlretrieve function, urllib module, 309, 320
URLs filter
    instant markup project, 418
urls.txt file
    XML-RPC file sharing project, 534
Usenet, 453
Usenet groups, 597
user parameter
    connect function, Python DB API, 296
UserList/UserDict/UserString
    subclassing list/dict/str types, 185
users
    getting input from users, 14–15
users dictionary, 479
UTF-8, Python 3.0, 600, 605
util.py block generator
    instant markup project, 406

None, 37
    seeing all values stored in objects, 157
    special values, Python DB API, 297, 304
values method, dictionaries, 80, 100, 586
    changes in Python 3.0, 605
van Rossum, Guido, 278
variables, 13, 29, 131, 569
    all variable, 219
    altsep variable, 224
    argv variable, 222, 223
    environ mapping, 223, 224
    environment variables, 216
    global variables, Python DB API, 294–295
    linesep variable, 224
    modules mapping, 222
    naming conventions, 13
    nonlocal variables, Python 3.0, 602
    path variable, 222
    pathsep variable, 223, 224
    platform variable, 222
    rebinding variables in outer scopes, 133
    scopes, 140
    scoping, 131–133
    sep variable, 223, 224
    stderr stream, 222
    stdin stream, 222
    stdout stream, 222
vars function, 131, 584
VERBOSE flag, re module functions, 249
version control
    remote editing with CGI project, 497
versions, Python DB API, 294
view.cgi script
    bulletin board project, 506, 508–510
        link from main.cgi, 507, 508
        link to edit.cgi, 508
        testing, 513
    remote editing with CGI project, 497
views
    dictionary views, Python 3.0, 603
virtual tea party *see* chat server project
VisualWx environment, 6

**■V**
ValueError class, 163
values
    literal values, 579

**■W**
Warning exception, Python DB API, 295
warnings, 173
Weave, 370

web application frameworks, 343, 347

web development

mod_python, 336–343

web forms *see* forms

web pages

dynamic web pages with CGI, 328–336

adding pound bang (#!) line, 329

CGI script, 331

CGI security risks, 330

debugging with cgitb, 331–332

HTML form, 334–336

invoking CGI scripts without forms, 334

preparing web server, 328–329

setting file permissions, 329–330

using cgi module, 333

screen scraping, 321–328

Beautiful Soup module, 327–328

Tidy, 322

using HTMLParser, 325–327

using web services, 344–346

XHTML, 325

web programming

dynamic web pages with CGI, 328–336

mod_python, 336–343

screen scraping, 321–328

Beautiful Soup module, 327–328

Tidy, 322–324

using web services, 344–346

web server

dynamic web pages with CGI, 328–329

Web Service Description Language (WSDL), 345

web services, 344–346, 347

remote procedure calls with XML-RPC, 345

RSS, 345

service provider, 344

service requester, 344

SOAP, 346

web sites

generating from single XML file, 435

XML parsing project, 437

web tutorial, Python, 569

web.py, 344

web-based bulletin board *see* bulletin board project

webbrowser module, 225

website element, XML parsing project, 437

website.py file, XML parsing project, 448

website.xml file, XML parsing project, 438

WebsiteConstructor class, 449, 451

Webware, 341, 344

Weight class, arcade game project, 558

weight.png file, arcade game project, 554, 556

weight.pny file, arcade game project, 554

whence parameter

seek method, files, 266

while loops, 98, 569

ignoring return value of raw_input function, 238

iterating over file contents with read(), 270

iterating over file contents with readline(), 271

while statements, 592

while True/break idiom, 104–105

iterating over file contents with read(), 271

whitespace

handling for DOS, 225

VERBOSE flag, re module functions, 249

who command, chat server project, 480, 485

widgets

wxPython GUI toolkit creating, 281

widgets, text editor

Bind method, 286

width of field, string formatting, 56, 57, 59

WikiCreole, 424

WikiMarkupStandard, 424

wikis

remote editing with CGI project, 489

wiki-style markup systems, 424

Wikitext, 424

wildcards, regular expressions, 242

Windows

installing mod_python on, 337

installing Python on, 1–3

setting environment variables, 216

windows *see* frames

Windows Installer file, 3

Wingware environment, 6

wininst format

bdist command, Distutils, 387, 388

with statement, 267

changes in Python 3.0, 605

closing files, 267, 274

context managers, 268

with statements, 593
wrapper code
    SWIG, 372, 375, 380
    wrapping legacy code, 366
wrapping modules as archive file, 386, 387
write method
    save event, wxPython, 286
write method, files, 264, 269
write method, stdout class
    writing Twisted server, 318
write mode, open function (files), 262
writeback parameter, shelve.open function, 239
writeFooter method
    XML parsing project, 446, 448, 451
writeHeader method
    XML parsing project, 446, 448
writelines method, files, 267, 269
    XML parsing project, 451
writing files, 264, 274
    closing files after writing, 267
    updating files after writing, 268
writing lines, files, 266, 274
WSDL (Web Service Description Language), 345
wx module
    importing, 280
    method naming conventions, 281
    style facets, 284
    using keyword arguments with wx constructors,
        282
wx.ALL flag, 285
wx.App class
    creating application object, 280
    GUI client project, 538
    MainLoop method, 281
wx.BoxSizer class
    Add method, 285
    building text editor, 284
    horizontal or vertical style, 285
    style argument, 285
    using relative coordinates, 284
wx.Button class
    adding button to frame, 281
    label argument, 282
    parent argument, 281
    pos (position) argument, 283
    size argument, 283

wx.EVT_BUTTON symbolic constant, 286
wx.EXPAND flag, 285
wx.Frame class
    building text editor, 281
    parent argument, 281
    Show method, 281
    size argument, 283
    title argument, 282
    windows as instances of, 281
wx.HORIZONTAL/wx.VERTICAL values, 285
wx.HSCROLL value, 284
wx.LEFT/wx.RIGHT flags, 285
wx.Panel class
    building text editor, 284
    SetSizer method, 284
wx.PySimpleApp class
    creating application object, 281
wx.TE_MULTILINE value, 284
wx.TextCtrl class
    building text editor, 283
    style parameter, 283
wx.TOP/wx.BOTTOM flags, 285
wxDesigner environment, 6
wxGlade environment, 6
wxPython GUI toolkit, 277, 291, 597
    building text editor, 279–288
        creating application object, 280
        creating frames (windows), 281
        creating widgets (components), 281
        event handling, 286
        importing wx module, 280
        improving layout, 284–285
        interface elements, 280
        minimal requirements for, 279
        positions and sizes, 283
        titles and labels, 282
        using relative coordinates, 284
    choosing between GUI toolkits, 278
    demo distribution, 279
    downloading, 278
    example illustrating, 289
    GUI client project, 537
    installing, 279
wxWindows platform
    wxPython GUI toolkit, 277

## ■X

%X, %x conversion specifiers, 57
XHTML
    advantages over HTML, 325
XML, 435
    uses of, 436
XML parsing project, 435–452
    creating content handler, 439
    creating HTML pages, 442–444
    creating simple content handler, 441
    dispatcher mix-in classes, 444, 446
    events/event handlers, 439–441, 448–450
    factoring out header/footer/default handling,
        446
    further exploration, 451
    goals, 436
    handling special characters, 450
    implementations, 438–451
    installing, PyXML, 437
    parsing XML file, 439
    preparations, 437–438
    SAX parser, 436
    Simple API for XML (SAX), 435, 438
    support for directories, 447
    tools, 436–437
xml.sax module
    parse function, 439
xml.sax.handler module
    ContentHandler class, 439
XMLDestination class
    news gathering project, 468
XML-RPC
    remote procedure calls with, 345
XML-RPC file sharing project, 517–535
    adding GUI client, 537–545
    avoiding loops, 518
    connecting to nodes, 518
    creating client interface, 527–528
    exceptions, 528–529
    further exploration, 534
    implementations, 519–534

Node class, 520–525
node communication, 518
preparations, 519
requirements, 518
tools, 518
validating file names, 529–534
XML-RPC server
    SimpleXMLRPCServer module, 310
xmlrpclib module, 310, 518
    XML-RPC file sharing project, 520, 527
        Fault class, 528, 529
XPath, 325
xrange function, 100, 101, 112, 584
    changes in Python 3.0, 606
xreadlines method, files
    lazy line iteration with, 272

## ■Y

YAML
    markup systems and web sites, 424
yield expression, generators, 198, 199
yield statement, generators, 195, 198
    generator-function, 198, 207
yield statements, 590

## ■Z

Zawinski, Jamie, 242
ZeroDivisionError class, 161, 163, 576
    catching with more than one except clause, 165
    muffling, 164, 165
zero-padding, string formatting, 58
zeros
    numbers containing leading zeros, 70
zfill method, strings, 588
zip files
    sdist command, Distutils, 387
zip function, 101, 112, 584
    changes in Python 3.0, 605
    constructing PolyLine objects, 430
"zlib not available" warning, 429
Zope, 341, 343, 344
ZSI, SOAP toolkit, 346

# You Need the Companion eBook

**Your purchase of this book entitles you to buy the companion PDF-version eBook for only $10. Take the weightless companion with you anywhere.**

We believe this Apress title will prove so indispensable that you'll want to carry it with you everywhere, which is why we are offering the companion eBook (in PDF format) for $10 to customers who purchase this book now. Convenient and fully searchable, the PDF version of any content-rich, page-heavy Apress book makes a valuable addition to your programming library. You can easily find and copy code—or perform examples by quickly toggling between instructions and the application. Even simultaneously tackling a donut, diet soda, and complex code becomes simplified with hands-free eBooks!

Once you purchase your book, getting the $10 companion eBook is simple:

❶ Visit **www.apress.com/promo/tendollars/**.

❷ Complete a basic registration form to receive a randomly generated question about this title.

❸ Answer the question correctly in 60 seconds, and you will receive a promotional code to redeem for the $10.00 eBook.

THE EXPERT'S VOICE™

233 Spring Street, New York, NY 10013

Offer valid through 3/11.